Boulder City Cemetery

Boulder City, Clark County, Nevada

1942 to June 2000

Volume Three: Obituaries & Legislative Reports

Diane E. Greene, AG
Accredited Genealogist
(Eastern States)

WILLOW BEND BOOKS
2007

WILLOW BEND BOOKS
AN IMPRINT OF HERITAGE BOOKS, INC.

Books, CDs, and more—Worldwide

For our listing of thousands of titles see our website
at
www.HeritageBooks.com

Published 2007 by
HERITAGE BOOKS, INC.
Publishing Division
65 East Main Street
Westminster, Maryland 21157-5026

Copyright © 2007 Diane E. Greene

Other books by the author:

Boulder City Cemetery, Boulder City, Clark County, Nevada, 1942 to June 2000
Volumes 1–3

Mary Eliza Easton Diary, Loudon, Franklin County, Pennsylvania

Nevada Civil War Claims, Legislative Reports

The Civil War Diary of Lieutenant Robert Molford Addison, Co. E,
23rd Wisconsin Volunteer Infantry, December 24, 1863–December 29, 1864

All rights reserved. No part of this book may be reproduced or transmitted in any form or by any means, electronic or mechanical, including photocopying, recording or by any information storage and retrieval system without written permission from the author, except for the inclusion of brief quotations in a review.

International Standard Book Number: 978-0-7884-4089-6

Contents

Introduction . . . . iv.

Obituaries   1

Newspaper Articles 341

Legislative Reports 355

Boulder City Municipal Code 365

Index 369

Introduction

When I compiled the two volume set of *Boulder City Cemetery 1942 to 2000*, I included obituaries from the Cemetery Clerk's files and from the biography files at the Boulder City / Hoover Dam Museum. This volume contains the obituaries for most ones that were missing. *The Boulder City News* is a weekly newspaper, which comes out on Thursdays. I checked for obituaries two weeks after the death date and I was able to locate many more obituaries, but some were not found.

The background of the cemetery is described in detail by Elton Garrett in the 28 Nov 1947 issue of the *Boulder City News*. It is on page 346 of this book.

For more information on the history of Boulder City Cemetery, see *In the Beginning . . . : A History of Boulder City, Nevada*, by Dennis McBride (Boulder City, NV: Boulder City/Hoover Dam Museum, 1992), pp.83-85. Photocopies of the Cemetery Clerk files are in Manuscript Collection #MS 72 at the Boulder Dam / Hoover Dam Museum, 1305 Arizona Street, Boulder City, Nevada. The Boulder City Cemetery Clerk can be contacted at City of Boulder City, 401 California Avenue, Boulder City, Nevada 89005.

Diane E. Greene, AG

Adair, Teresa
Boulder City News, Thursday, 17 Mar 1960, 1:5.
INFANT ADAIR SERVICE HELD
Graveside services were conducted last Saturday for Teresa Adair, two-month old daughter of Mr. and Mrs. Dallas Adair. Bishop Bert Whitney officiated. The infant was born Dec. 29, 1959 and besides her parents, is survived by a brother, Donald and a sister, Connie, and grandparents. Mr. and Mrs. G. R. Strong and Mrs. Esther Adair, all of this city

Adams, Fern Ada
Boulder City News, Thursday, 11 Nov 1976, 8:1-3.
Fern Ada Adams Passes Away
Fern Ada Adams homemaker, 819 East Mesquite Avenue, Las Vegas, passed away at the Boulder City Hospital Nov. 1, 1976. In the earlier days, when she first came to Las Vegas, she lived in the Old Morman Fort which is now preserved as a monument. Later one, she was married on the Old Ranch which was on the Old Morman Fort Property. She and her husband, Frank, moved to Boulder City in 1932 and resided at 1109 Avenue K. Frank Adams was an Automotive Mechanic Foreman at the Government garage. They moved to Las Vegas when he retired March 31, 1972. Fern Adams was born August 9, 1915 in Delta, Utah, to Samuel Hood Smith and Mary Addie Wilkins Smith. She was a member of the Rebekahs, Cactus Lodge No. 40, and a member of the Boulder City Mothers' Club. She is survived by her husband, Frank George Adams of Las Vegas; a daughter, Ann Elizabeth Boyce of Boulder City; her mother, Mary A. Smith, St. George, Utah; a brother, James W. Smith of North Las Vegas; a sister, Naida Clarice Myers of St. George, Utah; and two grandchildren. Raymond Scott Boyce and Rebecca Dawn Boyce, Boulder City. Funeral services were held in the Chapel of the Church of Jesus Christ of Latter-Day Saints at 10 a.m. November 5, 19767. Family Prayer was given by John Myers; Bishop Bryant Solomon conducted the service; Invocation by Osborne Traasdahl; Eulogy by Harvey Walter Boyce. Organ Selections by Nancy Murphy; President Leonard Stubbs. Speaker; Monte Morris, Benediction. Pallbearers were Melvin R. Moore, Louis Gebbs, Dale Imlay, Don Harmer, Frank Davis, and Harvey Wood Boyce. Honorary Pallbearers were: Tony Jensen, Kurt Bohn, Leo Dunbar, Hobert Blair, Neil Holmes, Ben Flandrers, Joe Kine, A. A. Wascher, Elmo Johnson, Jack Swartz, and Mel Moore. Dedication of Grave, Bishop Solomon. Interment was at the Boulder City Cemetery.

Adams, Frank G.

Boulder City News, Thursday, 16 Feb 1995, 8:1-2.

Frank G. Adams of Boulder City, died Feb. 2, 1995, in Henderson. He was born April 18, 1907 in Nebraska City, Neb. A resident of Southern Nevada since 1935, he spent most of those years in Boulder City. He is survived by his daughter, Ann E. Boyce of Boulder City; son-in-law, Harvy Walter Boyce and grandson, R. Scott Boyce, also of Boulder City; and grand-daughter, Rebecca Daw Edelmann of La Jolla, Calif. Adams was a retired foreman of the Bureau of Reclamation's automotive garage. He was preceded in death by his wife, Fern A. Adams, 5 brothers and 2 sisters. While employed by the Bureau, he served as fire captain and assistant fire chief of the Federal Fire Department and was instrumental in purchasing fire equipment that is now the property of the Boulder City Museum. A charter member of the Boulder City Lodge No. 50 of the Independent Order of Odd Fellows, he served in all elected offices and was past grand master. He was also a member of the Cactus Rebekah Lodge. Adams was also a member of the Grand Encampment of the IOOF for Nevada, serving as district deputy grand master and district deputy grand patriarch. Adams began his automotive career in the 1930s with two brothers at the Adams Brothers' Garage at 6th and Stewart St. in Las Vegas, where the building is still standing and remains an automotive shop today. He was known for his hobby of studying, identifying and photographing desert wildflowers and for his wide range of nature photography, particularly Nevada's desert scenery. Services were held Feb. 6, at the Boulder City LDS Chapel with interment at the Boulder City Cemetery, next to his wife, Fern.

Adams, Frank M.

Boulder City News, Thursday, 13 Aug 1981, p.2:4-6.

Frank M. Adams passed away Aug. 9 in Boulder City. He was born June 18, 1903 in Grand Blanc, Mich. He had been a resident of Boulder City for 11 years. A retired engineer in the aircraft industry, he is survived by a stepson Bruce Teague of Chattsworth, Ca.; step-daughter Loretta Paxson of Las Vegas; sisters Doris Adams, Purcell, Mo., and Phyllis Christensen of Aptos, Ca.; nine grandchildren and 13 great grandchildren. Funeral services will be at Palm chapel today at 10 a.m. in Henderson. Burial will be in the Boulder City Cemetery.

Adams, Mark Charles
Boulder City News, Thursday, 1 May 1986, p.1:2-6.
Boulder City man killed in Monday construction accident
A Boulder City man was killed Monday morning in an accident at a construction site in Green Valley, according to Henderson Police. HPD sergeant, James J. Avery said Mark Adams "was checking the grade and the grader backed over him" shortly before 11 a.m. yesterday. Adams worked for Central Grading Company, a subcontractor for Lincoln Property Company. David Cooper, spokesman for Lincoln, said the project under construction is a new phase of Pueblo Verde Apartments on Green Valley parkway. State industrial insurance System officials were notified immediately by the company. Police said investigation into the death was continuing. Central Grading owner Gary Stewart drove the Caterpillar's operator away from the site about an hour after the accident. Stewart also notified the victim's Bishop, who went to the widow's home to tell her of the tragedy. Stewart mentioned Adams was a member of the Church of Jesus Christ of Latter Day Saints.

Boulder City News, Thursday, 1 May 1986, p.35:1-2.
Mark Charles Adams, 36 of Boulder City, died Monday in Henderson. He was born Sept, 18, 1949, in Detroit. A resident since 1979, he was a grading supervisor. He is survived by his wife, Kathy; son Ryan, both of Boulder City; daughters, Marlene and Michelle; parents, Marilyn and Charles; brother, Matthew, all of Long Beach, Calif. The funeral will be at 10 a.m. Thursday in Boulder City LDS Chapel. Burial will be in Boulder City Cemetery. Palm Mortuary, of Henderson, is handling arrangements.

Adcock, Betty R.
Boulder City News, Thursday, 24 Jul 1980, p.10:1-2.
Betty R. Adcock
Services were held last Tuesday at Grace Community Church for Betty R. Adcock, 60, who died July 18 in Boulder City. The Reverend Mel Pritts officiated. Mrs. Adcock was born April 17, 1920 in Mt. Vernon, Illinois and was a six year resident of Boulder City. She and her husband were cottage parents at the Southern Nevada Children's Home in Boulder City. She is survived by her husband, Earl Adcock of Boulder City; a son, Mark Adcock of Orange, California; brothers, Charles Lockhart of Boulder City, Sidney Lockhart of Urbana, Illinos, and Malcom Lockhart of Sugar Grove, Ill.; and a sister, Dione Johnson of Boulder City. Interment was at Boulder City Cemetery.

Ahern, Katherine

Boulder City News, Thursday, 14 Apr 1994, p.11:1.
Katherine Ahern 84, died April 6, 1994, at a local convalescent home. Born Sept. 24, 1909, in Mulberry, Kansas, she had been a resident of the Boulder City area for 17 years. She is survived by two sons, William Ahern of Boulder City and Don Ahern of Seal Beach, Calif. Services were held Saturday. Arrangements were handled by palm Mortuary in Henderson.

Alvarez, Andy

Boulder City News, Thursday, 1 Apr 1976, p.8:6-8.
Heaven now has one more man to play beautiful music and paint the clouds with sunshine! Andrew T. "Andy" Alvarez, 66, died early Monday morning after a long, brave fight with cancer. He was a patient at the Valley Hospital. Rosary will be recited tonight at 7:30 p.m. at Palm Chapel in Henderson. The funeral mass will be said at 9 a.m. tomorrow at St. Andrew's Catholic Church. Father Hugh Smith will officiate. Burial will be in the Boulder City Cemetery. Andy was born July 30, 1090 [sic] in Magdalena, New Mexico. After living in other small towns in that state, he moved as a child to Holbrook, Arizona. From there he came to Boulder City in 1942. He was employed by the U. S. Bureau of Reclamation from Jan. 1944 to July 20, 1971, when he retired. He also did odd jobs around town, giving them a chance to make more friends. Andy and Jennie did practically all the work in building their lovely home at 12 Valley View Lane, in lakeview – the first house inside the "Town Limits." Andy also loved to care for the flowers in the yard. Ask most Boulder City people what they remember about Andy, and they will answer "His music!" His electric guitar was a popular instrument for dancing, and he helped at the beginning square dance groups. Andy played with many of the musicians, including Billie Bates, Jim Murchison, Bill Trelease and Henry Ramsey. Others of us knew Andy as an artist, and his most outstanding paintings were on black velvet. His horse pictures were particularly good, and we are proud to have one of the last ones he painted, which he completed for John to receive as a Christmas present. Andy is survived by his wife, Jennie, 12 Valley View Lane; a daughter Carmen, of Las Vegas; a brother, Frank Alvarez, Phoenix, Ariz.; two sisters, Stella Mata and Leonides Paddilla, both of Phoenix; and one grandchild.

Anderson, David
Boulder City News, Thursday, 1 Nov 1984, 11:1.
David Anderson, 84, died Thursday, September 6, 1984 in Henderson. He was a resident of Boulder City and the immediate area for over 40 years. Mr. Anderson was born September 28, 1898 in Newark, New Jersey, and was an accountant. He was a Past Commander of the American Legion, member of the Mason Wyandotte Lodge No. 3 for over 50 years, and a member of the DAV. David Anderson is survived by his wife, Gwendolyn Anderson, and stepson, Donald G. Estes, both of Boulder City.

Anderson, Irene
Boulder City News, Thursday, 23 Apr 1987, 30:1.
Irene Anderson, age 90, passed away Thursday, April 16, 1987 in Henderson. She was born Aug. 16, 1896 in New York. She was a housekeeper and an 11 year resident of Boulder City. She leaves her daughters, Irene Spillian of Boulder City, Margaret O'Connel of Nanaugatuck, Conn.; sister, Margaret Beck of Margate, N. J., six grandchildren and ten great grandchildren. Interment was in Boulder City Cemetery.

Anderson, Juanita B.
Boulder City News, Thursday, 21 Sep 1995, 8:1-2.
Juanita B. Anderson, 76, of Boulder City, died Sept. 16, 1995, in a local hospital. She was born Oct. 5, 1918, in Webb City, Mo. She is survived by her husband, Ira E. of Boulder City; a son, Bill Anderson; her mother, Gladys Hurst; a brother, Howard Hurst, all of Henderson; six grandchildren, and one great grandchild. Services were held Wednesday. Arrangements were handled by Palm Mortuary in Henderson.

Anderson, Merril V.
Boulder City News, Thursday, 2 Nov 1978, 8:1-2.
A Requiem mass was conducted last Monday, October 30 at t. Andrew's Church for Merril V. Anderson, 81, who died October 26 in Boulder City. Mr. Anderson was born in Reading, Pennsylvania and had lived in Boulder City for two years. He had been an elevator constructor. Survivors include his wife, Irene of Boulder City; daughters, Margaret O'Connell of Fairfield, Connecticut and Irene Spillan of Boulder City; sisters, Jennie Bash and Lucy Keplinger, both of Pennsylvania; six grandchildren and six great grandchildren. The Reverend Joseph Anese officiated at the service and interment followed at Boulder City

Cemetery.

Anderson, Walter Eugene "Moose"
Boulder City News, Thursday, 17 Jul 1980, p.9:5.
Graveside services were held last Monday in Boulder City Cemetery for Moose Anderson, 20, who died July 9 in Boulder City. Pastor Gary Moore of the Bethany Baptist Church officiated. Mr. Anderson was born July 10, 1959 in National City, California. He was a laborer and had lived in Southern Nevada since 1962. He is survived by his wife, Dana Anderson of Missouri; his mother, Norma Tougas of Boulder City; father, Orville G. Anderson of California; brothers, Mark and Eric Anderson of Boulder City; stepfather, David Tougas Sr. of Boulder City; and two grandmothers, Elizabeth Anderson and Irene Figueroa, both of California.

Andrews, John Stanley
Boulder City News, Thursday, 2 May 1974, 2:4.
John Andrews Services Held
Funeral services were held Tuesday afternoon for John Stanley Andrews, 74, at the Palm Chapel in Henderson. The rites were conducted by Wilfred T. Voss, past grand master of the Masons of Nevada. Burial followed in the Boulder City Cemetery. Pallbearers were Art Hurt, Carl Merrill, Nick Havrilla, Horace Ward, Marvin Wood and Henry Pelham. Mr. Andrews died Friday the 26th in Sunrise Hospital, following a long illness. He was born August 29, 1899 in Chicago, Ill. He enlisted in the U. S. Navy in 1916 as a musician, and was appointed band master in 1933. He retired from Service in 1942 and came to Boulder City. He worked as a guide at Hoover Dam, and as a guard under Chief Charles Peterson. Under the G. I. Bill, he took training as a watch repairman, and was employed by Marshall Field Co. in Chicago, until he retired because of ill health. Later, he returned to Boulder City with his wife Helen (Hunter), whom he married Aug, 7 1929 in Philadelphia, Penn. He joined the St. Paul's Lodge No. 14, F&AM in Newport, Rhode Island, Dec. 28, 1936, and affiliated with Boulder Lodge No. 37 on Nov 7, 1972. He was an active member of Boulder City Elks Lodge No. 1682, and had belonged to the Veterans of Foreign Wars in Iowa. He is survived by his wife, Helen, 619 Ave. C (Apt. 1); Brother Frank Andrews of Pennsylvania; sister Helen Snyder, Vancouver, Canada; and several nieces and nephews.

Apple, Donald Walter
Boulder City News, Thursday, 13 Oct 1994, 9:3-4.
Donald Walter Apple died Wednesday, oct. 5, 1994, at a North Las Vegas Care Center. He was born Feb. 1, 1905 in Dayton, Ohio, and worked for 40 years at NCR. He moved to Nevada in 1973. His wife of 64 years, Vera Gray Apple, died April 1, 1994. He is survived by two son; Peter Gilbert Apple of Clarence, NY, and Timothy Scott Apple of Las Vegas, NV; a daughter, Cynthia Apple Harris of Boulder City, NV; also 8 grandchildren and 4 great grandchildren. Memorial services are private. Burial will be in Boulder City, NV. Donations may be made to Bethany Baptist Church Youth Group in Boulder City.

Arnold, Jack
Boulder City News, Thursday, 27 Jan 1977, 5:4-5.
Jack Arnold Passes Away
In April of 1940, they moved to Boulder City as he had accepted a temporary position of guide at the Hoover Dam. Later he transferred to the position of clerk with the Boulder Canyon Project. With the outbreak of World War II. Mr. Arnold reenlisted and served in the Navy until 1945. Upon returning to B. C., he resumed his work with the Bureau of Reclamation. For a brief while beginning in 1951, he and Mabel returned to Oklahoma to try their hand at farming, only to return in 1953 and permanently settle in B. C. His wife preceded him in death in 1963. After twenty-six years of Federal service, he retired in 1966 and later married his second wife, Hazel. Mr. Arnold is survived by his wife, Hazel, a sister, Mrs. A. D. Williams of Hobbs, New Mexico and two cousins, Edith Arnold of Hobbs N. M. and Gussie Arnold of Oklahoma. Funeral services were held for Noah "Jack" Arnold on Wed., Jan. 26, 2 p.m. at the Boulder City Masonic Lodge. Mr. Arnold, a retired guide at the Hoover Dam, had resided in B. C. For thirty-seven years and died January 24, 1977. He was born Oct. 12, 1896 in Izard County, Ark., but his family moved to Southeastern Texas when he was a small child. On July 2, 1917, he enlisted in the United States Navy and served aboard the U. S. S. Des Moines. Throughout his early life, he worked in a chemistry laboratory, as a carpenter, and teaching school. Mr. Arnold eventually completed his higher education studies with a Bachelor of Arts Degree in 1927 and a Masters in American History during 1936. Prior to this, in 1922, he married Miss Mable Fields. They settled for a time in Oklahoma where he taught as well as serving as Superintendent of Public Schools.

Atwood, Robert E.
Boulder City News, Thursday, 12 Apr 1979, 1:4-7
Robert E. Atwood
Graveside services will be held Friday at 10 a.m. at the Boulder City Cemetery for Robert E. Atwood, 53, who passed away April 10 in Boulder City. The Reverend Joseph Anese of St. Andrew's Catholic Church will officiate. Mr. Atwood was born August 19, 1925 in Great Falls, Montana and had resided in Boulder City for a number of years. He was employed at Hoover Dam as a tour guide. He was a Navy veteran of World War II and a member of the D. A. V. In Las Vegas. Survivors include his wife, Janet, of Boulder City; a son, Terry Atwood of Boulder City; a daughter, Robin Stultz of Pleasanton, Calif.; a brother, Chester J. Atwood of Grants, New Mexico; sister, Katherine Lovell of Havre, Mont. and two grandchildren.

Austin, Gene Douglas
Boulder City News, Thursday, 8 May 1975, 23:4.
Gene Austin Services
Funeral services were held Tuesday afternoon for Gene Douglas Austin, 45, who died April 27 at the Sunrise Hospital. The rites were conducted by Bishop Kenneth Simkins at the Church of Jesus Christ of Latter-Day Saints in Boulder City. Burial was in Boulder City Cemetery. In lieu of flowers, donations may be made to the Steven Chadwick's Mission. Mr. Austin was born December 20, 1930 in Paonia, Colorado and lived in Southern Nevada for 20 years. He had been the owner-operator of the former Hancock Service Station. He is survived by his wife, Leona Mae, 655 Ave. C; son Rocklyn Gene Austin, Bowman, North Dakota; daughter, Vicki Lynn Doll, Torrence, Calif.; his mother, Edith Austin, Price, Utah; sister, Joy Schideler, Warner, Okla.; Betty Gerth, Henderson, Nevada; and Ruby Gale, Roosevelt, Utah; brothers, William Austin, Price, Utah; Richard, Mickey and James Austin, all of Las Vegas; and 5 grandchildren.

Baker, William Emmett "Bake"
Boulder City News, Thursday, 25 Nov 1971, 8:7-8.
Rites Held For William Baker Here Tuesday by Esther Shipp
William Emmett "Bake" or TWA Baker, 69, was laid to rest in the Boulder City Cemetery, Tuesday afternoon after a long and interesting career in the field of pioneer aviation. He had been in poor health since a heart attack in 1867, and died Friday in Corona Del Mar, California. Bishop Jake Williams officiated at the funeral services at the local church of Jesus Christ of Latter-Day Saints. My files contained four articles about Bake - a long, feature story with pictures, written by the late Don Ashbaugh: a letter written by Bake during his long tenure as a member of the Board of Trustees of the Southern Nevada Memorial Hospital: a short announcement of his retirement from TWA in December, 1958: and an item from my column of April 6, 1967, telling of his critical illness. So – this obituary will be quoting from them, without the customary quotation marks. In 1927, Major C. C. Moseley, vice-president of the fledgling Western Air talked Baker into deserting the roofing business and joining the company's small staff at old Vail Field east of Los Angeles. He assured him that some day "Western Air will be bigger than Union Pacific." At that time, Vail Field was in a hay field. Baker's first job was as an apprentice mechanic, watchman and truck driver. He slept at the hangar, and was permanently on duty! When Lindbergh made his famed flight across the Atlantic in 1927, the smart company officials found him anxious to be connected with airline expansion. (This feature has a photograph of Bake, and others, in front of Lindy's "Spirit of St. Louis"). They formed another company called Transcontinental Air Transport, designed to span the nation, by planes in daylight and trains at night! Baker had received his certificate as an engine and aircraft mechanic. The new company sent him to Holbrook, Arizona to prepare a field where planes could be refueled. With him was Herbert Hoover Jr. When the first plane got there, much of the equipment had failed to arrive, and Pearl Baker had to sew a windsock to hoist atop a telephone pole. T. A. T. and Western Air merged, and the station was moved to Winslow, Arizona. Baker was to be on hand for the first air mail flight on Dec. 1, 1929. However, the night before, he suddenly received orders to go to Kingman and take charge. Pearl and Bake, with daughters Lena and Dorothy, loaded their dog and clothing into a car and drove all night to await the arrival of the initial mail flight. They stayed there 7 years. Then C. A. A. gave TWA a direct route to San Francisco through Las Vegas, so Baker was sent there in 1937 to the old McCarran Field. Next, in 1938, he was assigned to Boulder City to set up a southern Nevada terminal. Baker

stayed in Boulder City for 12 years. The girls went to school and married. Bake became one of our leading citizens. He was a member of the Rotary Club, was president of the Chamber of Commerce in 1947, belonged to the old Sportsman's Association, and was charter member of the Boulder City Elks. He was first elected to the Clark County hospital board in 1946, and was re-elected several times. Bake was responsible for many "firsts" – including the present lighting system at night, and the very first upper air observation ever used outside fo the military services. He rode thousands of miles in TWA aircraft of every kind from the original Douglas —2 to the present modern planes. The CAA intervened in 1950, and Bake moved back to Las Vegas. He was district passenger service manager at the time of his retirement in December, 1958. Later, the Bakers moved to Costa Mesa, California, but the married daughters stayed in Nevada, living in Boulder City until the past few years. Lena still works here for the U. S. Bureau of Reclamation. Survivors include his widow, Pearl, Santa Anna, California: daughters Lena (Mrs. Art) Hurt, and Dorothy Haney, both of Las Vegas: three grandchildren and one great-grandchild.

Ballard, Joan
Boulder City News, Thursday, 10 Aug 1967, 2:3.
Ballard Services Today
Funeral services were conducted Tuesday at 11 a.m. for Joan Ballard, 33, with Bishop Jacob Williams of the LDS Chapel officiating. Burial was in Boulder City Cemetery. She passed away Friday in the Boulder City Hosptial. Bunker Brothers Mortuary was in charge of arrangements. Mrs. Ballard resided at 632 Avenue M and was born in Salt Lake City Nov. 27, 1933. Survivors include her husband, Hirschi; a son, Michael Wolfenstein; two daughters, Shelly Ann and Lynette Marie Ballard, all of this city; parents, Mr. and Mrs. Victor Angell, Sr., Hurricane, Utah; two brothers, Clairmont Angell, La Puente, Calif., and Victor Angell, Jr., of Wyoming; and two sisters, Mrs. Doris Underwood, St. George, Utah.

Balmer, Kathryn E.
Boulder City News, Thursday, 17 Nov 1994, 9:2.
Kathryn E. Balmer, 79, died Nov. 12, 1994. Born July 18, 1915, in Marble, Colo., she had been a resident of the Las Vegas area since 1955. She is survived by her husband, Eugene Balmer of Las Vegas; two sons, Michael H. and Larry J. Balmer of Las Vegas; and seven grandchildren. Prayer service will be held at 6 p.m. today at St. Andrews in Boulder City, and a 10 a.m. Mass will be held Friday, Nov. 18 also at St. Andrews Catholic Church in Boulder City. Arrangements were handled by Palm Mortuary in Las Vegas.

Banks, Nellie A.
Boulder City News, Thursday, 14 Jul 1994, 9:1-2.
Nellie A. Banks, 84, died July 7, 1994, in Boulder City Care Center. He was born November 11, 1909, in Des Moines, Iowa, and had been a resident of the Boulder City area for four years. He is survived by a daughter, Virginia Lilly of California; nine grandchildren and 22 great grandchildren. Services will be private. Arrangements were handled by Bunker Mortuary.

Banks, William "Bill" W.
Boulder City News, Thursday, 30 May 1991, 9:3.
William "Bill" W. Banks, 80, died Monday. He was born Feb. 10, 1911 in Des Moines, Iowa, and was a member of the Moose Lodge and the Painter's Union of Las Vegas. He is survived by a wife, Nellie of Boulder City and a daughter, Virginia Lilly of Las Vegas and nine grandchildren and 15 great grandchildren. Services will be held today at 2 p.m. at the Bunker Chapel. Arrangements were handled by Bunkers.

Barbera, Tina Marie
Boulder City News, Thursday, 8 Mar 1990, 12:1-2.
Tina Marie Barbera 31, passed away Feb. 25. She was born Feb. 3, 1959 in Montgomery, Alabama. She had attended grade school and spent part of her high school years at Boulder City High School. She was presently a homemaker in San Bernadino, CA. She leaves her husband Michael Barbera, daughters Jessica and Nicole of San Bernadino, CA. Her mother Diane Cowan Anglade of Victorville, CA., father Walter Gaines of Travelers Rest, South Carolina. Two brothers Michael and Mark Gaines both of Boulder City. A sister Casey Gaines of Ogden, Utah. Her grandfather was Robert A. Cowan, a Boulder City pioneer. Memorial

services will be held at 1 p.m. on Friday at the First Baptist Church, Ave. B in Boulder City.

Barrineau, Harry James
Boulder City News, Thursday, 25 Mar 1982, 8:6-7.
Funeral services were held yesterday for Harry James Barrineau, 32, who passed away in Boulder City Sunday, March 21. Mr. Barrineau was born September 14, 1949 in Stockton, Ca. He was a maintenance man for Clark County Parks and Recreation department. He is survived by his mother, Mary, of Boulder City; daughter, Tanya K. of Boulder City; son James R. of Sparks, Nevada, and brother Steve, of Silverton, Oregon. Funearl services were held at Palm Chapel in Henderson with the Reverend John Osko, for the Henderson First Baptist Church officiating. Burial was in Boulder City Cemetery.

Bartlett, Donald E.
Boulder City News, Thursday, 25 Sep 1958, 8:4-5.
V.F.W. Military Rites Held In B.C. For Donald E. Bartlett
Military graveside rites for Donald E. Bartlerr, 24, were conducted on Saturday afternoon September 20, at the Boulder City Cemetery with the V.F.W. Basic Post 3848, officiating. Bartlett died in a mine accident at Montrose, Colorado on September 17. The deceased and other workers at the mine were repairing a defective water pump in the mine shaft and Bartlett was electrocuted, according to the findings of the Montrose County Corner's inquest. Bartlett was born May 26, 1934 in Ogden, Utah and is a former resident of Pioche, Nev. where he was graduated from High school. He was a veteran of the Korean War. Before going to work at the Camoose Uranium Mine in Colorado, he resided in this area. Survivors include his mother Mrs. Thelma Bird of 55C Victory Village; his father, William E. Bartlett of Salt Lake City; an infant daughter of Naturita, Colorado; two brothers, Bud Bartlett of Richmond, Utah and Elton Bartlett of Moab, Utah; two sisters, Mrs. Dorene Cole of Bolder City and Mrs. Jeanette Davis of Beaver, Utah; a step-father, Lavon Bird of Victory Village; and a step-sister, Mrs. Home Englestead of 115 Joshua Street. Conducting the rites for the V.F.W. Basic Post 3848 were Homer Englestead, Commander; Walt Walters, Senior Vice Commander; Joel Zander, Junior Vice Commander; Aubrey Weese Officer of the Day; Kenneth MacEachern, Chaplain; and Bill Goodale, Color Bearer. Taps was sounded on the bugle by Al Klann. The Marine Firing Squad from the Lake Mead Base and Color Guard from the Nellis Air Force Base also participated. The sermon was delivered by the Bishop of the Boulder City

L.D.S. Church.

Bates, Russell Elliot
Boulder City News, Thursday, 20 Jan 1994, 11:3-4.
Russell Elliot Bates, 89, died January 17, 1994 at Nathan Adelson Hospice in Las Vegas. He was 51-year resident of Boulder City. He was born in Skidmore, Nodaway county, Missouri, Oct. 11, 1904, the son of Fredrick Elliot and Laura Ernestine Bates. He came to Boulder City in 1942 to work as a rigger, constructing transmission towers at Hoover Dam, for furnishing electric power to Basic Magnesium plant as a part of the World War II effort. After that, he worked in Nevada and California as a Heavy Equipment Operator, running bulldozers, blades, tournspulls and other dirt moving equipment in the construction of highways and airports. He was married to Beulah M. (Billie) Mitchell in Aldrich, Mo., July 26, 1936. He was a 33-year member of the International Union of Operating Engineers, Local 12. Other organizations include the National Rifle Association, Boulder City Aero Club, Operating Engineers Retirees, and American Association of Retired Persons (AARP). Besides his wife, survivors are Cornelia Bates Madsen of Provo, Utah and Laurel Jeanne Bates Peart of Arden, N.C. There are 18 grandchildren and five great grandchildren. Services are at 10 a.m. Monday in the Boulder City Ward of the Church of Jesus Christ of Latter-Day Saints, with burial in Boulder City Cemetery. Arrangements were handled by Palm Mortuary in Henderson.

Bayo, Dave J.
Boulder City News, Thursday, 24 Mar 1988, p.30.
Dave J. Bayo, age 15, died Tuesday, March 22 in Las Vegas and was a life time resident of Boulder City. He was born on Dec. 7, 1972 in Boulder City and was a high school student. He is survived by his mother Katherine Bayo of Boulder City; brothers Darin of Laughlin, Daniel of Battle Mountain; sisters Diane Dehm of Battle Mountain, Karen Rogers of Winnemucca, Linda Romero of Elko and Kerry Holton of Oklahoma. He is also survived by aunts and uncles Mr. and Mrs. William Stevenson of Syracuse, and Mr. and Mrs. C. Montclair of Parish, both from New York. Palm Mortuary of Henderson is handling the arrangements. Visitation begins Thursday, March 24 from 2 to 8 p.m. A Rosary will be said Thursday at the Palm Chapel in Henderson at 6 p.m. Graveside service will be Friday, March 25 at 3 p.m. at the Boulder City Cemetery with Father Joe Annese of St. Andrew's officiating.

Bayo, Peter J.
Boulder City News, Thursday, 25 Dec1986, 17:1-2.
Peter J. Bayo, 64, of Boulder City, died Saturday in Boulder City. He was born Aug. 15, 1922, in New York, N. Y. A 16 year resident, he did maintenance work at UNLV and was a veteran in the U. S. Army during World War II. He is survived by his wife, Katherine of Boulder City; sons, Darin of New Jersey, Daniel of Laughlin, and Dave of Boulder City; daughters, Diane Dehm of Battle Mountain, Karen Rogers of Winnemucca, Kerry Holton of Oklahoma, Linda Romero of Elko; one sister in Texas and 11 grandchildren. Service will begin at 1 p.m. Saturday in Palm Chapel, Henderson. Interment will be in Boulder City Cemetery.

Beck, Thomas David
Boulder City News, Tuesday, 14 May 1953, 1:6.
Thomas Beck Funeral Rites Held Friday
Funeral services were conducted Friday afternoon for Thomas David Beck, who died late Wednesday night following a lingering illness. The Boulder City Elks were in charge of the rites which were in the Elks hall. Interment followed in the local cemetery. Beck was born July 3, 1881, in Grenada, Mississippi, and was a veteran of the Spanish-American war. He was in government service for 45 years at the time of his retirement in 1948. Mr. and Mrs. Beck moved here four years ago and have been living at 644 Avenue K. He became ill a year ago and spent a long period in the Wadsworth General hospital in California. Recently he has been in the Boulder hospital. Survivors include his widow, Cora Cook Beck; a brother, Bays Beck of Grenda; and a sister, Florrie Holland of Batesville, Mississippi.

Bees, Lester Hoyt
Boulder City News, Thursday, 26 Feb 1970
Les Bees Service is Today, by Esther Shipp
Lester Hoyt Bees, 69, died suddenly Sunday night at his home 724 sixth Street. William Belknap Jr., C.S., will read the services at 1:30 this afternoon at Palm Mortuary in Henderson. Interment will follow at the Boulder City Cemetery, under auspices of the Christian Science Society. Pallbearers will be L. R. Douglass, Tommy Nelson, Robert Sparks, Albert Hartley, Dee Towne and Sterling Lewis. Lester Bees was born May 10,1900 at Sharon, Pennsylvania, and graduated from high school there in 1919. He was employed as an engineering assistant by the Sharon Steel

Hoop Company for a year, and then was a field representative for the Salisbury Iron Company in Lime Rock, Connecticut. Les moved to Los Angeles in 1924 and worked there until 1941, when he moved to Las Vegas, Nevada to join the McNeil Construction Company at Basic Magnesium Plant as field accountant. He remained with them as head of that section until the completion of the buildings. At that time, he joined, the Bureau of Reclamation Boulder Canyon Project as a clerk and was progressively promoted. Dec. 28, 1958, he was reassigned to the Region 3 office as an accountant in the Finance Branch, and later held the position of operation accountant until his retirement in July, 1963. Lester Bees and Lucile Willis were married in 1932, in Long Beach, Calif. Their son, William Robert "Bob" Bees, graduated from Boulder City High School, the US Naval Academy, and is now living with his wife Carolyn in Tampa, Florida, where he is a power -sales engineering manager with Tampa Electric Company. Les used to work with Cub Scouts when Bob was that age, and for two years helped Bob with the Soap Box Derby. He enjoyed sports, especially football, and was usually found at the games. Following his Government retirement, he continued to do accounting and bookkeeping in his home. Lucile has been a popular music teacher for many years. Carolyn and Bob arrived from Florida early this week. Also staying with Lucile is her cousin, Edra Ogsbury of Sun City, Arizona.

Bees, Lucile E.
Boulder City News, Thursday, 28 Apr 1977, 4:5.
Services Held For Lucile Bees
Graveside services were held last Friday for Lucile E. Bees who died April 19 in Las Vegas. Mrs. Bees was born in Allen, Kansas and was a retired music teacher. She had resided in the area since 1944. She lived at 724 Sixth St. in Boulder City. Her only survivor was a son Bob Bees of Clearwater, Florida. Palm Mortuary was in charge of the arrangements.

Beggs, Terry N.
Boulder City News, Thursday, 11 Mar 1982, 6:3-6.
Terry N. Beggs, of Boulder City died Tuesday, March 8, 1982. Born on September 21, 1935 in Hollywood, California, he had been an area resident since 1973. He was employed by TWA, as an aircraft mechanic and had worked for the airline since 1973. He was a member of the B. C. Elks Lodge and the interline Club. Survivors include his widow Bernice; sons, Chuck Beggs of Sacramento, Calif., and Michael Upchurch of Boulder City; daughters Peggi Beggs of Sacramento, Nancy Stickles of Las Vegas, Nevada, and Debbie Fabre of Carson City, Nev. He also

leaves his father, Charles Beggs, of Boulder City; a sister, Roberta Reay of Las Vegas, an aunt, Sadie Patrick of Los Angels, and a granddaughter, Heather Fabre.

Bell, Vernon J. "Dutch"
Boulder City News, Tuesday, 13 Jul 1967, 1:1-2.
Graveside Rites for Dutch Bell
Private graveside services for Vernon J. (Dutch) Bell, 73 were held at B. C. Cemetery Sunday with Elks Lodge 1782 officiating. In lieu of flowers the family requested that donations be made to the Nevada Heart Association. Mr. Bell, husband of Postmaster Laura Bell, passed away last Friday morning at his home, 636 California Ave. He had been a resident of this city for 24 years. Bell, a retired mining engineer, had followed mining as a career which started at Buckskin, a family mine north of Winnemucca, and culminated at Managanese, Inc., in Henderson. In the 1920's, he and his brother Forrest, who died several years ago in Winnemuca and Harold Hagar leased the Bucksin property shipping out some of the richest ore ever found in Nevada. On July23, 1927 he married Laura Webb of San Diego who was then employed as a reporter for the Humbolt Star in Winnemucca. The Bells left Winnemucca in 1942 for Hawthorne, moving to Boulder City in May of 1943. Here Dutch Bell was employed by the Bureau of Mines and later became traffic superintendent for Manganese, Inc., in Henderson. He retired in 1956 after suffering a severe heart attack. Bell attended school in Winnemucca and Santa Clara University in Santa Clara, California. A veteran of World War I he served in France. Survivors besides his wife include two daughters, Mr. R. N. (Dorothy) Ruby of Santa Cruz, California, and Mrs. Paul (Judy) Seigel of Ann Arbor, Michigan, and a son Norman, serving in the army at Fort Bliss, Texas, a brother, Norman E., San Diego and four grandchildren. Bell was the uncle of Mrs. Cliff Segerblom and Mrs. Merle Lyon, both of Boulder City.

Bellor, Elizabeth "Betty"
Boulder City News, Thursday, 7 May 1992, 7:3-4.
Elizabeth "Betty" Bellor, 84, died Saturday in Boulder City. Born May 6, 1907 in Jerome, Ariz., she has been a resident of Boulder City since 1943, and a homemaker in her own home. She is survived by her daughter, Patricia J. Pennock of Fullerton, Calif.; and her son, James R. Bellor of Falls Church, Va. The family suggests donations be made to the Boulder City Hospital, 901 Adams Blvd. in Boulder City, Nev. 89005. Services were held in Boulder City. Arrangements were handled by Palm Mortuary

of Henderson.

Boulder City News, Thursday, 7 May 1992, 7:1-2.
Friends and Family Remember Betty Bellor as a Joyful Spirit
By Teddy Fenton
Laid to rest Tuesday, May 5, 1992 at the Boulder City Cemetery was Elizabeth "Betty" Bellor. Her birthday fell on the very day of her services. She would have been 85 years old, her family had planned a celebrations, they were coming for the occasion, instead they must go on without her. She was a dream mother, her love held them together, she visited them on every occasion, there are 5 grandchildren and five great grandchildren. Across the United States she would travel, to be at their parties, to just hug them and love them. Her life was blessed with two children. They are Pat Bellow Pennock, Fullerton, Calif., and James Bellor of Falls Church, Va. How do friends remember her? I spent an afternoon making calls. Beginning with Ester Morris, who to the end stood by, and always when Betty no longer drove her car, Esther was happy to take her everywhere. Here then is Ester: "Betty was fun to be around. Sharing and giving was as natural for Betty as breathing. She adored children, remembering her as "Aunt Betty" by the children of Gordon and Dorothy Miles, both parents had professional lives, to Betty they took their small children. Their girls, Nancy and Barbara, spent so much time with Betty Bellow that she was heard to say on more than one occasion. "I raised those girls." Bob and Irene Parker, was so grateful that Betty could "baby sit" the children, Bobby and Sherie, Irene said it was a relief to leave them with someone who loved them as her own. To write this tribute I contacted friends, who have known Betty all the years (dating back to the arrival of the family to Boulder City in 1937). She had clean and wonderful hobbies, collected purple bottles on the desert, loving the seasons, nature was a religion for her, her gardens around her home on Colorado St. Was a source of pleasure. . .

Beneda, Lawrence R.
Boulder City News, Thursday, 5 Oct 1989, 30:4.
Lawrence R. Beneda, 71, of Las Vegas, died Friday. He was born April 19, 1918, in Goodland, Kansas, he was an auto mechanic. Survivors included his wife, Melba Beneda of Las Vegas; his two daughters, Cail Garicia of Oroville, Calif. and Dolores Peters of Baton Rouge, La. Services were held. Palm Mortuary handled the arrangements.

Beneda, Stanley Robert
Boulder City News, Thursday, 30 May 1974, 22:6.
Funeral services were held Saturday for Stanley Robert Beneda, 56, at the Palm Chapel in Henderson. Rites were conducted by the Reverend Guy Holliday of Grace Community Church. Burial was in the Boulder City Cemetery. Pallbearers were Sid Eaton, Dale Raynor, Ronnie Beard, Richard Tarter, Leland Sullivan and Robert Strehlow. Mr. Beneda died Thursday in the Boulder City Hospital, after a short illness. He was born July 4, 1917 in Oberlin, Kansas. He began working fo the U. S. Government on July 6, 1955 as an engineering draftsman in Cody, Wyo. He was promoted to physical science technician in Geology, and the family moved to Boulder City on June 30, 1965 from Sulpher, Okla. He transferred to Coulee Dam, Wash. in 1968, but returned to Boulder City and retired in 1971. He was a charter member of the Boulder City Golf Club. Survivors are his wife Nellie, 604 California Ave., sons, Earl, James and Joseph of Boulder City and Robert of Henderson; a sister, Louise Wastenberg, Yreka, Calif.; and several grandchildren. A son Louise (?) was killed in an automobile accident in 1969.

Bennett, Haley Samantha
Boulder City News, Thursday, 1 Jan 1987, 1:1.
Haley Samantha Bennett, age 3, died Monday, Dec. 29 in Toledo, Ohio. She lived in Boulder City since her birth on Dec. 17, 1983. She is survived by her parents Randy and Barbara Bennett of Boulder City; sisters Andrea and Elizabeth of Boulder City; paternal grandparents Waldo and Jane Bennett of Lafayette, Ohio and maternal grandparents John and Elaine Budd of Boulder City. The funeral service will be held at Grace Community Church of Boulder City on Saturday, Jan. 3, at 11 a.m. Father Herbert Ward of St. Jude's Ranch will officiate. Interment will be at the Boulder City Cemetery. Arrangements are being made by Palm Mortuary in Henderson.

Bennett, Sarah Bessie
Boulder City News, Wednesday, 21 June 1944, 4:1.
Mrs. Bennett Dies Following Operation
Mrs. David Bennett, 38, a resident of McKeeversville for the past two years, died Monday morning, a week after she underwent a serious operation. She was in poor health for some time. Surviving are her husband, Dave, Bakersfield, California; and daughters, Virginia Crane, 19, McKeeversville; LaJoy Huffstedler, 17, 628 Avenue B; Bobbie Ellen,

12, and Betty Sue, 6. They lived in Sloan, Nevada, before establishing residence in McKeeversville. The funeral will take place Wednesday at 4 p.m., at the Grace Community church.

Benson, Lucille "Billie"
Boulder City News, Thursday, 9 Nov 1989, 7:1-2.
Lucille "Billie" Benson, 83, a Boulder City resident since 1947, died Saturday, Oct. 29 in a local hospital. Born in Brigham City, Utah, on July 15, 1906, she was a housewife. She was a member fo the First Ward, Church of Jesus Christ of Latter-day Saints. She is survived by her son, Don Benson of Salt Lake City; two brothers, Earl Benson of Huntington Beach, Calk\if., and Paul Frampton also of Salt Lake City; and three sisters, Elva Pulsipher of Boulder City; June Stock of Montpelier, Idaho, and Joyce Pulver of Las Vegas. Funeral services were held at noon, Friday in the LDS Chapel in Bolder City. Palm Mortuary handled arrangements.

Benson, Taft
Boulder City News, Thursday, 6 July 1989, 8:1-4.
Taft Benson laid to rest at the Boulder City Cemetery.
By Teddy Fenton
Pioneer Taft Benson, a resident of Boulder City for 42 yars was honored at a beautiful service at the LDS chapel on 5th St, in Boulder City. He was 80 years of age, an Army Veteran, a member of the 1st Ward LDS Church, BC. His death on June 25 is a loss to our community. His services were conducted by La Grande Neilson. His widow, Lucille, "Bille" Taft was surrounded by the family that she had loved along with her husband of 62 years, devoted and close the union could not have been happier. They were blessed with a son, Don Benson, who arrived in Boulder City with his wife, Lenoe. Their home is in Hong Kong, China. Their children are Craig and Steven Benson and Susan Andrew. There are six great grandchildren. Family members arrived from far and near. Dr. Well Stock and his wife, June arrived from out of town as did Billie's brothers, Paul Frampton. Musical numbers were by Wally Murray, accompanied by Nancy Gregerson. La Grande Neilsen, accompanied by Nancy Gregerson. An organ and a piano was used, one for each number. Three members of the LDS choir sang. They were La Grande Nielson, Larry Gregerson and Richard Murphy. Steven Benson, the opening prayer, and Lenoe Benson the Eulogy. The closing prayer was by Susan Andrew. The pall bearers were Craig Benson, Robert Pulver, Dean Pulsipher, Ed Nelson, Tommy Nelson, and Claude Grant. Honorary pall

bearers were Earl Frampton, Michael Andrew and Adam Andrew. The latter are Taft and Billie's grandchildren. All Mormon services include remembrances by friends and family. William Pulver, and Taft and Billie's son Don recalled humourous and unforgettable moments from the past. It is necessary also to name the songs that made the services so memorable. They were "I need you every hour" and "How Great Thou Art." To the family and to Billie Benson, the town has loved you. Your family has honored you. The stories you two could share with us is incredible. Billie and Taft arrived in Eldorado Canyon in 1933. There to join Alma and Dean Pulsipher. The girls cooked six meals a day with absolutely no luxuries of any kind. Don Benson their son, was 4 years old. Now he too has a story to tell. Imagine being a citizen in Hong Kong, China. Don and Lenoe will remain with Billie for as long as it takes to help her with business. Our story today is not what I had planned. I tried to make it accurate in every detail. I wrote it three times! My need to share more history was overpowering. To you all, a family so close, you are blessed. Blessed as well that La Grande Neilson officiated. He is a family friend and took part in the service as a member and as a close friend. When a member of the LDS Church leaves us, he or she is accompanied to his fainal rest by tributes from a large church membership. No matter how busy all of you are, you don your bet clothes, and you say goodbye with grace and beauty. Blessed? I am blessed to be asked to do this story. Our community extends its sympathy.

Bicknell, Deborah S.

Boulder City News, Thursday, 29 Sep 1983, 2:1-3.
Deborah S. Bicknell, 21, Boulder City, died Friday in Henderson. She was a seven-year resident of the area. She was born Sept. 26, 1961, in Ely and was a homemaker. She is survived by her husband, Charles of Boulder City; daughters, Amy and Deborah, both of Boulder City; parents, Jim and Dee Petersen both of Boulder City; and brothers, David, Don and Mark Bush, all of Boulder City. Services were at 10 a.m. Tuesday in the 2nd Ward Chapel of the Church of Jesus Christ of Latter-day Saints, Boulder City. Burial was in Boulder City Cemetery. Palm Mortuary is handling arrangements.

Bierce, Walter B.

Boulder City News, Thursday, 25 Jan 1973.
Funeral services were conducted yesterday morning at the Masonic Temple in Boulder City for Walter B. Bierce, 89, who died Saturday night in the Boulder City Hospital. Officiating at the Masonic Rites by Boulder Lodge No. 37 and burial at the local cemetery was Harry Overbey, past grand master of Nevada. Pallbearers were Albert Hartley, William French, Michael Laux, John Nunner, George Day and John Pilant. Honorary pallbearers were Morgan Sweeney, Gene Wellman, Dean Pulsipher, LeRoy Burt, Robert Denning, Lee Tilman, Douglas Moore and Ralph Ligion. Walter Bierce was born January 9, 1883 in Hamilton, New York. He joined the Masons in Chicago, and later became a charter member of Ely Lodge No. 29, F & AM in Nevada. He was a 50 years member of the Royal Arch Masons, and belonged to the Commandry. An electrician, he belonged to the IBEW. The Bierces came to Boulder City in 1931, and he worked on the Dam. He was a maintenance foreman at the time of his retirement from the USBR in 1953. He is survived by his widow, Marguerite M. Bierce, 509 Wyoming St., and a sister, Lula Oakes of Hamilton, N. Y.

Bisbee, Clair. A. "Biz"

Boulder City News, Tuesday, 6 June 1944, 1:1-2.
C. A. Bisbee, Pioneer Boulder Newsman, died in Trailer Near Boulder
Boulder City has lost her "Uncle Biz." Hundreds of friends of "Biz" in the armed forces who got great satisfaction out of the letters he sent them about the home town will mourn the passing of C. A. Bisbee, who died some time late last week in his trailer near McKeeversville. Heart trouble was said to have caused death. One of Boulder's best-loved citizens, "Biz" has been a part of the spirit of the city ever since its founding, thirteen years ago, having been one of the pioneers of the days of dust and the sound of hammers. He was found dead Sunday at about 10 a.m., by G. Orton and Bob Lewis, of the post office, who had wondered at his not having gotten his mail since Wednesday. Roy Bisbee, brother of Biz, arrived last evening from Rancho Sespe, at Fillmore, California, and Betty Garnett, one of his daughters, is expected to arrive today from Redondo Beach. Word is awaited from Gail Bisbee, who is at Mineola, New York; Mrs. Earl Carnes (Royanna); Mrs. R. B. Welsh of Washington, D. C. (Peggy), son and daughters of "Biz," before funeral arrangements are announced. C. A. Bisbee was born March 11, 1877, in Chardon, Ohio, and attended Oberlin college at Oberlin, Ohio, from which he was graduated. He was engaged in sales work and

administrative work with International Correspondence Schools, and also sold insurance, for many years. He met Hazel Butzerin in Montana, and they were married there, having four children, all of whom are now living. Bisbee came to Boulder City at the inception of the Boulder project, as circulation manager in Boulder City for the Review-Journal. Biz' column, "Bunkhouse Bunk," was started during construction days, and continued from time to time, in the Review-Journal, later in the Boulder City News. He once published the best of his writings in booklet form, for sale to tourists. With the exception of a few times when he was away on other work and on trips, he has made Boulder City his home during most of the existence of the city. For several years he lived in his trailer at the lake and at Railroad Pass. A few weeks ago, shortly after having quit his strenuous work for a well-earned rest, he moved his two trailers to a spot between McKeeversville and Bootleg Canyon. It was there that Orton and Lewis found his body, in bed, Sunday morning. Biz had told his friend Lee Hayward that "if anything should happen" he should find a note in his pocket. The note was there, giving names and addresses of relative and ending with: "Luck, fellow. We had fun, didn't we? Thanks for everything. Biz." Bisbee's dog, "Bunk," had been locked in the car, but it was Biz' custom to leave plenty of water, so she was in good condition even though it apparently has been Thursday that Bisbee has been last seen in Boulder City. A. G. Boynton talked with Biz on the post office steps Thursday at about 9 a.m., and was perhaps the last person to talk with him. The body is at the Garrison mortuary in Las Vegas.

Boulder City News, Tuesday, 13 June 1944, p.3:3.
Final Rites Held for C. A. Bisbee
Funeral services were conducted Saturday evening at 5 o'clock at Grace Community church for C. A. Bisbee who passed away several days ago. Reverend Winston Trever conducted the services both at the church and at the cemetery. Mrs. William Getts sang "Abide With Me" and "The Old Rugged Cross," with Miss Helen French at the organ. Pallbearers were: Elton Garrett, J. C. Manix, E. P. Bryant, G. Orton, Bob Lewis, and R. W. Brann. Interment was in Boulder City cemetery. Mrs. James Garnett, Mr. Bisbee's daughter, and her husband, Air Cadet James Garnett, left immediately after the services for their home in Redondo Beach, California. Gail Bisbee arrived Sunday form Mineola, New York, too late to attend services for his father. He and his uncle, Roy Bisbee, expected to leave last night or this morning for California. Gail is in radar research work in Mineola, and will return there after visiting his sister at Redondo Beach.

Blackwell, Nora E.
Boulder City News, Thursday, 3 Oct 1985, 6:1-2.
Nora E. Blackwell, 66, of Boulder City, died Wednesday, Sept. 25 in Boulder City. She was born in Indianapolis, Ind. Nov. 24, 1918. She was a 32-year resident of Boulder City. She leaves her husband, John of the home; daughter Jaci Saunders and grandson, Jason, all of Goodyear, Ariz.; sisters Oneita Brisendine of Clovis, Calif. and Anna Boehmer of Fresno. A graveside service was held Tuesday in Boulder City Cemetery.

Blair, Esper Mills
Boulder City News, Thursday, 9 Oct 1958, 5:6.
Esper Blair Final Rites Held Tuesday
Funeral services for Esper Mills Blair, 53, were held on Tuesday afternoon at Grace Community Church, with the Reverend Earl Fox officiating. Eastern Star final rites were also held at the same time, conducted by Roberta Sutherland, worthy matron of Desert Chapter No. 22, OES, and Nick Havrilla, substitute associate patron. Sylvia Legler provided background music on the Stevenson Memorial organ. Mrs. Blair died Friday, October 3 at her home. She had not been feeling well, and had just completed a series of tests at a Las Vegas hospital a few days before. Esper Mills was born August 1, 1905 in Knoxville, Tennessee. She and her husband, Hobart Blair, moved here from Idaho in 1931 and were "one of the families who helped shape the community." In addition to her husband, she is survived by her son Edgar, 710 9th street, grandchildren Bonnie Lynn and Douglas; her father, William Mills of Washington, three brothers, Home of Washington, Amos and Otis of Idaho; and 2 sisters Geneva Elsenson, Washington and Marie Durden, Idaho. Mrs. Blair was a member of the Eastern Star, the Hoe and Grow Garden club, and the Women's Association of Grace Community Church. Pallbearers were Leo Dunbar, Marwood Doud, Frank Adams, Otto Littler, Clarence Arp and Robert Cowan. Interment was in the Boulder City Cemetery.

Bochmann, Bessie D.
Boulder City News, Thursday, 15 May 1980, 2:3-6.
Services for Bessie Dena Bochmann, 90, were conducted Wednesday at Palm Chapel with the Reverend Ron Mayer of Christ Lutheran Church officiating. Mrs. Bochmann was born August 3, 1889 in Illinois and died May 11 in Las Vegas. She had been a resident of Southern Nevada for 32 years. A homemaker, she was a member of the Order of Eastern Star in Boulder City. She is survived by her husband, Karl H. Bochmann of

Boulder City; a daughter, Gloria Nickell of Las Vegas; son, Roland Nienkamp of California; and three grandchildren. Burial was in Boulder City Cemetery.

Bochmann, Karl H.
Boulder City News, Thursday, 17 Jul 1980, 9:6-8.
Graveside services were conducted last Monday in Boulder City Cemetery for Karl H. Bockmann, 92, who died July 11 in Boulder City. Pastor Ron Mayer of Christ Lutheran Church officiated. Mr. Bochmann was born July 15, 1887 in Rosita, Colorado. He was a machinist and had lived in Southern Nevada for 32 years. He is survived by his daughter, Gloria Nickell of Las Vegas; step-son, Roland Nienkamp of California; and three grandchildren.

Bogart, Frederick L.
Boulder City News, Thursday, 30 Nov 1995, 12:3-4.
Frederick L. Bogart, 71, died Saturday, Nov. 25, 1995 in a local hospital. Born Sept. 11, 1924 in Los Angeles, Calif., he had been a resident of Boulder City for 27 years. He was a retired rendering plant manager, a member of the Boulder City American Legion, also a member of the Boulder City Seventh Day Adventist Church, and a veteran of the U.S. Army, having served in World War II. He is survived by his wife, LeFay of Boulder City; two daughters, LeGay Bailey of Boulder City and Nancy Johnson of Las Vegas; mother, Mamie Bennett of Boulder City; one grandson, Joshua Bailey of Boulder City; two grand-daughters, Allison Johnson of Las Vegas and Ginny Bailey of Boulder City. Visitation will be from 11 a.m. to 5 p.m. today at Palm Mortuary-Henderson. Funeral services will be held at 10 a.m. Wednesday at the Seventh Day Adventist Church in Boulder City, followed by graveside services at the Boulder City Cemetery.

Boris, Beatrice
Las Vegas Review-Journal, Saturday, 24 Jan 1998
Beatrice Boris, 64, died Thursday. A computer operator, she was born May 18, 1933, in New York and was a 10-year resident of Las Vegas. She is survived by her sons, Ron and Marshall, both of Las Vegas; brothers, Henry Maiman and Ira Maiman, both of New York, and Milton Maiman of Israel; sister, Dorothy Goldsmith of New York; 11 grandchildren; and six great-grandchildren. Graveside services will be at 2 p.m. Monday in Boulder City Cemetery. Hites Funeral Service handled arrangements.

Bourget, June S.
Boulder City News, Thursday, 22 Mar 1984, 11:6-8.
June S. Bourget, 49, of Boulder City, died Sunday. She was born April 21, 1935, in Lakin, Kan. A one-month resident, she was a bowling alley owner. She is survived by her daughter, Janelle, and son, Jeffrey, both of Boulder City, and father, Boyd Stehwien of Boise, Idaho. The funeral was held at 2 p.m. Wednesday in Palm Chapel in Henderson. Burial will be in Boulder City.

June Bourget Served as Editor of the NEWS, by Teddy Fenton
Services were held for June Bourget yesterday. She is buried at the B.C. Cemetery. June was the city-editor of the *Boulder City News* for only a short time. Her contribution to the NEWS was unique and different. Obviously a poet, and one who admired Boulder City and revered the desert would not be forgotten by the people who enjoyed her poetry . . . one column in particular was so complimentary to our town, our desert and our people that it will be run again . . . a beautiful memorial to a lovely woman. Our Boulder City people (with a long memory) will also remember that she owned the Potts Paint business. It was located where now the Oaklane Preschool Academy at 1308 Wyoming St. June loved people. Her column was dedicated to a report on people who came into the NEWS office. It is a lazy habit of our writers to always mention the same well-known citizens all through the year. June wrote about people whose name had never been in print before and probably not after she left our paper. June felt that everyone was important. Then a stanza of Poetry within the column made such an impression that she earned a brand new set of readers for the NEWS. We regret her passing. The family is welcome to call 293-171_ with more information.

Boyer, Winifred N.
Boulder City News, Thursday, 8 Sep 1982, 3:3-4.
Winifred N. Boyer, 60, of Boulder City, died Thursday, in Boulder City. Mrs. Boyer was born Aug. 9, 1921 in Beaver County, Ill. She was a homemaker. She is survived by her husband, Carle, and daughter, Sandra Jane, both of Boulder City; brothers, LaVerne Bass of Pinckneyville, Ill.; Andrew Bass of Steelville, Ill., and Melvin Bass of DuQuoin, Ill. The graveside services will be at 11 a.m. Monday in Boulder City Cemetery.

Bozzano, Bernice M.
Boulder City News, Thursday, 20 Jul 1995, 8:3-4.
Bernice M. Bozzano, 78, died Saturday, July 15, 1995, in an Arroyo Grande, Calif. convalescent hospital. Born Feb. 15, 1917 in Chicago, Ill., she had been a resident of Boulder City for about 18 years, after which she moved to Arroyo Grande. She was a retired credit manager for Sears in Los Angeles. She enjoyed Las Vegas, cooking and sewing. She is survived by one daughter, Sylvia Rowan and husband Gerald, of Arroyo Grande; one son, Leonard and wife, Carole of Henderson; six grandchildren and 10 great grandchildren. Graveside services were held at the Boulder City Cemetery, Boulder City. Arrangements were handled by Marshall-Spoo Sunset Funeral Chapel in Grover Beach, Calif.

Bozzano, Silvio
Boulder City News, Thursday, 2 Feb 1984, 23:1-2.
Silvio Bozzano passed away Jan. 26 in Las Vegas. He had lived in Boulder City for five years. He was born Sept. 9, 1917 in Chicago, Ill., and was a member of the United Transportation Union. He is survived by his wife, Bernice of Boulder City; a son Leonard of Boulder City; daughter Sylvia Rowan, Arroyo Grande, Ca.; three sisters, Mary DeMaggio, Wisconsin; Dolly Donat, Chicago, Ill., Theresa Stoller, Chicago, Ill., and brother, Leonard Bozzano, Chicago, Ill; five grandchildren. Rosary was recited at Palm Chapel Monday at 6:30 p.m. and Mass was held in Boulder City at St. Andrews Catholic Church Tuesday at 10 a.m. Interment was at Boulder City Cemetery.

Bradley, Deveda
Boulder City News, Thursday, 10 Sep 1981, 2:4-7.
Deveda Bradley died September 6, 1981 at her home in Boulder City. She was born August 4, 1919 in Texhoma, Oklahoma. She was an office services supervisor for the U. S. Bureau of Reclamation at Boulder Dam. She was a 22 year resident of Boulder City. Services will be held Thursday at 10 a.m. at Grace Community Church in Boulder City with Reverend Mel Prittz officiating. Burial will be in Boulder City Cemetery. Survivors include husband, Bob; son Robert of Las Vegas; daughter, Anne Vance of Madera, CA. Nancy Heersema of San Dimas, Ca; four sisters, Irma Smith of Upper Sandusky, Ohio, Wenona Vanderhoofven of Las Vegas, Verlene Jansen of LaMar, Col, Velma Auten of Auberry, Ca,; five brothers, Merle Hass of Richcrest, CA.; Bruce of Espanola, N.M., Darell of Oxnard, CA., Vernet of South Carolina, Gary of Liberalk,

Kansas; mother, Vira Hass of Boulder City; six grandchildren. Memberships include Order of Eastern Star, Desert Chapter, No. 22, Henderson Toastmistress Club, and Grace Community Church of Boulder City.

Brandt, Joseph Norma

Boulder City News, Thursday, 17 Jan 1974, 9:4.
The funeral Mass was held Monday morning for Joseph Norma Brandt, 80. The Reverend Hugh Smith officiated at St. Andrew's Catholic Church. The Rosary had been Sunday night at Palm Chapel in Henderson. Burial was in the Boulder City Cemetery. Pallbearers were Everett Wacaser, Romy Rodriquez, Robert Bender, George Ball, Robert Littleton and Walt Wood. Mr. Brandt died Friday in the Boulder City Hospital, after four years of failing health. He was born July 16, 1893 in Curdsville, Kentucky. He enlisted in the U. S. Navy in 1918 and served until 1921. He was a member of Post No. 127 of the American Legion in Glendale, California. He worked as a painting contractor in the construction business for many years. Joe and Florence were married Sept. 1, 1928. They traveled all over the United States, to Central America, and to Europe. For a long time, they enjoyed trips in their trailer, and came to Boulder City ten years ago because they like fishing. Their activities have been limited in the past two years. His is survived by his wife, Florence Brandt, 616 Don Vincente, Boulder City.

Brayton, Sharon L.

Boulder City News, Thursday, 12 Jan 1995, 8:2.
Sharon L. Brayton, 52, died Monday, Jan. 9, 1995 in Boulder City. She was a 16-year resident of Boulder City. She was born Dec. 12, 1942 in St. Louis, Mo. and had served as Supervisor for the city of Boulder City. She is survived by her husband Dennis Brayton of Boulder City; four daughters, Patti Schultz, Dennise Novoselek, and Kimberly Brayton, all of Boulder City and Michelle Hampststen of Las Vegas; her mother Helen Schultz of Boulder City; and four grandchildren. Services will be held at Grace Community Church in Boulder City at 10 a.m. Thursday, Jan. 12. The family requests donations be made to National Cancer Research. Arrangements were handled by Palm Mortuary of Henderson.

Brenbarger, William P.
Boulder City News, Thursday, 6 Aug 1987, 12:1.
William P. Brenbarger, age 71, died Aug. 2 in Boulder City. He was born in Oakland, Calif., on Jan. 21, 1916 and was a resident of Boulder City for the past 20 years. He was a retired Engineer in the U.S. Government, and a veteran of the Army Air Corps. He is survived by his wife Evelyn of Boulder City; his son Todd of Boulder City and his sister Louise Theemiling of El Toro, Calif. Graveside services were held Aug. 5 at the Boulder City Cemetery.

Brennan, Richard P.
Boulder City News, Thursday, 22 May 1986, 7:1.
Richard P. Brennan, age 76, passed away Tuesday May 13, 1986. He was born August 25, 1909, in Fort Dodge, Iowa. He was an employee of Los Angeles City, a member of the Knights of Columbus and a 31 year resident of Boulder City. He leaves his wife, Margaret of the home; daughters, Mary Laswell of Las Vegas, Judy Newby of Boulder City, Kathleen Rhodes of South Pasadena, Calif. and Pat Harris of Arlington, Texas; 18 grandchildren and 16 great grandchildren. In lieu of flowers, the family requests donations to a charity of your choice.

Brennan, Margaret
Boulder City News, Thursday, 7 Oct 1993, 9:1-3.
Margaret Brennan died Friday, Sept. 24, 1993. She was 78. She was born Dec. 19, 1914, in New York and had been a resident of Boulder City for 39 years and was a homemaker. Survivors include four daughters: Patricia Harris of Arlington, Texas; Kathleen Rhodes of South Pasadena, Calif.; Mary Laswell of Las Vegas, Nevada; Judy Newby of Boulder City, Nevada; also nine grandchildren and many great-grandchildren. Memorial services were held Sept. 28 in the Christian Center. Palm Mortuary handled arrangements.

Brown, Kimberly Susan
Boulder City News, Thursday, 1 June 1978, p.8:6-8.
Kimberly Susan Brown Surrounded Herself With Music And Poetry
Kimberly Susan Brown, daughter of the late Robert Brown and Loeta Brown was buried at the Boulder City Cemetery on Tuesday at the age of 17. She had suffered since she was 13 with an incurable disease. In spite of that she went into the writing of poetry during her last years, deep and wonderful compassion is evident in every written line. She also composed

her own songs and set to music she played them on her guitar. Just before her death she had been presented with a new guitar which was a source of great joy. Some of her poems were recited by her brother Ernest at her funeral at the LDS Church. Kimberly was so professional on her violin that she won first place in Kingman at a concert in competition. She also crocheted and did rare and beautiful embroidery. Kimberly is the grand daughter of the colorful and pioneer family, Jay and Ruby Nicks, 206 Lakeview Drive. She was present when a family reunion was held in 1978 with relatives coming from far and wide. Noteworthy was an aunt who was 104 years old, yet able to fly out to attend a reunion and then to fly home again. Ruby said there were 6 generations present at the reunion and the only reason the story did not appear in the NEWS was because Esther Shipp, her favorite correspondent was on vacation. Kimberly was the only girl among a family of five. Her brothers are Ernest and Robert, Las Vegas and Larry and David, Boulder City. If ever a girl was loved and idolized by the large Nicks family it was Kimberly. Their relatives stretch across the United States with many of them living in Boulder City. Friends and neighbors extend the hand of sympathy to the family.

Brown, Mary

Boulder City News, Thursday, 25 Jul 1985, 9:1-3.
The NEWS regrets that a belated mention of the tragic passing of Mary Brown (Mrs. Bob) was delayed because of materials not reaching us in time to tell her friends that Mary had gone into the hospital for surgery. Her unexpected death stunned us all. Mary will not be forgotten. The phone has been ringing as friends asked why her death had not been mentioned in the NEWS. Her husband, Bob, her daughter, Barbara, her son-in-law Ben Gowan and other members of her family will help us tell of a glorious life . . . one in which she left beauty behind her, the hobby she loved, painting exquisite ceramic treasures . . . beginning with china in its raw form, and coating it . . . placing it in the oven. . . the collection she left for her family, the gifts to her friends, all will be treasured. Tracy Towne talked to us about Mary for a long time. They were best friends. Dee and Tracy and Bob and Mary attended Bureau of Reclamation events together. Until her untimely death the two women, who had known one another for close to 50 years, kept track of each other. Mary struggled with a dreadful illness, Tracy has been having a rough time also, the two could sympathize and understand the ordeals of life . . . and show how much they cared. Bob, we know it is hard to bear, losing a companion such as Mary. Our community share you loss. . . and that of the members of your family. Mary's services were three weeks ago. Please call Teddy,

193-1716 with your memories of a beautiful citizen who made Boulder City proud to claim her as a resident. Bob and Mary Straus were married in 1934. She had worked for Ham and Taylor, the famous lawyers in Las Vegas for years. She leaves a daughter, Barbara and 4 grandchildren.

Bunker, Archie Wendell
Las Vegas Review-Journal, Sunday, 23 Aug 1998
Bunker, Water District Pioneer, Dies at 87. A. Wendell Bunker, a former Las Vegas city councilman who played a major role in the development of the original Las Vegas Water District, died Saturday of an undisclosed illness. He was 87. "I think his family instilled in my father the importance of civic duty early on and he carried that with him through his entire life," his son Richard Bunker said. "He liked people, wanted to help them out, and he was very committed to the development of Southern Nevada." Wendell Bunker, who served on the City Council from 1948 to 1958, was one of the council members responsible for transferring the water district, once run by the Union Pacific Railroad, over to local government. "He was always concerned that private industry might use the scarce resource of water for means other than what it was really needed for," his son said. He also was credited with playing a role in the creation of what is now known as the Las Vegas Convention and Visitors Authority, the agency responsible for luring tourists and conventions to the area. "They actually bought the old Joe Brown Racetrack, and that is where the Convention Authority now sits today," Richard Bunker said. Wendell Bunker was born in St. Thomas on Aug. 18, 1911. The Southern Nevada town was later covered by water when Hoover Dam was built and Lake Mead was created. He moved to Las Vegas in 1925 and graduated from Las Vegas High School in 1929. He was employed for several years by Union Pacific and served as chief deputy county recorder and auditor for six years. In addition, he worked as a title researcher at the Pioneer Title Insurance Co. He also worked as a real estate broker and was a co-founder of Nevada Savings and Loan. Bunker spent 25 months in the Army during World War II, including 16 months in the South Pacific. He was a member of the Las Vegas Kiwanis Club, the Boulder Dam Area Council and the Boy Scouts of America. Bunker is survived by his wife, Marion Mott Bunker; sons, Richard, Gary and Robert, all of Las Vegas; a daughter, Susan Johnson of Boulder City; seven grandchildren and 16 great grandchildren. Services will be held at the Church of Jesus Christ of Latter-day Saints, East Stake Center, at Gateway Road and Wyoming Avenue, on Tuesday at 11 a.m. Visitation will be held an hour before the services at the church. Interment will be at Boulder City Cemetery. The

family asks that donations be made to Primary Children's Hospital in Salt Lake City.

Bunting, Warren Robert
Boulder City News, Thursday, 3 Mar 1988, p.31.
Warren Robert Bunting, 59 died Friday, Feb. 26 at Orem, Utah. He had been a resident of Boulder City area since 1984. He was born in Hollywood, Calif. on July 16, 1928 and was the co-owner of a drive-in theater in Orem, Utah. He was a U.S. Army veteran. Survivors include wife LaRue Bunting, Orem, Utah; sons L. Don Bunting, Phoenix, Ariz., Anthony Robert Bunting, Morro Bay, Calif.; daughters LuAnna Rae Anderson, Springville, Utah and Sandra Lee Bunting, San Luis Obispo, Calif.; brothers Gordon P. Bunting, Morro Bay, Calif. and Roger C. Bunting, Monterrey, Calif.; 3 grandchildren. Funeral services were held Wednesday, march 1 at 1 p.m. in the Boulder City Cemetery. Officiating were the BPOE and VFW. Interment was in the Boulder City Cemetery, Boulder City.

Burgan, Glynn Hyde
Boulder City News, Thursday, 29 Aug 1957, p.1:4.
Rosary Rites For Mrs. Burgan To Be Tonight
Rosary will be said tonight at 8 o'clock at the Palm Mortuary in Las Vegas for Mrs. Glynn Hyde Burgan, 53, who died of cancer at Rose de Lima Hospital in Henderson Monday night. Mrs. Burgan, a resident of Boulder City for the past eight years, had been in the hospital for the past 11 months. Funeral service will be held in St. Andrew's Church Friday at 11 a.m. and burial will be in the Boulder City Cemetery. She underwent surgery at the Boulder City Hospital three and a half years ago, and again at Southern Nevada Memorial Hospital in Las Vegas, where she was a patient for some time before returning home. She was the mother of Mrs. John (Carolyn) Russell and Mrs. Homer (Marilyn) Medlin of Boulder City. She is survived by her mother, Mrs. Frances Jane McCoy of Springfield, Mo., a sister, Maurine Bowers of Ft. Monmouth, N. J., and five grandchildren, Jane, Genevieve, Charlotte, and Glynna Sue Russell, and Victor Medlin of Boulder City. She also leaves her former husband, Paul Burgan, of Cactus, __ will be among those __. Mrs. __. She came here from Billings, Mo., and was active in St. Andrew's Altar Society, and in Red Cross, Cancer and heart Fund drives until her illness. She made her home with the Russells, 50 Lakeview, and the Medlins, 44 Lakeview.

Burk, Mertie T.
Boulder City News, Thursday, 11 May 1972, 4:3.
Services Held For M. Burk
Graveside services for Mertie T. Burk, were at the Boulder City Cemetery Friday with the Reverend Russell Fincher of the Bethany Baptist Church, conducting the services. Mrs. Burk died May 2 at the Boulder City Hospital. She was born Sept. 11, 1904, in South Dakota, and resided at 1305 Wyoming street. She had lived in this area for five years. She is survived by a son Vern Burk, of Boulder City; sister, Miss Carlis Thompson, Bellefourche, S.D. and four grandchildren. Palm Mortuary was in charge of arrangements.

Burnett, Clayton Claude
Boulder City News, Thursday, 16 Jul 1992, 7:1.
Clayton Claude Burnett, 77, died Wednesday. He was born May 25, 1915, in Galax, Va., and had been a resident of the Boulder City area for 12 years. He is survived by his wife, Atrice O. Burnett of Boulder City; two daughters, Treca Bivins of Alta Loma, Calif., and Hope Bailey of Pasco, Wash.; three sisters, Flora Burnett of Rifle, Colo., Myrtle Harmon of Galax, Va., and Ila Patton of Galax, Va., and six grandchildren and four great grandchildren. Services were held Monday, and arrangements were handled by Palm Mortuary in Henderson.

Burr, John L.
Boulder City News, Thursday, 23 Oct 1975, 9:1.
Boulder Lodge #37, F & A.M. will conduct graveside services in Boulder City Cemetery at 2 p.m. tomorrow, for John L. Burr, 77, Mr. Burr died Tuesday morning after a long illness. He was born May 1, 1898 in Cincinnati, Ohio, but later moved to Kentucky, when he became a member of Covington Lodge #109, F. & A.M. he was owner of a retail furniture store. Mr. Burr and his wife Gladys moved to Boulder City 5 years ago. They designed and built the beautiful house at 1108 Avenue I. When he became ill, and had to use a wheelchair, they sold their home and moved to an apartment at 870 Avenue B. In addition to his wife, he is survived by a daughter, Dorothy Cahill, of Las Vegas; a sister, Alma Hahn, Holiday, Florida; and a grandson, Lonnie Burr, of Los Angeles.

Burt, Elmo D.
Boulder City News, Thursday, 24 Sep 1970.
Funeral services were held Wednesday at 10 a.m. at the LDS Chapel in Boulder City for Elmo D. Burt who died Saturday night at his home, 565 Sixth St. after a long illness of almost 10 years. Bishop Jake Williams conducted the service, Leonard Stubbs gave the eulogy and music was presented. Burial was in B. C. Cemetery. Mr. Burt was born May 10, 1914, in Junction, Utah, the son of the late Thomas and Olive Burt. He married Zella Trollope in Salt Lake City in June 1936 and moved to Boulder City that September. When Mr. Burt first came to this city he worked for his father who was a building contractor and later was employed by the Bureau of Reclamation where he was a journeyman electrician at the time of his leaving in 1946. In 1948 be became an employee of Reynold Construction C. at the Nevada Test Site where he was an electrical supervisor until his illness in 1961. He is survived by his widow, Zella, this city; a step-son, Robert Trollope, San Francisco; a stepdaughter, Vivian T. Cagle, Las Vegas; two step great grandchildren; five brothers, Wildon, Las Vegas; Aldon and Leroy of Boulder City; Ted, Bullhead City, Arizona, and Don, Renicin, Wash,; two sisters, Mrs. Carlyle Sprague, Reno, and Mrs. Shirley Vinson, Harlingen, Texas.

Bush, Samuel E.
Boulder City News, Thursday, 21 Dec 1989, 12:1-2.
Samuel E. Bush, a long-time resident of Boulder City died Monday, Dec. 11, 1989. He is survived by his wife, Helen Toye-Bush, a son, Stanley E Bush, seven grandchildren, and five great grandchildren. He moved to Boulder City from Thorntown, Indiana, in February of 1948 where he built his home next to the Boulder Cam Federal Credit Union. Sam was noted for is green thumb, winning several gardening awards. Many residents will also remember his avid interest in photography. He shared his films of the fourth of July parades which he took without fail every year. He also shared with the senior and his many friends his films of flowers, sunsets, and his many travels. He was famous for his Sweet Shop in the Boulder Theatre Building from 1948 to 1952 in the spot now occupied by Electronics Unlimited. While he owned this establishment, there was seldom an empty booth. He also opened the Ice Cream Bar where Edie's Flowers now stands, wit just as much success. Sam was an active member of Grace Community Church and a Mason of Lodge No. 37 for many years. Services were held at Palm Mortuary in Henderson on Dec. 16.

Cacace, Fortunate "Forty"
Boulder City News, Thursday, 12 Mar 1981, 27:1-2.
Graveside services will be held this morning at 11 a.m. at Boulder City Cemetery for Fortunato "Forty" Cacace, 79, who died March 8 in Upland, California. He was born July 26, 1901 in Cairo, Egypt and was a retired representative for Mobile Oil Company in New York. Mr. Cacace is survived by his wife, Gladys of Boulder City; a son, Cyril Cacace of Boulder City; one granddaughter, Caren Wagner of Wahoo, Nebraska; and a great-granddaughter, Jessica Wagner, also of Wahoo.

Cacace, Gladys
Boulder City News, Thursday, 20 Jul 1995, 8:1-2.
Gladys Cacace, 90, died Tuesday, July 18, 1995 at a local hospital. Born June 5, 1905 in Longford, Ireland, she had been a homemaker in Boulder City for 15 years. She was a member of the Daughters of the British Empire and Claremont Women's Club in California. She is survived by her son, Cyril of Boulder City; one brother, Norman Smith of Ashford, England; one grandchild and three great grandchildren. Services will be held at 10 a.m. Saturday, July 22, 1995 at the Palm Mortuary Chapel, Henderson. Interment will be at the Boulder City Cemetery. Arrangements were handled by Palm Mortuary of Henderson.

Campbell, Delmar
Boulder City News, Thursday, 19 Jan 1995, 9:2-3.
Delmar Campbell, 52, a 1½ year area resident, died Sunday, Jan. 15, 1995 in a local hospital. He was born Oct. 28, 1942 in Corning, N.Y. and was a banking maintenance engineer. He is survived by his daughter Heather Campbell, Syracuse, N.Y.; two sisters, Sherry Oswalt of Las Vegas and Lonnie Campbell of Orange County, Calif.; and an uncle, George Hogan of Syracuse, N.Y. Graveside services will be held at 9:30 a.m., Friday, Jan. 20, 1995 in the Boulder City Cemetery. Palm Mortuary handled arrangements.

Campbell, Steel E.
Boulder City News, Thursday, 17 Mar 1977, p.9:5-7.
Graveside Service Held for S. E. Campbell
Graveside services for Steel E. Campbell, 54, who passed away March 13 in Las Vegas, were held at the Boulder City cemetery Wed. at 2 p.m. Mr. Campbell was born Nov. 11, 1922, in White Township, Pa. He was a retired trainman for the railroad and resided at 979 El Camino Way in

Boulder City. He had lived here two years. A veteran of World War II in the air force, he was a member of the Acacia Lodge 355 of the F&AM in Blairsville, Pa.; Coudersport Consistory of Coudersport, Pa., and Brotherhood of Railroad trainmen. He is survived by his widow, Kathryn; daughter, Melinda Rudibaugh of Phoenix, Ariz.; and a brother, Carson Steel of Butler, Pa.

Candelaria, Rafael
Boulder City News, Thursday, 21 Oct 1976,10:2.
Mr. Rafael Candelaria of 601 Avenue L, passed away October 15th at the Southern Nevada Memorial hospital in Las Vegas. He was a resident of Boulder City over eight years. Mr. Candelaria was born October 22, 1897, in Concho, Arizona. He was a farmer. He is survived by his wife, Julia Candelaria; three daughters, Sophia Sanchez of Boulder City, Elsie Cruz of Phoenix, and Julia Fowler of Garden Grove, Calif.; three sons, Gilbert Candelaria of Henderson, Pete Candelaria of Phoenix, Cesario Candelaria of Crestline, California; eighteen grandchildren, and eighteen great grandchildren. It was his wish that, in lieu of flowers, donations be made to the Helen J. Stewart School in Las Vegas. There was prayer service Monday, Oct. 18, at 7 p.m. Palm Chapel in Henderson, and Mass at St. Peter's Catholic Church in Henderson, on Tuesday at 10 a.m. Father Caesar Caviglie officiated. Interment at the Boulder City Cemetery.

Caniglia, Andrew
Boulder City News, Thursday, 24 Nov 1994, 7:1-2.
Andrew Caniglia, 92, died Friday, Nov. 18, 1994, at a local hospital. Born Nov. 7, 1902, in Rivisondoli, Italy, he had been a resident of Boulder City for one and one-half years. He was a retired owner and operator of a shoe repair business. He is survived by his wife, Fannie Caniglia of Boulder City; one son, Donald Caniglia, also of Boulder City; one brother, Emido Caniglia, of Cleveland, Ohio; and two grandchildren. A Mass was said at St. Andrews Catholic Church, in Boulder City at 10 a.m. Tuesday. Arrangements were handled by Palm Mortuary of Henderson.

Carl, Ermgard

Boulder City News, Thursday, 15 Feb 1990, 20:1-4.
By Teddy Fenton
On Sunday, Feb. 18, 1990, graveside services will be conducted by Father Joe Annese at 2 p.m. It is hoped that the many friends of the Carl family will join Maud Kathryn Crowell, Dr. Ernest Carl and Sonya Gillighan to the memory of their mother Ermgard Carl who lived with her husband, famous author, Hugo Carl right next door to the home of Lloyd and Lillian Morrison on I St. Ermgard led an enchanted life. The book (memoirs) of her life was loaned to me by Lillian Morrison. In it she shared her philosophy, every word is a jewel. She adored life, she had reason to, a happy and exciting life with her husband Carl, enjoyment beyond belief with her three children, and an exquisite joy in grandchildren. Sonya, Lisa, and Eric, Andrea, Julie, Jeffrey, Joseph and Richard. The above are the children of her three children. Ermgard arrived from Germany while it was at the height of its beauty. The Black Forest was untainted (now it is being destroyed by a blight). She expressed her love for all things of nature, trees, flowers, animals, her childhood was marked by "pets" and her own children were to enjoy the desert creatures here in Boulder City. She called her book "A Life" and it would make the finest tribute ever to her if it could be repeated in full. Maud Kathryn wrote "Hi Teenager" for the BC News 1948-49. She said to tell her classmates "hi" and she will welcome their presence at her mother's services.

Carlson, Marie

Boulder City News, Thursday, 21 Apr 1994, 6:2.
Marie Carlson, 76, a 15-year Boulder City resident died Tuesday, April 19, 1994 in a local convalescent home. She was born on Nov. 30, 1917 in Omaha, Neb. and was a homemaker. She is survived by her husband, Herbert J. Carlson of Boulder City; a daughter, Judy Olson of Rio Verde, Ariz.; two sisters, Helen __ of Laguna Hills, Calif.; and Donna Groberk of Concord, Calif.; three brothers, Michael Zoroya of St. Louis, Mo.; Ted Zoroya of Mesquite, Texas; and one grandchild. Services were held. Palm Mortuary handled arrangements.

Carney, Louie J.

Boulder City News, Thursday, 6 Sep 1973, 18:4.
Graveside services were a0 a.m. Saturday at the Boulder City Cemetery for Louie J. Carney, 75, 300 E. Tropicana, Las Vegas, who died Thursday in a local hospital. Mr. Carney, who was born in Ashland City, Tenn., on Feb. 27, 1898, was a construction worker. He is survived by his wife, Frances Carney, Las Vegas; a son, Jerome D. Carney, Mojave Valley, Ariz.; a brother, F. M. Cantrell Nashville, Tenn.; a sister-in-law, Katherine Fomsbee, Kingman, Ariz.; a nephew, Arleigh Watson, Henderson, and two grandchildren. Bunker Brothers Mortuary is handing arrangements.

Carroll, Barry Wayne

Boulder City News, Thursday, 24 Feb 1983, 2:4-7.
Barry Carroll killed in auto accident
Boulder City resident Barry Wayne Carroll, 19, was killed in a vehicle accident on U.S. 15 Tuesday night as he was returning home from San Diego, California. He lived with his grandparents, Herb and Veda Oliver, who were driving a second vehicle behind Carroll. They did not witness the accident. The victim apparently fell asleep and lost control of his car which struck an embankment. Carroll survived the crash but wandered onto the highway where he was struck by a truck and killed. His is the son of Gary Carroll of Oregon and Joann Carroll (deceased). He also leaves an uncle, Bob Oliver, and great uncle, Vern Oliver. Carroll had graduated from automotive school and had attended UNLV. No funeral services were available at press time. Palm Mortuary is in charge of arrangements.

Boulder City News, Thursday, 3 Mar 1983, 2:1-4.
Barry Wayne Carroll, 20, of Boulder City, died Tuesday in Barstow, Calif. Mr. Carroll was born Nov. 21, 1962, in Tampa, Fla. He was a student. His is survived by his father, Gary of Hillsboro, Ore,; grandparents, Herbert and Vada Oliver, and uncle, Robert Oliver, all of Boulder City, and half-brother, Kelly of Las Vegas. A graveside service was held last Friday in Boulder City Cemetery. Palm Mortuary handled arrangements.

Carse, Clifford C., Sr.
Boulder City News, Thursday, 17 Nov 1983, 7:1.
Graveside services will be held Friday at 11 a.m. in the Boulder City cemetery for Clifford C. Carse, Sr., who passed away November 15 in Boulder City. He was 79. He was born May 13, 1904 in Long Beach, Ca., and resided in Boulder City for nine years. He was a retired cement mason. Mr. Carse is survived by sons Clifford, Jr., of Boulder City and Edward M. of Las Vegas; daughter Betty Finmark, Torrance, Ca., nine grandchildren and seven great grandchildren. He was a member of BPOE Chapter 1682 of Boulder City.

Carson, Charles T.
Boulder City News, Thursday, 11 July 1946, p.1:1
Body of Charles Carson, Who Disappeared May 9, Found Near Lake Mead
The body of Charles T. Carson, 78-year-old Boulder City man who disappeared last May I, was found yesterday afternoon n a ditch about a quarter of a mile west of Lake Mead lodge, beyond the highway and toward the hills. The body was found by Chief Ranger Donal J. Jolley and Ranger W. F. V. Leicht of the National Park Service, who joined Bureau of Reclamation rangers in a search after a motorist reported to Chief C. F. Peterson that an odor was noticeable along the highway near that point. The remains were discovered at 2:56, according to Jolley's record, about half a mile from where Carson was last seen alive by Mrs. Ray Poyser, who reported having seen him walking near the highway west of the lodge the afternoon of the day he disappeared from his home here. Papers in his pockets and his clothing tallied with descriptions given when he was reported missing. He was the father of Mrs. N. R. Moller, 664 Avenue G. And had lived with the Mollers for about a year precious to his disappearance. He had lived in Seattle previously and when he wandered away from home here, as he sometimes did, one of his first answers to questions was that he was "going to Seattle." It was thought, after his disappearance, that he might have gotten a ride with tourists and returned to Seattle, though no trace of him could be found there. National Park Service and Bureau of Reclamation rangers searched the lake shore and hills for a week or two after his disappearance seeking him in the vicinity of where he was last seen. In his pockets when he was found was a notebook with a note on one page, "I live at 664 Ave. G. My phone 95. My name is Charles Carson, father of Elyse Moller." On another page was the name Karl Kelty, and on another "Elyse Moller, 664 Ave. G." Rangers removed the notebook, two photographs, a keyring with keys and

a tie clasp for identification purposes and burned the clothing, which consisted of a dark grey coat and pants, blue shirt, black low shoes. He wore no hat. The remains were taken by ambulance accompanied by Lester Burt and George Corcoran to the Bunker-Burt mortuary in Las Vegas. While the aged man had no pocketbook or money with him, there were three neckties, and extra pair of socks and a hair brush in his pockets. Present at the time rangers removed the effects from his pockets were Deputy Coroner C. A. Savage, Carl Eliason, manager of Lake Mead lodge, Donald L. Linck, John S. Ward. It is expected that the latter two, with Leicht will act as coroner's jury at the inquest which will be held at the police station Friday at 5 p.m. Dr. D. M. MacCornack, who was called to the scene, said death appeared to be from natural causes. The deceased man leaves a son, Charles Victor Carson of San Francisco; two daughters, Mrs. May Renaud of Long Beach, and Mrs. Moller, as well as a number of grandchildren and great grandchildren. Mrs. John Pilant, Henderson, is a granddaughter and her two sons, John and Richard, are among the great grandchildren. Funeral arrangements will await the return of Mrs. Moller, who is visiting her sister in Long Beach.

Carver, Benjamin S.
Boulder City News, Friday, 5 Mar 1948, p.1
"Dad" Carver Dies Of Heart Attack; Funeral Tomorrow
Funeral services for Benjamin S. Carver will be held at 10 a.m. tomorrow at Grace Community Church. Reverend Winston Trever will officiate. "Dad" Carver died of a heart attack yesterday at his home, 604 California Ave., where he lived with his daughter-in-law, Mrs. Georgia Carver. He was 80 years of age. He also is survived by a son, Edwin, who is expected here today from his home in San Bernardino; a grandson, Bud Carver of Onyx, Calif.; a granddaughter, Mrs. George Lowe of Hawthorne, Calif.; and two great granddaughters. "Dad" came here 14 years ago after having been a building contractor for many years in California. He spent much time with flowers, and his yard and garden are a showplace in Boulder City. He occasionally worked for Mort Wagner at Desert Lodge. Yesterday as he was eating a late breakfast he complained of feeling unwell. Mrs. Carver called Dr. Robert L. Fenlon, but "Dad" died about an hour later.

Cavis, Arthur B.
Las Vegas Evening Review-Journal, Thursday, 20 Apr 1944, 7:3.
Boulder Notes - Funeral services for A. B. Cavis who died Sunday morning, were held Wednesday evening at 5:30 o;clock, at Grace community church. Music was furnished by Miss Madelaine Elwell, at the Stevenson memorial organ. The Reverend Winston who officiated, spoke briefly on the life and character of the deceased and concluded with scripture reading and a prayer. Graveside services were conducted by the Boulder City V. F. W. post, as Cavis was a member of the Spanish War veterans organization. Four comrades of post number 10 acted as pallbearers. R. G. Hanson, post commander was in charge, with Thomas Godbey as chaplain. A military salute was fired and taps were sounded by Dennis Whalen. Cavis is survived by his wife, Vergie Cavis, one daughter Mrs. James Peasley, of Tracy, California, and a son Grant Cavis of Summit City, California and five grand children. He was born in Maysville, Ohio, in June 1881 and moved to Boulder City in 1932, where he began work for Six Companies.

Cavis, Vergie
Boulder City News, Friday, 19 May 1950, 8:4.
Funeral Sunday For Mrs. Cavis
Vergie Cavis, who had lived in Boulder City since construction days until recently, died in her sleep Tuesday night, apparently of a heart attack. Her body will be sent to the Palm Funeral Home on Saturday. Mrs. Cavis had just purchased a trailer house, and was visiting at the home of her son Grant in Hermiston, Oregon. She also has a daughter Ardeen, Mrs. James Peasley, in Los Banos, California. Mrs. Cavis worked at the Visitor's Bureau for several years. She was a member of the Business and Professional Women's Club, the Rebekah lodge, and is the first charter member of the local B. P. O. Does grove to die. She was a member of Grace Community Church, where she used to teach Sunday school. Olaf Stoeve, pastor of Community Church, will conduct the funeral services on Sunday at 2:30 p.m. She will be buried beside her husband in the Boulder Cemetery.

Chamberlain, Gary C.
Boulder City News, Thursday, 7 Feb 1980, 6:1-3.
Funeral services were held last Tuesday at Bethany Baptist Church for Gary C. Chamberlain, 47, who died February 2 in Las Vegas. The Reverend Gary Moore officiated. Born April 17, 1932 in Salt Lake City, Utah, Mr. Chamberlain had resided in Boulder City for two years. He was manager of a recreational vehicle showroom. He is survived by his wife, Louise Chamberlain of Boulder City; a daughter, Debra Wilkerson of Livermore, Calif.; a son, Kevin Chamberlain of Ventura, Calif.; sister, Peggy Pankey of Castro Valley, Calif.; brother, Cal Chamberlain of Redding, Calif.; and his mother, Irma Chamberlain of Redding. Interment was at Boulder City Cemetery.

Chamberlain, Lamar E.
Boulder City News, Thursday, 15 Apr 1982, 35:4-5.
Lamar E. Chamberlain, 69, died Wednesday, April 14, 1982 in Boulder City. He lived here for thirty years. He was born in Cedar Fort, Utah, December 29, 1912. He was a welder for Pacific Engineering. Survivors are his wife, Leone H. of Boulder City; a son, Jaron of Cerritos, California; daughters, Shirley Jacobson of Henderson, Terry Payne of Boulder City and Judy Chamberlain of Boulder City. Three brothers, Afton of Cedar Fork, Utah, Roy of American Fork, Utah and Cecil of Lehigh, Utah. Six grandchildren and three great grandchildren. Services will be held Saturday at 11 a.m. at the Boulder City LDS Chapel, with Bishop Bruce Alder of the second ward LDS officiating. Entombment will be Palm Mausoleum in Boulder City.

Chambers, Clement W.
Boulder City News, Thursday, 19 Jan 1995, 9:3-4.
Clement W. Chambers, 90, retired U.S. Bureau of Reclamation employee and early pioneer in Boulder City and later one of the first settlers of Page, Ariz., died Jan. 12, 1995 of heart failure at Fairfax Hospital, Va. He lived with his daughter in Vienna, Va. He arrived in Boulder City in 1931 where he first lived in a tent for 11 months until houses were built. He worked for Six Company on the Boulder Dam Project and later for the U.S. Bureau of Reclamation as a rigger, and structural steel iron worker. He also worked on the diversion tunnels. He was a resident of Boulder City until 1956 when he moved to Arizona to be a member of the team that laid out and began construction of the city of Page. He later worked as a powerhouse mechanic on Glenn Canyon Dam. A long-time resident

of Page he was active in city government, serving on the city council. He was also a member of the Page volunteer fire department. He moved from Page to Vienna, Va., in 1992. His wife of 69 years, Leila McCollum Chambers, died in 1992. Survivors include one daughter, Dolores Westfield of Vienna, Va.; four grandchildren, five great grandchildren and also his Brothers-in-law Alton McCollum and Irwin McCollum who are still residents of Boulder City. He was a member of Grace Community Church of Boulder City. Friends may call on Friday, Jan. 20 from 1 to 2 p.m. when funeral services will be held at the Palm Mortuaries and Memorial Parks on Boulder Highway in Henderson. Interment will follow the service at the Boulder City Cemetery. Arrangements were handled by Palm Mortuary of Henderson.

Chambers, Leila M.
Boulder City News, Thursday, 23 Jan 1992, 9:2.
Leila M. Chambers, 88, died Friday. She was born Sept. 4, 1903, in Missouri, and was a resident of Boulder City from 1931 to 1956. Her ususal place of residence was Page, Ariz. She is survived by her husband, Clement Chambers of Page, Ariz.; one daughter, Dolores Westfield of Vienna, Va.; two brothers, Alton McCollum, both of Boulder City; also four grandchildren and four great grandchildren. Services were held Tuesday. Arrangements were handled by Palm Mortuary in Henderson.

Chapman, Elwood C.
Boulder City News, Thursday, 26 Apr 1973, 3:2.
Services Mon. At Palm For Elwood Chapman
Funeral services were held Monday at 2 p.m. at Palm Chapel in Henderson for Elwood C. Chapman, 38, who died April 20. Mr. Chapman was born June 17, 1935 in Harrison, Maine. He resided in Boulder City at 628 Avenue M. He was a pump operator for the Bureau of Reclamation. He is survived by his wife Gicela; daughters Valerie and Gloria, son Clifford, all of Boulder City; brother, Clyde of West Brook, Maine; sister, Janice Charest, Westbrook; parents, Mr. and Mrs. Clifford Chapman, Gorham, Maine. Interment was at Boulder City cemetery.

Cheadle, Margaret Weller Titus
Boulder City News, Thursday, 14 Jan 1965.
Margaret Weller Titus Cheadle, 85, died Friday morning, Jan. 8, at the El Jen Convalescent Center, after a long illness. She had lived in Boulder City since 1941. Mrs. Cheadle was born June 28, 1880 in Glenwood, Ohio. At the age of 10 she moved with her family to Telluride, Color., where her father bought the Ballard Gold Mine. She was one of nine children, all of whom preceded her in death. She was married to Edgar Snow Titus of Rockland, Maine, and they had one child, the late Ruth L. Baker, who lived for many years at 655 Avenue G. Mr. Titus, a mining engineer, perished under mysterious circumstances in Death Valley in July, 1905. The Titus Canyon is named after him. Later she married Carl Cheadle of Telluride, who died in 1936. Mrs. Cheadle preferred being a homebody. She had no other vocation and did not belong to any organizations. She is survived by two granddaughters, Shirley (Mrs. William L.) Phillips, 647 Avenue G; and Barbara (Mrs. Robert C.) Sansom of Kearns, Utah; also four great-grandchildren and numerous nieces and nephews. Graveside rites were held Tuesday afternoon at the Boulder Cemetery, with the Reverend Guy Holliday officiating.

Cheney, Louise O.
Boulder City News, Thursday, 21 Sep 1989, 29:1-2.
Louise O. Cheney, 54, of Boulder City, died Friday. She was born Dec. 27, 1934, in San Jose, Calif. She was Branch Manager for Title Company. Survivors included her husband, David Cheney of Boulder City; her father, Frank Sanchez of Modesto, Calif., two daughters, Debbie Wilkerson of Livermore., Calif. and Tomi Cheney of Laguna Hills, Calif.; three sons, Kevin Chamberlain of Babylon, New York, Steven Cheney of San Diego, Calif. and Michael Cheney of Boulder City; two brothers, Louie Conrad of San Jose, Calif., Warren Conrad of Novato, Calif. and a sister, La Vern Teel of Las Vegas and two grandchildren. Services were held Monday. Palm Mortuary handled arrangements.

Chesley, John Albert "Bert"
Boulder City News, Thursday, 20 Oct 1988, 6:4-6.
John Albert "Bert" Chesley passed away at his home on Avenue M on Wednesday, Oct. 12, 1988. He was 90 years old. Bert was born near Pima, Ariz., in 1898 and came to Boulder City in 1943 and worked at Central Market for 28 years, (beginning at the old original store located on Wyoming Street where Boulder City Clinic is located today). He was a lifelong member of The Church of Jesus Christ of Latter-day Saints. Bert is survived by his wife, Opal, two daughters, Janella Chandler of Henderson and Velda Rusch of Boulder City, and one son Dave Chesley of Las Vegas, one sister Alice David of Safford, Ariz. and by 13 grandchildren and nine great-grandchildren. Graveside services were held on Monday, Oct. 17 at Boulder City Cemetery with counselor Heber Tobler presiding.

Chesley, Opal
Boulder City News, Thursday, 13 Apr 1995, 14:3-4.
Opal Chesley, 88 of Boulder City, died April 10, 1995. Born July 22, 1906, in Safford, Ariz., she was a homemaker. She is survived by two daughters, Janella Chandler of Henderson, and Velda Ilene Rusch of North Terrytown, N.Y.; a son, Dale A. of Las Vegas; one sister, Ethel Adams of Scottsdale, Ariz.; 11 grandchildren and four great grandchildren. Visitation will be at 3 p.m. today and viewing until 7 p.m. Graveside service will be at 1 p.m. Friday at Boulder City Cemetery. Palm Mortuary in Henderson handled arrangements.

Childress, Esther
Boulder City News, Thursday, 16 May 1974.
Esther Childress Services
by Esther Shipp
Esther Childress, 73, died May 8. She was laid to rest Tuesday, beside her husband in the Boulder City Cemetery. At her request, no services were held. Esther Christina Wing was born June 1, 1901 in Whitehall, Wisconsin. As a young woman, she joined the Whitehall Rebekah Lodge No. 23. She and Leslie Pryor Childress were married Aug 4, 1920 in Yakima, Washington. She was a founder and past president of the PTA in Yakima, Wide Hollow School District No. 26, and a state representative of the Chekola Women's Club of Yakima. The family moved to Boulder City in 1940. She joined Desert Chapter no. 22 O.E.S. in 1942, used to belong to the Bookmarker's Club, and had membership in the Community

Concert group of Las Vegas. For many years she was active in the Women's Association of Grace Community Church, but was also affiliated with the First Church of Christ Scientist. Mr. Childress died in August 1960. She is survived by a son L. Earl Childress, 519 Don Vincente, Boulder City, son Stanley, Yakima, Wash.; four grandchildren and a sister, Bernice Wing Taylor, of Seattle, Wash.

Chilson, Harry Orville
Boulder City News, Thursday, 14 Nov 1968.
Funeral services were conducted Tuesday at 10 a.m. for Harry Orville Chilson, 74, of 1501 Nevada Highway who died Nov. 6 at Boulder City Hospital. The Reverend Hugh Smith of St. Andrew's Catholic Church officiated and Bunker Brothers was in charge of arrangements. Mr. Chilson was born Jan. 14, 1894 in Rockwood, S.D. and had lived here for seven years. He was a retired mortician. He is survived by his widow Rose of this city, and a daughter, Mrs. Evelyn Flemmer, Libby, Mont.

Christianson, Hans J. and Gudrun
Boulder City News, Thursday, 11 Jun 1981, 2:4-5.
Something beautiful happened in the lives of Hans and Gudrun Christianson for together they had come to the United States from Denmark to make new lives over 50 years ago. They married in Denmark, had celebrated their 50th wedding anniversary last year in Boulder City, had lived in an apartment here since leaving Little Valley, New York 3 years ago, coming here to be close to their beloved daughter, Mary Timme, and when they could not take care of each other in their home, they chose to take a room at the B.C. Care center where they died just 5 hours apart last Sunday. Hans, 81, was used to being "head of his household" and he preceded his bride of 50 years by 5 hours. So close in life they now join hands to go through the next adventure behind the curtain we know they welcomed, since they both lived an active life. They were known by the good friends who served them "Meals on Wheels" while they lived in the apartment. They were loved at the Care Center and Mary, their daughter, said to thank this wonderful community for caring for her parents. Mary Timme and her husband Glen were so happy when her parents left New York to come here where they loved the warm climate. Hans had worked in a factory in Little Valley where the product was dry milk shipped all over the world. Mary and Hans traveled back to their homeland, Denmark, on several occasions but their real home was always the United States. A son, Paul, preceded them in death. His children are Kay Glover, Lyn and Gayle Christanson. Mary and

Glenn Timme have children Anne Marie and Glenn, Jr. On June 17,1981, Gudrun would have been 79 years old. Reverend Mel Pritts conducted the graveside services. He said he felt as the family died, that the celebration of life as the Christiansons had know it, was continued with absolute joy in the fact that they were never separated.

Clair, Clifford R.
Boulder City News, Thursday, 19 Apr 1973.
Clifford R. Clair died yesterday at his home at 1501 Nevada Highway, lot 29. He was 70 years of age. He was born on February 18, 1903, and was the owner-operator of a drive in business. Survivors include his widow Frances; four sons, Gilbert D., Wichita, Kansas, Charles R., Independence, Kansas, Marvin L., and Orville D., both of Oklahoma City, Okla.; a brother Allen D., Olean, N.Y.; two sisters, Sarah Burton, San Juan Capistrano, and Emily Hixon, Stanton, Calif.; also eight grandchildren and two great grandchildren. He was a member of the Boulder City F. and A.M. Services will be held Saturday at 11 a.m. at Palm Mortuary Chapel conducted by the Masonic Order. Burial will be in Boulder Cemetery.

Clark, Cleo F.
Boulder City News, Thursday, 4 Sep 1986, 30:1.
Cleo F. Clark, age 91, a 15 year resident of Boulder City, passed away Wednesday, Aug. 27. She was born July 15, 1895 in Oklahoma. She had been a housewife. She leaves nieces Fern Griffith of Boulder City, Helen Dowty of Roseville, Calif., and Hazel Hull also of Roseville. Nephews, Vern Messner of Joplin, Mo., and Bob Messner of Hawthorne, Nevada. Graveside services were held Tuesday, Sept. 2 with the Reverend Steve Nueezley officiating. Interment was in the Boulder City Cemetery.

Clark, Erle Douglas "Pop"
Boulder City News, Thursday, 2 Nov 1967, 1:1.
Community Loses Pioneer
Erle Douglas "Pop" Clark, another Boulder City pioneer, died Saturday. Funeral services were conducted Tuesday morning at Palm Chapel in Henderson by the Reverend Guy Holliday of Grace Community Church. He was born June 29, 1892 in Dixon, Calif., and worked in the construction field all of his life. The Clarks came to Boulder City in March 1932, and he was employed at Hoover Dam until 1948. He worked on Davis Dam from 1949 to 1951, at Mercury from 1951 to 1954, and at

Lake Mead Naval Base from 1954 until his retirement in 1960. Not content to be idle, "Pop" helped his daughter's family to renovate their home at 648 Avenue G. Mabel and Erle were married Oct. 18, 1916 in Camrose, Alberta, Canada, and last year celebrated their Golden Anniversary. They were the parents of four children, one deceased. "Pop" is survived by his widow, Mabel, 648 Avenue H; two sons, Winfield R. at 624 Seventh St., Boulder City and Lowell E. "Tex" Clark of Tampa, Fla.; daughter (Mrs. Donald) Russell, 648 Avenue G; 9 grandchildren and 3 great-grandchildren. Also a sister, Janet Robben of Dixon, California.

Clark, Guy W.
Boulder City News, Thursday, 26 Aug 1982, 9:7-8.
Guy W. Clark, 71, of Boulder City, died last Wednesday in a local hospital. Mr. Clark was born on may 5, 1911, in Pangutich, Utah. He was employed with the U. S. Post Office, and retired as superintendent of the Airport Station; he was a member of the LDS church, BPOE, and the Association of Retired Postal Workers. He is survived by his wife, Wilba "Billie" Clark, and his daughter, Connie Stewart, both of Boulder City; son, Robert of Las Vegas; brother, James of Panguitch; sisters, Mrs. Gal C. Jordan of Sun City, Arizona; Mrs. R. Gene Fitzgerald fo Midvale, Utah and Mrs. Mary Alvey of North Las Vegas, and eight grandchildren.

Clark, Jack J.
Boulder City News, Thursday, 30 Sep 1971.
Clark Interred In Boulder
Jack J. Clark, 44, was interred in the Boulder City Cemetery yesterday morning, following funeral services held at the Palm Chapel in Henderson under the auspices of the Masonic Order. He died Saturday in Henderson. Clark was born January 19, 1927 in Cheyenne, Wyoming. He has lived in Nevada for 10 years. He was a member of Las Vegas Lodge No. 21, F & AM, Malta Commandery Knights Templar, the Royal Arch Masons, and the Zobud Council of Royal and Select Masters. Mr. Clark is survived by his wife, Elaine, 291 Nebraska, Henderson; step-daughters Cindy Scout and Susan Kramer. Step-son Fred Kramer all of Henderson; and step-son Don Kramer of Camp Pendleton, California.

Clark, Robert C. "Sparky"
Boulder City News, Thursday, 9 May 1968.
Elks Conduct Clark Rites
Robert C. "Sparky" Clark, 57, died Wednesday afternoon in the Boulder City Hospital. Funeral services were conducted Saturday morning by officers of BPO Elks Lodge No. 1682, which he had joined in 1961. Background music was provided by Lena Hurt, a BPO Doe. Exalted Ruler Phil Wagner was also in charge of graveside rites at Boulder City Cemetery. Mr. Clark was born Aug. 21, 1910 I Cottonwood, Calif., and he worked for the late Earl Brothers at a theater in that state. His mother and step-father, Mr. and Mrs. Charles Elder, came to this area in 1931, and his sister taught in the first little school building erected by Mr. Elder. "Sparky" followed his family here in 1932, and was manager of the Boulder City Theater for several years. For two years before World War II he operated one of the souvenir stands near Hoover Dam. In 1941 he was employed by the U.S.B.R., Boulder Canyon Project, as an apprentice electrician. After his return from military service, he completed his apprenticeship in April, 1954, and was promoted to electrician, maintenance. He was presented with the Department of Interior 20-year service emblem in March 1961. He was fondly known as "Uncle Bob" top his three nephews, Earl Jr., Robert and Charles (Chuck), and to their children. He is survived by his brother Earl Clark Sr., a Boulderite for many years, who now lives with wife Lena in Red Bluff, Calif.

Clegg, Blanche F.
Boulder City News, Thursday, 21 Apr 1977, 5:4.
Blanche F. Clegg Passes Away
Services were held yesterday at Palm Mortuary for Blanche F. Clegg who passed away April 16 in Boulder City. Mrs. Clegg was born March 23, 1892 in Baldwin, Kansas and had resided in Boulder City for 3½ years. She lived with her husband William at 632 California St. Shw as a member of the Royal Neighbors of America. Beside her husband she is survived by daughters Dorothy Durante of Costa Mesa, Calif. and Mary L. Behr of Boulder City; sons Jack Clegg of Holliday, Florida and Arnold Clegg of Petaluma, Calif. a sister Nell Jess of Council Bluffs, Iowa and brother Jack Snethen, Denver, Colorado, ten grandchildren and 10 great grandchildren. Interment followed at Boulder City Cemetery.

Clegg, William
Boulder City News, Thursday, 20 Jun 1985, 33:1-2.
William Clegg, passed away Tuesday, June 11 at home at 501 Hopi Place, Boulder City, Nev. He was born November 27, 1895 in Belfast, Ireland. A resident of Boulder City for 11 years. He is survived by his daughters, Mary L. Behr, 501 Hopi, Boulder City, Nev.; Dorothy Durante, Costa Mesa, Cal.; sons, Jack Clegg, Holliday, Florida and Arnold Clegg, Petaluma, Cal. Brother, John Clegg of Portland, Ore. 10 grandchildren and 10 great grandchildren.

Clements, James Alfred
Boulder City News, Thursday, 8 June 1972.
Graveside Services For J. Clements
Graveside rites will be held this morning at 11 o'clock for James Alfred Clements, 56. They were be conducted at the Boulder City Cemetery by the Reverend Gene Holman of the Foursquare Gospel Church, with military honors by American Legion Post 31, of which Clements was a member. Mr. Clements was killed instantly when he lost control of his car in the southbound lane on Boulder Highway near Sturm Street, Monday noon, and was hit by a pick-up truck traveling in the north-bound lane. James Clements was born March 7, 1916 in Florida. He served in the U. S. Navy. He has been a cook for many years, and came here from Reno in 1970. He was employed as a chef at the Rainbow Club in Henderson. Survivors are his wife Marie (They were married Christmas, 1971), 203 Mead Way, Boulder City; a son, Michael Clements, Manchester; his mother, Kathleen Nelson, Durham, North Caro.; a brother, Bernie Clements, Chapel Hill, N. C.; and three grandchildren.

Coffin, Helen C.
Boulder City News, Thursday, 3 Mar 1988, p.31.
Helen C. Coffin, 91 died Wednesday, Feb. 24 in Boulder City. She had been a resident of the Nevada area since 1919 residing in Boulder City since 1932. She was born in Providence, R.I. on Dec. 16, 1896 and was a owner and operator of a gift shop. Survivors include son Don Belding, Boulder City; four grandchildren and seven great-grandchildren. Visitation began Thursday, Feb. 25 at 2 p.m. at Palm Mortuary in Henderson. Rosary was recited at 6 p.m. Thursday and Mass was said on Friday, Feb. 26 at 10 a.m. both at St. Andrew's Catholic Church in Boulder City. Father Joe Annese of St. Andrew's Catholic Church officiated. Interment was in the Boulder City Cemetery, Boulder City.

Coggins, Clyde A.
Boulder City News, Thursday, 24 Sep 1970.
A graveside service will be conducted Friday at 2 p.m. at Boulder City Cemetery for Clyde A. Coggins, 69, who died Tuesday morning at Southern Nevada Memorial Hospital of a lingering illness. He was born Oct. 22, 1900 in Salisbury, N. C. and had been in Boulder City since 1956. Mr. Coggins was a retired railroad telegrapher and station master. The deceased is survived by two sons, Russell of Henderson, and Michael of San Diego, Calif.; two daughters, Mary Pratt of Bishop, Calif., and Carol Hilliard of San Antonio, Tex.; and 16 grandchildren.

Cole, Elsie Dorene
Boulder City News, Thursday, 25 Feb 1971, 1:8.
Bishop Jacob Williams conducted services Tuesday at 1 p.m. for Elsie Dorene Cole, 43, at the Boulder City L.D.S. Chapel. Interment was in the B. C. Cemetery. Palm Mortuary was in charge of arrangements. Mrs. Cole died of cancer shortly after midnight Saturday at Rose de Lima Hospital. She was born Aug. 11, 1927 in Ogden, Utah and had lived here for 19 years. At the time of her death she was the secretary of the chief ranger of the National Park Service. Mrs. Cole is survived by her husband, J. E. Cole, Sr., 525 Utah St.; two sons, J. E. Jr., and Steven, Boulder City; a daughter, Candace Thiriot of Las Vegas, her father, William Bartlett, Salt Lake City; her mother, Mrs. Thelma Bird of Las Vegas; a brother, Elton Bartlett, Washington; a sister, Mrs. Janet Rollins, Las Vegas and four grandchildren.

Cole, Etta S.
Boulder City News, Thursday, 7 June1973, 3:4-5.
Funeral Set For Etta S. Cole, by Esther Shipp
Funeral services will be held today for Etter S. Cole, 77, who died Tuesday at the Desert Retreat Hospital in Las Vegas. The rites are scheduled for 2 p.m. at the Palm Mortuary in Henderson, and burial will be in the Boulder City Cemetery. Reverend Robert Richards will conduct the service. Etter Steele was born Dec. 29, 1895, in Prescott, Arkansas, and circumstances made it difficult for her to get an education. This limited her activities in many ways. Later she moved to Wichita, Kansas, where she married Peter N. Cole, a veteran. A plumber, Cole was the tenth man on the payroll of the Six Companies the first day they started operations. Etter and Pete were among the earliest pioneers in the tent village of "Ragtown." Eventually they moved into 600 Ave. F, a house

Pete helped to build. In 1948, Laura Bell wrote up Pete as a Boulder Builder. He died a couple of years later. Etter like to sew, and made many of her own clothes. She also kept her yard full of flowers, and like to dance. She is survived by two sisters, Florence Cooper of Winniewood, Okla.; Mrs. J. B. Mathews, Sapulpa, Okla., and a niece, Gladys Ericksten of Las Vegas.

Collins, Lillian
Boulder City News, Thursday, 12 Feb 1981, 3:1-8.
The Bright Spirit of Lillian Collins Was Felt By Everyone
by Teddy Fenton
Lillian Collins died last Sunday morning. She was in her 80th year. Her birthday was Aug. 26. No one will every say that her 80 years on this earth went unused. Her bright spirit touched people young and old. There was a need for her volunteer work for she believed in doing whatever there was to do to alleviate suffering from any form of illness and disease. Her forte was working with the March of Dimes. For years she served as the state advisor from Nevada for the March of Dimes. Funds raised in Nevada was under her leadership. Finally the break-though. The Salk Vaccine was discovered and while the long hard fight to stop the deadly attacks of polio did not disappear entirely, certainly one seldom heard of a stricken child. Lillian was so lovely and had such presence at a microphone that she was called on to act as narrator for the annual fall fashion show staged by the Woman's Club. One could know that when she belonged to an organization she always did her share of the volunteer work. She was president of the Woman's Club and through it developed a work program that enabled the entire group to become known for their civic work. Lillian married Ray in 1925. Their anniversary was always a cause to celebrate. Her good friend, Esther Shipp, would print the item in the Nov. 22 anniversary list. Lillian watched the list for weekly birthdays and anniversaries and would either send a card or make a personal call. The cards mailed out from the Collins residence would reach toward 2000 a year until postage became too high. It would seem watching her volunteer work all the years we knew her that young people activities were her favorite project. She headed the B.C. Girl Scout Council for over 10 years. When the Scouts were reorganized and all became a part of Clark County, Lillian then became president of the Frontier Girl Scouts. Politically she became involved as the most active woman in the Republican movement other then her good friend Anna Wartman. She held an open house for candidates seeking office, she ran for assemblywoman from District 22 and was defeated by a narrow margin.

Whatever she did, she did with all the enthusiasm she possessed. She was forever being photographed for news stories and her famous hats were gorgeous. She became a familiar figure to Nevada politicians who served in Washington D. C. During World War II. She attended a conference of the Woman's National Advisory Committee for the bond of the month campaign. A newspaper clipping shows her there while Congressman Cliff Young, Republican-at-large purchased a bond from her. When the Polka Dot Haven teenage center was organized complete with officers 1952 her guiding hand was felt all through the years it existed. She praised the youngsters "who worked for their own recreation" endlessly and it was her persuasion that brought to fruition the necessary funds to build the Polka Dot Haven skating rink. Its cement slab serves even today as a base for one of the tennis courts. The teenage club burned to the ground after serving our youngsters for several years. She loved her family. Each big event, birthdays, anniversaries, Thanksgiving and Christmas they were all together. Her daughter, Diana, was so glad her parents lived in Boulder City all during her years in school. Lillian and Ray were active in all the "worlds" of Diana as she grew up in Boulder City. Beside Diana there is a son, Kenneth Taylor, granddaughters, Leslie Adams and Maureen Calvin, and Ann Laughran, and the dear little great great grandchild is Vanassa Calvin. A grandson is K.V. Taylor, Riverside, Cal. Friends who remember he great love for children can repay that loyalty by donating to her favorite cause which is St. Jude's Ranch for Children. Her great friend, Father Ward, who conducted her memorial services at Palm Mortuary yesterday, is the Executive Director at the ranch. Contributions can be mailed to Box 985 Boulder City, Nevada 89005.

Collins, Ray
Boulder City News, Thursday, 26 Jan 1984, 20:1-5.
By Teddy Fenton
Ray Collins, a resident of Boulder City beginning in 1943 died of dread cancer last Friday. He was home being well cared for by his beloved wife, Leona, and by his family and a family friend. Nathan Adelson hospice donations named by family. Before going into the remarkable career of bank manager, Ray Collins, the family wanted us to emphasize the importance of the Nathan Adelson Hospice volunteers. It was with the help of that amazing group that Lillian Collins, who also died from cancer, was able to remain home until her tragic death. To the memory of Ray and the late Lillian Collins we will next week write a feature story about their work. A true miracle. Ray and Lillian arrived in Boulder City

in 1943. It doesn't seem possible that the Collins and their family arrived in Boulder City when the town was 12 years old. To us who depended upon them and revered them it seemed like they had grown right out of the earth beneath the town they both served so generously. Don Ashbaugh, in 1947, wrote a feature story about Ray Collins that began, "Ray Collins is the most famous man in her profession." What Don referred to was the Ray drove away armed robbers on several occasions. He never killed a man but he certainly captured three different criminals. The last successful capture almost cost his life. To the end of his days Ray limped because the robber shot him. Bank manager Ray Collins spent 44 years of his life as a bank manager. None were ever robbed. The active life of the Collins in Boulder City. In 1943 A. R. Collins became the second bank manager of the Bank of Nevada on Arizona St. (It is now Pilgrim's Nevada Drug). How many Boulder City people owe their start in life to that wise man. In 1946, as an example, Ray Collins trusted Steve and Teddy Fenton with an $8,000 loan when Steve did not even have a job. With that money we raised the house at 663 Ave. "D" and put apartments below our own quarters. Had he not trusted us then it would be impossible for Teddy to make a living renting the apartments. Ray began his banking career in 1922. In Los Angeles, where Don Ashbaugh worked for the L.A. Times (as a reporter) he worked for the small Western State Bank, owned by Trans America Corp (the forerunner of B. & A.) He took a job as bookkeeper. He moved right up the ladder, teller, assistant cashier, secretary and then manager 10 years later in 1932. Boulder City welcomes Ray and Lillian. They moved to a small house on Wyoming St. Soon Lillian was entertaining to such an extent that they had to enlarge the house. Ray joined BPOE 1682, but he also served as a member of the B. C. School Board, was the treasurer of the Rotary Club, Secretary of the Elks Club, treasurer of the Community Chest Drive, the local OPA chief and chairman of innumerable loan drives for War Bonds, infantile paralysis, Red Cross, etc. We thank the late Don Ashbaugh for the above material. He admired Ray without reservations. Ray Collins was a great man and a friend to thousands of people in his lifetime. In a later story it is mentioned that Ray was president of the B.C. Rotary Club, and was treasurer of the Salvation Army. He transferred to Las Vegas in 1956. He and Lillian purchased a house on Fairway Drive in Henderson. There they continued their community volunteer work. Ray was an avid golfer. Even with his injured leg he kept playing golf. One could certainly write a book about Ray Collins. A memorial to the Boulder City Museum Foundation has been given by Teddy Fenton and Bill Harbour. Lillian Collins has also been named to the BCMHA memorial by her daughter, Diane Adams. Ray remarried in 1983. To Leona Collins, his widow, we express deep sorrow that your beautiful union was to end so soon. You made Ray a happy man when you came to Henderson to share his last years. Ray left a family that had been close for all his years. Diane Adams, his daughter, a stepson, Kenneth Taylor, of Ridgecrest, Cal. Four grandchildren and one great grandchild.

Conger, Ethel F.
Boulder City News, Monday, 13 Jan 1947, 4:2.

Mrs. Ethel F. Conger of Boulder City passed away at her home at 8 a.m. Friday morning from a heart ailment. She was the daughter of Mr. and Mrs. Francis L. Horn, and was born Nov. 20, 1880, at Stromsburg, Neb. She became the wife of Isaac N. Conger in 1902 at Stromsburg. They were engaged in farming and dairying there. To this union were born three children, Francis L. and Charlotte M. and one son who died in infancy. Her husband passed away April 19, 1913. She was united in marriage to William E. Conger Nov. 19, 1914, at Polk, Neb. He is the brother of her former husband. To this union three sons and one daughter were born, namely William P., Joe, James and Mary E. Joe died in infancy. They made their home in Nebraska until January 1943, when they came to Boulder City. Mrs. Conger was baptized and joined the Baptist Church as a girl. She was an active member in the Ladies Aid Society and W. C. T. U. at Polk. They moved from there to Ericson, Neb., where she was interested in Christian affairs. Later they moved to Grand Island, where she was a member of the Ladies Self Help Center until her health failed. In her declining years she has enjoyed listening to the sermons and gospel singing over the radio. Mrs. Conger was a kind, loving and understanding wife and mother. She was loved by all who knew her because of her friendly personality and neighborly deeds. Her absence will be felt by the community in which she lived as well as by her loved ones who mourn her passing. The funeral services will be held Tuesday at 2 p.m. at the Grace Community Church, Boulder City. She lies in state at the Palm Funeral Home in Las Vegas, which has charge of the arrangements. Reverend Winston Trever will preach the funeral sermon. Helen Haley will sing "Asleep in the Arms of Jesus" and "Sweet Bye and Bye," both favorites of Mrs. Conger. William E. Conger, Frank Conger, William Conger, James Conger, Charlotte Hora, Mary E. Peterson.

Conners, Myrtle F.

Boulder City News, Thursday, 5 Nov 1970.
Graveside services will be conducted at 10 this morning for Myrtle F. Conners, 79, who died Sunday in a rest home. The Reverend Guy Holliday will officiate at B. C. Cemetery. Prior to entering the rest home Mrs. Conners lived at 619 Ave K. She was a retired cook. She held membership in the B. C. Women's Club and the Women's Association of Grace Community Church. She was born Jan. 21, 1891 in Falmouth, Mich. Mrs. Conners is survived by a son, Robert and two daughters, Shirley Marshall and Lois Pavlich, all of Boulder City; a brother, A. N. Barber, Gig Harbor, Wash.; a sister, Agnes Magis, Seattle, Wash.; six grandchildren and six great grandchildren.

Connor, Jeremiah

Boulder City News, Thursday, 5 July 1973, 17:1-2.
Jeremiah Connor Services Here
Jeremiah I. Connor died June 22 in Boulder City. He was 54-years of age. Born on September 28, 1918, in Altura, California, he was a resident at 537 Avenue I, Boulder City and has been an area resident for the past 10 years. Jerry, as he was called, came to Boulder City in 1964 and went to work for the City in the maintenance crew of public works. He was one of the crew of men who went to Bullhead City, Arizona, to obtain the palm trees that are so attractive along Nevada Highway. He was noted for being a fine gardener, but worked where ever he was needed. Funeral services were held at the First Ward of the L.D.S. Church in Boulder City, Monday, June 25th at 2 p.m. Bishop Jacob Williams officiated. The speaker was Osborn Trasdahl, with music by Margie Leavitt. Pall bearers were, Charles Denshire, Clifford Denshire, Mitchell Carlgren, Vernon Bradley, Mark Perry and Leonard Baldwin. Jerry was buried in the Boulder City Cemetery. Survivors include his widow, Eva; a daughter, Catherine Raddatz of the family residence; step-daughters Jeanne Hibbard, Yerington, Nev., and Betty Harris of Midvale, Utah; his parents, Mr. and Mrs. Jeremiah Connor sr. of Boulder City.

Cook, Ina
Boulder City News, Thursday, 25 Sep 1975, 11:7.
Graveside services for Mrs. Ina Cook, 89, were held Mon., Sept. 15 at 3 p.m. in Boulder City. Mrs. Cook passed away Sept. 13 in the Boulder City Hospital. She was born Oct. 10, 1886 in Troy, Tenn., and had resided in Boulder City since 1952. She is survived by a daughter-in-law, Constance Cook in Boulder City, two grandchildren and three great grandchildren.

Cook, Sue
Boulder City News, Thursday, 18 Jun 1992, 10:3-4.
Sue Cook, 45, died Saturday, June 13, 1992 in a local hospital. She was an 18-year resident of Boulder City. She was born March 22, 1947, in Bart, Okla. She had been a clerk at Shopper Stopper for 11 years and most recently was employed as a clerk at the Boulder City Hospital. She is survived by her husband, Jerry and son, Royce of Boulder City; daughter, Tammy Turner of Las Vegas; mother, Sue Weaver and brother, Bill Weaver, both of Boulder City. A sister, Mary Linch of Lake Isabella, Calif. Services were Wednesday at Palm Mortuary in Henderson. Burial was held in the Boulder City Cemetery.

Cooper, Frank D.
Boulder City News, Thursday, 11 Nov 1971, 2:3.
Frank Cooper Services At Local Church
Funeral services will be held at 11 o'clock this morning for Frank D. Cooper, 61, who died Tuesday morning after a long illness. The rites are to be conducted by Father Robert Batemann at St. Christopher's Episcopal Church, where Frank was a member. The family requests that donations be made to the memorial fund at the church, instead of flowers. Frank was born October 31, 1910 in Beach, North Dakota. He attended the Benjamin Franklin University, Washington, D. C., school of accounting and business administration. He began his service with the U. S. Government in 1930, with the Bureau of Census, and later served with the U. S. Tariff Commission, Treasury Department and Federal Power Commission. He transferred to the U. S. Bureau of Reclamation at Casper, Wyo., in 1948 as an accountant on the North Platte River Projects office of region 7. He and his family moved here in 1956. In 1959, he was promoted to the head of the Field Accounting and Reports Section of the USBR Region 3 Finance Office, and provided technical guidance to accounting personnel through out the region. Frank received a 40 year pin

for the government in 1970, and retired in January, 1971. He was a member of the BPO Elks Lodge, and shared an interest in sports with his family. Frank is survived by his wife, Hazel, 603 Ave. H; sons, Frank D. Cooper, III, San Jose, Calif,; a daughter, Rhonda Winfrey, Oklahoma; sever grandchildren. Also his mother, Della H. Cooper, and brother James, both of Rushville, Ill.; and a sister, Mary Elizabeth Jesmer, North Hollywood, Calif.

Corderman, Edith E.
Boulder City News, Thursday, 23 May 1985, 36:1-3.
By Teddy Fenton
From our midst a beautiful soul joined her husband Eugene in that home of eternal rest. Eugene died on May 5, 1979, Edith, on May 6, 1985. She was 80 years old. During her long illness her family kept her at home where she remained until the final day of her life. She died in the Boulder City Hospital. There is a long story to relate about the Senior Cordermans. Edith led a quiet life but had been involved in outside activities that benefitted this community. Eugene had been the best friend possible to Grace Community Church. We remember both of them at the church but Eugene had a title! It was "caretaker" but it was so much more than that. He served as a volunteer for more hours than his paycheck. He was a natural born gardener and the grounds around historic Grace Community Church was a fitting monument to his love for the land. In this, his wife shared a pride for all things beautiful. So now they are both named as "Memorials" for the church they loved. Do be generous in your donations to their memory. We miss our wonderful parents. The family they left behind are sons: Richard, B.C.; Gerald, Concord, Cal.; and daughters Sissy, Raini, and Marti, all of Boulder City. When we had a family reunion there were a lot of young people there. Our parents enjoyed 11 grandchildren and 12 great grandchildren. We know Mom and Dad are happy in their continuing joy in one another. Thank you all again for being their friends.

Corderman, Eugene
Boulder City News, Thursday, 10 May 1979.
Graveside services were held Tuesday at Boulder City Cemetery for Eugene Corderman, 74, who passed away May 5 at a local hospital. Reverend Mel Pritts officiated at the service. Mr. Corderman was a long time resident of Boulder City and had worked at Central market as a meat cutter for a number of years. From 1968 until February of this year he was custodian of Grace Community Church as well as being a member of the

church. He was born January 11, 1905 in Sac City, Iowa. Mr. Corderman is survived by his wife, Edith, of Boulder City; daughter, Marti Corderman, Lorraine Dunbar and Eleanor Lyon, all of Boulder City; sons, Richard Corderman of Boulder City and Gerald Corderman of Concord, California; a brother, Ralph Corderman of Storm Lake, Iowa; sisters, Leona Bloyer of Spirit Lake, Iowa, Velma Rodman of Sac City and Marie Bloyer of Schaller, Iowa; ten grandchildren and ten great-grandchildren.

Cordova, Dan L., Dr.
Boulder City News, Thursday, 16 Jan 1964, 1:4-5.
Dr. Dan Cordova's Rites Planned Today
Graveside service will be conducted today at 2 p.m. in the Boulder City Cemetery for Dr. Dan Cordova, 73, who died Monday at the Boulder City Hospital after a lingering illness. Dr. Cordova will be interred at the cemetery following a service conducted by William Belknap, of the Christian Science Church. He has no known survivors. The pioneer resident was a financial expert and served many wealthy retired persons as an investment counselor and finance manager. He was considered an expert in the field of taxes by many Las Vegas lawyers and was often called upon to conduct research in legal cases involving such matters. Dr. Cordova received a doctor of philosophy degree as an actuarian from the University of Madrid in Spain and gained national recognition as chief secretary to the famed Oliver Wendell Holmes when the latter served as chief justice of the United States Supreme Court. One of the most colorful aspects to the doctor's life as a youth was the fact that he was raised in the home of the famed Western lawman, Wyatt Earp, when Earp was in his last years. Doctor Cordova handled several area accounts as an accountant, including, for many years, the Railroad Pass Casino. He resided at the Uptown Apartments. Funeral arrangements were made through Bunker Brothers Mortuary.

Cotterill, John R.
Boulder City News, Thursday, 11 Sep 1986, 29:3.
John R. Cotterill, 75, died Monday, September 1 in Boulder City. He was born Oct 2, 1910 in Anthony, Kan. A two-year resident, he was a former Navy photographer. He is survived by his son, John R. Cotterill, Jr., of Los Angeles; daughter, Shirley Evans of Laguna Beach, Calif.; four grandchildren and one great grandchild. Graveside services were held at 9:30 a.m. Friday in Boulder City Cemetery. Palm Mortuary, Henderson, handled the arrangements.

Cowan, Edna
Boulder City News, Thursday, 11 May 1978, 3:5-8.
Edna Cowan Was Loved by Everyone
Edna, the beloved widow of Harry Cowan, was buried yesterday after a beautiful service at the Community Church. Her friends, her family, and her pastor, Reverend Guy Holiday attended in loving memory to one of the kindest, most Christian, and uncomplaining angel ladies to ever come to reside in this city of Boulder City which she loved with unabating loyalty. Her children were all with her. They are John, Anita, Ben, Phyliss, and Carolyn. She had fourteen grandchildren and one great grandchild. Her family gave her undying joy. Anita lived with her and Ben lived close by in Henderson. Caroline said that each and every one of them managed to see their parents at every possible occasion. It is important for everyone who remembered her ready smile and her love for religion that she truly lived for the Lord, and in His name she worked unstintingly for the Community Church. Everyone agreed that she couldn't give up on any task for the church until it was finished to her satisfaction. She served in many offices, she was President of the Community Church "Ladies' Aid" in 1944. She belonged to PEO Chapter K and she taught the Young Matron's Club at the church. Edna Cowan was hilariously funny whenever she presented a one-woman skit to the Young Matrons. She could imitate each character and when one was supposed to sing, she stopped everything and made believe she was a professional entertainer. Nothing pleased her anymore than to see everyone laughing so hard the tears were flowing down their cheeks. Bless her forever for having the joy to spread, the strength to serve, the unselfishness to care more about others than she cared about herself. When Caroline arrived to the hospital on the evening before her mother's passing, she said it was so typical of Edna Cowan to look up and explain in joy at seeing her child standing there, but then: Ph! But Caroline you should not have left your husband and your boys for me." She rests in peace now. It was her solemn belief that the Lord called when he was ready and that it was cause to celebrate. She would be so happy to hear her friends say that it was this way for her and that she would have it no other way. She so seldom talked about herself that it is doubtful that many people knew that she was the valedictorian of her class. In her humbleness she always talked for the newspaper about her family and not about herself. The Ester Shipp files are filled with items about the 5 children that belonged to Edna and Harry Cowan but not one story appeared about Edna. If the humble and un-selfish inherit the earth there is no doubt that a very special heaven will become Edna's home. Our

community thanks you, dear friend, for being our friend. Your friends and family were blessed beyond words to have known you and enjoyed you. God Speed dear friend and mother.

Cowan, Harry Welrose
Boulder City News, Thursday, 27 Jun 1974, 16:3.
Harry Welrose Cowan, 91, was buried Saturday morning in the Boulder City Cemetery. The Reverend Guy Holliday conducted the funeral services at Grace Community Church, where Harry was a member. Nita Kay Pong played old favorite hymns on the organ; and in quoting favorite Bible passages, Holiday likened Mr. Cowan to "A tree planted by the stream, that bringeth forth its fruit in due season and its leaf does not wither." Pallbearers were Leo Dunbar, Elton Garrett, Ralph Ramsey, Joseph Kine, Nicholas Havrilla and Buckley Howard. Harry was born June 23, 1882 in Baldville, West Virginia, and was a certified Public Accountant. He had a 25 year certificate from the New York Life Insurance Co., and in Manila, Arkansas, was a bank executive. The family moved to Nevada during construction of "Basic" and he was employed as an accountant for the McNeil Co. Harry and Edna Rundberg were married Feb. 16, 1917. They liked people, and their home was always a pleasure to visit. In Boulder City, they bought the former P.S. Webb residence at 738 Park St., which was one of the first really nice individually owned houses built here in town. One of the memories the children have, is that Harry and his father cut the stones for and constructed the beautiful Methodist Church in Manila. Although he did not participate in sports, he enjoyed watching them. Mr. Cowan had several bouts with illness and injuries, and died June 19th at the St. Rose de Lima Hospital. Donations in his memory may be made to the Grace Community Church Memorial Fund. Survivors are his wife, Edna, and daughter Anita Mooring, 738 Park St; sons John R. Cowan, Leeton, Missouri, and Ben Cowan of Henderson; daughters Phyllis Gabriel, Dayton, Ohio, and Carolyn Stakely, Montgomery, Ala.; 14 grandchildren; and a sister, Bessie Sweet, Memphis, Tenn.

Cowan, LuElla Meldrum
Boulder City News, Thursday, 21 Jan 1988, 8:1-2.
A tribute to LuElla Meldrum Cowan
On March 8, 1904, LuElla Meldrum was born in Provo, Utah, the eighth of twelve children. She lived on a five acre fruit and vegetable farm that her father owned. There was always work to do but when it was done her father would take the family and friends on a hay rack, pulled by horses,

to Utah Lake Resort where they would picnic. LuElla records in her journal, "There are advantages in having one's life span from horse and buggy days to the jet age. It is only by contrast that we can fully appreciate the things we have and enjoy today. I can recall in my very early day the wood burning stove, no running water, taking baths in a tub near the kitchen stove." In 1919, her father died in the great flu epidemic, leaving her mother and older children to care for the family. In spite of these obstacles LuElla was still able to continue and complete her schooling. A business course led to her first employment at Dixon Taylor Russell Furniture Store in Provo. On July 2, 1932 she married Eugene Cowan in Salt Lake City, Utah. They made their first home in Boulder City in the fall of that year. They have had a home here since, except for four years living in Northern California. At that time, Eugene had been laid off by the government due to an influx of WWII veterans who were given job preferences, even though he himself was a WWI veteran. To help bring in money, LuElla took in babysitting and then began working as a secretary at Titanium Metals Corp in Henderson. During these early years in Boulder City, two daughters, LuJean and Jacqueline were born to them. Eugene was finally transferred to Shasta Dam, California, where he worked as a crane operator. In the fall of 1950, Eugene was transferred back to work at Hoover Dam. LuElla started working as a secretary in January 1952 for the U. S. Government for different department heads, which included the Bureau of Mines for the Bureau of Reclamation. Soon after Eugene retired in 1960. They decided to do some traveling. They made a flying trip to Alaska to visit their daughter. A couple of years later they went to Hawaii. The latter part of 1969 LuElla retired early because of Eugene's health was declining and he needed her home with him. Eugene passed away February 1972 and LuElla records in her journal that " his passing left a vacant spot in my life. There were many adjustments to be made and I experienced many lonely times. I decided to keep busy and forget about myself, which was a good solution to loneliness." She then began to do some real traveling all over the world. Her travels took her to Europe, Canada, the Caribbean, South America, Mexico, Spain, Morraco, Egpyt and the Holy Land. During all these years she was very active in the LDS church, serving as secretary in various church organizations and doing genealogical work. She also was an active member of NARF. LuElla was very proud of being a pioneer in Southern Nevada and regularly attended meetings for the Boulder City Museum, for she left it important to preserve the heritage of Boulder City.

Cowely, Margaret

Boulder City News, Thursday, 21 Sep 1978, 6:3-4.
Margaret Cowely Is Buried In Boulder City Cemetery
In Boulder City there are hundreds of people who once knew Margaret Cowely of Las Vegas who was buried last Monday in the Boulder City cemetery. Her services were conducted from the Four Square Gospel Church with Reverend Margery Homan officiating. Our picture will illustrate all too clearly what was meant when Margaret's friends referred to her as a great beauty. She worked at the office in the old Boulder City hospital during the years Fanny Connolly was supervising the famous center. Her best friend to the end of her days was Lola "Mrs. Doc" Jensen. Lola nurses thru the same time period and Doc Jensen was a familiar "volunteer" during those happy years for all three of them. Margaret was married to the late Bill Cowely. He retired from the Bureau of Power and Light in the early 60's. They went to Florida and Canada for a few years but after Bill's tragic death, a lonely Margaret returned to Las Vegas and entered the business world. Her daughter, Kathy Stien, said admiringly of her mother. She could do anything. She managed a China and Crystal Store, she was so active in Civil Defense that they named her State President. Her last job was as a check. She was known state wide as Toastmistress gatherings as being an exceptional speaker. She excelled in interior decorating. Margaret Cowely was born in Oakatoks, Atberta, Canada on Oct. 1, 1915. She came to Las Vegas in 1955. During her last illness she lived with her daughter, Marji Ann Mercereau of Las Vegas. Other survivors are a granddaughter, Kathy Stienback, Las Vegas, Jerry Bray, Lancaster and Laura Bray, Dillon, Colo. Also a brother, Jerry Long. This is the way Lola Jensen described the need of beautiful Margaret Cowely's Need to Return Home. She called this tribute.
RETURN
Take Me Back by Boulder Highway
Down through the shady glen
Carpet my grave with violets
Say a small prayer and then:
Leave me to peace and silence
In the town I love best of all
Where the Elm trees whisper softly
And the wild things gently call.
In memory of my friend.
By Lola B. Jensen

Crain, Jacob A.
Boulder City News, Thursday, 5 Oct 1995, p.12:1-2.
Jacob A. Crain died Tuesday, Sept. 26, 1995 at a local hospital. Born Sept, 26, 1995 in Henderson, he was the son of Timothy and Kristin Crain, of Boulder City. He is survived by his parents; maternal grandmother, Virginia Allen, and paternal grandparents, Al and Dell, all of Boulder City; and was preceded in death by his grandfather, Buster Allen. Graveside services were held Friday, Sept 29, 1995 in Boulder City. Arrangements were handled by Palm Mortuary of Henderson.

Crossley, Harda R.
Las Vegas Review-Journal, Tuesday, 25 Aug 1964, 9:3.
Crossley, Harda R., 52, of 119 Magnesium, Henderson. Died Aug. 23 in Boulder City Hosp. Born, March 28, 1912, in Dallas, Texas. Member Eastern Star of Henderson. Survivors: husband, Joy D. daughter, Ardeen Derrick; son, Patrick, all of Henderson; brother, Aron Bolton, Grants Pass. Ore.; sisters Eunice Burson, Receda, Calif.; Mebra McCord, Billings, Mont. Services: Wednesday, 3 p.m., Palm Chapel of All Faiths, Henderson, with Eastern Star officiating. Interment, Boulder City Cemetery.

Crossley, Joy D.
Boulder City News, Thursday, 1 June 1978, p.8:3-5
Longtime Area Resident Passes Away
Joy D. Crossley 76, passed away May 30 in Henderson. He had lived in the area since 1934, first in Boulder City, later in Henderson and had just recently moved back to Boulder City. Mr. Crossley was born March 8, 1902 in St. Joseph, Missouri and was retired from Stauffer Chemical Company where he had been employed as a heavy equipment operator. He was a past treasurer for Mt. Moriah Lodge No. 39 F & AM; a Past Worthy Patron of Sunrise Chapter No. 38 OES; a member of the Starlight Shrine No. 1 Order of White Shrine of Jerusalem; an Honorary Board member of the Henderson Assembly No. 17 or Rainbow Girls and a member of the Operating Engineers Local No. 12. In lieu of flowers the family has requested that memorials be made to St. Rose de Lima Hospital Tumor Board. Survivors include his wife, Ann of Boulder City; a daughter, JeDean Derrick of Henderson; one son, Patrick Crossley of Semi Valley, California; a sister, Helen Sullivan of Vancouver, Washington and three grandchildren of Henderson. Services will be held Friday, June 2 at 11 a.m. at Palm Chapel under the auspices of Mt. Moriah Lodge. Interment will follow at the Boulder City Cemetery.

Culp, Stuart Jr.
Boulder City News, Thursday, 16 Apr 1987, p.32:1.
Stuart W. Culp Jr., age 60, passed away Thursday, April 9, 1987. He was a 22-year resident of Boulder City. He was born Feb. 22, 1927 in Chicago. He was a fireman for the Los Angeles Fire Department and a U. S. Marine Corps veteran of the Korean War. He was also an active member of the Boulder City Elks. He leaves his daughters, Julie and Sonia, both of Apple Valley, California. Palm Mortuary handled the arrangements.

Cummings, Artie B.
Boulder City News, Thursday, 14 May 1987, 16:1-2.
Artie B. Cummings, age 88, of Boulder City, passed away Wednesday May 6, 1987 in Las Vegas. She was born August 2, 1898 in Nebraska. She was a homemaker and a 43 year resident.

Curry, Gertrude
Boulder City News, Thursday, 1 May 1975, 5:3.
Graveside services will be held today at 2 o'clock for Gertrude Baker Curry, 90. They will be conducted by the Reverend Guy Holliday of Grace Community Church. She will be interred in Boulder City Cemetery, where her husband Harry is buried. Mrs. Curry died Tuesday in the Beverly Manor Convalescent Hospital. She had been hospitalized previously in Boulder City, following a fall. For many months Gertrude has been using a walker, because of a broken hip, but was "Fiercely Independent" and continued to do most of her won work at her apartment at 539 Avenue C. Her friend, Vivian Perkins, did as much as she was allowed. Gertrude was born Dec. 5, 1884 in Warren, Pennsylvania. She and her husband moved to Boulder City from back East in 1946, and they lived on Avenue D. She was a popular "Baby Sitter" for many years. She was as active as she could be, with poor health, at Grace Community Church and the Women's Association. She always appreciated it when she was given rides by her many friends. Her only survivor is a niece, Jeanette Harvey, in Warren, Penn. Getrude was overjoyed when this only living relative visited her in 1974.

Curry, Harry E.
Boulder City News, Thursday, 7 May 1953, p.10:1-3.
Harry Curry Funeral Held
Funeral rites were held for Harry E. Curry, 77, on Saturday afternoon at the Church of Jesus Christ of Latter-Day Saints, with Bishop Leonard Stubbs officiating. Monreve Hardy and Letty Jo Ness sang two solos, accompanied by Jeanne Ear. The two sisters also sang at the interment services at the Boulder cemetery on Sunday. Curry died late Thursday night at the Boulder City hospital, following a heart attack early Thursday morning. He was born July 27, 1875, at Elk City, Pennsylvania. Curry did heavy duty machinist work before retiring in 1944, and his last employment was at the Central Market here. Mr. and Mrs. Curry have lived in Boulder City for seven years, making their hoe in an apartment at the Howard residence at 644 Avenue D. Survivors include his widow, Gertrude; a daughter, Nita Curry of Akron, Ohio; a son, Dr. Herbert L. Curry, who is a professor os speech at Central Michigan College at Mt. Pleasant, Michigan; three grandchildren, three brothers and a sister. Arriving here for the funeral were Mrs. Bowman and her nephew, Dennis Curry.

Curtis, Henry Starr
Boulder City News, Thursday, 8 Oct 1987, 12:3-4.
Henry Starr Curtis, born July 19, 1970 in Belpre, Ohio, died October 3, 1987 in Boulder City. Curtis was reared in Ohio and graduated from Ohio State University in Chemical Engineering in 1933. His engineering and management positions took him to Alabama, Ohio, Texas, and Nevada. He was a registered Professional Engineer in Ohio, West Virginia and Nevada. He moved to Nevada in June 1956. He retired in 1971 as manger of Keer McGee's Henderson plant. He served in the Army Chemical Corps during World War II and was awarded the Soldier's Medal for heroism for saving the lives of co-workers. He continued service in the Army Reserve and retired as a Lieutenant Colonel. Henry had a life-long commitment to the Boy Scouts of America, stemming from his youth as an Eagle Scout. He served as president of the Boulder Dam Area Council in 1961. He was a long-time member of the Henderson Rotary Club and served as its president in 1976-77. Curtis served as a Boulder City Councilman from July 1967 to May 1969 and at his death, served on the Boulder City Civil Service Commission. He sorely missed his wife of 46 years, Violet Brown Curtis, since her death in 1982. He will be missed by his family and friends. He is survived by his daughter Gail Gaterburg in Austria; his son, Starr Curtis, of Henderson and five grandchildren, Jesse,

Julie, Christian, Nathaniel and Maren. Service will be at Grace Community Church, 1150 Wyoming, Boulder City, on Thursday, Oct. 8 at 2 p.m. In lieu of flowers, donations may be made to Boy Scouts of America – Boulder Dam Area Council, or the Nathan Adelson Hospice Foundation. Interment will be at the Boulder City Cemetery. Arrangements by Palm Mortuary of Henderson.

Curtis, Vi

Boulder City News, Thursday, 12 Aug 1982, 2:1-3.
Vi Curtis Services to be held Friday
Vi Curtis passed away on Aug. 10, 1982, in her home after a lingering illness of over a year. At her bedside were her husband, Henry, and their children Starr Curtis and Gail Gatterberg. She was 71 years old. The services will be at Grace Community Church in Boulder City tomorrow at 9 a.m. The minister will be Reverend Willcom Kirtsman. MOST IMPORTANT: In lieu of flowers please donate to the Nathan Adelson Hospice Program. The address is 3201 S. Maryland Parkway, Las Vegas, Nevada. Vi Curtis was one of the outstanding volunteers in our town. Always with Henry, her husband, at her side, the tow just gave to our community until it became a habit to "ask Vi" and she seldom said "no." Her smiling face was a legend at the B. C. Hospital for she was active in all phases of the Women's Auxiliary. Her story will be told in full with the help of her beloved family. The files that were collected by Esther Shipp have many great moments in this life of a wonderful community volunteer. The Hospice Program allowed our dear friend to die at home for the tender care she received was absolutely a miracle. If you prefer give your donations directly to Henry Curtis, 523 Ave. M, Boulder City, 89005.

Dake, Leo "Pete"

Boulder City News, Thursday, 26 Mar 1992, 11:1.
Leo "Pete" Dake died Tuesday in a local hospital. He was born March 28, 1932, in Eufaula, Okla., and had been a resident of the Boulder City area for four years. Dake was a veteran of the United States Army serving during the Korean conflict. He is survived by his wife, Joreena M. Kae of Boulder City; two daughters, Janice Cunningham of San Diego, Calif. and Linda Case of Garden Grove, Calif.; two sisters, Billie Wood of Checotah, Okla., and Pat Dake of Little Rock, Ark.; four brothers, Ed Dake and Jack Dake, both of Tulsa, Okla., Finis Dake of Cherry Valley, Calif., and Ron Dake of San Fernando Valley, Calif.; also three grandchildren. Viewing services are being held today from 8 a.m. to

noon. Graveside services will be at 1 p.m. today at the Boulder City Cemetery. Arrangements were handled by Palm Mortuary in Henderson.

Dana, Florence W.
Boulder City News, Thursday, 9 Mar 1972.
BC Pioneer Dies In Falls Church
Funeral services for Florence W. Dana, 92, who lived in Boulder City during construction days of the Dam, were held yesterday at 4 p.m. at the Covington-Martin Funeral Home in Falls Church, Ca. Interment will be in Boulder City cemetery. Mrs. Dana died Sunday, March 5. Mrs. Dana's husband, the late Lee H. Dana, was an engineer in the construction of Boulder Dam, between 1931 and 1949. She was born April 26, 1879 in Pennsylvania. She is survived by a daughter, Mrs. L. J. Synder, Falls Church, Va.; son David W. Dana, St. Thomas, in the Virgin Island, eight grandchildren and 15 great grandchildren.

Danneberger, Marion "Dan"
Boulder City News, Thursday, 22 Sep 1983, 29:7-8.
Marion "Dan" Danneberger, 75, of Boulder City, died Saturday in Las Vegas. Mr. Danneberger was born July 20, 1908, in Cowden, Ill. A 42-year resident, he was the owner of Danneberger Plumbing in Henderson. He is survived by his wife, Ruth; son, Robert, both of Boulder City; daughter, Dalley Harris of Loma Linda, Calif., and four grandchildren. A graveside service was held at 10 a.m., Tuesday in Boulder City Cemetery. Palm Mortuary handled arrangements.

Danneberger, Ruth
Boulder City News, Thursday, 30 Dec 1993, 9:4.
Ruth Danneberger, now of Riverside, California, died Wednesday, Dec. 22, in Riverside. She was 82. She was born Nov. 17, 1911, in Ohio, and had been a resident of Boulder City for many years. She had been active in the BC Women's Club, serving as its president. She also was active for many years in collecting the items left from the annual Grace Community Church Country Store and taking them to the Indian missions in Four Corners. Survivors include a daughter, Sally Harris of Riverside; a son, Robert, of Henderson; four grandchildren, Jill Harris and Timothy Harris, both of Riverside, and Cretia Christos, both of Placentia, California. Graveside services were held Tuesday, Dec. 28, at Boulder City cemetery in Boulder City, Nevada. Palm Mortuary, Henderson, handled arrangements.

Davidson, Wanda Mae
Boulder City News, Thursday, 12 Jan 1989, 16:2.
Wanda Mae Davidson, 63, a resident of Boulder City since 1973, died Jan. 5 in Henderson. Born in Portland, Ore., on Dec. 15, 1925, she was a retired accounting technician and a member of Christ Lutheran Church in Boulder City. She is survived by daughters Sandra Boero of Boulder City, Marsha Buesgens of Tacoma, Wa., and Sheila Allen of Sibley, Iowa; brothers Leonard J. Brooks of Portland, Ore., and Daniel L. Brooks of San Mateo, Calif.; and seven (7) grandchildren. Services were handled by Palm Mortuary of Henderson on Jan. 9 at Christ Lutheran Church with Pastor Steve Cluver officiating. Interment was in Boulder City Cemetery. Memorials may be sent to the American Lung Association or Christ Lutheran Building Fund.

Davies, Morris E.
Boulder City News, Thursday, 31 Mar 1983, 2:2.
Morris E. Davies, 76, a former resident of Boulder City, died Thursday in El Cajon, Calif. He was born July 4, 1906, in Utah and was a hardware salesman. He is survived by his daughters, Barbara Ellertson of El Cajon, Colleen Keith of Vancouver, Wash., Lola hunt of Las Vegas and Mary Kaye Jones of Salem, Ore.; son, Paul of Provo, Utah; one brother; six sisters; and nine grandchildren. Services were at 10 a.m. Wednesday in the Boulder City chapel of the Church of Jesus Christ of Latter-day Saints. Burial was in Boulder City Cemetery. Palm Mortuary handled arrangements.

Davis, Amelia
Boulder City News, Thursday, 12 Jul 1984, 21:1.
Services for Pioneer Amelia Davis today at 8 a.m., by Teddy Fenton Family and friends will gather today to bid farewell to Amelia Davis who died peacefully last Sunday. Amelia was at Central park on July 4, 1984, with her sons and members of her family. None could have guessed that she would not be back next year for she enjoyed the hour-long concert with a broad smile on her face the entire time. She would not want us to grieve. Her happy nature is what we will all remember, that and her service to her family, her church, her friends and her community. Amelia was born on March 25, 1901, in Eureka, Utah. 43 years of her life was spent in Boulder City. Her husband of over 50 years was a giant in our community. He was Leonard Davis, a leader in every sense of the word. Their children are sons, Joseph and Henry, of Las Vegas, Bill of Boulder

City and Leonard of Berea, Calif., and 13 grandchildren and three great grandchildren. She will be buried beside her husband in the Boulder City cemetery. Amelia said coming to Boulder City was the wisest move the family ever made. Every day she said prayers and gave thanks for her many blessings and for her family who had given her so much pleasure. All of her sons made marvelous careers and her grandchildren and great grandchildren gave her equal reasons to be proud. No wonder she smiled all the time! The above paragraph is from a story by Esther Shipp. It was her career as a community servant that she left a mark that will last forever. She served a 4 year term on the school board. She took the appointment seriously. She studied every book she could find, and she was active also during the war years on the local USO, and was a PTA president, she helped organize citizen participation in USO work, she was president and secretary of the American Legion Aux. President of St. Andrews Altar Society, and was a charter member of the BPO Does. She was the chairman of the committee which paved the way for revival of the Recreation Association and she worked to obtain funds for Boulder City's first paid recreation director. She was secretary of the B. C. Community Chest Assoc. She was chairman of the board which administered the Duane S. Laughery memorial Fund from which a scholarship was named annually to a graduate of the Boulder City High School. A graduate of St. Mary's College, Notre Dame, Ind., she held a bachelor's degree in history and economics.

A Memorial Named to the Boulder City Museum

As spokesman for the family a request has been made by her son, William "Bill" Davis that a Memorial Fund to gifted to the B. C. Museum Building Fund be given in lieu of flowers. Amelia was an historian and her home is rich with books and memories. Amelia would want this story to include a paragraph on her husband, Leonard Davis. He was known as one of the old school that belonging to an organization, a man must live by the rules of that organization. Therefore we share a story that had a headline in a L.V. paper. It read "Thousands Attend Elks Barbecue at Helldorado Village." A total of 3500 persons, or a thousand more than expected, attended a barbecue that was chaired by the Boulder City Elks Lodge No. 1682. Profits from the event totally surprised the Elks. Leonard P. Davis was the exalted ruler at the time. He said the proceeds would be divided between the general fund for charitable work, and the building fund. Leonard and Amelia, you are united again to go forth doing community service in another land. We revere the memories of both of you.

Davis, Donna Marie

Boulder City News, Thursday, 24 June 1993, 7:1-3.
Donna Marie Davis, 47, a five year Boulder City resident, died Wednesday, June 16, 1993 in a local hospital. Born March 14, 1946 in Kankakee, Ill., she was a homemaker. She was a member of the Christ Lutheran Church in Boulder City and a past Sunday School Superintendent. She was a substitute teacher for the Clark County School District and a past president of the PTA at the Kenny Gwinn School. She is survived by her husband, Jon F. Davis, a daughter, Andrea Leigh Davis and two sons, Clint Michael Davis and Kyle Clifton Davis, all of Boulder City; mother, Alice Swanson of Henderson, Ky.; four sisters, Jean Overfield of Hopkinsville, Ky.; Palm Skaggs of Henderson, Ky.; Karen Schmidt of Bay Village, Ohio and Christie Goolsby of Evansville, Ind.; and three brothers, Joe Swanson, Jim Swanson and Bill Swanson, all of Henderson, Ky. The family requests donations be made to the Gift Fund National Cancer Institute, Bethesda, Md. 20893 for breast cancer research or to the Christ Lutheran Church, 1401 5th Street, Boulder City, Nevada 89005. Palm Mortuary handled arrangements.

Davis, Ralph

Boulder City News, Thursday, 25 May 1978, 9:1-2.
Ralph Davis Buried Tuesday
Funeral services were held for Ralph Davis, 701 Elm St., last Tuesday at the Four Square Church with Reverend Margery Holman officiating. Mr. Davis was buried at the Boulder City Cemetery. He is survived by his widow, Velma and his daughter Debbie Davis Cattoir. Mr. Davis died from a stroke. It was so sudden the family was in deep shock. Velma said it is hard to understand but her belief in the workings of the Lord is so firmly a part of her religion that she feels very confident of being able to rebuild her life as a volunteer and an important part of this community that her husband had loved so deeply. Debbie was the light of Mr. Davis's life. She was the only child and she in turn adored her father. The community extends sympathy and prayers to the little family. Ralph Davis was a Maintenance Custodian at Hoover Dam. He has served at the dam for 25 years. He was a Veteran of the Korean War. He dearly loved gospel music and he was an avid fisherman. He and Val had been married for 23 years. Out of town relatives coming for the funeral were Mrs. Vicky Lopez, Mrs. Barbara Thomas, Calif. and Lonnie Pope from Las Vegas.

Davis, Robert R.
Boulder City News, Thursday, 11 June 1970.
Services were held Wednesday at 10 a.m. at Palm Chapel, Henderson, for Robert R. Davis, Navy veteran who died Sunday at his home in Eldorado Trailer Park. He was 59. Mr. Davis had lived here for eight years and was a stationary equipment operator for the Bureau of Reclamation. Burial was in the B. C. Cemetery. He is survived by his widow, Nona, daughter, Mrs. Ted (Patricia) Brown, both of this city; a son, Robert of Logandale and three brothers, Richard of San Clemente, Donald of Sacramento and James of Olwine, Ia. He also leaves five grandchildren.

Davidson, Marshall W.
Boulder City News, Thursday, 11 Nov 1976, 8:7-8.
Marshall W. Davidson, 56, died early Sunday morning in the local hospital. Mr. Davidson, long time resident of Marina, Calif., came to Boulder City three years ago. He was a retired Army Master Sergeant WWII veteran of 25 years in the Postal Service at Marina. He is survived by his loving wife, Wanda M. and devoted daughters, Marsha M. Nelson, Sandra K. and Sheila F. Davidson; granddaughter, Rachael Ann Nelson, all of Boulder City. Funeral services were conducted Wednesday morning at the Christ Lutheran Church. Pastor Ronald Mayer officiated. Interment was at the Boulder City Cemetery.

Dawson, John S. "Jack"
Boulder City News, Thursday, 6 Aug 1992, 10:1-2.
John S. "Jack" Dawson died Aug. 3, 1992 in Kelowna, British Columbia. He was 74. A resident of Boulder City, he was born April 5, 1918, in Detroit, Michigan. His parents were Charles Earl Dawson and Ina Jean Smith Dawson. He was a noted actor, director and producer for CBS-TV in New York for 30 years. For eight years he was the producer of the Hill Curnorah Pageant for the Church of Jesus Christ of Latter Day Saints. Following his move to Nevada, he was prominent in southern Nevada theatrical and musical activities. He was an ordinance worker at the Las Vegas LDS Temple. Survivors include his wife, Patricia Ann Clawson Dawson of Boulder City, NV; a daughter, Sharon Jean Brooks of Eohnert Part, CA; sons, John C. "Jake" Dawson of Concord, CA; J.A.C. Redford of LaHabra, CA; Patrick A. Redford of Salt Lake City, UT; also 12 grandchildren. Services will be conducted Saturday, Aug. 8, at the 1st Ward LDS Church, 916 Fifth St., Boulder City at 1 p.m. Interment will be in Boulder City Cemetery.

Deane, Amalee Estelle
Boulder City News, Thursday, 27 Nov 1986, 12:2-4.
Amalee Estelle Deane, age 80, of Boulder City passed away Tuesday, Nov. 18. She was born Oct. 24, 1906 in Oskalla, Texas. She leaves her son, Donald W. of Las Vegas; daughter Anne C. Miller of Reno; sisters, Irene Duncum of San Antonio, Texas, Alva Cathey of Charlotte, North Carolina and Ruth Brennan of Marble Falls, Texas; a brother Wilson Story also of Marble Falls, Texas; three grandchildren and six great grandchildren. Interment was in the Boulder City Cemetery.

Amalee Deane Remembered by Esther Shipp
Amalee Estelle Deane, 80, was buried Friday in the Boulder City Cemetery, next to her husband, William. Funeral services were conducted at the Palm Chapel in Henderson by Father George Gerard of St. Timothy Episcopal Church who had also officiated at William's funeral in 1974. Amalee Estelle was born Oct. 24, 1906 in Oskalia, Texas to Fannie and William Story. Later, she moved to San Antonio, Texas. When William obtained a job as a ranger at Hoover Dam in 1942, he had to come here ahead of his family. Amaleee drove all the way to Boulder City alone, with her children Anne and Don. Anne was graduated from BCHS in 1948, and Don in 1949. Amalee worked for the late Leonard Atkison at Desertwear for many years. Her grandson, Jerry Deane, says, "I remember that she was very outgoing. She liked to work with the public, was very courteous, and helped women chose the right type of clothing to wear," Jerry continued, "She did alterations, and many women came to her for this expert service." Amalee like to play golf with Ann Nickell, and was a charter member of the Golf Association. She belonged to the Boulder City Women's Club, and liked to travel. She is survived by her son, Donald W. Dean, Las Vegas; daughter, Anne C. Miller, Reno, Nevada; sisters, Irene Duncum of San Antonio; Alva Cathey of Charlotte, North Carolina; Ruth Brennan, Marble Falls, Texas; brother, Wilson Story, Marble Falls; three grandchildren and six great-grandchildren.

Debbold, Irving E.
Boulder City News, Thursday, 9 Feb 1989, 22:3.
Irving E. Debbold, 77, a 16 year resident died Tuesday, Feb. 7 in Las Vegas. Born in Syracuse, N.Y. on March 24, 1911, he was the owner-operator of Marine Hardware Manufacturer. He was a Coast Guard veteran of World War II, a Boulder City Lodge No. 1682 member, 1 30 year member of Rotary International. He was a pioneer in the neon sign business in Los Angeles, Calif. and was a world record holding boat racer

in the 1940s. He was Clark County delegate to the Republican National Convention in 1976, a former Boulder City planning commissioner and Boulder City Charter Commissioner. He is survived by his wife Hazel L. of Boulder City; a son Lester I. of Chicago, Ill.; a daughter Marlene Phillips of Las Vegas; a granddaughter Carol Mlawsky of Las Vegas and a grandson Steven Osborn of Quartz Hill, Calif. Graveside services are scheduled at 1 p.m., Friday Feb. 10 in the Boulder City Cemetery.

DeGrosa, Joseph John
Boulder City News, Thursday, 18 Oct 1979, 3:2.
Joseph John DeGrosa, 74, a past resident of Boulder City, passed away October 15 in North Las Vegas. He was born January 27, 19905 in Brooklyn, New York and was a retired plumber. He is survived by a son, Gary DeGrosa of Las Vegas and sisters, Mary Gallo and Jean DeSalvio of New York City and Nellie DeGrosa of Ft. Lauderdale, Florida. A Rosary will be said Friday night at 7 p.m. at Palm Chapel and Saturday at 10 a.m. a Mass will be held at St. Andrew's Catholic Church. Burial will be at Boulder City Cemetery.

Denison, Arlene M.
Boulder City News, Thursday, 24 Dec 1987, 8:1.
Arlene M. Denison, 73 died Thursday, Dec. 17 in Las Vegas. She had been a resident of the Boulder City area for the past 20 years. She was born in Eau-Claire, Wis. on May 13, 1914 and was a medical assistant. She was a U.S. Army veteran of World War II, past president of Drove No. 34, Boulder City Does, served in World War II First Contingent of WACS, past president of Southern Nevada Medical Assistant Association, a member of the Motor Maids of America (ladies motorcycle club), member of the VFW no. 1047 Auxiliary, North Las Vegas and the American Legion Post no. 311. Survivors include husband Arthur Denison, Boulder City; daughter Marvel Clark, Escondido, Calif.; seven grandchildren and eight great-grandchildren. Funeral services are scheduled for Tuesday, Dec. 22 at 11 a.m. in the Palm Chapel in Henderson. Interment will be in the Boulder City Cemetery.

Denison, Eugene Everett "Gene"
Boulder City News, Thursday, 14 Nov 1974, p.7:1-4.
Eugene Denison Services [note: obituary printed wrong, missing sentences]
Boulder City – Funeral rites were held yesterday afternoon at Palm Chapel in Henderson for Eugene Everett "Gene" Denison, 57. Burial was in the Boulder City Cemetery. Gene died Nov. 10 in the Dixie Hospital in St. George, Utah, of a heart attack. He was born March 2, . . . appointment as a laborer and truck driver. He served in the U.S. Army in World War 2. His government job became permanent on July 16, 1946 and he was a foreman 2 of mixed gang maintenance when he transferred to the city on Jan. 3, 1960. Gene was superintendent of Public Works for Boulder . . . March 3, 1972. The family had purchased their government house on Avenue B, but sold it when they moved to Grant's Pass, Oregon "to travel." Later, when former Boulderites, the Beebes, opened a trailer park in Washington, Utah, the Denisons moved there into a mobile home. . . wife Elizabeth "Betty" Denison, Washington, Utah; two daughters, Sheila Ann (Mrs. Robert) Enright, Westminister, Calif.; and Darla (Mrs. John) Reo, Las Vegas; four grandchildren, and a brother, Arthur Denison, North Las Vegas.

Denzer, Gene V.
Boulder City News, Thursday, 10 Oct 1974, p.23:3-4.
Gene Denzer Services
Funeral services will be held at 2 p.m. Saturday, for Gene V. Denzer, 53, at the Palm Chapel in Henderson. Officiating will be Pastor John Martinson and Pastor Lee Thoni of the Calvary Lutheran Church in Las Vegas. Mr. Denzer died early Tuesday morning at the Sunrise Hospital, where he had been a patient under intensive care for a week. Previously, he had been in St. Rose de Lima. He was born Dec. 29, 1920 in Minnesota City, Minnesota. Gene and Jeanette were married May 20, 1944 in Lewiston, but lived for several years in Milwaukee. They moved to Boulder City in 1953, and he was employed as a crane repairman for Titanium in Henderson. Their daughter Konye was Damboree Queen in 1963, and was in the top 10 of the Miss Nevada Contest. Survivors are Jeanette, 1328 Colorado St.; daughter Konye (Mrs. Gary) Wright, Phoenix, Ariz.; a brother, Oak Denzer, Wisconsin; brothers Ray, George, Alvin, Dale and Neil Denzer, all of Minnesota; a sister, Beulah Dickman, Minn.; and three grandchildren.

Detrick, Orzal L.
Boulder City News, Thursday, 2 Apr 1981, p.12.
Orzal L. Detrick, 68, died last Friday in Boulder City. A chief inspector for a foraging plant, Mr. Detrick was born December 17, 1912 in Swanington, Indiana. He was an eight-year resident of Boulder City. He is survived by his wife, Josephine Detrick of Boulder City; son, John S. Detrick of Wheaton, Illinois; daughter, Anna M. Long of Boulder City; sisters, Orpha Hartley of Remington, Ind. and Elnora Sims of Clovis, California; brother Virgil of Oak Forest, Ill.; and four grandchildren. Graveside services were conducted Monday morning in Boulder City Cemetery.

Diebold, Walter Harvey
Boulder City News, Thursday, 26 Sep 1991, 7:3.
Walter Harvey Diebold, 76, a Boulder City resident since 1950, died Saturday in Las Vegas. Born Oct. 11, 1914 in Winnetka, Ill., he was a maintenance engineer in the Boulder City Schools for 25 years. He is survived by his wife, Linda F. Diebold of Boulder City and two sons, John Diebold of Pensacola, Fla. and Daniel Diebold of Leachburg, Pa.; a brother, Roger Diebold of Boulder City and three grandchildren. Graveside services were held. In lieu of flowers donations may be made to the memorial fund at Boulder City Credit Union. Bunker Mortuary handled arrangements.

Donovan, Teresa A.
Boulder City News, Thursday, 5 Dec 1991, 10:1-2.
Teresa A. Donovan, 81, died Saturday in a local hospital. She was born Oct. 15, 1910, in New York, and had been a resident of the Boulder City area for seven years. She is survived by one daughter, Patricia Morra of California, and two grandchildren. Mass Services will be held at St. Andrew's Catholic Church today at 9 a.m. Arrangements were handled by Palm Mortuary in Henderson.

Dorr, Victor A.
Boulder City News, Thursday, 1 Sep 1983, 9:1-2.
Former Boulder City resident, Victor A. Door, 59, died Sunday in Phoenix. A resident of Kingman, he was born April 15, 1923, in Bangor, Maine, and was a self-employed house painter. He is survived by his wife, Anna of Kingman; step-sons, Jim Wammack of Boulder City, Eddie Wammack of El Cajon, Calif,; and Roger Wammack of La Mesa, Calif.; and six grandchildren. Graveside services will be conducted at 11 a.m. Thursday in Boulder City Cemetery. Bunker Mortuary is handling arrangements.

Dosch, Autumn Regina
Boulder City News, Thursday, 17 Feb 1977, 3:3-4.
Services Held For Child, Autumn Dosch
Funeral services were held Monday at Palm Chapel in Henderson for three-year-old Autumn Regina Dosch, who passed away Feb. 11 in Boulder City. The child was born July 24, 1973 in Los Angeles, Calif. She resided at 430 Birch street. She is survived by her parents, Mr. and Mrs. Paul A. Dosch; a sister, Brooke Dosch; brother, Paul Jr.; grandparents, Mr. and Mrs. Charles Burkhart, Saline, Mich. Interment was at the Boulder City Cemetery.

Dosch, Paul
Boulder City News, Thursday, 1 Oct 1987.
Paul A. Dosch, 46, died Monday. He was a resident of Boulder City since 1976. A veteran, he was born June 27, 1941, in Brynmawr, Pa., and was an operator for a water and power company. He is survived by his wife, Kathleen; daughters, Brooke and Amanda; son Paul Jr., all of Boulder City; brother, John of Florida. Services were Wednesday at Bethany Baptist Church in Boulder City. Burial was in Boulder City Cemetery. In lieu of flowers, the family requests donations be sent to Christian Center School of Boulder City, or Boulder City Department of Parks and Recreation. Palm Mortuary handled arrangements.

Dubois, Eugenie

Boulder City News, Thursday, 1 Sep 1988, 10:3.
Eugenie Dubois, mother in law of Dr. John Rousseau, pastor of Grace Community Church passed away Monday, August 22, 1988 in Honolulu at Lehei hospital where she had been staying for the last four years. Born in France, she was 92 years old. Cecile Rousseau was her only child and Eugenie followed the Rosseaus when they moved to the U.S.A. in 1967. She helped them greatly in raising their two adopted sons, James and John, who live in Hawaii. Her ashes will be deposited at the Boulder City Cemetery. A memorial service will be held for her at Grace Community Church, Tuesday, September 6 at 5 p.m. Instead of flowers a memorial gift could be made to the church.

Dunlap, Lola B.

Boulder City News, Thursday, 3 Mar 1988, p. 31.
Lola B. Dunlap, 80, passed away Feb. 29 in Boulder City. Resident of the community for 38 years, she was born on July 30, 1907. She was a long-time member of the Does Drove 34 in Boulder City and was active in many Senior Center activities. Survivors include a daughter, Dorothy Cleveland; a grand-daughter Melissa Higginbotham; a grandson Burl Cleveland; also two great-grandsons; all of Ventura, Calif. Palm Mortuary is in charge of arrangements. Viewing will be at Palm Chapel, Henderson, today from 2 to 9 p.m. Services will be at Palm Chapel, Henderson, Friday at 10 a.m. Burial will follow in Boulder City cemetery. In lieu of flowers, the family requests that donations may be made to the Boulder City Elks fund for new chairs in the lodge room.

Dunagan, James H.

Boulder City News, Thursday, 28 June 1979, p.4:3.
Funeral services were held Wednesday morning at Palm Chapel for James H. Dunagan, 54, who passed away Sunday in Henderson. A long-time resident of Boulder City, he was a retired high scaler for the Bureau of Reclamation. A U. S. Navy World War II veteran, he was born march 11, 1925 in Oklahoma. Mr. Dunagan is survived by his daughters, Debra Sue Kail and Lisa Dunagan, of Mt. Rose, Colorado; mother, Lucy Dunagan of Boulder City; brothers, Charlie Dunagan of Las Vegas and Ray Dunagan of San Diego, California; sisters, Hazel Friday and Ethel Romine of

Guthrie, Oklahoma; Dollie Haskett of Boulder City, Mae White of Wilcox, Arizona and Melba Jordan of Jacksonville, Florida. Burial was at Boulder City Cemetery.

Dunagan, Lucy Jane
Boulder City News, Thursday, 11 Oct 1990, 7:2-3.
Lucy Jane Dunagan, 95, a 44-year Boulder City resident, died Oct. 4, in Boulder City. Born in Arkansas on May 18, 1895, she was a housewife. She is survived by five daughters, Dollie Haskett of Boulder City; Hazel Friday of Guthrie, Okla; Ethel Romine of Baker City, Ore.; Mae White of Willcox, Ariz.; Melba Jordan of Jacksoncille, Fla.; two sons, Charles Dunagan of Las Vegas and Ray Dunagan of Boulder City; a sister, Carrie Johnson of Bethel, Okla; and 21 grandchildren, several great-grandchildren and 3 great-great grandchildren. Services were held. Palm Mortuary handled arrangements.

Dunbar, Harry Edgar
Boulder City News, Thursday, 12 June 1952, p.1:4.
Services Held For Dunbar; Early Pioneer
Funeral services were held Tuesday at Grace Community Church for Harry Edgar Dunbar, who passed away on Friday at the age of 87. Members of the Boulder City Elks Lodge assisted in the services. Dunbar, who died at the home of his son, leo, at 1329 Denver Street, had been in poor health for the past year. A native of Owasso, Michigan, he had come to this area during the early days of construction of Hoover Dam. When the job was finished, he returned to his former home in Montrose, Colorado. About five years ago, he and his wife came back to Boulder City to live with their son. In addition to his widow and son, Dunbar is survived by a daughter Mrs. Robert Archer of Wichita, Kansas. Mr. and Mrs. Harry Edgar Dunbar had recently observed their sixty-fifth wedding anniversary.

Duncan, Charles R.
Boulder City News, Thursday, 17 Feb 1966, 1:1.
ELKS CONDUCT DUNCAN RITES
Funeral services were conducted at 1 p.m. yesterday afternoon for Charles R. Duncan, 607 Avenue D, at the Boulder City Elks Lodge with the Elks officiating. Palm Mortuary of Henderson was in charge of arrangements and burial was in Boulder City Cemetery. Mr. Duncan was born Nov. 20, 18890 in Cherry County, Neb. He was a painter in construction work by trade, and had lived in Boulder City since 1946. There are no known survivors.

Dunlap, Burl T.
Boulder City News, Thursday, 11 Mar 1982, 6:1-3.
Dunlap Graveside Services Held
Graveside services were held Tuesday at the Boulder City cemetery for long-time Boulder resident Burl T. Dunlap, who passed away Thursday, March 4 in Boulder. Mr. Dunlap was born Feb 25, 1907 in Quinton, Okla. He was a retired broilermaker for Stauffer Chemical Co. He had lived in this area since 1950. He is survived by his wife, Lola, Boulder City; daughter Dorothy Cleveland, Ventura, Ca.; brother Jack Dunlap; Olive Hill, Ky.; sister Monnie Attig, Bellflower, Ca.; two grandchildren and one great grandchild. He was a member of the Elks Chapter 1682 of Boulder City and Boilermakers Local No. 92. Palm Mortuary was in charge of arrangements and interment was at the Boulder City cemetery.

Dunlap, Lola B.
Boulder City News, Thursday, 10 Mar 1988, 6:1.
Lola B. Dunlap, 80, died Monday, Feb. 29 in Boulder City and had been a resident since 1950. A homemaker she was born on July 30, 1907 in Boise, Idaho and was a member of the Boulder City Senior Center and the BPO Does, Drove 34 of Boulder City. She is survived by her daughter Dorothy Cleveland of Ventura, Calif. and two grandchildren Melissa Higginbotham and Burl Cleveland both of Calif., and also two great grandchildren. Funeral service were held at Palm Chapel in Henderson on March 4 and interment was in the Boulder City Cemetery.

Dunphy, James T.
Boulder City News, Thursday, 5 Apr 1973, 9:5-6.
James Dunphy Service Held
The funeral Mass for James T. Dunphy, 55, was said Monday morning at St. Andrew's Catholic Church, with burial following at the Boulder City Cemetery. The Rosary was recited Sunday night at Palm Mortuary Chapel in Henderson. Mr. Dunphy died March 29 in St. Vincent's Hospital of Los Angeles, after a long illness. He was born August 26, 1917 in Jamestown, R. I. He saw action with the U.S. Navy during World War 2. Mr. Dunphy began work as a machinist with the U.S. Bureau of Reclamation on the Yellowtail Project in Fort Smith, Montana, on Sept. 9, 1966. He was transferred to Boulder City on Dec. 29, 1968, and retired on disability in December, 1972. He was a member of the Knights of Columbus in Billings, Mont.; the Benevolent and Protective Order of Elks in Boulder City, and the American Federation of Government Employees. Survivors are his widow, Mary, of Lake Shore Trailer Village; son James T. Jr.; daughters Connie and Janice, all of Boulder City; daughters Thersa, Boulder, Mont.; Mary K. Oliver, Washington, D.C.; and Jean Bornhoft, Billings, Mont. Also his mother, Helen G. Dunphy, Arlington, Va.; brother Robert, Annapolis, Md.; and sister Helen Dunphy of Arlington, Va.

Dyson, Albert W.
Boulder City News, Thursday, 19 Feb 1987, 27:6.
Albert W. Dyson, age 65, a 15-year resident passed away Tuesday, Feb. 10. He was born July 5, 1921 in Ohio and was a technician for the city of Boulder City. He leaves his wife, Virginia of Boulder City; daughters, Mrs. Virginia Luther of Ohio and Charlene Anderson of Boulder City; brother, Bernard Dyson of Ohio and three grandchildren.

Eads, Evelyn Francis
Boulder City News, Thursday, 21 Oct 1976, p.10:2.
Mrs. Evelyn Francis Eads, homemaker and six-year Boulder City resident, 633 Avenue K, passed away Friday, October 15, 1976, in the Boulder City Hospital. Mrs. Eads was born March 24, 1903, in Ishpeming, Michigan, to James Williams and Sarah Brown Williams. She is preceded in death by two husbands. Mrs. Eads is survived by her

daughter, Betty Rovacchi of Boulder City; a son, William Sampson of Detroit, Michigan; a brother, Clifford Williams of Detroit; a sister, Doris Torongeau of Floral City, Florida; seven grandchildren; and two great grandchildren. Services were held at Palm Chapel in Henderson on Monday, October 18, at 10 a.m. Reverend Guy Holliday of Grace Community Church officiated. Interment was at the Boulder City Cemetery.

Echols, Orbin Ira
Las Vegas Review-Journal, Tuesday, 16 May 1950, p.2:2.
Conduct Rites
Funeral services were conducted this afternoon at the Grace Community Church in Boulder City for Orbin Ira Echols, 62, former Boulder City resident who died last Wednesday in Richmond, California, where he was visiting his son, James Echols. The Reverend Olaf Stoeve, pastor of the church, conducted the service and interment took place in the Boulder City cemetery where Echols' wife was buried a few years ago.

Eddy, Florence
Boulder City News, Thursday, 10 Sep 1964, 6:3-4.
Funeral services were held Tuesday afternoon for Florence Eddy, 74, at Grace Community Church. The rites were conducted by the Reverend Guy Holliday. Burial followed in the Boulder City Cemetery. She died in the Boulder City Hospital, after an illness of several months. Pallbearers were Al Fisher, Joseph Kine, Jack Heyward, Fred Rader, Leo Dunbar and Sylvia Legler played background music on the organ. Florence Meisner was born in Crete, Nebraska, March 5, 1890. She married Claud Sleeper on Christmas Day, 1909, and they celebrated their 47th wedding anniversary a month before his death in January 1957. The Sleepers homesteaded in Wyoming with friends of school days, the Eugene Eddys. Florence and Claud came to Boulder City in 1936 with their two daughters, Marjorie (now Mrs. Jack Gagliolo of Boulder City), and Betty (Mrs. Jack Garehime Jr. of Las Vegas). At first, Claud managed the Lake Auto Court, which belonged to Florence's brother, Lou Meisner. Later, he was employed by the government. For awhile, Florence was manager of the motel, and she was a friendly hostess to many of us. After Claud died, Florence visited back in Nebraska. Gene Eddy was a widower. The two

lonesome old friends were married June 20, 1957 at the First Methodist Church in Las Vegas. Florence lived at 620 Avenue F for nearly 20 years. She dearly loved flowers, and shared those which she grew in her yard. The whole family enjoyed sports, and followed our local activities. She was a member of Cactus Rebekah Lodge No. 40, I.O.O.F., served for many years as a courier for the Boulder Hospital, belonged to the Women's Club, the Martha Circle of the Women's Association of Grace Church, and was a past secretary of the Retired Government Employees Association. She is survived by her husband Eugene Eddy, 620 Ave. F; her two daughters as mentioned above; a sister, Mrs. Francis Pasner of Las Vegas; four grandchildren – Shirley (Mrs. Ramon) Williams of Bakersfield, Calif.; Roger Likens of Colorado; Sannene and Kurt Garehime of Las Vegas; and three great-grandchildren, Debbie, Danny and Robin Williams. In lieu of flowers, the family requested that donations be given to fight cancer.

Eller, Agnes Emma
Boulder City News, Thursday, 31 Aug 1995, 12:1-2.
Agnes Emma Eller, 80, died August 23, 1995, in a local hospital. Born April 17, 1915, in Chicago, Ill., she had been a Boulder City area resident since 1977. She is survived by two sons, Phillip and John Sampson, both of California; and two grandchildren. Services were held Monday. Arrangements were handled by Palm Mortuary in Henderson.

Eller, Leroy Charles
Boulder City News, Thursday, 22 Feb1990, 9:5-6.
Leroy Charles Eller, 81, a long-time resident of Boulder City, died Tuesday, Feb. 13, 1990. He was born June 28, 1908 in Mansfield, Ohio. He was a salesman. Survivors include his wife Agnes Eller of Boulder City, a daughter, Precious Mehr of Medford, Ore.; a brother, Dale Eller of Sunland, Calif. and one grandchild. Private family services were held. Palm Mortuary handled arrangements.

Ellis, James H. "Jim"
Boulder City News, Thursday, 3 Jul 1975, 9:7.
Funeral services will be held for James H. "Jim" Ellis at 11 a.m., Saturday, at the First Ward of the Church of Jesus Christ of Latter-Day Saints. They will be conducted by Bishop Kenneth Simkins, and burial will be in the Boulder City Cemetery. Jim took sick suddenly Monday, and died immediately at the Boulder City Hospital. Jim was born October 12, 1911, in Tooele, Utah. He was employed by the U. S. Government from 1939 to 1952 in Ogden, Utah, and was foreman of the maintenance shop when he left there. The family moved to Nevada in 1953 and he operated a garage in Henderson. He became blind in 1955, but was active on the board of directors of the Nevada Federation of the Blind and the Southern Nevada Sightless. He and his wife, Opal, made daily trips to the Blindcraft headquarters in Las Vegas, where he became an expert at caning chairs and taught Braille. In 1966, Jim was president of the Nevada Federation of the Blind. At this time, the family lived in Boulder City, in Lakeview. With the combined help of the Radelph-Sheppard VendirStand Act (giving preference to blind persons the operation of vendi stands on Federal property), the Soroptimist Club of Las Vegas, and the Bureau of Services of the Blind of Nevada, the first refreshment stand on Hoover Dam was constructed in 1960, and the Ellis family ran the Dam Snacketeria on the Nevada side from the time it was built, until now. In January, 1971, they purchased the Dam Café which later became "Mario's." Jim is survived by his wife, Opal, 309 Lakeview Drive; sons John Brad Ellis, Boulder City; William H. Ellis, zTehran, Ira Rolland B. Clift, with the U.S. Army at Fort Carson, Colo.; Harvey J. Clift and Barry L. Clift, Las Vegas; daughters, Barbara (Mrs. Desmond L.) Garvin, and Beverly (Mrs. Billy) Parl both of Henderson; Katherine (Mrs. Arthur) Wright, Las Vegas; and Darlene (Mrs. Ray) Wilson, Chilcoot, Calif.; One brother, Walter "Babe" Ellis, Ogden, Utah; 3 grandchildren and __ great.

Ellis, Opal N.
Boulder City News, Thursday, 6 Sep 1979, 8:16-17.
Services will be conducted Friday, Sept. 7 at 10 a.m. at the LDS Chapel in Boulder City for Opal N. Ellis, 60, who died September 3 in Las Vegas. She was born February 14, 1919 in Rirle, Indiana and was a member of the First Ward of the Church of Jesus Christ of the Latter Day Saints. Mrs. Ellis is survived by daughters, Katherine Wright, Barbara Garvin and Beverly Park, all of Henderson, and Darlene Wilson of California; sons, Rolland Clift of Hawaii, Harvey Clift of Cedar City, Utah, Barry Clift of Pahrump, John Ellis of Boulder City and William Ellis of Texas; 28 grandchildren and several great grandchildren. Palm Mortuary is handling arrangements.

Emerich, William A.
Boulder City News, Thursday, 12 Oct 1978, 8:1-2.
William A. Emerich Passes Away
Services were held last Monday for William A. Emerich, 61, who passed away October 6 at the Boulder City Hospital. A machinist and a World War II veteran of the U.S. Army, Mr. Emerich was born May 22, 1917 at Whitebird, Idaho. He was a member of the Boulder City Masonic Lodge and the Scottish Rite of Long Beach, California. Surviving are his wife, Bernice Emerich of Boulder City; a son, William W. Emerich; daughters, Linda L. Arden and Cheri G. Center, all of Las Vegas; and six grandchildren. The Reverend Marjorie Holman of the Four Square Church, and the boulder City Masons officiated at the service held at Palm Chapel. Interment followed at Boulder City Cemetery.

Engle, Charlotte June
Boulder City News, Thursday, 24 Sep 1953, 3:1.
Funeral Rites Held Tuesday For Charlotte Engle
Funeral services were held Tuesday afternoon for Charlotte June Engle, 5 months old daughter of Mirl and John Engle, who died Saturday after an illness of a few months. At the time of the infant's death, the Engles were visiting relatives in Fremont, Mo., after attending a church convention in Tennessee. Charlotte June was born April 29, 1953, in Boulder City. She is survived by her parents, her sisters, Kathie, Mary and Johnny Lou, and a brother Jackie. She was the granddaughter of Martha Holt and the

recently deceased C. E. Holt of Lakeview Addition. The Reverend Guy Olmstead conducted the services in the yard of the family home at the Boulder City cemetery. Graveside rites were led by Brother Jesse Griffen. Mr. and Mrs. Criffen sang two numbers, "Further Along" and "Won't It Be Wonderful There."

Engle, LeRoy
Boulder City News, Thursday, 31 Dec 1987, 8:1.
LeRoy Engle, 55, died Wednesday, Dec. 23 in Boulder City. He had been a resident of the Boulder City area since 1974. He was born in Slick, Okla. on July 29, 1932 and was a staff sergeant in the United States Army. Survivors include mother Lottie Burns, Boulder City; brothers John Engle, Las Vegas; James Engle, Henderson; Charles Engle, Prior, Okla.; Derald Burns, Coleman, Texas; sisters Geraldine Herron, Clarkston, Wash,; Helen Wilcoxon, Clarkston, Wash,; Martha Stanton, East Las Vegas; Brenda Burns, Boulder City and Judy Keehn, Stevens Point, Wis. Visitation was held Monday Dec. 28 at noon with funeral services held Dec. 29 at 1:30 p.m. in the Palm Chapel in Henderson. Interment was in the Boulder City Cemetery.

Eno, John A.
Boulder City News, Thursday, 29 May 1975, 9:8.
Funeral services will be held at 10 o'clock, this morning, for John A. Eno, 74, who died May 26 in the North Las Vegas Hospital. The Reverend Guy Holliday will officiate at Grace Community Church, and burial will be in the Boulder City Cemetery. He was born March 20, 1901 in Exeter, New Hampshire, and was a retired X-ray technician. He has lived in this area for 15 years. Mr. Eno is survived by his wife, Martha, 1425 Ingraham, Las Vegas; a daughter, Andrea (Mrs. Bruce) Anderson, 636 Avenue H, Boulder City; a brother, Jerone Eno, Skowhegan, Maine; two sisters, Antoinette Bouchard, Haverhill, Mass.; and Adelina Basiliere, Waterville, Maine; and three grandchildren. Mrs. Anderson, who works for Blair Realty, says that her mother plans to move to Boulder City.

Eno, John
Boulder City News, Thursday, 29 May 1975, 11:1.
Eno, John A., 74, of 1425 Ingraham St., died Monday in a local hospital. Resident 15 years. X-ray technician. Survivors: wife, Martha; daughter, Andrea C. Anderson of Boulder City; sister, Antoinette Bouchard of Haverhill, Mass. and Adelina Basiliere of Waterville, Maine; brother, Jerome of Skowhegan, Maine; three grandchildren. Services 10 a.m. Thursday at the Grace Community Church with the Reverend Guy Holliday officiating. Burial in Boulder City Cemetery. Palm Mortuary Henderson.

Ernst, Georg
Boulder City News, Thursday, 29 June 1978, p.2:5-6
Georg Ernst To Be Buried in Boulder City
Graveside services will be held Saturday, July 1 at 10 a.m. at the Boulder City Cemetery for Georg Ernst, 70, who died June 13 in Peekskill, New York. Survivors include his wife, Carola of Peekskill; sons, Peter Ernst of San Bernardino, Calif., and Hugo Ernst of Houston, Texas; daughters, Anneliese Caruso of Boulder City, Ursula Ernst of Peekskill and C. Lisette of W. LaFayette, Indiana and five grand-children.

Evans, Alma
Boulder City News, Thursday, 8 May 1975, 6:1.
Alma Evans, 78, was laid to rest Tuesday afternoon in the Boulder City Cemetery. Funeral services were held previously in the Bunker Brothers Chapel in Las Vegas, by Chester Hooper, minister of the Church of Christ in Boulder City, where Mrs. Evans was a member. She died May 3 in the Vegas Valley Convalescent Center in Las Vegas. She was born March 13, 1897 in Peoria, Ill,; but lived in Missouri many years. While there, she learned to work with pottery, from the family of her husband, Arthur Evans. In 1940 they moved to Boulder City, where other members of the Evans family already resided. There little pottery shop developed into the famous Desert Sands. Although the store was sold in 1953, Arthur continued to work there. He died in 1966. Mrs. Evans was employed in the kitchen of the Boulder City Hospital, while it was under Government administration. She is survived by her daughter, Dorothy (Mrs. Raymond) Thurston, with whom she had been living at 108 Forest Lane in Boulder

City; a son, Ferrell Evans, who now operates the Desert Sands Pottery in Barstow, Calif.; a brother, Ray Williamson, Warrenton, Missouri; two grandchildren and two great grandchildren.

Evans, Arthur
Boulder City News, Thursday, 7 Aug 1966, 1:1-2
Evans Rites. Famous Pottery Craftsman Dead.
Funeral services for Arthur Evans, 78, were conducted yesterday morning by the Reverend Ralph Aycock of the Church of Christ and by the local Masonic Lodge. Burial followed in the Boulder City Cemetery. He died at home Monday, of heart failure, following a siege of flu. Mr. Evans was born February 10, 1988, in Dexter, Mo. When he was a young boy in the Ozark Mountains, he learned the family skill of making hand-turned pottery from native clay. The Evans family came to Boulder City in 1940, because they felt that the many tourists might appreciate their distinctive craftmanship. They use ordinary desert clay from such places as Searchlight, Chloride and the Valley of Fire, coloring it with pigments of minerals (red from iron ore, blue from cobalt, etc.). They first opened business in a small "work shack" but in four years expanded to the Desert Sands Pottery shop on Nevada Hwy. In 1953, Terrill Evans (Arthur's son) sold the town's unique manufacturing industry to Mr. and Mrs. George Allen and Mrs. Ruth Rousey, but his father remained as the company potter. Thousands of tourists and townspeople have enjoyed watching members of the Evans family making the large variety of items. Many Girl Scout troops have had the art demonstrated to them by the skilled artists — including daughter Dorothy Thurston and niece Lucille Dossett. Mr. Evans belonged to the Church of Christ. He was a member of Dexter Lodge No. 532, F&AM. He is survived by his widow, Alma, 108 Forest Lane, Boulder City; daughter Dorothy (Mrs. Raymond) Thurston, 531 Cherry Street; son Terrell, Barstow, Calif,; grandchildren, Raymond and Lois Thurston. Also, a brother, Randell Evans, Dexer, Mo.; sisters, Mollie Grissom, Pocatello, Idaho; Lennie Noland, Cape Girardeau, Mo,; and Amy Tucker, Bloomfield, Mo.

Evans, Lawrence E.
Boulder City News, Thursday, 24 Aug 1989, 25:6.
Lawrence E. Evans, 75, a resident since 1979 of Boulder City, died Aug. 12 in Las Vegas. Born in Hubbard, Neb., on Jan. 26, 1914, he was a financial secretary for a Plumbers and Pipefitters Local. He is survived by his wife, Lois H. Evans of Boulder City; three daughters, Marlene K. Jordahl of Portland, Ore., and Sharol L. Gibbons and Annette Evans, both of Boulder City; two brothers, Edward Evans of Freemont, Neb. and Joy Evans of La Measa, Ariz.; a sister, Charlotte Tindeland of Laporte, Minn,; and 11 grandchildren and eight great grandchildren. Services were held. Palm Mortuary handled arrangements.

Evans, William McKinley "Bill"
Boulder City News, Thursday, 23 Jan 1969, 1:5.
Legion Rites for W. Evans Today in BC
Graveside services will be conducted at 2 p.m. at the B.C. Cemetery for William McKinley "Bill" Evans, 72 who died suddenly Sunday at his home in Newcastle, Utah. The rites will be in charge of American Legion Post 31, of which he was a member. Mr. Evans was born March 29, 1896, in Redwood Falls, Minn. He spent some time in 1916 on the Mexican border with the National Guard; served with distinction as a 1st lieutenant with the 2nd Minnesota Infantry Regiment in World War I; and re-entered the Army in World War II as a lieutenant and company commander of the 797th Military Police Battalion. He later became an escort guard officer, Prisoner of War Section, for Meade, Md., from where he was discharged. The veteran began his career with the U. S. Government in 1923 as a mail carrier. He and his wife came to Boulder City in 1932, during construction of Hoover Dam and he worked as a pipefitter. He was a pipefitter foreman for the Boulder Canyon Project, and received a 30-year emblem award in Sept. 1957, He was secretary of the Project Apprenticeship Training Program from the time of its inception until his retirement. The Evanses lived at 647 Avenue G for 26 years. He like to garden and successfully experimented with growing citrus fruits in his yard. They moved to Utah a few years ago. He is survived by his widow, "Willie," of Newcastle; three sisters – Florence Evans and Mary Van Kamp of Salem, Ore. and Pearl Jane Yeager of Sioux Falls, S.D. He is the uncle of Fred Holland, Boulder City; and the brother-in-law of former Boulderites Hazel Lueking and Fred Holland, Las Vegas, and Tom

Holland of Newcastle.

Fagan, Celeste Browne
Boulder City News, Thursday, 23 Jun 1988, 15:5-6.
Celeste Browne Fagan, 86, died Saturday, June 18 in Boulder City. She had been a resident of Boulder City for one year. She was born in Union County, Ky on June 25, 1901 and was a homemaker. Survivors include daughter Arleen Marks and son-on-law Jack, Boulder City; granddaughter Vicki Marks Yeley, Orangeburg, SC; great grandchildren, Ryan and Ann-Marie Yeley, Orangeburg, SC; sisters Angela Browne and Rosemary Stockton, both of Morgan Field, Ky. Prayer service was held Sunday, June 19 at 4. P.m. mass was held Monday, June 20 at 11 a.m. both at St. Andrews Catholic Church in Boulder City. Interment was in the Boulder City Cemetery.

Finigan, Lawrence
Boulder City News, Thursday, 13 Feb. 1969.
Funeral services were conducted last Saturday at 10 a.m. at Palm Chapel, Henderson, for Lawrence Finigan who died Feb. 5 in Boulder City Hospital following a heart attack. Mr. Wes Lieurance of the Church of Christ officiated and burial was in the local cemetery. The deceased was born March 28, 1909 in San Angelo, Tex. and lived at 639 Avenue D. He was a self-employed painter and had been a Boulderite for 18 years. He is survived by his widow, Evelyn, Boulder City; a daughter, Mrs. Peggy M. Kohler, Point Arkansas, Tex.; three grandchildren; three sisters, Mrs. Kathryn Deres, San Antonio, Tex.; Mrs. Norine Huegele, Portland, Ore. and Mrs. Betty Krafft, Spokane, Wash.

Fiscus, Alice
Boulder City News, Thursday, 20 Oct 1988, 6:1-3.
By Teddy Fenton
Alice Fiscus died on Oct. 14, 1988, after a short illness. Her services were at Grace Community Church. Reverend White of Bethany Baptist officiated. She was 49 years old. Born at Clovis, New Mexico on Sept. 6, 1959. The family arrived in Boulder City in 1942. No housing was available. The camped at the government camping grounds until a small house was purchased in McKeeversville (now Lakeview). It was mid-

summer and Mildred would take her children to Wilbur Square (known also as Government Park) and all summer long the cool grass and growing trees was a second home. Alice was a brilliant child. She was in a car wreck at the age of three. The injury was to hamper her career. She was known as a person who loved good books, history was a favorite. Her entire schooling was in Boulder City. She attended summer classes at UNLV majoring in her favorite subjects. She learned typing and took a business course at the Dana McKay Center at UNLV. Alice was born to wonderful parents. The late John and Mildred Fiscus. By sheer luck they lived at the edge of the desert at 402 Lakeview Dr. The lot was planted with fruit trees and vegetable gardens. To it arrived every desert animal imaginable. Alice and her brothers and sister fed them all. Inside the house there were canaries and other tame species of birds. Long walks into the desert, it was a setting dear to a child's heart. It explains the gentle nature of Alice who was loved by all who knew her well. For a livelihood she was a treasure to many hard working business people. She not only cleaned their homes, she babysat their pets and she was sought after as a baby sitter. County Store will begin tomorrow. She would be there working as she did for many years. She loved to shop and Country Store was her favorite yard sale. There she built her library, there she found antiques and rare furniture. At her death it took two storerooms which she rented to hold her valuables. She worked for Mazie Delonney, also Mrs. Curley Smith, Rosemary Whalen, and her loyalty, dependability, honesty and her good mind impressed, not only her employees but her friends as well. Her family, her mother Mildred, brothers Lee, John and Floyd are finding this death hard to bear. She was so special and caring. There is no much more to write about her. This tribute is not enough in the way of homage to salute the total Alice Fiscus. A memorial is established at the Boulder City Museum and her name will be printed in gold on a bronze platelet. For all the visitors at the museum at 444 Hotel Plaza that memorial will be very special to friends and family. To friends who wish to donate a donation can be left with a volunteer at the museum any day of the week. Please know we will miss her and we sympathize with the family who loved her and that love was returned full fold.

Fiscus, John Carpenter
Boulder City News, Thursday, 23 Oct 1986, 13:3-4.
John Carpenter Fiscus, 89, died Tuesday Oct. 14 in Boulder City. He was born in Audubon County, Iowa, Dec. 13, 1896. A farmer, he was a U.S. Army veteran. Fiscus is survived by his wife, Mildred of Boulder City; daughters, Alice and Frances Mayfield, both of Boulder City; sons, Lee Conine of Denver, John Jr. of Henderson, Floyd of North Las Vegas; sister, Ruth of Taloga, Okla.; 16 grandchildren and eight great-grandchildren.

The Passing of John Fiscus Sr. Requires a Longer Story
by Teddy Fenton
It is press time as this is being written. The passing of big John Fiscus ends a legend. As Pastor Franklin White, Bethany Baptist Church remarked, John ha a foot in two centuries. He would have been 90 on Dec. 13. His birth place, even the adventure of a lifetime was told to the family and to Pastor White. It was fascinating material and a story our readers will want to hear. John now rests at the Boulder City Cemetery. John was known throughout Clark County as the beeman of Boulder City. His money even now is stored on many a pantry shelf. Mildred told us that when John had a massive heart attack in 1952, then years after the family arrived in Boulder City, he could no longer do the heavy work he needed to earn a living. One incident that actually introduced me to John was when a swarm of bees settled onto the late Clyde Coggins cabin at 663 Ave. D. All tenants became instantly alarmed except Claude. He calmly called John and was fascinated by the costume including head gear that allowed John to see out but the bees could not fly in. In no time John captured the swarm and took them home. John and Mildred were married 57 years. The celebration of their Golden Anniversary was recorded in a feature in the *News*.

Fiscus, Mildred
Boulder City News, Thursday, 14 Apr 1994, p.11.1
Mildred Fiscus, 91, died April 12, 1994, in Boulder City. Born Oct. 20, 1902, she had been a resident of Boulder City for 51 years. She was a homemaker and a member of the Bethany Baptist Church. She is survived by a daughter, Frances Mayfield of Boulder City; three sons, Lee Conine of Dolan Springs, Ariz., John Fiscus Jr. of Boulder City and Floyd Fiscus of North Las Vegas; two sisters, Lela Beevers of Sacramento, Calif., and Leola Merchant of Oroville, Calif,; three brothers, Otis Towner of Oregon, Everett Towner of Benton, Ark. and Earl Towner of Sorcorro, New Mex.; 14 grandchildren. Viewing services will be held from 2 p.m. to 6 p.m. tonight in the Palm Henderson mortuary. Funeral services will be held at 2:00 p.m. Friday at Bethany Baptist Church. Arrangements were handled by Palm Mortuary in Henderson.

Flury, Benjamin F.
Boulder City News, Thursday, 12 Feb 1953, p.1:1-2.
Masonic Rites Held For Pioneer Ben Flury Yesterday
Masonic funeral rites were conducted yesterday evening at Community church for Benjamin F. Flury, construction and maintenance superintendent for the USBR, who died Saturday of a heart attack after being hospitalized with influenza. Past grand worthy master Wilfred Voss directed the services, and the Reverent Olaf Stoeve delivered the eulogy. Interment followed in the Boulder City cemetery. The pallbearers, all members of Boulder Lodge No. 37 F&AM, were A. E. Hamilton, A. L. Sharrow, Bruce Eaton, Mike Laux, Clarence Watson and Earl Musgrove. Honorary pallbearers were old friends E. G. Nielsen, James Bellor, William P. McGonigle, Claude Moore, Paul Bonnell, Ben Vaughn, Harold Carpenter, Laurence Barnson, Steve Wenta, George Clark, Scott Wood, R. L. Francis, Morgan Sweeney, Richard Dickens, Osborne Traasdahl and Louis Pulsipher. Mrs. Everett Carpenter was soloist during the service. Flury was born in Sparta, Ga., on February 22, 1897. He came to Boulder City in construction days to work for Babcock and Wilcox, installing giant pipes in the tunnels at the dam. In 1936 he transferred to the Reclamation. In addition to his widow, Florence, he leaves two stepdaughters, Bette Alyce and Linda Wadsworth, of Boulder City; a daughter, Mrs. Louis Serventi, and grandson, Don Serventi, of San Francisco; a sister, Mrs. Leon Williams, Boulder City, and a sister and

two brothers in Georgia. He was a member of the Sportsmen's Association, the Bureau of Reclamation Bowling league, and the Circle 8 square dance club, in addition to being an active member of the Masonic lodge. Among those here from out of town for the services are Mrs. Serventi and son, Miss Wadsworth from Tucson, Arizona, where she is a student at the University of Arizona; Mrs. Clyde Baker of Los Angeles, and Mr. and Mrs. Frank Wadsworth of Las Vegas.

Foley, Aline
Boulder City News, Thursday, 5 Feb 1987, 31:1.
Aline Foley, age 76, passed away Wednesday, Feb. 4, 1987. She was an 11-year resident of Boulder City. She was born Dec. 7, 1910 in Grove, Oklahoma, and was active for many years in the Boulder City community.; She is survived by her husband Joseph and son Roger, both of Boulder City; two grandsons, David of Henderson and Daniel of Philippines; two great granddaughters, Sara of Henderson and Naomi of the Philippines; and one great grandson David, Jr. also of Henderson. Visitation will be Friday from 3 to 7 p.m. at Palm Mortuary. Graveside services will be held Saturday at 11 a.m. at the Boulder City Cemetery. In lieu of flowers, donations may be made to the American Heart Association.

Foster, Baby
Boulder City News, Friday, 28 Dec 1945, 1:2.
Foster Baby Dies, Funeral Saturday in Boulder City
Funeral services for the four-months-old son of Mr. and Mrs. George Foster will be held at the L.D.S. church Saturday, December 29, at 2 p.m., according to Mr. and Mrs. Clifford Reid, 512 Arizona street, parents of Mrs. Foster. Bishop Owen Gibson will be in charge of the service and G. C. Spilsbury will be speaker. Burial will be at the Boulder City cemetery. Mrs. Foster, who formerly was Geraldine Reid, awoke Christmas morning to find her baby dead in his crib. Cause of death was designated as thymes lymphatrous. Mrs. Reid flew to Bellflower, Calif., where the Fosters make their home. Mr. Reid and Dave Black followed by automobile. They returned to Boulder City Thursday morning with the body, and accompanied by Mr. Foster's father. Foster's mother rushed back to Boulder City from Nebraska, where she was visiting her family. She was accompanied by her youngest son, Bob Foster. Mr. and Mrs.

George Foster live at 409 E. Maple, Bellflower.

Fourno, Joyce Carroll
Boulder City News, Thursday, 12 Dec 1991, 7:2.
Joyce Carroll Fourno, age 60, died Friday, Dec. 6, 1991, in the Henderson Convalescent Hospital. She was a resident of Boulder City for the past four months. She had been suffering from a lung disease called pulmonary fibrosis for the past year. She is survived by her daughter, Marian Vince of Boulder City; her son, Frank Fourno of Vancouver, Wash.; twin grandchildren, Thomas and Ashley Vince of Boulder City; and several cousins including Cliff Carse of Boulder City. She was born Joyce Carroll Carse on January 31, 1931, in Palisade, Neb. In 1948 she moved to Washington state where she lived until moving to Boulder City this past August. She retied from the State of Washington having worked as a nurse for over 20 years. Graveside services will be held at 2 p.m. on Thursday, Dec. 12, at the Boulder City Cemetery, with Reverend Richard Smith officiating. Arrangements were handled by Palm Mortuary in Henderson.

Fowler, Richard Kenneth
Boulder City News, Thursday, 22 Oct 1964, 1:6.
Kenneth Fowler Rites Pending
Funeral services are pending for Richard Kenneth Fowler, 7, who died oct. 16 in Japan, where his father is stationed with the Navy. Richard was born January 30, 1957 in Watsonville, California, and has traveled with his family. He is survived by his parents, Buck Wayne Fowler, MMCA, and wife Catherine Violet, his brother, Buck Wayne Jr.; his maternal grandparents, Mr. and Mrs. Clarence Simpson of 1009 Nevada Hwy., and two aunts, Sandra and Jaylene Simpson. Mr. and Mrs. Fowler were flown back to the United States immediately, and are now waiting for arrangements to be completed.

Fowler, Smitty G.
Boulder City News, Thursday, 14 Jul 1994, 9:1-2.
Smitty G. Fowler, 82, died July 8, 1994 in a local hospital. He was born Oct. 28, 1911, and had been a resident of the Boulder City area for 20 years. There are no known immediate family members. Services were held Wednesday. Arrangements were handled by Palm Mortuary in Henderson.

Fritz, Herbert L.
Boulder City News, Thursday, 30 July 1970, p.1.
Herbert Fritz Service Saturday
Funeral services will be conducted at Palm Mortuary Saturday at 10 a.m. for Herbert L. Fritz, 92, who died Tuesday in Las Vegas. Mr. Fritz, had been a resident of Boulder City for 20 years and until recently lived at his home, Happy Camp, 544 Sixth St. He is survived by a daughter, Mrs. Edith Taylor, Lake San Marcos, Calif., a sister, Edna Fritz, Three Rivers, Calif., a grandson, Richard Taylor, St. Clair Shore, Mich. and a granddaughter, Barbara Bommarito, Detroit, Mich. Cremation will follow the services with ashes interred in B. C. Cemetery.

Fuller, Grace E.
Boulder City News, Thursday, 31 Mar 1994, 15:1.
Grace E. Fuller, 93, died March 23, 1994. Born July 6, 1990, in Boulder County, Colo., she had been a resident of Henderson area for 50 years. She is survived by three daughters, Katherine Smith of Henderson, Grace L. Guyette of Las Vegas and Mary Elms of New Mexico; sister Edna Strawn of Arizona; five grandchildren, eight great grandchildren and one great-great grandchild. Services were held Saturday. Arrangements were handled by Bunker Mortuary.

Furticella, Eva P.
Boulder City News, Thursday, 1 Aug 1991, 10:1.
Eva P. Furticella, 69, died Friday in a local hospital. She was born July 21, 1922, in Cababria, Italy and had been a resident of the area for 10 years. She is survived by her husband, Nicholas R. of Boulder City; one son, Nicholas A. of San Clemente, Calif.; two sisters, Ann Maglish of Griffith, Ind., and Marge Giusto of Vernon, Conn.; one brother, Joseph A. Sposato of San Clemente, Calif.; and three grandchildren. Viewing services are today at Palm Henderson Mortuary from noon to 4 p.m. Scripture services at St. Andrew's Catholic Church will be held today at 6 p.m. and Mass services will be at St. Andrew's Catholic Church Wednesday at 10 a.m. Palm Mortuary of Henderson handled arrangements.

Gabriault, Jerome
Boulder City News, Thursday, 7 Feb 1980, 4:3-4.
Funeral services were held Monday, Feb. 4th, at St. Andrews church in Boulder City for Jerome Gabriault, 64, who died at his home Thurs. Jan 31st. Interment was in Boulder City Cemetery. Mr. Gabriault retired to the area three years ago from Detroit, Mich., where he worked as a supervisor for Detroit, Diesel Allison Div. of General Motors. He was a native of Calument, Mich., in Michigan's Upper Peninsula. He is survived by his wife Margaret of Boulder City; a daughter, Sharon Szetela of Dearborn Hgts, Mich., a son, Stephen Gabriault of Detroit, two grandsons and one granddaughter. A brother, Elzear, of Merced, Ca. also survives, plus numerous nieces and nephews.

Garbat, Agnes V.
Boulder City News, Thursday, 19 Sep 1991, 10:4.
Agnes V. Garbat, 76, died Saturday, in Phoenix, Ariz. She was born Dec. 31, 1914, in Chicago, Ill., and had been a resident of the area for nine years. She is survived by two daughters, Patricia Buxton of San Francisco, Calif., and Margaret Cadaret of Phoenix; one son Dennis Garbat of Boulder City; nine grandchildren; and eight great-grandchildren. Services were held Monday at Boulder City Cemetery. Arrangements were handled by Palm Mortuary in Henderson.

Gardner, Misty Ann
Boulder City News, Thursday, Mar 1982, 6:3-4.
Misty Ann Gardner, one year old, died Saturday, March 6, 1982 in Las Vegas. She was a resident of Boulder City for the year of her life. She was born, January 29, 1981. She is survived by her parents, Michael and Vicki Gardner, brothers Mikie and Tony Gardner, and paternal grandmother, Dorothy M. Gardner, all of Boulder City. Paternal grandfather, John B. Gardner of Norwalk, Ca. and Maternal Grandparents, Mr. and Mrs. W. D. Jones of Norwalk, CA. Great-grandparents, Mr. and Mrs. C. E. Curry of Lubbock, Texas. Services were held Wednesday, March 10, 1982, at noon in the Boulder City LDS Church, with Bishop Bruce Alder fo the 2nd ward officiating. Interment followed in the Boulder City cemetery.

Garrett, Theodore Robert
Boulder City News, Thursday, 24 Apr 1980, 5:4-5.
Graveside services will be conducted today at 2 p.m. in Boulder City Cemetery for Theodore Robert Garrett, 81, who died Tuesday. He was born November 25, 1898 in Overbrook, Kansas and was a retired regional property officer of the U. S. Bureau of Reclamation and an Army veteran of World War I. He was a 50-year member of the American Legion and life member of the Ottawa, Kansas Lodge No. 18 A.F.& AM. Mr. Garrett is survived by his wife, Perle Garrett of Boulder City; son, Theodore R. Garrett, Jr. of Dansville, California; brothers, Frank Garrett of Mindon, Kan., Ralph Garrett of Denver and Clyde Garrett of Alhambra, Ca; sisters, Ruth Owens of Lawrence, Kan., Marjorie Badger of Brownsvile, Texas, Myrtle Brown of Anaheim, CA; and four grandchildren. The family requests that no flowers or plants be sent. Donations may be given to the Candlelighters of Clark County, c/o the American Cancer Society, 953 E. Sahara, Las Vegas, Nevada.

Georgeson, R. L. "Pop"

Boulder City News, Thursday, 14 Jan 1954, 1:5-7.
Funeral Rites for Popular "Pop" Georgeson Saturday
Boulder will say farewell to one of its best loved residents, R. L. "Pop" Georgeson Saturday. The rites will be held at 10 a.m. in the Masonic Temple. Pop died yesterday at 5 a.m. in Pasadena where he had been hospitalized since suffering the first of two strokes on November 18, the wedding anniversary of he and his wife of nearly half a century, Adelin. The passing of the popular pioneer merchant saddened the entire community. Pop had been one of the community's most active citizens since coming here from Ventura, California, and purchasing the Emporium, later selling it to Mrs. Paul Wilson. He was one of the most active members of both the Boulder City Elks lodge and the Rotary club. Just last year the Elks presented him with his 55-year badge of membership. He was a charter member of Brainerd, Minnesota lodge when it was founded in 1890. When the Boulder City lodge was instituted in 1945 Pop admitted here and became a charter member, serving as chairman of the first board of trustees and heading the project of acquiring the lodge's present building. Rotarians from all over the world have been greeted by his jovial smile as chairman of the reception committee for many years. He had been a devoted Rotarian since joining the organization in 1942. Pop was born in Wick, near Aberdeen, Scotlandon November 14, 1878. He was the son of William and Robina Georgeson. His father, a sea captain, died aboard his ship in Africa while Pop was very young and his mother brought him to Brainerd where he attended school, grew up, worked for the railroad and in a bank, and when 21 opened his first store. He later moved to St. Paul and managed a large store there. In 1917 he moved with his family to Venture and engaged in the variety store business. At the height of the depression he visited Boulder City, like its prospect and has been here since. He transferred his long time Masonic membership to the Pointsettia lodge in Ventura while there and had retained it at that place. He was the central figure of a large celebration there in 1949 when he was presented with his 50 year membership pin in masonry. Both Georgeson and his wife remained active in social life, even though he had retired from active business several years ago. They were constant attendants at social events and when they left for the coast in November to visit their daughter's family none here realized it was his last farewell to his wide host of friends. In

addition to his widow and son, Robert W. Georgeson, of Boulder City, he leaves a daughter, Mrs. George Farrell of Pasadena and two brothers, William D. of Los Angeles and Jack W. of St. Paul. Interment will be in the Boulder City cemetery.

Gieck, Fred
Boulder City News, Thursday, 22 June 1978, 2:3.
47 Year Resident Passes Away
Graveside services will be held this afternoon at 2 p.m. at the Boulder City Cemetery for Fred Gieck, 84, who passed away June 19 in Boulder City. Mr. Gieck was born August 9, 1893 in Osage County, Missouri and had resided in Boulder City since 1931. He was a retired diamond driller from the U.S. Bureau of Reclamation. He was an Army veteran of World War I and a member of the Boulder City VFW. Survivors include his wife, Oris of 701 Elm St., Boulder City; a son, Fred Gary Gieck of El Segundo, California; a brother, John D. Gieck of Boulder City; sisters, Nora Burger of Lawton, Oklahoma, Florence Lehman of Ukipa, Calif., and Grace Penrod of Bloomington, Indiana; two granddaughters, Debora and Kimberly Gieck. Palm Mortuary is handling the arrangements.

Gieck, Oris
Boulder City News, Thursday, 17 Mar1994, 13:1.
Oris Gieck passed away Mar. 9, 1994, in Torrance, California. She was 78 years old. She was born June 26, 1915. She worked at the Boulder City Hospital for 20 years. She was preceded in death by her husband, Fred Gieck. Survivors include a son Gary Gieck of Torrance; a sister Wanda Nay of Parma, Idaho; a sister, Ann Gieck of Boulder City NV; also two grandchildren and four great-grandchildren. Services were private.

Giesey, Darlene Alma
Boulder City News, Thursday, 26 Jul 1990, 10:1-2.
Darlene Alma Giesey, 90, a Boulder City resident, died July 23 in a local hospital. Born Mar. 7, 1990, in La Moille, Illinois, she was a Boulder City resident for over 50 years. She is survived by one daughter, Barbara J. Wood, four granddaughters and six great grandchildren. She was preceded in death by her husband William Jay Giesey, a 40-year employee of Los Angeles Department of Water and Power as a power line builder during the construction of Hoover Dam and a lineman after the construction years. The Gieseys were sponsors of the local USO during WWII and she was an active member of the Does until recently. A private family service was held with Palm Mortuary handling arrangements.

Giesey, William Jay
Boulder City News, Thursday, 5 Dec 1974, 3:6.
William Giesey Services Held
by Esther Shipp
Funeral services were held Tuesday afternoon for William Jay Giesey, 75, at the Elks Hall. They were conducted by B.P.O. Elks Lodge No. 1682, of which he was a member. Burial was in the Boulder City Cemetery. Jay died Saturday in the Boulder City Hospital, after a long illness. Jay was born June 21, 1899 in LaMoille, Ill., the first of 3 children. He lived in this town until shortly after his marriage to Darlene Maloy, Sept. 28, 1920, in Princeton, Ill. They had a double wedding with friends. When the young couple moved to California, Jay started working in the electronics field. In February, 1927, he was hired by the City of Los Angeles Department of Water and Power, and was a structural steel worker (Boulder 287KV) involved in building the transmission lines from Boulder Dam to Los Angeles. In August, 1937, he was assigned to the Boulder City Headquarters, and in December, 1937, was promoted to tower lines mechanic. In December, 1949, he was promoted to line foreman. He retired in June, 1964. He belonged to the I.B.E.W. The Gieseys purchased the house at 603 Ave. D, and renovated it to live in when they left the Department house. They also enjoyed spending the summer in their cabin at Mammoth Creek, Utah. One grandchild says she can remember that Jay was always clever at making things, and could improvise whenever necessary.

Gifford, William Thomas
Boulder City News, Thursday, 2 Nov 1967, 7:6-8.
Elks Conduct Gifford Rites
Boulder City Elks conducted funeral services Monday at 2 p.m. for William Thomas Gifford who died in Boulder City Hospital Oct. 26. The rites were held in the lodge hall and interment was in Boulder City Cemetery. Mr. Gifford was born July 13, 1892 in Olive Hill, Tenn. and had lived in this area for 40 years. At the time of his death he was a resident of Moore's Trailer Park. The deceased was a retired railroad engineer and a charter member of BPOE 1704, Hawthorne. Survivors include his widow, Estella, this city; a daughter, Beatrice Sanders, Las Vegas; a son, W. T. Gifford, Tucson, Ariz., and five grandchildren.

Gilbert, Roy E.
Boulder City News, Thursday, 31 Mar 1977, 27:5.
Roy E. Gilbert Passes Away
Funeral services were held last Monday at Palm Mortuary for Roy E. Gilbert, who died March 24 in Escondido, Calif. He was 83. Born October 26, 1893 in Shelbyville, Missouri, Gilbert resided at 3700 E. Broadway in Las Vegas. He was a 14 year resident of the area. A veteran of World War I, Gilbert was a retired interior decorator. Survivors include a daughter, Rita Barrow of Boulder City and sons John Gilbert of Poway, Calif. and Roy Gilbert of Wallace, North Carolina. Interment followed at Boulder City Cemetery.

Gilger, Archie
Boulder City News, Thursday, 8 May 1980, 8:1-2.
Graveside services will be held Friday at 11 a.m. at the Boulder City Cemetery for Archie E. Gilger, 73, who died last Friday in Las Vegas. A 31 year resident of the area, Mr. Gilger was born July 24, 1906 in Parowan, Utah. He was a member of the Masons. Mr. Gilger is survived by his wife, Lyle Gilger; seven sons and daughters and numerous grandchildren.

Gilger, John Allen
Boulder City News, Thursday, 9 Nov 1989, 7:1-2.
John Allen Gilger, 25, a lifetime resident of Boulder city, died Sunday. He was born on July 29, 1964; he was a prep cook and a U.S. Army Veteran. Survivors include his parents, Mr. and Mrs. Roy D. Gilger of Boulder City; two sisters, Shellee Gilger of Henderson, Cindy Gilger of Boulder City and his grandmother, Kittie Kivett of Boulder City. Graveside services will be held at BC cemetery at 1 p.m. today. Palm Mortuary will handle arrangements.

Gilmore, Leah
Boulder City News, Thursday, 7 Feb 1985, 28:1-2.
Leah Gilmore (85) passed away Feb. 5 Mrs. Gilmore lived in Boulder City since 1936. She was a homemaker. She was born Oct. 14, 1899 in Atwood, Ill. She is survived by her 3 children, Earl Gilmore, Albuquerque, N.M., Leonard Gilmore, Livermore, CA., Betty Nickell, Boulder City, NV, 7 grandchildren, 1 great grandchild. Services will be at Grace Community Church, Feb 8, 11 a.m. Boulder City.

Gilmore, Patrick Edward
Boulder City News, Thursday, 13 Mar1980, 5:1.
Services were conducted last Saturday at Palm Chapel for Patrick Edward Gilmore, 53, who died March 6 in a local hospital. The chief engineer for the Boulder City hospital, Mr. Gilmore was born June 17, 1926 in Thermopolis, Wyoming. He served in the Navy and had resided in Southern Nevada for five years. He was a member of the Masons of Stockton, California and Veterans of Foreign Wars of California. Mr. Gilmore is survived by his wife, Connie Gilmore of Las Vegas; three sons, Patrick Kevin and Bruce Gilmore, both of California, and Brad Cudlip of Boulder City; two daughters, Kathleen Rae Gilmore of California and Lori Gilmore of Las Vegas; sister, Vida Smith of Utah; his mother, Irene Gilmore of Boulder City; and one grandchild. Burial was at the Boulder City Cemetery.

Glass, Donald
Boulder City News, Thursday, 7 Aug 1969, 1:3
Don Glass Funeral Set Today
Funeral services will be conducted today at 10 a.m. at St. Andrews Catholic Church for Donald Glass, 57, who died of a heart attack while enroute home to Boulder City following a vacation in Sturgeon Bay, Wisc., with his wife and daughter. His death occurred last Friday in Hay springs, Neb. He will be buried in B. C. Cemetery and Palm Mortuary in Henderson is in charge of arrangements. Besides his widow, Clara of Boulder City, he is survived by his daughter, Mrs. Helen Stecker of Carson City, and his mother, Mrs. Lillian Glass of Sturgeon Bay. Mr. Glass owned and operated Don's Hamburgers on Avenue C. He went into business here in July 1953.

Glazier, Charles "Chick"
Boulder City News, Thursday, 28 Oct 1965, 2:5.
Funeral services were conducted Tuesday at 10 a.m. for Charles (Chick) Glazier, 75, who died last Friday after 32 years in Boulder City. The rites were conducted at the Masonic Temple. Mr. Glazier was born Feb. 8, 1890 and was a retired electrician. Besides his membership in the Masons, he belonged to the Veteran of Foreign wars and the international Brotherhood of Electrical Workers. He is survived by his widow, Lois, and daughters Beverly Hughes and Helen Stagner, this city; a son, Theodore, Ogden, Utah; and 12 grandchildren and nine great-grandchildren.

Godbey, Thomas M.
Boulder City News, Thursday, 25 Aug 1977, 1:2-4.
Services For Boulder Pioneer to be Held Tomorrow
Funeral services for Boulder City Pioneer, Thomas M. Godbey, will be conducted tomorrow at 10 a.m. in the Palm Mortuary Chapel in Henderson. Godbey, who arrived in Boulder City in May of 1931, will be buried in the Boulder City Cemetery with a graveside service by the American Legion Post 31 and Veterans of Foreign Wars. Services will be conducted by the Reverend Guy Holliday of Grace Community Church. Godbey was influential in drafting the charter which incorporated Boulder City in the late 50's and early 60's. Prior to that time he served several

term in the state legislature. He is survived by his wife Irma, two sons, Thomas W. Godbey of Utica, N.Y., and James of Las Vegas; three daughters, Laura Kelly and Alice Koontz of Boulder City and Ila Clements, Warren, Pa.; sisters Esther Hayes, Asheville, N. C. and Pearl Murphy, Las Vegas. He is also survived by 17 grandchildren and two great grandchildren.

Boulder City News, Thursday, 25 Aug 1977, 3:3-6.
Story of Tom Godbey Triumphant Journey 1899-1977
By Teddy Fenton
In 1955 a story appeared in the Boulder Journal by a great writer named Don Ashbaugh. He had been the editor of the Boulder City News and had come to know Tom and Erma Godbey very well. He wrote a story in the "Boulder Builder" section and it is from that story that the NEWS will present today a look back at a remarkable career. The funeral arrangements will be contained in another part of the NEWS and suffice to say Tom Godbey will be sorely missed by our town for he represented as no other man we have known that rare quality called loving kindness. Tom was never too busy to care for a sick friend. His guidance as a youth worker was never to falter until Tom's collapse and death at the Boulder City Hospital. Erma would want us to say that Tom had a smile on his face to the very end and was joking with her and with the nurses and doctor just before he died. We also want to say that one does not write a story about Tom without linking his name with his sweetheart of 55 years, that brave and wonderful partner and wife. Erma Godbey, and they together raised five children who were to carry on the unselfish service to this town they loved. Two sons, Tom Jr. and Jim, three daughters, Ila, Laura and Alice, the latter being born in Eldorado Canyon. Don Ashbaugh was to write: "Whenever the subject of Tom Godbey comes up the old-timers say that the family who worked the most for the betterment of the town are the Godbey's. The story has been told in print many times about their one-family service club for soldiers during the war for the Godbey's held open house every weekend for men stationed at a multitude of army camps. During the period of W.W.2 the Godbey's hosted a total of 500 soldiers in their home with cots spread out in the backyard. Food was supplied somehow. Tom himself, a lifelong worker with his beloved American Legion, was to serve in the navy. After his discharge he worked in a tobacco factory. During this period he attended a high school graduation. Erma Drumm, the class valedictorian, caught

his eye and his heart, he told a friend, "I am going to marry that girl," two months later Erma and Tom began the journey that benefitted every community they lived in. Boulder City became their home in 1931 and as a team they made it a better place by working on committees for building the first cemetery, the first library and even the first schools were funded by parents for the government had not set aside funds for ball parks or any of the necessary functions mentioned above. Tom and Erma must have put in half of their working lives as volunteers. Tom Mayborn Godbey was born in Salem, Mo. May 17, 1899. His homes were to be Flat River, Mo., St. Louis, Silverton, Colo., Miami, Ariz., and lucky for us, Boulder City. Williamsville "Ragtown" was to be the first home for Erma, Tom and their 5 children. Erma has been taped and also a book has been written containing the memoirs of those hard living conditions when the Godbeys first arrived. The book and the tape is at the "Special Collections" dept. at UNLV. Tom is a charter member of American Legion Post 31 and the Veterans of Foreign Wars. He served two terms in the State Assembly. During the months of drafting the city charter in 1959, Tom was proud to be asked to serve on the committee that laid out the ground work for incorporation. In 1975 the crown that Tom and Erma had earned with a life-time of civic work was given by the beloved American Legion Post 31. They were named Mr. and Mrs. Hometown, USA. See them now in the lead car of the Damboree parade, Erma waving to a multitude of friends while Tom sat in dignified splendor with a smile that never left his face that day. Later they were to be enthroned on the speaker's stand at the park and we camera bugs took a hundred pictures of that splendid glory. It was seemly and right that the American flag waved in bright sunshine behind the stand. If the NEWS had space we could fill 16 pages with the life of Tom and Erma Godbey and the family they raised. The grandchildren are carrying on the tradition. They were blessed to have such a father, and grandfather, and Erma, bless you and keep you.

Goodwin, Joseph P.
Boulder City News, Thursday, 30 Sep 1971, 1:5.
The funeral Mass was held yesterday morning at St. Andrew's Catholic Church for Joseph P. Goodwin, 48, who died suddenly Monday. The Rosary was recited Tuesday Evening, at Palm Chapel in Henderson. Burial was in the B. C. Cemetery. Mr. Goodwin was born November 21, 1922 in East Boston, Massachusetts. He was a first torpedo man in the U. S. Navy, and served his country from 1940 to 1961. He belonged to the American Legion, VFW and to the Fleet Reserve in Washington, D.C. Since the family moved to Boulder City, he has been working at Nellis AFB as a grounds and greens keeper. Mr. Goodwin is survived by his wife, Constance, 701 Elm St. A daughter Constance Jefferson of Boulder City; a half-brother James; and a cousin Francis Perrault, also of Boulder City.

Gordon, Berry
Boulder City News, Thursday, 23 May 1968, 1:3-4.
NC Man Killed
Funeral services for Berry Gordon, who was fatally killed at midnight Monday near Railroad Pass as he walked toward Boulder City. He was struck by a truck driven by James Clark of Carson City. The victim, knocked 163 feet by the impact, was declared dead on arrival at Rose de Lima Hospital shortly after the accident. Palm Mortuary in Henderson is handling the funeral arrangements. An autopsy was performed when the victim's blood soaked shirt was found in a garage can near Pittman and his wallet was missing. Mr. Gordon resided at 623 California St. with his wife, Gloria and was a bus boy at a Strip Hotel. He was born Dec. 22, 1932 in Inkom, Idaho, and was a veteran of the Korean action. Besides his widow he is survived by a daughter, Pamela, Pocatello, Idaho; his mother, Mrs. Mabel Gordon, a sister, Mrs. Louise Olsen and a brother, Bill, all of Las Vegas.

Goyette, Cecile
Boulder City News, Thursday, 4 Nov 1993, 6:3.
Cecile Goyette, 77, died Friday, Oct. 29 in Boulder City. She was a five-year resident of Boulder City. She was born Oct. 19, 1916 in Three Rivers, Mass. and was a retired cook. She is survived by her daughter, Walleen a Lukowski of Boulder City; a sister, Jeanne Panebianco of Methuen, Mass,; two granddaughters, Diana and Michelle A. Lukowski both of Boulder City; and two other grandchildren. A Mass service was held at St. Andrews Catholic Church. Arrangements were handled by Palm Mortuary of Henderson.

Graff, Karl Hardy
Boulder City News, Thursday, 31 Jan 1991, 10:2.
Karl Hardy Graff, 55, died Thursday, Jan. 24. He was a 28-year resident of Boulder City. He was born March 11, 1935 in Hurricane, Utah. He was a high school teacher for 30 years in the Clark County School District; a member of VICA for 18 years; a member of LDS 1st Ward in Boulder City; a varsity Scout Leader in Boulder City and coached baseball in Boulder City. He is survived by his wife Beryl of Boulder City; four sons, Mark and Scott both of Boulder City, Todd of Twin Falls, Idaho and Brad of Cedar City, Utah; two daughters, Tona Graff of Boulder City and Shauna Kerr of Encinitas, Calif.; two brothers, Stanley of Las Vegas and Kenyon of Orem, Utah; two sisters, Dorothy Winder of Las Vegas and Joyce Snow of Provo, Utah; and six grandchildren. Services were held Monday at the Boulder City LDS Ward Chapel. Arrangements were handled by Palm Mortuary of Henderson.

Gray, George
Boulder City News, Thursday, 8 Sep 1955, p.1:5.
Funeral Rites for Late George Gray Scheduled Today
Funeral services for George Gray, 65, will be held at 9 o'clock this morning, at Palm Funeral Home, 132 S. First Street, Las Vegas. They are to be conducted by a minister of the Episcopal Church. Saturday, Gray was found dead in his room in the Hillside Dormitory, where he died in his sleep. He was employed as an assistant electric plant operator by the City of Los Angeles Department of Water and Power, and was due to retire at the end of this month. He came here seven years ago from

California. Gray was born September 3, 1890 in Texas. He was a veteran of the Navy. He belonged to the Blue Lodge, Colage No. 211 F. & A. M., and was a member of the Indian Consistory, Valley of South McAllister, Orient of Oklahoma. As a pastime, he enjoyed the study of astronomy, mineralogy and drafting. Of a quiet nature, he was well liked by both his fellow workers at the Dam and those at the Dormitory. Gray is survived by a son, Rex, who came here from Baldwin park, California, to make funeral arrangements. Also a brother Lawrence in the state of Washington; a half-brother Lawton Barry, and their mother, Ada, both of Compton, California.

Gray, Mary
Boulder City News, Thursday, 20 Jan 1983, 2:6-7.
Mary Gray, 69, a resident of Boulder City, died Jan. 14. She was born on Sept. 29, 1913, and was a homemaker. She is survived by her husband, Albert, of Boulder City; sister, Mabel Walters, of Arkansas and brother, Ernest Tagert, of Seattle. Services were conducted Monday, Jan. 17 and were handled by Palm Memorial. Interment was at Boulder City Cemetery.

Greene, Buford S.
Boulder City News, Thursday, 12 Apr 1988, 10:1.
Buford S. Greene, 66, died Tuesday, April 12 in Las Vegas. He had been a resident of the Boulder City area for nine years. He was born in Austin, Texas on Aug. 15, 1921 and was a bioanalyst. He was a veteran of World War II serving in the Navy. Survivors include wife Mary Jane Green, Boulder City; daughter Mary Jane Marx, Burney, Calif.; brothers Malbone W. Greene, San Diego, Calif.; William E. Greene, San Gabriel, Calif,; sisters Minnie Laura Matthews, Pico Rivera, Calif.; Mary Eleanor Davis, San Gabriel, Calif.; ten grandchildren. Visitation was held April 17 at noon. Graveside services were held Monday, April 18 at 11 a.m. with Father Joe Annese of St. Andrew's church officiating. Interment was in the Boulder City Cemetery.

Gresh, Bertha
Boulder City News, Thursday, 11 Dec 1975, 1:2-5.
Beautiful Bertha Gresh Rests in Boulder City Cemetery
By Teddy Fenton
They called her "The Queen Mother of Eldorado Canyon" and it has become a common sight to see her ever-youthful face framed with a cloud of perfectly groomed hair, her tiny 5 foot frame dressed in an immaculate dress, often posed before her prize oleander tree, or among her fruit trees and , even more fitting to her way of life, we would see Bertha at her shrine. "Our Lady of Eldorado Canyon." Bertha lived in a cabin in Eldorado Canyon. Her nearest neighbors were ground squirrels and lizards. Her idea of riches was to have all her barrels filled with rain water. On her frequent trips to Boulder City where she spent weekends with Leonard and Amelia Davis, she always brought her containers and filled them with water. She was never unhappy at the inconveniences, she would say, "No one is going to take me away from my home." At 93 she left for the last time. Services were conducted by Father Hugh Smith at the St. Andrew's Catholic Church on Wyoming St. Probably no one on early was more surrounded by so many friends who truly revered the woman who remained beautiful all her life. The Friendship that Began with a Quest for Bitter Licorice. The first time Amelia Davis ever saw her lifelong friend, Bertha Gresh, they were both shopping at Central Market. Bertha asked for bitter licorice. There was non. Amelia, not to be outdone in the friendship department, approached the tiny woman and engaged her in conversation, found out where she lived, then Amelia and Leonard went to Las Vegas, purchased the bitter licorice and took it to Bertha in Nelson. Found out that she was going to be alone at Christmas time . . . brought her home to what was to be hundreds of visits and attendance to St. Andrews down thru the years. We do not know when Bertha first came to our town to church but St. Andrews was built in 1932 and Bertha came to Nelson in 1918 with her husband, Cyrus, so perhaps she is the member with the longest attendance. She is definitely the unique individual who lived longer in Nelson than any other woman or man. Bertha loved her canyon and the famous cabin was the center of a stream of visitors. If there was a single thread of history to be related about the "Wall Street Mine" which adjoined the Gresh property Bertha told it best. Although Bertha was never to benefit from a rich gold strike on her patented claims, she loved to tell the story of the $4 million dollar

stream of gold from the Bull Frog or from the Techatticup just over the hill from Nelson. Bertha, 93 years young, her kind will not ever seen again, most anyone would say "they threw away the pattern." Murl Emory, in deep admiration said at the gravesite," she had a great journey." Here to settle her effects was her beloved niece, Isabel Smith, from Cedarberg, Wisconsin. As Bertha would have wished, her historical material will be donated to the UNLV "Special Collections." We wish we could put down all the history of this once in a lifetime pioneer, alas, space forbids. Suffice to say, her own words were she would live it all again.

Griesbaum, Teresa Matilda
Boulder City News, Thursday, 7 June 1979, 5:3-4.
A requiem mass was said at St. Andrew's Catholic Church last Monday morning for Teresa Matilda Griesbaum, 69, who died May 31 in Boulder City. She had been a homemaker and a member of St. Andrew's Altar Society. She was born July 17, 1919 in Missouri. Mrs. Griesbaum is survived by her sons, Dan Griesbaum, of Boulder City, Richard Griesbaum of Bridgeview, Illinois, and Robert Griesbaum of Hickory Hills, Illinois; daughters, Luella Jarvill of Quincy, Illinois, Mary Zwiersybki and Sue Garbat, both of Boulder City; and a brother, Frank Fruenner of Peoria, Ill. Interment was at the Boulder City Cemetery.

Griffin, Lamar
Boulder City News, Thursday, 22 Oct 1992, 13:1.
Lamar Griffin was born Oct. 7, 1908 and died after a lengthy illness on Oct. 21, 1992. Lamar was born in York, Neb., and lived in Colorado most of his life. He and his wife, Grace moved to Boulder City several years ago. He is survived by his wife, Grace Griffin; daughter, Rita White; son, Gary Griffin and seven grandchildren. He was a retired pharmacist and an active member of Bethany Baptist Church. Viewing will be held Saturday, Oct. 24 from 9-11 a.m. at Bethany Baptist Church, 210 Wyoming St. in Boulder City. Graveside services will be at 11:30 a.m. at Boulder City Cemetery. The family requests that in lieu of flowers that donations be made to Bethany Baptist Church.

Griffith, Glen G.
Boulder City News, Thursday, 20 Aug 1970, 1:4.
Graveside services were conducted Tuesday at 10 a.m. for Glen G. Griffith, 66, owner of Griff's Barber Shop. He had been an area resident for 34 years and was a native of Independence, Kans. He was born Nov. 17, 1905. Mr. Griffith died last Friday. Elks Lodge 1682, of which the deceased was a charter member, officiated at the burial service and Palm Mortuary was in charge of funeral arrangements. He is survived by his widow, Fern, 667 Avenue D; a daughter, Mrs. John (Mary Lou) Fielding, Henderson; a stepfather, Roy Waite of Boulder City and two granddaughters.

Grimes, Annie Edna
Boulder City News, Thursday, 2 Jul 1964.
Funeral services were held at graveside Tuesday at the local cemetery, for Annie Edna Grimes, 83, who died last Friday at the Boulder City Hospital. Officiating was the Reverend Guy Holliday of the Grace Community Church. Mrs. Grimes was born on Sept. 17, 1880, in Cape Elizabeth, Maine. She had lived in Boulder City for two-and-a-half years with her husband, William O. Grimes. In addition to her husband, she is also survived by three sons, Stanley M. Grimes, Conrad, Iowa; Robert J. Grimes, from Boulder City; and Walter L. Grimes, Winthrop, Wash. She is survived also by ten grandchildren and one great-grandchild.

Grimes, Wiliam Oliver
Boulder City News, Thursday, 3 Oct 1968, 1:8.
Grimes Rite At Graveside
Graveside services at B.C. Cemetery were conducted Sept. 27 at 11 a.m. by the Reverend Neal Myers, pastor of First Southern Baptist Church, for William Oliver Grimes, 80, who passed away Sept. 23 while enroute from Battle Mountain to his home here. Mr. Grimes lived at 664 Eighth St. and had been a Boulderite for seven years. He was born in Arizona Dec. 22, 1887. A widower, he is survived by three sons – Stanley M. of Conrad, Ia; Robert J, Boulder City and Walter L, Winthrop, Wash. Palm Mortuary of Henderson was in charge of arrangements.

Grinstrom, Carol

Boulder City News, Thursday, 13 May 1965, 10:5.
Mrs. Grinstrom Buried Friday
Funeral services were conducted last Friday at 10 a.m. at Palm Mortuary in Henderson for Carol Grinstrom, 53, 638 Ave. M with the Reverend Guy Holliday of Grace Community Church officiating. Mrs. Grinstrom was born July 31, 1901 in San Francisco, Calif. She is survived by her husband, Gustas, Boulder City; mother, Sue Wilson, Los Angeles; a sister, Mrs. Clyde Johnson, Albuquerque, N. M.; a brother, Wilbur Wilson, Los Angeles and one grandson. Burial was in Boulder City Cemetery.

Gurney, Robert J.

Boulder City News, Thursday, 22 Apr 1976, 5:6.
Robert Gurney Services Held
Graveside services were held at the Boulder City cemetery, Tuesday morning, for Robert J. Gurney, 52. Officiating was the Reverend Hugh Smith of St. Andrew's Catholic Church. Mr. Gurney died Wednesday at the Boulder City Hospital, where he had been a frequent patient. He was born Dec. 30, 1923, and lived in this area for several years. He was employed as a janitor by the U.S.B.R. when the agency hired out this type of work. He was also a bartender at Herb's Recreation Tavern for awhile. Survivors are unknown.

Gustad, Sophie

Boulder City News, Thursday, 21 Nov 1957, 5:2.
Sophie Gustad Funeral Held
Funeral services were held on Monday afternoon for Gunda Sophie Gustad, 78, who died at the Boulder City Community Hospital Thursday, after a long illness. The Reverend Earl S. Fox officiation at the rites at Grace Community Church. Mrs. Rudolph Legler, at the Stevenson Memorial organ, played Norwegian compositions which were favorites of Mrs. Gustad. Pall bearers were Robert Welsh, Byron Miller, Lloyd Hudlow, LeRoy Nicholson, Custis Bowser and Roy Gear. Burial was in the Boulder City Cemetery. Mrs. Gustad was born December 1, 1878, in Drammen, Norway. She came to the United States in 1905, and was married in St. Paul, Minnesota, where her husband Ingemar died in 1934.

She moved to Boulder City in 1944, to live with her daughter, Eleanor and son-in-law, Arleigh B. West, 308 Nevada Hiway. While here was active in the Women's Association, until her health became poor. In addition to her daughter, survivors are grandsons, John and Richard West, and a sister, Mrs. Elmine Olson in Norway.

Gutierrez, Samuel E.
Boulder City News, Thursday, 24 Sep 1987, 14:1.
Samuel E. Gutierrez, 76, passed away September 21 in Las Vegas. A resident of Boulder City since 1945, he was born July 22, 1911, in Albuquerque, New Mexico. He worked for 30 years for the U.S. Bureau of Reclamation and retired in 1972. He served in the U.S. Army as a military policeman from 1941 to 1945 and saw action in Normandy, northern France, Germany and central Europe. He was awarded many decorations and citations including European, African and Middle East ribbons, five Bronze Stars and the American Defense Service Medal. He was a member of the Disabled American Veterans. Survivors include his wife Rose, whom he married on Nov. 12, 1940; also eight children, Sally Yeoman, Sam Gutierrez, Jr., John Gutierrez, Marilyn Bourne, Nancy Walser, Rose Marie Tinger, Leah Ulivarri and Linda Gutierrez; also 15 grandchildren and one great grandchild. A rosary was conducted Wednesday evening at St. Andrew's Church. A funeral Mass will be held today at the church at 9 a.m.

Hagen, Mickie
Boulder City News, Thursday, 13 Apr 1995, 14:1-2.
Mickie Hagan, 61, died Tuesday, April 11, 1995 at a local hospital. Born Jan. 5, 1934 in London, Ohio, she was a resident of Las Vegas for two years, after moving from a seven-year residency in Boulder City. She was a retired cottage parents, having worked in child care. She worked at the Southern Nevada Children's Home; was on the board of directors of the Faith Lutheran High School; in 1968 she was named one of the "Outstanding Women of the Year" in Who's Who of America; a member of XI MU Chapter of Beta Signa Phi; a Red Cross volunteer; a Foster Parent for 25 years; and was a lifetime member of London High School Booster Club. She was preceded in death by her daughter, Rosemarie. She is survived by her husband, Delbert Hagen Sr., of Las Vegas; one daughter, Devra Betts, also of Las Vegas; one son, Delbert Hagen II, of

Albuquerque, N.M.; one sister, Martha Boggs, of London, Ohio; four brothers, Melvin Cooper, Ronald Cooper, and Theodore Cooper, all of London, Ohio; and three grandchildren. Services will be held at 1 p.m. Saturday, April 15, 1995 at Christ Lutheran Church in Boulder City. Interment will be at the Boulder City Cemetery. The family suggests that in lieu of flowers, donations be made to Christ Lutheran Church, 1401 5th St., Boulder City, NV 89005 or ; the Faith Lutheran High School, 1251 Robin, Las Vegas, NV 89106. Arrangements were handled by Palm Mortuary of Henderson.

Hall, Douglas
Boulder City News, Thursday, 27 Oct 1966, 1:8.
Hall Rites Today
Military graveside services will be conducted at Boulder City Cemetery at 10:30 this morning for Douglas Hall, 20, who died Monday shortly after having been admitted to B. C. Hospital suffering from a self-inflicted gunshot wound. The deceased, born Aug. 3, 1946, was the son of Mr. and Mrs. Harry C. Hall and the shooting occurred at the family home, 817 Fifth St. Representatives from Lake Mead Naval Base will officiate and arrangements are by Palm Chapel in Henderson. Mr. Hall is survived by his parents, a brother, Harry E. Hall and a sister, Mrs. James (Marilyn) Patton, all of Boulder City.

Halleck, Eulah
Boulder City News, Thursday, 8 Mar 1979, 5:5.
Services were held last Monday for Eulah Halleck, 81, who passed away March 2 in Boulder City. Mrs. Halleck was born March 9, 1897 in Calhoun, Michigan and had been a resident of Boulder City for many years. A sister-in-law, Mary Peters of Boulder City is her only survivor. The services were held at Palm Chapel and interment followed at Boulder City Cemetery.

Halleck, Harold G.
Boulder City News, Thursday, 27 Jul 1972.
Funeral Held Monday For Harold Halleck
Funeral services were held Monday for Harold G. Halleck, 74, at the Palm Chapel in Henderson. The rites were conducted by the BPO Elks Lodge, of which he was a member. Burial followed, in the Boulder City Cemetery. Mr. Halleck died Friday, in the Boulder City Hospital. He was born July 4, 1898 in Ramson, Michigan. He was a retired test board man for the Northwest Bell Telephone Company. Mr. Halleck served in the U. S. Navy in World War 2. He belonged to the Masonic Order. Mr. Halleck is survived by his wife, Eulah, 820 Cheryl Lane, Boulder City; and a sister, Roseland Lacoe, Dimondale, Mich.

Hamdorf, Eugene H.
Boulder City News, Thursday, 25 Dec 1990, 19:1-2.
Eugene H. Hamdorf, 75, a long-time resident of Boulder City died Friday. Born Aug. 14, 1914 in Corley, Iowa, he was a heavy construction supervisor. He was a member of BPOE No. 1682 Boulder City and Ted Lawson Chapter Retirees Club of Operating Engineers No. 12. The family suggests memorials be made in his name to St. Christopher's or St. Jude's Ranch for Children. Survivors include his wife, Mary Alice Hamdorf of Boulder City; a daughter, Sandy Christiansen of Boulder City; two sons, Alan Hamdorf of Banning, Calif., and David Hamdorf of Placentia, Calif.; a sister, Helen Jensen of Hemet, Calif.; two brothers, Marlan Hamdorf of Beaumont, Calif., Frank Hamdorf of Hemet, Calif.; and four grandchildren. Services were held. Palm Mortuary handled arrangements.

Hamilton, Dorothy Ellen May
Boulder City News, Thursday, 30 Oct 1975, 8:2-3.
Dorothy Hamilton Services, by Esther Shipp
Funeral services were held yesterday afternoon for Dorothy E. M. C. Hamilton, 59, at the Palm Chapel in Henderson. The rites were conducted by the Reverend Guy Holliday of Grace Community Church. Burial was in the Boulder City Cemetery. Dorothy died Sunday in the St. Rose de Lima Hospital in Henderson, after a long illness. In lieu of flowers, the family requested that contributions be made to the radiology laboratory at that hospital. Dorothy Ellen May Moore was born Oct. 6, 1916 in

Ellsworth, Iowa, and was graduated from high school there. She attended the Iowa State Teacher's College. Later, she moved to California and attended the Pasadena City College. She was employed in a real estate office in El Monte. Dot came to Boulder City, and was employed by the City of Los Angeles Department of Water and Power from Oct. 6, 1947 until January, 1953. January 8, 1953, she started working for the U. S. Bureau of Mines as a clerk-stenographer. She was secretary to the Chief for several years before her retirement on disability June 29, 1973. Dorothy Colhopp and Lloyd Hamilton were married Aug. 30, 1960 by J. P. Chet Tyree. She belonged to the Boulder City Bowling Association, and was a life member (and past state officer) of the Nevada Women's Bowling Association. Dot is survived by her husband, Lloyd, 701 Elm St., Boulder City; and her daughter DeeAnn Van Hatten, Las Vegas.

Hammer, Marguerite Louise "Betty"
Boulder City News, Thursday, 4 Oct 1984, 6:1-3.
By Esther Shipp
Funeral services were held Tuesday afternoon for Marguerite Louise "Betty" Hammer, 67. The Reverend Steve Neesley officiated at the First Southern Baptist Church, of which Betty was a member. She died September 30, at Sunrise Hospital, after a long fight with cancer. Pallbearers were Claude Smith, Ernie Eskam, Carl Cowan, John Stednick, Bob and Jim Jones. The organist was Cobie Seymore, Glenda Neesley, wife of the pastor, sang "Overshadowed." The hymn "I am living in Canaan's Land" was sung by Claude and Juanita Smith. Julie and Stephen Barrick and Keith Barrick. Keith also concluded the services with "The Lord's Prayer," as a solo. Betty was born November 23, 1917 in Wellington, Texas. She studied music for 12 years, and played the piano for glee clubs at school and for her churches. The family moved to Boulder City in 1965 from New Mexico. There was a vase of 18 red roses on the piano, representing the 18 years she played piano at the First Baptist Church. As the pastor said in the eulogy, "Make a joyful noise unto the Lord" expressed Betty's feelings about music and her life. Betty was a member of Cactus Rebekah Lodge No. 40, IOOF, and sometimes served as the musician. Betty is survived by her husband, Glenn, of Boulder City; son Bill of Las Vegas, son Kenneth of Scottsdale, Ariz; three grandchildren; two brothers, Dallas Keller of New Mexico, Charles Keller of California; and two sisters, Helen Williams, of California, and

Mildred Card of Idaho.

Hammer, William Glenn
Boulder City News, Thursday, 24 Jan 1991, 6:1-2.
William Glenn Hammer, 71, a 26-year-resident died Monday, Jan. 21 in Boulder City. Born Oct. 11, 1919 in Rocky Ford, Colo., he was a Naval World War II veteran. He is survived by two sons, Bill C. Hammer of Las Vegas and Kenneth W. Hammer of Scottsdale, Ariz.; a brother, Donald Hammer of Albuquerque, N.M. and a sister, Laura May Allen of Solano, N.M. Services are scheduled at 2 p.m., Saturday, Jan. 26 at the First Baptist Church in Boulder City. Interment will be in the Boulder City Cemetery. Arrangements were made by Palm Mortuary.

Hannig, Juilus L.
Boulder City News, Thursday, 18 Jan 1990, 26:5-6.
Julius L. Hannig, 81, a long-time resident of Boulder City died Monday. Born December 20, 1908 in Washington, Utah, he was a produce manager. He was a member of First Ward LDS Church, Boulder City. Survivors include his wife, Lavera Hannig of Boulder City; five daughters, Doris Purcell of San Jose, Calif.; Florence Reynolds of Phoenix, Ariz; Sharline Voss and Joan Mueller of Reno, Sandra Newman of Boulder City; a son, Heber J. Tobler of Boulder City; three brothers, Smith Hannig of Henderson, Max Hannig of Pioche, Ross Hannig of Las Vegas; 22 grandchildren and 24 great grandchildren. Viewing will be from 10 a.m. through 11 a.m. today at Boulder City Lds Relief society room. Services will be at 11 a.m. today at Boulder City LDS Chapel. Palm Mortuary will handle arrangements.

Harbin, Woody W.
Boulder City News, Thursday, 30 Mar 1995, 8:1-2.
Woody W. Harbin, 80, of Boulder City died March 24, 1995, in a local hospital. Harbin was born Nov. 11, 1914, in Grandview, Texas and had been a member of the Bethany Baptist Church. The family request donations be made to the Boulder City Hospital, Long Term Care. He is survived by his wife, Ethelleen Harbin of Boulder City; two daughters, Dorothy Molin of Boulder City and Jeanette Rowe of Naperville, Ill.; and three grandchildren. Services were held Tuesday. Arrangements were

handled by Palm Mortuary-Henderson.

Hardcastle, John Anthony
Boulder City News, Thursday, 11 July 1953, 3:1.
Hardcastle Funeral rites Held Tuesday
Funeral services were held Tuesday morning for John Anthony Hardcastle, 55, of St. Christopher's Episcopal Church. Father Joseph Hogben conducted the requium eucharist and the burial office which followed. Interment was in the Boulder City cemetery. Pallbearers were Bruce Bulloch, Kay Morley, Marcel Pace, George Petroff, Tom Porter and Gordon Jones. Mr. Hardcastle has been in poor health for several months. He entered the local hospital, Wednesday morning, and died Saturday afternoon of a complicated illness. Mr. Hardcastle was born July 21, 1908, in Harrowgate, England, and later moved to Canada. The Hardcastle family came to Boulder City from Toronto, six years ago, under the sponsorship of Mrs. Hardcastle's brother, Stanley Gaffin. The Hardcastles helped Mr. Gaffin to mange the Brown Derby Motel, on their arrival. His current employment was driving a checker taxi in Las Vegas. Survivors are his widow, Lena, and daughters Louise and Maureen, all of 524 Seventh Street; a brother George of Vancouver, British Columbia; sisters Ann Harris and Helen Stypick of Niagara Falls, N. Y.; Minnie Rennie of Brantsford, Ontario; and Sheila Hardcastle of Scarborough, Ontario.

Harding, Mary H.
Boulder City News, Thursday, 18 Aug 1994, 6:4.
Mary H. Harding, 76, a 21 year resident of Boulder City, died Aug. 16, 1994 in a local hospital. Born June 30, 1918 in Brookville, Penn., she was a retired oil refining executive secretary. She was married to her husband Charles for 60 years. She was a member of the Boulder City Community Club and American Legion Auxiliary of Boulder City. She is survived by her husband Charles Harding of Boulder City and a sister, Louise Overbeck of Finger Lakes, N.Y. In lieu of flowers the family requests donations be made to the American Cancer Society. Services will be held at 10 a.m. today, at the Palm Chapel in Henderson. Arrangements were handled by Palm Mortuary of Henderson.

Hardy, Legrande "Blackie"
Boulder City News, Thursday, 19 Feb 1976, 12:5-8.
Legrande "Blackie" Hardy Services
Funeral services were held Monday afternoon for LeGrande Laird "Blackie" Hardy, 75, who died at his home last Friday of natural causes. Officiating was Bishop Kenneth Simkins of the Boulder City First Ward of the Church of Jesus Christ of Later-day-Saints. Others taking part in the program were Stake president, Leonard Stubbs; Dale Imlay who gave the eulogy; Second Ward Bishop Jake Williams, and Alton Burt. Burial was in the Boulder City Cemetery. Pallbearers, all members of the family, were Edward "Ted" Pike, Idaho Falls, Idaho; Dr. Thomas Hardy, Reno; Dr. William Pike, Radny Pike, Douglas Pike, and Bill Hardy, all of Las Vegas. Osborne Traasdahl dedicated the grave. Graveside rites were conducted by members of Boulder City Elks Lodge 1682, of which Blackie was a charter, lifetime member. It was at one of the early Helldorados that he won the nickname "Blackie" because his was the blackest beard in whiskers contest! LeGrande was born June 20, 1900 in Salt Lake City, Utah, the son of Mary and William B. Hardy. His father died in 1914, and his mother in 1961. He came to Nevada from Salt Lake City. He and Ruth were married Jan. 14, 1935 in Las Vegas. They had one son, Larry, who was graduated from Boulder City High School in 1959, and from Brigham Young University in 1962. Blackie was one of the original guides at Hoover Dam, beginning in 1936, and was one of the popular because of his sense of humor. Somehow, this led to his appearing on the television show of Groucho Marx. He worked with every other guide in the 34 years until his retirement in 1970, and there were 79 people at his retirement party! Some of the former fellow-workers attending still in the Las Vegas area, were Clarence Bruce, Jerry Seible, Wayne Kelley, Art Olson and Mark Swain. Blackie like sports, playing cards, and was a "Late bloomer" artist of oil paintings! Before his eyesight grew poor, he was a champion pool player! He is survived by his wife, Ruth, 639 Ave. F; a son Larry, Reno; grandson Derek Hardy, Reno; brothers Dr. Stanley Hardy, Las Vegas; and Joseph Sulser, San Mateo, Calif.; two sisters, Sophia Roberts, Richmond, Va.; and Genevieve Dangerfield, Salt Lake City.

Hardy, Ruth
Boulder City News, Thursday, 2 Apr 1981, 3:1-3.
Ruth Hardy was one of the Shining Spirits
Ruth Hardy will be missed by her neighbors on "F" St. for she was such a gentle smiling friend that it was a joy just to say hello to her. Several years ago the NEWS did a Sr. Citizen story about her which will be used as a base to do another "goodbye" story for her next week. This is press time and the tribute her neighbors, friends and family would want us to do would be too hard to get her story "right" for she was a generous and loving wife, friend, neighbor, sister and above all, she loved her only son and her grandchild to the point of her great heart bursting. Derrick, her grandchild, would come for Christmas to help Grandma decorate the tree. Ruth would tell stories about her grandchild for hours! Larry, her son, was raised at 639 Ave. F from the day of his birth. His year by hear birthdays were recorded by his mother in photographs. There are no end to the sick beds (from every faith) that Ruth Hardy visited. She seemed to make a friend feel better just coming in the door. No greater love has ever been expressed by one woman. Her story next week will bring pleasure to her memory and to her family. Her faith was so strong that she would want all of you to believe that she is in the best of all worlds. LeGrande and Ruth Hardy ... you will not be forgotten. Bless you both.

Harnedy, Lulu May
Boulder City News, Thursday, 10 Dec 1953, 3:6-7.
Death Takes Mrs. Tim Harnedy At Southern California Hospital
Funeral services were held Saturday afternoon for Lulu May Harnedy, 73, who died suddenly Wednesday at Loma Linda Hospital in California, where she had been undergoing treatments for ten days. The rites were conducted by the Reverend Earl Fox at Grace Community Church. Mrs. Harnedy was buried beside her husband, in the Boulder City Cemetery. The death came as a shock to the many friends "Lu" made I the three years she lived here. Lulu May Harnedy, 73, died yesterday morning in the Loma Linda Hospital in California, where she had been undergoing treatments for the past 10 days. The death came as a shock to the many friends which "Lu" has made in the three years she has lived in Boulder City. Mrs. Harnedy resided at 627 Avenue G. Making their home with her, since the passing of her husband, Tim Harnedy, in July 1952, have been her sister Elsie Bates of Excelsor Springs, Missouri, and their

brother, Leo F. Eddy of Yakima, Washington. Mrs. Harnedy was born December 17, 1881 in Franklin County, Kansas. She moved west with her husband many years ago, and the couple were pioneer residents of Indian Springs, Nevada, building the first service station there. They came to Boulder City to retire. She has been active in the Women's Association of Grace Community Church, and was chairman of the Martha Circle this year. Survivors include a daughter, Virginia Dane of North Las Vegas, three grandchildren, Maurine Leland and Tim Dane; Mr. Eddy, her brother; Mrs. Bates, her sister; and another sister, Rose Newson of Aroyo Grande, California. Funeral arrangements are pending. It is expected that Mrs. Harnedy will be buried beside her husband, in the Boulder Cemetery. At the request of the family, friends were requested to contribute to the American Cancer Society instead of sending flowers for the funeral.

Harris, Muran W.
Boulder City News, Thursday, 1 July 1982, 11:5-6.
Murran W. Harris, 65, of Boulder City, died Monday in Las Vegas. Mr. Harris was born March 14, 1917, in Iowa. He was a counselor and a World War II Navy veteran. He is survived by his wife, Gail of Boulder City; son, Bill of Minnesota; sister, Nancy Willette of Boulder City, and three grandchildren. The graveside service will be at 10 a.m. Wednesday in Boulder City Cemetery.

Harvey, Margaret Splawn
Boulder City News, Thursday, 23 Jan 1992, 9:1.
Margaret B. Splawn Harvey died Thursday, Jan. 16, 1992 in a local hospital. She was 81. She was born June 5, 1910 in Banks, Arkansas, and was a member of the Central Christian Church. She had resided in Clark County for 43 years and has been a 16-year resident of Boulder City. She worked in Idabel National Bank in Idabel, Oklahoma, for 18 years. Survivors include her husband Lewis of Boulder City; a son, James of Las Vegas. Services were conducted Tuesday at Palm Mortuary in Henderson with burial following in Boulder City cemetery. The family requests that donations may be made to the Lydia Circle of Central Christian Church.

Haser, Frances
Boulder City News, Thursday, 9 Oct 1958, 5:4.
Graveside funeral services were held Saturday at the Boulder City Cemetery for Frances Haser, 72, who died Thursday at the Boulder City Hospital. The rites were conducted by the Reverend Thomas Daly of St. Paul's Independent Lutheran Church of Las Vegas. Mrs. Haser was born April 24, 1886 in Austria, Hungary. She and her husband moved to Boulder City from Ohio in the spring of this year and lived at 635 Avenue G. She had been a semi-invalid for a long period and was cared for by her late husband Vincent, who died suddenly two months ago. She is survived by a daughter Teresa Helene Cook of 636 Ave. H; son John Harry and Steven Skerce of Chicago, Illinois, and George Skerce of Pasadena, Cal.; 3 stepsons, Frank Haser of Cal.; Rudolph and Vincent Jr. of Ohio; stepdaughter Katherine Sedwick of California and seven grandchildren.

Hatcher, Ella Pearl
Boulder City News, Thursday, 3 Nov 1988, 30:2.
Ella Pearl Hatcher, 87, died Friday, Oct. 28 in Henderson and was a resident since 1973. She was born in Bluefield, Va., Nov. 16, 1900 and was a homemaker. She is survived by daughters Frances Roberts of Las Vegas, Faye E. Fisher of Williamsburg, Va. and three grandchildren. Viewing and visitation were held from noon to 5 p.m. on Nov. 1 Private services and interment were held at Palm Mortuary of Henderson.

Hatfield, Alfred W.
Boulder City News, Thursday, 30 May 1968, 1:8.
Services were conducted at Calvary Foursquare Gospel Church at 2 p.m. Wednesday for Alfred W. Hatfield, 92, of 202 Donna Way who passed away Monday in B.C. Hospital. Mr. Hatfield was born Sept. 18, 1875 in Missouri and had lived in Boulder City for 27 years. He worked at Hoover Dam and Luke Whalen was his supervisor. He and his wife Susie were married Jan. 10, 1910 in DuPew, Okla. and celebrated their 50th wedding anniversary in 1960. The Reverend Gene Holmar conducted the service and Bunker Brothers were in charge of funeral arrangements. Besides his widow he is survived by a son, Richard J., Boulder City; three daughters, Nora Ritter, Guthrie, Okla., Carmen Ritter, this city, and Ruby Brasuell, Sunnyside, Wash.; 24 grandchildren and 23 great grandchildren.

Hatfield, Susie
Boulder City News, Thursday, 8 Jan 1970.
Funeral services were conducted last Saturday at 2 p.m. at Calvary Foursquare Church by the Reverend Gene Holman for Susie M. Hatfield, 76, 202 Donner Way who died Dec. 30 at home. She was born Dec. 24 1893 in Missouri and just before her late husband's death the couple celebrated their 50th wedding anniversary. Mrs. Hatfield is survived by a son, Richard of this city; three daughters, Nora Ritter, Godfrey, Okla., Carmen Ritter, this city and Ruby Brassel, Seattle, Wash.; two sisters, Mrs. Laura Gore, Las Vegas and Mrs. Beulah Mooney, this city and two brothers, James and Walter Nicks, also of Boulder City. Palm Mortuary was in charge of funeral arrangements and interment was in B. C. Cemetery.

Hawkins, Nellie Emma
Boulder City News, Thursday, 16 Jun 1988, 10:3.
Nellie Emma Hawkins, 59, of Boulder City, died Monday in Boulder City. She was born Aug. 28, 1928 in Mutual, Okla. A two-year resident, she was a seamstress. She is survived by one son, Glen Hawkins of Burbank, Calif; two sisters, Belle Roberts and Eula Wettengel, both of Ventura, Calif.; two brothers, Louis Wettengel of San Diego, Calif. and Lester Wettengel of Gloverdale, Calif.; two grandchildren. Graveside services will be held at 10 a.m. Thursday, June 16 in Boulder City Cemetery. Palm Mortuary of Henderson is handling the arrangements.

Hayes, Donald H.
Boulder City News, Thursday, 9 Oct 1975, 2:5-6.
Funeral services will be 10 a.m. Thursday at Masonic Hall in Boulder City for Donald H. Hayes, 50, 2783 S. Torrey Pines, Las Vegas, who died Monday here. Mr. Hayes, born in Long Beach, Calif., July 3, 1925, he had lived in Boulder City and this area for the past 23 years. He was an assistant dispatcher for Nevada Power Co. He is survived by his widow, Frances Hayes of Las Vegas; two sons, Phillip Hayes of Las Vegas; William Hayes of Orangevale, Calif.; a daughter Nancy Hayes of Las Vegas, and a sister, Mary Newquist of California. Burial will be at Boulder City Cemetery. Palm Mortuary is handling arrangements.

Heller, James I.
Boulder City News, Thursday, 29 Oct 1992, 10:2.
James I. Heller, 83, a 15 year Boulder City resident, died Saturday, Oct. 24 in a local hospital. Born Oct. 27, 1908 in Bigelow Township, Minn., he was a retired agent for the federal government. He was a past president of the National Association of Retired Federal Employees, Boulder City Chapter. He is survived by his wife, Luella Heller and a daughter, Dolores Sorensen, both of Boulder City; a sister, Doris Heil of Pebble Beach, Calif. Services were held. Palm Mortuary handled arrangements.

Heller, Luella E.
Boulder City News, Thursday, 14 Dec 1995, 10:1-2.
Luella E. Heller, 86, died Sunday, Dec. 10, 1995, in a local hospital. A Boulder City resident since 1977, the homemaker was born Dec. 9, 1909 in Sleepy Eye, Minn. Survivors are her daughter, Dolores Sorensen of Boulder City; and two brothers, Morris Sheppard of Madison Lake, Minn., and Finely Sheppard of Youngstown, Fla.; seven grandchildren and eight great grandchildren. Services will be held at 11 a.m. Friday, Dec. 15, at the Palm Mortuary-Henderson Chapel. Interment will be private. Palm Mortuary-Henderson handled the arrangements.

Helms, Gaylord Sumner
Boulder City News, Thursday, 3 Feb 1994, 11:3-4.
Gaylord Sumner Helms, 89, died Jan. 24, 1994 in Boulder City. Born March 28, 1904 in Ithica, Mich., he was a resident of Boulder City for 31 years. He had worked as a Utility Clerk for 48 years for the Department of Water and Power of Los Angeles, Calif., and in Boulder City. He is survived by his wife, Murl D. Helms of Boulder City; one son, John G. Helms, of Palo Verdes Estates, Calif.; one daughter, Mary M. Hill of Boulder City; three grandchildren and one great grandchild. Services were held Jan. 27. Arrangements were handled by Nevada Funeral Service, a division of Nevada Cremation and Burial Society, of Las Vegas.

Henderson, Clyde Jr.
Boulder City News, Thursday, 21 Aug 1986, 35:1.
Clyde Henderson, Jr., 72, of Boulder City, died Wednesday in Las Vegas. He was born April 17, 1914, in Moberly, Mo. A 14-year resident, he was a plant operator and Army veteran. He is survived by his wife, Emily of Boulder City; son, Nicholas; daughter, Nancy, both of Los Angeles; sister, Mary Riley of Redlands, Calif.; one grandchild. A graveside service will be at 10 a.m. Saturday in Boulder City Cemetery. Palm Mortuary, Henderson, is handling the arrangements.

Henderson, William A.
Boulder City News, Thursday, 2 Apr 1981, p.12.
William A. Henderson, 57, died March 27 in Boulder City. A recent newcomer to the city, he was born December 14, 1923 in Chicago, Ill. He was recently retired as a pilot with TWA and had also served with the U. S. Air Force as a pilot. Mr. Henderson is survived by his sister, Agnes Ward Randolph of Boulder City; two nieces, Vinita Super of Phoenix, Arizona, and Cathleen Ward of Chicago; and two nephews, William Ward and Louis Beuschlein, both of Chicago. Private cremation services were held with internment at Boulder City Cemetery.

Hendricks, Dona E.
Boulder City News, Thursday, 21 June 1984, p.33:1-2.
Dona E. Hendricks passes away June 18 in Las Vegas. She was born March 29, 1916 in Albany, Minnesota. She had lived in the Boulder City area for the past five years, and was a member of the Boulder City Does, VFW Auxiliary and St. Andrews Catholic Church. She is survived by her husband, John W. of Boulder City; sons Ronald J. Scherer, Las Vegas, Dallan J. Scherer, also of Las Vegas; daughter, Carolyn Nohner, Watkins, Mn.; Rosemary Gardner, Canoga Park, Ca., Arleen Bohte, Canoga Park, Ca.; brother Jerry Bohte, N. C.; 11 grandchildren and five great grandchildren. Funeral services will be held tonight at 7 p.m. at Palm Chapel in Henderson. Officiant will be Father Joe Anese of St. Andrew's Catholic Church. Interment will be in the Boulder City cemetery.

Hendrickson, Matilda Priscilla

Boulder City News, Thursday, 27 Apr 1967, p.5:5.
Hendrickson Rites April 18
Matilda Priscilla Hendrickson, 78 died Apr. 15 in Whittier, Calif., while on a visit to her daughter. She was buried April 18 in the Boulder City Cemetery, beside her husband. Graveside services were read by Robert Broadbent. Mrs. Hendrickson moved here eight years ago and lived at 600 Avenue C with her sister, Chloe Reed. She was born Nov. 24, 1888, in Salt Lake City, Utah, but lived most of her life in California. A homebody, Mrs. Hendrickson belonged to no organizations, preferring to stay home and cook and sew for her once large family. She was still making baby clothes for great-grandchildren, the week before her death. Four children preceded her in death. She is survived by two daughters, Florence (Mrs. Lloyd) Hudlow, 312 Nevada Highway; and Alice Baker, Pico Rivera, Calif.; six grandchildren, nine great-grandchildren; her sister, Chloe, 600 Avenue C; two brothers William and Joseph Reed, Salt Lake City, Utah.

Hengler, William A.

Boulder City News, Thursday, 12 Feb 1980, 11:1-4.
A Requiem mass was said yesterday morning at St. Andrew's Catholic Church for William A. Hengler, 61, who died February 16 in Las Vegas. The Reverend Joseph Anese of St. Andrew's Catholic Church officiated. A retired truck driver, Mr. Hengler was born in Wheeling, West Virginia on April 20, 1918. He was a member of the Boulder City Knights of Columbus and Teamsters Local 420 in Los Angeles. He is survived by his wife, Anna Hengler of Boulder City; son, William Hengler, Jr. of Huntington Beach, Calif.; daughters, Mary Ridenour of Bolder City and Suzanne Harter of Davenport, Iowa; brothers, Edwin Hengler of Seal Beach, Calif., and Charles Hengler of Cleveland, Ohio; sister, Irene Harwat of Monterey Park, Calif.; and four grandchildren. Burial was at Boulder City Cemetery.

Heywood, Anne C.
Boulder City News, Thursday, 16 Sep 1976, p.5:1-2.
Anne C. Heywood Passes Away
Funeral services for Anne Catherine Heywood who passed away Thursday, September 9, in the Boulder City Hospital, were held at 10 a.m. Monday September 13, at Palm Chapel in Henderson, Nevada, with Robert Broadbent officiating. Mrs. Heywood was a resident of the area since 1932, residing at 1349 Denver Street in Boulder City. A daughter of Gottfried and Lydia Loose, Anne was born in Kraft, Russia on July 22, 1906. The Loose family which included daughter Lydia, Anne and Catherine, and son, David, migrated to the United States in 1913. The family settled in Bruch, Colorado, a small farming community east of Denver. Coming to Boulder City in the early nineteen thirties, she maintained a home and supported her two sons, Murvyn and George by working as a sales clerk and as a beautician. Her oldest son, Murvyn, was killed in action during the "Battle of the Bulge," near the Rhine River in March 1945. After her marriage to Jack Heywood in September 1945, she turned her attention to homemaking. Among her many talents was the ability to covert a modest home to a thing of beauty. She took great pleasure in growing and arrangements of plants and collecting inexpensive jewelry and creating beautiful ornaments. She was proud of her grandchildren, Doug, in radio announcing at KUOY FM, Yuma, Ariz. Gregg, Art Director for TV Channel 12 in Phoenix; Jeff and Janie, in high school; John and Wendy in elementary school. Her family was able to visit her during the period of her illness. Mrs. Heywood was active in the community. Her memberships included the Boulder City women's Club where she was Committee Chairman for many events; the Boulder City Women's Golf Association; Boulder City Bridgers, the Hospital Auxiliary; the American Legion Auxiliary, and the Gold Star Mothers. Mrs. Heywood is survived by her husband John Heywood of Boulder City; a son, George Brannan of Buckeye, Arizona; two sisters, Lyudia Foos of Brush, Colorado; Catherine Crincic of Denver, Colorado; one brother Dave Loose of Las Vegas; and six grandchildren. Pallbearers were Doug, Gregg and Jeff Brannan, Joe Brincic, Neil and Gardiner Heywood. Graveside services were conducted by the American Legion Auxiliary. Interment was at Boulder City Cemetery. Palm Mortuary handled the arrangements.

Heywood, Grace Sharp
Boulder City News, Thursday, 18 Mar 1982, 37:3-4.
Grace Sharp Heywood Remembered as an Indomitable Spirit
A special Tribute will be written about Grace Sharp Heywood in the NEWS next week. By the time the NEWS gathered the early day reminiscences of her friends of nearly 50 years, Perle Garrett in particular, it was late Tuesday and too late to gather it into the kind of story she deserved. Her sons carried her beautiful coffin to its final resting place at the B. C. Cemetery. The services were beautifully handled by Father Don Stivers of the Episcopal Church. A lesson was read by Reverend Margery Holman of Christian Center Church. Grace will be remembered for many reasons for she kept her old friends and added to that list over the years. She played the organ for her beloved church for over 30 years. Her hands were strong and sure and she played for the Feb. 14, 1982 church party at Collie's restaurant. Reverend Don Stiver said she will be missed at all occasions for she never siad "no" when asked to supply the music. Before her death she had donated $200.00 to the B.C. Museum and Historical Assoc. Memorial Fund. Her name and Everett Sharp, also Jack and Ann Heywood will be placed on the Memorial Plaque. Grace donated two cardboard boxes of early 1900 sheet music to the UNLV "Special Collection" room. She was a special and generous volunteer in every way.

Heywood, John L.
Boulder City News, Thursday, 22 Nov 1979, 6:3.
Graveside services were held last Tuesday at Boulder City Cemetery for John L. Heywood, 75, a former Boulder City resident who passed away November 15 in Phoenix, Arizona. Mr. Heywood was born June 8, 1904 in Panguitch, Utah. He was one of the original workers for the Six Companies and he was a veteran of World War II serving with the United States Air Force. Mr. Heywood is survived by his wife, Grace Heywood; brothers, Gardiner Heywood of Hurricane, Utah, Reid Heywood of Salt Lake City, Neil Heywood of Las Vegas and Joseph Boyd of St. George, Utah; sisters, Maude Sandall of Portland, Oregon and Edna Knight of St. George.

Hill, Fred

Boulder City News, Thursday, 18 Aug 1983, 23:1-8.

Fred Hill, a member of the Boulder City community for 50 years was buried in the Boulder City Cemetery Tuesday. His services were conducted by Bishop Carl Snow. The beautiful eulogy was spoken by a friend of 49 years, Tommy Nelson. The family and friends who revered this fine man, husband, father and friend, were proud beyond words when the love and caring in the following eulogy rang over the beautiful church. No one on earth can speak more sincerely than Tommy Nelson. We of this community extend our sympathy to Fred's widow, Ruby Hill, and to his son, Dr. Fred Hill, Jr and to his grandchildren, for their were six, all residents of Tucson, Ariz. Every single one of them have made their grandparents and parents mighty proud. Family members of the immediate family were also here to say goodbye to a man who had reached the wise age of 80 years. By Tommy Nelson . . . we were lifelong friends. It is indeed an honor for me to pay tribute to a long time friend. Alfred V. Hill was born in Amasa, Michigan, July 8, 1903. His parents immigrated from Vora, Finland which was a Swedish speaking part of Finland. Fred was raised in Bingham Canyon, Utah, where his father worked as a miner. Bingham is now part of the vast Kennecot Copper Pit and no longer exists. Fred and Ruby Rasmussen were married in Oakland, Cal. Fred was employed there as a machinist for the street car transit co. There he remained during 1930-31. In July of 1934 Fred and Ruby came to Boulder City. Fred went to work for Six Co's Inc. This was the famous contractors who build Hoover (Boulder) Dam. Upon the completion of the dam Fred transferred to the U.S.B.R. along with many other men who were employed by Six Co's Inc. Fred was one of first machinists haired by the government. Upon his retirement he had 35 years of Civil Service at the Dam. The secret of his success was that he was energetic, ambitious, and a master craftsman who took pride in his work. Any job he was assigned to was done in a professional manner. There was no half way methods with Fred. It had to be done just so. He was one to give an honest day's work for a day's pay. I well recall Fred being assigned to an intricate sheet metal duct project. It was a challenge but Fred met it and did it well. There after Fred was proud to be assigned sheet metal work and as usual did it so well that whenever sheet metal work was to be done, Fred was their man. Fred got on well with all his fellow workers. He was a member of the International Association of Machinists and belong to N.A.E.F.E. My wife Grayce and I and Fred and Ruby met in the year of 1934 when we lived in a triplex apartment bldg. at 661 Ave. "M". We shared with them the same bathroom, laundry facilities, clothes line, etc. When young Fred was born Grayce and I were part of the action with Grayce pacing the floor. Ruby gave birth to the baby in Las Vegas. A fine son, Dr. Frederick James Hill. He has given his parents much love, pride, joy and happiness, with six wonderful, fine looking children and a lovely daughter-in-law. They were many adventures ahead for our two families. Little could we know or guess what the daming of the Colorado would accomplish. Unquote from a touching eulogy, May Fred Hill find the joy in his journey that he gave to friends and family in this one.

Hill, Gerri M.
Boulder City News, Thursday, 11 Aug 1983, 27:1-4.
Memorial fund established in memory of Gerri Hill
As a consoling release of the recent tragic death of our granddaughter, Gerri M. Hill, daughter of George and Nancy (Farris) Hill of late Cave Junction, Oregon, and great granddaughter of Florence and George Deem, (famed peanut-ling) of Early Reading, Penn. Marian and I are happy on being able to set up this Memorial Fund of $200.00 to our Boulder City, Nevada library. Gerri, this small token to you could have and should have been for that college or career you often spoke to us about but "The Book" says, "Thy will be done." As an addendum, to our grief, our good neighbor, Mr. and Mrs. Clifford Brignall elected to be the first donors to the fund with $50.00. Gratuitously, allow me to quote an old Chinese philosophy to each and all. "Often times the beauty and fragrance of the dowers remains in the hands that gave them." Til we meet again, Gerri. Marian and Mahlon Hill

Hilton, Claude E.
Boulder City News, Thursday, 12 May 1987, 10:1-3.
Services Held For Claude Hilton by Teddy Fenton
The gentle spirit of our neighbor, Claude Hilton rests and he is at peace. He died last Sunday after an illness that left him unable to pursue the hobbies he loved so well. He loved his family and included his children, Edna Hilton Martenson and his son Ralph, in all pursuits enjoyed by the group. He married Emily Mae Baker in Endiott in 1914. The twin tragedies brought him closer to his daughter, Edna if this is possible. For

Edna said losing him is so hard to bear for they were closer than words can describe. He was her pal, her friend and she turned to him for everything. Edna was widowed when her son Thern Martenson was in college. Then will be a rock to lean on during this dreadful loss. He was close to his grandfather who in turn was proud of him. Claude Hilton was born on Aug. 2, 1894. Until he came to Boulder City his entire lifetime was spent in Endicott, New York. For 47 years he worked for Endicott Johnson, a company that manufactures shoes. It employed 25,000 people throughout its plants. Clause was in charge of the elevators. He traveled from plant to plant to supervise the people who in turn were in charge of the elevators. The company tanned its own leather and purchased the hides from South America. As a neighbor it is important to share the way it was to observe Clause for all the years he and Emily lived on Wyoming St. Even though he had a car he would walk down my alley to go visit his best friend, Edna, a daughter who returned the esteem. In his hands might be a plumbers "snake" and he would stop to chat with the news of the day. His conversation would be about animals. How he loved all critters including on ei n particular. Her name was "Honey" a doggie with only three legs. She died and she is buried in the Eldorado Valley pet cemetery (now forbidden to people wanting to place pets there). There was such a child-like wonder about the way Claude decorated Honey's grave. Toys made of rubber, little animals and toys that Honey would have played with as a puppy. The grave is surrounded by a little white picket fence. In his latter years Claude was active in his garden, having a lawn that was the best on the street. In was hard to bear when he could no longer keep it that way. He had a beautiful hedge all around his property. But as he grew towards the last years he had a block wall constructed. He was a veteran, WWI. A member of the Aviation Signal Corps. He watched the first airplane fly, saw all the wonders of a changing world from horse drawn carriages to cars of every price and description. Edna has beloved daughter, was a Field Representative in the Social Security Office in Las Vegas. It was to be near her that he moved to Boulder City. Behind them, Claude and Emily left a beautiful home in Endicott that Claude had built after his war service ended. The American Legion conducted the graveside services. Reverend Ron Mayers officiated. He is buried beside Emily in the Boulder City Cemetery. The family of Claude Hilton have asked friends and neighbors to make donations to the BC Hospital. Send checks or donations to the hospital on Adams Blvd., in Boulder City. Claude was taken there during his final illness. He told his daughter no hospital could equal our hometown facility for its loving kindness and wonderful care.

Hilton, Ralph D.
Boulder City News, Thursday, 7 Oct 1976, 10:6.
Ralph D. Hilton who resided at 1101 Wyoming Street, passed away October 3rd in the Boulder City Hospital. Mr. Hilton was born June 19, 1919, at Union, New York, and had lived in the Boulder City area sixteen years. He was Deputy Veteran Affairs Commissioner with the State of Nevada. Mr. Hilton was a Veteran of WWII Navy. His parents are Mr. and Mrs. Claude E. Hilton of Boulder City. He was a member of the Las Vegas Kiwanis Club, Disabled American Veterans, the VFW, the American Legion Post #8 and the Veterans of Foreign Wars. He is survived by his parents, Mr. and Mrs. Claude E. Hilton, his sister, Mrs. Edna Martenson of 1217 New Mexico Street, and a nephew, Thern Maretenson also of Boulder City. Graveside services were held Wednesday, October 6, 1976, at 10 a.m. at the Boulder City Cemetery. The Reverend Mike Friedman of the North Las Vegas First Baptist Church, together with the American Legion Post #8 and other Veteran groups, officiated.

Hind, Edward W.
Boulder City News, Thursday, 4 Jul 1991, 7:3.
Edward W. Hinds, 75, died Thursday, June 27, in Kingman, Ariz. He was born June 17, 1916, in Los Angeles, Calif. and had been a resident of the area for 16 years. He is survived by his wife, Julie of Boulder City; four daughters, Kathleen Miller of Laguna Beach, Calif., Sharon Criswold of Pinold, Calif., Doreen Savage of Vacaville, Calif., and Gloria Savage of Fallbrook, Calif.; one sister, Edith Bell of San Marcus, Calif,; 11 grandchildren and 2 great grandchildren.

Hinderer, Ida Alice
Boulder City News, Thursday, 25 Oct 1973, 2:3.
Mrs. Ida Alice Hinderer, a 25-years resident of Boulder City, passed away Oct 20 in Las Vegas and graveside services were held Tues. at the Boulder City cemetery. Mrs. Hinderer was born Nov. 17, 1890 in Newmansville, Pa. She resided at 604 Ave. G, and was a member of the Grace Community Church. She is survived by a son Harold of Port Orange, Florida; daughter Helen Ursin, Las Vegas; sisters Lottie Holabaugh, Emma Sliker, and Martha Magee, all of Pa.; a brother Ernest Sliker.

Hodgkin, John F.
Boulder City News, Thursday, 6 Jul 1995, 13:1-2.
John F. Hodgkin, 84, died Saturday, July 1, 1995 in a local hospital. A local resident for 43 years, be was born Aug. 7, 1910 in Enid, Okla. A life-time member of the BPOE of Boulder City, he had been a retired power generation control room operator. Survivors include his wife, Kathleen, and his son, David, both of Boulder City; a sister, Nell Palmer of Denver, Colo.; three grandchildren; and four great-great grandchildren. Services were held. Arrangements were handled by Palm Mortuary-Henderson.

Hoffman, Edward John
Boulder City News, Thursday, 2 Dec 1971.
Heart Attack Claims Life of E. Hoffman
by Esther Shipp
Edward John Hoffman died Thanksgiving Day at his home, 1005 Adobe Circle, after a long illness. Graveside rites were conducted Tuesday morning at the Boulder City Cemetery by the PBO Elks Lodge N. 1682, of which Ed was a member. His wife, Gladys, preceded him in death on his 70th birthday, November 8. Since then, Ed couldn't find enough to do to keep him occupied, and his heart had been bothering him again. He had written a very nice letter on the 18th, thanking me for the obituary of Gladys. Ed was born Nov. 8, 1901 in Colby, Wisconsin, and lived in that state many years. He was in the restaurant business in Napa, California, before moving to Boulder City in 1959. He and Gladys owned and operated the Coffee Cup until 1965, when they decided to take a rest for

health reasons. In 1969, they once more took over the proprietorship of the Coffee Cup, enlarging and modernizing the interior. When Gladys became very ill, they again sold the café permanently. The two were members of the Chamber of Commerce. Ed is survived by his stepchildren, Alvin Bing of Las Vegas, and Imogene Acosta of Phoenix, Arizona; four grandchildren; a brother, Tony Hoffman, Strafford, Wis., and a sister, Clara Schommer, Marshfield, Wisconsin.

Hoffman, Gladys M.
Boulder City News, Thursday, 11 Nov 1971, 1:6.
Funeral Held Wednesday For Mrs. Hoffman by Esther Shipp
Gladys M. Hoffman, 71, was laid to rest in the Boulder City Cemetery, yesterday morning after a long fight with cancer. She died at Sunrise Hospital early Monday morning, following an illness of 18 months. Funeral services were conducted at Christ Lutheran Church by the Reverend Paul W. Egertson of Calvary Lutheran Church of Las Vegas. Gladys had belonged to the Prince of Peace Lutheran Church in Boulder City. Pallbearers were Al Bornhoft, Jack Doty, Elton Garrett, Matt Ruth, Jack Caldwell and Don Linck. Gladys Murry was born on March 9, 1990 in Belgrade, Montana. She had a son and daughter by her first marriage. She and Ed Hoffman were married in 1957, and ran a restaurant in Napa, Calif., before moving to Boulder City in 1959. They owned the Coffee Cup Café, and ran it until 1965, when they decided to take a rest. However, they took the café back in 1969 and modernized the enlarged interior of the building. Last year, the couple finally retired and live in a mobile home at 1000 Adobe Circle in the Coronado Estates. Gladys belonged to the Oder of Eastern Star in Vista, California. In Boulder City she was active in the Chamber of Commerce and the Business and Professional Women's Club. She had many capabilities and one of her favorite past times was writing poetry. Her verses were frequently printed in the magazine section of the *Review-Journal*. In addition to her husband, Ed, she is survived by her daughter Imogene Acosta, of Phoenix, Ariz., son Alvin Bing Las Vegas; four grandchildren; a brother, Pat Murry, and a sister, Pauline McConald of San Diego, California. In lieu of flowers, the family requested contributions to the Clark County Cancer Society.

Holberg. Charles Oscar

Boulder City News, Thursday, 6 June 1946, 1:1.
Charles Holberg Dies After Long Illness; Funeral To Be Friday
Charles Oscar Holberg died yesterday at 10:30 a.m. at the family home, 617 Avenue M, after a lingering illness of more than a year. A few weeks ago Holberg enjoyed a visit from all five of his sone and daughters at a family reunion here. Since that time he has remained at the family home, though he had spent much time during the last year at Basic hospital. Mrs. Carmen Burkhardt of Miami, Ariz., nurse and friend of the family, came to Boulder City three weeks ago, to help care for Holberg. She was accompanied by her small son. Funeral services will be at 5 p.m. Friday at Grace Community church, with the Reverend Winston Trever in charge. Mrs. Ruth Getts and LaVon Stokes will sing and Mrs. Madelaine Garrett will play the organ. Members of the Knights of Pythias, of which organization he was an active member, will act as pallbearers, and the lodge will conduct graveside ceremonies. Pallbearers will be Lee Hayward, Everett E. Sharp, John White, Clyde Moses, Art Minish and Fred Rader. Phyllis Holberg, granddaughter, who is a nurse cadet at Great Falls, Mont., flew to Boulder City recently for a visit with her grandfather, and Mrs. Dorothy Gise, another granddaughter, flew to Boulder from her home in Nyack, N. Y., returning three days ago. Charles Holberg was born in Denver, Colo., December 1, 1876, and completed high school in Denver, after which he took carpentry apprenticeship at the Denver and Rio Grande railroad shops, learning the trade there with his father. He was married at the age of 22, and built mills and did millwright work throughout the west and Mexico, going then into contracting work in Miami, Arizona. Later he did millwright work in Colorado, Wyoming and Nevada, coming to Boulder City in 1935, where he has had his won carpenter and cabinet shop, at 617 Avenue M. Called by his friends "pop" and "Charlie," he was known among acquaintances for his wit and humor, and had as hobbies hunting and fishing. He was a member of Elks lodge 1410, Miami, Ariz., and Lake Mead lodge Knights of Pythias. Mr. Holberg is survived by his widow, five children, 15 grand-children and five great grandchildren. The children are Mrs. O. N. Stephens of La Junta, Colo.; Mrs. S. A. Sullivan of Baynard, N. M.; W. C. Holberg of Lyons, Ga.; Clarence A. Holberg, Cherry Lynn apartments, and Lloyd D. Holberg, 615 Avenue M, Boulder City.

Holmes, Grace L.
Boulder City News, Thursday, 4 Oct 1990, 2:4.
Grace L. Holmes, 57, an 11 and one-half year resident of Boulder City died Sept. 25, in a local hospital. Born in Inglewood, Calif. on Jan. 21, 1933, she was a vice president for a boat company. She was a member of the national jet boat club and was very active in boat races. She is survived by her husband, William H. Holmes, Sr. of Boulder City; and four sons, Richard Holmes, David Holmes and Howard Holmes, all of Las Vegas and William Holmes, Jr. of Texas and two sisters, Frances Hostitler of Scaro, Calif. and Mildred Stewart of Boise, Indiana; and a brother, Larry Miller of Corkland, Calif. Services were held. Palm Mortuary handled arrangements.

Holmes, Helen Hazel
Boulder City News, Thursday, 12 Dec 1991, 7:3.
Helen Hazel Holmes, 85, died Dec. 4. She was born Feb. 24, 1906, in Harrison, Neb., and had been a resident of the Boulder City area for 60 years. Holmes was a member of Cactus Rebekah Lodge No. 40, Ladies Auxiliary __ Militant, Boulder City 31'ers, and NARFE, and was affiliated with Grace Community Church for many years. She is survived by two daughters, Doris Sullivan of Fresno, Calif., and Carol Peckenpaugh of Jeffersonville, Ind.; one sister, Clara Tibbits of Lusk, Wyo.; eight grandchildren and one great great grandchild. Arrangements were handled by Bunkers Mortuary.

Holt, Bert
Boulder City News, Thursday, 3 Apr 1969.
Services will be conducted at 2 p.m. today at Foursquare Gospel Church for Bert Holt who died at his home in Lakeview March 29. The Reverend Gene Holman will officiate and interment will be in Boulder City Cemetery. Bunker Brothers Mortuary is in charge of arrangements. Mr. Holt was born Jan. 15, 1921 in Depew, Okla. He was never married. He is survived by his mother, Mrs. Martha Holt, Boulder City; four brothers, William W., Olympia, Wash.; Charles, Lawndale, Calif.; Junior, Boulder City and Woodrow, Gardener, Okla. He also leaves four sisters, Ruby Nicks, Boulder City; Mirl Engle, Las Vegas; Cora Gore, Westminster, Calif.

Honeycutt, Lillian

Boulder City News, Thursday, 19 Jun 1980, 2:4-7.

Lillian Honeycutt, A Beloved Educator is Laid To Rest by Teddy Fenton Lillian Votaw Honeycutt, 81, was surrounded by her friends and family yesterday as final rites were held for her at Grace Community Church. She was buried at the B.C. Cemetery. The services were conducted by Reverend Pritts. The warm friendships she formed with students and faculty members was known by everyone. Her sisters, Mabel Condit of Tucson, Arizona, and Olive Stansmore of Boulder City want to thank her neighbors and friends for standing by all through the hardship of a lingering illness that ended in her death last Saturday. Lillian will lie beside her husband, Bill Honeycutt, at the B.C. Cemetery. Mrs. Honeycutt died on July 1, 1968. Lillian's parents, Ida and William Votow, also lie in the local cemetery. Lillian brought her parents to Boulder City and they lived in one half of the Honeycutt duplex. It, like her present home on 5th St., was constructed by Bill Honeycutt. Bill and Lillian came from Kingman, Arizona. She was a teacher there. It is hard to believe that at first she was unable to get a position as an educator in the B.C. school system. Luckily for all the children whom she taught in that long career the rules were changed, those being that a married lady could not teach, and she not only became one of our most beloved and popular instructors, she served as the Dean of Girl students and later became the vice-principal of the Boulder City High School. Students were to salute her in many instances, as a favorite teacher. There has seldom been a class reunion that she doesn't appear and the long ago students of that long career told her the debt they owed her. She taught with love and the discipline of trust and guidance. When she lost her husband she did not sit at home with folded hands. She began a journey that went around the world. Her adventures were told many times in the NEWS. We will miss her. She was purposely put on this earth to serve as a friend of all who knew here. She belonged to so many organizations that it would be impossible to tell of the vast good that was done with her volunteer work and willingness to make our town and the world around her a better place because she lived here. . .

Hood, Lori J.
Boulder City News, Thursday, 17 May 1990, 8:4-6.
Lori Janine Hood, 28, a life-time Boulder City resident, died Saturday in Boulder City;. Born on July 23, 1961, she was an assistant chef in a restaurant. She was graduated from Boulder City High School in 1979 and attended Apollo Business School in Henderson. Survivors include her husband, Rich Hood; son, Justin Hood; father, Robert E. Bellis; sister, Tina Bellis and step-mother, Helen Bellis; all of Boulder City. Other survivors include sister, Barbara Porter; step-sister, Nancy Whiting both of Las Vegas; brother, G. Mike Bellis of New Zealand and grandmother, Maude Bellis of Wheatland, Wyo. Memorial services will be held at 3:00 p.m. Friday at Palm Chapel in Henderson. Interment will be at Boulder City Cemetery.

Horton, Elaine Abercrombie
Boulder City News, Thursday, 3 Jan 1951, 1:3.
Final Rites For Elaine Horton Held Monday
Elaine Abercrombie Horton was buried Friday afternoon in the Boulder City cemetery beside her father, John Abercrombie, Boulder City Pioneer who died in 1942. Funeral services were conducted by the Reverend Olaf Stoove at Grace Community Church. Janet Carpenter sang "Going Home," accompanied by Sylvia Legler on the Stevenson Memorial organ. Pallbearers were Jack Wheeler, Jr., Porter Bassett, Bill Nickell and Lawrence Goen of Boulder City; Lionel Leonard of Victorville, and James Bradshaw of Reno. Honorary pallbearers were B. W. Cowan, James Godbey, Tom Godbey, Jr., Donald Whalen, Jack Hurt and Larry McSwain. Mrs. Horton was taken sick at the home of her mother Helen Abercrombie, 603 California Ave. when she and her husband Robert were here for the holidays from their home in Florence, Arizona. She was taken to the hospital December 26 and died two days later. Also visiting Mrs. Abercrombie at the same time were her son John and his wife of Los Angeles, and son Fred of Evanston, Illinois. Horton's sister Betty of Reno, came to town for the funeral services. Mrs. Horton was born October 5, 1928, in Chicago, and came to Boulder City when she was three years old. While in high school here she wrote the words to the "Alma Mater" song and upon graduation was awarded a Smith scholarship to the University of Nevada. At Reno she was an honor student and president of the Pi Phi sorority. She graduated from the

University and was married to Robert Horton graduate mining engineer, on Sept. 1, 1949 at Community Church. They made their home in Reno until recently.

Hoskins, John K.
Boulder City News, Thursday, 20 Feb 1992, 9:1-2.
John K. Hoskins, 82, died Thursday in a local hospital. He was born March 24, 1909, in Minneapolis, Minn., and had been a resident of the Boulder City area for one month. He is survived by his wife, Lena S. Hoskins of Boulder City; three daughters, Mary Fulle of Alta, Calif.,Catherine Kothe of Boulder City, and Bernice May of Tujunga, Calif.; one sister, Mary Merrill of Fresno, Calif.; one brother, Howard Hoskins of Minneapolis, Minn.; nine grandchildren, and 13 great grandchildren. Services were held. Arrangements were handled by Palm Mortuary in Henderson.

Howard, William Arlow
Boulder City News, Thursday, 25 Nov 1993, 10:2-3.
William Arlow Howard died Nov. 22, 1993, in Boulder City. He was 83. He was born Aug. 8, 1910, in Colorado Springs, Colorado, and had been a resident here for 29 years. He was retired from the city of Boulder City where he had worked in the landscape and maintenance department. A veteran of WWII, he served in the Army Air Corp, as a pilot/paratrooper, serving in the European Theater of Operation. He was a member of American Legion Post 31 in Boulder City. Survivors include his wife of 46 years, Cecilia; a son, William R. Howard; a daughter-in-law, Kristen Howard; three grandchildren, Clay and Liann Bounty and Sarah Howard, all of Boulder City, NV. Arrangements were handled by Nevada Funeral Services of Las Vegas.

Huddleston, Daisy Moyer

Boulder City News, Thursday, 20 Jan 1966, 2:3.
Funeral services were held Sunday afternoon for Daisy Moyer Huddleston, 77, with the Reverend Guy Holliday officiating at Grace Community Church. Burial followed in the Boulder City Cemetery. Pallbearers were her sons Paul and Mill Lively, and grandsons Billy Johnson, Tim and Michael Kilpatrick, and Bob Lively. Mrs. Huddleston died in her sleep, early Thursday morning. Following a short illness she had been brought to Boulder City, Wednesday night to stay with her daughter Agnes Johnson, a registered nurse. She had previously visited the Johnson home, many times. She was born February 15, 1888, on a farm in Bradley County, Tennessee. In recent years she lived in Victorville, Calif., where she was a member of the Senior Citizens Club. She was the mother of nine children, five of whom survive. They are Agnes (Mrs. Clarence) Johnson, 421 Birch Street; Deanne (Mrs. Bud) Kilpatrick, Independence, Calif.; sons, Paul Lively, Independence; Bill, Arcardia, Calif.; Jim, Mathis, Texas. She is also survived by a sister, Grace Lewis, Cleveland, Tenn.; nine grandchildren and 7 great-grandchildren.

Hudlow, Florence E.

Boulder City News, Thursday, 16 Mar 1978, 2:5-8.
40 Year Resident Passes Away
Pioneer resident Florence E. Hudlow, 66, passed away Tuesday, March 14 at Sunrise Hospital. She had resided at 312 Nevada Highway. She had lived in Boulder City for 40 years and worked for the U.S. Bureau of Reclamation as assistant purchasing agent. Mrs. Hudlow was born February 26, 1912 in Salt Lake City. She was a member of the Order of Eastern Star and Grace Community Church, and had been instrumental in the formation of the church in its early stages. Survivors include her husband, Lloyd J. Hudlow of Boulder City; daughters, Linda Fox of Las Vegas, Bette A. Dickhaus of Columbia, Missouri, and Joanne Hudlow of San Diego; one son, Grant B. Hudlow of Arizona; a sister, Alyce Baker of Boulder City and grandchildren, Martin Queenan of San Diego, Karl Eric Kickhaus of Columbia, Mo., Christopher H. and David E. Fox of Las Vegas and a great grandson, Sean Queenan of San Diego. Graveside services will be held Friday, March 17 at 2 p.m. with the Reverend Earl Fox, former pastor of Church and now retired, officiating. In lieu of

flowers that family has requested that donations may be made to the Kidney Foundation or the American Cancer Society, Clark County Chapter. Palm Mortuary is in charge of the arrangements.

Hudson, Dr. Jewel Norman
Boulder City News, Thursday, 9 Jan 1992, 6:1-2.
Dr. Jewel Norman Hudson passed away January 1, 1992 at St. Rose Dominican Hospital in Henderson. He was 85 years of age. Private family graveside services were conducted in Boulder City January 3, 1992 with Reverend David Brown of Desert Hills Baptist Church officiating. A native of Marion County, Ark., he retired to Boulder City after 26 years as a Civil Service Attorney Advisor in the Federal Trade Commission in Washington, D.C. He held Bachelor's and Master's of Science degrees from the University of Arkansas, and a Juris Doctor of Law from Iowa State University, graduating with high honors, and was awarded the coveted Order of the Coif. Dr. Hudson was the author of a published genealogy of the Jesse Hudson and Related Family, a copy of which is of record in the Library of Congress. He was a member of the First Baptist Church of Washington, D.C. Upon retiring to Boulder City in 1970, he transferred his membership to the First Baptist Church and later to Grace Community Church. He was a charter member of AAPR and the Senior Citizens Organization. Dr. Hudson is survived by his wife, Ouida (Weda) May, of the home, a foster son Mr. Merle Turley and wife, Dorothy of Boulder City, a sister Rue Allena Burbridge and a nephew William Coleman Emery, both of whom recently retired from California to their native state of Arkansas, two grand nieces and one grand nephew. Arrangements were handled by Palm Mortuary of Henderson.

Hueftle, Bernice M.
Boulder City News, Thursday, 3 Sep 1987, 10:4.
Bernice M. Hueftle, 83, died Friday Aug. 28 in California. She was a resident of Boulder City for 15 years. She was born March 20, 1904 and was a housewife. She is survived by her son Leroy Hueftle of Huntington Beach, Calif.; daughter Barbara Layne of Boulder City; brother Roy Rohrbacker of Grant, Neb.; six grandchildren and eleven great grandchildren. Graveside services will be at Boulder City Cemetery at 10 a.m. on Sept. 3. Pastor Ted Godwin from Grace Community Church will officiate. Palm Mortuary of Henderson are handling arrangements.

Huening, Fred H.
Boulder City News, Thursday, 1 Aug 1968.
A funeral mass was held at 9 a.m. last Saturday morning for Fred. H. Huening who died July 24 at B.C. Hospital. He had been making his home with his son, Theodore and family at 716 Eighth St. Burial was in the B.C. Cemetery. Father Hugh Smith officiated. Mr. Huening was born Oct. 27, 1881 in Essen, Germany. He was engaged in the wholesale tobacco and liquor business in that country. After moving to New York he owned and operated a farm. The deceased is survived by three sons, Theodore, Boulder City; Fritz, Staten Island, N.Y. and Alphonse H. Frankfort, N.Y. Palm Mortuary in Henderson was in charge.

Hughes, William E.
Boulder City News, Thursday, 19 Jan 1989, 25:3.
William E. Hughes, 72, a resident for 45 years, died Jan.16 in Boulder City. Born in McDonald, Ohio, on July 22, 1916, he was a truck driver and a World War II Army veteran. He is survived by his wife, Mildred B. Hughes of Boulder City; daughters, Bille A. Lazaro of Las Vegas and Unita M. Rowe of Boulder City; brothers Richard L. Hughes of Las Vegas, Ronald R. Hughes of Sandy Valley and Jack Hughes of Winston, Ore.; sister, Joan Zumwalt of Portland, Ore.; and five grandchildren and three great grandchildren. Palm Mortuary of Henderson is handling the arrangements. Visitation is Thursday from 4 p.m. to 9 p.m. Funeral services will be at 11 a.m. Friday with an officiant from Nellis AFB. Interment will be in Boulder City Cemetery.

Hunt, Howard C.
Boulder City News, Thursday, 24 May 1979, 10:7-8.
Funeral services were held last Monday at Palm Chapel for Howard Clark Hunt, 66, who died May 17 in a Las Vegas hospital. Mr. Hunt was born August 20, 1912 in Franklin Grove, Illinois and was a 22-year resident of Boulder City. He was a veteran of World War II and the owner and operator of a landscape business. He is survived by his daughter, Anita Bybee of Springfield, Illinois; sisters, Mattie Peevy of South Beloit, Ill, Shirley Harris and Clara Swayze both of Santa Rosa, Calif., Betty J. Kinnaman of Chicago, and Ruth Sutherland of Imperial Beach, Calif. Interment was at the Boulder City cemetery.

Huntley, Monte G.
Boulder City News, Thursday, 16 Mar 1978, 10:6.
Graveside services will be held today for Monte G. Huntley, 64, who passed away March 13 in Boulder City. Mr. Huntley was born May 6, 1913 in Scranton, Pennsylvania and was a retired upholsterer. He had been residing at 524 Birch Street with friends Bill and Dorothy Kamrowski at the time of his death. He was a veteran of World War II. There are no known local survivors. The Reverend Guy Holliday of Grace Community Church will officiate at the 2 p.m. services at Boulder City Cemetery.

Hurt, Robert H.
Boulder City News, Thursday, 6 Mar 1980, 4:6-8.
Services will be held at Palm Chapel, Henderson, at 11 a.m. today for Robert H. Hurt, 60, who died March 3 in Las Vegas. Members of the Boulder City Masonic Lodge will officiate. Mr. Hurt was born November 8, 1919 in Gadsen, Alabama and had resided in the area since 1932. He was a graduate of Las Vegas High School, was a member of the Carpenter's Local #1780, the Boulder City Masonic Lodge, #37, and of American Legion Post 8 in Las Vegas. Mr. Hurt was a veteran of World War II and was a member of the LDS E. Tropicana Church. He had been a carpenter at the Tropicana Hotel. He is survived by his wife, Ora Hurt of Las Vegas; and brothers, Art Hurt of Las Vegas and Jack Hurt of Sacramento, California. Interment will be at the Boulder City Cemetery.

Imlay, James Fenton
Boulder City News, Thursday, 4 Aug 1966, 1:7.
Services for James Fenton Imlay, who died Sunday in Boulder City Hospital, were held Wednesday at the LDS Chapel at 1 p.m. Burial was in the local cemetery. A 25-year resident here, Mr. Imlay lived at 1117 New Mexico St. He was a retired blacksmith and belonged to the B. C. Elks Lodge 1682. He was born Dec. 29, 1907 in Cedar City, Utah. Survivors include his son, Dale F. Imlay; grandchildren, Sidney Lynn and Darin F. Imlay, this city; four sisters, Mrs. La Grande Hardy, Boulder City, Mrs. James Boners, Salt Lake City, Mrs. Charles Gillespie, Bishop, Calif. and Miss Luetta Imlay, Hurricane, Utah; and three brothers, George, Hurricane; Kenneth, Cedar City and John, Salt Lake City. His wife,

Wilma DeMille Imlay, preceded him in death.

Isenberg, Richard "Dick"
Boulder City News, Thursday, 24 Nov 1994, 7:1-2.
Former City Manager Richard Gene "Dick" Isenberg died Tuesday, Nov. 15, 1994, at his home in Boulder City. He was 67. Isenberg was the city manager of Boulder City from 1970 to 1972, selected from a field of 67 applicants for the vacancy. He had previously served as the city manager in Turlock, California, from 1961 to 1968. A founder and charter member of the Boulder City Golf Course, he was instrumental in developing the plans for the course and have them come to fruition. He served on various committees for the Panasonic Las Vegas Invitational Golf Tournament which later became the Las Vegas Invitational. He was born Aug. 13, 1927, in Gary, Indiana. He had a bachelor's degree in science from Ball State University in Muncie, Indiana. He served in the U.S. Navy during WWII and later was a teacher prior to going into government service. He was a recreation supervisor in Bakersfield, California and later a recreation and parks director in Los Altos, California. Isenberg retired as Clark County Recreation Superintendent in 1991. He was a lifetime member of the Nevada Recreation and Parks Society and a member of the International Association of City Managers. He also was a member of the Rotary Club. Survivors include his wife, Alice, of Boulder City; sons Kurt Isenberg and Rick Isenberg, both of Palm Springs, Calif.; two step-sons, Steven Corry and David Corry, both of Boulder City, also five grandchildren. Services were private. Palm Mortuary in Henderson was in charge of arrangements. The family offered that donations may be made in his name to the Boulder Dam Hotel Association or KNPR - Nevada Public Radio 89.5 FM.

Jacobs, Gayle Maureen
Boulder City News, Thursday, 1 May 1986, p.35:1-3.
Gayle Maureen Jacobs passed away Friday, April 18, 1986, in Scottsdale, Arizona. She was 70 years of age. Born in Bear River City, Utah, on August 28, 1915, she was a homemaker. She lived in Boulder City from 1939 to 1956 when she moved to Las Vegas until 1976 when she moved to Fairview Park, Ohio. She had visited Las Vegas for the past three winters. Survivors include her husband James of Fairview Park; sons Gordon Roberts of Salt Lake City, Utah, John Roberts of Hillsborough,

Calif.; a daughter Shelia Roberts of Scottsdale, Arizona; brothers Vear Jenson, Max Jenson, both of Salt Lake City, Floyd Jenson of Brigham City, Utah, Frank Jenson of Bear River City, Utah; a sister Donna Wright of Northridge, Calif,; also 10 grandchildren. Services were conducted at Palm Valley Chapel on Saturday, April 26.

Jacot, Francis H.
Boulder City News, Thursday, 1 Oct 1987.
Francis H. Jacot, 57, died Sept. 2, 1987, in Glendale, California. He was a long-time resident of Boulder City. A Navy veteran of the Korean War, he was born December 30, 1929, in Los Angeles, California and was a resource specialist for the National Park Service. He is survived by his wife, Mary Jean, of Boulder City; son Daniel of Los Angeles; daughter Suzanne Villareale and son-in-law Christopher Villereale of Las Vegas; mother, Berthe of Los Angeles; one grandson. Services were held at the Church of the Recessional in Forest Lawn Mortuary in Glendale, Calif. Burial will be in Boulder City. There were no local services.

Jenne, Wilma H.
Boulder City News, Thursday, 19 Dec 1991, 11:2-3.
Wilma H. Jenne, 75, died Saturday. She was born Dec. 25, 1915, in Lewiston, Utah, and had been a resident of the Boulder City area for 52 years. She was a school teacher and a member of LDS Church in Boulder City, First Ward. She is survived by her husband, Floyd L. Jenne of Boulder City; two daughters, Nancy Fielding of Shelley, Idaho, and Joan Rogers of Boulder City; one son, Floyd (Rick) Jenne of Sandy, Utah; 12 grandchildren and 1 great grandchild. Services will be held Friday at LDS Chapel 1st Ward, Boulder City at 2 p.m. Visitation is from 1-4 p.m. today and one hour prior to service in Relief Society Room. Bunker Mortuaries handled arrangements.

Jensen, Jeffrey Allen
Las Vegas Review-Journal, Tuesday, 21 Jan 1969, p. 19:4.
Jeffrey Allen, one-month-old, 617 School Dr., died Thursday at Sunrise Hospital. Born Boulder City Dec. 14, 1968. Survivors: parents, Mr. and Mrs. Roy Jensen; and three sisters, Tina, Cathy and Tracey Jensen, all of Las Vegas. Graveside services: held Monday at Boulder City, Cemetery. Fr. Hugh Smith officiating.

Johnson, Christopher Dean
Boulder City News, Thursday, 25 Apr 1991, 8:1-2.
Christopher Dean Johnson, 19, died Saturday in a local hospital. He was born March 25, 1972, in Fairmont, Minn. and had been a resident of the area for two and a half years. The family requests memorials go to Christ Lutheran Church, 1401 5th St., Boulder City, Nev. 89005, in memory of Christopher. Johnson is survived by his parents Mr. and Mrs. Allan Johnson; two sisters, Carissa and Cheyenne; and a brother Kyle, all of Boulder City; paternal grandmother, Lucille Johnson of Trimont, Minn.; maternal grandparents, Mr. and Mrs. Howard Stade of Trimont, Minn.; and great grandparents Mr. and Mrs. Paul Stade of Welcome, Minn. Viewing services will be held today from 1 to 7 p.m. and funeral services will be at Christ Lutheran Church Thursday at 2 p.m. Arrangements were handled by Palm Mortuary of Henderson.

Johnson, Harry E.
Boulder City News, Thursday, 15 Jan 1970
H. E. Johnson
Graveside services were conducted at 3 p.m. Tuesday by the Reverend Guy Holliday at Grace Community Church at the B. C. Cemetery for Harry E. Johnson, 67, who died while fishing at Kingman Wash last Saturday. He was born Sept. 19, 1902 in Hamilton County, Ill. The deceased and his wife, Deon, his only survivor, lived at Moore's Trailer Park. Mr. Johnson was a veteran of World War II, and retired from a State of Arizona position.

Johnson, John Eric
Boulder City News, Thursday, 23 Aug 1951, 1:5.
Funeral For Johnson Boy This Afternoon
A short funeral service will be conducted at 5 o'clock this afternoon at Grace Community church for John Eric Johnson, only son of Mr. and Mrs. Lyle Johnson, 857 Avenue G. This will be followed by a graveside service at Boulder Cemetery. The rites will be performed by the Reverend Ford Gilbert, pastor of the Henderson Community Church. An organ music background will be played at church by Madelaine Garrett, and the soloist will be Gwenn Chubbs. Pallbearers are to be Pete Smilanick, Howard Musser, John Phillips, and Jim Walkden. Johnny was born June 25, 1949 in Dixon, Illinois. He was accidentally drowned on Monday in a small stream in Zion National Park, where the family was on vacation. His body was brought to the Palm Funeral Home in Las Vegas on Tuesday night by family friends Ros Salter and Leo Price. Johnny is survived by his parents, both of whom work for the Reclamation project, a sister Sandra, his grandmother Mrs. Grace Trost who lives with the family, and a grandmother Mrs. Hilma Johnon, of Illinois. Mr. and Mrs. Jack Trost of 506 Avenue M are his aunt and uncle, and there are four uncles and an aunt in Illinois.

Johnson, Traci C.
Boulder City News, Thursday, 2 Nov 1978, 8:1-2.
Services were held at Palm Chapel last Tuesday for Traci C. Johnson, 7, who died October 28 in Las Vegas. The daughter of Mr. and Mrs. Dale Johnson of Boulder City, Traci was born June 19, 1971 in Boulder City. Besides her parents she is survived by three brothers, Scott, Rhett and Todd Johnson of Boulder City; a sister, Tami Johnson of Boulder City; maternal grandparents, Mr. and Mrs. Ernest Sass of Boulder City; and paternal grandparents, Mr. and Mrs. Vernon Johnson of Wells, Minnesota. The family has requested that in lieu of flowers donations may be made to the American Cancer Society.

Johnson, Veva
Boulder City News, Thursday, 23 Sep 1971.
By Esther Shipp
Graveside services were held Monday evening for Veva Johnson, 56, who died Saturday morning, Sept. 18, at her home. The rites were conducted by the Reverend Guy Holliday, at Grace Community Church, where Veva was a member. Relatives and a host of friends were in attendance. Veva Templer was born June 25, 1915 in Kansas. She and her husband Morris Johnson, and their tiny daughter Thea came here from Denver, Colorado., in 1952, when "Johnny" was employed by the U. S. Bureau of Mines. She worked in Girl Scouting when Thea was of that age, belonged to the American Legion Auxiliary, was active in the Women's Association of Grace Church, and was editor of the Church newspaper. All of this despite the fact that she suffered many illnesses, injuries and family tragedies. Thea Childers, a newlywed, was killed in 1965. The family formerly lived at 673 Ave. M, 1213 Ave. K, and in 1968 moved into a mobile home at 700 Elm Street. Veva is survived by her husband, Morris, Space 13, Eldorado Trailer Park; Milo Templer, Anaheim, Calif., and Richard, Oxnard, Calif.; nieces and nephews including Darryl L. Templer of San Diego, who used to live here with the Johnsons a few years ago.

Jonasen, Walter A.
Boulder City News, Thursday, 16 Dec 1976, 8:3-5.
Walter (Wally) A. Jonasen of 605 Don Vincente Drive, and a resident of Boulder City for the past 40 years, passed away in the Boulder City Hospital on Thursday, December 8, 1976, at 7:10 in the morning. He had suffered from cancer for some time. He was 67. A native Nevadan, he was born in Goldfield on September 21, 1909, to Jonas (Joe) E. Jonasen and Karen Frederikke Andersen Jonasen. Following the Goldfield Fire in 1923, he moved with his parents, to California where he finished his education and joined the Los Angeles Department of Water and Power as a Power Plant Operator. He moved to Boulder City in 1936 when the Department of Water and Power Commenced operating Boulder Dam, and was a member of the crew on the first operating shift. Mr. Jonasen retired in 1972 with 42 years of service, having risen to the Post of Chief Electric Plant Operator. He was a member of the International brotherhood of Electrical workers. He was a member of the Grace

Community Church in Boulder City. Mr. Jonasen was active in the masons, holding memberships in the Boulder City Lodge number 37, where he served as Treasurer, and the Motezuma Lodge number 30 of Goldfield. He was a member of the Scottish Rite of Free Masonry and the Zelzah Temple AOONMS, both of Las Vegas, as well as the boulder City Shrine Club where he also served as Treasurer, and Desert Chapter number 22 Order of the Eastern Star in Boulder City. Other associations included Life Membership in the National Rifle Association and the Nevada State Rifle and Pistol Club; membership in the Boulder Riffle and Pistol Club, and the California Rifle and Pistol Association. He is survived by his widow Bernice Jonasen; two sons, Robert W. of Temple City, California, and Frederick A. of Ridgecrest, California; a daughter, Shirley Kennedy of Colorado Springs, Colorado; a brother, Gordon P. Jonasen of Boulder City; and 8 grandchildren. Services were held at Palm Chapel in Henderson on Saturday at 11 a.m., December 11. 1976 Reverend Guy Holliday officiated; Bill Voss, Past Grand Master, assisted and interment, following cremation, was in the Boulder City Cemetery.

Jones, Albert R.
Boulder City News, Thursday, 23 Mar 1978, 7:4-5.
Graveside services were held last Monday, march 20 at Boulder City Cemetery for Albert R. Jones, 71, who passed away March 17 in Las Vegas. Mr. Jones was born March 24, 1906 in Jamestown, North Dakota and had resided in Boulder City since 1971. He was retired from the oil refining industry and lived at 1000 La Mesa Way. Survivors include his wife, Clara of Boulder City; one son, Al Jones of Fullerton, California; a daughter, Betty Ryerson of Boulder City; a sister, Myrtle Cysewski of Riverside, California and four grandchildren.

Jones, Clifford R.
Boulder City News, Thursday, 5 Dec 1985, 31:3.
Clifford R. Jones, age 70, of Boulder City, died Saturday, Nov. 30, in Boulder City. He was born in Ohio on May 1, 1915. He was a resident for the last five years. He was a Navy veteran of World War II and a baker. He leaves his wife, Beatrice of the home; daughters Jeannine Schwab of Boulder City, Linda of Erlanger, Ky. and Jackie Hippensteel of Mattawan, Mich,; a son, Clifford R. Jr. of Kalamazoo, Mich.; and six grandchildren. Services were held Tuesday at Grace Community Church.

Memorial donations may be made to the American Cancer Society.

Jordan, Maxine V.
Boulder City News, Thursday, 15 Sep 1994, 10:4.
Maxine V. Jordon, 69, died Thursday, September 8, 1994 in Boulder City. Born Nov. 6, 1924 in Webster County, Mo., she was a homemaker in Boulder City for 11 years. She is survived by one daughter, Patsy I. Ashbaugh, of Boulder City; one brother, Wayne Packard, of Arlington, Texas; four grandchildren and four great grandchildren. Arrangements were handled by Palm Mortuary of Henderson.

Kaiser, Otto H., Sr.
Boulder City News, Thursday, 18 May 1967, 1:5.
Kaiser, Sr. Buried Here
Funeral services were held recently for Otto H. Kaiser, 79, at St. Andrews Catholic Church. Mr. Kaiser had been making his home with his son, Otto, Jr. at 508 8th st. Burial was in Boulder City Cemetery. Mr. Kaiser had been a druggist in Chicago for 40 years and retired eight years ago in Beaumont, Calif. Survivors are three sons, Otto and Frank of this city and John of El Cajon, Calif.; two daughters, Mrs. Agatha Edmonds, Hilliard, O., and Mrs. Dorothy Baker, El Cajon; five sisters, three brothers, eight grandchildren and three great grandchildren.

Katchadoorian, Billie Sue
Boulder City News, Thursday, 7 Oct 1993, 9:1-2.
Billie Sue Katchadoorian, 57, died Sunday, Sept. 26 in a local hospital. She was a nine-year resident of the area. She was born Feb. 3, 1936 in Vienna, Ill. She is survived by her husband Harry Katchadoorian of Boulder City; two daughters, Kelly Hill and Jo Ann Katchadoorian both of Boulder City; two sons, David Katchadoorian of Las Vegas and Harry Katchadoorian of Boulder City; her mother, Verna Moore of Dearborn, Mich.; two sisters, Ruth Bezaire of Dearborn, Mich. and Coleen Lins of Grosse Ill, Mich,.; one brother Richard Moore of Detroit, Mich.; and one grandchild. Viewing services will be held at Palm Henderson Mortuary Thursday from 9 to 11 a.m. with services following at 11 a.m. Arrangements were handled by Palm Mortuary.

Katchadoorian, Harry Sr.
Boulder City News, Thursday, 30 Mar 1995, 8:1-2.
Harry Katchadoorian, Sr., 68, of Boulder City, died March 25, 1995. He was born Oct. 19, 1926, in Detroit, Mich. Katchadoorian is survived by two daughters, Kelly Hill and Joann Katchadoorian, both of Las Vegas; two sons, David of Las Vegas, and Harry of Boulder City; and one grandchild. Services were private. Arrangements were handled by Palm Mortuary-Henderson.

Keillor, Kathi
Boulder City News, Thursday, 13 Apr 1978.
A Tribute to Kathi
Kathi was admired by many students at BCHS for her courage and inner strength in her fight against cancer. There were many times when Kathi was in extreme pain yet the other students never knew. She could make a person feel so comfortable and relaxed even though she was not. The many activities Kathi was interested in during high school she could not participate in, yet she attended many and her spirit was overwhelming. During the fall and the Homecoming ceremonies, Kathi was thrilled to be queen. At that time her health was fairly stable and she was an absolutely beautiful queen. Kathi left many friends and acquaintances at BCHS who will remember he always. Kathi's parents loved her dearly and showed this in many ways, by providing and caring for her many needs during her sickness. Though Kathi's death was foreseen by her family, they all had hope and encouraged her to pursue life to its fullest extent. Kathi was loved and admired deeply by her family and friends, and will be in our hearts in the years to come.
Patty Koontz
Laurie Boucher

Keisling, infant
Boulder City News, Friday, 6 Dec 1946, 1:4.
Funeral services were held this morning at 10 o'clock at St. Andrew's Catholic Church for the infant son of Mr. and Mrs. John Keisling. Interment was in Boulder City Cemetery.

Kelly, Earl J.
Boulder City News, Thursday, 26 Jul 1979, 5:3.
17 Year Resident Passes Away
Graveside services will be held this morning at 10 a.m. at the Boulder City cemetery for Earl J. Kelly, 79, who died Monday. He was a 17 year resident of Boulder City and as an electrical contractor. Survivors include his wife, Dorothy, of Boulder City; a son, Jim Kelly of Boulder City; a daughter, Mary Lou McJilton, of Torrance, California; and four grandchildren.

Kelly, William R.
Boulder City News, Thursday, 8 Mar 1990, 12:1-2.
William R. Kelly, 50, a long-time resident of Boulder City, died Friday, March 2, 1990. He had resided in Las Vegas for eight months. He was born May 21, 1939 in New York City, NY. He was a commercial artist. Survivors include his wife, Barbara A. Kelly; two sons, William R. Kelly Jr. of Jacksonville, Fla. and Paul Kelly of Boulder City; a daughter, Jennifer Kelly of Boulder City; a sister Helen Zinggone of Valley Cottage, NY; and his step-mother, Theresa Kelly of Clearwater, Fla. Mass was held at 10 a.m. Tuesday March 6, 1990 in St. Andrews Church in Boulder City. Palm Mortuary handled arrangements.

Kemp, Allan Richard
Boulder City News, Thursday, 28 Oct 1993, 11:3.
Allan Richard Kemp, 79, died October 19 in a local hospital. A retired Aerospace Engineer Kemp was born April 2, 1914, and had been a resident of the Boulder City area for one year. He was a member of P.B.O.E. He is survived by his wife, Laura B. Kemp Sonerson of Brion Rouge, La.; a son, George Paul Kemp of Cocketsville, Md.; a sister, Louis Kemp Hart of Oceanside, Calif.; a brother, Norman Paul Kemp; and two grandchildren. Arrangements were handled by Palm Mortuary in Henderson.

Kennedy, Addie
Boulder City News, Monday, 9 Jun 1947, 1:4.
Funeral Held for Mrs. R. E. Kennedy
Funeral services for Mrs. Robert E. Kennedy were held at 4:30 p.m. today at Grace Community Church. Interment was at Boulder City Cemetery. Reverend Winston Trever officiated. Pallbearers were Elton Garrett, Carl Vetter, John Stanley, Marvin Diamond, William Campbell and Leo Courtney. Relatives who came here for the services included Mr. and Mrs. J. Irl Pritchard, Sheridan, Wyo.; Mr. and Mrs. Ralph D. Mercer and daughter Anita, Hyattville, Wyo.; Cortez Pritchard and Mrs. Clara McGary, Powell, Wyo.; Mr. and Mrs. Roger Kennedy and sons Charles, Bruce and Keith, Estes Park, Colo. With Mrs. Kennedy at the time of her sudden death early Friday were her husband, Robert E. Kennedy; her son R. Evans Kennedy, and Mrs. Kennedy, and Mr. Kennedy's sister Winifred Kennedy of Denver. Other survivors include a daughter, Mrs. Marguerite Huey, Albany, N.Y. two brothers, Cortez and Irl Pritchard; four sisters, Mrs. McGary, Mrs. Mercer, Alice Pritchard and Mrs. Lucy Noll. Mrs. Kennedy was born Addie M. Pritchard, in West Virginia. She was next to the oldest child in her family. When she was 16 years old her parents became ill and she assumed the care of her brothers and sisters, and reared them to maturity. She obtained a teachers certificate and supported the family with her earnings. In 1910 she married Mr. Kennedy in Hyattville, Wyo. In 1917 his family was struck by a series of tragic deaths that left only two children, Roger and Winifred, his half brother and half sister. Mrs. Kennedy took them into her home and reared them along with her own children. Winifred Kennedy now will remain here to keep house for Mr. Kennedy.

Keough, James J.
Boulder City News, Thursday, 3 Apr 1958, 1:5.
James Keogh Sr. Funeral Tuesday
Funeral services for James J. Keough, Sr., 76, were held on Tuesday morning at the Bunker Brothers Chapel in Las Vegas, with the Reverend Glen Tudor of the First Christian Church officiating. Interment was beside his wife in the Boulder City Cemetery. Keough, who resided in an apartment at 804 Wyoming St., was admitted to the Community Hospital on March 15. He died Saturday the 29th. He was born December 13, 1881 in Arlington, Mass. and was a retired Lumber Camp Sawyer. He and his

wife Lillian moved to Boulder City two years ago from Chicago, Ill. Mrs. Keogh died here Dec. 24, 1957, and close friends report that he wanted to join her. They are survived by one son, James J. Keough, Sr., who operates the Snak Bowl at 546 Nevada Hwy., and lived at the B. C. Trailer Park; also as grandson, James D. Keough of Westminister, Cal.; and two great-grandchildren. The couple did not take an active part in community affairs because of their heath, but they were known by sight to the neighbors and like by all the children to whom they spoke as they strolled together on their daily walks.

Keough, Lillian Kay
Boulder City News, Thursday, 2 Jan 1958, 1:7.
Funeral Held For Mrs. Keough
Funeral services for Lillian Kay Keough, who died Tuesday at her home, were conducted Thrusday morning in the Bunker Brothers Chapel in Las Vegas. The Reverend Glen Tudor officiated. Mrs. Keough was buried at Woodlawn Cemetery. Mrs. Keough died the day before her 70th birthday, as she was born Dec. 25, 1887, in Rochester, New York. She has lived in Boulder City for a year. Survivors are her husband, James of 804 Wyoming St., one son, James Jr. of Boulder City; one grandson and two great-grandchildren.

Kerzmann, Albert E.
Boulder City News, Thursday, 17 Dec 1992, 10:4.
Albert E. Kerzmann, 88, died Dec. 8, 1992, in a local convalescent home. He was born Aug. 15, 1904, in Philadelphia, Pa., and had been a resident of the Boulder City area for 30 years. He is survived by his wife, Victoria E. Kerzman of Boulder City; a son, Jack A. Kerzman of Glendora, Calif.; a sister, Marg Leuke of Philadelphia, Pa.; and 4 grandchildren. Services were held Tuesday. Arrangements were handled by Palm Mortuary in Henderson.

Kesterson, Pauline O.
Boulder City News, Thursday, 8 Jan 1953, 1:3.
Funeral For Pauline Kesterson Is Saturday
Funeral services for Pauline O. Kesterson, 76, one of the town's most beloved pioneers, will be conducted at 1:30 p.m. Saturday at the Grace Community church, with the Reverend Olaf A. Stoeve officiating. Burial will follow in the local cemetery. Mrs. Kesterson died Tuesday at the Souther memorial hospital in Las Vegas, where she has been a patient for more than a month. She suffered a stroke last July and has been hospitalized here, in Phoenix, and in Las Vegas ever since. Pauline Oberweiser was born July 10, 1876, in Menasha, Wisconsin, where her family had lived for 130 years. She was graduated as a registered nurse from Hahnemann hospital in Chicago in 1903. She served in army hospital in the Canal Zone from 1910 to 1918 and there met Sgt. J. N. Kesterson, who she married in Asheville, North Caroline, in 1919. Their only child, Robert, lived at 509 Avenue M. The Kestersons came to Boulder City in 1931 and at first lived in a tent at Railroad Pass, where Mrs. Kesterson drove the first nail in the first schoolhouse in the area. For many years she lived by preference on a little farm in dry lake. Her green pickup truck, which she learned to drive when 65 years old, while Bob was in the navy, was recognized by everyone when she drove to town every day for water, to see her son, and to visit friends. Mrs. Kesterson was a charter member of Cactus Rebekah No. 40, and in May was awarded a jeweled badge and the title of "Lady of the Decoration of Chivalry." which is the highest honor that can be given by the Rebekah lodge. She belonged to the American Legion auxiliary and was also a charter member of the Norman Ready Navy Mothers' club of Las Vegas and of the Boulder Dam chapter. For many years she devoted herself to bringing comfort to service men, especially those in the navy, and has made hundreds of hospital slippers, wheel chair robes, jelly cakes, cookies and other items for "her boys." She instituted the annual observance of placing a wreath on the waters of Lake Mead every Navy Day in memory of those who had lost their lives. During Work War II she helped furnish the recreation room here at Camp Sibert, which was named after an old friend of hers from Panama days, Colonel Sibert. She also worked as a consultant with the Girl Scouts. At the funeral, members of the Canton branch of the Odd Fellow order will serve in uniform as pallbearers, and a chorus of Rebekah lodge members will sing a hymn.

Madelaina [sic] Garrett will play the organ.

Kickbush, Anselm Harold Charles
Boulder City News, Thursday, 4 Nov 1993, 6:4.
Anselm Harold Charles Kickbush, 74, died Saturday, Oct. 30 in a local hospital. He was a three-year resident of Boulder City. He was born June 11, 1919 in Alma, Mich. and was a retired photographer. He was a member of Kiwanis in Tujunga, Calif. from 1944 - 1977 and from 1977 - 1990 in Kaneohe, Hawaii having served as President of the Kaneohe Club. He also served as Lt. Gov. of all Hawaiian clubs. He was a professional photographer in Tunjunga, Calif. for 33 years. He is survived by his wife, Virginia Rose Kickbush of Boulder City; a son, Bill Edward Kickbush of Las Vegas; a daughter, Denita Lynn Burns of California; a sister, Leota Kickbush of Owosso, Mich,; and five grandchildren, Brandon of Las Vegas, and Brian, Richard, Autumn and Sharlene of Lancaster, Calif. Graveside services were held. Arrangements were handled by Palm Mortuary of Henderson.

Kilday, Duncan McKenzie "Irish"
Boulder City News, Thursday, 25 Jan 1973.
By Esther Shipp
Duncan McKenzie "Irish" Kilday, 73, was laid to rest Saturday afternoon in the Boulder City Cemetery, with military rites by American Legion Post 31, of which he was a member. The funeral service had previously been conducted at the Elks Hall by BPOE Lodge 1682, to which he also belonged. Active and honorary pallbearers were Paul Klann, Herb Knauss, George LeFevre, Herbert Quinn, Winfield Clark, Lee Maddox, Oliver Leone, Antone Rua, Guy Brungardt, Denzie Pease, LeGrande Hardy, Marwood Doud, Perlie Morris, Tom Godbey and Ed Friedlan. Music was provided by Rosa Wagner and Linda Cooper. Irish died last Tuesday night at the Boulder City Hospital, after a full life which began in Dundee, Scotland, Jan. 3, 1900. The Kilday family moved to the United States when Irish was a small child. He attended school in New York and Connecticut. He joined the U.S. Army in 1918, and became a naturalized citizen while at Camp Seveir, South Carolina. He served in the 90th infantry division until the end of World War I. He worked as a mechanic's helper in New York City, then re-enlisted in the Army in the Motor Transport Repair Unit 306 and was stationed in Maryland and New York. After his discharge, he returned to Connecticut, but later helped in

the wheat harvest in the midwest before moving to Texas. From 1923 to 1930, he was employed by Ford Motor Co. in Dallas as packer, stock clerk, and order filler. Next, he owned a service station in Ballinger, but closed it to go with construction companies in Waco, Texas; Long Beach, Calif.; and finally, Las Vegas, Nevada. From 1933 until 1936 he worked for Six Companies during construction of Hoover Dam. March 2, 1936, he was hired by the Bureau of Reclamation as jackhammer operator, and was transferred to the position of storekeeper in 1939. From storekeeper and clerk, he was promoted to garage superintendent in April, 1950. Next he became general supply clerk, the position he held until he retired in September, 1965. Ten years ago, Irish had radical surgery to remove a lung, but, after a necessary "vacation," he continued to work and remain active in community affairs. After his retirement, one favorite recreation was playing cards with his many friends. He is survived by his widow, Stella, 424 Avenue B; two daughters, Dorothy Kirby and Duncann Tyson, both of Phoenix, Ariz.; three grandchildren and two great-grandchildren. Also two sisters, Peg Duplaine of Norfolk, Va., and Louise Kirby of Los Angeles, Calif.

King, Ethel C.
Boulder City News, Thursday, 3 May 1990, 22:3.
Ethel C. King, 77, a Boulder City resident since 1976, died April 24. Born on July 25, 1912 in Barstow, Calif., she was a housewife. She is survived by a daughter, Claudia Colyar; two granddaughters, Jeni Colyar and Julie Harris; a grandson, David Colyar; three great grandsons, Jesse Colyar and Adam Beach, all of Boulder City. Private services were held. Palm Mortuary handled arrangements.

Kinney, Herbert Clyde
Boulder City News, Thursday, 16 Nov 1972.
Graveside services were held yesterday at Boulder City Cemetery. Palm Mortuary was in charge of arrangements. Herbert Clyde Kinney, 644 Avenue L, died Monday in a local hospital. He was born in Minneapolis, Minnesota, on March 13, 1895, and had lived in the area for six years. He was a retired heavy equipment operator, a veteran of WWI and a member of V.F.W. Post 3574 of Boulder City. Survivors include his widow, Ina, of the family residence; two daughters, Vivian Gustafson, of Seattle, Washington, and Charlotte Betlack, Cary, Illinois; a son, Clyde E., of

Bowie, Maryland; a sister, Louise Logue, Spokane, Washington; also six grandchildren.

Kirchman, John Robert
Boulder City News, Thursday, 15 Feb 1990, 20:1-2.
John Kirchman, age 77, passed away Sunday February 11, 1990 in a local hospital. He was an 18 year resident of Boulder City, born September 25, 1912 in Wahoo, Nebraska. He was a retired records clerk for the U.S. Government and a World War II Army Veteran. He had been employed for the Department of Agriculture for 25 years, the Office of Defense Mobilization for 3 years and for the Veterans Administration in Washington, D.C. He leaves two sisters Jane Dailey of Boulder City, Arlene Garrett of Dallas, Texas and a nephew James Dailey. A Rosary Service was held in Palm Chapel Henderson on Tuesday with graveside services on Wednesday at the Boulder City Cemetery.

Kirchman, Lila A.
Boulder City News, Thursday, 13 Oct 1977, 5:7-8.
Lila A. Kirchman, 91 passed away October 12. She was born August 12, 1886 in Weston, Nebraska and had resided in Boulder City for the past five years. Mrs. Kirchman lived at 840 Cottonwood and was a homemaker. She was a member of the Altar Society at St. Andrew's Church. Survivors include a son, John Kirchman of Boulder City; daughters, Arlene Garrett of Dallas, Texas and Mary Jane Dailey of Boulder City; brothers, Donald D. Campbell of Monterey, California and James R. Campbell of Wahoo, Nebraska; seven grand children and 18 great grandchildren. Rosary will be said this evening at 7:30 p.m., Palm Chapel and a Mass will be celebrated at 10 a.m. Friday at St. Andrew's Church. Interment will take place at Boulder City Cemetery.

Kirkpatrick, Josephine C.
Boulder City News, Thursday, 8 July 1976, 3:8.
Josephine C. Kirkpatrick, 85, died July 1 in the Boulder City Hospital. Rosary was held Monday night at Palm Chapel in Henderson, and the Funeral Mass was conducted Tuesday morning at St. Andrew's Catholic Church in Boulder City. Father Hugh Smith officiated at both services. Burial was in the Boulder City Cemetery. Mrs. Kirkpatrick was born May

18, 1891 in St. Louis, Missouri. For many years she was a seamstress and also worked in the interior decorating field. She has lived in this area for 13 years. She was a member of the St. Andrew's Altar Society, and the Third Order of Saint Francis. She is survived by her daughter, Jane Sullivan, with whom she resided at 621 Kings Place, three grandchildren (including Suzanne Sullivan), and seven great-grandchildren.

Klann, Elsie M.
Boulder City News, Thursday, 2 Sep 1993, 10:3-4.
Elsie M. Klann, 83, died Tuesday, Aug. 24, in a local convalescent home. She was a 51-year resident of Boulder City. She was born Sept. 2, 1909 in Thompsonville, Mich. She was a retired treasurer/manager of the Boulder City Credit Union having worked there over 20 years. She was a volunteer and treasurer of Boulder City Hospital Auxiliary, a member of the Credit Union Executive Society, and director of the Nevada Credit Union League and Credit Union National Association. She is survived by two son, Gary Klann of Henderson, and David Klann of San Antonio, Texas; four grandchildren; and one great-grandchildren. Services were held Saturday at Palm Henderson Chapel. Arrangements were handled by Palm Mortuary of Henderson.

Klemmer, Raymond
Boulder City News, Thursday, 16 May 1974, 5:4.
Raymond Klemmer Services Held
Funeral services were held Wednesday at the Palm Chapel in Henderson for Raymond Klemmer, 53. The rites were conducted by Father Clark Tea, of St. Jude's Ranch. Burial was in the Boulder City Cemetery. Mr. Klemmer died Sunday morning of an apparent heart attack. He was born August 1, 1920 in New York City, N.Y., but moved west many years ago. He and Patricia Keith met and married in Phoenix and lived there before coming to Boulder City three years ago. Mr. Klemmer was employed by the Dura-Kool Awning Co. in Las Vegas, and also worked as a part time bartender at Herb's Recreation Tavern in Boulder City. Pat is a nurse in the office of Dr. John Connolly. They bowled in the local Monday league, and like to go fishing. He is survived by his wife, Pat, of Lakeshore Trailer Village; two sons, Raymond of Phoenix, Ariz. and Brent, Boulder City; three daughters, Deanna Page, Kathleen Scherrer and Janet Moen, all of Phoenix; two stepsons, Richard Keith III and William Keith, also of

Phoenix; and 9 grandchildren.

Klinger, John A.
Boulder City News, Thursday, 14 Feb 1985, 32:1.
John A. Klinger, 80, passed away February 11 in Henderson. He was born Feb. 11, 1905 in McCarthay, Pa. He lived in Boulder City and was a former scrap metal dealer. He is survived by his wife Bessie of Buffalo, NY.; daughter Jean Dumais, Buffalo, NY; several nieces, nephews, and grandchildren. Graveside services will be held Friday at 11 a.m. at the Boulder City Cemetery.

Klinger, Roy Arthur
Boulder City News, Thursday, 29 Mar 1990, 11:3-4.
Roy Arthur Klinger, 56, died March 20, 1990, in Boulder City. A lifeline resident of the community, he was born in Boulder City on March 1, 1934, and was a machinist/machine shop operator. He was a veteran, having served in the U.S. Army. He was a member of the B.P.O. Elks. Survivors include his mother, Sarah Klinger; three sisters, Patricia Klinger, Betty Smith and Doris Gault; a brother, son Michael Klinger, a daughter, Kristina Klinger, all of Boulder City, Nevada. Graveside services were held on Mar. 22 at the Boulder City cemetery. Arrangements were handled by Palm Mortuary, Henderson.

Knauss, Herbert
Boulder City News, Thursday, 24 Mar 1980, 3:6-8.
Long-Time Boulder Resident Passes Away
Services will be conducted at 10 a.m. Friday at Palm Chapel for Herbert "Herb" Knauss, 68, who died Tuesday in Boulder City. The Reverend Joe Anese of St. Andrews Catholic Church will officiate. Other officiants include members of the Elks Lodge, Veterans of Foreign Wars and the American Legion. Mr. Knauss was born in Salt Lake City March 18, 1912. He was the owner of Herb's Recreation Tavern in Boulder City and have lived in Southern Nevada since 1942. He served in the army during World War II. He was a member of Elks Lodge No. 1956, Veterans of Foreign Wars Port No. 3574, American Legion Post No. 31, the Boulder City Chamber of Commerce and United Commercial Travellers. Mr. Knauss is survived by his wife, Frances Knause of Boulder City; two sons, Clark of Sparks, Nevada, and Richard of Arizona; a daughter,

Gretchen Thomas of Las Vegas, a stepson, Roger Stahl of Las Vegas; a sister, Afton Dresskell of Colorado; and three grandchildren. Burial will be in Boulder City Cemetery.

Knauss, Minnie E.
Boulder City News, Thursday, 4 Nov 1976, 9:1-2.
Mrs. Minnie E. Knauss, of 712 Ave. B, passed away in the Boulder City Hospital during the morning hours of October 31, 1976. The mother of Herbert H. Knauss, she had resided in Boulder City two years. Most of her life was spent in Butte, Montana. She was a homemaker; a member of the American Legion Auxiliary of Boulder City; and a charter member of the United Congressional Church of Butte, Montana, in which Guild she was active until moving to Boulder City. She was predeceased by her husband, Herbert Knauss, who died October 20, 1934. She was born to Mr. Crellin and Annie Henzie Crellin, Sept. 3, 1882, in West Point, Nebraska. Survivors are; one son, Herbert H. Knauss of Boulder City; one daughter, Mrs. Afton Dresskell, Denver, Colorado; two sisters, Mrs. Nellie Gale of Spokane, Washington, and Lillie Stoecker, Butte, Montana; five grandchildren; and 6 great grandchildren. Services were held Wednesday, Nov. 3, at 10 a.m. at Palm Chapel Henderson. Father Herbert A. Ward, Jr., of St. Jude's Ranch for Children, in Boulder City officiated. Burial was at Boulder City Cemetery in Lieu of flowers, please send donations to the Boulder City Hospital.

Knighton, Howard H.
Boulder City News, Thursday, 5 May 1966, p.1:3.
H. Knighton Rites Today
Funeral services will be conducted at 2:30 this afternoon at Grace Community Church for Howard H. Knighton, 66, 615 California Ave., who passed away Monday. Mr. Knighten was born in Fairfield, Neb., Feb., 1900, was a retired diamond core driller and had lived in this area for 27 years. He was a member of Collinsville Lodge 132, A. F. & M. Survivors are his widow, Madeline; sons Howard Jr., Christmas Mine, Ariz., and Kirk, Las Vegas, daughter, Mrs. James McGee, of Las Vegas; brother, A. R., Collinsville, Okla.; sisters, Mrs. Hazel Bunch, Collisnville; Mrs. Charles Hendrick, San Diego; grandson, James McGee, Jr., Las Vegas. Reverend Guy Holliday will officiate at the service and burial will be in the local cemetery.

Koenig, Arnold "Joe"

Boulder City News, Thursday, 28 Jul 1983, p.2:4-7.

Boulder City resident Arnold C. "Joe" Koenig passed away the morning of July 22, 1983 after a brief illness at Southern Nevada Memorial Hospital. Funeral rites were held at Palm Mortuary in Henderson, Nev. on Monday July 25 and were attended by many of Joe's friends, associates and family. Eulogy was delivered by Reverend John Osko of Henderson, Nev. Survivors include his sons John Koenig of Littleton, Colorado, David Koenig of Henderson, Nevada and two grand-daughters of Yreka, California and Sepulveda, Calif. Joe was born in Knox County, Indiana on Feb. 9, 1909 to John and Hester Koenig, also of Indiana. Although his family had extensive coal mining interests in the area, Joe moved from Indiana to So. Calif. with the advent of World War II in 1941. Joe worked in the defense industry with Douglas Aircraft until the end of World War II, following which he established a tree removal and trimming business. Joe moved to Boulder City in 1962 where he acquired property, was active in civic affairs, and established Boulder City Tree Service and Boulder City Building Materials. Joe quickly acquired a reputation for fairness and honesty with those he dealt with and earned the respect of his fellow businessmen for his strict adherence to a code of ethics and honor and for trust in his fellow man. Frequently, many of his business agreements were sealed in the time honored tradition of a simple handshake. John had a penchant for dawn-to-dusk hard work at 100% effort and efficiency which resulted in many of his younger employees astonishment. Keeping alive the "good Samaritan" tradition, Joe frequently took in many unfortunate people stranded in the area. Joe loved the community and the good people in it. His business interests will be assumed by his son John and Davis, who ask for the patience of Joe's many customers and business associates during the transition while they try to fill a very large pair of shoes. Inquiries should be addressed to : P. O. Box 422, Boulder City, Nevada 89005.

Koerner, Charles A.
Boulder City News, Thursday, 15 Feb 1979, 36: 5-7.
A requiem mass will be held this morning at St. Andrew's Church at 9 a.m. for Charles A. Koerner, 75, who passed away in Boulder City on Tuesday. Mr. Koerner was born June 16, 1903 in Waterloo, Iowa. He had resided in Boulder City for 15 years and had been employed as an electrical engineer for the Bureau of Reclamation. He was a member of the Boulder City BPOE. He is survived by his wife, Eva, of Boulder City; one son, Charles A. Koerner, Jr. And six grandchildren. The Reverend Joseph Anese will officiate at the services and interment will be at Boulder City Cemetery.

Korfman, Michelle
Henderson Home News & Boulder City News, Thursday, 21 June 1984, p. 24:1-4
Many attend services for Michelle Korfman
St. Andrews Catholic Church was filled beyond capacity Tuesday as a crowd estimated at 700 persons gathered to pay final tribute to 17 year old Michelle Korfman who disappeared from the Meadows Mall in Las Vegas on April 1 following a fashion show. Believed to be a victim of mass murderer Christopher Wilder who shot himself to death after being cornered in New Hampshire on April 13, the body of the popular teenager was discovered on May 11 by two hikers in the Angeles Mountains northeast of Los Angeles. However, positive identification was not made until last Friday morning. Fr. Joe Annese officiated at the services which were attended by schoolmates, friends and many who had assisted in the many weekend searches since Michelle's disappearance. Pallbearers included Mike Polignone, Mike Ramsey, Joe Kervrat, Tony Kerbrat, Ron Maloney and Dick Robinson. Interment was in Boulder City Cemetery. Scholarship established. A scholarship fund has been established in Michelle's name at the Boulder City branch of Valley bank. Korfman says the fund will be used to give scholarships to graduating seniors at Boulder City High School. Michelle was an honor roll student at BCHS and participated on the volleyball and drill teams. She was a member of the senior graduating class.

Korn, Vada Lou
Boulder City News, Thursday, 10 Dec 1964, 1:2.
Services To Be Friday For Mrs. Vada Korn
Funeral services for Mrs. Vada Lou Korn will be held Friday at 2 p.m. at the Masonic Temple. Members of Eastern Star of which Mrs. Korn was a member will conduct the services. Burial will be at the Boulder City Cemetery with Reverend Larry Hendrickson officiating. Mrs. Korn died Dec. 8 at Boulder City Hospital at the age of 53. She is survived by her husband Bill Korn and one daughter, Cynthia Lou, both of Boulder City, also a brother, V. C. Youngblood of Portland, Ore. Mrs. Korn was also a member of B.P.O. Does No. 34. The Korns had lived in Boulder City for seven years. They owned the Desert Trails.

Kowalski, Edward Bernard
Boulder City News, Thursday, 3 May 1979, p. 7.
Edward Bernard Kowalski, 55, passed away April 25 at the Boulder City Hospital. He had been a resident of Boulder City since December of 1977. Mr. Kowalski was born July 25, 1923 in LaSalle, Illinois and was a superintendent in the aircraft industry. He was a World War II Navy veteran and he was also a member of the Society of Veterans at Pearl Harbor. He is survived by his wife, Rose Marie, of Boulder City; a daughter, Sharon Beebe of Phoenix, Arizona; sisters, Katherine Pagora and Eleanor Scerini, both of Illinois, and Virginia Falk of California; and two grandchildren. Services were held last Saturday at St. Andrew's Catholic Church with the Reverend Joseph Anese officiating. Burial was at the Boulder City cemetery.

Krause, Beverly
Boulder City News, Thursday, 30 Oct 1986, 13:3.
Beverly Krause, 66, died Sunday, Oct. 26 in Boulder City. She was born in Los Angeles, Calif., on Sept. 21, 1920 and had resided in Boulder City for the past 12 years. Survivors include three sisters, Carol Weaver of Portland, Ore.; Janet Acquist of Los Angeles, Calif.; also two brothers, William Baird of Glendale, Calif. and Walter Baird of Azusa, Calif. Services are scheduled at Palm Mortuary in Henderson at 7 p.m. tonight. Private graveside services will be held Friday.

Lamb, Clarence I.
Boulder City News, Thursday, 15 Feb 1990, 20:1-4.
Clarence I. Lamb, 84, a long-time resident of Boulder City, died Tuesday, Feb. 6, 1990. Born March 1, 1905, in Ballard, Wash., he was an engineer. He was a member of the Knights of Columbus, 4th degree. Survivors include his wife, Edith Lamb, of Boulder City; three sons, Michael Bartlett of Orange County, Calif., Walter Bartlett of Riverside, Calif. and Frank Bartlett of Costa Mesa, Calif.; eight grandchildren and one great grandchild. Services were held. Palm Mortuary handled arrangements.

Lamb, Marvin D.
Boulder City News, Thursday, 11 Mar1992, 10:1-2.
Marvin D. Lamb, 44, a six year Boulder City resident, died Tuesday, March 10 in a local hospital. Born in What Cheer, Iowa on April 24, 1948, he was a contract specialist with the Bureau of Reclamation. He was a U.S. Air Force veteran of the Viet Nam war. He is survived by his wife, Dahlene C. Lamb and a son, Brandon Lamb, both of Boulder City; his mother, Lucy Lamb of Des Moines, Iowa; a sister, Susan Andeway of Anchorage, Alaska; a brother, Lyle Lamb of South English, Iowa; and a father-in-law, John Westen of Boulder City. Viewing services will be held from 12 to 5 p.m., Friday, March 12 at the Palm Henderson Mortuary. Funeral services will be a 1 p.m., Saturday, March 13 in the Palm Mortuary Chapel. Interment will be in the Boulder City Cemetery. Arrangements were handled by Palm Mortuary of Henderson.

Lanska, David
Boulder City News, Thursday, 20 Jan 1994, 11:3-4.
David Lanska, 20, a Henderson resident, died Jan. 11, 1994. Lanska was born Oct. 11, 1973, in Picayune, Miss. He was a 1992 graduate of Boulder City High School and was employed by a local restaurant. He is survived by his mother, Noy Lanska of Henderson; father, Charles Lanska of Boulder City, a brother, John Lanska and a sister, Chelsea Caless of Las Vegas and his stepmother Beverly Lanska of Boulder City.

LaPlante, Adrian
Boulder City News, Thursday, 21 Apr 1994, 6:1-2.
Adrian LaPlante, 87, died April 15, 1994, in a local hospital. Born Sept. 27, 1906, in New Bedford, Mass., he had been a resident of the Boulder City area since 1966 and was a veteran of the United States Army serving during World War II. He is survived by his wife, Olive LaPlante of Boulder City; a daughter, Marilyn Buckhart of Boulder City; a sister, Loretta Eagan of Hartford, Conn.; two brothers, Joe LaPlante of Jewett, Conn. and Emile LaPlante of New London, Conn.; and three grandchildren. Prayer services were held yesterday. Mass services will be held at 10 a.m. today at St. Andrews Catholic Church. Arrangements were handled by Palm Mortuary in Henderson.

Leavitt, Margie F.
Boulder City News, Thursday, 29 June 1978, 2:4-6.
Margie F. Leavitt, 605 Wyoming Street Boulder City, beloved wife of Grant J. Leavitt passed away June 27 in Boulder City. Mrs. Leavitt was born at Pima, Arizona on Nov. 5, 1922. She was married and sealed to Grant J. Leavitt on Dec. 21, 1946 at the St. George Temple. Mrs. Leavitt was very active in the L.D.S. Church with particular emphasis in music. Survivors include her husband, Grant; sons Danny and Earl; daughters Bonnie and Cherie; also seven grandchildren. Funeral services will be held at the Church of Jesus Christ of Latter Day Saints, 5th Street Boulder City, Nevada. Date and time is pending. Funeral arrangement will be made through Bunker Brothers Mortuary.

Leavitt, Mary Ann
Boulder City News, Thursday, 13 Nov 1975, 2:3.
Funeral services were held Saturday morning for Mary Ann Leavitt, 26, who died Tuesday at the Boulder City Hospital, after a long illness. The rites were conducted by Bishop Kenneth Simkins at the Boulder City Ward of the Church of Jesus Christ of Latter-Day Saints. Burial was in the Boulder City Cemetery. Mary Ann Hooper was born May 18, 1949 on Staten Island, New York, but later moved to the southern states. The Hooper family came to Nevada from Tennessee on Aug. 6, 1961. She did clerical work for the U. S. Navy. Mary Ann and Earl K. Leavitt (the son of Grant Leavitt) were married July 4, 1970, in Boulder City. In addition

to her husband, she is survived by three sons, Mathew David, Michael Earl, and Mark Andrew, all of 612 Avenue C. Also her parents, Mr. and Mrs. Ralph Hooper of Bridgeport, W. Va.; brothers Jim, Cerritos, Calif.; William, Knoxville, Tenn.; Eugene, Maytown, Penn.; Ralph, Bridgeport, W. Va.; two sisters, Charlene Powers, Simi Valley, Calif.; and Rozanne Hooper of Bridgeport, West Virginia.

Lechner, Sara L.
Boulder City News, Thursday, 21 Dec 1978, 2:7.
Sara L. Lechner Dies
A funeral mass was held last Tuesday for Sara L. Lechner, 73, who passed away December 15 at a Las Vegas hospital. Mrs. Lechner had been a housekeeper at the rectory at St. Andrew's Catholic Church in Boulder City three years. She was born November 18, 1905 in Oklahoma. Survivors include a daughter, Lela Mulligan of Boulder City; a son, Orville D. Dyer of Galt, California; a sister, Kathy Scholl of Huntington Park, California; three grandchildren and five great-grandchildren. Interment was at the Boulder City Cemetery.

Leonard, John
Boulder City News, Tuesday, 1 Jul 1947.
Funeral services for John Leonard were held at 10 a.m. today at St. Andrews Catholic Church. Reverend John J. Ryan officiated at the low mass, and preached a brief sermon. The choir sang hymns, and Mrs. Joe Manix and Mike Slattery sang solos. Pall bearers were Harry Rayner, Luke Whalen, Roy Cole, William Dossett and R. W. Manning. Burial was in Boulder City Cemetery. Leonard died last Thursday of heart disease at the age of 59. He is survived by three daughters, Mrs. Rulen G. Ostensen of Boulder City, Mrs. John Munds of Torrence and Laberta Leonard of Corona, Calif., and a son, Lionel Leonard, a student at University of Nevada.

LeSchander, Ruth S. MacPherson
Boulder City News, Thursday, 18 Jan 1990, 26:2.
Ruth S. MacPherson LeShander, 82, a long-time resident of Boulder City died Wednesday. Born Nov. 23, 1907 in Rehrersburg, Penn., she was a bookkeeper and dental hygienist. She was a member of Eastern Star. Survivors include her daughter, Kay M. Chipman of Boulder City; four grandchildren and three great grandchildren. Services will be held at 10 a.m. Saturday, Jan. 20 at Boulder City Cemetery. Nevada Cremation and Burial Society will handle arrangements.

LeVan, William Mack
Boulder City News, Thursday, 8 Mar 1990, 12:1-2.
William Mack LeVan, 60, a resident of Boulder City since 1988, died Thursday, March 1, in Boulder City. Born in Sidney, Ohio, on May 17, 1929, he was an operating engineer in the construction industry. He is survived by his wife Stella Levan of Boulder City; and sister Pat Kingsley, Mesa, Ariz. Memorial Mass was held at St. Andrews Catholic Church in Boulder City on Friday. The family suggests that memorials be made in his name to: The American Lung Association.

Lewis, Anne
Boulder City News, Thursday, 16 Aug 1956, 4:4.
Final Rites Held For Mrs. Lewis
Final rites for Mrs. Anne Lewis, 55, of 612 Avenue G were held last Friday at the St. Andrews Catholic church. Burial was in the Boulder City Cemetery and pall bearers were Russell Farnsworth, Paul Wilson, Doc Hiller, Al Burt, Don Jones and John Layton. Mrs. Lewis passed away Aug. 8 in the Boulder City Community Hospital where she had been confined for about 10 days for treatment of a heart ailment. She and her husband, Frank, local carpenter, had been residents of Boulder City for 23 years. In addition to her husband, survivors include two sons, Edward Snyder of Boulder City and Roy Snyder of the state of Washington; a daughter, Mrs. Fred Jess, of Washington; and a sister, Mrs. Beth Stoker of Boulder City.

Lewis, Beverly E.
Boulder City News, Thursday, 15 Jan 1981, 4:8.
Funeral services for Beverly E. Lewis, 88, were held last Sunday afternoon at Palm Chapel. Bill Belknap, Christian Science Reader, officiated. Mrs. Lewis died January 9 in Boulder City. She was born September 28, 1892 in Syracuse, New York, and had lived in the Vegas Valley area for 45 years. She was a member of the Christian Science Church of Boulder City. She is survived by one granddaughter, Sheila Huff of Texas; a nephew, Ervin J. Nelson of Las Vegas; four great-grandchildren and one great grandchild. Interment was in Boulder City Cemetery.

Lewis, Bob
Boulder City News, Thursday, 1 Feb 1979, 11:1-8.
The sun came out and the day was the kind Nevada is famous for as friends of Bob Lewis for close to 50 years filed in the chapel at the Palm Funeral Home in Henderson to say goodbye to a brave soldier who had led a long and courageous career as a civic worker and volunteer par excellence for his entire life in Boulder City. Bob Lewis was buried last Monday with many honors. Helen Lewis, his widow, Beverly Mackie, his daughter, his three sisters, Irma Anderson, Chula Vista, Cal. Ireta Banks and Ellen Thomas of Spanish Oaks, his brother-in-law, Bishop Banks, four grandchildren and four great grandchildren, were visibly touched by the impressive services that had been arranged by his brothers of the Knights of the Pythias, and the eulogy by his friend, Leonard Stubbs, was awe inspiring. Bob left us on Jan. 25, 1979. He was born July 26, 1900 in Spanish Fork, Utah. His long life had held more happiness than most people can say about their own. Every honor that fell his was well-earned and given with a full and generous heart. In this story of his career and his dedication to his beloved family and to his hundreds of close friends, we will see a repeated pattern of loving kindness, of Goodwill to Men. A never to be forgotten funeral service. From the time of the orders beginning, the Knights of Pythias have bed goodbye to their fallen brothers with a service conducted by a funeral team from among its highest officers. For Bob Lewis, there was something special added. From Reno there arrived Past Grand Chancellor, William Hyde, Past Grand Chancellor, Robert Hess, and with the assistance of Bob's dear friend, LeRoy Burt, all of them remembering Bob with love and appreciation for

his long years of service to their order, they poured their very deep emotions into every word and gesture. Past Grand Chancellor, Teague Well sang "How Great Thou Art" and after his splendid voice has stilled there was a long silence, a pin could have dropped and been hears. When the services were over every one crowded around Teague saying they never heard the song express such a wonderful meaning for an occasion. Pall Bearers were LeRoy Burt, Arthur Patton, Joe Gallio, his grandson, Joe Kine, McWane Stucki and Hermany Guidry. Leonard Stubbs, a long time Bishop of the Mormon Church, but now elevated to Present of the Henerson, Nevada stake, is a friend and admirer of Bob Lewis, the relationship dates back to when Leonard was a growling youth and Bob was assistant postmaster of the Boulder City Post Office. Helen Lewis and Leonard Stubbs shared memories of her beloved companion. The eulogy was straight from President's Stubbs memory of a good and decent man. The NEWS acknowledges the loan of President Stubb's material while at the same time we know space will not permit the full use of every word. The wedding of the young people, on Aug. 8, 1923, was followed by Bob's transfer from the McGill postoffice to the Boulder City P.O. in the early 30's. We have a picture of Bob Lewis surrounded by his co-workers, among them Pops Doolittle and Jimmie Lee (both of whom had served as postmasters of the Boulder City P.O.) and on either side there were young women helping cancel the first day issue of the "Boulder Dam" stamp with a picture of the dam emblazoned across its face. Bob belonged to the Knights of the Pythias for 39 years. He was the Grand Chancellor, the highest rank at a state level, and Supreme Outer Guard, which is a National Rank. He took great pride in the organization and he and his wife, Helen, traveled, not only though out Nevada but to all the bordering states as well. Their companions and closest friends on every trip were Lucille and LeRoy Burt. The two men held down the same ideals. The couples shared, also a great love of sports, and attending a ball game was as natural to Bob and his friends as it was to do a good deed for a neighbor in need. It was at a ball-game that Bob first spotted his wife to be, Helen Shupp, known to her friends as "Tiny" or "Squirt" and sitting beside her, and introducing himself, our Bob swept her off her feet and right to the marriage that was to end in death after 56 happy years. Leonard was to say this: "To the old timers of Boulder City, Bob is a legacy of friendship and love. As a youth I remember experiencing a feeling of thanks for his kind "hello" as he would greet us at work or on the street, and he remembered us all by our first name. Loved and enjoyed us without hesitation. With him we think of Dusty Rhoades, Mr. Orton, Bryce Ballard and my own father, Mr. Al Stubbs. Those men so long remembered for their work at the post office, taught us integrity, dependability, and trust, by setting the example. Bob worked for the Federal Service 31 years. He worked his way thru two years at the U. of Utah. His first job was at the smelter plant at Ruth, Nevada where he assayed the ore. After retiring from the B.C. postoffice as assistant postmaster, Bob went to work for the state employment office. The driving aggravated him and he eagerly accepted employment for the late Johnny Manis, manager of Earl Brother's Tourist Bureau and his station at Hoover Dam became known by tourists far and wide. His knowledge of this area plus his always friendly willingness to serve the public was to make a lot of friends for Nevada while he worked as a volunteer public relations friend to the visitors. Bob was a charter member of Lake Mead Lodge No. 37 Knights of the Pythias and a charter member also of the Lion's Club, for which he served as the first president and served as the first Chancellor Commander of the Knights of the Pythias. Bob was active in Boy Scout work, serving on the executive board of the Boulder Dam Area Council. He served on the local hospital board and at one time headed the Boulder City Welfare Board. This salute from the Esther Shipp files shows several impressive pictures of Bob in various public service. The B. C. Welfare Association was formed to give emergency relief from the United Fund. In 1858, Bob was elected president, taking over the office from the late, great Chief (Charles Peterson. Bob is buried in the Boulder City Cemetery. From Spanish Fork, Utah, Robert Lewis's brother-in-law, Bishop Banks dedicated the grave. Helen Lewis, you have been so brave through out this long illness. We will remember Bob forever. Your wish that all of us give to our favorite charity, of the library, or the Boulder City hospital will be honored. However, let us remember Bob's devotion to the Knights of the Pythias Retarded Children's Project. A donation to that worthy cause would be his favorite. Helen would want us to thank everyone for the concern they have shown for Bob and for her own welfare. The NEWS could not have printed this wonderful tribute to Bob Lewis without the help of his close friends, LeRoy and Lucille Burt. The warmth he spread everywhere and the journeys the families made to serve the Knights of the Pythias would cover our entire paper. We pioneers will not be long joining Bob Lewis and all the other friends who lie in the Boulder City graveyard, We can only say, "Until We Meet Again."

Lewis, Clair Raymond

Boulder City News, Thursday, 19 Oct 1972.

Funeral services for Chaire Raymond Lewis, 56, who died Monday at Boulder City Hospital, will be 11 a.m. Thursday at Bunker Brothers Chapel. Interment will follow in Boulder City Cemetery. Mr. Lewis, an electrician at Hoover Dam, was born Dec. 24, 1915 in Lincoln, Ia. He had lived in this area the past 30 years, his last address being 131 Elm, Henderson. He served in the Army during World War Two. He is survived by his wife, Jean E. Lewis of Henderson; brother, Don Lewis of Albert, Ia.; and four sisters, Dorothy Moyer of Seattle, Helen Wilson and Stella Lewis of Des Moines and Cathy Husman, who lived in Texas.

Lewis, Jessie

Boulder City News, Thursday, 12 Jul 1979, 6:5.

Graveside services were held Monday morning at the Boulder City Cemetery for Jessie Lewis, 90, who passed away July 4 in Las Vegas. She was born May 8, 1889 in Stockton, Illinois, and was a homemaker and a member of the Eastern Star, Desert Chapter #22. Mrs. Lewis is survived by William Bishop of Elizabeth, Illinois and Earl Michael of Atchison, Kansas. Dr. Melvin Pritts of the Grace Community Church officiated.

Lewis, Sterling

Boulder City News, Thursday, 7 Feb 1980, 6:3.

Funeral services will be held Saturday at Palm Chapel at 2 p.m. for Sterling Lewis, 65, who passed away February 5 in Boulder City. Mr. Lewis was born May 12, 1914 in Manmouth, Utah and had been a resident of Boulder City for 18 years. He had been a funeral trust salesman. He is survived by his wife, Beverly Lewis of Boulder City; brothers, J. Earl Lewis of Provo, Utah, Kenneth and Dean Lewis of Salt Lake City; sister, Emily Natella of Salt Lake City; a nephew, Dr. Ervin Nelson of Las Vegas; and a niece, Janice Moyle of Salt Lake City. Interment will be at the Boulder City Cemetery.

Likens, Rodger Gene
Boulder City News, Thursday, 26 Jun 1980, 6:1-3.
Graveside services were held Thursday, June 19, in Boulder City for former Boulder City man Rodger Gene Likens, who passed away at his home in Portland, Oregon June 13. Mr. Likens was born in Kimball, Nebraska, January 2, 1936. The family moved to Boulder City when he was six months old. He graduated from Boulder City High School in 1954 and the Air Force Academy at Colorado Springs, Colorado Springs, Colorado in 1961 as a Second Lieutenant. While attending Boulder City High School, he was prominent in sports and was captain of the football team and co-captain of the basketball team, earning many honors in both sports. At the time of his death, he was owner of the Oregon Value and Fitting, Inc., an electronics company. He is survived by his mother, Margie Heaton, Boulder City; sister, Shirley Parker, San Francisco; Aunt and Uncle, Betty and Jake Garehime, Las Vegas, and several nieces and nephews. Pallbearers at the graveside services were William McCormick, Gordon Mills, Jack Caldwell, Ramon Williams, Herber Tobler, Russell Coggins, and honorary pallbearers, Dick Voss and Harry Torrence.

Linck, LaVona E.
Boulder City News, Thursday, 18 Mar 1992, 10:3.
LaVona E. Linck, 87, died March 10, 1993. Born July 14, 1905, in Midvale, Utah. Linck was a resident of the Boulder City area for 52 years. She was a member of the Boulder City LDS Chapel 2nd Ward, Bolder City Bridgers, and the Boulder City Women's Club. Linck is survived by her husband of 68 years, John H. Linck; a daughter, Luana L. Shamo; a son, Donald L. Linck, all of Boulder City; a brother, W.D. Clark of Salt Lake City, Utah; four grandchildren and 18 great grandchildren. Services were held Monday. Arrangements were handled by Palm Mortuary in Henderson.

Littler, Helen S.
Boulder City News, Thursday, 19 Sep 1985, 29:1-2.
Helen S. Littler, a resident since 1939, passed away Friday, Sept. 20. She was born Jan. 19, 1902 in Carlyle, Ill. and was a homemaker. She leaves two sons, William of Boulder City and Theodore of McKinleyville, Calif.; five grandchildren and seven great-grandchildren. A rosary was said Sunday at St. Andrews Catholic Church. The funeral mass was Monday morning. Interment is in the Boulder City Cemetery.

Littler, Shirley
Boulder City News, Thursday, 30 Sep 1976, 12:4-5.
Mrs. David F. Littler of 1315 Colorado Street, passed away in the Boulder City Hospital on September 15, 1976, in the afternoon. Shirley Littler was born in Portales, New Mexico, September 3, 1934. She attended school in Avenal, California. She was a member of the Women's Bowling League, the B-Sharps of Las Vegas, the Rolling Boulders Travel Club, and Vegas Rolling Wheels Travel Club. Mrs. Littler is survived by her husband, David Littler; 2 sons, Danny Kitchens of South Carolina, and Charles (Chuck) Littler of Boulder City; 1 daughter, Linda Diann Carlton; 1 granddaughter, Amy Carlton; her mother, Mrs. W. E. Deatherage of Taft, Calif.; 3 brothers, Bill Bousman of Phoenix, Larry Bousman of Santa Barbara, and Jerry Bousman of Atascadero, California. Other out of town persons who attended the funeral were Mr. Littler's mother, Lydia Littler of Denver; Mr. Littler's brother, Otto Littler, Ignacio, Calif.; and Mrs. Littler's friend from Susanville, Calif., Joannie DeCamp. Family and friends from Boulder City and Las Vegas, and organization members also paid last respects at the funeral Saturday, Sept. 18, at 10 a.m. Reverend Holliday, of Grace Community Church, officiated at graveside services. Interment was at Boulder City Cemetery. Arrangements by Palm Mortuary, Henderson.

Littler, William S.
Boulder City News, Thursday, 16 Sep 1976, 1:3-4.
Bill Littler Passes Away in Las Vegas
William S. Littler, age 76, 1204 Fifth street, passed away at Sunrise Hospital Wed. morning. A resident of Boulder City for 37 years, he was a veteran of World War I. He was a retired government worker and has been retired for 17 years. He was born Feb. 15, 1900 in Cayuga, Ind. Survivors include his wife, Helen; sons Paul and Ted of Los Angeles, Bill, Jr. of Boulder City; five grandsons, four great grandchildren; sister, Ruth Hines, Englewood, Fla. Graveside services will be held Friday morning at 10 o'clock at the Boulder City cemetery.

Locks, Helen M.
Boulder City News, Thursday, 22 Apr 1993, 8:1.
Helen M. Locks, 72, died Thursday, April 15, 1993, in a local hospital. She was a homemaker and a resident of Henderson for 16 years. She is survived by four daughters, Carol Hall, Bullhead City, Ariz. Jeannie Higgins, Boulder City, Arlene Hendrickx and Luanna Locks Hauver of Seattle, Wash.; three sons, Ed, Las Vegas, Alan, Ketchikan, Alaska, and Tom, Wichita, Kans.; and 14 grandchildren. Arrangements were handled by Palm Mortuary.

Locks, Stephen J.
Boulder City News, Thursday, 4 Apr 1985, 20:5-6.
Stephen J. Locks, 71, passed away April 1 in Boulder City. He had lived here for the past seven years. Mr. Locks was born Dec. 29, 1913 in Minnesota. His usual occupation was laborer. He is survived by his wife, Helen M. of Boulder City; sons Leonard, San Francisco, CA., Ed, Las Vegas, Allan Ketchikan, Alaska, and Tom of Wichita, Kansas; daughters, Carol Hall, Bullhead, Az., Jeanne Higgins, Reno, Arlene Hendrikx, Seattle, Wa., and Luanne Hauver, Ketchikan, Alaska; and five brothers and sisters. Private services were held and interment was in Boulder City Cemetery. Palm Mortuary was in charge of arrangements.

Long, Charles W.
Boulder City News, Thursday, 26 Jul 1979, 3:2-3.
Funeral Rites Set for Charles W. Long
Charles Wm. Long, 41 years of age will be buried Friday July 27th in Boulder City. The funeral will be held at Trinity Temple, 1000 E. St. Louis, L.V. at 10 a.m. Graveside rites will then follow at B. C. Cemetery at 12 noon. Chuck was a partner in the El Rancho Boulder Motel and Claremont Heights Land Development. He was a member of Trinity Temple and a 16 yr. resident of So. Nevada. Surviving him are his wife, Olynnda, sons; Kevin 20 yrs. and Mahlon 13 yrs. His parents are Mr. and Mrs. Wm. Long and sister Judith Orr, of Battle Creek, Mich. The family asks that in lieu of flowers contributions be made to K.I.L.A. Christian Radio, Las Vegas.

Long, Frank Leo, Jr.
Boulder City News, Thursday, 24 May 1984, 30:4-7.
Frank Leo Long, Jr., a 48-year resident of Boulder City, passed away May 22 in Boulder City. Mr. Long was born in Missouri Dec. 30, 1909 and was the retired superintendent of the City of Los Angeles Department of Water and Power in Boulder City. Funeral services will be at 9:30 a.m. at the Boulder City Masonic Lodge. Burial will be in Boulder City Cemetery. Survivors include his wife, Pauline M. of Boulder City; daughter Paula G. Lemke of Las Vegas. He was a member of the Masonic Lodge No. 37 of Boulder City, and the Las Vegas Chapter of the Red Rock Audubon Society.

Long, Frank Leo, Jr.
Boulder City News, Thursday, 31 May 1984, 8:1-3.
Frank Long was a pioneer of Boulder City since 1936. In those years he was a happy man and in every way a valuable volunteer. In one clipping, 1953, an article mentioned that on June 18 "Frank Long, assistant resident Power Company Engineer was named to fill a vacancy left by the resignation of Dr. D. M. MacCormich. Other men serving on the school board were Ray Collins, L. R. Douglass, Peggy Hyde, and Elbert Edwards. The latter being Supt of Schools as well as the secretary of the School Board. Everett Cunningham was the board president. Mr. Lord and his wife Paula were known for their work in Rotary and Masonic

affairs the article stated. To Paula, and to your family, our entire community extends sympathy. To you and to Frank our town owes so much. The story that follows was on file at the Bureau of Power and Light. Your family will remember that happy day when Frank retired. "Boulder City – Frank L. Long, who has been superintendent of the Hoover Power Plant and Boulder System since October 1, 1966, was guest of honor at a retirement party Monday, at the Assembly Hall. He received a gift from his fellow workers and a memory book. Charles M. Hunter, assistant superintendent, was in charge. Long was born Dec. 30, 1909 in Doe Run, Missouri. He attended the Pasadena Junior College, then went to University of Southern California to receive his B.A. degree in Electrical Engineering in June, 1934. June 15, 1934, he began employment with the City of Los Angeles Department of Water and Power at San Francisco Canyon. September 1, 1936, he was transferred to the Hoover Power Plant in Boulder City. In June, 1942, he became Chief Operator, and in August 1953, was chief operator in charge of operations. In March, 1953 he became assistant superintendent and was promoted to superintendent in October 1966. The family has moved from No. 3 Hillside Dr. to their home at 500 Ave. M. Frank and his wife Pauline (Polly) have both been active all these years, and their daughter Paula is a graduate of Boulder City High School. The Longs belong to the Boulder Bridgers, and Frank photographs birds in correlation with Polly's expert knowledge in this field. She has served offices in the Hoe and Grow Club as well as the Women's Club and the Eastern Star. Frank has been active in the Rotary Club and the Masonic Order, and in 1953 was named to the Boulder City School Board."

Lucero, Lloyd
Boulder City News, Thursday, 30 Dec 1971.
Lloyd Lucero Dies In Utah Crash
Lloyd Lucero, 37, 504 Utah street, a former employee of Titanium Metals Corp., was found Tuesday near St. George, Utah, after the vehicle which he was driving, dropped about 150 feet over an embankment. Mr. Lucero had been missing since about Dec. 21 when he left to take Christmas presents to relatives in Utah. His brother, Reuben, also of Boulder City, said they had contacted the Highway Patrol, and other officials when he did not return home because he was always careful about telling them when he would be late or delayed. Services are pending at the LDS

Church, and arrangements are expected to be handled by Palm Mortuary in Henderson. Mr. Lucero had worked at TMCA for 19 years, but had recently been ieled by the layoffs there. He was working at the Rainbow Club in Henderson as a part-time dealer. He is survived by a wife Patricia; two brothers, Reuben and Fidel of Boulder City; and two sisters, Cora Jones, Las Vegas and Teresa Archuletta, Salt Lake City, Utah.

Lucero, Rosalie A.
Boulder City News, Thursday, 9 Mar 1995, 11:1-2.
Rosalie A. Lucero, 54, died Saturday, March 4, 1995. Born, Mary 13, 1940 in Moquah, Wisc., she was a resident of Boulder City for 26 years. She was a retired clothing manufacturing clerk. She is survived by her husband, Albert G. Lucero, of Boulder City; three daughters, Jo Ann Taylor, also of Boulder City; Debi Ells and Kim Herndon, both of Henderson; one son, Ricky, of Boulder City; seven sisters, Inez Trubachik, of Heppner, Ore.; Tillie Lunda, of Moquah, Wisx.; Georgia Sigl and Mary Trubachik, both of Hood River, Ore.; Helen Elinger, of Wstacada, Ore.; Lillian Russell, of South Bend, Wash,; and Susan Valasity, of Portage, Mich.; three brothers, Rudy Misun, of Moquah, Wisc.; Jack Misun, of Two Rivers, Wisc. Johnny Misun, of Ishpeming, Mich.; and five grandchildren. Arrangements were handled by Palm Mortuary of Henderson.

Lueking, Carl Leslie
Boulder City News, Thursday, 11 Sep 1958, 1:1.
Funeral services were held yesterday afternoon for Carl Leslie Lueking, 62, who died on Saturday at the Veteran's Hospital in Salt Lake City, after a long illness. The Reverend Walter Hanne of the First Presbyterian Church of Las Vegas officiated at the First Presbyterian Church of Las Vegas officiated at the Bunker Bros. Chapel. Interment followed at the Boulder City cemetery, with the graveside rites conducted by Post No. 31 of the American Legion. Lueking was born June 24, 1896 in Hustonia, Missouri. The Luekings came to Boulder City in early construction days, and for many years lived at 902 Wyoming Street until they moved to Paradise Valley a few years ago. A veteran of World War I, he was a charter member of the local Legion Post and the Boulder City 40 et 8 Club. He worked most recently at the Nellis AFB as a maintenance engineer. Lueking is survived by his wife Hazel, Rt. No. 1, 6025

Chapperal Road, Paradise Valley; two brothers, Fred of Los Angeles, California and G. W. of Kansas City, Missouri; and a sister, Mrs. V. W. Cerrington of Los Angeles. Pallbearers were Messrs. Fields Watts, G. Kuhle, Clarence Harris and Wallace of Nellis; and Walter Wright of Boulder City.

Luizzi, Nicola
Boulder City News, Thursday, 13 Oct 1983, 14:3-4.
Nicola Luizzi, 77, died Tuesday in Las Vegas. He was a resident of Boulder City for four years. Born in Los Angeles, CA on Nov. 24, 1906, he was a retired painter. Survivors include wife, Madeline, of Boulder City; son Frank, of Los Angeles; daughter, Stella Hengler, of Huntington Beach, CA; sister Rose Kempf, of West Covina, CA; brother Jack, of Hemet, CA; and two grandchildren. Mass is scheduled this morning at 10 a.m. at St. Andrews Church in Boulder City. Burial will be in Boulder City Cemetery.

Lyons, Helen Zetta
Boulder City News, Thursday, 30 Nov 1989, 14:2.
Helen Zetta Lyons, 45, passed away Nov. 21 in Boulder City. She was born on Sept. 16, 1944, and had lived in the area for 20 years. She was a school bus driver for the Clark County School District and a member of the Christian Center Church in Boulder City. Survivors include a daughter, Rebecca Decker of Boulder City; two sons, Robert M. Lyons and John E. Lyons, both of Boulder City; her mother, Zevesta Z. Scott of Phoenix, Arizona; a sister, Betty Pogue of Missouri. Services were held at the Christian Center Church on Nov. 25, the Reverend Jim Kitchell officiating. Interment was in Boulder City Cemetery. Palm Mortuary in Henderson was in charge of arrangements.

Lytle, Edythe A.
Boulder City News, Thursday, 7 Feb 1991, 7:3-4.
Edythe A. Lytle, 77, died Thursday, Jan. 31, in a local hospital. She was a 50-year resident. She was born in Calumet, Minn., on April 11, 1913. She was a retired owner-operator of the Mother Goose store in Boulder City. She was married for 49 years. She is survived by her husband Paul of Boulder City; and a son John Paul of Boulder City. Services were held.

Arrangements were handled by Palm Mortuary of Henderson.

MacDonald, Richard G.
Boulder City News, Thursday, 21 Sep 1944, p.1.
R. G. MacDonald Passes Away; Funeral Services Set for Friday Afternoon
Relatives and friends of the late Richard G. MacDonald, who passed away early Wednesday morning, will pay tribute to his memory at funeral services Friday afternoon at 4 o'clock at Grace Community church. The Rev Winston Trever will officiate, and burial will be at the Boulder City cemetery. MacDonald was found dead in his bed early yesterday by Mrs. MacDonald. He had been at home for the past five days on account of a heart ailment. Death was believed to have some sometime between 5 a.m. and 7 a.m. Wednesday. His last official act as assistant director or power was attendance at the meeting of Bureau of Reclamation officials Saturday in Boulder City. Fine tributes to MacDonald were given at yesterday's meeting fo the Boulder City Rotary club, of which he was a member, by H. O. Watts and Director of Power E. A. Moritz. "In Mr. MacDonald's death," said Moritz, "I feel deeply that I have lost a most loyal assistant and sincere friend." Richard G. MacDonald was born in Quirida, Colorado, on October 7, 1884, and attended public schools and high school at Florence, Colorado. He continued his education at Utah State Agricultural college at Logan, Utah; Iowa State college, Ames, Iowa, and Bliss Electrical school, Washington, D. C. MacDonald's early career was occupied with electrical and mining work in the western part of the United States. He was general superintendent of Western States Gas and Electric company at Eureka, California, for a number of years. He entered the service of the United States Bureau of Reclamation in 1936, as an engineer. On April 1, 1940, he was appointed to the position of assistant director of power, the position he held at the time of his death. Mr. MacDonald was prominent in civic affairs, being an active member of the Boulder City Rotary club and of the Southern Nevada Technical society. He is survived by his wife, Mrs. Irene MacDonald; his mother, Mrs. Ann Nicolls, of Florence, Colorado; two cousins, Mrs. E. W. Rockwell and Grayson Meyers, and an aunt, Mrs. Josephine Meyers. Robert Foreman of Oakland, California, son of Mrs. MacDonald, is expected to arrive in Boulder City soon.

Boulder City Cemetery: Boulder City, Nevada   181

Boulder City News, Friday, 22 Sep 1944, p.6.
MacDonald Funeral Rites at 4 O'clock Today
The Funeral service for the late R. G. MacDonald, who died early Wednesday morning at his home at 301 Utah street, will be held at 4 o'clock this afternoon at Grace Community church. The Reverend Winston Trever will be in charge of the funeral, with Miss Jean Dunbar playing the Stevenson Memorial organ and Mrs. Shirley Boyd singing. Burial will be at the Boulder City cemetery. The Palm Funeral home is in charge of arrangements. Mr. MacDonald, who was assistant director of power for the Boulder project, died following an illness of a few days, commencing Saturday, when he suffered a heart attack.

Boulder City News, Saturday, 23 Sep 1944.
Hundreds Honor Memory of R. G. MacDonald at Funeral Friday Afternoon
With fitting tribute to the late Richard G. MacDonald, both as a man and as engineer on the Boulder Dam project, whose efforts on behalf of the project have been important and of lasting value, the funeral of the late assistant director of power was conducted yesterday by the Reverend Winston Trever, but R. G. MacDonald truly put it into practice. He was never too busy to stop and help someone in need of help. Though R. G. MacDonald has gone into the Great Beyond, the work he did here will live on, he said, and what he taught us will continue with us with enduring value down through the years. The reverend Trever recounted that MacDonald was born October 7, 1884, and that he died early Wednesday, September 20, at his home at 301 Utah street, in Boulder City. Miss Jean Dunbar played the Stevenson Memorial organ and Mrs. Shirley Boyd sang. Pallbearers were E. A. Mortiz, Robert H.; Rose, R. V. Sprague, Ernest P. Bryant, A. G. Boynton and Lloyd Hudlow. The body was laid to rest at the Boulder City cemetery. Arrangements were under direction of the Palm Funeral Home.

MacLeod, William "Bill"

Boulder City News, Thursday, 14 Feb 1980, 4:1-5.
By Teddy Fenton

Surrounded by family and friends, the graveside services for one of Boulder City's most beloved friends were conducted by the Masonic Lodge and also by Reverend Melvin Pritts of the Grace Community Church. His sorrowing family told of the father they had lost. His kindness and wonderful nature had been obvious to all who knew him and his wife, Margaret, his daughter, Ann, and his son, Tom, said he was the same gentle man, loving to be with his family above all else, in his role as husband and father. Tom in particular, said he had never heard his father speak an unkind word about anyone. Shana, his granddaughter, said he was a perfect grandpa. The shock of his tragic death at the age of 66 was felt all the more because he had enjoyed wonderful health. A non-smoker, a swimmer, a man who had won trophies bowling, and was on a speaking base with hundreds of Boulderites because of his long walks each day, how could he leave us so suddenly? Was on the lips of his family and friends. Bill died in his home. Like a fallen tree we can examine the life of this friend to man, and in telling him goodbye we can say that Boulder City was lucky to have him here and his family also. Bill was born in Westmister, B.C. on Nov. 3, 1913. His Scotch bloodline was obvious in that kind face and in that name! He was a friend to all who knew him. That wide-open smile was a trade-mark. Bill and his brother, Don were young when the family moved to Boise, Idaho. His marriage to Margaret Hultgren was Sept. 24, 1941. He soon entered W.W.II. His daughter Ann was born during that war. Bill's first job after the war (he was a Staff Sgr.) was in Montana. One would have to know the country around Hungry Horse Dam in Montana to realize how much the family enjoyed its scenic beauty while Bill worked as an account for USBR at the Hungry Horse Project. A few miles away lay the great Glacier National Park. No where on earth do mountain streams abound with trout as that area in Montana. In spite of the scenic wonderland and the fishing, the snow and cold became uncomfortable chore. Bill asked for a transfer and luckily his next post was Boulder City, Nevada. His accounting career continued with the USBR. His immediate superior was Floyd Lindeberg. Their friendship lasted from the first day until the tragic death last weekend. Bill and Margaret were feted at a retirement party in 1972. Bill loved to sing. His tenor voice added depth and beauty to the Grace

Community Choir for over 20 years. Other ways he enjoyed life was by bowling. He won several trophies. He was also a strong swimmer. The family lived at 703 Ave. B. The lawns looked like a park. In one corner of the backyard he had a small garden. He also had fruit trees. Bill was chosen as the Worthy Patron for Eastern Star this current year. It is the highest honor accorded by the Eastern Star to a brother Mason. He was willing to do any service they asked him to do. He also belonged to the Elk's Lodge No 37 F & AM. He was a charter member back in Boise, Mont. of the Elks Gleenman. Pallbearers at his services were Al Bourne, John Layton, Doug Robinson, Walter Diebold, Floyd Lindeberg, and John Pilant. Boulder City extends its sympathy to Margaret and to her children. Residents since 1979, each contributed their share of kindness and service to this community. Bill will be missed. We wish him God-speed.

Mace, George R.
Boulder City News, Friday, 17 Feb 1950, 1:3.
Funeral Services For George Mace Tomorrow at 2 p.m.
Funeral services for George R. Mace will be held Saturday afternoon at 2 o'clock at Grace Community Church with the F. & A. M. Masonic lodge No. 37 in charge. Interment will be in the Boulder City cemetery. Mr. Mace, a well known and well like resident of this community since 1937, passed away at the Wadsworth hospital in Los Angeles February 12 at 12:10 p.m., from a lingering illness. He was born at Norborne, Missouri April 8, 1892. He was a member of the Highland Park. Masonic lodge No. 382, Highland Park, California. Survivors are three brothers – Terrill, who formerly lived here, now of Free Water, Oregon; Ben of Kansas City, and Archie of Chicago, and one sister who resides in Minnesota. Terrill Mace came to Boulder City immediately upon receiving word of his brother's death. Bunker Brothers have made arrangements for the funeral.

MacGregor, Verna Mary
Boulder City News, Thursday, 31 Oct 1985, 29:1-2.
Verna Mary MacGregor, a six-year resident of Boulder City, passed away Monday, Oct. 21. She was born June 27, 1918 in Detroit. She was a retired legal secretary. She leaves her husband Bruce of the home; son John W. Walker of Landing, Mich; brothers Bill Du Charme of Roseville, Mich; Ronald Du Charme of Clarkston, Mich.; and Gordon Du Charme of

Mt. Clamens, Mich. Burial was in Boulder City Cemetery. Memorial donations can be made to the American Diabetes Foundation.

Maddox, Doris C.
Boulder City News, Thursday, 30 Jul 1992, 8:3-4.
Doris C. Maddox, 82, died Sunday in Boulder City. Born Feb. 22, 1910, in Whitesburg, Ga., she had been a resident of Boulder City since 1952. She was a retired sales manager, working in pottery retail. She was a member of Desert Chapter #22 Order of the Eastern Star; Early Member of First Baptist Church of Boulder City. She is survived by her daughter Marion Derby of Boulder City; one son, Jackson Maddox of Las Vegas; one sister, Inez Banner of Blairsville, Ga.; and one brother William Camp, of St. Simons Island, Ga.; and four grandchildren. Services will be held at 9 a.m. today at the First Baptist Church, Boulder City. Arrangements were handled by Palm Mortuary of Henderson.

Maddox, Lee
Boulder City News, Thursday, 5 Aug 1976, 5-6.
Funeral services for Lee Maddox, who passed away July 28, were held Saturday at the First Baptist Church in Boulder City. Mr. Maddox was born Aug. 20, 1905 in Zebalon, Ga. He was a retired welder for the U. S. Bureau of Reclamation in Boulder City. He had resided here for 24 years, and lived at 701 Ave. B. He is survived by a wife, Doris; son Jackson P. of Las Vegas; daughter, Marion Derby of Palm Springs, Ca.; sister, Belle Gill of Atlanta, Ga., and grandchildren Mike and Kent Derby and Terra Maddox. Interment was at Boulder City cemetery.

Mallot, Jeanne P.
Boulder City News, Thursday, 25 Mar 1992, 6:4.
Jeanne P. Mallot died in Boulder City on Mar. 17, 1993. She was born oct. 31, 1905, in the Territory of Oklahoma. Her home was in California where she and her husband were accountants. He preceded her in death. Jeanne was employed in 1944 in Henderson, Nevada, where she worked for Basic Magnesium. She is survived by her sister, Rae M. Royer of Boulder City, Nevada, with whom she was visiting at the time of her death. The Reverend Dr. Richard Smith of Grace Community Church in Boulder City conducted her services on Mar. 22, 1993.

Malmsten, Georgia H.
Boulder City News, Thursday, 18 Sep 1975, 2:2.
Mamsten Services Set
Graveside services for Georgia H. Malmsten, 88, who died Sept. 14 at Southern Nevada Memorial Hospital, will be held this morning at 10 a.m. at Grace Community Church in Boulder City. Guy Holliday will officiate. Mrs. Malmsten, who resided at 608 Bryant Court, Boulder City, for the past eleven years, was born Nov. 30, 1888 in Barlington, Wisconsin. She was a housewife and member of Grace Community Church. Survivors include her husband, Roland, a daughter, Mrs. Virginia McGrath of Boulder City, one grandchild and one great grandson.

Maltby, Alta Grace Elridge
Boulder City News, Thursday, 3 Aug 1961, 9:6-7.
Mrs. Maltby's Funeral Tuesday; Buried in Boulder City Cemetery
    Funeral services were held Tuesday for Alta Grace Elridge Maltby, 59, who died Friday in the local hospital after a prolonged illness. The Reverend Guy Holliday conducted the rites at the Grace Community Church and interment followed in the Boulder City Cemetery. The Maltbys joined Grace Church in June, transferring from the First Presbyterian Church of Hollywood. The pallbearers were Charles Sweet, Robert Austin, Leo Dunbar, Raynard Lundquist, James Schaack and Ralph Ramsey. Mrs. Maltby was born March 16, 1902 in Detroit, Michigan. She and her family have lived in the west for many years. Mr. and Mrs. Maltby, ardent rock hounds, displayed their beautiful minerals, jewelry and rock pictures in fairs throughout the west. They moved to Boulder City in 1960, when Mr. Maltby retired. The deceased was a member of the Rebekah Lodge in California. She is survived by her husband, Clifford of 688 Eighth Street, two sons, Richard A. of Pullman, Washington; and Donald T. of Los Angeles; and three grandchildren.

Maltby, Josephine F.

Boulder City News, Thursday, 8 Jan 1987, 8:3-4.
Josephine F. Maltby, 85, of Boulder City died Wednesday in a local hospital. She was born Feb. 1, 1901 in Santa Paula, Calif. A 24-year resident, she was a homemaker. She is survived by her children, Dale E. Fletcher of Las Vegas, John F. Fletcher of Laguna Nigel, Calif.; brother, William "Bud" Knick of Taft, Calif.; 10 grandchildren and 10 great-grandchildren. Services and burial were private. Family requests memorial donations be made in her name to First Church of Christ Scientist, Boulder City, Nev. Davis Funeral Home is handling arrangements.

Manning, Ivy

Boulder City News, Thursday, 2 Apr 1981, 12.
Ivy Manning, 87, died Tuesday in Boulder City. She was born May 14, 1893 in Barbados, West Indies and had been a resident of Boulder City for a year and a half. Mrs. Manning is survived by two sons, Larence of Boulder City and Basil of Brooklyn, New York; four daughters, Karmen McCullough of Boulder City, Eldra Conides of Lake Havasu, Arizona, Leslie Enid Manning of Boulder City and Vere Peterson of Queens, N.Y.; sisters, Winnie Simmons of New Orleans, Louisiana and Vivian Nilsen of Las Vegas; 10 grandchildren and 15 great grandchildren. Funeral services will be conducted at 10 a.m. Friday at Palm Chapel. Burial will be in Boulder City Cemetery.

March, Fred

Boulder City News, Thursday, 12 Jan 1995, 8:2.
Memorial services were held for Fred March on 1/6/95 at Palm Memorial Mortuary in Henderson. Mr. March passed away on January 2 after a lengthy illness. He was born in Transcona, Canada. At the age of 17 he enlisted in the Canadian Army and served overseas combat duty during World War II. He moved to the United States and became a citizen after the war. He was employed for 36 years by Pitney-Bowes as a field and branch manager. Upon retirement he moved to Boulder City and took an active roll in politics. He is survived by his widow, Marijean, two sons, Ron of Henderson, and Patrick of Valencia, Calif.; three granddaughters and three great grandchildren; two brothers and two sisters who reside in

Canada.

Martin, Essie L.
Boulder City News, Thursday, 26 May 1994, 16:1-2.
Essie L. Martin, 87, died Thursday, May 19, 1994 in a local hospital. She was a 24-year resident of Boulder City. She was born Jan. 29, 1907 in Denton, Texas and was a homemaker. She is survived by her son Claude H. Martin of Henderson; six grandchildren; and eight great grandchildren. Graveside services were held Saturday. Arrangements were handled by Palm Mortuary of Henderson.

Martin, Richard
Boulder City News, Thursday, 19 Aug 1993, 11:1.
Richard Martin, 53, died Monday after a lengthy illness. He was a four year resident of Boulder City. Martin was employed with the Los Angeles Water and Power Company for 23 years. He came here in 1989 to install a new microwave system for LA Water and Power. Martin was a ham radio operator and he liked to work on all phases of telecommunication systems. He also liked to help with marriage and family/life counseling. He leaves a wife, Caroline, son Richard, both of Boulder City, daughter Lori Ann and mother Corrine, both of Huntington, Calif. Arrangements were handled by Palm Mortuary of Henderson.

Martz, Lloyd P.
Boulder City News, Thursday, 6 July 1978, 8:3-4.
Services were held yesterday at Palm Chapel for Lloyd P. Martz, 55, who passed away July 3 at Echo Bay. Mr. Martz was a 20 year resident of Echo Bay and was a maintenance foreman for the National Park Service. He was born July 30, 1922 in South Whitley, Indiana. Survivors include his wife, Irma of Echo Bay; father, Claude Martz of Columbia City, Indiana; daughters, Collette Lusson of Phoenix, Arizona, Sandra Waldie and Linda Martz of Las Vegas and Paula Hoover of Boulder City; brothers, Dick and DeWayne Martz of Columbia City, Harold of Miami, Florida, Esta of Cameron, Wisconsin and Alvin of San Diego, Calif,; sisters, Jackie Duggins of Columbia City and Patsy Alwood of Bakersfield, Calif.; and eight grandchildren. Cremation followed the services.

Mather, Robert Lee "Bob"

Boulder City News, Thursday, 7 Aug 1969, p.1:2.
Funeral services were held yesterday morning for Robert Lee "Bob" Mather, 74, Boulder pioneer who died Sunday night in the Boulder City Hospital, following a long illness. The services were conducted at the First Baptist Church, of which Bob was a member, by the Reverend Louis Gerdes, pastor of the Southern Baptist Church in Henderson. (The Reverend Neal Myers accepted a call to a church in Arizona two weeks ago.) Pallbearers were Robert Guyette, Clifford Heddens, Herman Raynor, Robert Jones, Richard Daniel and Will Hinkens. Burial was in the Boulder City Cemetery, where his wife Mae was interred in March. Mr. Mather was born September 25, 1894 in Hodgensville, Kt. He was an apprentice and journeyman painter until he was 21, when he tried working for the Louisville and Nashville Railroad. Then he left Kentucky for Akron, Ohio, to employment at the Goodyear Rubber Company. He served his country during World War I in France and in Boulder City was a charter member of Post 3574, Veterans of Foreign Wars. Following his discharge in August 1919, he returned to Ohio to his former job, but during the depression he once again began painting. Like thousands of others, Bob traveled to Nevada to help with the construction of Hoover Dam. His first job was driving a team of mules across the desert to help complete the access road. Later, he started painting again, and switched from the Six Companies to the Bureau of Reclamation in 1936. He earned a Superior Performance Award before his retirement in the winter of 1962. Most of the years, Bob and his family lived at 643 Avenue D. He was preceded in death by his wife, his step-son Leslie, and Leslie's daughter, Linda. He is survived by his son, Robert L. Mather, Jr. in Las Vegas; and one sister, Anna Mae Walker, Macon, Ga.

Mathias, Albert A.

Boulder City News, Thursday, 20 Sep 1979, p.11.
Graveside services will be held at 2 p.m. this afternoon at the Boulder City Cemetery for Albert Arthur Mathias, 85, who passed away September 18 in Boulder City. Mr. Mathias was born February 18, 1884 in Michigan City, Indiana. He had been a resident of Boulder City for 15 months. He was a veteran of World War I, a member of the Porter Lodge No. 137 F & AM of Valparaise, Indiana, and Scottish Rite Bodies Valley of South Bend, Indiana. Surviving are his wife, Alma Mathias of Boulder

City; daughters, Helen Anderson of Fullerton, California, Norma Barth of Boulder City, and Mary L. Kindy of Elburn, Illinois.

Matulic, Milan D.
Boulder City News, Thursday, 19 Feb 1987, 27:5.
Milan D. Matulic, age 67, passed away Wednesday, Feb.11 in Boulder City. He was born Nov 8, 1919 in Milst, Yugoslavia. He was a three-year resident, a long-shoreman and a World War II Navy Veteran. He leaves his wife, Geraldin of Boulder City; son Sam Playa of Del Rey, Calif.; daughter Yvone Lorke of Boulder City; father Sam of an Pedro, Calif.; sister, Margaret Elich of Rolling Hills, Calif., and two grandchildren. Interment was in Boulder City Cemetery.

Maugham, Mardella "Delle" Coy
Boulder City News, Thursday, 8 Sep 1977, 8:1-5.
Services for Della Maugham Held Tuesday
One of Boulder City's most beloved citizens, Mardella "Della" Coy Maugham, died at the Boulder City Hospital on September 2, 1977 of a lingering illness. She was a resident of Boulder City since early 1968. Her son, Gregory began school in Boulder City. Della began her professional career locally in the Boulder City Hospital as a nurse's aid in 1968. Later she checked out groceries at the new Safeway store and her last job was as a clerk at Leo Dunbar's Central Market. Della was one of ten children of Ben and Florence Tabor. Her mother is still alive but her father died several years ago. Three of the ten children preceded Della in death. They were Lloyd Ben Tabor, Alta Marie Tabor, and Violet Esther Tabor. Della was born in Oncno, Nebraska on May 19, 1933. She is survived by her children, Winona Esther Stevens, Chris Maugham, Jr. and Gregory Ray Maugham. Greg, 14, has attended the Boulder City school system from kindergarten. She is also survived by her sisters, Beaulh Daniels, Prescott, Arizona; Christine Hewett, Flagstaff, Arizona; Barbara Corwell, Phoenix, Arizona; Rosella Jean Cleef, Pasa Robles, California; Melody Lea, Springfield, Illinois; and a brother, Walter Garland, San Antonio, Texas. Her mother Florence Tabor lives in Buckeye, Arizona. Pallbearers were Steve Cole, Jay Cole, Pete Bennett, Dallas Harrison, Kem Strickland and Bob Stevens. She was buried in the Boulder City Cemetery.

McBride, Alvis E.
Boulder City News, Thursday, 31 Oct 1985, 29:1.
Alvis E. McBride, 83, died Friday in a local hospital He was a 23-year resident of Boulder City. He was born June 10, 1902, in Arkansas and was a miner. He is survived by his sons, Bobby of Henderson and J. O. Ray of California; daughters, Mary Daniel of Boulder City, Darnell Walker of Henderson and Tommy Honer of Oregon; brothers, Delmos and Willie, both of Arkansas, and Tommy of California; sister, Clara of St. Louis; 16 grandchildren; and 21 great-grandchildren. Visitation is scheduled for 3-9 p.m. Monday in Bunker Mortuary. Services were at 10 a.m. Tuesday in First Baptist Church, Boulder City. Burial was in Boulder City Cemetery.

McCarthy, Francis L.
Boulder City News, Thursday, 24 May 1979, 10:7-8.
Private services were held for Francis L. McCarthy, 67, who passed away May 20 at the Boulder City Hospital. Born August 23, 1911 in Auburn, New York, Mr. McCarthy was a roofing contractor in the roofing business. He had lived in Boulder City since August of 1976. He is survived by his wife, Agnes McCarthy, of Boulder City; a son, Patrick McCarthy of Arizona, and two grandchildren. Interment was at Boulder City Cemetery.

McCarty, Pamela
Boulder City News, Thursday, 18 Oct 1956, 1:5.
Pamela McCarty Killed Instantly When Hit by Car
Boulder City's record of no traffic fatalities within the city limits in almost 20 years ended Monday afternoon when 7-year-old Pamela McCarty was struck by a car at New Mexico and G streets while riding her bicycle and killed instantly. Final rites will be held at the Grace Community church Friday morning at 10 o'clock with the Reverend Earl Fox officiating. Burial will be in the Boulder City Cemetery with Bunker Brothers of Las Vegas in charge of arrangements. Pamela was born in San Francisco and would have been 8 years old on Dec. 3. She was a second grade student at the Boulder City elementary school. Survivors include her parents, Mr. and Mrs. Kenneth McCarty of 649 Nevada Highway and a sister, Mea, age 2½. Driver of the car involved in the fatal accident was Mrs. Frances Talley of 668 California, Boulder City housewife, according

to police officials. Both Mrs. Talley and Mrs. McCarty have been confined to the Boulder City Community Hospital for treatment since the accident but were released Wednesday. Mrs. McCarty (Kathleen) is employed by the Bureau of Reclamation in the irrigation division as a secretary of A. S. West. Mr. McCarty is a musical composer employed in Las Vegas. The McCarty's have been residents of Boulder City since 1954. According to the Chief of Police Lloyd Jenne, the accident occurred shortly before 4 o'clock Monday afternoon. The police chief said he has been unable to locate any witnesses to the accident but an investigation showed that the little girl probably was dragged about 47 feet after initial impact. Death was due to a skull fracture, according to Coroner Charles Peterson. Peterson said the inquest would be held this afternoon in the Advisory Council chambers at 2:30. Two of the three members of the coroner's jury will be Andrew Mitchell, principal of the school Pamela attended, and Lloyd Morrison. A third member of the jury was to be named this morning. Chief of Police Jenne reported he had not questioned Mrs. Talley concerning the accident. No charges have been filed against the driver of the car, he said and Clark County District Attorney George Dickerson will determine if charges would be filed after the inquest is held.

McClure, Myron Cook
Boulder City News, Thursday, 6 July 1972.
Funeral services for Myron Cook McClure, 85, will be held at 10 a.m., tomorrow (July 7) at Palm Mortuary in Henderson. The rites are to be conducted by the BPO Elks Lodge, of which he was a member, and burial will be in the Boulder City Cemetery. Mr. McClure was born January 27, 1887 in Sparta, Illinois. From August, 1947 until September, 1960, he was a foreman for the CMFTTMP Railroad in Deer Lodge, Montana. He was employed by the City of Boulder City in September, 1960, in the electrical division, and was a lineman foreman at the time of his death. He had been a member of the B_W for 42 years. For recreation, he was very fond of fishing. He died Monday, July 3, in the Redlands Community Hospital, after taking ill while visiting a daughter. Mr. McClure is survived by his wife, Ruby Space __, 701 Elm St., Boulder City; a son Larry, of the same address; sons Mike and Vincent of Las Vegas; daughter Patricia Mahanay of Redlands, Calif.; and Marlene Smithee, Flint, Mich., and 5 grandchildren. Also a brother Jack McClure,

Chester, Ill; and sister Margie Simmington, B_ingame, Calif.

McCollum, Daniel Luther
Boulder City News, Thursday, 11 Dec 1952.
Daniel Luther McCollum, 84, was buried yesterday in the Boulder City cemetery beside his wife, who died seven years ago. Services were conducted by the Reverend Olaf Stoeve, at Grace Community church where McCollum was an active member and student of the Adult Bible class. A retired farmer from Meadville, Mo., Mr. McCollum came here 12 years ago. Since his wife's death he made his home with his son-in-law and daughter, Mr. and Mrs. C. W. Chambers, 615 Ave. B. He became ill late last week and was taken to the hospital Friday night. He was born August 4, 1868, in Winnigan, Mo. He and Wardie Genevra Riddle were married February 22, 1900, in Wasco, Mo. In addition to his daughter in Boulder City, he leaves another daughter, Mrs. J. N. Felts of Coulee Dam, Washington, and four sons, A. H. McCollum, 639 California avenue; O. E. McCollum of Bakersfield, Calif., and N. E. and I. A. McCollum in Washington. He leaves seven grandchildren.

McCollum, Orland E.
Boulder City News, Thursday, 5 Jan 1967, 3:5.
O. E. McCollum Rites Monday
Orland E. McCollum, 56, died Thursday of emphysema. Funeral services were conducted at the Palm Chapel in Henderson, Monday afternoon, and he was buried in the Boulder City Cemetery. He was born July 9, 1910, in Linn County, Mo. A heavy equipment operator, he was one of the workers on construction of Hoover Dam. Mr. McCollum had been making his home in Atascadero, Calif., but for the past few months lived with his sister, Leila (Mrs. Fred) Chambers at Page, Ariz. The Chambers family also lived in Boulder City until Glen Canyon Dam started. He is survived by three brothers, Alton H. McCollum of the Paulah Motel, 809 Nevada Highway; Irwin of Othello, Wash.; Norvell of Oroville, Calif.; and two sisters, Lucille Field of Coulee Dam, Wash., and Mrs. Chambers. There are also several nieces and nephews, including Larry McCollum of 909 New Mexico Street.

McCollum, Pauline
Boulder City News, Thursday, 3 May 1973, 5:5.
Graveside Services Held for Pauline McCollum
Private graveside services were held Tuesday morning for Pauline T. "Polly" McCollum, 58, at the Boulder City Cemetery with the Reverend Guy Holliday officiating. In lieu of flowers, the family requested contributions to the Cancer Fund. Polly died Sunday in the Sunrise Hospital, after valiantly fighting cancer for many months. Pauline Trammell was born Sept. 6, 1914 in McCauley, Texas. She was married to Alton H. "Mac" McCollum, and they lived in California before moving to Boulder City in 1945. Not a "joiner," she was family oriented and enjoyed sewing and homemaking. However, she helped her husband with office work at Mac's Garage (now owned by son Larry) and managed the old Paulah Motel, which was renovated into the new Sand's Motel at 809 Nevada Highway. She is survived by her husband, Mac, and daughter Martha McCollum, 809 Nevada Hwy; son Lawrence, 809 New Mexico St.;daughter Mildred Williamson, Austin, Tex.; six grandchildren; brother, John Trammel, Washington, D.C.; six sisters, Bessie Edwards, Santo, Tex.; Minnie Black, Oakridge, Tenn.; Lucille Black, Las Cruces, New Mex.; Helen Richardson, St. Paul, Ore.; Daisy Aikens, Bloomington, Calif.; and Estelle McArthur, Riverside, Calif.

McCollum, Wardie Genevera
Boulder City News, Thursday, 28 Dec 1945, 1:3.
Mrs. McCollum Dies at Home of Daughter
Mrs. Wardie Genevera McCollum passed away from a cerebral hemorrhage Wednesday night, Dec. 26, about 11 o'clock at the home of her daughter, Mrs. Clement W. Chamber, 615 Avenue B. She had been ill for the past six weeks. Mrs. McCollum was born March 8, 1875 in Milan, Missouri. She is survived by her husband, D. L. McCollum, Boulder City; two daughters, Mrs. J. N. Fields of Coulee Dam, Washington, and Mrs. Chambers; and four sons, Norvell McCollum of Boulder City, Alton McCollum of Henderson, Orland McCollum of Oceanside, Calif., and Irwin McCollum, who is with an engineer combat battalion in Austria. Funeral arrangements have not yet been completed. The body is at the Palm Funeral home in Las Vegas.

McCoy, Mary Ellen
Boulder City News, Thursday, 7 Nov 1968, 1:3.
McCoy Rites Today at 9
Requiem mass will be conducted at 9 this morning in St. Andrew's Church for Mrs. Mary Ellen McCoy who died Monday night at B.C. Hospital. Father Hugh Smith will officiate and burial will be in B. C. Cemetery. Palm Mortuary is in charge of arrangements. Mrs. McCoy was born Dec. 9, 1908 in Youngstown, N. Y. She lived at 528 Date St. and had been a resident of Boulder City for 19 years. She was past president of St. Andrew's Altar Society and the Confraternity of Christian Doctorine. The deceased is survived by her husband, Raymond K. and John, all of Boulder City, and two brothers, Jack Cody of Kenmore, N.Y. and James Cody of Niagara Falls, N.Y.

McCuin, Luella G.
Boulder City News, Thursday, 30 Dec1982, 2:4.
Luella G. McCuin, 78, a resident of Boulder City since 1948, died Saturday in Las Vegas. She was born Feb. 22, 1904, in Little Rock, Ark. and was a homemaker. She is survived by her husband, Clarence of Boulder City; sister, Irma Cooke of Roger, Texas; and brother Gustaf Hegberg of Little Rock. Graveside services will be at 2 p.m. Thursday in Boulder City Cemetery. Palm Mortuary is handling arrangements.

McDonald, Delores
Boulder City News, Thursday, 15 Nov 1990, 11:1-2.
Delores McDonald, 62, died Sunday, Nov. 4 in Boulder City. She was a 40-year resident. She was born Aug. 10, 1928 in Grand Island, Neb. and was a retired secretary. She is survived by her mother, Selma McDonald of Los Angeles, Calif.; and a brother, Lt. Col. Gerald McDonald of Selma, Ala. Memorial services were held at St. Andrews Catholic Church. Arrangements were handled by Palm Mortuary.

McDuff, Mrs. Kate Files
Boulder City News, Friday, 10 Sep 1948, p.14.
Hold Funeral Service Here Today For Mrs. Kate Files McDuff
Mrs. Kate Files McDuff passed away Wednesday afternoon at 2:50 o'clock at the home of her daughter, Mrs. M. L. Chappell, 608 Avenue D, from a lingering illness of several months. Funeral services will be held at Grace Community Church this evening at 5 o'clock with Reverend Winston Trever officiating. The Eastern Star of which Mrs. McDuff had been a member for over 49 years will have charge of the services at the graveside. Interment will be in the Boulder City cemetery. Pall bearers will be Dr. J. C. Roberts, Harry Fuller, Barney Gino, Charles Bridgman, S. A. Curley and Jack Heywood. Bunker Brothers of Las Vegas are in charge. Mrs. McDuff was born June 1, 1872, in Files Valley, Texas where her grandfather settled and for whom the valley was named. She married J. W. McDuff September 3, 1893, in Grandview, Texas. Mr. McDuff passed away there November 12, 1926. Survivors are her daughter, Mrs. Chappell; a son, J. W. McDuff Jr., Dallas, who is expected to arrive with his wife for the services; a sister, Mrs. W. H. McCall, Itasca, Texas, and three grandchildren, Sally Ann and Jimmy McDuff, and Benny Crowell, Mrs. Chappell's son.

McEwan, Gwen
Boulder City News, Thursday, 3 Jan 1980, 2:5-8.
By Teddy Fenton
Jack Williams delivered the impressive Eulogy at the Mormon Church on Dec. 31, 1979, for beautiful Gwen McEwan. His first words were: "Gwen asked me months ago if I would do this for her." What followed was a testimony of courage that all who had known Gwen knew to be true. Her courageous battle to live a normal life in spite of the sad fact that dread cancer had begun fifteen years before her tragic death. The word "tragic" would apply to Gwens pain and suffering, but the word "joy" is always used when death occurs within the church of the Latter Day Saints. Brother Williams said, "Gwen has gone home, her family and departed friends were waiting for her and yet today her presence is here with us. She would not want us to be sad." Lying in state, Gwen McEwan was resting in a casket that was the most beautiful tribute to love ever seen by the friends and family who filled the Sanctuary to capacity. It had been built entirely by the skilled hands of her daughter, Leslie Grain. The color

of the lining was Gwen's favorite Bergundy Velour. We can see those shining brown eyes, so filled with expression as she saw the casket where it had been store three weeks prior to her death. Palm Mortuary was proud of it and showed it to so many admirers that they called it a monumental sharing of a moment that might never happen again and had not happened before in the history of Palm Mortuary. Her daughter, Leslie who was a home-ec teacher, and who had taken a course in woodworking, and who was allergic to "Mahogony Wood" from which the casket was fashioned, had determined that her mother would rest in the beauty with which she had surrounded her family all her life and this came true as all who saw the casket at Palm Mortuary and later at the final services, can witness. It is the magnificent work of a talented creator who obviously inherited her mother's talents. Leslie and her mother, traveled a month together each year. The joy of those family oriented trips, visiting John Jr.'s growing family of 7 grandchildren, having with them Leslie's son, it was memorable and as all who knew her. Gwen did not spoil a single moment of the joy by letting her always present cancer spoil those summer adventures. When John and Gwen went to Afghanistan, where John was transferred by the Bureau of Reclamation, Gwen was able to decorate their spacious house with the treasurers of the country. These now grace the home she left, "for a land more kind than home, more large than earth" and we know she will be remembered for the beauty she spread everywhere. Jake Williams spoke of the hundreds of friends whose life was touched by Gwen's love for older people, and for the suffering of all people in hospitals or confined to their homes, she especially became known for her compassion and willingness to sit by the friend's bedside. She was especially close to Della Maugham during her final months of dying from dread cancer. Bishop Alder of the Second Ward of the Mormon Church opened the Services and carried forth the same message that was followed by Brother Jake Williams. A salute to the greatest courage any of us who knew her had witnessed for 15 years. It is as sure as life on earth that the miracle of keeping Gwen alive and sometimes free from pain will find its way into the medical history. Gwen was sure a cure for cancer was in the near future and her case history almost made it happen during her lifetime. That is something to remember her for above other facets of her life of sharing her love with her neighbors, family and friends. She was a true example to all of us. As a neighbor she could not be praised enough. She would see someone new moving into the neighborhood. Immediately she made the first overture of friendship. A loaf of bread, or something out of her home - canned pantry of garden vegetables and fruit, she was "first" and she loved it. We want to close this tribute with a smiling memory of an evening at City Council. New laws were coming for Home Occupancy business permits. As Leslie Grain put it, her mother could have sold Hoover Dam but in this case she was selling miniature vacuum cleaner called the Hokey and it was a gem. She was glowing with triumph as she showed council its workings. Her role was actually that of a great actress and her voice carried clearly in the chambers. We were all laughing. Gwen, no salute will do justice to your life. Just know that your example should be followed by those of us, less kind, less compassionate, less beautiful of soul, and certainly less courageous. The closing prayer was given by brother Eugene Gregerson. Pallbearers were Curly Frances, Jerry Morley, Gilbert Wood, Fred Neilson, Charlie Hunter and John McEwan, Jr. Council John McEwan and his beloved wife had been married 41 years and one day at the time of her passing. Their union was blessed with years of work with the Mormon Church and the community they cared for. God Bless and Keep You, Dear Gwen.

McEwan, William C.

Boulder City News, Thursday, 26 Aug 1982, 9:5-6.
William C. McEwan, 90, died Sunday evening at Valley Hospital. He was a Boulder City resident since 1942. Mr. McEwan was born on February 14, 1892, in Provo, Utah. He graduated from Brigham Young University and was a pilot and veteran of World War I. During his residence in Boulder City, McEwan was the Manager of the Manix Department Store and also worked for the Bureau of Mines. Mr. McEwan retired from the Bureau of Mines when he reached the age of 70. He was also the Charter President of the Boulder City Lyons Club. McEwan is survived by his sons, William S. McEwan of Ridgecrest, California, and John S. McEwan of Boulder City. Services will be held today at 10 a.m. at the LDS Chapel in Boulder City.

McHugh, Judith Ellen
Boulder City News, Thursday, 6 Jan 1966, 1:3.
Requiem For Judy McHugh
Requiem Mass was sung at 10 yesterday morning for Miss Judith Ellen McHugh, 26, of 643 California Ave. who died Sunday. Father Gerard Fanning officiated at St. Andrew's Church and interment was in Boulder City Cemetery. Judy, as she was known to residents of Boulder and Henderson, had lived here 19 years, having been born to Richard T. and Eileen McHugh, in Oak Park, Ill. Besides her parents she is survived by two sisters, Mrs. Patricia Weir, Henderson and Maureen McHugh, this city; two brothers, Kenneth and James P. and her maternal grandparents, Mr. and Mrs. C. A. Scranton, Chicago, Ill. Rosary was recited for the deceased at Palm Chapel on Tuesday night.

McIntyre, Bertha E.
Boulder City News, Thursday, 13 Jan 1983, 2:3.
Bertha E. McIntyre, 71, passed away Monday Jan. 10, in Sunrise Hospital. Born January 24, 1911, in Wisconsin, Bertha had lived in Las Vegas for 20 yrs. before moving to Boulder City 2 months ago. She leaves a husband, Sherman, a son and 2 daughters, Douglas McIntyre of Shelton, Washington, Emily Littler of Boulder City and Elaine Galbraith of North Las Vegas. Sisters Mary Sowers of Miles City, Montana, Elizabeth Spencer of Joliet, Montana, 4 grand children and 1 great grandchild. Graveside services will be at the Boulder City Cemetery Friday at 11 a.m.

McKenzie, Ethel E.
Boulder City News, Thursday, 12 Dec 1968.
A funeral mass will be held today at 10 a.m. at St. Andrew's Catholic Church for Ethel E. McKenzie, 537 Hopi Place, who died Dec. 8 at Rose de Lima Hospital in Henderson. The deceased was born Feb. 2, 1901 in Corbin, Mont. She was a longtime resident of Boulder City, moved away, and returned two years ago. She was a member of Boulder Dam Post Veterans of Foreign Wars Auxiliary. She is survived by her husband, John D. of Boulder City; three sons, Roe Bassett of California, Carlter Bassett of Montana and Porter Bassett.

McKinnis, Gary Phillip
Boulder City News, Thursday, 1 Feb 1973.
Gary Phillip McKinnis, 40, died January 26 in a local hospital. A resident of the area for 16 years, he was born in Salem, Oregon, on November 24, 1932. A resident of 701 Elm St., Space 56, he was a cook by profession, and had been working at the Temple Bar Resort in Temple Bar, Arizona. He was a veteran, having served in the U. S. Army from 1957-59. Survivors include his parents, Mr. and Mrs. George McKinnis of Boulder City; a brother Clarence of Las Vegas; a sister Patricia J. Burgess of Las Vegas; two sons, Phillip of Portland, Oregon, and Kelly, Houston, Texas. Services were held Tuesday at 11 a.m. at the Four-square Gospel Church in Boulder City, the Reverend Gene Holman officiating. Interment was in Boulder City Cemetery. Palm Mortuary was in charge of arrangements.

McLaughlin, Charles J.
Boulder City News, Thursday, 23 Apr 1992, 8:1-4.
Charles J. McLaughlin, a teacher at Basic High School for 20 years, was remembered Wednesday during graveside services at the Boulder City Cemetery. McLaughlin, 76, died Friday in a local hospital. He was born in Riverside, R.I., on Dec. 23, 1915. His parents were Charles M. and Helena F. (Sullivan) McLaughlin. A retired lieutenant commander in the U. S. Navy, McLaughlin served as an officer aborad the USS Hale during the Korean conflict. He was a graduate of Rhode Island College and earned a master's degree from Boston University. After his active military service, he resided in Rumford, R.I., and taught at East Providence High School for 12 years. He lived in Las Vegas from 1960 until he moved to Boulder City three years ago. He was a counselor and teacher at Basic High School for 20 years until his retirement in 1980. He is survived by his wife, Margaret E. (Hanson) McLaughlin of Boulder City; son Charles J. McLaughlin Jr. of Henderson; and nephew, Joseph L. Clair of Hollywood, Fla. Donations in his name may be made to Boulder City Hospital, 901 Adams Blvd, Boulder City, Nev. 89005.

McNair, Jessie Lee
Boulder City News, Thursday, 7 Feb 1985, 28:1-2.
Jessie Lee McNair, 76, passed away January 29, 1985, in a hospital in Mesa, Arizona. Born February 22, 1908, in Rock Springs, Texas, she was a 30 year resident of Boulder City prior to moving to the Phoenix area for the past six months. Survivors include: 1 daughter; Mrs. Norma J. Palmer, Phoenix, AZ. 1 son; Ben McNair of Boulder City, Nevada. 2 sisters: Rosabelle Dean of Grants Pass, Oregon and Lora Chapman of Phoenix, AZ. 1 brother; James Waddell of Henderson, Nevada. Four grandchildren and four great grandchildren. Funeral services were held Friday, Feb. 1, 1985 at Grace Community Church. Interment at Boulder City Cemetery. Arrangements handled by Tempe Mortuary, 405 East Southern Avenue, Tempe, AZ.

McNeil, Robert John
Boulder City News, Thursday, 12 Dec 1974.
Funeral services for Robert John McNeil, a long-time Henderson and Boulder City resident, will be held today at 10 a.m. at Palm Chapel. Burial will be in Boulder City.

Manning, Leslie Enid
Boulder City News, Thursday, 12 May 1988, 6:1-2.
Leslie Enid Manning, 76 died Saturday, April 30 in Boulder City. He had been a resident of the Boulder City area for the past eight years. He was born in Barbados, West Indies on Jan. 22, 1912 and was an inspector for Gyroscope Manufacturing. Survivors include brother Lawrence Manning and sister Eldra Conides both of Boulder City, brother Basil Manning of Reseda, Calif.; and sisters Carmen McCullough of Boulder City and Vere Peterson, Queens, N.Y. Funeral services were held on May 4 at 11 a.m. in the Palm Chapel in Henderson with Doug McCready of the Christian Science Church officiating. Interment was in Boulder City Cemetery.

Marks, Arleen
Boulder City News, Thursday, 30 Dec 1993, 9:3.
Arleen Marks died Monday, Dec. 27, 1993 at her home. Marks was born Nov. 30, 1929, in Oak Park, Ill. She was the daughter of Celeste Browne Fagan and Arthur Samuel Fagan. Shw married Jack Fisher Marks May 1, 1950. She was a member of Colonial Dames of the 17th Century, Daughters of the American Colonist, Descendants of Washington's Army at Valley Forge, the Germanna Foundation, and a very active member of St. Andrew's Community. She was Lady Grand Cross of the Equestrian Order of the Holy Sepulachre of Jerusalem. She was the Nevada State National Society Daughters of the American Revolution Chaplain at the time of her death. She is survived by her husband Jack Fisher Marks; daughter, Victoria Marks Yeley; grandson, Ryan Marks Yeley, and granddaughter Ann-Marie Yeley. Wake services was held Monday and funeral Mass Tuesday. Arrangements were handled by Palm Mortuary in Henderson.

Markus, Ruth
Boulder City News, Thursday, 1 Sep 1988, 10:2.
Ruth Markus, 73, died Friday, Aug 26, Las Vegas. She had been a resident of the Boulder City area for the past nine years. She was born in Bellingham, Washington on Nov 30, 1914 and was a retired draftsman. She was a U.S. Navy World War II veteran. Survivors include husband Alfonsas E. Markus, Boulder City; sons John Markus, Fairfax, Va.; James Markus, Henderson and daughter Linda Markus, Phoenix, Ariz.; four grandchildren. In lieu of flowers donations may be made to the American Lung Association. Rosary was recited Monday, Aug. 29, 7 p.m. at St. Andrew's Church. Mass was held Tuesday, Aug. 30 at 10 a.m. at St. Andrew's Church. Clergy was Father Thomas Phillips. Interment was in the Boulder City Cemetery, Boulder City.

Mecham, Forrest Ray
Boulder City News, Thursday, 28 May 1987, 24:1-3.
By Esther Shipp

Forest Ray Mecham, 67, was buried Saturday in the Boulder City Cemetery. He died Wednesday after a long bout with cancer. The Odd Fellow's funeral service was conducted at Palm Chapel by Grand Master Manuel Souza of Hawthorne, past Grand Master John H. Shipp and PDDGM Joseph L. Kine. Rebekah Assembly solist Linda Cooper sang "The Old Rugged Cross" and "Whispering Hope." Pallbearers were Arthur Denison, Merle Mitchell, Frank Turner, Glen D. Bicknell, J. E. "Bob" Cole and Charles "Chuck" Bicknell. Honorary pallbearers were Neil H. Homes, Dr. Hiram Hunt, Marion Beall, Frank Adams, Wayne Fehler and Gerry Smith. American Legion Post 31 was in charge of the military rites at the cemetery. Those taking part were commander Clayton Glenn; Chaplain Fay Johnson; Marilyn Nelson; Ed Hagen, colorguard; Phil Wagner; Ted Palmer; John Softchin; Sherl Stice; John Dent; Jason VanDenBosch and Orville P_kett, firing squad members who gave the 21-gun salute; and Tommy Nelson, who played taps. Fay presented the American flag from the coffin. Ray was born September 3, 1919 in Lockerby, Utah. His family moved to Arizona when he was a child. He was graduated from Globe High School, and the Northern Arizona Teacher's College in Flagstaff. Ray's parents were active in the Independent Order of Odd Fellows and Ray was initiated into Rescue Lodge No. 12, Globe, in 1936. Later he transferred to Boulder Lodge No.50, I.O.O.F. in Boulder City. Ray moved to Nevada in 1944. He started working for the U.S. Bureau of Reclamation as a draftsman, but was a realty specialist when he retired Jan. 11, 1980. He served with the U.S. Air Force during World War II and is a past commander of American Legion Post 31. Ray and Marjorie were married February 29, 1956. He was transferred to Phoenix, Arizona where they became active in the U.S. Coast Guard Auxiliary. He served as commander of Flotilla 10-4. Later, he was transferred to Idaho Falls, Idaho. When they moved back to Boulder City, they had a home built on Esther Drive. They liked to travel and owned a fifth-wheeler RV. Two years ago Ray was elected Grand Master of the Grand Lodge of Nevada, I.O.O.F. and became ill while making his official visits. He helped deliver Meals on Wheels, a project sponsored by Cactus Rebekah Lodge No. 40, I.O.O.F., of which he was a member. He also belonged to Gateway Encampment No. 23,

I.O.O.F. , the BPO Elks, NARFE, AARP and served on the board of the Boulder City Senior Center. He is survived by wife Marjorie of Boulder City; daughter Patsy Asher of Fredericksberg, Virginia; son Russell Mecham of Concho, Arizona; son Robin Mecham and daughter Becky Struthers, both of Susanville, California; 8 grandchildren, 3 great-grandchildren; brother Leland Mecham, Tucumcari, New Mexico; sisters Maxie Corey, Durango, Colorado and Evelyn Freeman, Farmington, New Mexico; and many, many friends.

Medlin, Armine
Boulder City News, Thursday, 11 Oct 1979, 2:4.
Armine Medlin, age 71, died in the Boulder City Hospital, October 2, after a long illness. Burial was in the Boulder City cemetery. He was a World War II veteran and served with the SeaBees Division of the Navy in the South Pacific. Mr. Medlin was born September 23, 1908 to Vale Hoag of Joplin, Missouri. They met and were married while they both were employed by The South West Bell Telephone Company there. They moved from Missouri in the 30's to El Monte, California. He was employed by the Acme Santa Fe Tank Company of Los Angeles for many years. After World War II they came to Boulder City, Nevada and he worked for the Bureau of Reclamation until his retirement in 1970. His wife, Vale, preceded him in death in 1967. He was also preceded in death by his parents: Lucy Ellen and Thomas Hardy Medlin and an older brother, Eugene Medlin. His surviving relatives are: two sisters: Miriam Kennedy of Boulder City, Nevada; Mildred Batson of Raytown; three brothers: Homer Medlin of Tuscon, Arizona, James Medlin of Billings, and John Medlin of Raytown.

Medlin, Val Martha
Boulder City News, Thursday, 11 May 1967, 1:6.
Val Medlin Rites May 4
Funeral services for Val Martha Medlin, 60, were held Thursday afternoon at Palm Chapel In Henderson, with the Reverend Guy Holliday of Grace Community Church officiation. She was interred in the Boulder City Cemetery. Monday at midnight, when Mr. Medlin came home from work, he found his wife dead in her chair, still holding a pencil and crossword puzzle, with the television on. She was born May 9, 1906 in Joplin, Mo. She and her husband moved here from El Monte, Calif., and

he is employed by the U.S.B.R. She loved the desert and Boulder City. Mrs. Medlin is survived by her husband Armine, 640 Avenue M; a daughter, Bonnie Marie Swimley; a sister, Yea Coolbaugh; brother, Gene Quin Blanset; aunt, Martha Dixon; and 3 grandchildren, all from California. Also many friends.

Merrill, Betty
Boulder City News, Thursday, 10 Mar 1988, 6:2.
Betty Merrill, 69, passed away Sunday, March 6. She was born March 7, 1919. She had lived in Boulder City many years but had recently moved to Cayucos, Calif. While in Boulder City she was active in the Horsemans Assoc. She leaves two daughters, Gail Galloway of Calif.; and Diane Verser of Las Vegas and a son Glen Merrill, also of Calif., eight grandchildren and two great grandchildren. Graveside services will be Friday at 3 p.m.

Merritt, Earl
Boulder City News, Thursday, 12 Feb 1959, p.1.
Our City Mourns The Loss Of One Of Its Most Loved And Highly Honored Citizens. Capt. Earl Merritt
Capt. Merritt Passes Away After Heart Attack
One of Boulder City's best loved citizens, Capt. Earl Merritt, of the Rangers passed away yesterday morning at the local hospital at the age of 52. He suffered a heart attack last Friday afternoon at his home and was rushed to the hospital where he was put in an oxygen tent. Capt. Merritt was born in Moselle, Miss., Sept., 3, 1906, the son of Mr. and Mrs. James Merritt, both deceased. He was one of hour sons and four daughters, all of them living. In 1943 he was united in marriage to Gertrude Jetnnette Boyer who also survives him. The captain served two hitches in the Armed Forces – the U. S. Marine Corps from December 1924 to December 1928 and was a sergeant in the Military Police of the U. S. Army from February 1943 to September 1945. Between his duties in the military service he became a Ranger and was promoted to his present rank in 1942. Capt. Merritt was a member of the Boulder City Elks lodge, the Veterans of Foreign Wars, the American Legion and the Boulder City Sportsmen. He was also a member of the First Baptist Church. Funeral services are incomplete, pending the arrival of members of his family. But, it is known that he will be buried in Boulder City. Harold Corbin,

City Manager, when told of his death states: "He was a very loyal and sincere man and will be missed by everyone in the community." Elton Garrett voiced the thoughts of many when he stated that he will be a tremendous loss to all of us. He cited the fact that when the chief of the Bureau of Reclamation Rangers was away, Capt. Merritt was in charge and always gave splendid cooperation to Garrett in his position as U. S. Commissioner. DeWitt Tracht summed up the thoughts of everyone when he expressed the admiration people felt for Capt. Merritt in his work and his helpfulness to everybody.

Michaels, Frederick Andrew
Boulder City News, Thursday, 12 Dec 1974, 3:4-5.
Frederick Michaels Services Today
by Esther Shipp
BOULDER CITY - Military funeral services will be held at 2 p.m. this afternoon for Frederick Andrew Michaels, 57, who died Monday of a heart attack. The rites will be conducted at Palm Chapel in Henderson by Bill Hamilton and Harold Knox, officers of Post 3574 Veterans of Foreign Wars. Burial will be in the Boulder City Cemetery. Known by the various nicknames of Fred, Andy and Mike, he was born March 20, 1917 in Chicago, Illinois. He worked for 21 years on the police force in Chicago, and was a captain. In World War 2, he served as a radio section chief in the 24th Signal Company of the U.S. Army, and was a Staff Sergeant when discharged in 1945. He earned a bronze star medal for operations against the enemy in Mindanao, Philippine Islands. The Michaels Family came to Boulder City in 1962, and Mike was employed by the Boulder Natural Gas Company, until he retired. He was active in the VFW, holding a life membership in Post 3574, by which he was elected commander four times, beginning in 1966. He held the office this term. He was an active member of the Ham Radio Citizens Radio Station, and the Men's Commercial Bowling League. Mike was also a member of the Boulder City First Nighters, playing a bit part in "Deadwood Dick." He built the set for this "Mmellerdrammer" and "You Can't Take It With You." He liked to play cards in the afternoons, with several buddies. Survivors are his mother, Ida Michaels, 636 Ave. F; a daughter, Jayne (Mrs. Steve) Forman, Mountain Home, Idaho; and a brother, Randolph "Randy" Michaels, the former Boulder City finance officer now in Central Point, Oregon.

Milam, Charles August "Gus"
Boulder City News, Thursday, 19 Aug 1976, 8:1-5.
Charles August "Gus" Milam Passes Away
A four year resident of Boulder City, Charles August "Gus" Milam, who resided at 1209 new Mexico Street, passed away Friday August 13, 1976, in the Boulder City Hospital. Mr. Milam was born September 22, 1907, in Leitchfield, Kentucky. He was an active member in the First Baptist Church, Boulder City, and a member in good standing in the Masonic Lodge and the order of Eastern Star in Boulder City. A wholesale grocer clerk by trade, he retired at the age of 63 and not long thereafter he and Mrs. Milam moved from Phoenix to Boulder City. Mr. Milam is survived by his wife, Etta; a son, Charles A., Jr., of Flagstaff, Ariz.; a brother, Ernst of Leitchfield, Kentucky; three stepdaughters, Ila Craft of Glendale, Ariz,.; Shirley Frazier, Milledgeville, Tenn.; Patricia Forrest, Patagonia, Arizona; and eighteen grandchildren. Out of town friends and relatives who attended the funeral were: Mr. and Mrs. Wm. Craft and sons, Glendale, Ariz.; Mr. and Mrs. Richard Morris, Phoenix, Ariz.; Mr. and Mrs. Chas. A. Milam, Jr., Flagstaff, Ariz.; Mr. and Mrs. Quinten Brown, Independence, Mo.; Mr. Miller Brown, Independence, Mo; and Mr. and Mrs. Udell Brown, Richland, Wash. Arrangements were with Palm Mortuary, Henderson. Services were at the First Baptist Church in Boulder City, Monday, August 16, 1976, at 11 a.m. with the Reverend Ray Magruder officiating. Masonic Services were held at graveside, and interment was in Boulder City Cemetery.

Milka, John H.
Boulder City News, Thursday, 14 Feb 1980, 19:3.
A funeral mass will be said Friday at 9 a.m. at St. Andrew's Catholic Church for John H. Milka, 57, who died February 12 in Henderson. Father Joe Anese will officiate. Mr. Milka was born October 9, 1922 in Chicago, Illinois and was a retired painter. He had lived in Boulder City for two years. He is survived by his wife, Eleanor Milka of Boulder City; a son, Robert Milka of Park Ridge, Ill.; daughter, Joan Gilligan of Haughton, Louisiana; a brother, Edward Milka of Chicago; and seven grandchildren. Interment will be at Boulder City Cemetery.

Miller, Charles R.
Boulder City News, Thursday, 12 Jun 1980, 3:6-9.
Charles R. Miller, 66, of Boulder City, died Thursday in Boulder City. He was a four-year resident of the area. He was born Sept. 16, 1913 in Ohio City, Ohio, and was an auto salesman. He was also a veteran of World War II. He is survived by his wife, Jeanette of Boulder City; daughters, Sharalee Schwecheimer of Lander, Wyo., and Joan West of San Jose; nine grandchildren and three great-grandchildren. Funeral services were held Saturday in Palm Chapel, Henderson. The Reverend Stephen Neesley of First Southern Baptist Church in Boulder City officiated. Burial was in Boulder City Cemetery. Palm Mortuary in Henderson handled arrangements.

Miller, Doris Mather
Boulder City News, Thursday, 26 Jan 1978, 8:5-6.
Doris Mather Miller, 80, passed away January 19 in Boulder City. She had lived in the area for 27 years and was so well known by many Boulderites for the many years she worked at the Boulder City Hospital as a Registered Nurse. Ms. Miller leaves beloved friends, Amelia Hanmore and Ketch Wilson. She was born November 30, 1897 in Manawa, Wisconsin. She had resided at 612 Ave. F. Graveside services were held last Monday at Boulder City Cemetery.

Miller, Frederick Nathan, Sr.
Boulder City News, Thursday, 11 Dec 1952.
At the request of Frederick Nathan Miller, Sr., 64, funeral services will be conducted by the Church of Jesus Christ of Latter-day Saints this afternoon at 2:00 p.m., with Jerry Morley officiating. Bishop Leonard Stubbs is the speaker, with the invocation by Glade Stubbs. Miller Lawrence Barson will dedicate the grave, and Leroy Burt will offer the closing prayer. Interment will be at the Boulder City cemetery. Miller came to Boulder City about six years ago to recuperate from an injury received at Davis Dam, according to his neighbors. He kept close to his home at 95 Lakeview and followed his hobby of gardening. Miller was born in Florence, Arizona, September 2, 1888, and married Artie Surrie on March 23, 1910, in Bisbee, Arizona. He was a retired miner. He is survived by his widow, one son, Edward N. Miller of Cedar City, Utah;

three sisters, Mrs. Edith Cummings, Wilcox, Ariz., Al Miller, Phoenix, Ariz., Mack Miller, St. David, Ariz., and Warren Miller, St. David, Ariz.; and one grandson, Eddie Miller of Cedar City, Utah.

Mills, Marguerite J.
Boulder City News, Thursday, 18 Feb1988, 27:6.
Marguerite J. Mills, 73, died Sunday, Feb. 14, 1988. She was a resident of Boulder City for the past four years. She was born July 26, 1914 in Washington, D.C. and was a dental hygienist, retiring in 1961. She is survived by her daughters, Alberta Ellis, Boulder City and Suzanne Berry of Cupertine, Calif.; son, Thomas a'Becket of Millersville, Md.; brother, George Jeager of Tacoma Park, Md.; and sever grandchildren. Memorial services will be Friday, Feb. 19 at 3 p.m. in Grace Community Church, Boulder City. Burial is private, Palm Mortuary, Henderson handled arrangements. In lieu of flowers, the family requests donations be made to Grace Community Church of a favorite charity.

Mills, Ralph E.
Boulder City News, Thursday, 20 Nov 1975, 3:2.
Ralph E. Mills Services Held Mon. At Palm
Ralph E. Mills, 64, passed away Nov. 13 in Las Vegas. He was born May 14, 1911 in Brookline, Mass, and was a resident of 1305 Monterrey Drive in Boulder City. He was a six months resident of this area and was a past master at the Boston Lodge A F&AM. He is survived by his widow, Edith; daughters Linda Mills, Las Vegas, Anna of Waltham, Mass. and Jane Bowler of Peabody, Mass,; stepsons, Robert Chandler, Billingham, Mass., Richard Chandler of Oxford, Conn., stepdaughter, Shirley Clarahan of Manchester, Conn., 12 grandchildren. Funeral services were held yesterday at Palm Chapel with interment at the Boulder City cemetery.

Mitchell, Benjamin F.
Boulder City News, Thursday, 29 Aug 1985, 33:1-2.
Benjamin F. Mitchell, 71, of Boulder City, died Aug. 20. He was born in Big Springs, Texas on March 4, 1913. He was an operating engineer and had been a five-year resident. He leaves one brother, Al of Oregon. The funeral was held Friday in Palm Chapel, Henderson, with burial in the

Mooney, Beulah E.
Boulder City News, Thursday, 4 Feb 1993, 8:1-3.
Beulah E. Mooney, 74, a 51-year Boulder City resident died Tuesday, Jan. 26 in a local hospital. Born July 19, 1918 in Depew, Okla., she was a homemaker. She is survived by her daughter, Nell Gutierrez of Tempe, Ariz. and five sons, Dywen Mooney of Coleville, Wash., Hugh Mooney and Denzil Mooney, both of Boulder City, Cecil Lloyd Mooney of Nelson and Hershel Mooney of Boulder City; and a brother, Walter Jefferson Nicks of Boulder City and seven grandchildren and three great-grandchildren. Services were held. Palm Mortuary handled arrangements.

Mooney, Trenie Leon
Boulder City News, Thursday, 22 Mar 1979, 10:5.
Services were held yesterday at Palm Chapel for Trenie Leon Mooney, 19, who died March 18 as the result of an automobile accident. Mr. Mooney was born December 31, 1959 in Boulder City and had been a lifetime resident of the city. He was employed by State Industries in Henderson. He is survived by his father, Dywen Mooney, of Boulder City; mother, Mary Johnson, of Los Angeles, Calif.; and grandparents Mr. and Mrs. Cecil Mooney of Boulder City and Mr. and Mrs. Joseph Archuletta of Farmington, New Mexico. Interment followed at Boulder City Cemetery.

Moore, Alexander Leslie
Boulder City News, Thursday, 16 Nov 1961, 7:5.
A. L. Moore Buried Today
Alexander Leslie Moore, 73, died late Monday night, after an illness of several years. He had been in the Southern Nevada Memorial Hospital for a week. Mr. Moore has been living in Boulder City since 1954, with his daughter Marjorie (Mrs. Ray) Mecham. Mr. Moore was born April 25, 1888, in Helena Mont. He escaped death as a young man, when he was buried alive in a gravel pit, and lived to survive 7 brothers. He was an electrician by trade, and worked as a high-line man in Washington. He once managed an apartment house in San Francisco. He is survived by his wife, Elizabeth, of San Francisco; a son, James R. Moore of Palo Alto,

Calif.; and three daughters, Marjorie Mecham of 1120 Fifth St., Boulder City; Marian Moore of San Francisco, and Jean Mayden of San Jose, California. Graveside services will be conducted today at Boulder City Cemetery.

Moore, David G.
Boulder City News, Thursday, 2 Feb 1967, 15:8.
David Moore Buried Here
Funeral services were conducted Jan. 25 at 11 a.m. at St. Christopher's Episcopal Church for David G. Moore, 611 Ave F, with Father Robert Nicholas officiating. Burial was in Boulder City Cemetery. Mr. Moore was born Oct. 22, 1910 in Colorado and had been a local resident for nine years. He was employed as an operating engineer, and a member of Local 12. He is survived by his widow, Connie, this city; two sons, David, of Spring Valley, Calif., and Patrick of Imperial, Calif.; two stepsons, Howard Clarke, Boulder City, and Robert Clarke of Garden Grove, Calif,; one stepdaughter, Jean Isham, Binghamton, N.Y., and a sister, Mrs. David Law, Grants Pass, Ore.

Moore, Gaylen A.
Boulder City News, Thursday, 7 Dec 1995, 9:1.
Galen A. Moore, 41, died Sunday, Dec. 3, 1995 in a local hospital. Born Oct. 29, 1954 in Boulder City, she had been a resident for 11 years. She was an oral health care merchandiser; most recently with the Pizer Co. In 1962 she moved to Yuma, Ariz., and completed her education. She was married in 1975 and resided in Phoenix until returning to Boulder City. An outdoor enthusiast, one of her favorite things was camping. She had a great sense of humor. Witty and funny, and in the most dire circumstances could evoke laughter. Even in the last days of her illness, she was joking with those around here. She is survived by her husband, David W.; two daughters, Kaycee and Karee; parents, Bill and Ardeen Sears, all of Boulder City; and two sisters, Karen Dejoria and Jayme Phillips, both of Henderson. Graveside services will be held at 11 a.m. today at the Boulder City Cemetery. Arrangements were handled by Palm Mortuary of Henderson.

Moore, Harold G.

Boulder City News, Friday, 23 Apr 1948, 1:2.
Harold Moore Dies After Long Illness; Funeral Tomorrow
Harold G. Moore, resident of Boulder City for 14 years, died yesterday noon. Funeral services will be held at 10 a.m. tomorrow in Grace Community Church. Reverend Winston Trever will officiate. Burial will be in Boulder City Cemetery. Graveside ritual will be performed by Veterans of Foreign Wars Post No. 3574, of which Moore was a member. Death came in Boulder City Hospital, where Moore had been under treatment for Addison's disease. The deceased is survived by his mother, Mrs. W. A. Moore, with whom he lived at 651 Ave. D; two brothers, Eugene T. Moore, also of 651 Ave. D, and Claude Moore, 668 Ave. K; and three sisters, Mrs. Hurlburt Smith of Independence, Ore.; Mrs William H. Wells, Twin Falls, Idaho, and Mrs. A. V. Slater, Burley, Idaho. Mrs. Smith arrived here early yesterday; the other two sisters were en route. Moore was born May 20, 1914, in Twin Falls. He came to Boulder City in 1934 and operated a small locomotive for Six Companies. In 1937 he went to work for the Bureau of Reclamation as a rigger. During the war he spent three years in the Army's chemical warfare service, European theatre. After the war he returned to his job here, but left it last July when his illness began. He and his brothers about that time began building an auto court at 804 Nevada Highway. It was opened for business a few days ago, but Harold was unable to see it.

Moore, Ivetta

Boulder City News, Thursday, 13 Nov 1969, 1:1.
2 Locals Killed In Crash
Chester William Brinkerhoff, 45, of 680 Eighth St. and Mrs. Ivetta Moore, 33, of 657 Seventh St., died instantly Tuesday in a one-car crash on the North Shore Road. He was pinned beneath the car which skidded 98 feet, left the road and flew 34 feet in the air before striking a bank and digging a nine-foot trench. The car then flew another 34 feet uphill and struck a second time at the top of a small knoll. Mrs. Moore was thrown 10 feet from the car to the right. Robert Strenge of 2001 E. Tonopah, Las Vegas, a witness, said he was going west when the Brinkerhoff car came head-on over a rise in the middle of the road. Strenge told the Nevada Highway Patrol that Brinkerhoff swing back to his won side of the road, but swung too far. Funeral services have been set for Mr. Brinkerhoff at 9

a.m. Saturday at the LDS Church in Boulder City with Bishop Jake Williams officiating. Services will follow at 2 p.m. in Virgin, Utah, and burial will be at the Virgin cemetery. Mr. Brinkerhoff was born Aug. 11, 1924, in Virgin, Utah. He was a meat cutter. He is survived by a wife Delora, son Stephen; daughter Cheryl; mother Mrs. William Brinkerhoff, of Virgin; sisters Clara Spendlove, Luella Thompson, and Verna Brown of Richland, Washington; Brother Kay Brinkerhoff, Salt Lake City. Services for Mrs. Moore will be held Monday at 11 a.m. at the Calvary Foursquare Church in Boulder City. She was born Jan. 21, 1937 in Gilbert, Ariz. She is survived by her husband, Eldon, daughter Donna; sons Marvin and Jerry; parents, Mr. and Mrs. Walter J. Nicks; sisters Loeta Shafer, Georgia Standfield; brothers, Willie J., Louis T, Charles and Robert and a grandmother Martha Holt. Interment will be at the Boulder cemetery.

Moore, Minnie
Boulder City News, Thursday, 24 Jul 1975, 8:1.
Minnie L. Moore, 92, was laid to rest Tuesday morning, in the Boulder City Cemetery.; Funeral services were held by Pastor Ray Magruder at the Southern Baptist Church, of which Mrs. Moore was a charter member. Pallbearers were John Forrester, Dick Porter, Wesley Nicholson, Herb Seymore, Robert Parker and Clifford Sailor. She died July 18 in the Boulder City Hospital, where she had been a patient 6 weeks. She was born Feb. 19, 1883 in Aurora, Missouri. Minnie and her husband, W. A. Moore, lived in Idaho many years. They were parents of three sons and three daughters. In 1936 they moved from Filer, Idaho, to Bolder City, where two of their sons were helping in construction of the dam. Their home on Avenue D attracted many visitors with cameras, because of her beautiful flowers. Mr. Moore died in 1945, their son Harold died in 1947, and Eugene in 1962. Minnie is survived by her son Claude, owner of Moore's Trailer Park, with whom she has been living at 611 Bryant Court; her daughters, Pearl Smith, 647 Ave. D, and Thelma Wells, 655 Ave. I, both of Boulder City; and Mildred Slater, Reno. There are 4 grandchildren, 10 great grandchildren, and 4 great-great grandchildren.

Morlang, Henry "Red"
Boulder City News, Thursday, 17 Nov 1994, 9:2.
Henry "Red" Morlang, 81, died Thursday, Oct. 27, 1994 at a local hospital. Born March 23, 1913 in Max, N.Dakota, he had been a resident of Boulder City for five years. He was a retired heavy duty equipment mechanic. He is survived by his wife of 60 years, Mary R. Guido, of Boulder City; two daughters, Nancy Carlyle, of Boulder City; Betty Rocha, of Lake Havasu City, Ariz.; two sisters, four grandchildren and two great grandchildren. Services were held. Arrangements were handled by Palm Mortuary of Henderson.

Morris, Jesse D.
Boulder City News, Thursday, 14 Jul 1994, 9:1-2.
Jesse D. Morris, 75, died July 8, 1994. He was born Aug. 14, 1918, in Hillsboro, Ill., and had been a resident of the Boulder City and Caliente areas for 52 years. He is survived by two daughters, Betty Whitener of Corvallis, Ore., and Jeanie Robinson of Las Vegas; a son, J. Dan Morris MD of Prescott, Ariz.; and six grandchildren. The family requests donations be made to Nathan Adelson Hospice, 4141 S. Swenson, Las Vegas, Nevada. Services were held Wednesday. Arrangements were handled by Palm Mortuary in Las Vegas.

Morris, Dr. Ray Vernon
Boulder City News, Thursday, 7 Oct 1971.
Funeral services were held for Dr. Ray Vernon Morris, 76, at Christ Lutheran Church. The rites were conducted by the Reverend Dan Gimbel, and burial followed in the Boulder City Cemetery. Dr. Morris died Tuesday, Sept. 28, in the Boulder City Hospital. Ray Morris was born Dec. 20, 1894 in Sheldon, Missouri, but spent most of his life in Oklahoma. He as a podiatrist for 40 years in Oklahoma City, before retiring and moving to Nevada in 1961. He is survived by his widow, Shirley, 659 California Avenue; sons Ray V. Morris Jr., Oklahoma City, and Thomas H. of Palo Alto, Calif; daughter Jeanne R. Ray, Tallahasse, Fla, 12 grandchildren and 1 great-grandchild.

Moritz, Cora Trimble
Boulder City News, Thursday, 7 Jun1977, 5:4.
Cora Moritz Services Today
Local services will be held today at 9 a.m. for Cora T. Moritz, former Boulder City resident, who died June 6 in Fallbrook, California. Mrs. Moritz was born April 3, 1891 in Denver, Colorado. She is survived by a daughter, Maxine Wylie of Fallbrook and a brother, Max Ferguson of Las Vegas. Interment will follow at Boulder City cemetery. Palm Mortuary is in charge of arrangements.

Moritz, Cora Trimble
Boulder City News, Thursday, 7 Jun1977, 5:6-7.
Lovely Cora Trimble Moritz Dies in California
by Teddy Fenton
All friends who remember Cora Trimble Moritz will not forget her lovely presence in Boulder City. A tiny queen-like figure with a halo of silver hair always lying about her lovely face in perfect condition, she walked with an upright grace that no other woman in our town could match. It was easy to compliment her appearance although we were inclined to take her for granted for she never left the home unless attired as if she was going to a great ball. As this is being written no details of the services have been relayed so we will count on an announcement in the NEWS and carry forth some of the instances for which she will long be remembered. On Dec. 3, 1947, a fine writer named Fanny Connelly did a bang-up job capturing the role played by the then widowed Cora Trimble. Her husband, Bill Trimble became chief ranger of Boulder City in 1933 and held that position until 1940 when he died of a heart attack. Cora became a landlady and she did all of her own scrubbing as the rentals vacated. She bought into the Boulder City Sweetshop where now stands the "Sun Circle" Art Gallery. Famous for its many flavors of ice cream she really made a wide circle of friends among the townsfolk but she sold out to accept the position f the "hostess at the castle" which was the DWP lodge on the hill across from our big water tank. Cora was perfect for that job. She was indeed the queen that fate had intended her to be. She presided at dinners for honored guests, she was ideal for the job and became famed for the way she put the guests at their ease. She had formerly been employed by the USBR as matron for the Government guest house and dormitory and she knew the engineers from every state.

Cora Trimble married "Mr. Boulder City" and began another kind of life. He was E. A. Moritz, former reclamation director of Boulder City but known throughout Bureau of Reclamation circles as "Mr. Reclamation." They lived at 1024 Wyoming St. On the walls of their home, especially in the study, there were dozens of awards given to Mr. Ernest Moritz. Life had been a real challenge for Cora Moritz for she loved serving people. As long as she acted as hostess at the Dept. of Water and Power lodge, she took charge of the dinner parties and prepared the food herself. Heavy cleaning, work was done by maintenance men. She will be buried at the Boulder City cemetery.

Moritz, Ernest A.
Boulder City News, Thursday, 28 Aug 1975, 1.
Mr. Reclamation Ernest A. Moritz Dies at 92
Funeral services were held Monday morning for Ernest A. "Ernie" Moritz, the grand old man known as "Mr. Reclamation." He would have been 93, Saturday. The rites were conducted at Palm Chapel in Henderson by the Reverend Clark A. Tea of St. Christopher's Episcopal Church in Boulder City. Interment was in the Boulder City Cemetery. Pallbearers were Arleigh B. West, Louis R. Douglass, Henry Pelham, William J. Williams, Roy Gear and William Phillips. Ernest Moritz was born August 30, 1882 in Sheboygan, Wisconsin, the son of Anna (Bidgenbach) and Louis Moritz. He received a B.S. degree from the University of Wisconsin in 1904, and was awarded a scholarship to complete his civil engineering degree in 1905. That year, he accepted a summer job with the new Reclamation Service, and was assigned to Garden City, Kansas. In the fall, he returned to the University where he was instructor in applied mathematics for three semesters. For awhile, he worked in Chicago, Ill. in bridge building. However, in 1907 he went back to the Reclamation as assistant engineer on the Yakima Project in Washington. Soon he became engineer in charge, and the structures he built in those early years continued sound, and were one of the most successful Reclamation projects. He married Avera C. Flint on June 30, 1909. They were the parents of two sons and a daughter. She died April 25, 1948, in Boulder City. In 1912, as a side duty, he became editor of the monthly publication which was the forerunner of the present Reclamation Era. On the Washington staff, in charge of engineering plans, specification and contract analysis, he was the first to recognize the value of experimental

investigation – an activity now carried out in USBR Denver Laboratories. In 1914 he authored the volume "Working Data for Irrigation Engineers." In August, 1915, Moritz transferred to the newly established office of design and construction at Denver. In March, 1920, he became project manager of the Flathead project in Montana. He resigned in April, 1921, to engage in private business with his brother, C.J. Moritz of Effingham, Ill., dealing in municipal engineering and heavy construction work on buildings, highways, sewers, bridges and dams. In 1934, he once again returned to the U.S. Bureau of Reclamation as engineer at Parker Dam (then the world's deepest). In 1938, he was construction engineer on Marshall Ford Dam near Austin, Texas. When it was finished in 1941, he became Director of Power, Boulder Canyon Project, at Hoover Dam, in Boulder City. When the U.S.B.R. was regionalized in 1943, Mortiz was named director of Region 3, comprising California, Southern Nevada, most of Arizona, small portions of Southern Utah and Western New Mexico. He was a member of the American Society of Civil Engineers, Tau Beta Pi Fraternity, and was active in the Rotary Club for many years. On September 16, 1949, he married Cora S. Trimble, who had come to Boulder City in 1933 with her husband William, and was chief ranter for the USBR until his death in 1940. For several years she was the hospitable hostess of the Department of Water and Power Lodge on Hillside Drive. In April, 1952, Mortiz retired and was awarded the Distinguished Service Medal of the Department of the Interior, sanctioned by Congress for outstanding governmental service. Here for the occasion were Undersecretary of the Interior Richard Searles, Commissioner Michael Straus, Arizona Congressman Harold Patten and Arizona Senator (Democratic Majority Leader) Ernest McFarland. In October, 1953, he was recipient of one of the two life memberships in the National Reclamation Association, at ceremonies in the University of Nevada (Reno), attended by Secretary of Interior Douglas McKay. In June, 1954, he spent five weeks at the University of California Hospital, undergoing two critical operations for spinal blocks which threatened to paralyze his legs. At that time, he was serving as chairman of the Boulder City advisory council. He resigned from this in April, 1958. For a year, in 1953-54, Mortiz was a member of the Clark County grand jury. Governor Charles Russell appointed Moritz to a post on the Colorado River Commission in August, 1954. He worked on this until his declining health forced him to curtail his activities. He and his wife moved to Las Vegas not long ago. Although all of these positions have been serious, the "grand old man" was also known for his wit and humor. He is survived by his widow, Cora, 4255 Spencer St., Las Vegas; sons Holly Moritz, Centerville, Ohio, and Robert Mortiz, Dallas, Texas; daughter Betty (Mrs. G. L.) Jones, Austin, Texas; stepdaughter Maxine (Mrs. L.F.) Wylie, Fall Brook, California; and seven grandchildren.

Morley, M. Marie
Boulder City News, Thursday, 6 Jan 1994, 10:1-2.
M. Marie Morley, 92, died Tuesday, Dec. 28, 1993 at a local hospital. Born May 21, 1901 in Victor, Colo., she was a resident of Boulder City for 46 years. She was a retired dry cleaning seamstress. She was preceded in death by her husband, Claude and her son Kay. She is survived by two sons, Robert E. Morley, and Jerry H. Morley both of Boulder City; three sisters, Willa Caldwell, also of Boulder City; Melva Young, of Folsom, Calif,; and Callie McMurdy, of Salt Lake City, Utah; 14 grandchildren, 30 great grandchildren, and two great great grandchildren. Services were held Monday. Interment is at the Boulder City Cemetery. Arrangements were handled by Palm Mortuary of Henderson.

Moser, Alpha L.
Boulder City News, Thursday, 2 June 1983, 33:1-2.
Alpha L. Moser, 76, died Monday. She was a __ year resident of Boulder City. She was born Jan. 6, 1907 in Colorado and was a homemaker. She is survived by her husband, John Moser of Boulder City; daughters, Maxine McLean of Northridge, Ca. and Kay White of Provo, Utah; brother, Perry Moore of Canada; 10 grandchildren; and 13 great-grandchildren. Services were 3:00 p.m. Wednesday at the Boulder City Christian Center Church. Burial followed in Boulder City Cemetery.

Moya, Moises
Boulder City News, Thursday, 21 Srp 1989, 29:1.
Moises Moya, 78, a resident of 6 years of Boulder City, died Friday in Las Vegas. He was born Jan. 16, 1911 in Frisco, New Mexico. He was a truck driver for a freight company. He was a member of the Teamsters Local #103 Phoenix, Ariz. He was a member of the Saint Andrews Catholic Community, Boulder City. Survivors included his wife, Ruby Moya of Boulder City; a sister, Adelina Sedillo of Flagstaff, Ariz.; three

sons, Moses Moya of Phoenix, Ariz., Jake Moya of Torrence, Calif,; and Jimmy Anthony Moya of Rancho, Calif, and his daughter, Ruby Reid of Boulder City; his 13 grandchildren and six great grandchildren. Services were held. Palm Mortuary handled arrangements.

Mull, William Robert
Boulder City News, Thursday, 10 Mar 1988, 6:1.
William Robert Mull, 70 died Tuesday, March 1 in Las Vegas. He had been a resident of the Boulder City area for the past six years. He was born in Middletown, Ohio on June 27, 1917 and was the owner of a tavern. He was a major in the United States Army. He belonged to BPOE No. 1682 of Boulder City and the VFW of Middletown, Ohio. Survivors include wife Ruth, Boulder City; daughters Roberta Sue Williams, Dayton, Ohio; Linda Sue Wilson, Fairfield, Ohio; Eve Mae Holder, Corona, Calif.; Darleen Koppin, Franklin, Ohio; Dawn Rene Hill, Middletown, Ohio; sons Robert Lester Mull, Lebanon, Ohio and Ray Gayhart, Franklin, Ohio; sister Jane McCandless, Middletown, Ohio. Visitation began Thursday, March 3 at 3 p.m. with funeral services at 2 p.m. March 4 in the Palm Chapel in Henderson. The family suggests memorials be made to BPOE No. 1682 of Boulder City.

Myers, Arthur L., Jr.
Boulder City News, Thursday, 2 Mar 1956, 20:1.
Arthur L. Myers, Jr., 64, a Boulder City resident for the past ten years, died Wednesday, Feb. 22 in Las Vegas. Born in Warren, Ohio, on Nov. 4, 1924, he was a shipping clerk for a tire manufacturer. He is survived by his wife, Victoria Myers of Boulder City, and three sisters, Jean Fisher, Bonnie Seretko and Delores Biddlestone, all of Warren, Ohio

Myers, Leona
Boulder City News, Thursday, 8 Nov 1956, 12:4.
Final Rites Today For Mrs. Meyers
Final rites are being held this afternoon at 3 o'clock in the Church of Christ in Henderson for Mrs. Leona Meyers who died Monday evening in the Boulder City Community Hospital where she had been confined for three days. Friends are invited to attend. Mrs. Meyers had lived in Boulder City for the past 11 years, coming here from Muskagee, Okla.

She was 84 years old and resided at 528 ½ Avenue K. Widowed, Mrs. Meyers is survived by two sons, Jack Alldridge of 700 California in Boulder City, and Alvin Alldridge of Lancaster, Tex. and six grandchildren and 11 great grandchildren.

Myers, Victoria
Boulder City News, Thursday, 22 Feb1990, 9:1-2.
Victoria Myers age 62, of Boulder City passed away Sunday Feb 18, 1990 while visiting family in Warren, Ohio. She was a 12 year resident of Boulder City. Her husband Arthur preceded her in death. She leaves a twin sister Virginia Dyson, of Boulder City, sisters Elizabeth Spangenberg, Julia Capito, Arelene Rutan and Alice Rutan all of Warren, Ohio; Olive Lane of Cerritos, CA., and Eleanor Kountz of Modesto, CA., numerous nieces and nephews. Services were held in Warren, Ohio. Burial was in Boulder City cemetery.

Neely, Elenore E.
Boulder City News, Thursday, 11 Aug 1994, 8:3.
Elenore E. Neely, 82, died Aug. 3, 1994, in a local convalescent home. Born July 26, 1912, she had been a resident of the Boulder City area since 1971. She is survived by her son, Brian Hurt, of Valencia, Calif. Arrangements were handled by Palm Mortuary in Henderson.

Neilson, Dustin
Boulder City News, Thursday, 19 Mar 1981, 31:8.
Dustin Neilson, age 2, passed away Tuesday at Sunrise Hospital. He was the son of Kent and Lisa Neilson of Henderson. Mrs. Neilson is the former Lisa Goodbar of B. C. Grandparents are Katy Elgin of Boulder City and Mr. and Mrs. Byron Neilson of Henderson. Graveside services will be Friday in Boulder City.

Nelson, Larry Leroy
Boulder City News, Thursday, 12 Jul 1990, 6:1-2.
Larry Leroy Nelson, 55, a 21-year resident of Boulder City, died Wednesday, July 4, in a local hospital. Born June 30, 1935, in Bellview, Missouri, he was a senior patrolman for a utility company. He is survived by two sons, Michael Nelson and Randall Nelson of Boulder City; and a

daughter Joy Lynn Le-Clair of Arcadia, Missouri; and four grandchildren. Memorial services were held Saturday, July 7 at 1 p.m. in Palm Chapel in Henderson. Arrangements were handled by Palm Mortuary of Henderson.

Newbanks, Alma R.
Boulder City News, Thursday, 13 Apr 1978.
Alma R. Newbanks, 66, passed away April 6 in Boulder City. She has resided in the area since 1945. Mrs. Newbanks was born August 17, 1911 in Plainview, Arkansas. She lived at 701 Elm Street. Survivors include daughters, Alma Hatfield and Janiece Tyrell of Boulder City; sons, Mack Newbanks and Ray Torrence of Huntington Beach, California; stepdaughters, Ida Mae Callazo and Maxine Apadaca of Van Nuys, California; 18 grandchildren and 11 great grandchildren. Services were held last Monday at the Four Square Gospel Church. Interment followed at the Boulder City Cemetery.

Newbanks, Mack
Boulder City News, Thursday, 18 May 1972, 5:8.
B. C. Pioneer, M. Newbanks Dies Here
Mack Newbanks, a 40-year resident of Boulder City, died Tuesday at the Boulder City Hospital. Mr. Newbanks, age 69, was born Oct. 1902, and was living at 701 Elm St., space 36. He is survived by his wife, Alma, son Mack, Jr., both of Boulder City; daughters Alma Hatfield, Boulder City; Idie Callaco, Van Nuys, Calif.; Maxine Apadec, Calif.; stepdaughter, Janiece Tyrell, Henderson; step-son, Ray Torrence, Huntington Beach, Calif.; 14 grandchildren and two great-grandchildren.

Newman, Emma Nathalia
Boulder City News, Thursday, 2 Apr1987, 7:3.
Emma Nathalia Newman age 82, of Boulder City passed away Friday, March 27, 1987. She was born April 7, 1904 in Lincoln, Neb. She was a nine-year resident, and a retired school teacher. She leaves her daughter, Shirley Nutter of Boulder City; grandsons, Steven Nutter of Moapa and Darrell Nutter of Oklahoma City, Okla.; granddaughter, Ida Haxton of Phoenix, Ariz., and eight great grandchildren. Services were Tuesday in Boulder City Cemetery.

Nicholson, Hallie O.

Boulder City News, Thursday, 10 Sep 1992, 10:3-4.
Hallie O. Nicholson, 91, a 46 year Boulder City resident died Wednesday, Sept. 2. Born Jan. 12, 1901 in Paola, Kan., she was a homemaker. She was a member of Christ Lutheran Church in Boulder City. Survivors include a daughter Louise Voehlker of Prescott, Ariz., a brother, Albert McHenry of Mt. Shasta, Calif.; two grandchildren and four great-grandchildren. She was preceded in death by Wesley Nicholson. Services were held. Palm Mortuary of Henderson handled arrangements.

Nicholson, Leonard

Boulder City News, Tuesday, 1 Dec 1942, 1:2.
Military Honors at Rites for L. Nicholson Today
Funeral services for Leonard Nicholson, aviation cadet who was killed in a plane crash last week at Ft. Stockton, Texas, will be at 2 p.m. today at Grace Community church, and military honors will be accorded at the graveside service, according to T. L. Nicholson, father of the deceased. The service at the church will be conducted by the Reverend Winston Trever, and arrangements have been made for a military salute to be fired at the graveside by enlisted men from Camp Williston. The body was due to arrive at 8 o'clock last evening, having bee delayed by train service. Nicholson, who had been in the army for a year and a half, was completing his qualification for rating of second lieutenant when he was killed in a plane crash during his final solo flight, at Ft. Stockton. Members of the DeMolays will act as pallbearers for the service.

Boulder City News, Wednesday, 2 Dec 1942, 1:2.
Leonard Nicholson Is Laid To Rest with Taps
Relatives and friends of Leonard Nicholson, killed recently in a plane accident while in army service at Ft. Stockton, Texas, attended services at which he was laid to rest with military honors at the Boulder City cemetery yesterday afternoon, following funeral services at Grace Community church. An army guard of honor from Camp Williston fired the salute and taps were sounded from the graveside and echoed by another bugler atop the hill. The Reverend Winston Trever conducted the services at the church and at the grave, and Mrs. C. E. Roark played appropriate music on the organ. Pallbearers were Millard Spearman, Dick Chase, John Pilant, Leo Downing, Melvin Sharp and Bill Downing,

Melvin Sharp and Bill Ewing, members of the DeMolay, to which Leonard Nicholson belonged as a member. Nicholson was killed last week when the plane in which he was making his last solo flight as a navigation cadet to qualify for his commission, crashed at Ft. Stockton.

Nicholson, Wesley Omer
Boulder City News, Thursday, 19 Feb 1976, p.12:5-6.
Wesley Nicholson Services Held
Funeral services were held Tuesday for Wesley Omer Nicholson, 75, who died last Thursday at the St. Rose de Lima Hospital. The Reverend Ray Magruder officiated at the First Baptist Church, of which the Nicholsons were charter members. Pallbearers were members of Boulder Lodge No. 37, F & A.M. to which Wesley belonged. Burial was in the Boulder City Cemetery. Wesley was born April 28, 1897 in Mars, Pennsylvania, but his folks soon moved to a ranch in Arizona. He joined the U. S. Navy in 1917. When he was discharged in 1919, he was a member of the Naval Reserve while working on the experimental farm for the University of Arizona. Wesley and Hallie were married May 19, 1918. Later, they lived in Oklahoma, where Wes worked in the oil fields. Next, they went to New Mexico. In 1931, Wes Signed with the Six Companies as labor foreman at the Dam site, and the family moved to the Nevada desert, from Texas. The Nicholsons were active in the formation of Grace Community Church, and Hallie helped Zona Courtney start the Cradle Roll, which later became the base of the present Boulder City Mothers' Club. In later years, Wes served on the Council. They both belonged to the Adult Bible Class. When the Hoover Dam was completed in 1935, the Nicholsons returned to Texas for a few years. In 1942, Wesley was employed by the U. S. Bureau of Reclamation at the water treatment plant in Boulder City, and the family lived at 1354 Denver St. He was filter plant operator when he retired in July 1962. Their daughter Louise, who was an infant when they first came to Nevada, was graduated from Boulder City High School in 1948. She had been active in Christian Endeavor, Sunday School at Community Church, and sang in the choir. She was employed by the U. S. B. R. Until her marriage at Edward Voelker, Sept. 16, 1951, and the couple moved to Flagstaff, Ariz. Ed is employed by the U. S. Geological Survey. When Grace Community Church expanded, several denominations built their own sanctuaries. The Nicholsons were second on the list to help found the First Baptist Church, on Avenue B. Leaving

the "government house," the Nicholsons moved to a lovely new home at 718 Ninth Street. They both belonged to AARP, NARFE, and Wesley was a member of American Legion Post No. 31. They had a beautiful garden, enjoyed working in their yard, and took pride in the fruit trees. Wesley is survived by Hallie; his daughter Louise Voelker, Flagstaff, Ariz.; two grandchildren; a sister, Cora Riggs, St. Mary's West Virginia; two brothers, Floyd Nicholson of Portland, Oregon; and Joe Nicholson of Fontana, California.

Nickell, Wilbur Dent
Boulder City News, Thursday, 2 Nov 1972.
Funeral services will be held at 1 o'clock this afternoon for Wilbur Dent Nichell, 58, at the Boulder City Ward of the Church of Jesus Christ of Latter-Day Saints. Bishop Jake Williams will officiate. Burial is to be in the Boulder City Cemetery. Mr. Nickell died Saturday, October 28, in the Rose de Lima Hospital. He was born Dec. 12, 1913 in Bates County, Missouri. He worked as a transmission man for the Bell Telephone Company, which transferred him to Boulder City from Los Angeles, 20 years ago. Survivors are his wife, Mildred, 813 Utah St., son Roger with the U.S. Navy in Vietnam, a daughter, Tamara Nickell of Los Angeles, and one grandchild. Also a brother, Charles L. Nickell of Mississippi, two sisters, Cicele Sargent of Urich, Mo., and Helen York of Butler, Mo.

Nixon, Bessie Jane
Boulder City News, Thursday, 15 Apr 1992, 12:2-3.
Bessie Jane Nixon, 88, died Tuesday at a local hospital. Born Sept. 12, 1904 in Brown, Ill., she was a homemaker in Boulder City for three years. She was a member of the Boulder City LDS Church, 3rd Ward. She is survived by two daughters Rose Thomas of Boulder City and Belva Horton of Lake Elsinore, Calif.; two sons, William F. Thomas of Alma, Wash., and Grover L. Thomas of Dundee, Ore.; 11 grandchildren and 13 great grandchildren.

Noble, Florence Virginia
Boulder City News, Thursday, 2 Feb 1978, 4:4.
Funeral services were held last Tuesday for Florence Virginia Noble, 67, who passed away January 28. Mrs. Noble was born May 11, 1910 and at the time of her death was residing at 3738 Pilgrim Street in Las Vegas. She is a former resident of Boulder City and had lived in the area since 1942. Survivors include a daughter, Phyllis Pendergrass of Las Vegas; one brother, Robert Simpson of Billings, Montana; and a sister, Iva Clark of Belfry, Montana; four grandchildren and one great grandchild. The services were held at Palm Chapel with interment following at the Boulder City Cemetery.

Norman, Bert Jr.
Boulder City News, Thursday, 8 Nov 1990, 17:3.
Bert Norman Jr. died Nov. 2 in a local hospital. He was 72. He was born June 2, 1918 in San Pedro, Calif. and had resided in Boulder City for six of the 34 years in Nevada. He is survived by his wife, Helen. Two daughters Julie Burt, of Las Vegas and Christine Nay of Boulder City; and a son Bert Norman, III of Chino, California.

Norman, Charles R.
Boulder City News, Thursday, 28 June 1973, p.10:4.
Accident Kills Charles Norman
Charles R. Norman, 17 year-old son of Leonard M. and Deon W. Norman was killed in a motorcycle accident near San Bernardino, Calif. at 4:15 a.m. Monday. He was riding on a cycle driven by Kenneth Eckhoff of 4613 Alpine Place, Las Vegas. Funeral services for Eckhoff, who was returning to his post with the U. S. Navy in San Diego at the time of the crash, are pending in Redlands, Calif. Norman was a passenger on the cycle with Eckhoff when it hit a freeway overpass guardrail on Interstate 15 and threw the youths 25 feet to the street below the overpass. The cycle was traveling at a high speed at the time of the crash, the California Highway Patrol reported. He was born in Framington, New Mexico, July 29, 1955. He was a Boy Scout, member of the LDS Church, played in the Boulder City High School land and was a graduate with the 1973 class. He is survived by his parents, a brother John, of Boulder City; Grandparents John and Pearl Williams of LaVerkin, Utah, and Mrs. Floy

B. Norman, of Santa Barbara, Calif. Funeral services under the direction of Bunker Brothers Mortuary, will be held at the LDS Church in Boulder City today at 10 a.m. Burial will be at the Boulder City cemetery. Bishop Bryant Solomon and Stake President Leonard Stubbs of the LDS Lake Mead Stake, will officiate.

Norman, Helen M.
Boulder City News, Thursday, 19 Sep 1991, 10:4.
Helen M. Norman, 60, died Tuesday in a local hospital. Born March 1, 1931, in Northville, S.D., she was a resident of Boulder City for 18 years and she had been a bookkeeper with a construction firm. She is survived by two daughters, Julie Burt of Las Vegas; Chris Nay of Boulder City, and one son, Bert Norman of Chico, Calif. Services will be held at 1:30 p.m. today. Arrangements were handled by Palm Mortuary of Henderson.

Novasconi, James
Boulder City News, Thursday, 20 Dec 1979, 5:6.
James Novasconi, 89 years. Long time resident of Boulder City passes away Monday at the Veteran's Hospital in Prescott, Arizona after a lingering illness. He was a Veteran of World War II, serving in the Asiatic-Pacific Theater. His survivors include: a sister, Mrs. John (Helen) Crim of Ouray, Colorado; two step-sons, Harold Barrell of Salt Lake City, Utah and Gene L. Barrell Sr., of Boulder City; a step-daughter, Judith Hefty, of Montana; fourteen grandchildren and two great grandchildren; and Frances and Flora Coughlin of Ventura, California, an Aunt and Uncle. Mr. Novasconi's wife, Lucille, preceded him in death. Services will be conducted by the Boulder City American Legion Post #31, under the direction of Commander Billie Ward at the Boulder City Cemetery. Father Joe Annesse of St. Andrews Church will officiate at the graveside services. He was a veteran of the New Guina, Bismark Archipelago Western Pacific, So. Philippine, Luzon, and Papuan-Battles and Campaigns. He held rank of Staff Sergeant with the 71st Bombardment Squadron - 38th Bombardment Group. Services will be held Thursday, December 20 at 11 a.m. at the Boulder City Cemetery with Palm Mortuary officiating.

Novasconi, Lucille
Boulder City News, Thursday, 26 Oct 1967, 1:1.
Novasconi Rites Set Friday
Services will be held tomorrow at 2 p.m. at Palm Chapel in Henderson for Lucille Novasconi, 47, who passed away in Boulder City Hospital last Tuesday. Mrs. Novasconi had been a resident of Boulder City for the past six years and lived at 701 Elm St. She was a member of the Gem Club. She is survived by her husband, James; daughter, Judy Hefty, Las Vegas; sons, Harold L. Barrell, Carter Lake, Iowa; brothers, Edward L. Green, Boulder City and Earl L. Green of Victorville, Calif.; father, Ernest L. Green, Boulder City, and five grandchildren. Reverend Paul W. Pfankuch of the Prince of Peace Lutheran Church will officiate and interment will be in Boulder City Cemetery.

O'Hara, William "Bill"
Boulder City News, Thursday, 13 Aug 1953, p.1:1-2.
Bill O'Hara Passes Away, Funeral Held Tuesday
Funeral services for William "Bill" O'Hara, prominent local resident, were held Tuesday evening at St. Christopher's Episcopal church. Reverend Jack Fredricks conducted the rites. Interment was in the Boulder City cemetery. Mr. O'Hara passed away Friday at the Marcus L. Lawrence Hospital, Cottonwood, Arizona, following an illness of three years. He had been a patient at the Cottonwood hospital for almost a month. His wife was with him at the time of death. He was born August 11, 1891, Princeton, Kentucky. He married Hattie Schart in Pagosa, Colorado, in 1916. They moved to Boulder City in 1932 and were among the first residents of the community. Mr. O'Hara operated a cleaning and tailoring shop until 1946. Following his retirement from the tailoring-cleaning business, he became a real estate broker. For many years he was a member of the Chamber of Commerce. He was active in the Elks lodge having a 41-year membership and was a charter member of the organization. He held membership in the Masonic Lodge and Episcopal church. The Masons and Elks attended the rites in a group. Surviving besides his widow are four children, Mrs. J. H. (Joysa) Spann of Fort Knox, Kentucky; Mrs. J. E. (Joanne) Harris of Waco, Texas; Bill O'Hara Jr., of Fontana, Calif.; and A. J. O'Hara of Long Beach, Calif., and nine grandchildren. All the children will be here for the service. He also had two brothers, Phil O'Hara and Grady O'Hara both of Knoxville,

Tennessee. Pall bearer were Joe Lappin, Phil Noble, George Van Horn, Charles Kimball, Carl Merrill and Jack Alldridge. Honorary pall bearers were Clarence Watson, A. G. Boyton, Frank Lewis, Albert Franklin, Jack Kleindeinst, F. C. Nelson, Lawrence Barnson, W. A. Nicholson, O. L. Gray, J. E. Turner, Richard Warren, Frank Baker, Harry Smith, Claude Nichols and D. A. Jones.

Olson, Bernice
Boulder City News, Thursday, 10 Dec 1987, 19:1.
Bernice Olson, aged 89, died Sunday, November 29 in Boulder City, where she had been a resident for the past ten years. She was born in Bishop Hill, Illinois on May 16, 1898 and was a dance teacher before her retirement. She had no local survivors. Graveside services were held and arranged by Palm Mortuary of Henderson on Dec. 2 in Boulder City Cemetery.

Orchard, Charles L.
Boulder City News, Thursday, 24 May 1979, 10:7-8.
Charles L. Orchard, 71, passed away May 21 in Boulder City. He had been a resident since 1973. Born January 27, 1908 in Minneapolis, Minnesota, Mr. Orchard had been employed as a dispatcher for the U. S. Post Office. He was a member of the V.F.W. post of Boulder City. Survivors include his wife, Yvonne Orchard of Boulder City; a daughter, Charmion Woofe of Bellmont, California; a son, Anthony K. Orchard of Italy; and eight grandchildren. A rosary service will be held Thursday at Palm Chapel at 6:30 p.m. and a funeral mass will be said at St. Andrew's Catholic Church on Friday at 10 a.m. Interment will be at the Boulder City Cemetery.

Orchard, Yvonne C.
Boulder City News, Thursday, 14 Apr 1983, 2:5-7.
Yvonne C. Orchard, who had resided in Boulder City since 1973, passed away in Belmont, Ca. April 12. She was born Dec. 28, 1908. She is survived by a daughter Charmion Woofe of Belmont, Ca.; a son Anthony K. Orchard of Italy and eight grandchildren. Rosary services will be held tonight at 5:30 at Palm Chapel in Henderson, and Mass will be held Saturday at 11 a.m. at St. Andrews Catholic Church in Boulder City.

Father Joe Anese will officiate. Interment will be in the Boulder City cemetery.

Osborn, Guy H.
Boulder City News, Thursday, 15 Sep 1983, 29:1-2.
Guy H. Osborn, 79, died Thursday September 1, 1983 in Boulder City. He was a resident 1 month. Mr. Osborn was born November 4, 1903 in Berneyville, Oklahoma. He was a retired welder from Steamfitter, Pipefitter local 250 of Gardena, Calif., and a member of the Seaside Lodge. He leaves a wife Ida Mae; son Ralph Osborn and grand daughter Carolyn of Lakewood, California. A brother; Hugh Osborn, of East Polock Pines, Calif., a sister Ruby Martin of Tulare, Calif., and a nephew John Myers of Las Vegas, Nevada. Services were conducted by the Boulder City Masonic Lodge with determent in Boulder City Cemetery.

Ott, Helen Elizabeth
Boulder City News, Thursday, 31 Jan 1991, 10:1.
Helen Elizabeth Ott, 71, died Saturday, Jan. 26 in a local hospital. She was a 12-year resident of Boulder City. She was born April 25, 1919 in Kenosha, Wis. She was a member of the Boulder City Senior Center and Community Club and was married 45 years to Charles. She is survived by her husband Dr. Charles W. Ott of Boulder City; three sons, Charles W. Ott III and Roger Ott, both of Illinois and Christopher Ott of Washington; two daughters, Cynthia Lee Malinowski of Indiana and Linnea Ott of Las Vegas; a brother Hjalmar Peterson of Texas; and three grandchildren. Services were held Tuesday at Palm Henderson Chapel. Arrangements were handled by Palm Mortuary of Henderson.

Pace, Stella K.
Boulder City News, Thursday, 9 Sep 1971.
Services For Stella K. Pace
Graveside services will be conducted by the Reverend Guy Holliday tomorrow at 10 a.m. for Stella K. Pace, 88, who died at the Boulder City Hospital Wednesday. She lived with her daughter, Ruth Pesout, at 300 Navaro Ct. The deceased is also survived by two sisters, Mildred Weaver, Pleasanton, Kans., and Kilene Davis, Springdale, Ark. Palm Mortuary is in charge of arrangements.

Rader, Ruth O.
Boulder City News, Thursday, 23 Jul 1985, 10:1.
Ruth O. Rader, age 92, of Boulder City, passed away Sunday, July 19, 1987 in a local hospital. She was born Aug. 26, 1894 in Central City, Colorado. She was a homemaker and a 47 year resident. She leaves her stepdaughter, Julie Cleland of Manhattan, Kansas. Graveside services were held in Boulder City Cemetery.

Palmer, Alice H.
Boulder City News, Thursday, 20 Aug 1964, 1:4.
Friends Pay Last Respects To Mrs. Palmer
The Funeral Mass was said Tuesday morning for Alice H. Palmer, 67, who died in her sleep Friday night at her home, 520 Fifth Street. The Rosary was recited Monday night by Father Gerald Fanning at St. Andrew's Catholic Church. Mrs. Palmer had lived in Boulder City 22 years. In January, 1962, she retired as chief cook for the Boulder City Hospital, where she had worked 15 years. She was a member of the Altar Society at st. Andrew's. Mrs. Palmer was born March 21, 1897 in Turber, Texas. She is survived by her daughter, Marie Lawellin of 809 New Mexico Street, Boulder City; a son, Thomas of Northridge, California, and seven grandchildren.

Palmer, Thomas
Boulder City News, Friday, 26 Aug 1949, 6:5.
Final services were held Monday for the late Thomas Palmer, who died Friday at the Boulder City hospital after a long illness at the age of 60. The Rosary was recited Sunday evening at St. Andrew's church by the Reverend Florence Flahive, who conducted the funeral mass yesterday morning at 9 o'clock in the church and the graveside services at the Boulder City Cemetery. Members of the Boulder City Elks lodge, of which Palmer was a long time member, acted as pallbearers for both services. Sunday evening Phil Harrigan, C. A. Savage, Alfred Fisher, W. T. Manning, Barney Gino and Joe Lappin officiated the Rosary service. For the funeral service and at the graveside, the pallbearers, with the exception of Leading Knight Chester Widner, were all lodge brothers residing in the same block with Palmer on Fifth street, George Campbell, Glen Muchow, William Williams, Phil Harrigan and I. J. Robicheaux.

Palmer, after residing here several years, went to the coast for his health, returning to his Boulder City home about six months ago. His condition steadily grew worse and he was taken to the hospital, where Mrs. Palmer is a member of the staff, on last Thursday. In addition to the widow he leaves a daughter, Mrs. William Lawelin, and a son, Thomas Palmer, Jr., of Los Angeles, and four grandchildren.

Palumbo, Marilyn E.
Boulder City News, Thursday, 26 Oct 1965, 12:1-2.
Marilyn E. Palumbo, 50, of Boulder City, died Oct. 21, 1995. She was born June 14, 1945, in Chicago, Ill., and was a member of St. Andrews Catholic Community of Boulder City. The family requests donations be made to Stop DUI, 3321 Sunrise Ave. Suite #107, Las Vegas, NV 89101. She is survived by two sons, David M. of Henderson, and John A. of Boulder City; two daughters, Angela M. of Boulder City, and Laura M. of Henderson; her father, Al E. Kepler of Chicago, Ill.; and a brother, Ed Kepler of Rochester Hills, Mich. Services were held Wednesday. Arrangements were handled by Palm Mortuary in Henderson.

Park, Preston Ray
Boulder City News, Thursday, 29 Jul 1965, 1:4.
Lakeview Youth Killed
Preston Ray Park, 18, 402 Lakeview Dr., was killed early Sunday morning when his lightweight motorcycle collided with the rear of a car near East Las Vegas. Highway patrol officers said the youth was attempting to avoid the pursuit of a sheriff's deputy. Investigating officers said the sheriff car reached speeds up to 80 miles an hour in following Park when the collision occurred. The driver of the car was absolved from all blame for the accident. The youth was rushed by ambulance to Southern Nevada Memorial Hospital where he was pronounced dead on arrival. He was born March 26, 1946 in Santa Rita, N.M. and was employed as a salesman. Survivors: mother, Mrs. Mildred Bailey, North Las Vegas; father, William Park, Ely; brothers, Billy and George, Henderson; sister, Mrs. Rosemary Hetrick, Jamestown, N.Y. and maternal grandmother, Gertrude Trayler, Texas. The Reverend William Bromley, Jehovah's Witnesses, officiated at services in Bunker Brothers Mortuary at 2 p.m. Wednesday and interment was in Boulder City Cemetery.

Parker, Elizabeth Anne

Boulder City News, Thursday, 16 Oct 1986, 12:1.
Elizabeth Anne Parker, 97, of Boulder City, died Thursday, Oct. 9 in Boulder City. She was born June 3, 1889 in Wilmington, Indiana. She is survived by her daughter, Margaret Day of Boulder City; sister, Mary E. Polley of Indio, Calif.; grandchild David of __; and two great grandchildren.

Parmelee, Thelma

Boulder City News, Thursday, 20 Feb 1975, 8:1-2.
Catholic funeral services were held Friday afternoon for Thelma G. Parmelee, 70, who died Wednesday in Las Vegas. Father Theodore Can Skee, chaplain at St. Rose de Lima Hospital, officiated at Palm Chapel in Henderson. Burial was in the Boulder City Cemetery. Thelma Garrett was born Jan. 31, 1905 in Missouri. She received her BA degree from the University of Wyoming, and taught in that state for seven years. She and her husband, Thomas L. Parmelee, came to Boulder City from Phoenix, Ariz. in 1948, when he transferred here as realty assistant for the USBR Region 3 irrigation division. Their three children were born here. He passed away in January, 1969. Thelma taught first or second graders in the Boulder City Elementary School for nearly 10 years. In 1959 she was awarded the American hearing Society's Kenfield Memorial Scholarhsip, which entitled her to necessary training to teach lip-reading to children with a hearing loss. She earned her MA from northern Arizona University in the field of special education, and did extra work in speech and hearing at San Francisco State and Los Angeles State. She received a scholarship for this from the Emblem Club. She held an elementary life certificate to teach in Wyoming and Nevada. In 1960, she began teaching the newly organized class for the aurally handicapped in Henderson. For her outstanding success, she was given a plaque when she retired in 1970. Thelma had moved to Las Vegas in recent years. She is survived by her son Fred Parmelee and daughter Sue Pearson, both of Las Vegas; a son Charles Parmelee, Ridgecrest, Calif.; a sister, Ione Tamasi; brothers, James and William Garrett, all three of Des Moines, Iowa.

Parmenter, Marylyn
Boulder City News, Thursday, 8 May 1987, 10:5-6.
Marylyn Parmenter, age 2, of Boulder City, passed away Monday, April 28. She was born Sept. 27, 1983 in Boulder City. She leaves her parents, Richard and Janice; brothers, Richard, Sean, Scott, and Bryan; sister, Janalyn, Kayelyn and Caralyn, all of the home. Grandparents, Frank and Mary of Darby, Mont. and Orpha and Donald Ream of Las Vegas. Memorial donations may be made in her name to Model Developmental Learning Center, UNLV.

Pate, Sarah C.
Boulder City News, Thursday, 9 Apr 1981, 11.
Sarah C. Pate, 74, died April 6 in Boulder City. She was born December 6, 1906 in Nova Scotia, Canada and had been a resident of Boulder City for 10 years. Mrs. Pate is survived by sons, William Pate, Jr. of Boulder City; Ernest Baker of Panbrook, Mass., Kenneth Baker of Cypress, Ca., Harold Baker of Redwood City, CA, and Phillip Baker of Clayton, WA; daughters, Sally Caven of Norwald, CA and Bonnie Harris of Framington, Mass; sisters, Eleanor Tohlen of Las Vegas, Irene Ketterer of Costa Mesa, CA and Gervis Hartling of New Hampshire; 27 grandchildren and several great-grandchildren. A Rosary was recited Tuesday at 7 p.m. at Palm Chapel and a funeral Mass was said Wednesday at 10 a.m. at St. Andrew's Catholic Church. Interment will be in Boulder City Cemetery.

Pelham, Helen Jane
Boulder City News, Thursday, 3 Oct 1991, 9:4.
Helen Jane Pelham, 76, died Monday. She was born Aug. 21, 1915, in Ogden, Utah, and had been a resident of the area for 45 years. She was a member of St. Christophers Episcopal Church, Chapter "K" PEO in Boulder City, Desert Chapter #22 Order of the Eastern Star, Past Matrons Club, Daughters of the Nile, Trustee Boulder City Hospital Board Organ Club, and Boulder City Womens Golf Association. Donations may be given to the Nathan Adelson Hospice. She is survived by two daughters, Carol Dockter of Sierra Vista, Ariz., and Patricia Fairchild of Lawrence, Kan.; one son, George Pelham of Reno; and seven grandchildren. Services will be held at St. Christopher Episcopal Church today at 10 a.m. Arrangements were handled by Palm Mortuary in Henderson.

Pellow, Florence M.
Boulder City News, Thursday, 8 Aug 1991, 9:2-3.
Florence M. Pellow, 92, died July 29, in a local hospital. She was born March 20, 1899 in Calumet, Mich., and had been a resident of the area since 1979. She was a member of the American Legion Auxiliary Post 61, Alter Society, D of I Circle #413, 3rd Order of St. Francis, Charter Member Senior Citizens, all of these lodges are in Calumet, Mich. Pellow is survived by a daughter, Margaret Gabriault of Boulder City; two sons, R. James Longpre of Boulder City and William Longpre of Canton, Mich,; one sister, Gladys Vertin of Boulder City; one brother, Cecil Toms of Boulder City; two step-children, 12 grandchildren, 18 great grandchildren and many nieces and nephews. Arrangements were handled by Palm Mortuary of Henderson.

Pendlebury, James
Boulder City News, Thursday, 7 Apr 1983, 10:2-3.
James Pendlebury, 72, of Henderson, died in Las Vegas. Mr. Pendlebury was born Nov. 20, 1910, in Massachusetts. He was an electrician. He was a member of the BPOE of Kingman, Arizona. He is survived by his wife, Martha of Henderson; son Thomas of Oxnard, Calif.; daughters, Priscilla Horne of Henderson and Mary Jane Gray of Bristol, Conn.; 10 grandchildren, and four great grandchildren. A graveside service was held in Boulder City Cemetery. Palm Mortuary handled arrangements.

Penny, Randy
Boulder City News, Thursday, 8 Sep 1988, 13:5-6.
Randy Penny, 66, a resident for the past eight years of the Boulder City area, died Sept. 3 in Boulder City. Born in Beach Grove, Ark., on July 28, 1922, he was a plasterer for Viking Builders, Inc. He is survived by daughters Rhonda L. Thormodsgaard of Boulder City and Betty Sheek of Buena Park, Calif.; son Larry Parks of San Diego, Calif.; sisters Mary Charrette of St. Louis, Mo. and Wanda Waddell of New Orleans, La.; brothers Stanley Penny and Johnny Penny both of Denver, Colo.; eight grandchildren Neil Jr., Tad, Rhonda and Kari Thormodsgaard, Cory and Kyle Sheek, Kimberly and Brian Parks. Funeral services were held at 10 a.m. on Wednesday, Sept. 7 in the Palm Chapel in Henderson. Officiating was Pastor Jim Ketchell for the Christian Center in Boulder City.

Interment was in the Boulder City Cemetery.

Pesout, Ruth Pace
Boulder City News, Thursday, 30 Jul 1987, 8:1.
Ruth Pace Pesout, age 78, passed away Saturday, July 25, 1987, in Boulder City. She was born January 25, 1909 in Addington, Okla. She was a retired elementary school teacher and a 19-year resident of Boulder City. She leaves her daughter, Joan Northrop of Boulder City; son, Donald of Livermore, Calif.; seven grandchildren and three great grandchildren. Services were held Tuesday in Boulder City Grace community Church in Boulder City. Interment was in the Boulder City Cemetery.

Peters, Mary A.
Boulder City News, Thursday, 1 Jan 1987, 1:1.
Mary A. Peters, 76, of Boulder City, passed away Thursday, Dec. 25, 1986 in Boulder City. She was born April 30, 1910, in Michigan. A longtime resident, she was a retired teacher. She is survived by her brother, George Brady of St. Charles, Mich.; and sister, Nora Bow of Merrill, Mich. Private services were held. Interment will be in Boulder City Cemetery.

Petersen, Ellis Fritz
Boulder City News, Thursday, 11 Aug 1977, 6:1.
Retired Navy Officer Dies
Ellis Fritz Peterson, 62, was buried with military honors, Monday morning, in the Boulder City cemetery. The rites were conducted by Chaplain David W. Fahner of Nellis Air Force Base. Mr. Peterson died Thursday at home, after a long illness. He was born January 4, 1915, in Salt Lake City, Utah, and worked as an asphalt foreman before his retirement. He and Lucille, his wife of 38 years, came to Boulder City five years ago. A Chief Warrant Officer in the U. S. Navy, Peterson served at Pearl Harbor. He had belonged to the American Legion, but did not join locally. He and his wife were charter members of the Rolling Boulders Chapter of the Good Sam Club. They enjoyed the outdoors, and he participated in many sports. He is survived by Lucille, 512 Don Vincente Court; a daughter, Nancy Estrada of Clarement, California;

mother, Anna Petersen of Las Vegas; brothers Ivan Peterson, Las Vegas; sister Anna Thoreson, Houston, Texas; and three grandchildren. Contributions in his name may be made to the Cancer Society.

Petersen, Lucille A.
Boulder City News, Thursday, 1 Jun 1989, 22:3.
Lucille A. Petersen, 72, a former 15 year resident of Boulder City, now residing in Redondo Beach, Calif., died Friday, May 26 in Redondo Beach, Calif. Born in Oklahoma, on April 3, 1917, she was a homemaker. She is survived by a daughter, Nancy of Redondo Beach, Calif.; a son, Fred, of Carson City; a brother, Ray Stagner of Mt. Aries, Ga.; and five grandchildren and four great-grandchildren. Services are scheduled for 11 a.m. today at Grace Community Church. Officiating will be Dr. John Rousseau. Interment will be in Boulder City Cemetery.

Petroff, Mary J.
Boulder City News, Thursday, 26 May 1988, 15:2.
Mary J. Petroff, 89, died Friday May 20 in Boulder City. She had been a resident of the Boulder City area for one month. She was born in Poland on Jan. 29, 1899 and was a homemaker. Survivors include daughter Dorothy Caputo, Boulder City; brothers Frank Dubell, Masontown, Pa. and Walter Dubell, Weatherly, Pa.; six grandchildren and six great-grandchildren. Visitation and viewing were held Sunday, May 15 from 6 p.m. to 9 p.m. at 800 South Boulder Highway in Henderson. Rosary was said Monday, May 28 at 7 p.m. with mass on Tuesday, May 24 at 10 a.m. both at St. Andrew's Catholic Church. Father Joe Annese officiated. Interment was in the Bolder City Memorial Park in Boulder City.

Phillips, John Henry
Boulder City News, Thursday, 11 Jan 1973.
Graveside services are tomorrow at 11 a.m. at B.C. Cemetery for John Henry Phillips, 79, who died late Tuesday night in the Boulder City Hospital. He had been in poor health for several years. Burial will be in Boulder City. Mr. Phillips was born in Colorado Springs, Colo. on August 25, 1893. He moved to Nevada in 1899 and lived in Ely for many years. He and his wife Susan had been married 49 years when she died in 1966. They had four children, one son dying in 1960. An electrician, Mr.

Phillips began working for the USBR in Boulder City on March 2, 1942. The family lived at 533 Hopi Place.

Pickard, Minnie C.
Boulder City News, Thursday, 13 Mar 1975, 8:7-8.
Funeral services were held Tuesday, March 4, for Minnie C. Pickard, 55, at the Palm Chapel in Henderson. Officiating was the Reverend Robert W. Richards of Henderson Community Church. Mrs. Pickard died Feb. 18 in the Boulder City Hospital. Minnie Christensen was born April 7, 1919 in Pioche, Nevada. She was married to George William Pickard, who passed away in October, 1962. The Pickards moved to Henderson during World War II, then came to Boulder City in 1957. They lived at 645 Avenue M, but in recent years she has resided at 701 Elm St. She is survived by three daughters, Marsha Rose Tomey, 701 Elm; Sharon Baker and Valene Leavitt, both of Las Vegas; three sons, Leonard Pickard, San Diego, Calif.; George W. Pickard, Florence, Arizona; and Raymond Pickard; seven grandchildren. Also a brother, Frank Christensen, Miami, Ariz.; and three sisters, Rose Rowland, 1001 Colorado St., Boulder City; Louise Showacy, 623 Ave. D, Boulder and Eva O'Brien, Las Vegas. Son Leonard composed the following verse to be inscribed on the headstone of her grave, beside her husband, in the Boulder City Cemetery: Mamma never got all that she should, The breaks in her life were too small. By many of us she was misunderstood, But Mama knew she was loved by us all.

Pilant, Jean H.
Boulder City News, Thursday, 16 Jan 1992, 7:1.
Jean H. Pilant of Boulder City died Monday, Jan. 13, 1992 in a Las Vegas hospital. She was 66. She was born April 20, 1926 in Seattle, Washington and had worked as a secretary for the State of Nevada prior to her retirement. She attended school in Boulder City and graduated from Boulder City High School. She was a member of Desert Chapter No. 22, Order of Eastern Star and Daughters of the Nile and the Social Order of the Beauceant. She was a member of Grace Community Church in Boulder City. Survivors include her husband, John W. of Boulder City; three sons, John R. of Boulder City, Richard N. of Las Vegas, Daniel C. of Kerns, Utah; a daughter Theodora Reed of Las Vegas; a brother Wilburt Parrott of Renton, Wash. Services will be conducted today;

Thursday, at 2 p.m. at Grace Community Church in Boulder City, the Reverend Richard Smith officiating. Burial will follow in Boulder City Cemetery. The family requests that in lieu of flowers, donations may be made to the Jean Pilant Memorial Fund, Desert Chapter 22, Order of Eastern Star in Boulder City.

Pilant, John Robert "Butch"
Boulder City News, Thursday, 11 Aug 1994, 8:1-2.
John Robert Pilant, 50, died Aug. 6, 1994. Born Sept. 14, 1943, in Las Vegas, he had been a resident of the Boulder City area for 20 years. He was a mail handler and a past member of Clark County Re-Act. He is survived by his father, John W. Pilant, of Boulder City; a daughter, Terri J. Reed of Las Vegas; two brothers, Richard N. Pilant of Las Vegas and Daniel C. Pilant of Kearns, Utah; an aunt, Cuba C. Pilant, and an uncle, Robert L. Pilant, both of Riverside, Calif. The family requests that donations be made to the Shriners Crippled Childrens Hospital. Services were held Tuesday. Arrangements were handled by Palm Mortuary in Henderson.

Pilant, John W.
Boulder City News, Thursday, 26 Dec 1994, 6:1.
John W. Pilant, 71, died Sunday, Dec. 25, 1994 at a local hospital. Born April 9, 1923 in Spokane, Wash., he was a retired construction electrician. He was also a veteran of the U.S. Army, having served in World War II. He was a member of I.B.E.W. Local #357; a past master of Boulder City Masonic Lodge #37 F&AM; a member of Scottish Rite Body of Las Vegas; a member of Zelzah Shrine Temple; a member of Boulder City Shrine Club; a past master of Lodge of Research #3; and a past grand patron of the Order of Eastern Star. He is survived by his wife, Lula Pilant of Boulder City; one daughter, Terri Reed, of Las Vegas; two sons, Dan Pilant, of Kerns, Utah; Richard Pilant, of Las Vegas; two brothers, Richard Pilant, of Sacramento, Calif.; Robert Pilant, of Riverside, Calif.; eight grandchildren and one great grandchild. Viewing will be from 12 p.m. to 7 p.m. today, and 8:30 a.m. to noon Friday. Services will be held at 2 p.m. Friday, at the Grace Community Church in Boulder City. Interment will be at Boulder City Cemetery. Arrangements were handled by Palm Mortuary of Henderson.

Place, Adolf Edwin
Boulder City News, Thursday, 9 Nov 1972.
95-Year Old A. E. Place Dies After Long Illness
Adolf Edwin Place, 95, of 531 Avenue L, died Nov 6 at his home following a lengthy illness. Rosary was scheduled last night at Palm Chapel in Henderson, and funeral services are scheduled for today at 2 p.m. at Palm Chapel. Mr. Place, who had a long and distinguished career as a mining engineer, was born Dec. 21, 1876 in Hamburg, Germany. His father was Harry P. Place and his mother, Antonio Schareer. Mr. Place's father was connected with banking in American and his mother immigrated to the U.S. in 1873. He attended the Technical universities of Karsrube and Braunschmeig. Later in America, he graduated from the Massachusetts Institute of Technology in 1903. He also passed the Civil service examinations as an engineer. He was employed as an engineer by the U.S. Geological Survey until 1907, when he resigned to take charge of his father's mines in Southern Mexico. Mr. Place and Buena Vertura Aispuro were married Oct. 15, 1936 in Mexico. They have been "second parents" to eight nieces and two nephews- most of whom went to school in Boulder City. He has been associated with mining all of his life, and during 1948 to 1960, was in Chihuahua, Mexico. He is survived by his wife of Boulder City, three daughters, Alberta Horn, Henderson; Tetra Gome, Henderson; Elvira Cuppa, Las Vegas and ten grandchildren.

Poncin, George Peter "Pete"
Boulder City News, Thursday, 2 June 1955, 1:3.
"Pete" Poncin Passes Away
This area today was mourning the death of one of its older residents – George Peter "Pete" Poncin whose familiar little real estate building was a landmark in the Pittman ward of Henderson. Poncin, 81, passed away yesterday afternoon after a brief illness. Funeral services will be held Friday afternoon at the Boulder City cemetery with Father David Wilson presiding. The rites will be private. Poncin is survived by two daughters, Mercedes Manis, wife of John Manis, Boulder City, and Eulila Beatty of Port Orchard, Washington. Poncin came to Nevada in 1935 as an employee of the Park Service and moved to Southern Nevada after retiring from the Park Service and then started his real estate business in 1942.

Potter, Roy Willard

Henderson Home News and Boulder City News, Thursday, 18 Dec 1980, 31:5-6.
Services for Roy Willard Potter, 78, owner of Photographic in Boulder City were held last Monday at noon in Bunker Chapel. Mr. Potter and his wife, Irene, were married in Calgary, Alberta, Canada, on March 22, 1921. They had lived in Warm Springs from 1954 until moving to Boulder City three years ago. Mr. Potter is survived by his wife Irene and several nieces and nephews. The Reverend Frank Hutchinson officiated.

Poulos, Charles

Boulder City News, Thursday, 23 May 1985, 36:2.
Charles Poulos, 80, of Boulder City, died Friday in Henderson. He was born Sept. 17, 1904 in Greece. An 18-year resident, he was a machinist. He is survived by his wife, Flossie of Boulder City; daughter, Christina Kosappis of La Canada, Calif,; son, Basil of Anaheim, Calif.; eight grandchildren and three great-grandchildren. A graveside service was Monday in Boulder City Cemetery. Palm Mortuary, Henderson handled the arrangements.

Price, Ethel R.

Boulder City News, Thursday, 19 Jan 1989, 25:3-6.
Ethel R. Price, 63, a resident of Henderson of 33 years and a resident of Boulder for 24 years, died Jan. 11 in Henderson. Born in Terryville, S.D. on June 4, 1924, she was a homemaker and a member and past matron for the Order of Eastern Star Desert Chapter 22 in Boulder City and a member of the Henderson Presbyterian Church. She is survived by her husband, Leo of Henderson; sons Ronald and Gary both of Henderson; daughters, Vicki Carlman and Patti Presquez of Henderson and Debbi Wythe of Las Vegas; mother Lucille Salter of Henderson; sisters, Ruth Knox of Arlington, Texas and Aileen Wells of Houston, Texas; brothers Tom Cooper of Boulder City; stepmother, Wilma Cooper, also of Boulder City; and 13 grandchildren. Palm Mortuary of Henderson handled the arrangements.

Price, Leo Edward
Boulder City News, Thursday, 3 Jan 1991, 7:3-4.
Leo Edward Price, 71, a 50-year resident of Henderson, died Saturday, Dec. 19/ Born in Gillespie, Ill. on Aug. 25, 1919, he was an electrician and veteran of the U.S. Army. He is survived by his three daughters, Vicki Carlman of Henderson; Debbi Wythe of Las Vegas and Patti Fresquez of Lancaster, Calif.; two sons, Ronald Price of Ririe, Idaho and Gary Price of Henderson; his mother, Ival Price of Boulder City; a brother Bill Price of St. Louis, Mo.; two sisters, Joyce Bywater of Boulder City and Opal Dunn of San Francisco, Calif.; and 13 grandchildren. Memorial services are scheduled at 1 p.m. today, in the Henderson Presbyterian Church. The family suggests memorials in his name be made to Nathan Adelson Hospice in Las Vegas. Arrangements were handled by Palm Mortuary of Henderson.

Puckett, Audrey M.
Boulder City News, Thursday, 17 Apr 1980, 12:7-8.
Services were held Tuesday at Palm Valley View Chapel for Audrey M. Puckett, 61, who died April 10 in Boulder City. The Reverend Ethan Gebauer of Mt. View Lutheran Church officiated. A resident of Las Vegas she has lived in the area since 1945. She was born December 19, 1918 in Chicago, Illinois and was active in a marriage encounter group. She was a homemaker. Mrs. Puckett is survived by her husband, Charles Puckett of Las Vegas; sons, Ken Frejlach of Covina, Calif. and Gary Puckett of Long Beach, Calif.; daughters, Karen Langley of Covina, Bonnie Tucker of Las Vegas and Charlene Dunford of Reno; a brother, Wally Frank of Henderson; sisters, Jerri McBriade of Lombard, Ill., and Elinor Collins of Chicago; and ten grandchildren. In lieu of flowers, donations may be made to the Arthritis Foundation. Interment was at Boulder City Cemetery.

Pulleyn, Leon W.
Boulder City News, Thursday, 13 Dec1979, 7:7-8.
Graveside services were haled Wednesday afternoon at the Boulder City Cemetery for Leon W. Pulleyn, 85, who passed away December 8 in Henderson. The Reverend Gary Moore of Bethany Baptist Church officiated. Mr. Pulleyn was born September 16, 1894 in Castile, New York. He is survived by his wife, Olive, of Boulder City; sons, Ronald Pulleyn, of Boulder City, Arthur Pulleyn of Magnolia, Delaware, and David Pulleyn of Ithica, New York.

Pulleyn, Olive D.
Boulder City News, Thursday, 15 Dec1988, 10:1-2.
Olive D. Pulleyne 88, died Wednesday, Nov. 30. She was born in Sugar Run Penn., and a 24 resident of Boulder City. She is survived by her sons, Ronald of Boulder City, Arthur of Magnolia, Del, and David of Ithaca, N.Y. Eleven grandchildren and four great-grandchildren. Graveside services were officiated by Pastor Frank White of Bethany Baptist Church. Interment was in Boulder City Cemetery next to her husband Leon, who preceded her in death by nine years. Anyone interested may make donations to the Boulder City Care Center, Activity Fund, in her memory. Checks may be made out to BCCC Activity Fund, 601 Adams Blvd, Boulder City.

Pumphrey, Beatrice E.
Boulder City News, Thursday, 30 May 1974, 3:3.
Funeral services were held Friday afternoon for Beatrice E. Pumphery, 77, at the Palm Chapel in Henderson. Michael Thorn of the Salvation Army officiated. Interment was in the Boulder City Cemetery. Beatrice Cooper was born Sept. 26, 1896, in Granger County, Texas. A retired operator of a rest home, she came to this area in 1971, and lived at 816 Cheryl Lane. She is survived by four brothers – Clarence L. Cooper, 1408 Monterey Dr., Boulder City; Harold Cooper, Ferguson, Mont.; Robert M. Cooper, Burbank, Calif.; and Edgar E. Cooper, Dennison, Tex.; three sisters, Jane Seiber, Mary Gotchall and Jemima Boston, all of Jacksonville, Ill.

Puryear, Nelie

Boulder City News, Thursday, 30 July 1970.
Graveside services at B. C. Cemetery will be conducted by the Reverend Guy Holliday Friday at 10 a.m. for Nelie Puryear of 521 Avenue K who died Tuesday at B.C. Hospital. She was born Dec. 26, 1882 in Mobeetie, Tex., and has been a resident here for 27 years. Mrs. Puryear is survived by two daughters, Mrs. Rae Royer, 521 Avenue K, this city, and Mrs. Billie Mallot of Woodlake, Calif.; a son, Tom Puryear and a brother, Harry T. Frye, both of Wheeler, Tex., also three grandchildren and one great great grandchild. Friends may pay their respects at Palm Mortuary in Henderson throughout today and in lieu of flowers are asked to contribute to their favorite charity.

Quinn, John "Jack"

Boulder City News, Thursday, 3 Sep 1992, 10:4.
John "Jack" Quinn died Wednesday, Aug. 26, 1992 in San Bernardino, Calif. He was 54. He was a former long-time resident of Boulder City. He graduated from Boulder City High School in 1957. He was an army veteran and had worked for Cal-Nev pipeline for 27 years. He is survived by his brothers, Herbert and Michael, both of Boulder City, Nev., and his sisters, Fran Gordon, Mary Peterson and Martha Phillips, all of Las Vegas, Nev. In lieu of flowers, the family requests donations to the American Heart Association, American Cancer Society or a favorite charity of the donor's choice. Graveside services were held Wednesday at Boulder City Cemetery.

Raddatz. John Walter

Boulder City News, Thursday, 25 Aug 1977, 10:3-4.
Accidental Shooting Claims Boulderite
John Walter Raddatz, age 24, died of an accidental shooting Saturday August 20 at his place of employment, AA Row Wrecking and Salvage. He was born in Merced California where he lived until he was 8. He them moved to Las Vegas where he lived and met and married Cathy Conner. They made their home in Boulder for 2 years. He worked at the Husky and Big K Car Wash while living in Boulder. He and his family moved to Las Vegas where they have made their home for the past 3 years. He is survived by his wife, Cathy, his daughter, Eva, his parents Mr. and Mrs.

Robert Grunwald of Caliente, and his mother-in-law, Mrs. Eva Conner.

Ramsey, Henry L.
Boulder City News, Thursday, 25 Dec 1990, 19:1-2.
Henry L. Ramsey, 70, a resident of Boulder City since 1945, died Jan. 21 in Boulder City. Born in Ely, Oct. 22, 1919, he was retired. He is survived by his wife, Ursula Ramsay, of Boulder City; a son, Jerry L. Ramsay, and daughter, Judy K. Rowland, both living in Boulder City; also a brother, Wendel S. Ramsay, of St. George, Utah; a sister, Ella Belleville, of Gabbs, Nev.; six grandchildren and one great grandchild. Services will be held at 2 p.m. today, in the Boulder City LDS chapel. Interment will in the Boulder City Cemetery. Arrangements are handled by Palm Mortuary.

Ramsey, Nina
Boulder City News, Thursday, 17 Apr 1980, 12:7-8.
Services were held last Monday at Grace Community Church for Nina Ramsey, 71, who died April 11 in Boulder City. The Reverend Mel Pritts officiated. Mrs. Ramsey was born September 27, 1908 in Indiana and had lived in Boulder City since 1951. She was a homemaker. She is survived by her husband, Ralph Ramsey of Boulder City; son, Douglas K. Ramsey of China; brothers, Haldah, Harry, Donald and Forrest Garton, all of Ft. Wayne, Indiana; and a sister, Lucy Shaw of Abingdon, Maryland. In lieu of flowers, the family has requested that donations may be made to St. Jude's Ranch for Children or the Southern Nevada Children's Home, both in Boulder City. Interment followed at Boulder City Cemetery.

Ray, Helen Pherrin
Boulder City News, Thursday, 23 Dec 1993, 11:3-4.
Helen Pherrin Ray, 85, died December 18, 1993, in a local hospital. Perrin was born Dec. 19, 1907 in Central City, Iowa. She had been a resident of Boulder City for 40 years and was a member of Phi Mu Sorority O.E.S. #22, Desert Chapter. She is survived by her son, Donald V. Ray of Las Vegas; five grandchildren and seven great grandchildren. She was preceded in death by her father, J.B. Pherrin and her mother Jessie Morton. Services were private. Arrangements were handled by Nevada Funeral Service in Las Vegas.

Rayford, Brooks
Boulder City News, Thursday, 12 Dec 1974, 8:5.
Brooks Rayford Dies in Las Vegas
Former Boulder City resident Brooks Rayford died December 6 in a Las Vegas Convalescent home. Born in Cleveland, Ohio, on July 9, 1888, he was member of the Masonic Lodge, Scottish Rite and Shriners. He had lived here for the past two years. There are no local surviving relatives. Graveside services will be conducted at Boulder City Cemetery at 2 p.m. Monday.

Raymond, James Nelson
Boulder City News, Thursday, 2 Oct 1986, 10:1-2.
James Nelson Raymond, 58, of Boulder City, died Thursday, Sept. 25. He was born July 14, 1928, in Pittsburgh, Pa. A five year resident, he was an auto manufacturing engineer and a World War II Marine Corps veteran. He is survived by his wife, Doris of Boulder City; son, James N., Jr., of Manteca, Calif,; brother, Charles A. of Pittsburgh, Pa.; sister, Mary Gesaley of Pittsburgh, Pa and one grandchild. Services were held Monday in Grace Community Church, Boulder City. Interment was in Boulder City Cemetery. Palm Mortuary handled the arrangement.

Reddington, Mary L.
Boulder City News, Thursday, 14 Aug 1986, 9:1.
Mary L. Reddington, age 49, of Boulder City, passed away Friday August 8 in Las Vegas. She was born Nov. 11, 1938 in San Francisco, California. She was a homemaker. She leaves her husband Walter of Boulder City, daughter Ellen Tudor of Pahrump, brother David Bradley of Las Vegas and three grandchildren. Interment will be in the Boulder City Cemetery.

Reding, Nellie
Boulder City News, Thursday, 5 Mar 1959, 8:6.
Mrs. Nellie Reding Passes Away Here After Short Illness
Requim Mass was celebrated Monday at 10 a.m. for Mrs. Nellie Reding, at St. Andrews Church. The deceased, 89, passed away Saturday at the local hospital after a short illness. Msgr. John M. Sibon officiated at the service and interment was in Boulder City Cemetery. Mrs. Reding was born march 16, 1898 in Johnsburg, Minn., and has made her home here

for the past year at 541 Seventh St. She is survived by three daughters, Mrs. Marie Gleason and Esther Wengert, this city, and Mrs. Agnes Warren, Mt. Rose, Ala. She also leaves two sisters, Mrs. William Long and Mrs. Emna Decker, as well as 4 grandchildren and 13 great grandchildren.

Reece, Erasmia Renee
Boulder City News, Thursday, 9 Apr1992, 9:3.
Erasmia Renee Reece, 85, an 11 year Boulder City resident died Sunday, April 5, 1992 in a local hospital. Born, June 26, 1906 in Greece, she was a retired owner-operator of a nursing home. She is survived by her husband, Howard W. Reece of Boulder City; and two daughters, Elizabeth Limverakis of Philadelphia, Penn.; Despina Tannacakis of West Lake Village, Calif.; two sons, James Constantine, El Toro, Calif. and Charles Troupe of Vacaville, Calif.; a brother, Socrates Reeves of Calais, Calif. The family requests donations be made to the Boulder City Hospital, 901 Adams Blvd., Boulder City, Nev. 89005. Services were held Palm Mortuary handled arrangements.

Reese, Bertrand "Bert" Samuel
Boulder City News, Thursday, 4 Mar 1976, 3:3.
Bertrand Reese Services
Funeral services were held Monday morning at the Bunker Chapel in Las Vegas for Bertrand "Bert" Samuel Reese, 87. Officiating was Bishop Kenneth Simkins of the First Ward of the Boulder City Church of Jesus Christ of Latter-Day Saints. The eulogy was given by his grandson, John Reese. Burial was in Paradise Memorial Gardens in Las Vegas. Pallbearers were grandsons Jack Cockrum, Lynn McDonald, Richard Kendall, Douglas, Robert and Leslie Reese. Mr. Reese was born Dec. 21, 1888 in Electric, Montana, and was one of the National Park Service Naturalist-Rangers who helped in the formation of Yellowstone National Park. His first wife was Ethel Marble. She died in 1959. He married Margaret Reese in 1961. The Reese family came to Boulder City from Montana in 1944. He was employed by the U.S.B.R. until his retirement at the age of 70. His last job was that of dog catcher – who liked and was liked by dogs! He enjoyed working in his rose garden, and playing cards. Having served in World War I, he became a member of VFW in Livingstone, Montana. He belonged to American Legion Post No. 31 and

VFW Post 3574 in Boulder City. He is survived by his wife, Margaret, 701 Elm St.; four sons, Edward L. Reese, 528 Hopi Pl.; Chester R. Reese, 643 Ave. G, both Boulder City; James Reese, Missoula, Mont.; and Robert, Sunnyvale, Calif,; two daughters, Jessie Hargrove, 701 Elm, Boulder City; Helen White, Elko, Nev.; 24 grandchildren and 30 great-grandchildren.

Reese, Margaret C.
Boulder City News, Thursday, 8 Nov 1990, 17:4.
Margaret Curdy Reese died Oct. 31 in Boulder City. She was 98. Reese was born Feb. 17, 1892 in Streeter, Ill. She had been a local resident for 23 years and was a homemaker. She is survived by three sons; Edward and Chester of Boulder City and Robert of Sequim, Wa. Two daughters; Jessie Hargrove of Boulder City and Helen White of Elko. 23 grandchildren, 56 great grandchildren and 17 great great grandchildren. Arrangements were handled by Bunker Chapel.

Reinmiller, Weldon R.
Boulder City News, Thursday, 9 Dec 1993, 8:1-2.
Weldon R. Reinmiller, 74, died Wednesday, Dec.1 at a local hospital. Born March 26, 1919 in Staplehurst, Neb., he was a resident of Boulder City for 15 years. He was a retired owner-operator of a hotel, retiring after 30 years and was a veteran of the United States Army, having served in World War II. He is survived by his wife, Mary R. Reinmiller, of Boulder City; one daughter, Ricki Van Hoorebecke of Huntington Beach, Calif.; two sons, Lee Reinmiller of Boulder City, and Roger Reinmiller of Saudi Arabia; and four grandchildren. Services were held and interment in the Boulder City Cemetery. Arrangements were handled by Palm Mortuary of Henderson.

Remington, Edith H.
Boulder City News, Thursday, 8 Nov 1956, 11:6.
FINAL RITES ARE HELD FOR EDITH REMINGTON
Final rites for Edith H. Remington who died suddenly at the Lake Mead Lodge Oct. 31 were held Sunday afternoon at the St. Christopher's Episcopal church. Mrs. Remington, who was 56, was employed at the Lake Mead Lodge at the time of her death. Survivors include a half sister, Sally Packenham of Lafayette, Calif. and a former Boulder City resident; a daughter, Mrs. Edith Hallard of Compton; three sisters, Marjorie Brown of Missoula, Mont., Daisy Carter of Morristown, N.J. and June Hileman of Libby, Mont.; and two grandchildren.

Renaud, Margueritte Louise
Boulder City News, Thursday, 8 Dec1988, 15:1.
By Ester Shipp
Marguerite Louise Ashton Renaud was laid to rest Friday afternoon. She died at home Monday night, Nov. 28, following a long illness. The Reverend John Osko of the First Baptist Church in Henderson officiated at the funeral service conducted at the Palm Chapel. Also at the graveside in Boulder City Cemetery. participating in the ceremony by Cactus Rebekah Lodge No.. 40, Independent Order of Odd Fellows, were Marjorie Mecham, Ardeen Sears, Dolores Gatlin and Clara Turner. Margueritte, better known as "Marge" to her many friends, was born May 6, 1912, in Highland Park, Mich. She lived in that state most of her life, but loved to travel. Marge was a homemaker until 1960, when circumstances forced her into the business world. She went back to school to start a career, and became manager of the Paul Revere Insurance Co. Marge moved to Boulder City in 1976, and lived in the Gingerwood Park. Her mobile home was filled with lush plants, showing that she must have had a "green thumb." She was an excellent game player, and had a wonderful sense of humor which stayed with her until her final hours. Marge always kept herself well groomed and dressed like a lady. Her illness distressed her partly because she was unable to keep up appearances. Marge joined Cactus Rebekah Lodge No. 40, IOOF April 25, 1979. She held several appointed offices. She was elected vice grand, but was unable to continue on to noble grand. She enjoyed visiting lodges in other towns, and was an interesting and pleasant traveling companion. She is survived by her daughter Joy Piche of Las Vegas, whom Marge

sincerely appreciated for all of her constant, loving care for so any months. Also a daughter Deloris Harris of Tenton, Mich; six grandchildren and one great-grandchild. Joy's feelings about her mother were expressed in the following quotation: "Some people come into our lives and quickly go. Some people stay for awhile and leave footprints on our heart and we are never the same."

Rennie, Mary A.
Boulder City News, Thursday, 19 Sep 1985, 29:1-2.
Services were held Friday in St. Andrew's Catholic Church for Mary A. Rennie, 80, who passed away on Sept. 11. She was born June 7, 1905, in St. Ignace, Mich. She had been a piano teacher and a resident of the area for 17 years. She leaves a son Don of La Habra, Calif.; daughter, Marilou Burrill of Laguna Beach, Calif.; eleven grandchildren and seven great-grandchildren. A funeral mass was said on Saturday with burial in the Boulder City Cemetery.

Reynolds, Trevis Fenton
Boulder City News, Thursday, 21 Sep 1978, 6:5-6.
Trevis Fenton Reynolds Passes
Services were held last Tuesday for Trevis Fenton Reynolds, 79, who passed away September 16 in Boulder City. Mr. Reynolds was born January 19, 1898 in Roseberg, Oregon and was a retired teacher. He was an Army veteran of World War I and a member of F and AM in Sanger, California. Survivors include his wife, Andree of Boulder City; son, Wayne Alan Reynolds of Winnepeg, Canada and a sister, Zelda M. Edwards of Corvalis, Oregon. Services were held at the boulder City Masonic Lodge and interment followed at the Boulder City Cemetery. Palm Mortuary handled the arrangements.

Richey, Charles A.
Boulder City News, Thursday, 30 July 1970.
This Morning Richey Service At St. Andrew's
A Requiem Mass will be said today at 10 a.m. at St. Andrew's Church for Charles A. Richey, 66, who died Saturday night at Rose de Lima Hospital in Henderson. Rosary was recited Wednesday evening at Palm Chapel in Henderson and interment will be in Boulder City Cemetery. Mr. Richey

was born May 16, 1904 in Iowa and until his retirement Jan. 24, 1969, had been superintendent of the Lake Mead National Recreation Area for more than 14 years. He had been an employee of the Department of the Interior for 37 years and held the department's Distinguished Service Award. A graduate of Iowa State University with a degree in landscape architecture and with graduate work at Lake Forest Foundation for Architects and Landscape Architects. Richey first became associated with the NPS in 1931 when he was employed as a junior landscape architect in San Francisco. In that position, he was a member of the first team selected to prepare master plants for the development of national parks and monuments in the west and south-west. He was transferred to Santa Fe, New Mexico in 1935 as an associate architect in the Branch of Plans and Design. In 1940 he was promoted to the position of assistant superintendent and later to superintendent of Southwestern National Monuments, administering 28 areas in four states. Three years later he was named assistant director of the service's regional office in Santa Fe and in that capacity was instrumental in working out the details of a merger of Southwestern National Monuments into the regional organization. In 1947 he was elected to serve as an advisor to the supreme commander of the Allied Powers and the Japanese government on the reorganization and replanning of the Japanese national parks. Before leaving Washington in 1954 to assume the Lake Mead superintendency, he prepared a report on land acquisition which has evolved into a statement of policy on this phase of national park administration. Mr. Richey was one of the original members of the Boulder City Planning Commission and since 1955 of the executive board of the Boulder Dam Area Council, Boy Scouts of America which he served as a commissioner. In addition he was a member of the American Society of Landscape Architects, Rotary Club, Arizona Park and Recreation Association as a member of the executive board, Nevada Park and Recreation Society and the Alpha Phi Chapter of Pi Kappa Alpha fraternity. He was also a member and helped organize the Southern Nevada Unit of the Coast Guard Auxiliary. Mr. Rickey is survived by his widow, Ruth A., 609 Fifth St., Boulder City, and two sons, Charles A., of Las Cruces, New Mexico, and Mark A. of Honolulu, Hawaii. In lieu of flowers friends are asked to make donations to the Clark County Cancer Society. Pallbearers will be D. J. Boaz, James R. Brotherton, L. L. Garrison, Cal L. Keele, Dan Wilson and William M. Loftis.

Richey, Ruth
Boulder City News, Thursday, 21 Aug 1986, 35:1.
Ruth Richey passed away last Sunday, August 17 at a local care center. She had been a resident of Boulder City since 1954. Her late husband, Charles, was Superintendent of National Park Service here for many years. Survivors include two sons; Charles of Mojave, Calif., and Mark of Boulder City; also three grandchildren. A rosary will be recited at St. Andrew's Catholic Church on Friday at 7:30 p.m. Services at St. Andrew's will be at 8 a.m. Saturday. Burial will be in the Boulder City Cemetery. In lieu of flowers, it is requested donations be made to the American Cancer Society.

Richmond, Maurice Albert
Boulder City News, Thursday, 30 Aug 1984, 10:1-2.
Maurice Albert Richmond, Sr., 87, a resident of Boulder City for 34 years, died Thursday at Henderson Convalescent Hospital. He was a lifetime member of the International Brotherhood of Electrical Workers and the American Legion, with many good friends in Boulder City. A loving husband and parent, he is survived by his wife Susan Casazza Richmond, his son Maurice Albert Richmond, Jr., Zaragosa, Spain, and daughter Joan Miriam Richmond Kunde, of Redwood City, California. He also leaves to granddaughters, Two grandsons, and two great-grandchildren. Maurice Richmond was born January 15, 1897, in Mudville, Iowa, the second of four sons born to Albert G. and Caroline E. (Bradley) Richmond. About 1902 the family moved to Washington State, and Maurice grew up in the farming and logging villages north of Spokane. On June 28, 1918 he enlisted in the Navy, and served in the north Atlantic during World War I, attaining the rank of Fireman Second Class. After his discharge on August 1, 1919 he lived in Spokane for a few years, then moved to California. There he got the first of many jobs in his lifelong profession as an electrician, supervising the lighting during construction of the Philbrook Earth Dam near Stirling City. In 1928 Maurice met and married his wife in San Francisco, where both his children were later born. He moved to Honolulu in 1935 and found employment first with the Hawaiian Electric Company, and then the Naval Base at Pearl Harbor. He helped organize the first effective union of electrical workers on Oahu. In the wake of the Japanese attack of December 7, 1941, Maurice was part of a rescue crew which saved sailors

from the capsized Oklahoma warship. He himself was instrumental in preserving the lives of several men. Maurice continued to work at Pearl Harbor through most of the war. The Richmonds removed to Long Beach, California, in 1944. He worked at Terminal Island Navy Yard there until it was closed in 1950. Shortly thereafter he took a position with the Bureau of Mines in Boulder City, which he retained until his retirement in 1959. After Maurice retired he and his wife traveled widely throughout the United States, Canada and Europe. Following several years of increasing weakness, Maurice's last illness was brief. Memorial services were held Tuesday at the American Legion Hall. Further ceremonies will accompany the interment of the ashes at Boulder City Cemetery in November.

Richmond, Susan Casazza
Boulder City News, Thursday, 30 May 1991, 9:1-2.
Susan Casazza Richmond, 91, wife of the late Maurice Albert Richmond, Sr. and a resident of Boulder City for 38 years, died Thursday, May 16, 1991 at Devonshire Oaks care center in Redwood City, Calif. She is survived by her son, Maurice Albert Richmond, Jr. of Victorville, Calif., daughter Joan Miriam Sue Richmond Kunde of Kwajalein, Marshall Islands, and four grandchildren; Lynda Sue Richmond Lektorich of Garden Grove, Calif., Ellen Claire Richmond of Fullerton, Calif., Robert James Kunde of Bakersfield, Calif., and Brian Phillip Kunde of Redwood City. She also leaves a sister, Mrs. Josephine Casann Marks of Waterford, Calif., and two great-grandchildren. Susan was born Assunta Casazza on July 31, 1899 in the North End of Boston, Mass. Her parents were Sabato and Michelina (Mercadante) Casazza, immigrants from Avellino Province in Southern Italy. She looked back fondly on her early years in Boston, particularly the rich educational and cultural opportunities the city accorded. Susan left home to work while still in her teens. As a young woman she went to Southbridge, Mass., and joined the work force of the American Optical Company. She remained there several years, rising from a file clerk to a Dictaphone transcriber, and ultimately to a patent researcher with her won office in the legal department. She moved to California with her sister Josephine in the mid-1920s, out of a desire to see the West. She was in San Francisco when she met her future husband, Maurice. They were married there on April 1, 1928, Palm Sunday. In 1935, with work hard to find in California due to the Great Depression,

the Richmonds moved to Honolulu. There Maurice found a position with the Hawaiian Electric Company. Later he worked for the naval base at Pearl Harbor. In the wake of the Japanese attack of Pearl Harbor. In the wake of the Japanese attack of December 7, 19141, while Maurice helped with rescue efforts at Pearl Harbor, Susan sheltered friends who had fled from the devastation and prepared her household for the invasion that was feared imminent. During the war she served on a draft board while Maurice continued to work at the naval base. The Richmonds returned to the mainland in 1944. Maurice was employed by the Terminal Island Navy Yard in Long Beach until it was closed in 1950. Soon after he received a job offer from the Bureau of Mines in Boulder City, and they came to Nevada. The Richmonds spent their first night in Boulder City camping under a large tree by Lake Mead. They were among the first homeowners on Eighth Street, then a new development at the edge of the desert. After Maurice retired from the Bureau of Mines in 1959 the Richmonds traveled widely thoughout the Southwest, and toured much of North America and Europe. Susan was active in the community as a member of the American Legion Auxiliary and Grace Community Church. After her husband died she remained in their home until 1988, when she moved to a small care home operated by a friend in Boulder City. Later that same year she went to Redwood City to be nearer to family. There she spent her remaining years. Her final illness was brief. She lived a full and good life, and will live on in the hearts of those who knew and loved her. A private memorial service for family and friends was held at Boulder City Cemetery on May 24, where he ashes will be interred with those of her husband. Memorial donations should be made to St. Judes Ranch for Children in Boulder City.

Riggs, Ivan W.
Boulder City News, Thursday, 29 Jun 1989, 27:1.
Ivan W. Riggs, 83, of Boulder City, died June 25, in Boulder City. He was born Dec. 15, 1905, in Murrayville, Ill. A 14-year resident, he was a welder. He is survived by his daughter, Emma Lee Sneed of Boulder City; a sister, Martha Beck of Las Vegas; two grandsons, John H. Sneed III of Los Angeles and Andrew Sneed of Boulder City; and one granddaughter, Cheryl L. Sneed of Boulder City. Visitation is scheduled from 2 p.m. to 9 p.m. today at Palm Memorial, Henderson. Services will be at 2 p.m. Friday at Grace Community Church, Boulder City. Dr.

Swinburg will officiate. Burial will be in Boulder City Cemetery.

Riggs, Thomas A.
Boulder City News, Thursday, 18 Jan 1990, 26:1-2.
Thomas A. Riggs, 64, a long-time resident of Boulder City, died Friday. Born May 18, 1925, in Cushing, Okla, he was a truck driver and a U. S. Navy veteran. Survivors include his wife, Pat Riggs of Boulder City; two sons, Thomas Riggs, Jr. of Boulder City and Tony Riggs of Vernon, Utah; a daughter, Patty Rainey of Boulder City; a brother Dean Riggs of Cushing, Okla.; and four grandchildren. Services were held. Palm Mortuary handled arrangements.

Rignell, Paul M.
Boulder City News, Thursday, 22 June 1978, 5:1-5.
Death Of Paul Rignell Saddens Boulder City
On Father's Day, June 18, Paul M. Rignell of 609 7th St. in Boulder City died from a lingering illness. One of the tragedy's of his passing was that his final illness prevented him for accompanying his wife, May, to view with pride the graduation from the U of Utah, their son, Paul, a full fledged doctor of medicine. Paul, a graduate of the Boulder City schools has registered at the LDS Hospital in the Residency Program. He is majoring in internal medicine. Paul Rignell was 78 years old at the time of his passing. He was a retired electrician from the test site. Previous to that during World War II he had been employed at BMI and was known and admired by many pioneer electricians from the Boulder Canyon Project. Paul never joined the local Elks but remained with the Las Vegas Elks membership. He worked on Cashman Field and took part in many Helldorado Day projects. May Rignell, well known Boulder City surgical nurse was happy in a marriage that lasted 38½ years. She described her husband as, "kind, gentle soft spoken and a wonderful father to our son, Bob." When Bob played his freshman year at the U of Wisconsin, his brilliance on the field reached the attention of Morry Zenoff (also a graduate from Wisconsin U) and he had Bobby on his program on Radio Station KBMI. Paul Rignell was so proud when his son decided to pursue a career in medicine. For this a transfer was made to the U of Utah where Bob graduated with full honors. (That story has been released to the NEWS and will appear in another part of our paper). Paul came from a family who lived rich long lives. He was born Oct. 3, 1899, in

Minneapolis. He is survived by his brothers, Eddie of Minneapolis, Carl of Chicago, sister, Mildred Cooper from Minneapolis, his son, Bob, his daughter, Joyce Schwandenberg, of Klamath Falls, Ore. There are six grandchildren and one great grandchild. May Ringell said to tell her friends and Bobby's classmates from the Boulder City school system that this town was just exactly what she and Paul had hoped it would be as a fine place to raise their only son and to welcome to their home grandchildren and now a wee great grandchild. She especially wanted to thank coach Kenneth Andree for the way he inspired her son to excel in sports. She mentioned other teachers and other coaches as being responsible for the fun the family had as a unit for the parents never missed a ballgame in which Bobby participated. One knows that Paul Rignell was a happy husband, brother, son and father and above all a happy husband with May at his side. We wonder? Will Dr. Bob Rignell come back to Boulder City when he graduates from the LDS Hospital? Paul was buried in the Boulder City cemetery Wednesday. The Reverend Lee Thoni, pastor of the Calvary Lutheran Church officiated.

Rismiller, Ervin E.
Boulder City News, Thursday, 1 Sep 1983, 9:1-3.
Ervin E. Rismiller, 65, died August 23 in Boulder City. A resident of Boulder City, he was born Oct. 11, 1917 in Iowa. He as a retired carpenter and member of the Boulder City Veterans of Foreign Wars. He is survived by his wife, Gertrude, of Boulder City; brothers Robert of Detroit, MI, Walter, of Tipton, IA, and Donald, of Georgia; and sisters Dorothy Freece and Jean Van Duren, both of Georgia. Private cremation services were held.

Robertson, Ricky
Boulder City News, Thursday, 14 July 1977, 13:4.
Former Boulder Youth Succumbs
Former Boulder City resident, Ricky Robertson, died of injuries sustained in an automobile accident, July 8, in Petaluma, California. Robertson, age 17, was the son of Mr. and Mrs. Everett Robertson, also residing in Petaluma. The youth also leaves a sister, Mrs. Steve Madrigal, of Boulder. Funeral services and burial will be conducted at the Palm Mortuary in Henderson, taking place Friday (July 15) at 2 p.m.

Robison, Susan
Boulder City News, Thursday, 24 Jan 1952, 1:7.
Graveside Rites Held Tuesday For Susan Robison
Graveside services were held Tuesday afternoon at the Boulder City Cemetery for Susan Kay Robison, one year old, who died Friday afternoon in the Boulder City hospital. Bishop Herman Nelson, of the Latter-day Saints Church, officiated. "Whispering Hope" was sung by Marjorie Kelley and Della Ostergard, accompanied by Alice Shanahan on the violin. Verlene Sullivan, of Henderson sang, "Somebody We'll Understand." Talked were given by A. R. Palmer of Boulder City, Eldon S. Leavitt of Las Vegas, and Walter Cannon of St. George pronounced the benediction. The grave was dedicated by Bernard Cannon of Henderson. Susan Kay, daughter of Mr. and Mrs. Rulon Robison, 600 Arizona Street, was born December 2, 1950. She became ill early last week and was taken to the hospital on Wednesday afternoon, with a virus infection. The youngster is survived by her parents, and two brothers Michael and David. Also her maternal grandparents, Mr. and Mrs. Claude Cannon, of St. George, Utah, who are at present living with the family of Mrs. Robison's sister, Mrs. Denny Pease at 1120 Fifth. Other immediate relatives at the funeral were Wilfred Robison, an uncle from Yerington; Mr. and Mrs. B. C. Cannon and Mr. and Mrs. L. E. Cannon, all aunts and uncles of Henderson; cousins Karvel and Kenneth Rose, of Boulder City, and more than 25 other relatives from Bunderville, St. George, Caliente, Mesquite, Logandale and Las Vegas.

Roche, Walter L.
Boulder City News, Thursday, 7 Sep 1978.
Walter Roche Dies
Walter L. Roche, 69, a five year resident of Boulder City, passed away September 5th in Las Vegas. He was born August 30, 1909 in Brooklyn, New York. Survivors include his wife, Dorothy of Boulder City and one daughter, Glencora Roche of Oakland, California. Memorial services will be held Friday, September 8 at 10 a.m. at Boulder City Cemetery.

Roush, William Leonard

Boulder City News, Thursday, 24 Dec 1970.
Funeral services were conducted at 11 a.m. Monday at Palm Chapel, Henderson, for William Leonard Roush, who died suddenly Friday. Burial was in B. C. Cemetery. A service was conducted Sunday night by the Elks. Mr. Roush, a retired partner of Young & Rue Storage Co., was born April 29, 1912 in Nooksack, Wash. He had lived here 39 years. He is survived by his widow, Elizabeth of this city; three brothers, Henry, Coulee Dam City, Wash., Wilber, Portland, Ore, and Lyle of Reno.

Royer, William Myrl

Boulder City News, Thursday, 8 Nov 1984, 18:1-2.
William Myrl Royer passed away November 2 in Las Vegas. He was 79. He was born in Casey, Illinois on June 9, 1905. He lived in Decatur, Illinois prior to coming to Boulder City in July 1954. He was employed as a Project Engineer by Titanium Metals Corporation after working for some years for A. E. Staley Company. Some of his inventions were patented by the companies for whom he worked. Mr. Royer was a 32nd degree Mason. He was a member of the Boulder City Masonic Lodge Number 37 and the Ancient and Accepted Scottish Rite of Freemasonry. He was a past president of the Masonic Acacia Club. He worked with the Boulder City Senior Citizen Organization serving one term as its vice president. He belonged and served as a director of the American Association of Retired Persons and he was a member of the National Association of Retired Federal Employees. Mr. Royer loved the desert and Boulder City. He had a great desire to keep Boulder City the small and unique town it was when he came here. Mr. Royer, is survived by his wife, Rae, of Boulder City, his son Reverend William M. Royer, of Hirscher, Illinois, Four grandchildren and four great-grandchildren of Arizona and Illinois and his sister, Mrs. William Atz, of Las Vegas, Nevada. His daughter, Willma, passed away June 29, 1984. Reverend Kenneth Criswell, of Grace Community Church and Boulder City Masonic Lodge Number 37 conducted graveside services at the Boulder City Cemetery, on Tuesday, November 6, 1984. If anyone wishes to make a gift in Mr. Royer's memory, please make a donation to the organization of your choice.

Rudd, Amanda Chamblin
Boulder City News, Thursday, 7 June 1990, 15:2.
Amanda Chamblin Rudd died May 26, 1990 in a local hospital. She was born March 19, 1990 at the family home in Boulder City. She is survived by her parents, Lauren and Daron Rudd of Boulder City; one sister, Erin Rudd of Boulder City; one brother, Bryan Rudd of Boulder City; grandmothers, Leslie Aschenbrenner of Novato, Calif., and Betty Lou Rudd of Boulder City; and grandfather, James Aschenbrenner of Novato, Calif. Services were held. Palm Mortuary handled arrangements.

Rudd, Gordon J.
Boulder City News, Thursday, 2 Jun 1988, 10:1.
Gordon J. Rudd, 48, died Monday, May 30 in North Las Vegas and was a resident of Boulder City for 18 years. He was born on Sept. 19, 1939 in Plymouth, Utah, and was the owner operator of Trucking for Construction and a member of Teamsters Local No. 631. He is survived by his wife Betty of Boulder City; son Daron J. of Boulder City; daughters Cindy Cascioppo and Jerrie Layne of Boulder City; sisters Doris Arelano of Plymouth and Rae Ola Deaking of Torrey both from Utah; brothers Derrell S. of Salem, Utah and Jeffery of Rock Springs, Wyoming and six grandchildren. Palm Mortuary of Henderson is handling the arrangements. The funeral service will be at 2 p.m. on June 2 at Boulder City LDS Chapel with Bishop Lasko as officiant. Interment will be in Boulder City Cemetery.

Ruth, Matthew
Boulder City News, Thursday, 24 Aug 1972.
Funeral Today For M. Ruth
Funeral services will be at 10 A.M., Saturday, for Matthew Ruth, 52, who died Tuesday in the Wesley Hospital in Los Angeles, Calif.; after a long illness. The rites are set at Palm Mortuary Chapel in Henderson. Burial will be in the Boulder City Cemetery. Matt the popular owner of the Boulder Bowl, was born Jan 14, 1890 (?) In Jefferson County, Arkansas. He and his family came to Boulder City in 1956 from San Diego, Calif., and he bought the bowling alley from Folke Hermanson in 1957. Since then he has renovated it to try to keep up with public demand for the sport. He belonged to the Bowling Proprietor's Association, and was a

member of the Eagle's Lodge. When he could get away from the bowling alley, his favorite occupation was exploring the desert with his dunes buggy. Matt is survived by his wife, Mary Ann, 520 Ave. A, who also runs the alley; a daughter, Linda (Mrs. Alan) Naegle, 625 Seventh St. Boulder City, who is a nurse at Sunrise Hospital; a son Warren Goedert, Annapolis graduate, now Deputy District Attorney in Reno; and four grandchildren. Also his mother, Lois Hawkins, Gardena, Calif, a brother John H. Ruth of Rome, Italy; and a sister Minnie Lou Powell, Magee, Arkansas.

Ryan, Archie D.
Boulder City News, Thursday, 22 Sep 1955, p.1:1-2.
Large Crowd Pays Final Tribute To Archie Ryan at Elks Rites
A crowd that filled the Boulder City Elks club to overflowing gathered Sunday evening to pay tribute to Archie D. Ryan, prominent local citizen, as officers of the lodge headed by Exalted Ruler Donald Swartz conducted ritualistic funeral services. Ryan, active and prominent in local affairs, died last Friday at the Boulder City hospital from injuries received the previous weekend when an automobile in which he was riding with Chester Tyree went off the new dam highway. Friends from all parts of the state attended the rites. Past Exalted Ruler L. W. Lappin paid tribute to Ryan's great legion of friends through-out the nation in an eulogy to the departed brother. His favorite songs, "I'll Take You Home Again, Kathleen" and "Home on the Range" were sung by Russell Farnsworth accompanied by Madelaine Garrett. Pallbearers were all close friends of his in the local lodge, Past Exalted Rulers Lappin, W. Phil Nobel, A. G. Klinger, Glenn Whilhelm and H. T. Wilhite. Graveside services in the Boulder City Cemetery also were conducted by the officers of the Elks. Joining the widow, Bernice, for the services, were his sons Kelly Ryan of Chicago and David of Reno; his daughter, Kathleen Ryan Anderson of Berkeley and his brother, George Ryan of Logan, Utah.

Safford, Blaine
Boulder City News, Tuesday, 19 Oct 1948, p.5.
Blaine Safford, 41. Dies Suddenly
Stricken with a heart attack Sunday afternoon, Blaine D. Safford, 41, died suddenly two hours later at the Boulder City hospital. Safford was employed as a truck driver for the park Service since 1946. He was born

April 7, 1907 at Idaho Falls, Idaho. He is survived by his widow, Mrs. Vee Safford, a son Richard Kelly, aged 4; a daughter Kerry Low, aged 6; and three sisters, Mrs. A. J. O'Hara Sr., of Boulder City; Thelma Beanush of Bingen, Wash., and Norma Jane Evans, Long Beach. The Saffords lived at 524 Avenue M. Funeral arrangements will be announced by Bunker Brothers mortuary.

Boulder City News, Wednesday, 20 Oct 1948, p.1.
Safford Funeral Services Today
Funeral services will be held this afternoon at 2 p.m. for Blaine D. Safford. Safford died suddenly Sunday afternoon at the Bolder City hospital. Services will be held at the L. D. S. Church with Bishop Owen Gibson officiating. Mrs. Herman Nelson and Mrs. Alton Roueche will sing "Sometime We'll Understand" and "Whispering Hope." G. C. Spilsbury will talk about Safford's life. The organ will be played by Mrs. Robert Denning. Pallbearers will be Hobson Beard, Fred Roder, Virgil Averett, Wayne Peters, Cal Kelley and Hyrum Nielson. The body will lie in state at the L. D. S. Church from 1:15 to 2 p. m. Following the services, Safford will be interred in the Boulder City cemetery.

Sallee, Harry James "Jim"
Boulder City News, Thursday, 11 Mar 1976, p.9:4.
Harry Sallee Services Today
Funeral services will be held at 10 o'clock this morning for Harry James "Jim" Sallee, 82. The rites will be conducted at the Bunker Chapel in Las Vegas by the Reverend John Dudeck of Bethany Baptist Church in Boulder City. Burial will be in the Boulder Cemetery. Jim died Monday night in the Las Vegas Convalescent Center in Las Vegas. He was born Jan. 7, 1894 in Long Island, Kansas. He farmed in that state, and also worked as a railroad fireman in Nebraska. He joined an Army engineer's group in Kansas in 1917, and entered the U. S. Army on March 5, 1918. He served as a motorcycle dispatcher (messenger) in the 89th Division at Xammes, France. On Oct. 4, 1918, his motorcycle ran over a mustard gas shell, and he was severely injured. His life was saved by a miracle – the shrapnel that went through his chest pocket was stopped by a German metal match box issued by Kaiser Wilhelm and given to Jim by a prisoner at St. Mihiel. Jim's right arm had to be amputated. In January, 1919 he was brought to Hampton, Va., then transferred to Walter Reed Hospital in

Washington, D. C. He earned a Purple Heart and an Honor Roll signed by Pres. Wilson. He was discharged March 24, 1919 and returned to Kansas. He learned to use his left arm rapidly, and did whatever work was available. Jim married Eulalia Penninger in 1919, and they moved to Fremont, Nebraska. They had three children. The family moved to Colorado, to California, and then in 1944 came to Boulder City for Jim's health. Jim and Eulalia were active in the community, were rock hounds, and belonged to the Gem Collectors Club. Jim cut and polished beautiful jewelry. Eulalia died of cancer in 1954. Him was a member of the Veterans of Foreign Wars, Boulder Dam Post 3574, and belonged to the Odd Fellows lodge for a few years. Jim married Mary Newcomb, and they continued collecting rocks and antiques, including old bottles. They lived in Moore's Trailer Park. Mary died in 1964, also of cancer. He is survived by a son Neal Sallee, Covina, Calif.; Daughter La Vada (Mrs. Kenneth) Paris, 304 Nevada Highway, Boulder City; daughter Dorothy Trevathon, Wamsutter, Wyo.; a brother, M. L. Sallee, Albuquerque, New Mex.; sisters Alice Goodrich, Loveland, Colo.; and Anna Haiste, Salina, Kansas; 8 grandchildren and 7 great -grandchildren.

Sass, Gladys L.
Boulder City News, Thursday, 20 Feb 1992, 9:3-4.
Gladys L. Sass, 96, a 15-year Boulder City resident, died Monday in a local hospital. Born on Jan. 2, 1896 in Omaha, Neb., she was a homemaker. She is survived by a daughter, Lois Johnson of Henderson and a brother, Max King of San Francisco, Calif.; two grandchildren and one great-grandchild. Graveside services are scheduled at 11 a.m. today in the Boulder City Cemetery. Arrangements were handled by Palm Mortuary of Henderson.

Schaap, Fremont O.
Boulder City News, Wednesday, 19 Feb 1947, 4:4.
Schaap Funeral Tomorrow
Funeral services for Fremont O. Schaap will be held at 10 a.m. tomorrow at Grace Community Church, followed by burial in Boulder City Cemetery. Schaap was born 59 years ago at Orange City, Iowa, and died in Boulder City Hospital Sunday. He had been employed here by the Bureau of Reclamation and National Park Service. Among the survivors

are two brothers, Cornelius J. Schaap of Flagstaff, Ariz., and Raae Schaap of Batavis, Java; and two sisters, Mrs. Charles S. Irwin of Sioux City, Iowa, and Mrs. Mary Severson of Randalia, Iowa.

Schaller, Mary M.
Boulder City News, Wednesday, 10 Sep 1985, 29:1-3.
Mary M. Schaller, 49, of Boulder City, died Monday in Boulder City. She was born May 16, 1936, in Mary's Mountain, Alaska. A resident since 1973, she was a homemaker. She is survived by her husband, John L. of Boulder City, sons, John and Alan, both of Boulder City and Conrad of Las Vegas; daughter, Mary Lynn of Las Vegas; brother, George Kakaruk of Nome, Alaska; sister, Theresa Noyakuk of Anchorage, Alaska; mother, Alice Kakaruk of Anchorage. A rosary will be said at 5 p.m. Thursday in St. Andrew's Catholic Church, Boulder City. The funeral Mass will be said at 9 a.m. Friday in St. Andrew's Catholic Church, Boulder City. Burial will be in Boulder City Cemetery. Palm Mortuary, Henderson, is handling arrangements.

Schlueter, Alfred H.
Boulder City News, Thursday, 5 Dec 1985, 31:2.
Alfred H. Schlueter, age 69, died Friday, Nov. 15 in Las Vegas. He was born Dec. 22, 1915 in Illinois. A five-year resident, he had been a purchasing agent and a World War II Army veteran. He leaves his wife, Esther of the home; Al Jr. of Jacksonville, Fla.; daughter, Heather Hellenbrand of Boulder City and four grandchildren. Services were in Christ Lutheran Church, Boulder City. Burial in the Boulder City Cemetery.

Schlueter, Marion Ann
Boulder City News, Thursday, 2 Sep 1982, 8:1.
Marion Ann Schlueter, 68, died Saturday in Boulder City. A housewife, she was born June 18, 1914 in Chicago, Ill. She was a two-year resident of Boulder City. She survived by her husband, Alfred; daughter, Heather Hellenbrand both of Boulder City; son, Alfred Jr. of Jacksonville, Fla; two brothers, Maurice Sullivan of Chicago, Ill. and James Sullivan of El Paso, Texas; one sister Dolores Sullivan of Chicago; and four grandchildren. Services were conducted at 10 a.m. Tuesday at St.

Andrews Catholic Church in Boulder City. Palm Mortuary handled all arrangements.

Schutz, Harry Oliver, Jr.
Boulder City News, Thursday, 4 Jun 1992, 11:1-2.
Harry Oliver Schutz Jr., 78, died Friday, May 29, 1992, in Boulder City Hospital. He was a 20 year resident of Boulder City. Born March 19, 1914 in Fresno, Calif., he is survived by his wife of 57 years, Clara, of Boulder City; son, Ivan Harold Schutz of Stockton, Calif.; daughter, Mary Catherine Schutz Romines of Auburn, Calif.; 6 grandchildren; and 5 great grandchildren. Harry and Clara moved to Boulder City in 1970 after Harry retired from San Joaquin Delta College in Stockton, Calif., where he was Chairman of Physical Science Dept., and a teacher for many years. He was a ground school instructor for the Navy Program in Carson City during World War II. He owned his own plane and instructed aeronautics while teaching in Stockton. He was a graduate of University of California at Berkeley. He was a member of the Sacramento Chapter of Phi Delta Kappa. He belonged to Grace Community Church. There will be no services at his request.

Schwartz, Benita Louise
Boulder City News, Tuesday, 17 Sep 1946, p.1:2.
Funeral Yesterday For Benita Louise Schwartz
Mass of the Angels was said at 9 o'clock Monday morning at the funeral services at St. Peter's Catholic church in Henderson for Benita Louise Schwartz, five months old daughter of Mr. And Mrs. Leslie Schwartz, former Boulderites, who died suddenly Friday afternoon at their home in Henderson. Interment was in the Boulder City cemetery.

Sears, Jeannie M.
Boulder City News, Thursday, 24 Nov 1977, 11:5.
44 Year Resident Jeannie Sears Dies
Long time resident Jeannie M. Sears passed away November 20 at the age of 80 in Boulder City. She was born April 13, 1897 in Livingston, Texas and had resided in Boulder City since 1933. She had been employed with the U.S. Bureau of Reclamation as a records supervisor. Survivors include sons, Robert C. Sears of Buena Park, California and William Sears of

Yuma, Arizona; sister, Ethel McCardell of Livingston and five grandchildren. Graveside services were held yesterday at Boulder City Cemetery.

Seiler, Mary L.
Boulder City News, Thursday, 11 Aug 1966.
Mary Seiler Rites Tuesday
Requiem mass was celebrated Tues. at 10 at St. Andrew's Catholic Church for Mary L. Seiler, 76, of 751 Avenue I by the Reverend Gerard Fanning. Burial was in Boulder City Cemetery with Palm Mortuary in charge of funeral arrangements. Mrs. Seiler was born Dec. 11, 1888 in Youngstown, Ohio, and died Aug. 6. She had lived here for eight months. Survivors include a daughter, Mrs. LaVerne Thomas, Boulder City; brother, Emmett Loney, Youngstown, Ohio; a granddaughter, Mary Ann Kania, Boulder City, and a grandson, Thomas W. Thomas, Las Vegas.

Seley, Samuel
Boulder City News, Thursday, 23 Feb1956, 8:4.
Samuel Seley Passes Sunday
Masonic services are pending for 79 year-old Samuel Seley who passed away Sunday in the Boulder City Hospital one week after he had been admitted for treatment of a heart ailment. Survivors include a step-daughter, Mrs. Madeline Henderson of 647 Avenue F and a niece and nephew of Chicago, believed to be enroute here for the funeral. Mr. Seley, who had lived at 631 Avenue I, came to Boulder City about four years ago from Ohio. He was a retired railroad man being formerly employed by the Belt Railroad in Chicago. He was a member of both the Shriners and Masonic order.

Sepka, Chester S.
Boulder City News, Thursday, 25 Jul 1985, 9:1.
Chester J. Sepka, 72, of Boulder City, died Sunday in Las Vegas. He was born Jan. 18, 1913, in Illinois. A resident since 1972, he was a check clerk for the railroad. He is survived by his wife, Marcella; son, Donald, both of Boulder City; brother Ted of Chicago; sisters Loretta Herlihy of Wheaton, Ill., Mary Shilkaitis of Melrose Park, Ill. Services were private. Interment was in Boulder City Cemetery. Palm Mortuary, Henderson, handled arrangements.

Settle, Glen William
Boulder City News, Thursday, 10 Jan 1952.
Glen Settle Rites Held Tuesday
Funeral services were held Tuesday afternoon for Glen William Settle, who died on Friday at the local hospital following a brief illness. Bishop Herman Nelson conducted the rites at the church of Jesus Christ of Latter-day Sts. J. Donal Earl gave the invocation and Woodrow W. Wagner the benediction. Richard Farrell, a brother-in-law of Settle, read appropriate poetry. A trio composed of Jeanne Earl, Marge Leavitt and Thora Nelson, accompanied by Teresa Denning, sang "Sometime we'll understand" and "Lead Kindly Light." Delpha Dodge, accompanied by Thora Nelson, sang "Going Home." Interment followed at the Boulder Cemetery. Settle was born September 15, 1912 in Bancroft, Idaho. He has lived in Boulder City for four years, and before that in Las Vegas for 15 years. Survivors are his widow Geraldine Engle Settle, 668 California Avenue, a two months old son, William Clyde; two step-sons, Harris Leroy Burns and Rex Burns; his parents, Mr. and Mrs. William Settle, of Sacramento, California; a brother Don Settle, of Henderson; and five sisters, Maxine Hanson, Wendell, Idaho; Helen Bird and Mary Rich, of Paris, Idaho, Mrs. Richard Farrell of Provo. Utah; and Mrs. Glen Bristo, of Renton, Wash.

Shafer, Claude
Boulder City News, Thursday, 22 Mar 1973.
"Cowboy" Claude Shafer is Missed, by Teddy Fenton
Around town Claude Shafer was accepted as a beloved character. Surely you saw him driving his little V.W. with his stetson placed squarely on his head and his head held high and straight. His attire was always jeans

and cowboy boots and he died when his little car ran off the road out by R. R. Pass "Died with his boots on" as he would have wanted to, said his son Randy. He liked to be called "Cowboy" and no wonder. He was a bareback rider, a stunt man, a man who loved horses (and all animals) with every inch of his slender frame. His children are Randy and Eddie and Martha. There were 9 grandchildren. He is buried in the Boulder City cemetery. At 16, Cowboy drove a 4 hitch team from Broodwater to Burell, Nebraska (his birth place 62 years ago). At 18 he competed in local rodeos in the western section of Nebraska. In Oregon he beat out the man who became the world champion. At 21 h3 moved into Southeastern Wyoming and entered bareback competition in bronc romping on the Cheyenne frontier (known as the grand daddy of them all). In Southern California Cowboy went to work on the Hoot Gibson ranch. He doubled in a movie for Hoot, "The Tenderfoot." There is a shot of Hoot tearing out of a shoot on a bucking bronco but it was Cowboy doing the riding. At 25 he showed up in Oregon (placer mining) and there married Goldie Baker in 1936. They had one son, Randy born in 1937. Later he came to California, and married for the second time to Hannah, and 3 children were born, Martha and Eddie. He worked in the shipyards in San Pedro and was kissed by Dorothy Lamour when she christened a war ship. Back in Laramie, Wyoming he worked for the Union Pacific, he had come to be known as "Spuds." His hobbies were haunting and fishing and shooting pool. He had a pool stick with his name on it, a gift from son Randy at the State Coach Saloon at the time of his death. (Dick and Lottie took up a collection which may be used to buy the 9 grandchildren identification bracelets). In hunting prowess he couldn't be topped. He would say, "I will hit the deer in such and such a place" and a bet was always won if anyone took him up on it. He loved to dance and his son Randy loved to hunt with his dad and their favorite state to do so was Wyoming. In 1953 he moved with his family to Pittman and for a short while stayed at the Polka Dot Motel. Known throughout the trade as an expert welder, all Cowboy had to do was to show a sample of his welding and a job was cinched. He worked for American Potash from 1953-61 at which time he was blown off a tank and was injured and fiven 100% disability. He moved his family to Lakeview (outside Boulder City) and there took such an interest in community affairs that he was the first to pass a petition for a playground and paved streets in the townsite. Though not a member of the VFW he almost called the post in Henderson his second home. He became involved in VFW projects. Sold poppies, carried petitions to get a V. A. Hospital which is now in use at Rose de Lima, was known for always giving of himself to anything that benefitted man. He lived at 607 Ave. D (Idyllic Retreats) and his friend Helen Leavitt, (Mrs. Stan) lives there as well. She broke her ankle one day, and Cowboy turned to his friends (VFW) and borrowed a wheelchair and crutches so Helen could get about.

Shanahan, Leland R.
Boulder City News, Thursday, 24 June 1982, 7:3-4.
Leland R. Shanahan, 72, a 39-year resident, died Friday in Boulder City. He was born Dec. 19, 1909, in Los Angeles and was an electrician. He is survived by his wife, Alice of Boulder City; daughter, Patricia of Las Vegas; and brother, Stanley of Sunland, Calif. Services were held at 10 a.m. Monday in Bethany Baptist Church. Burial followed in the Boulder City Cemetery. Palm Mortuary, Henderson, handled arrangements.

Shannon, James A. II
Boulder City News, Thursday, 14 Apr 1988, 6:1.
James A. Shannon II, 26, of Jefferson City, Mo., died Saturday in Jefferson City, Mo. He was born April 15, 1961, in Jackson, Calif. He was a construction supervisor. He is survived by his father and mother, James Sr. of Boulder City and Patricia Robles of Pine Grove, Calif.; a daughter and son, Shawn and Jason, both of Henderson; four sisters, Angel Farris of El Dorado Hills, Calif., Jamie, Jessica and Jennifer, all of Boulder City; four brothers, John of Hawaii, Joe and Jeffrey, both of San Jose, Calif. and Jeromy of Boulder City; grandparents Gilbert and Leona Jackson of Jackson, Calif.; a stepmother, Lyda and stepfather, Real Robeis. Graveside services were held in Boulder City with burial in the Boulder City Cemetery.

Shelton, Jessie F.
Boulder City News, Thursday, 2 Jan 1969, 1:3-4.
Jessie Shelton Buried Saturday
by Esther Shipp
Funeral services were conducted Saturday morning for Jessie F. Shelton, 68, one of Boulder City's pioneer women. The rites were conducted by the Reverend Guy Holliday at Grace Community Church, where the

Shelton family attended the beginning services in 1931. Pallbearers were Tom Godbey, George Talley, Jake Dieleman, Frank Jensen, Wilfred Voss and Clarence Neumann. Burial was in the Boulder City Cemetery. Jessie died Thursday, Dec. 26, at the Boulder City Hospital. She had been ill for several months. Jessie Foster was born oct. 12, 1900, in Pearsall, Texas. At the age of 16 she followed the footsteps for her mother and sister to become a telephone operator in San Antonio. She worked there through World War 1, until her marriage to childhood sweetheart Marcus Shelton, Jan. 10, 1923. The couple moved to Arizona, where their two sons were born. In July 1931, they came to Nevada and lived in one of the first Six tents in McKeeversville, when Shelton obtained a job at the dam. As soon as houses were available, they moved to 500 Avenue K, then in 1942 bought their home at 663 Avenue I. Shelton was killed in an automobile accident, and Jessie went back to work, beginning at the checking station at the west gate of the dam. When this was closed in 1945, she started her job as a local telephone operator, choosing the night hours so that she could be home with her sons to prepare their meals, etc. Her friendly voice gave comfort to the many distraught callers during the nighttime emergencies. Jessie retired in 1953. Jessie was justly proud of her sons. They were active in sports at the Boulder High School and earned important scholarships for college. They both served in the armed forces for their country, and both graduated with honors from college. Dr. Frank, a nuclear physicist, is married and lives with his wife and children in Colorado Springs, Colo. Warren, an electrical engineer, has been staying with his mother since her illness. Jessie was a charter member of the American Legion Auxiliary and the Ladies Auxiliary to the VFW. She also belonged to the Women's Association of Grace Community Church and Cactus Rebekah lodge No. 40. IOOF. She is survived by the two sons and three grandchildren.

Sheridan, Maude
Boulder City News, Wednesday, 26 Feb 1947, p.1:3.
Sheridan Funeral
Funeral services for Maude Sheridan will be held at 2 p.m. tomorrow at Grace Community Church with Reverend Winston Trever officiating. Burial will be in Boulder City Cemetery. Mrs. Sheridan died Monday of heart disease. She was a member of the pioneer Mormon family of northern Nevada and taught school there before coming here.

Sherrod, Carl B.
Boulder City News, Thursday, 28 Nov 1974, 7:6.
Verna Salisbury's Father Dies In California
Verna Lee Salisbury just returned from Hesperia, where she attended the funeral of her father Carl B. Sherrod. He passed away Nov. 15th at the Apple Valley Hospital. Services were held at Kerns Memorial Chapel. The Reverend Vernon Nybakken of the Assembly of God officiated. Interment was Thursday morning at Memory Gardens memorial Park, Brea, Calif. Mr. Sherrod, born in Texas, lived in Hesperia for the past 16 years. He came to Boulder City several times a year to visit his daughter. He had many friends here and enjoyed his visits very much. He is survived by his widow, Ruth of Hesperia, daughter Verna Salisburg, 2 sisters, one brother, 3 grandchildren, 4 great grandchildren.

Sherwood, Marguerite L.
Boulder City News, Thursday, 20 Aug 1987, 6:4.
Marguerite L. Sherwood, age 56, died Sunday, Aug. 16 in Boulder City and was almost a lifetime resident. She was born on Aug. 20, 1930 in Memphis, Tenn. and was a housewife and a member of the Professional Award Winning Trump Players Association. She is survived by her son, Dana Sherwood of Northridge, Calif.; mother Lillian Weiler of Boulder City; sister Dorothy Ragsdale of Sugarland, Texas; one grandchild and several nieces and nephews. Palm Mortuary of Henderson is handling the arrangement. The funeral services will be held at the Grace Community Church on Aug. 20 at 2 p.m. with John Rousseau officiating. Interment will be in Boulder City Cemetery.

Shields, W. I. "Bill"
Boulder City News, Thursday, 8 July 1982, 8:1-2.
W. I. "Bill" Shields, 63, an eight-year resident, died Monday in Boulder City. Mr. Shields was born Feb. 7, 1919, in Abia, Iowa. He was a tavern and restaurant owner and a World War II Army veteran. Survivors include his wife, Mayetta, of Boulder City; three sisters, Thelma Whittington of Boulder City, Ruth Searl of Newton, Iowa, and Darlene Johnson of Des Moines, Iowa. Graveside services were held Wednesday at the Boulder City Cemetery.

Shoemaker, Billie Jean
Boulder City News, Thursday, 6 July 1989, 8:1-2.
Services for Billie Jean Shoemaker, 21, a Boulder City resident who died Saturday in Las Vegas, are scheduled for 2 p.m. today in Palm Chapel, Henderson. The Reverend Richard Henry will officiate at the Episcopalian rites. A restaurant hostess, she was born in Mattoon, Ill., on Sept. 15, 1967, and had resided in Southern Nevada since 1968. She is survived by her parents Stanley L. and Marjorie R. Shoemaker of Boulder City; two sisters, Carolyn Hinkle of Henderson and Dolores Shoemaker of Boulder City; a brother, Gary, also of Boulder City; her grandfather, William Shoemaker of Las Vegas; and three nieces and one nephew. Interment will be in the Boulder City Cemetery. Palm Mortuary handled all arrangements.

Shope, Charles A.
Boulder City News, Thursday, 18 Oct 1973, 4:1-2.
Charles A. Shope, 65, died October 12, in Las Vegas. He was born August 26, 1908 in Redlands, Calif. He resided at 658 Ave. "D", Boulder City and had been employed as a warehouse clerk by Reeco. He is survived by his wife, Dolores; daughters, Nancy I and Mary F., of Boulder City; brothers, Herbert and Howard of Blaine, Wash, and a sister, Mabel Abernathy of Indio, California. He is a past Commander of American Legion Post No. 31, Boulder City. Graveside services were held Tuesday, 2 p.m. at the Boulder City cemetery. In lieu of flowers, donations should be sent to Boulder City Memorial Fund.

Shoppe, Mabel
Boulder City News, Thursday, 18 Jan 1979, 5:1-6.
By Teddy Fenton
Mabel Shoppe a pioneer of early day Boulder City moved from Boulder City in 1977 after having made her favorite town her home for more than 40 years. Last Saturday, Mabel was buried in the desert grave yard in her hometown of Boulder City. Her last wishes were to be brought back from her final home, Roy, Utah, where she resided with her sister, Josie M. Foley. The sisters had lived together in Boulder City until ill health forced them to sell Mabel's lovely house in order to move to Utah. Sister Josie is Mabel's only survivor. Mabel Shoppe, 84, was born in Ogden, Utah. She

was a former recording secretary of the Nevada Federation of Women's Clubs, Dist. No. 3; a charter member of both the Does 134 of Boulder City and the Boulder Dam Federal Credit Union and a member of Narfe. Mabel Shoppe would so much want to be remembered as an ardent golfer on the first course ever built in Boulder City. Records show that the old Six Companies Black Canyon golf association was formed in 1933. Over two dozen members met in Jan. 1933 and while no women headed the work force that soon formed with men from Babcock and Wilcox as well as many eager construction stiffs from the Six Companie's Inc. banded together, one can be very sure that Mabel Shoppe and her sister golfers were right there serving refreshments and eagerly polishing their golf clubs to get out there rain, snow, hail or sleet. Mabel is now buried at the Boulder City cemetery and chances are the grave she lies on was probably a part of the old course. If one is familiar with the old golf course, it is possible to see number one tee (in fact four of the tees are still to be seen, three are in fine condition, the fourth is falling back to nature.) The same of the "oiled" greens. One is occupied by a bee hive (the tee can be seen on the hill above it) Once one has been told the old Six Co's course is still partly intact there is a sense of excitement and a wish that at least one of the tee's could have a historical marker placed beside it. Housing developments have erased well over half of the course, soon, all traces of the course may be obliterated. Mabel Shoppe, Sammy Webb, Blanche Christianson, Mae Rudd, Mary Jane Burgett, Dot Hayward, Alice Doolittle, Mrs. Jack Higgins and Mary Higgins were some of the pioneers who played along with Mabel in those early years as were the younger generation of Elaine Reynolds and Ruthie Belding. Pictures exist of both men and women players. The course was a favorite with Clark County residents. They even had a crude club house and refreshments were served by Anderson Brothers who also served meals to the pioneer workers, who built Hoover Dam. Much more could be written about the love that Mabel Schoope felt for her favorite recreation. Until her move to Utah, Mabel had kept a cardboard box of newspaper clippings, golf scores and a number of pictures. Unfortunately for the sake of history, her entire collection was thrown away. How she regretted having done so when she heard the anguished remark by a local collector of history of early Boulder City. The library would have treasured every scrap and every picture for its historical records. Boulder City remembers with gratefulness the many volunteer projects that the late Irwin Schoppe and his wife involved themselves in. They really cared about his town and helped it become an active and caring community;. Their home on Colorado St. was the center of many groups meeting to discuss what was best for Boulder City. They will never be forgotten.

Shortle, John F.
Boulder City News, Thursday, 26 Apr 1973, 3:3.
John Shortle Services Held Mon.
Funeral services for John F. Shortle, 44, will be held Monday at Palm Chapel. Mr. Shortle died April 18 in Boulder City. He was born March 9, 1929 in Detroit, Mich., and was a gardener for the Dept. of Water and Power. He resided at 644 Avenue H. Survivors include his wife Margaret; three daughters, Sandra, Lori and Karen; brother Emett, Santa Ana; Robert, Long Beach; Michael, Long Beach, and Leo of Covina Heights; and sister Betty Sherwood, Detroit, Mich.

Shortt, Delmont M.
Boulder City News, Thursday, 30 May 1985, 35:1.
Delmont M. Shortt, 75, passed away Thursday, May 23 in Boulder City. He had lived in this area for 27 years and was a conductor for the Union Pacific Railroad. He was born Dec. 6, 1909 in Clearwater, Nebraska. He was past secretary of the Brotherhood of Railroad Trainmen. He is survived by his wife, Margaret Helen of Boulder City; daughters Beverly Shortt, Stockton, Ca., Georgia Daly, Tampa, Fla., Lynne Dee Shay, Boulder City, eleven grandchildren and one great grandchild. Funeral services were held Monday, May 27 at Palm Chapel in Henderson. Officiating was Reverend Ron Mayer from Christ Church Lutheran. Interment was at Boulder City Cemetery.

Schreeve, Oramel Victor
Boulder City News, Thursday, 19 Jan 1995, 9:1.
Ormel Victor Shreeve, 88, died Monday, Jan. 16. Born Jan. 29, 1906 in Reese, Mich., he had been a resident of Boulder City for 36 years. He was a retired owner/operator of a gas and appliance sales/service. He was a member of the Spiritual Assembly of the Baha'i of Boulder City. He is survived by three daughters, Susanne Shreeve, of Santa Barbara, Calif.; Karin Tadjiki, of Los Angeles, Calif.; and Machiel Moore, of Alpine, Texas; five grandchildren and three great grandchildren. Services were

held in Palm Chapel in Henderson. Arrangements were handled by Palm Mortuary of Henderson.

Shuck, Clarence C.
Boulder City News, Thursday, 22 April 1965. 5:8.
Lakeview Man Buried Saturday
Graveside services at Boulder City Cemetery were conducted Saturday afternoon for Clarence C. Shuck, 104 Walker Way, who passed away in Las Vegas last Thursday. Mr. Shuck was born June 20, 1883 in Lawrence, Kans. and had been a resident of this city for four years. He is survived by his wife, Ina, and one daughter, Marie Lee, this city; and two sons, Clarence Jr., Pomona, Calif. and Douglas, Roseville, Calif. Edler L. L. Dinwiddie of Seventh Day Adventist Church, conducted the service.

Shultz, John H.
Boulder City News, Thursday, 24 May 1956, 2:3.
John H. Shultz Rites Today at 10
Final rites for 53 year-old John H. Schultz will be held this morning at 10 o'clock at Grace Community Church with the Reverend M. K. Wilder, pastor of the Baptist church, officiating. Burial will be in the Boulder City Cemetery. A self-employed oil trucker, Mr. Shultz died at the Boulder City Hospital at 10:05 Saturday night, six hours after he had been admitted for treatment. He was born in Broadlands, Ill. Sept. 6, 1902 and came to live in Boulder City with his wife, Hannah, and 15 year-old son, Richard, about 2½ years ago from California. The family lives at 701 Elm St. in Moore's Trailer Park. Mrs. Shultz is a Boulder City high school teacher and Richard is a freshman student. Other survivors include another son, John, of Cincinnati; his mother, Hannah E. Shultz of Broadlands; a brother, Stanley of Chicago; a sister, Irene Dean of Phoenix; and a niece, Miss Nancy Dean of Phoenix.

Simpson, Anna M.
Boulder City News, Thursday, 21 Apr 1977, 3:5-6.
Long Time Resident Anna M. Simpson Dies
Services were held last Tuesday, April 19 at 10 a.m. at Palm Mortuary for Anna M. Simpson who died April 15 in Boulder City. Mrs. Simpson was born October 12, 1915 in Chicago, Illinois. She had been a resident of

Boulder City since 1942 and resided at 700 Elm St., No. 35. She was a member of the Boulder City B.P.W. Survivors include daughters, Kathryn Fowler of Boulder City, Kay Selby of Omaha, Nebraska, Sandra Ritter of Boulder City and Jaylene Carson, Garland, Texas; parents Mr. and Mrs. Raymond Schmitz of Chicago and Boulder City; brothers Raymond and Gerald Schmitz of Chicago and nine grandchildren. Interment was at the Boulder City Cemetery.

Singleton, Claude Lee
Boulder City News, Thursday, 10 Aug 1972.
C. Singleton Services Held Yesterday
Graveside services were held yesterday morning for Claude Lee Singleton, 84. The rites were conducted at the Boulder City Cemetery by the Reverend Robert Richards of the Community Church in Henderson. Mr. Singleton died Saturday at the Beverly Manor Convalescent Center in Las Vegas, where he had been a patient for a month. He was born June 24, 1888 in Simms, Texas, but also lived in Roswell and Las Cruces, New Mexico. His varied vocational life included ranching and hardware merchandising. Prior to coming to Boulder City, Mr. Singleton was a warehouseman, civilian employee for the U. S. Air Force in Salt Lake City, Utah, from 1952 to 1960. For many years he was a member of the Moose Lodge. Survivors are his wife, Cordie, 545 Date Street; a son, E. L. Singleton, 553 Elm St., Boulder City; a brother, Edward G. Singleton, Williamsburg, New Mexico, and two grandchildren.

Singleton, Cordie E.
Boulder City News, Thursday, 2 Mar 1978, 3:2.
Services were held for Cordie E. Singleton, 87, of Elm Street, who died last Thursday in a local convalescent hospital. The Reverend Guy Holliday of Grace Community Church officiated. A housewife, Mrs. Singleton had resided in the area for 18 years. She was born July 31, 1890 in Pioneer, Texas. She is survived by a son, E. I. Singlton of Boulder City; brother, Charles C. O'Neal of Roswell, New Mexico; sisters, Hettie, Leslie of Kermit, Texas, Alice Strange of Grand Prairie, Texas and Emoline Mann of Crane, Texas; and two grandchildren.

Sirkel, Edward Matthew
Boulder City News, Thursday, 23 Sep 1965, 2:6.
Sirkel Service By Masons
Funeral services were conducted Tuesday morning at the Masonic Temple for Edward Matthew Sirkel, 49, who died last Saturday. Mr. Sirkel was born May 16, 1916 in Austin, Tex. and had been a resident of Clark County for the past five years. Former Boulderites, he was living in North Las Vegas at the time of his death. He is survived by his wife, Helen Belle; his mother, Mary A. Bently, Denver; stepmother, Mrs. Herman Fare, Balmorath, Tex., two daughters, Mrs. Larry Roberts and Mrs. W. J. Van

Slack, Robin Joann
Boulder City News, Thursday, 26 Feb 1970
Baby Slack
Robin Joann Slack, 2 days old, was buried at the Boulder City Cemetery, Tuesday afternoon, with the graveside rites conducted by Bishop Jake Williams, of the Church of Jesus Christ of Latter-day Saints. Robin was born Wednesday Feb. 18, at the Boulder City hospital, and died Friday. Her parents are Rena and Richard Slack of Moore's Trailer Court. She is also survived by her sister, Amy; maternal grandparents, Mr. and Mrs. Lloyd Slack, 1319 Colorado Street.

Slaveck, Stephen
Boulder City News, Thursday, 7 Dec 1978, 12:7-8.
A requiem mass was said yesterday for Stephen Slaveck, 76, who died December 4 in Las Vegas. Mr. Slaveck was a resident of Boulder City and had been a superintendent for the U. S. Quartermaster Corps. He was a native of Chicago, Illinois. Survivors include his wife, Virginia of Boulder City; sons, Stephen of Crete, Illinois, and Richard and Raymond Slaveck, both of Henderson; daughters, Irene Scarpelli of Hoffman Estates, Ill., Dorothy Insalata of Boulder City and Lorraine Hovel of Chicago; sisters, Frances Daniel and Betty Sucaansky, both of Chicago; 19 grandchildren and five great-grandchildren. Burial followed at Boulder City Cemetery. Palm Mortuary handled the arrangements.

Sleeper, Claud

Boulder City News, Thursday, 31 Jan 1957, p.1:5.
Claud Sleeper Dies In Hospital; Final Rites Are Pending
Final rites are pending for Claud Sleeper, 68, who died yesterday morning at the Boulder City Community Hospital where he had been hospitalized since New Year's Day. Mr. Sleeper was stricken Jan. 1 at his home and taken to the hospital. He never regained consciousness. Members of the family said funeral services and burial would be in Boulder City. Bunker Brothers is in charge of arrangements. Mr. Sleeper, who lived at 620 Avenue F, had been a resident of Boulder City since 1936. He first managed the Lake Auto Court but later was employed by the Bureau of Mines and Bureau of Reclamation. He worked in the bureau's river control office at the time he was stricken. He was born in Red Cloud, Nebr., July 28, 1888 and grew up in that state, later moving to Wyoming before coming to Boulder City to live. He was a member of the Knights of Pythias and a former grand officer, and also of the IOOF. Survivors include his widow, Florence, of Boulder City; two daughters, Mrs. Jake Garehime, Jr., of Las Vegas and Mrs. Jack Gagliolo of Boulder City; a sister, Mrs. Carl Wright of Omaha; four grandchildren, Roger Likens, now attending school in Pueblo, Colo., Mrs. Ramon Williams of Boulder City, and Miss Sannene and Kurt Garehime of Las Vegas; and two great grandchildren, Debbie and Danny Williams of Boulder City.

Smee, Bert

Boulder City News, Friday, 1 Aug 1947, 1:5.
Dave Laughery, worshipful master of Boulder City Lodge No. 37, F. & A. M. Today requested that as many Masons as possible attend the funeral of Bert Smee at Grace Community Church at 4 p.m. Monday. Pall bearers will be Walter Swartz, Paul Webb, Robert Warner, Hobart Blair, John Manis and Garold Nellis. Reverend Winston Trever will officiate, and the lodge will be in charge of the services. Burial will be in Boulder City Cemetery. Smee died of heart disease Wednesday.

Smee, Lucy Florence "Grandma"
Boulder City News, Thursday, 20 Sep 1973, 3:8.
Lucy Smee Dies In Local Hospital
Lucy Florence "Grandma" Smee, 92, died Monday at southern Nevada Memorial Hospital, where she had been admitted with a broken hip. Desert Chapter No. 23, Order of Eastern Star, will conduct funeral services at 2 o'clock this afternoon in the Masonic Temple. Burial will be in the Boulder City Cemetery. She was born July 18, 1881 in Pike County, Indiana, but lived in Nebraska for many years. She and her husband, Bert, came to Boulder City in 1938, as their sons Pat and Mike already worked here. Her husband died in 1947, and son Pat in 1954. A homemaker, she was not active in any organizations, but kept up her membership in Emerald Lodge No. 291, O.E.S. Stapleton, Neb., for 50 years. When her health began to fail, she moved from Moore's Trailer Park to El Jen Convalescent Center in Las Vegas, for two years. Last year, she changed to the Las Vegas Convalescent Center. She is survived by her son Melvin R. "Mike" Smee, 2313 East McWilliams, Las Vegas; two daughters, Lucy Workman, Idaho; and Berta Dudley, Harrison, Montana; 10 grandchildren, 16 great-grandchildren. Also a sister, Fannie Clark, Costa Mesa, Calif.; and a daughter-in-law, Dorothy Smee, 513 Ave. I, Boulder City, Colo. The family suggested that donations to the Nevada Heart Association would be suitable memorial offerings.

Smee, Melvin R.
Boulder City News, Thursday, 8 Nov 1979, 16:6-8.
Funeral services for Melvin Robert Smee, 76, who died last Friday were held Monday at Bunker Chapel with Mount Moriah 39 of the Masonic Lodge officiating. Burial was at Boulder City Cemetery. Mr. Smee was born October 10, 1903, in Nebraska. He was a sanitation inspector and had lived in the area since 1931. He is survived by his wife, Vida A. Smee of Las Vegas; sons, Alvin B. Smee of Fullerton, California, and Melvin R. Smee, Jr. of Riverside, California. Sisters, Lucy E. Workman of Cardwell, Montana and Berta L. Dudley of Fallon, Nevada; nine grandchildren; and two great-grandchildren.

Smiley, Mary Louise
Boulder City News, Thursday, 11 Jun 1981, 2:4-5.
Mary Louise Smiley, 74, died Friday, June 5, 1981 in Boulder City. A resident of Boulder City for 25 years, she was a former switchboard operator. She was born in Chicago, Ill. on March 5, 1907. She is survived by her step daughter, Norma Moore of Boulder City and four nephews, William B. Milan of Washington, D.C.; Robert D. Milan of Sacramento, CA; Carline R. Milan, also fo Sacramento and Howard P. Milan of Los Angeles. Graveside services were held Wednesday, June 10, 1981 at Boulder City Cemetery, 2:30 p.m. with the Reverend Mel Pritts of Grace Community Church officiating. Interment followed at Boulder City Cemetery.

Smiley, William C.
Boulder City News, Thursday, 30 May 1974, 9:8.
William Smiley Services Pending
Funeral services are pending for William C. Smiley, 1304 Colorado Street, who passed away early Wednesday in a Las Vegas hospital. Services will be at 10 A.M. Friday at Palm Chapel. Burial will be in B. C. Cemetery.

Smith, Elton R.
Boulder City News, Thursday, 5 July 1984, 8:1.
Funeral services for Elton R. Smith of Boulder City were held last Wednesday at Foursquare Church in Boulder City. Mr. Smith passed away June 24 in Boulder City. He was born in Vernon, Texas, March 1, 1905 and was a retired U.S. Army Major. He is survived by his wife, Lois of Boulder City; daughters Linda Stauffer of Boulder City and Shirley Scown of Hehi, Utah; son Russell Smith of Diamond Bar, Ca. Reverend Marjorie Kitchell was in charge of the services and interment was at Palm Mausoleum in Boulder City.

Smith, Thomas C.
Boulder City News, Thursday, 30 Aug 1979, 8:8.
Thomas C. Smith Services Held Monday
Thomas Clyde Smith passed away August 23 in Boulder City. Funeral services were held Monday and interment was at the Boulder City cemetery. Mr. Smith was born March 21, 1907 in Providence, R.I. he had been a resident of Boulder City since 1966. He was a carpenter. He is survived by a son Thomas Smith, Jr., of North Las Vegas; sisters, Veronica Gaston, Phoenix, Ariz., and Winona Sullivan of Montebello, Ca.; brother, William of Salt Lake City, Utah; grandsons "Butch" Smith of Henderson, Terry Smith of Boulder City and Cory Smith of Gardena, Ca.; granddaughters, Wanda Hansen of North Las Vegas, and Laura Goldsberry of Ft. Lauderdale, Florida.

Smith, William A.
Boulder City News, Thursday, 5 Aug 1976, 5:6.
William A. Smith, of Boulder City, died last week at the age of 75. Born August 21, 1900, in Tipton, Iowa, Smith was a retired railroad conductor who resided at 12-1 Wyoming Street. He is survived by his wife, Nell; a son, Robert; granddaughters Vickie Beard and Susan Strechlow; and 5 great-grandchildren, all of Boulder City. Graveside services were held Friday, July 30, 1976.

Smoot, Charlesetta Layman
Boulder City News, Thursday, 20 Sep 1990, 1:3.
Charlesetta Layman Smoot, age 71, died Friday, Sept. 14, at the Dixie Medical Center in St. George, Utah. She was born December 19, 1919 in Venice, Ill. to William and Gusta Sparks Layman. She married Zeb Smoot Sept. 23, 1939 in St. Louis, Mo. She has lived in Los Angeles, Calif., Boulder City, and Beryl, Utah. Mrs. Smoot has given many hours of volunteer service to the hospital auxiliary at Boulder City Hospital. She was one of the founders of the Art Festival at Boulder City, raising much money for the hospital. She worked 10 years for the Bureau of Reclamation in Boulder City. She was an active member of the Escalante Valley Women's Club. Mrs. Smoot was active in 4-H and scouting. She was a member of the Beryl Baptist Church. Survivors include her husband Zeb Smoot of Beryl, two daughters Mrs. Can (Carol) Chisum and Mrs.

Ernest (Phillis) Eskam, two grandchildren, Eric Eskam, and Christi Chisum all of Boulder City, one sister Marcella Cohen of Pontoon Beach, Ill. Services were held at the Boulder City Cemetery under the direction of the Stilsbury-Desert Rose Memorial Chapel, St. George, Utah. In lieu of flowers the family suggests contributions be made to the memorial fund of the Beryl Baptist Church.

Smythe, Ida Mae

Boulder City News, Thursday, 19 Nov 1987, 34:1-2.
Ida Mae Smythe, 81 died Friday, Nov. 13 in Boulder City. She had been a resident fo the Boulder City area for the past nine years. She was born in Monroe County, Ind. on March 2, 1906 and was a homemaker. She was a member of Eastern Star, Desert Chapter No. 22 in Boulder City. Survivors include husband Arthur Smythe and daughter Marilyn Dart both of Boulder City; son Marlyn Smthe, DePoe Bay, Ore.; seven grandchildren and 10 great grandchildren. Visitation began Monday, No. 16 at 9 a.m. to 9 p.m. at Palm Mortuary in Henderson, 800 South Boulder Highway. Funeral services were Tuesday, Nov. 17 at 2 p.m. Interment was in the Boulder City Cemetery.

Soder, Marion C.

Boulder City News, Thursday, 5 Jan 1995, 8:14.
Marion C. Soder, 78, died Wednesday, Dec. 28, 1994 at a local hospital. Born Nov. 4, 1916 in Cheboygan, Mich.; she was a homemaker in Boulder City for 16 years. She is survived by her granddaughter, Shirley Curtis, great granddaughter, Robyn Curtis, one great grandson, Robert Curtis, all of Boulder City. Services were held. Arrangements were handled by Palm Mortuary of Henderson.

Softchin, Frances E.

Boulder City News, Thursday, 18 Aug 1988, 12:2-3.
Frances E. Softchin, 80, died Tuesday, August 9 in Las Vegas. She was a 20 year resident of the area. She was born in Brooklyn, New York May 13, 1906 and was a long distance telephone operator. Mrs. Softchin was a member of the American Legion Auxiliary Post No. 31 in Boulder City and a Senior Citizen's Kitchen KutUps band member as well as a member of St. Andrew's Church in Boulder City. She is survived by her husband

John P. Softchin of Boulder City, Niece Mary E. Gallaer of Woodhaven, N.Y. and nephews Billy Parker and Charles Parker both of Boston, Mass. Rosary service will be conducted Thursday, August 11 at St. Andrew's at 7 p.m. Mass will be Friday, August 12 at St. Andrew's Church at 10 a.m. Visitation will begin Thursday at noon at Palm Mortuary in Henderson. Interment will be at Boulder City cemetery.

Softchin, John Paul
Boulder City News, Thursday, 8 Feb 1990, 8:2-3.
John Paul Softchin passed away Feb. 1, 1990. He was born May 24, 1913 in Philadelphia, PA. He was a retired over-the-road driver and a member of many civic and fraternal organizations. He was Past Commander of Veterans of Foreign Wars, in Boulder City and worked in security in the general area. He was a veteran of World War II, U.S. Navy Construction Battalion, and served in North African Campaign. He was a member of the Church of Jesus Christ of Latter Day Saints, Boulder City Ward No. 2. He had lived in Boulder City for many years. His wife, Frances, preceded him in death. He leaves sisters Kay Ogden of Parkesberg, PA, Marianne Simone of New York City, Sovieny Klunk of Downingtown, PA, Julia Kaighn of Boulder City, and Nellie Softchin also of Boulder City. A brother Sam Softchin of Canton, PA. 15 nieces and nephews. Graveside services were Monday Feb. 5 with burial at Boulder City Cemetery.

Spangenberg, R. F.
Boulder City News, Thursday, 18 June 1964, 1:1-2.
Early AM Smash-Up
RR Pass Crash Kills Local Man
A Boulder City resident was killed early Friday morning when the car he was driving rolled over and smashed up in a spectacular accident on the Boulder Highway at Railroad Pass. Dead is R. F. Spangenberg, 39, who apparently was returning to Boulder City shortly after midnight.
According to a report from the Nevada Highway Patrol, his car was traveling toward town in the inside lane when it suddenly ran off into the area which divides the highway, skidded for 270 feet along the edge of the road, rolled completely over and skidded on its left side for another 60 feet, finally coming to rest on its wheels after tumbling yet another 151 feet. The vehicle landed on the inside lane of the northbound side of U. S. 93. Spangenberg's funeral services were conducted in the new Palm

Mortuary in Henderson on Monday, and were officiated by the Reverend Clyde O. Speas, of Bethany Baptist Church here. He was interred at the local cemetery. The local man was an employee of the Union Pacific Railroad in Henderson and lived with his wife, Dorothy, at 204 Rainer Court. He is also survived by three children, Margie, 13; Glenn, 11, and Jane, 4. He is also survived by his mother, Minnie Mae Fisher, of Los Angeles. He had no brothers and sisters. The victim and the family moved here six months ago from Whittier, Calif. He had been active in the local municipal tennis program and had served on a tennis committee in Las Vegas. The accident was covered by Patrolman Richard McDermott of NHP and occurred about 1:15 a.m. Spangenberg was taken to the local hospital where he was pronounced dead by Dr. Thomas White.

Spearman, Millard Joseph

Boulder City News, Thursday, 1 Mar 1973
Funeral Held Mon. For M. Spearman
Funeral rites were held Monday morning for Millard Joseph Spearman, 76, who died Feb. 22 after a long illness. The Reverend Hugh P. Smith of St. Andrew's Catholic Church officiated. Military graveside services were conducted at the Boulder City Cemetery by American Legion Post No. 31. Mr. Spearman was born July 8, 1896, in Keokuk, Iowa. He served in the U. S. Army in World War I. He was employed as an iron worker for the Guy P. Atkinson construction company in Ohio, before coming to Nevada during the building of the Dam. He worked for Six Companies, and Babcock & Wilcox. During World War 2, he was an iron worker at Henderson. In 1947, the Spearmans moved to Oregon and enjoyed farm life there for many years. Nina and Millard "Pappy" Spearman had two sons, who attended Boulder High School. Millard Jr. preceded his father in death. Nina and son Gordon live in Hermiston, Oregon. Other survivors are a brother, Harvey Spearman; a sister, Nellie Nelson; four grandchildren and five great-grandchildren. Nina was brought to Boulder City for the burial by Gordon and his wife June (daughter of Camilla Holtry Wait). Their mailing address is Rt. 3, Box 530, Hermiston, Ore. 97838.

Spellman, John Henry

Boulder City News, Thursday, 10 Dec 1987, 19:1.
John Henry Spellman, aged 67, died Friday, Dec. 4 in Boulder City. He was born in Hackensack, New Jersey on Nov 11, 1920 and was a resident of Boulder City for the past eight years. He was a fireman before retirement and was also a veteran of World War II and a life member of the American Legion Doremus Post Hackensack, N.J., International Order of Exempt Fireman of J.N. and State Retired Police and Fireman's Association. He is survived by his wife Natalie of Boulder City; daughter Karen Mauro of Hackettstown, N.J.; son John "Jack" F. of Flagtown, N.J.; brother Wilbur of N.J. and three grandchildren. The funeral arrangements were handled by Palm Mortuary of Henderson. Graveside services were held at Boulder City Cemetery on Dec. 7, officiated by Father Herbert Ward from St. Jude's Ranch Episcopal Church.

Spelts, Grant Ardell

Boulder City News, Thursday, 16 Mar 1978, 10:6.
Grant Ardell Spelts, infant son of Mr. and Mrs. William Spelts of 700 Fifth Street, passed away Sunday, March 12 in San Diego, California. The baby was born March 6 at St. Rose in Henderson. He is survived by his parents and one brother, Ryan B. Spelts; paternal grandparents, Mr. and Mrs. Ben Spelts of Idaho and maternal grandparents, Mr. and Mrs. Ardell Wolsey of Kingman, Arizona. Graveside services will be held this morning at 11 a.m. at the Boulder City Cemetery with Bishop Bryant Solomon of the LDS Church officiating.

Spickelmier, Robert

Las Vegas Review Journal, Sunday, 8 Aug 1965, 1:3.
Henderson Man Drowns in Mead
A young Henderson man drowned Saturday evening near Boulder Beach during a game of water baseball, the park service said. Bob Spickelmier, about 23, of 307 Atlantic Ave. was with a Jaycee group at the Special Events Beach, just north of Hemingway Harbor at the time of the accident.

Las Vegas Review Journal, Monday, 9 Aug 1965, 3:4.
Henderson Man's Body Recovered
The body of a Henderson man who drowned Saturday night near Boulder Beach was recovered Sunday morning by divers from the National Park Service. The victim was Robert Spickelmier, 23, of 307 Atlantic Ave. Officials said the victim was with members of the Henderson Jaycees on an outing at the Special Events Beach, just north of Hemingway Harbor. Members of the group and Spickelmier were engaged in a game of "water baseball" when he apparently waded into deep water and started to go down. Some in the party swam to his aid, but he fought them off in apparent panic. Funeral arrangements will be announced by Palm mortuary in Henderson.

Stead, Florence D.
Boulder City News, Thursday, 16 Aug 1984, 33:3.
Florence D. Stead, 89 passed away Aug. 13 in Boulder City. She was born Nov. 15, 1894 in Patterson, New Jersey and was a homemaker. She had lived in Boulder City since 1942. She is survived by daughters Ruth Bloomer and Elizabeth Craft of San Francisco, Ca., and Eleanor Fleck of Reno; six grandchildren and sic great grandchildren. Memorial services will be held at St. Christopher's Episcopal Church in Boulder City today at 4 p.m. Interment will be private. In lieu of flowers the family requests donations to St. Jude's children's home or St. Christopher's Church.

Steel, Paul L.
Boulder City News, Thursday, 20 Nov 1986, 16:3.
Paul L. Steele, age 74, died Monday, Nov. 17 in Las Vegas. He was born Oct. 11, 1912 in Redding, Kansas. A 23 year resident, he was a retired officer for the Bureau of Reclamation. He served in the U.S. Army during WWII, was also a Korean war veteran. He was a member of the American Legion, the Elks and the Knights of Columbus. He is survived by his wife, Esther of Boulder City; sons Pat of New Zealand and Mike of Las Vegas; daughter Bette Jean Bray of Fountain Valley, Calif; brother Kenneth, of Kansas; sisters Wanda Brewer, Lois Tanquary and Grave Moyer all of Kansas and eight grandchildren. Rosary will be said at St. Andrews Catholic Church in Boulder City Thursday at 6 p.m. Mass will be said Friday at 10 a.m. Burial will be in the Boulder City Cemetery. Palm Mortuary is handling the arrangements.

Steel, Paul L.
Boulder City News, Thursday, 27 Nov 1986, 12:1.
Paul L. Steele, a 23 year resident of Boulder City, received a Military Honor Guard Graveside ceremony at Boulder City Cemetery Friday, Nov. 21, 1986. Preceding the graveside services, a mass was said by Fr. Joe Annese at St. Andrews Catholic Church. Paul was born in Redding, Kan. and was a 29 year veteran of the U.S. Army serving in both WWII and Korea and retired in 1956 at the rank of Lt. Col. Paul, his wife, "Dedee" and their sons Pat and Mike arrived in Boulder City in 1963 when Paul was sales manager of Pomona Tile Company in Las Vegas. In the mid sixties Paul went to work as a guide at Hoover Dam then worked in Procurement until he retired in 1971. More recently Paul and "Dedee" have divided their time between Boulder City and Waikanae, New Zealand where their son Pat lives with wife Anne and children Samantha and Paul. Paul is survived by his wife, Dedee of Boulder City, sons Pat of New Zealand and Mike of Las Vegas, daughter Bette Jean Bray of Fountain Valley, Calif; brother Kenneth; sisters Grace Moyer, Wanda Brewer and Lois Tanquary of Arkansas City, Kas.

Steeves, Grace
Boulder City News, Wednesday, 13 Aug 1947, 1:2.
Mrs. Steeves, Early Resident of B. C., Dies Here at Age 72
Funeral arrangements were being made today for Mrs. Grace Steeves, wife of William Steeves, who died last night at her home, 635 Ave. F, after a lingering illness. Present besides her husband at the time of her death were her son Barry Steeves, 660 Ave. H, and Mrs. Steeves; and a daughter, Mrs. I. J. Searway, who arrived here Saturday from her home in Redding, Calif. Dr. J. C. Roberts was in attendance. The deceased also is survived by three other daughters, Mrs. R. L. Churchill of Baltimore, Mrs. W. N. Bernard of Wellsley, Mass., and Mrs. Marion Hall of Redding; a brother, Walter Carmichael of Preque Isle, Me,; a sister, Mrs. George Hutchinson, Boston; and five grandchildren, Nancy, Billy and Sandy Steeves, Brent Searway and Coralyn Bernard. Mrs. Steeves was born 72 years ago in New Brunswick, Canada. She was married to William W. Steeves in 1895. They celebrated their golden wedding anniversary here two years ago. Arrangements are in charge of the Palm Funeral Home of Las Vegas.

Steeves, William W.
Boulder City News, Monday, 17 Nov 1947, 1:5.
William W. Steeves Dies at Age 79
Funeral arrangements were being made today for William W. Steeves, long time resident of Boulder City who died in Boulder City Hospital yesterday at the age of 79. He had survived his wife, Grace, by three months and three days. The deceased leaves a son, Barry Steeves, 660 Ave. H; four daughters, Mrs. I. J. Searway and Mrs. Marion S. Hall, Redding, Calif.; Mrs. R. L. Churchill, Baltimore, and Mrs. W. M. Bernard, Wellesley, Mass.; and five grandchildren, Nancy, Billy and Sandy Steeves, Boulder City; Brenton Searway, Redding, and Carolyn Dawn Bernard, Wellsley. Mrs. Hall, Mrs. Searway and Brenton are expected here for the funeral, which the family said probably will be set for 3 p.m. Wednesday. The elder Steeves was born in Fort Fairfield, Me., and he and Mrs. Steeves were married 52 years ago in Maine. They celebrated their golden wedding anniversary here two years ago. They came to Boulder City in 1932 and Steeves worked as a watchman, first for Six Companies, then for the Bureau of Reclamation. He retired about two years ago. After his wife's death he continued to live at their home at 635 Ave F. until he fell ill two weeks ago and was taken to the hospital.

Stephens, Cecil W.
Boulder City News, Thursday, 11 Apr 1991, 10:1.
Cecil W. Stephens, 74, a 12-year resident, died Sunday, in a local hospital. Born in Pilot Point, Texas on June 24, 1916, he was a retired oil refinery foreman and a member of the Bethany Baptist Church. He is survived by his wife, Lee Stephens, of Boulder City; a daughter, Donna Disney of Shasta County, Calif. and a son, Gary Stephens of Orange County, Calif. Services were held. Palm Mortuary handled arrangements.

Stoker, Edna Beth
Boulder City News, Thursday, 19 Sep 1974, 9:3.
Edna Stoker Services
Funeral rites were held Saturday afternoon for Edna Beth Stoker, 33, at the Boulder City Church of Jesus Christ of Latter-day Saints. Bishop Bryant Solomon of Ward 2 officiated. Burial was in the Boulder City Cemetery. Pallbearers were Dale Imlay, Bill Slack, Kent McComb, Cullen Holyoak, Sherman and Douglas Hafen. Edna died Wednesday at the St. Rose De Lima Hospital, after a long illness. Edna Beth Talbot was born Feb. 17, 1941 in Salina, Utah. She was married to LaMar Stoker in the St. George Temple on Sept. 22, 1960. They moved to Boulder City 8 years ago from Panguitch, Utah, and he is a teacher at the Boulder City Elementary School. Until her failing health forced curtailment of her work, she was active in the church, serving as M.I.A. secretary, Primary Teacher and assistant secretary, and den mother for the cub scouts. She is survived by her husband, LaMar Stoker, 620 Kings Place; a son, Sterling; three daughters, Stella, Suzette and Stormie, of the same address; her parents, Mr. and Mrs. George Talbot, 1501 Nevada Highway; her paternal grandmother, Bessie Talbot, Panguitch, Utah; and her maternal grandmother, Edna Smoot of Henderson, Nev.

Stoneham, Leo B.
Boulder City News, Thursday, 13 July 1989, 33:4.
Leo B. Stoneham, 74, of Boulder City, died Sunday in Las Vegas. He was born Feb. 15, 1915, in Detroit. A two-and-a-half-year resident, he was a retired internal auditor and a World War II Army veteran. He is survived by his wife, Christine of Boulder City; two step-daughters, Frank Kish, also of Boulder City and Rita Walsh of Waterford, Mich.; a sister, Camille of Berkley, Mich.; and four grandchildren. Services will be held at 10 a.m. today in St. Andrews. Father Joe Annese will officiate. Burial will be in Boulder City Cemetery. Palm Mortuary is handling arrangements.

Stoner, Ezra
Boulder City News, Thursday, 21 Nov 1991, 9:12.
Ezra Stoner, 96, died Friday in a local hospital. He was born August 2, 1895, in Peru, Ind., and had been a resident of the Boulder City area for 13 years. Stoner was a veteran of the United States Army, serving during World War II, and a lifetime member of the American Legion. He is survived by one son, Charles A. Stoner of Hobart, Ind.; four sisters; five grandchildren and 13 great grandchildren. Arrangements were handled by Palm Mortuary in Henderson.

Stoney, Stephen Richard
Boulder City News, Thursday, 21 Aug 1967, 1:5.
Stoney Infant Buried Here
Graveside services were conducted Monday morning at Boulder City Cemetery for Stephen Richard Stoney with Bishop Jacob Williams of the LDS Chapel officiating. The infant was born Aug. 24 in Las Vegas and passed away two days later. He was the son of Mr. and Mrs. Stephen A. Stoney, Jr., 2943 Lawndale St. Survivors include his parents, and grandparents, Mr. and Mrs. Stephen A. Stoney of New Jersey and Mr. and Mrs. Richard L. Francis, Boulder City.

Stout, Glen
Boulder City News, Monday, 4 Nov 1946, 1:1
Glen Stout Died After Jump From Moving Truck Near Livermore, Calif.
Glen Stout, son of Mr. and Mrs. Walter Stout, 624 Avenue F, was killed Saturday night when he jumped from a moving truck on the highway near Pleasant, Cal., on the way from Oakland to Stockton. Pleasant is near Livermore. Details of the cause of his jumping from the truck were not definitely known, but he fell and apparently struck his head. Two different versions of the cause have been told, according to Willis Eaton of Corona del Mar, Cal, Glen's brother-in-law, for whom he has been working, as truck driver. One story heard by Eaton, who is now in Boulder City, was that there was a wreck on the highway ahead and that the other man, who was driving the truck, was slowing down to stop for this when Glen jumped. It was surmised that because of his right foot, which had been injured 10 or 11 years ago, he lost his balance and fell, though the truck was not going very fast at the time. The truck on which

he had been riding definitely was not wrecked. Word of Stout's death was phoned to Boulder City about midnight Saturday, the accident having occurred a short time before that. Eaton, who had seen Stout in Oakland at 2:30 p.m. Saturday, drove to Boulder City, arriving here at 5 p.m. Sunday, and did not learn of the death of his brother-in-law until his arrival here. Stout has lived in Balboa for the last three years. In addition to his parents and brothers and sisters, he is survived by his widow, whom he married in March, and her three-year-old daughter. Glen was born in Hinckley, Utah, 20 years ago, but went through school in Boulder City, having been an upperclassman in high school when he left. Funeral services will be held in Boulder City, Wednesday or Thursday, the body to arrive Tuesday morning at the Bunker Burt mortuary in Las Vegas.

Boulder City News, Tuesday, 5 Nov 1946, 4:4-5
Glen Stout Funeral to Be Wednesday at 2
Funeral services for Glen Stout, who died Saturday night after having jumped from a truck in central California, will be held at the L.D.S. church in Boulder City Wednesday at 2 p.m. Burial will be at Boulder City cemetery. The body will lie in state at the home of his parents, Mr. and Mrs. Walter Stout, at 624 Avenue F, from 10 to 12 noon Wednesday. Brothers and sisters of Glen are arriving from Idaho, California and other points, to attend the funeral. Archie Stout and Marwood Stout, two brothers, arrived Monday morning from Pocatello, Ida., accompanied by their wives and Mr. and Mrs. Archie Stout's one child and Mr. and Mrs. Marwood Stout's two children. Glen's widow, Shirley Stout, is expected to arrive in Boulder City this evening, with Mr. and Mrs. Merrill Dastrup of Ontario, Calif. Mrs. Dastrup is Glen's sister. Cardon Stout, another brother, is expected to arrive tonight from Boulder, Colo., and Nathan Stout is to arrive tonight from Great Lakes, Ill.

Strafford, Freddy
Boulder City News, Thursday, 2 Feb 1995, 9:1-2.
Freddy Strafford, 76, died Monday, Jan. 30, 1995 at a local hospital. Born May 16, 1918 he had been a resident of Boulder City since 1980. He was a retired owner/operator of a service station; a member of Boulder City Elks Lodge #1682; and was a veteran of the U.S. Navy, having served in World War II and the Korean War. He is survived by his wife, Donna B. Strafford, of Boulder City; one son, Chris Strafford, of Calif.; one sister,

Florence Berg, of Glendale, Calif.; one brother, Dick Strafford, of Grass Valley, Calif.; five step children; 11 step grand children; two grandchildren and two great grandchildren. The family suggests donations be made to St. Jude's Ranch for Children, in Boulder City. Services will be held at 11 a.m. today at Palm Mortuary-Henderson Chapel. Graveside services will follow at the Boulder City Cemetery. Arrangements were handled by Palm Mortuary of Henderson.

Stratton, Robert William
Boulder City News, Thursday, 9 Nov 1972.
Funeral Held Sat. For R. W. Stratton
Funeral services for Robert William Stratton, 60, maintenance engineer for the Boulder City Hospital, were held Sat. at 11 a.m. at Palm Chapel in Henderson. Reverend Guy Holliday of Grace Community Church, conducted the services. Interment was at the Boulder City cemetery. Mr. Stratton died Nov. 2 at the Boulder City Hospital. He was born Sept. 11, 1912 in Elyria, Ohio. His father was Harry Stratton and his mother was Ida May Beckwith. He was a member of the Rochston Lodge No. 316 F & AM of Kent, Ohio, and resided in Boulder City at 501 Ave. I for 15 years. He is survived by his wife, Dorothy C. Jones Stratton; a son, Robert L. of Kent, Ohio; daughter Patricia Berry Phoenix, Ariz; sister, Marian Swan, Cleveland, Ohio; brothers, Boyd Cook, LeGrange, Ohio and Charles Cook of Elyia, Ohio, and six grandchildren.

Strickland, Clifton
Boulder City News, Thursday, 30 Aug 1951.
Clifton Strickland, 54, was buried in the Boulder City cemetery on Monday evening, following Masonic funeral rites and graveside services, presided over by Wilfred Voss, past grand master of Nevada Masons. The rulogy was given by the Reverend John Eddings of the First Baptist Church. Lee H. Pickett acted as chaplain. Clarence Neumann was organist at the rites in the Masonic Temple, and accompanied two songs by quartet members Nicholas Havrilla, John Connolly, Harvey Johns and Leo Courtney. Pallbearers were John Masterson, Jack Swarts, Kenneth Swallow, Wesley Nicholson, Lloyd Morrison and Lloyd Wiggins. Strickland was a member of Prairie Lodge No. 465 at Hamburg, Arkansas.

Strickler, Minnie C.
Boulder City News, Thursday, 19 May 1977, 7:7-8.
Minnie C. Strickler passed away May 12 in Boulder City. Funeral services were held Monday at Palm Chapel and burial was at the Boulder City cemetery. Mrs. Strickler was born May 8 in Kentucky and she had resided at 659 Ave. B for two years. She is survived by a son Paul Bujarske of Boulder City, and Bernard Burjarske of Long Beach, Ca.; daughter Peggy Underwood of Dallas, Texas; two sisters, Mildred Matthews of Blytheville, Ark. and Hattie Holt of the same community; brothers Willis Caldwine, Jonoboro, Ark., and Ventrice of Harrison, Ark.

Stripling, Edwin C.
Boulder City News, Thursday, 15 Feb 1979, 5:1-3.
By Teddy Fenton
One of the finest citizens in Boulder City died this week. He was Edwin C. Stripling of 616 Ave. F. Ed was a landlord and was known for not charging his tenants as much as most of the other landlords in town. His many tenants over the years appreciated his friendship and thoughtfulness and he will be missed far more than anyone can tell at this sad time. Ed began buying rentals when property was priced very reasonably in Boulder City. He concentrated on Six Companie's cottages and he would update them as soon as he took possession. One night his rental at 659 Ave. F was entirely gutted when a tenant left a burning cigarette in an overstuffed chair. Ed had raised his fire insurance that same year and he remodeled the house and enlarged it with his insurance. His tenants would ask him for money for materials and paint and he never said he couldn't afford it. In his years as a landlord we heard many of his tenants say he was a good friend. His late sister, Myrtle Patton, also owned rentals and together they would trade labor and have a good time remodeling a property. He taught her his craft as a carpenter. They were close. Ed left behind two sons, Bruce Stripling, New Orleans, La, and David Stripling, Orlando, Fla. His mother lives in Florida, his brother, Clarence Stripling, in Sarasota, Fla., sister, Ruby Yerkes, Federal Way, Wash. and Ed had six grandchildren. We've lost a good neighbor and Boulder City could use more landlords as thoughtful as Ed was. To his family we say, "Whenever someone talks of death ... most people will not hear... they shut their ears and close their eyes...and hearts are filled with fear... and yet it's something everyone must surely someday do...each one of us must fade

away - and bid this life adieu." "But really friends, death holds no sting, just long eternal rest...our bodies die, our soul lives on... to this I will attest." From Sketches by Ben Burroughs. Ed was a World War II veteran. His Memorial Services were held at the Bunker Chapel last Tuesday.

Stukas, Leta A.
Boulder City News, Thursday, 3 Mar 1955, 8:6.
Funeral Rites For Mrs. Leta Stukas Scheduled Today
Funeral services for Leta A. Stukas, 52, will be held this afternoon at 2:30 at the Church of the Nazarene in Henderson. The Reverend Ralph Kaldenberg of Las Mesa, California, will officiate. Interment will be in the Boulder City Cemetery. Mrs. Stukas, wife of the Reverend R. H. Stukas, pastor of the Church of Nazarene in Boulder City, has suffered with multiple sclerosis since 1941, when the family lived in Roswell, New Mexico. She and her husband came to Henderson a year ago to live with their son and his wife, the Reverend and Mrs. Wilfred E. Stukas, pastor of the Nazarene Church there. Since coming to Boulder City, the Stukas family, including their 17-year-old son, Richard have resided at 901 Avenue K. Mrs. Stukas was born December 24, 1902 in Iowa. Other Survivors include two other sons, Capt. Robert Stukas now stationed with the armed forces in North Africa; Donald L. Stukas of Paramount, California; four grandsons, three granddaughters and four sisters, Lila Martin of Ventura, California; Ella Mendenhall of Oxnard, California; Ida Marshall of Hastings, Nebraska; and Leola Rundell of Long Beach, California.

Sullivan, Alice Mae
Boulder City News, Thursday, 11 Jun 1987, 16:3-6.
by Teddy Fenton
A gentle and unselfish friend to all who knew and loved her has passed from our earth. She was buried on Tuesday in the beautiful Boulder City Cemetery. Alice Mae Sullivan now rests beside her husband Joe, and other members of her beloved family who preceded her in death. Her rest was well earned. For ten years she has courageously endured arthritis in its most severe form. She was at the Boulder City Care Center when she passed to a better land, and with her was her niece, Ila Godbey Clements. Few families are as close as the Godbey clan. When a member becomes

ill, all the members rush to her side. For the seven years that Alice worsened she was never allowed to feel lonely. Her passing was so peaceful that Ila, who held her hand all through the night and the early morning, said she seemed to turn back to the days of her youth, her face so relaxed, all marks of pain entirely disappeared. There is so much can be said about the 97 years Allie lived upon our earth. How one small person could have done all she accomplished is hard to believe. . . she was a miracle. She cared so much for everyone. She was a teacher so special to the needs of her children. Tuesday, June 9, 1987, was a day chosen for the services of a beloved member of a grateful community. The Reverend John Rousseau of Grace Community Church officiated. Palm Mortuary conducted the arrangements. Erma (Mrs. Tom) Godbey spoke the eulogy. "My sister Allice Sullivan had a very busy and rewarding life. She was a Country School Teacher for 30 years in Colorado. A wife and mother, her son J. Monroe is with us today, her daughter, Sammette preceded her in death. She was a substitute teacher. She could teach a first-grader to read and she could also teach a high school students all subjects such as Latin, World History, Chemistry or Geometry. She was a wonderful needle woman. She excelled at embroidery, crochet, knitting, tatting, and was a superb seamstress. She is being laid to rest today in a dress she made herself. She took it on a trip around the world. She sewed for her many nieces, nephews and friends. Joe and Allie arrived in Boulder City in 1942. They bought a house at 664 Avenue C. Together they raised fruit trees, roses and before Allie left her home (because of illness) she had the entire yard front and back planted in flowers and all things green and beautiful. When Allie could no longer be alone she was befriended by her friend Delores Shope. There she lived until her illness progressed to having to be taken to the Care Center. Allie worked until she was 70 years old. She worked at the Bureau of Mines in the Cobolt Lab during World War II. She was timekeeper for a period after the war, still at the Bureau of Mines. She became an accountant, USBR in the last accounting office in the administration building. She worked with the late Marwood Doud. She did volunteer work for the Red Cross during the war and also in Colorado before coming to Boulder City. She knitted 150 shawls for "Bundles for Brittiany" then knitted countless sweaters for the servicemen. She made baby layettes for all the mothers in our family and for the friends she loved who were mothers. She was secretary for the Red Cross and in Boulder City she trained Red Cross swimming instructors for the volunteer swim program. In those days there was no swimming pool and the children were taken to Lake Mead. Alice accompanied them. After retiring at age 70, she became active in NARFE. She attended Grace Community Church and was a member of its Women's Circles. She was a member of the Rebecca Lodge in Durango, Colo.; and a PTA organizer for several counties. Erma explained that Allie was a half sister and a second mother to her. She was 14 years her senior. She baked the wedding cake when Erma's mother married Allie's father. When Erma was born Allie made some of the baby clothes. She was always like a mother to the nephews and nieces of the Godbey family and to all who knew her in the neighborhood where she lived. In particular she loved the children of Delores Shope. Mary Shope attended the services from California. Speaking for those of us who knew her and her large family of Godbey's – enmasse. We are proud of have known her. Rest in peace, beloved Allie, You will be missed.

Sullivan, Eileen C.
Boulder City News, Thursday, 2 Jun 1994, 12:1.
Funeral Mass for Eileen Sullivan, 87, a Buffalo woman who died May 30, 1994 at the Johnson County Memorial Hospital will be held at 8 a.m. Monday, June 6 at St. Peter's Catholic Church in Henderson. A Rosary will be recited Sunday evening at 7 p.m. at the Palm Mortuary. Burial will be in the Boulder City Cemetery. Friends may donate to the American Cancer Society in care of the Adams Funeral Home in Buffalo, who are in charge of arrangements in Wyoming. Sullivan was born on Oct. 8, 1906, in Edina, Mo., to John and Adelaide Byrne. As a young child, she moved with her family to Butte, Mont., where she grew up and received her education. She graduated from Butte High School in 1924 and was married in June of 1925 in Butte to James Sullivan. They made their home in Butte where Mr. Sullivan was in the wholesale grocery business and in 1958 they moved to Los Angeles, where Mr. Sullivan was an Air Quality Control enforcement officer. They retired in 1977 and moved to Boulder City where Sullivan died in August of 1978. In 1980, Eileen moved to Hesperia, Calif., to live with her daughter and her husband. In 1989, they moved to Buffalo where she had lived until the time of her death. She was a past member of the Soroptomist Club in Butte and St. John's Catholic Church in Buffalo. She is survived by two daughters, Donna Reep of Buffalo and Patrica Kooch of Everson, Wash., seven grandchildren. She was preceded in death by her parents, her

husband, one brother and one son.

Sullivan, James F. Sr.
Boulder City News, Thursday, 20 July 1978, 26:5.
Services were held Monday for James F. Sullivan, Sr., 73, who passed away July 13 in Boulder City. Mr. Sullivan was born January 14, 1905 in Butte, Montana and had resided in Boulder City for several months. He was a retired engineering inspector for Los Angeles County and a life member of the BPOE of Butte, Montana. He is survived by his wife, Eileen of Boulder City; a son, James F. Sullivan, Jr., of Las Vegas; daughters, Donna Reep of Hesperia, California and Patricia Kooch of Boulder City; a brother, Gerald of Butte; sisters, Sister Mary Lawrence and Sister Mary Louise of Levinworth, Kansas; seven grandchildren and five great-grandchildren. Services were held at St. Andrew's Church with interment following at Boulder City Cemetery.

Sullivan, Joseph Michael
Boulder City News, Tuesday, 26 Feb 1953, 1:4-5.
Joe Sullivan Funeral Rites Conducted Yesterday by Elks
Funeral services for Joseph Michael Sullivan, 62, were conducted yesterday afternoon by the Elks lodge, of which he was a member. Sullivan died of a heart attack Sunday afternoon, a few minutes after entering Boulder hospital. He had been in poor health for several years. Sullivan was born in Fort Lewis, Colorado on March 31, 1890, being one of twin sons of Michael and Annie Fielding Sullivan, who were both natives of Ireland. His parents and twin brother, James have been dead for several years. He came here from Durango in 1944, and worked for the Bureau of Mines until after the war. During the last three years he has been employed in the U. S. B. R. Regional reproduction department. Sullivan joined the Elks lodge in Durango in 1925, and served as club steward here in 1948. He also belonged to the Odd Fellows lodge in Colorado. The deceased is survived by his widow, Alice, a son, Joseph Monroe Sullivan of Mill Valley, California; and a daughter, Samette (Mrs. Jack) Moe, of Indian Springs. Mrs. Sullivan is the sister of Erma Godbey, on Avenue L. Those participating in the funeral rites were Don Ashbaugh, exalted ruler; L. S. Lappin, leading knight; Phil Noble, loyal knight; L. E. Clark, lecturing knight; Darrell L. Pitts, esquire; Charles Kimball, chaplain and Archie D. Ryan, secretary. The Reverend Ford L.

Gilbert, of Henderson, a member of the local lodge and Nevada state chaplain of the order, delivered the sermon. Assisting with the service were E. Paul Carter, inner guard; Walter Vreeland, organist and Charles O. Hiller, tiler. Russell Farnsworth sang two solos. Pallbearers were his close friends, John Shipp, John Fielding, Phillip Harrigan, L. P. Davis, Charles A. Shope and A. R. Wegren. Interment followed in the Boulder City cemetery. The Palm Funeral home had charge of the arrangements.

Suriani, Carmine
Boulder City News, Thursday, 19 Sep 1985, 29:3.
Carmine Suriani, 82, of Boulder City, died Monday in a local hospital. He was born Feb. 3, 1903, in Italy. He was an eight year resident. He is survived by his daughters, Ann Donald of Las Vegas and Rosemary Davis of Boulder City; five grandchildren and one great-grandchild. The funeral will be in Palm Mortuary in Henderson. Time and date are pending.

Sweeney, Morgan
Boulder City News, Monday, 11 Aug 1947, 1:3-4.
Morgan Sweeney Jr. Dies at Lake; Last Rites Wednesday
Requiem mass for Morgan Sweeney Jr. will be said at 9 a.m. Wednesday at St. Andrew's Catholic Church. Rosary will be recited at 7:30 p.m. tomorrow at the church. Morgan died Saturday evening when swimming at Boulder Beach with a party of friends. He is believed to have suffered a heart attack as he dived off a raft. He was the son of Mr. and Mrs. Morgan Sweeney, 718 park St. He was 21 years of age, having been born January 28, 1926. Morgan came to Boulder City 10 years ago and attended grade and high school here. He was a star athlete, playing on the football team and on the basketball team that won the Nevada state championship in 1946. During the late war he enlisted in the Navy, and later received a medical discharge. He was a member of the Knights of Columbus and American Legion Post No. 31. When he was attending University of Nevada he belonged to Lambda Chi Alpha fraternity. He was first president of the Teen Age Club here. In attempting to determine the manner of Morgan's death, Chief Ranger C. F. Peterson found that the group that included Morgan had been advised by lifeguard Jim Bellor to leave the water because dark was falling. When they came in, Morgan was missing. Bellor began to search for him, and spied him lying in eight feet of water. He recovered the body and attempted to revive the victim,

but without success. When the Ranger station was notified, Dr. E. A. MacCornack sped to the scene; Peterson dispatched the ambulance and provided a police car escort for Reverend Joseph A. Spitzig, pastor of St. Andrew's church. No water was found in the victim's lungs, and Lee Hayward as coroner listed the cause of death as a heart disease, as certified by Dr. MacCornack. Celebrant of the requiem mass will be Father Spitzig. Interment will be in Boulder City Cemetery. The body now is at the Palms Funeral Home in Las Vegas. Besides his parents, Morgan is survived by two sisters, Eileen, who is a student at University of Nevada, and Mrs. Sheila Hess of Pittsburg, Calif,; a grandmother, Mrs. Bridget Sweeney, and an aunt, Mrs. Zita McEwen, both of Los Angeles. A cousin, Miguel McEwen, is here from Los Angeles for the funeral rites, and a second cousin, Mrs. Mary Toomey of San Francisco, is en route from San Francisco.

Talbot, George B.
Boulder City News, Thursday, 25 Feb 1992, 8:3.
George B. Talbot, died Feb. 18, 1993, in a local hospital. He was born Oct. 28, 1916, in Panguich, Utah, and had been a resident of the Boulder City area for 19 years. He was a member of LDS 1st Ward in Boulder City. He is survived by his wife, Addie Talbot of Boulder City; two brothers, Robert of Kanab, Utah, and Ned of Parowan, Utah; four grandchildren, Sheila Rodman, Sterling Stoker, Suzette Sudweeks, and Stormie Baxter, and two great grandchildren. Talbot was preceded in death by a daughter, Edna Beth. Services were held Monday. Arrangements were handled by Palm Mortuary in Henderson.

Talley, Nancy Ethel
Boulder City News, Thursday, 27 Jun 1968, 1:1-2.
By Esther Shipp
Funeral services for Nancy Ethel Talley, 81, will be held at 3 p.m. tomorrow conducted by the Reverend Guy Holliday at Grace Community Church. Burial will follow in the B.C. Cemetery. Pallbearers will be Frank Jensen, Perlie Morris, John Shipp, Warren Kivett, Winfred Walker and Richard Slater. Honorary pallbearers are William Leicht, John Gieck, Joseph Wine, Ernest Courthey, William Plott and George Edwards. Ethel "Nanie" Winkler was born in a sod house in Lebanon, Kans. Sept. 15, 1886 and was a member of the Sons and Daughters of the Soddies. She

worked as a clerk in Kansas and later helped her first husband in their electrical appliance business. Following his death she moved to Boulder City in 1943 and lived with her sister, the late Violet LaCroix. Both sisters had a knack for arranging flowers and making corsages, and worked at Hayward's Flower Shop for many years. Ethel died Monday evening, June 24 at B.C. Hospital. She had surgery in the morning to insert a pin in a broken bone. She went to Winnemucca June 15 with a large delegation from Southern Nevada to see friend Alice Smiddy installed as Rebekah Assembly president. She fell Tuesday morning, June 18, and was taken to the hospital there. Thursday morning, June 20, Earl Leseberg piloted his place to Winnemucca to transfer Ethel to the hospital here. A nurse and friend, Lola Jensen, made the flight with them. Ethel Martin and George Talley were married Dec. 4, 1948. She received her 25-year jewel in the Rebekah Lodge in 1967. She was a member by transfer to Cactus Lodge 40, IOOF. Mrs. Talley was a past president of the ladies Auxiliary to Patriarchs Militant, Lake Mead Canton, IOOF and she was a past chief of Charleston Temple 2, Pythian Sisters. Mrs. Talley was also a member of the American Legion Auxiliary Post 31 and the 40 & 8. She belonged to Drove 34 BPO Does, the Women's Association of Grace Community Church and the Blind Center Society. She is survived by her husband George, Boulder City; a brother, Ralph Winkler, Hamilton, Mont. and a nephew, Guy Winkler, Corvallis, Mont. Her many friends remember her as one who followed the Bible precept – that it is more blessed to give than to receive.

Taylor, Edith B.
Boulder City News, Thursday, 25 Feb 1971.
Funeral services will be conducted Friday at 2 p.m. in Palm Chapel, Henderson, by the Reverend Guy Holliday for Mrs. Edith B. Taylor, 79, fo 700 Sixth St. She died Tuesday at her home. The deceased was born Oct. 9, 1891 and was a resident of Boulder City for 12 years. She was a member of Grace Community Church and in lieu of floral offerings, the family requests donation to the church. Mrs. Taylor is survived by her husband, Edward A.; a son, Edward B, both of Boulder City, an a son, of Woodland Hills, Calif.

Taylor, Thomas T.
Boulder City News, Thursday, 9 Apr 1970.
Funeral services will be held Friday at 11 a.m. at Palm Chapel for Thomas T. Taylor who was found dead Tuesday afternoon in his trailer in Moore's Trailer Park. Burial will be in B. C. Cemetery. Mr. Taylor was born Nov. 29, 1900 in Willow Springs, Mo. and was a member of the Carpenters Union. He is survived by two daughters, Barbara J. Wansley and Geraldine Tompson, both of Las Vegas.

Teal, Jean
Boulder City News, Thursday, 28 May 1992, 7:1.
Jean Teal, 87, died Monday in San Diego, Calif. She was born Nov. 15, 1904, in Sonora, Mexico, and was a former resident of Boulder City from 1970 - 1986. She is survived by a daughter, Margaret Vanderpool of Lake Havasu City, Ariz.; a son, William Jennings of Pasadena, Calif.; a niece Barbara Giberson of Spring Valley, Calif.; and several other nieces and nephews. Prayer services will be at 6 p.m. Friday at St. Andrew's Catholic Church, and Mass services will be at 10 a.m. Saturday at St. Andrew's Catholic Church. Arrangements were handled by Palm Mortuary in Henderson.

Thomas, George Franklin
Boulder City News, Thursday, 10 Feb 1955, 1:7.
IOOF to Conduct Final Rites Today for G. F. Thomas
Funeral services for George Franklin Thomas, 72, will be conducted at 2 p.m. today. (Thursday) at the IOOF hall, by officials of Boulder Lodge No. 56 IOOF. Thomas died early Tuesday morning in the Las Vegas Hospital after being seriously ill for two weeks. The interment will be in the Boulder City Cemetery. Mr. and Mrs. Thomas moved here from San Jose, California, last year and lived at 613 Avenue K. He had retired as a street car conductor, having served for 38 years in San Francisco. Thomas was a long time member of Bay City Lodge No. 71 IOOF, and was a past district deputy grand master. Mr. and Mrs. Thomas, who were married nearly 11 years, met at a lodge function. Thomas was born June 12, 1883 in Port Huron, Michigan. In addition to his widow, Clara, he is survived by a sister, Ella Campbell of Port Huron; and a brother, James, of Detroit. Marquerite Weston, 714 Park Street, is a step-daughter.

Thomas, Laurona Ruth
Boulder City News, Thursday, 16 Jan 1969.
Catholic graveside services were conducted Tuesday at 1 p.m. at Boulder City Cemetery by Father Hugh Smith for Laurona Ruth Thomas who died at her home, 520 Hopi Place last Friday. Mrs. Thomas was born Nov. 3, 1938 in McAlester, Okla. and until shortly before her death she was a resident of San Francisco. Her only survivor is her mother, Mrs. Ruth McCauley.

Thomas, LaVerne M.
Boulder City News, Thursday, 26 Dec 1996, 9:4.
LaVerne M. Thomas, 85, died Friday, Dec. 20, 1996, in a local hospital. Born May 31, 1911, in Youngstown, Ohio, she had been a resident of Boulder City for 48 years. She was a retired Bureau of Reclamation payroll clerk, and a member of the Alter Society at St. Andrews Catholic Church. She is survived by her son, Thomas W.; daughter, Mary Ann Morang, both of Boulder City; eight grandchildren and 25 great-grandchildren. Services were held. Arrangements were handled by Palm Mortuary-Henderson.

Thomas, Thomas Michael
Boulder City News, Thursday, 22 Dec 1994, 15:2-3.
Former Boulder City resident Thomas Michael Thomas, 33, died Wednesday, Dec. 7, 1994, in Lakeside, Arizona. He was born Oct. 2, 1961. Survivors include his mother, Janet Skogen; a sister, Pam Thomas; a brother, Marty Thomas, and daughters Evelynn and Miranda Thomas. Services were private.

Thomas, Timothy
Boulder City News, Thursday, 22 Mar 1979, 10:6.
Services were held yesterday morning at Palm Chapel for Timothy Thomas, 21, who died March 17 as the result of an automobile accident. Mr. Thomas was born March 2, 1958 in San Bernadino, California but had lived in Nevada for over 20 years. He attended Ruth Fife Elementary school and R. O. Gibson Junior-High School in Las Vegas before moving to Boulder City. He graduated from Boulder City High School with the class of 1976 before entering the U. S. Army. He had been stationed in

Germany until his discharge in September of 1978. Mr. Thomas had just reached his 21st birthday before his untimely death. He will be missed by many friends and by his survivors; mother and step-father, Janet and Ralph Arnts of Boulder City; a sister, Pam Thomas and two brothers, Tom and Marty Thomas; and a step-sister and a step-brother, Sherrie and Phil Arnts. Interment followed at the Boulder City Cemetery.

Thomlinson, Morris Dailey

Boulder City News, Thursday, 12 Apr 1972.
Morris Dailey Thomlinson, 58, died Monday in Boulder City. A resident at 523 New Mexico, he was born in Ironton, Missouri, and was a telephone installer for Centel. He was a member of the I.B.E.W., Twilight lodge F and A.M. in Columbis, Missouri. Survivors include his widow Elizabeth; three sisters, Zenobia Lorts, St. James, Mo, Mary Jones, Pilot Knol, Mo., Muriel McBroom, St. Ann, Mo., two brothers, Rate W. St. Louis, Mo., and Philip Potosi, Mo. Services will be held today at 2 p.m. at Palm Chapel conducted by the Boulder City F. and A.M. Interment will be in Boulder City Cemetery.

Thurston, Virginia Lee

Boulder City News, Thursday, 27 Aug 1992, 7:1.
Virginia Lee Thurston, 67, died Tuesday in Boulder City. Born Nov. 5, 1924 in Liberty, Mo., she was a retired artist working in hand pottery. She is survived by her daughter Lois Walker and one son, Raymond Thurston, both of Boulder City. Graveside services will be held at 10 a.m. Friday Aug. 28, 1992 at the Boulder City Cemetery. Arrangements were handled by Palm Mortuary of Henderson.

Tornquest, Emmil

Boulder City News, Thursday, 24 Jan 1952, 1:7.
Funeral Services Today for Mrs. C. H. Tornquist
Funeral services will be conducted at 10 o'clock this morning for Emmil Tornquist, who died Sunday morning. The Reverend Olaf Stoeve will conduct the rites at Grace Community Church. Interment will be in the Boulder City cemetery, where Mrs. Tornquist's husband Charles was buried a few years ago. Pallbearers will be Earl Brothers, Loren Johnson, Morgan Sweeney, Lloyd Hudlow, Robert Brown and Otto Litler. Mrs.

Tornquist was born in Monmouth, Illinois. She and her husband moved to Boulder City in construction days and Mr. Tornquiest helped to install machinery in the power house at the dam. His work later took him to other areas, but the couple moved back to Boulder City following his retirement. When her husband died Mrs. Tornquist lived with her daughter Mrs. Lloyd Compton in Las Vegas. For the past few months she had been staying in the Boulder Dam Hotel. Survivors are a daughter Jane Compton, grandchildren Clarissa Tyler, Nancy and Leslie all of Las Vegas, and a brother in Ill.

Tract, DeWitt
Boulder City News, Thursday, 28 Jun 1979, 1:2-6.
Outstanding Businessman and Pioneer DeWitt Tracht Laid to Rest
by Teddy Fenton
Dewitt and Violet Tract would have been married 49 years tomorrow but death claimed one of the outstanding citizens of Boulder City this week and Dewitt Tracht was buried yesterday morning at 9:30 a.m. at the B. C. Cemetery with Reverend Melvin Pritt officiating. Dewitt was a youthful 77 at the time of his passing. If the recipe for a long and happy life is hard work then his life is a testimony to success. He was a retired owner of Central Market which he had owned and managed for 32 years in Boulder City. With Violet, his widow, were their two sons, Dr. Kenneth Tract, Las Vegas, and Lawrence, Seattle, Washington. Their wives and the four grandsons were at the funeral as was Dewitt's sister, Auretta Bingham, Las Vegas. Pallbearers were all chosen from longtime employees of Central Market; Mads Gibson, Jack Caldwell, Lyle Hannig, Don Linck, Jay Salisbury, and Leo Dunbar, Jr. Dewitt Tract was a good and gentle man and we seldom saw him in a somber mood. He smiled his way to our hearts. His happy life as a husband and parent contributed to his long. He died while attending the outdoor play, "Oklahoma" after having returned from a trip to California. He attended Rotary in Henderson and was tanned and happy when he attended B. C. Rotary last Wednesday at Railroad Pass. Violet and Dewitt's family, in thanking their many friends for kindnesses beyond the norm, said to tell everyone that Dewitt died peacefully. His had been an outstanding journey. He was born April 8, 1902, in Crawford County, Ohio. His parents, with the four children, arrived in Cararra, Nevada. They moved to Las Vegas in 1918. Dewitt graduated from LVHS in 1921. He belonged and was active in the B. C.

Rotarian Club and also F. & A.M. He worked for years with the DeMolay's. He belonged to the B. C. Sportsman Club until it disbanded and he loved to hunt and fish. He and Violet spent happy weekends camping along Lake Mead shores. They owned a boat which the family all enjoyed. Central Market changed hands in 1941. Until 1941, Dewitt and his brother-in-law owned a modern food market on Fremont Street. The partnership of Bingham and Tract then extended to Boulder City when they purchased the original Central Market on Wyoming Street. "Bing" returned to his store in Las Vegas and the four members of the Tracht family became famous in our town as the store became known as the "Family oriented Central Market." It never lost the reputation! No man was happier than Dewitt was when Leo Dunbar, the 4th owner of historic Central Market, bought out Pete Taseo. Leo had worked at Central from his high school days. Under his guidance, and with a few of the old hands still working there, the store is still keeping people from shopping "out of town" because prices are competitive. Service with a smile is still evident as it has been since the beginning of its history. When Dewitt and Violet came to town there was no local bank. One of the best stories from the Tracht files (from the Shipp collection) is about Vi and her close friend, Cora Moritz, driving to Las Vegas to cash a $2,000 check for Central Market. After cashing the check at the old Boulder Club they found it had become dark and the fog had closed in. They could not even see the tracks of the Union Pacific crossing at Railroad Pass. When they reached the old guard shack at the entrance to Boulder City they breathed a sigh of relief. No paper would contain the long and unselfish service that was given to our community by Dewitt and Violet. They had been members of the Methodist church in Las Vegas but they transferred their membership to the Community Church of Boulder City. All Memorial donations can be given to the Heart Fund, the library, the church of your choice, or any favorite charity. Violet Tracht and her family said to extend their thanks to the friends who have been so good to them all through this said bereavement. She said that she could not have been happier than she was by the side of her husband of 49 years. They traveled with favorite friends all over the world after the store was sold. The town will miss Dewitt Tract. He set an example for all businesses to follow. It is called "SERVICE WITH A SMILE."

Troeger, Matilda Augusta

Boulder City News, Thursday, 29 Dec 1966, 11:1-2.
Death Separates Troegers After 64 Years of Marriage
Funeral services were held Tuesday afternoon for Matilda Augusta Troeger, 85, who died Christmas Day after a long illness. The rites were conducted at the Christ Lutheran Church by the Reverend Lavern Brack. Burial followed at the Boulder City Cemetery. She was born Jan. 20, 1881 in St. Charles, Mo. Matilda and Fred were married June 1, 1902 in Lincoln, Kans. They moved from the Sunflower state to New Mexico, where they raised six daughters on their farm. After 27 years, they went to live in Hawthorne for 5 years, and then came on down to Boulder City in 1946. The two were active in the construction and growth of the Christ Lutheran Church, and made many friends with their faithful support. They also voted in every election until Mrs. Troeger became a shut-in. Mrs. Troeger is survived by her husband Fred, 648 Avenue F; daughter, Esther (Mrs. John) Wingire of Bloomfield, N. M.; Lorna (Mrs. Howard) Hayes, Los Angeles, Calif; Oluma (Mrs. Carl) Griffin, Albuquerque, N. M.; Ella (Mrs. Paul) McCormick, Winslow, Ariz. Also her brothers, Fred and Herman Setmer of Broken Arrow, Okla,; William Detmer, Lincoln, Kans,; and sister, Hannah Gallo, of Kansas. There are also several grandchildren and great-grandchildren.

Tudahl, Herbert

Boulder City News, Tuesday, 28 Mar 1944, p.3:3
Herbert Tudahl Funeral Set for 2 p.m. Today
Funeral services for Herbert Tudahl, who passed away Friday evening at his home in McKeeversville, will be held at 3 p.m. today at Garrison's Funeral chapel in Las Vegas, with the Reverend E. A. Wessel officiating. A graveside dedication service will be conducted by the Reverend Wessel before burial, at the Boulder City cemetery.

Turcott, Patrick G.
Boulder City News, Thursday, 5 Feb 1987, 31:1.
Patrick G. Turcott, 70, of Boulder City, died Thursday, Jan. 29, 1987, in Boulder City. He was born July 8, 1916, in Boyne City, Mich. A three-year resident, he was a optometrist and a veteran of World War II. He is survived by his wife, Mary of Boulder City; daughter Cindy Le__mann of Monroe, Conn,; brothers, Willard of Boulder City, and Tomas L. of Petoskey, Mich; sisters, Sadie Conti of Port Charlotte, Fla. Rosary was said Friday in St. Andrews in Boulder City. Mass was Saturday in St. Andrews in Boulder City. Interment was in Boulder City Cemetery.

Turner, Lucie A.
Boulder City News, Thursday, 9 May 1991, 16:1-2.
Lucie A. Turner, 88, a 40-year resident of Boulder City, died Sunday. Born April 4, 1903 in Hereford, Texas, she had been a homemaker. She is survived by two sons, Thomas Turner of Bakersfield, Calif.; and Mathew Turner of Tonopah, Nev. The family suggests donations be made to Boulder City Hospital, 901 Adams, Boulder City, Nev. 89005. Viewing services will be held from 2 to 7 p.m. Friday. Funeral services are scheduled for 1 p.m., Saturday, May 11 at Grace Community Church in Boulder City. Palm Mortuary is handling arrangements.

Turner, Warren V.
Boulder City News, Thursday, 15 Dec 1983, 2:1-4.
Warren V. Turner, 85, of Boulder City, died Tuesday in Las Vegas. Mr. Turner was born Dec. 13, 1898, in Vethalto, Ill. A 35-year resident, he was a soil conservationist for the Bureau of Reclamation, a World War I and II Army Veteran and a member of the American Legion Post 31. He is survived by his wife, Lucie of Boulder City; sons, Fred of Henderson, Tom of Bakersfield, Calif., and Matthew of Boulder City; sister, Gladys Nisbet of Cave Creek, Ariz.; nine grandchildren, and 11 great-grandchildren. The funeral will be at 2 p.m. today in Grace Community Church in Boulder City. Burial will be in Boulder City Cemetery. Palm Mortuary in Henderson handled the arrangements. Family requests donations to the Grace Community Cabin Building fund.

Underwood, Ramona Wood
Boulder City News, Thursday, 16 Jul 1987, 31:5-6.
Ramona Wood Underwood 69, passed away July 8, 1987 in Hurricane, Utah. She was born April 11, 1918 in Hurricane. She had been a 40-year resident of Boulder City but had relocated to Hurricane in 1978. She was a medical secretary at the Boulder City Clinic for many years. She leaves a brother Dell Wood of Hurricane, a nephew Van Dell Wood of Las Vegas; nieces La Wauna Wood of Boulder City; LaRene Wood-Layton of Beaver Dam, Ariz. and Mrs. Ron (JoElla) Wisham of Boulder City. Also a sister in law Nathella Wood of Hurricane, Utah. Services were held in Hurricane, Utah with interment in the Boulder City Cemetery.

Valentine, Fred G.
Boulder City News, Thursday, 31 Dec 1992, 6:1-2.
Fred G. Valentine, Jr.; 56, died Dec. 24, 1992, in a local hospital. A 31-year resident of the Boulder City area, he was born June 30, 1936, in Norwich, Conn. Valentine was a veteran of the United States Marines serving in Korea, and was a member of the Airline Pilots Association. He is survived by his wife, Mary Ann of Boulder City; two sons Michael and Anthony "T.J." both of Boulder City and from a precious marriage a daughter, Diana Comeau of Plansville, Conn,; two sons, Frederick G. III and Rodney, both of Jewett City, Conn; and a sister, Barbara Valentine of East Haven, Conn. The family requests donations be made to the American Cancer Society, 1325 E. Harmon Ave., Las Vegas, Nev. 89119. Services were held Monday. Arrangements were handled by Palm Mortuary in Henderson.

Valentine, Mary Ann
Boulder City News, Thursday, 7 Jul 1994, 7:2.
Mary Ann Valentine, 48, a three year resident of Boulder City, died Monday, July 4, 1994 in Boulder City. She was born on March 22, 1946 in Mesa, Ariz. and was an airline flight attendant. She was a member of St. Andrews Catholic Church in Henderson. She is survived by two sons, Michael and Anthony Valentine, both of Boulder City; her parents, Manuel and Margaret Rosales of Mesa, Ariz.; two sisters, Viola Verdugo of Yuma, Ariz. and Josie Acosta of Mesa, Ariz.; three brothers, Morris Rosales, Conrad Rosales and Manuel Rosales Jr., all of Mesa, Ariz. Mass

services will be held at 9 a.m. today, July 7, 1994. Interment will be in the Boulder City Cemetery. Arrangements were handled by Palm Mortuary of Henderson.

VanZant, Ellen
Boulder City News, Thursday, 19 Feb 1976, 12:3-4.
Ellen VanZant Services
Ellen Mercy VanZant, who just turned 82, was laid to rest in the Boulder City Cemetery, Tuesday afternoon. The graveside rites were conducted by the Reverend Guy Holliday of Grace Community Church. Ellen died Feb.14 at Beverly Manor in Las Vegas, after a long illness. Ellen Mercy Clifford was born Feb. 9, 1894 in Wisconsin, in a tiny town that no longer exists. She became a school teacher. After she and Jack VanZant were married, they lived in various location in the mid-west, including many years in South Dakota, where they were close friends of the family of Wilma (Cooper) and Denny Pease. The couple had four children. Daughter June came to Boulder City in 1941, and the rest of the family followed soon after. June, who was one of the first employees at "Basic," was married to the late Jim Jordon. Ellen and Jack moved around a lot, always coming back to Boulder City. He died 10 years ago. When they lived here, they were active at Grace Church, and were members of the Adult Bible Class. Ellen also belonged to the Women's Association. Before ill health made it necessary to go to the Beverly Manor, Ellen lived with Bonnie and Don Linick. Ellen is survived by a son, Jack, Downey, Calif.; three daughters, June Jordon, 507 Utah St.; Bonnie Linck, 816 Eighth St.; and Patty Woodard, 604 Avenue G., all of Boulder City; seven grandchildren, and two great-grandchildren. Also two sisters, Rose Clifford of Sacramento, Calif., and Daisy Patton of Windham, Minnesota.

Vaughan, L. T.
Boulder City News, Thursday, 23 Dec 1948, p.1.
L. T. Vaughan, of Boulder City, died yesterday of myocaritis at the Boulder City Hospital.
Funeral services will be held at St. Andrew's Catholic Church Friday morning. Vaughan left his wife Gertrude and three sons, George, Richard, and Larry, none of whom live in Boulder, and his daughter Mary Ann Merrill. Vaughan worked for the 6 Companies during the early

construction days of the dam as a maintenance man. He had recently worked for the Bureau of Reclamation. The pallbearers at the funeral will be Joe Nicholson, Rawley Elsworth, Michael Slattery, P. J. Bolser, Tom Figgins, and Bert Thames.

VanDover, Clifford
Henderson Home News & Boulder City News, Thursday, 18 Dec 1980, 32:5.
Clifford E. VanDover of Boulder City passed away Friday, December 12th, at his daughter's home in Los Angeles. He is survived by his wife, Sigrid: his son, Darrell and Darren; his daughter, Miya and his many friends throughout the United States. Private services were held Tuesday in Boulder City. Burial was at Boulder City Cemetery.

Voorheis, James K.
Boulder City News, Thursday, 23 June 1977, 1:5-6.
One Killed, One Seriously Injured in Car Wreck
A high speed automobile accident claimed the life of one Boulder City youth and hospitalized another Monday night. James K. Voorheis, 19, was killed in the one car accident. Joe Ray was sent to Sunrise Hospital, where he is listed as being in "guarded, but improving" condition. The car, a 1972 El Camino, slid over 500 feet into a rocky embankment near the "Y" area, totally destroying the car. Ray, the apparent driver of the car, and Voorheis were still in the car when the first officers arrived on the scene.

Voss, Wilfred T. "Bill"
Boulder City News, Thursday, 14 Apr 1983, 6:5.
Bill Voss served his community with loyalty and 50 years of service
by Teddy Fenton
Wilfred T. Voss was born on June 26, 1903. He died on April 7, 1893. From the day of his birth until his death he served his community with all the strength of his loyal being. There is a story written about him that his wife Nadean wanted used for this farewell to "her Bill" a man she had been married to for 23 years. It is called "Sr. Citizen of the Week" and Nadean said it is accurate and Bill would love it if we didn't change one word. In Oct. 1965, his Honor Wilfred Voss was unanimously appointed

associate city judge, replacing L. R. Douglass. His name was admitted in nomination by Municipal Judge Alvin Wartman. Bill worked in conjunction with Judge Clifford Segerblom. At his services were such a large crowd of friends, family and members of the Masonic Lodge that no church in Boulder City or even Henderson could hold the expected crowd. Lynn Mobley, his stepdaughter, said it was impressive and heart touching to see 170 Masons, dressed in their customary robes, step up to Bill's coffin to say goodbye to a loyal Mason who put his lodge above himself. (See the story below). Survivors are his beloved Nadean, his son Richard, daughters, Dorothy Toulson and Ruth Schilberg (our of town) and his stepchildren, Lynn Mobley, Boulder City and Maury Laughery, Beaver, Utah. There are 11 grandchildren and six great grandchildren. Lynn said to remind everyone of how Bill used to referee at the baseball field behind the Legion Hall and later at Peterson Field. Nadean asked us to remember the gazeba on the first field!

Senior of the Week

On June 26, 1903 in Milwaukee, Wisconsin a son was born to Mr. and Mrs. Voss and they named him Wilfred T. He was the youngest of three children and had a delicate constitution. As a consequence in 1906 the Voss family moved to Goldfield, Nevada for reasons of health. They remained in Goldfield until 1912. After traveling for a while, the Voss's settled in Beowawe, Nevada where papa Voss was chief electrician and young Bill attended a 1-room school. In 1915 they moved to New Mexico for a year and then proceeded to Tempe, Arizona where Bill graduated from High School. He went on to attend the University of Arizona but for reasons of his won never finished that final year of college choosing to work instead. Marjorie Menser entered Bill's life in the latter part of the 20's. Their paths crossed during a visit and on July 15, 1927 Marjorie and Bill permanently pledged their lives together in the bonds of Holy Matrimony. Their fruitful union eventually produced 4 lovely children, two boys and two girls. In 1929 Bill and Marjorie went to South America and remained there for three years while Bill worked for Anaconda Copper. Their return to the States was prompted by the illness of Bill's mother. Bill has been a Boulder City resident since 1933 when he went to work for Six Companies and the government on the Dam and at BMI in Henderson. He entered the Navy in 1943 and he left the Navy as a lieutenant in 1945. During his naval service Bill took some correspondence courses in law which ultimately had a great influence in his later years. After the service he returned to government work and in

1952 he went to work for Nevada Power where he retired on July 30, 1968. Tragedy has struck twice in Bill's time, when he lost a son and when he lost Marjorie in 1959. He rediscovered love and life with the help of Nadean Laughery whom he married in March 1960. Good things continued to happen for Bill. In 1956 he became an associate municipal judge and has been one ever since. Next to his family, Bill's greatest love is Masonry. He has the distinction of being a 33 degree Scottish Rite Mason with 50 years as a member of Masons. He was a Master of the Boulder City Lodge in 1937 and Grand Master of Nevada in 1948. He is active in the Shine and belongs to the Legion of Honor. He has held six offices in the York Rite Bodies and is a Past Patron of Chapter 22 in the Order of the Eastern Star and is a member of Zelzah Temple. He is also active in the Demolay Legion of Honor and was recently presented with the Grand Cross Color awarded by the Grand Assembly of Rainbow Girls. In addition to Masonry, Bill still has time to enjoy baseball, basketball and boxing. His favorite activities are chess, checkers, and pool. And, the Voss's both like to travel and list Hawaii, Alaska and Mexico as some of their favorite trips. They just recently returned from a tour of the British Isles, and their future plans will always include travel as high on their list. Bill enjoys talking about his 11 grandchildren, four great-grandchildren and his son Richard and daughters, Ruth Schiberg and Dorothy Toalson. Bill and Nadean live at 647 California Street.

Vrooman, Thomas Edgar

Boulder City News, Thursday, 18 Feb 1965, 1:4.
Mystery Shrouds Fatality
Thomas Edgar Vrooman, 215 Wyoming St., who would have been 21 next month was fatally injured about 8:30 a.m. Tuesday in an explosion in a tool shed believed by Police Chief Richard Peterson and authorities of the Clark County Sheriff's office to have been caused by dynamite caps and an electrical battery. An investigation is still being conducted. The body was discovered around noon by his father, Barrent. The dead youth worked as a gardener for Thomas Companies on whose property the accident occurred at Utah street and Northridge drive. The blast decapitated him and severed his hand. His body was taken to Palm Mortuary in Henderson. Peterson and Chief Deputy Coroner Ken Elder remained at the scene of the explosion most of Tuesday endeavoring to piece together evidence as to what happened. Peterson states that the

young man was apparently in a squatting position with whatever cause the blast, resting on the blade of a shovel which was driven through the floor of the shed. The roof also showed evidence of having blown up and come down again. George Thomas of Thomas Companies told authorities that their building program does not require the use of explosives, and so was at a loss to explain their presence in the building. The victim and his father worked together, installing lawns and sprinkling systems for Thomas. The family came to Boulder City from California. He is survived by his parents, Mr. and Mrs. Barrent Vrooman, this city; two brothers, Ronald of San Diego, Calif, and Nicolas of Spring Valley, Calif. and grandparents Mr. and Mrs. George Pinkham, Vashon Island, Wash. and Mr. and Mrs. Earl E. Harris, Boulder City. Funeral services will be conducted at 7 tonight at Palm Chapel.

Walker, Cal Victor
Boulder City News, Thursday, 14 Dec 1978, 2:1-4.
Services will be held Friday, Dec. 15 at 11 a.m. at Palm Chapel, Henderson for Cal Victor Walker, 61, who passed away Dec. 13 in Las Vegas. Mr. Walker was born September 29, 1917 in Long Beach, California and had been a resident fo Boulder City for 40 years. He was a retired chief electrical operator with the City of Los Angeles, Dept. of Water and Power. He was also a U.S. Army Air Force veteran of World War II. Survivors include his wife, La Verne, of Boulder City; his mother, Bertha Walker of Laguna Hilla, Ca. and a brother, Frank Walker of Hernden, Virginia. Cremation will follow.

Wallace, Ronald Floyd
Boulder City News, Thursday, 25 Mar 1965, 1:7-8.
Violent Deaths Rock Boulder
Death struck with violence twice Tuesday in Boulder City - one was a verdict of suicide, the other murder. Both crimes were carried out with guns - both involved teenaged youths. Ronald Floyd Wallace, 18, was found dead early Tuesday afternoon at his home, 705 Utah St., by a friend, Steve Wheeler, who was expected at the home at 2 p.m. Robert Walker, 19, was found shot to death in the desert about 6:30 p.m. His murder is being investigated by Clark County authorities. Receiving no answer to a knock on the door, Wheeler entered and discovered the body of Wallace. He immediately went to the police station to report the death.

Clark County sheriff officers were also notified. Sgt. Larry Tabony and Officer Jerry Lewis answered the call. A canvass was made of the neighbors but no one could recall hearing any sound like a shot. Chief Deputy Coroner Kenneth Elder stated: "As far as I'm concerned, it's suicide." The youth was scheduled to appear in Municipal Court that afternoon on several charges, one of which was striking two parked cars belong to J. Elmer Cole three weeks ago. An 8 MM Mauser rifle, established as the death weapon, and a shotgun partially broken down, along with cleaning materials, were found beside the body. Police discovered a hole in the house roof where the bullet had gone through. Wallace is survived by his mother, Mrs. Betty Smith, a patient in Rose de Lima Hospital; a brother, Gerald Sprouse with the Army in Germany and a sister, Sharon Smith. Palm Mortuary in Henderson is in charge of funeral arrangements. Mysterious circumstances surround the death of Walker. Denzel Pease, head of the city electrical department, reported to police that he had noticed a car parked on the powerline road off Nevada Highway all day and though it should be checked out. Sgt. Tabony and Sgt. H. G. Smith found keys on the car seat. A later search revealed the body in the vicinity of the vehicle. Walker had been shot twice in the abdomen. Clark County authorities plan an autopsy and will make ballistic tests on one of the bullets found protruding from the body.

Walters, Gloria A.
Boulder City News, Thursday, 21 Mar1991, 9:1.
Gloria A. Walters, 64, a 29-year resident of Boulder City, died Saturday, March 16. Born in Los Angeles on Jan. 14, 1927, she was a retail grocery cashier. She was a member of the Retail Clerks Union. She is survived by her two daughters, Kathleen Walters and Sharon Castleberry, both of Boulder City; a son, Frank M. Walters, III of Las Vegas; her mother, Marquerite Clough of Reseda, Calif. and two sisters, Lorraine Maier of Reseda, Calif. and Joanne Mullens of Seal Beach, Calif. and five grandchildren. Those wishing to make donations in Gloria's memory may do so to Alzheimers Research. Rosary will be recited at 7 p.m. today. Funeral services will be at 10 a.m., Friday at St. Andrews Catholic Church in Boulder City. Bunkers Mortuary handled arrangements.

Ward, Harold V.
Boulder City News, Thursday, 13 Oct 1966, 1:4.
Funeral services were conducted Monday at 2 p.m. at Grace Community Church for Harold V. Ward, 40, who passed away last Thursday at Loma Linda, Calif. A maintenance man at the Bureau of Mines, he resided with his family at 721 Arizona St. He had been in the area for seven years. Mr. Ward was born June 3, 1926 in Garden City, Kansas and was a U. S. Army veteran of the Korean action. He leaves his wife, Betty Jo; daughters, Pamela Sue Goodard, Betty JoAnn Black, Becky Lea Black, all of Boulder City; son, Robert J. Black, U. S. Army; Darrell W. Black, Terry Allen Black and Jeffrey L. Ward, Boulder City; his parents Ray Ward and Mrs. George Wilson, this city, and a brother, Cecil Ward, this city. The Reverend Guy Holliday officiated at the church and burial was in Boulder City Cemetery.

Ward, John A.
Boulder City News, Thursday, 26 May 1977, 10:8.
Services for John War on Saturday
John A. Ward, 61, passed away May 23 at his home at 644 Ave. M in Boulder City. Born November 1, 1915 in Chicago, Illinois, he was a production controller in the diesel engineering manufacturing business. Mr. Ward was a Navy veteran of W.W.2, a member of the Boulder City B.P.O.E. and American Legion, AARP and United Auto Workers Local 719. He is survived by his widow Agnes, son William Ward of Chicago, daughter Kathee Jones of Chicago, brother William J. Ward and sister Mary Nolan, both of Chicago. Rosary will be recited at Palm Mortuary on Friday evening at 7:30 p.m. and a Mass will be held on Saturday morning at St. Andrew's Catholic Church at 10 a.m. with Fr. Baldus officiating. Interment will follow at the Boulder City Cemetery.

Ward, Theresa Othelia
Boulder City News, Thursday, 24 Jan 1980, 36:1-2.
Services were held last evening at Palm Chapel for Theresa Othelia Ward, 68, who passed away Monday in Las Vegas. Mrs. Ward was born in Kansas City, Missouri, and had worked as a receiving clerk for Macy's of San Francisco. She was a member of the Alter Society for St. Eugene's Cathedral in Santa Rosa, California. She moved here in 1978. She is

survived by her husband, Floyd E. Ward of Boulder City; a sister, Micki Kangas of Denver, Colorado, and 10 nieces and nephews. Burial will be in Boulder City Cemetery.

Wartman, Anna
Boulder City News, Thursday, 11 Feb1982, 13:1-4.
We Love You Anna Wartman
by Teddy Fenton
On Feb. 2, 1982, Anna Wartman slipped away from her earthly life. This is a tribute to her from a friend who knew her as someone who had loved her family above all else. But then, let us lead Anna Wartman into the life she loved so well outside her home. Her heart was touched by children who needed support from the public, St. Judes Ranch for Children was her main concern. Her memorial has been named at St. Judes for Children. The contributions we wend will be devoted towards the building of a new chapel. Anna's name will be immortalized there. The children who will become grown adults, looking back with gratefulness to Father Ward, and to all who work at his side, have reason to remember a great lady who belonged to the Las Vegas Auxiliary. That is undoubtedly the most successful fund-raising group of ladies in Clark County. They mail out a monthly newspaper, a report on the Thrift Market. A thank you to all who have donated time and money, a plea for more help. They have been responsible for building one cottage at St. Jude's, buying the furniture for all the cottages, the Swimming pool, the present chapel, the laundry room, the jungle gym, and other playground equipment, the office building, kitchen equipment, furnishing the dining room, and so many more donations in love and funding that it would take up several more pages. Anna was a Charter Member of the St. Jude Auxiliary. Her son, Al Wartman, has always fully supported St. Judes. He is on the Board of Trustees. His work as the lawyer for St. Judes Ranch for Children is donated. This brought Al and his mother together. Not for the first time! They had always supported public causes. When Boulder City incorporated, Al Wartman served as the lawyer without a salary. In all that he did as a volunteer his mother was either by his side or leading the way. This was particularly true in politics or as admirers of the Polka Dot Haven teenage center. Doris (Mrs. Al) came into the story later. This tribute is being written to tell our town that Anna Wartman was responsible for the attention the Polka Dot Haven received that made it a

famous teenage center throughout the county and even the state. She was office manager of the Boulder City News. It was 1952 when teenagers, answering a charge by then owner, Morry Zenoff, placed on the front page calling the local young people "dope heads" and no sooner was the paper on the streets than five of the young people, so accused, fired a letter to the editor, in it Morry was called a dopehead" and the names were signed for all to see who cared! On "D" St, lived Pat Fenton. Age 15. She was a friend of the five boys who had penned the letter to Morry. She rounded them up, added Don Douglass to the list, yanked her mother out of her lethargy, the lot of us arrived to the Camp Williston Barracks Bldg. where the hard-working Recreation Association Officers were holding a meeting. Bill McCullough, a leader in all recreation, was the president of the club. Bill listened to the complaints and placed the responsibility of getting the building turned into a teenage center where it belonged. On the heads of the young protestors. Enter Anna. There she was waiting in the wings. Our column, on the front page, called the Polka Dot Haven News surrounded by polka-dots on the masthead, became a weekly report of the kids! The young people had passed a petition around town asking for a meeting house, signed by 200 from all classes. It was a strong appeal to parents, to organizations. Yes! Anna was delighted. Morry gave the teens all the space they needed. The club became NEWS. Cliff Segerblom was our volunteer photographer. Donations poured in. The building bloomed. At last, at the end of summer, after as many as 50 young people worked on it at once, the Recreations Assoc, was proud as punch and let the kids paint polka dots to their hearts content. Yes! And fish on the ceiling and on the wall in the poolroom. Let us share that story later. It was Anna watching it all, taking all copy that came into the office and straightening out the grammar that is the subject here. She took in hand a young mother, a person so shy that she cried when first speaking to Anna Wartman and her bosum pal, Lillian Collins. Behind the scenes non knew they were about to groom "Teddy" a teenage director. Aided by Roberta Hudlow, How said to know they are all gone, yet how rewarding to write about them now, in utmost gratefulness. No one knows better than this writer how much good Anna Wartman did in this world. She was ready and willing to help any friend in running for office. She well knew that it was not easy to find precinct workers. She knew how to use her phone and fill her table with volunteer women licking envelopes, making appeals for money, etc. She did not want publicity. If members of her church wanted to do something for the good cases, her purse was always open. Father Don Stivers, and Father Ward, spoke of her with affection and admiration. They both respected her wish that her funeral be graveside services with only the family there. Anna Wartman did not like publicity. She refused to have the story of her long and happy marriage to Frank Wartman in the NEWS on the occasion of their 50th wedding anniversary on August 29, 1975. How we wish we had a picture of the young newly weds to run with this loving tribute. She was so proud of her husband, she called him "Pinky and told me of his career, his inventions, his dedication, but "NO! YOU CANNOT WRITE A STORY." When anna sais "No!" one listened! She loved her sons, her grandsons, her friends. No two women were ever so close as Anna and Lillian Collins. Many a time while on the run through town on an errand we would spot those two, so animated in conversation they scarcely realized they were in a public place. The welcome to this community of those two staunch civic workers was heart warming, There will never be another Anna Wartman not another Lillian Collins. There is something else they share in common. There are memorials to both of them at St. Jude's Ranch for Children. Anna left sons she absolutely worshiped, Judge Alvin Wartman and Peter, an outstanding Cartographer in Southern California. Anna was our Postmistress in Boulder City 1958-1960. Her contribution to the professional world was as a volunteer to the good of man. Her final illness took her from public view. Her private services were conducted by Father Don Stivers. May she rest forever for she has earned everlasting peace.

Wartman, Frank Secord
Boulder City News, Thursday, 14 Jul 1983, 1:2-6.
By Teddy Fenton
A tragic death occurred this week and Boulder City lost one of its greatest citizens. Las Saturday, July 9, 1983, Dr. Frank Secord Wartman joined his wife, Ana on that mysterious journey we call death. Their union began on Aug. 29, 1925. Anna left an empty place in the soul and heart of her husband when she died. Frank S. Wartman was born in the Territory of Arizona on August 2, 1899. Once in a while he would see a family friend, Mrs. Fran Butterfield, and they shared a common origin. Both had been born in the Territory of Arizona and both would proclaim to anyone within hearing distance that they were the only one in the room who could claim such a rare birthplace. Fate was to select this rare man to follow a career that would seek him out as a scientist and metallurgist. In

Boulder City the Bureau of Mines selected the present site to build its plant in 1936. Headlines in every local paper announced *An Ore Pilot Plant Set for Boulder City*. But it was W.W.II that sped up the research and development of the work by scientists and metallurgists which also brought the Wartman family to Boulder City in 1944. With them were their sons, Alvin and Peter. Both of the sons have gone on to successful careers. But the part of their lives that brought joy to Frank and Anna were the grandchildren. Al is the proud father of Franklin S. Wartman the 3rd and Alvin N. Wartman Jr. Peter's sons are Randall and Steven F. Wartman. Anna Wartman was to share the news of the grandchildren with all who knew her. Frank Wartman Loved Music And Books. Such a quiet man, a humble man, a man who did not seek people out for his life of 83 years was too short to waste one minute. This will surprise people outside his family, Dr. Wartman was an avid musician. At an early age he took violin lessons and besides the violin he played the guitar, the banjo and the family organ. His study was lined with books. The collection will be gifted to the UNLV Special Collection. Over 300 volumes of titanium and other precious metals. Suffice to say the entire family of Wartmans have helped put Boulder City on the map. Hear now the awards won by Dr. Frank S. Wartman. Frank Wartman, "Father" of Billion Dollar Titanium Process gets Nations Top Award. Rather than leave out a single line we will let our readers judge for themselves if any man or woman ever received such a tribute. This story appeared in the NEWS on Dec. 10, 1953. "WASHINGTON, Dec. 9 (Special) – Frank S. Wartman of Boulder City today was called one of the Department of the Interior's most outstanding employees and presented with the highest honor the department bestows - the Distinguished Service Award. . . For his part in developing a process for producing titanium the strong, lightweight "Wonder" metal desperately needed in the production of military and commercial aircraft. The honor was accorded Wartman, a long-time Bureau of Miens employee, during an impressive Tuesday afternoon ceremony in the auditorium of the interior building. On hand for the occasion were Secretary of the Interior Douglas McKay and Assistant Secretaries D. Otis Beasley and Felix Wormser. Among the several hundred spectators present for the occasion was Senator George W. Malone who recommended Wartman, for the award. Senator Malone was introduced during the program by Secretary McKay. Wartman was lauded by Assistant Secretary Wormser for his development of titanium, the light-weight, heat-resisting "Wonder" metal, by means of a magnesium reduction process. Wormser told Wartman that "Your development is the result of your pioneering efforts since 1938. The department is proud of your achievements and to show its appreciation is conferring on you its highest award - the citation for distinguished service." The citation pointed out that Mr. Wartman began investigating the technology of Titanium to determine its metallurgical possibilities when it was practically unknown. The citation read, "He also directed engineering development of laboratory and pilot plant scale necessary to place the process on a practical basis. Industry has substantiated Mr. Wartman's selection of the magnesium reduction process and it is expected that in the next two years the titanium metal industry will reach a billion dollar per year volume." Wartman, who flew from Souther Nevada to Washington for the ceremony, returned home last evening. He joined the Bureau of Mines on July 1, 1923 as a junior chemist. He received the degree of bachelor of science at the University of Arizona in 1921 and a master of science degree at the same institution in 1923." One cannot do justice to Dr. Wartman in a single tribute. He will not be forgotten ever by the men of science. Rare indeed as a person, he never sought publicity, was in fact "shy" and as Al Wartman told us this week. "My father had close friends with whom he corresponded. One can see them now. Pretend a group of fellow scientists were seated with my father. Once or twice an hour one might voice an opinion, but otherwise they would be seated together lost in thought." Until a week before his death he was active in his deep interest in research for he visited Carl Dewey, Director of the U.S. Bureau of Mines in Boulder City. He borrowed a catalog and discussed their common interests. On June 4, 1964 the following story appeared in the NEWS. It came from the combined collection of Esther Shipp and Laura Bell. You can judge for yourself the greatness of this uncommon plant. This was the first Honorary Degree given at the University of Nevada at Las Vegas. Uni. Honors Wartmand; Tabbed 'Father of Titanium.' Boulder City and Henderson residents this week are honoring Franklin S. Wartman, who yesterday received an honorary Doctor of Science degree during commencement exercises at the University of Southern Nevada in recognition of his long distinguished career as a metallurgist in Nevada. Wartman considered the "Father of Titanium," is presently senior consultant and engineer in charge of titanium research, as the U.S. Bureau of Mines here. He has become widely noted for his work in perfecting the necessary metallurgical advances in the Kroll process which made possible the production of pure titanium metal . . . now a vital material in the defense plans of America. For his outstanding work in this field, he was awarded a citation and a medal from the U.S. Department fo the Interior in 1953. He was honored with the Gold Medal Award when he was director of the local division of the Bureau of Mines. Many people who live in both area cities and are employed at Titanium Metals Corporation of America owe their jobs to Wartman's metallurgical research. The plant in Henderson and others throughout the country are a direct result of his efforts. Wartman, a resident of Boulder City since 1944, is a graduate of the University of Arizona. His family has been exceedingly active in community affairs for many years and several members have served in many important capacities as leaders of the community and developments are the area. Wartman's honorary degree was one of only two bestowed by the University of Nevada and the only one conferred during the commencement ceremonies at the Convention Center in Las Vegas.

Watkins, James Eric
Boulder City News, Thursday, 4 Aug 1994, 7:1-3.
James Eric Watkins, 22, was reported missing and presumed drowned at Lake Mead Friday, July 15, 1994. He was born Nov. 6, 1971, in Baxter Springs, Kas., and had been a resident of Boulder City for the past 3 ½ years. Watkins was a 1990 graduate of Riverton High School in Riverton, Kan. He had been a member of the Science Club, Drama Club, and Students Against Drunk Drivers. He lettered in baseball, and basketball. He attended Pittsburgh State University in Pittsburgh, Kan. He was affiliated with the Riverton Friends Church. Memorial services were held Saturday, Jul 23, in Southeast Kansas under the direction of Reverend Paul Snyder. Since moving to Boulder City, he has attended UNLV and was currently attending courses in criminology at Clark County College. He was employed as a security officer at Gold Strike Casino/Hotel near Hoover Dam. He had recently certified as an E.M.T. He just had received an invitation for membership to the Loyal Order of Moose No. 1928 in Las Vegas. Surviving are his parents, James L. and Dorothy Jean Watkins, a brother Paul L. Watkins, and a sister Margo L. Watkins, and a grandmother, Jean S. Cole, all of Boulder City. The remains were recovered Sunday, July 31, by Lake Mead Divers in conjunction with a special Marine camera funded by the K.C. Johnson Foundation. Family request donations be made to: The K.C. Johnson Foundation in care of

Cliff Johnson, 1710 East Lockwood St., Mesa, Arizona, 85203. Graveside services will be conducted today at 10 a.m. at the Boulder City Cemetery with the Reverend Marvin Gant officiating. Security officers from the Gold Strike will act as pallbearers. They include Peter Dunham, Robert Holloway, Rick Smale, Terry Mechtley, Terry Chastain, Rick Rybold, Manny Tofaya and Mark Novello.

Webb, Richard "Dick" Sidney
Boulder City News, Thursday, 29 Oct 1970, 2:6-7.
Mason funeral rites were held yesterday afternoon for Richard "Dick" Sidney Webb, 71, at the Palm Chapel in Henderson. They were conducted by Wilfred "Bill" Voss, past grand master of the Masons of Nevada; Harry Overbey, deputy grand master; and Robert "Bob" Parker, past master of Boulder Lodge No. 37 F. & A.M. They also officiated at the interment in Boulder City Cemetery. Pallbearers were N. W. Jack Arnold, William Art Hurt, John Layton, Horace Ward, Carl Merrill and Jack Caldwell. Dick was born October 23, 1899 in Kansas City, Kansas, and attended school in Ocean Park, Calif. He was a graduate of Purdue University with a degree in engineering, and joined Lafayette Lodge No. 123 F. & A.M. in Indiana. As a master Mason he belonged to the national Acacia Fraternity. Dick married Thelma "Sammy" Tilton, September 25, 1926. They had one son, Robert, born in Peru, where Dick worked for seven years at the Cerro De Pasco copper smelter in Aroya. After the Webb family moved to Boulder City in 1938, Bob attended the local schools and was a star athlete in high school. The whole Webb family was interested in sports, and "followed the team" out of town for many years. Dick and Sammy were on a hunting trip in the Ruby Mountains of northern Nevada when he became ill, oct. 13. He was given medical care in Ely, then brought by ambulance to Boulder City. Their trailer was brought back home by their son. Dick came to Nevada to do construction work with his brother, the late Paul S. Jim Webb, a Boulder pioneer, and many of the largest buildings in town were erected by them, as well as some of the nicer homes. When Jim died, Dick took over the Boulder Builder's Supply, with Sammy as his office assistant. The tow sold their business in 1968, and retired to travel around the state hunting, fishing and enjoying the beauty of the country. Dick is survived by his widow, Sammy, 644 California Avenue; his son Robert, San Ramon, Calif.; and four grand children, plus many friends who enjoyed listening to him

recount his experiences of past years.

Wegren, Angus
Boulder City News, Thursday, 2 May 1985, 24:5-6.
Angus K. Wegren, 79, of Boulder City died Sunday. He was a 45 year resident of the area. He was born Dec. 6, 1906 in Butte, Mont., and was a retired carpenter. He is survived by his wife, Frances of Boulder City; sons Carl of Reno and George of Boulder City; daughter, Sallie of Boulder City; and three grandchildren. Visitation was scheduled to begin Monday afternoon in Palm Mortuary, Henderson. Services were conducted Tuesday in Boulder City Elks Lodge. Burial was in Boulder City Cemetery.

Wegren, Frances
Boulder City News, Thursday, 29 Mar 1990, 11:3-4.
By Esther Shipp
Another friends was laid to rest, Tuesday morning. Frances Wegren died Saturday morning, a day after her 84 birthday. Viewing was Monday afternoon at Palm Chapel in Henderson. The Reverend Tim Walsh of the Baptist Church in Boulder City officiated at the graveside services at the Boulder City Cemetery. Frances Estelle Monroe was born March 23, 1906 in Los Angeles, Calif. She was graduated from the Fullerton High School. She and Angus "Bud" Wegren were married October 17, 1931 in the Rectory of the Presbyterian Church in San Bernardino. There golden wedding anniversary was celebrated at the Elk's hall in Boulder City. The Wegren family moved to Searchlight, Nev., in 1942, them came on to Boulder City in 1943. Myrtle and Doug Patton provided them a place to live. Bud worked at the Uptown Hardware Store and at the lumber yard. He died in 1985. Frances joined the Rebekahs in Coachella. Although she was not active here, she sis help the lodge with special projects. She was a Past President of the Mother's Club and headed the annual Mother's March of Dimes for many years. She served as a Girl Scout leader with the late Delores Shope. She was always busy with handcrafts, and passed her talents on to her daughter. She never became a member of the Does, but attended the Friday night dinners and supported the order in other ways. She was always helping other people. Bud and Frances enjoyed camping in their RV, and used to spend every summer at Wildhorse Reservoir, until 1984. She like sports. When her health became poor, and

she was nearly blind, she followed games on cable TV. She also appreciated the large type Bible and *Reader's Digest* given to her by her friend Ann Gieck. Frances is survived by her daughter Sallie and son George, who lived with her at 627 California Street; her son Carl, in Reno; granddaughters, Kathie Wegren and Kellie Barrett, Reno; grandson, Gus Wegren, Winnemucca; and great-grandchildren Ryan, Ray and Joey. Sallie and George respect the way the emergency crew handled the call when they came to the house, and thank them for their consideration.

Wegren, George Francis
Boulder City News, Thursday, 21 Oct 1993, 8:1.
George Francis Wegren, 58, died Tuesday, Oct. 19 in Las Vegas. He was born April 11, 1935 in Auburn, California and was a Boulder City resident for 51 years. He was a Teamster Laborer for 30 years working in convention services. He was a member of Knights of Pythias and Teamsters #631 and of BPOE #1682 in Boulder City. He is survived by his sister, Sallie Wegren of Boulder City; a brother, Carl Wegren of Reno; two nieces and one nephew. A memorial service will be held at 10 a.m., Oct. 23 at the Elks Lodge in Boulder City. Donations are requested to be sent to BPOE #1682 Charity Fund. Arrangements were handled by Nevada Funeral Service of Las Vegas.

Wehr, Harold "Lefty"
Boulder City News, Thursday, 8 Feb 1990, 8:1.
Harold "Lefty" Wehr, 80, a resident of Boulder City for 20 years, died Feb. 5. Born in Willingston, N.D. on Oct. 25, 1909, he was a retired project manager in construction. He was a member of Elks lodge in Ariz. He is survived by his wife, Charlotte Wehr of Boulder City; daughter Alberta Ewy of Las Vegas; granddaughter Norma Dennis, son-in-law Perry Dennis and great granddaughter Don Michelle Dennis all of Elko. Private family services were held.

Weiler, Marguerite
Boulder City News, Thursday, 27 Sep 1987, 11:1-3.
By Teddy Fenton
When the obituary was written in the *Boulder City News* about the passing of Marguerite Sherwood, we didn't realize she was a pioneer daughter of the late Jack Weiler. Her mother, Lillian Weiler, who was with her when she died. She died from an illness that had troubled her for years. Died in a house on "M" Street that her mother had purchased 40 years before. A rental, the tenants had run out without telling anyone, leaving unpaid rent, utilities and a terrible condition within the house and in the yard. Marguerite and her mother had been in Boulder City for several weeks coping with the problems. Dorothy Ragsdale lovingly refers to Marguerite as her "little sister," and while gathering material for this story, I interviewed Tommy Nelson, Elton Garrett and Madelaine Garrett. Tommy and Madalaine had taught Marguerite trumpet, taught her so well that she went into the world of entertainment, playing with famous bands. Pictures of her with the different bands are being sent. Dorothy Weiler Ragsdale lives in Sugarland, Texas, and is married to Harold Ragsdale, well-known musician who once played with area bands in Clark County including Tommy Nelson and Clark Higgins. When Dorothy arrived home after attending the services for Marguerite, she phoned saying she had found wonderful pictures of Jack and Lillian Weiler's early days with small daughters, Marguerite and Dorothy. Pictures with neighborhood children. They lived close to Erma Godbey (a street over) which explains why Laura Godbey Smith is a close friend of the family. So much to share . . . think a dozen pages of notes as shared by Dorothy. We are aware of the blow this sudden passing has been to the family.

Wellman, Erma Lorraine
Boulder City News, Thursday, 30 Mar 1972.
Erma Wellman Services Held At LDS Church
Erma Lorraine Wellman was laid to rest Tuesday at __, in the Boulder City Cemetery. Owen Gibson dedicated the grave. In the absence of Bishop Jake Williams, those participating in the funeral service at the Church of Jesus Christ of Latter Day Saints were Dale Brockett, Don Atkins, Leonard Stubbs, and Charles Hunter, all officers of the stake. Erna died Saturday in the BC Hospital after many years of suffering.

Theresa Denning provided prelude music on the organ Gwenn Chubbs sand "In the Garden" and "Abide With Me," accompanied by pianist Nancy Murphy. Pallbearers were John Stewart, Walter Wellman, Robert Forrest, Harold Stewart, Gerald Stewart, and Albert Dawson. Erma Stewart was born November 13, 1900 in Murray, Utah. She and Henry Eugene "Gene" Wellman were married February 19, 1921. Friends and relatives helped them celebrate their Golden Wedding Anniversary in Boulder City. They came here in 1942, from Ely, Nev. Erma was a good cook and worked in that capacity at several places, including the Boulder City Inn and the Nevada Drug Store. From 1952 to 1957 she leased the restaurant concession there from the Cunninghams and Opats. One of her other favorite occupations was making pixie dolls, with her mother. She was past president of the Auxiliary to VFW Post 3574, and belonged to the Relief Society, American Legion Auxiliary, Cactus Rebekah Lodge No. 40, and the F. O. Eagles Auxiliary. She is survived by her husband, Gene, 500 Sixth St.; a son, William Wellman, of Las Vegas; her mother, Emma Stewart, Boulder City; three brothers, Ernest Stewart, Loletta, Calif.; William Stewart, Fontana, Calif; and John Stewart, Upland, Calif. Also 8 grandchildren and 14 great-grandchildren.

Wells, Richard A.
Boulder City News, Thursday, 15 Mar 1979, 4:7.
Resident Dies in Car Rollover
Richard Wells, 23, of Boulder City, died March 9 when his vehicle failed to negotiate a curve on U. S. 93 above the Alan Bible Visitor Bureau and went off into the desert. Time of the accident is not know. The vehicle was spotted and reported to authorities at 7:__ a.m. Wells was pronounced dead at the scene. He is survived by his father, Curtis Wells, of Boulder City.

Boulder City News, Thursday, 15 Mar 1979, 17:5.
Graveside services were held last Sunday at the Boulder City Cemetery for Richard A. Wells, 23, who died in an automobile accident March 9. The Reverend Ron Mayer of the Lutheran Church officiated. Mr. Wells was born December 9, 1955 in El Paso, Texas and was employed as a laborer in construction work. Survivors include his father, Curtis Wells of Boulder City; mother, Carolyn Torres; brothers, Steven and Michael Wells and a sister, Paula Torres.

Whalen, Luke Arthur
Boulder City News, Thursday, 15 Nov 1973, 1:3-4.
Luke Arthur Whalen Services Here Today by Esther Shipp
This morning, family and friends will say good-bye to one of the town's most loved "old-timers" – Luke Arthur Whalen, 79, who died Monday night following a short illness. The Reverend Hugh P. Smith will officiate at the funeral mass at 10 a.m. at St. Andrew's Catholic Church. The Rosary was held by Father Smith last night at Palm Chapel in Henderson. Pallbearers will be Morgan Sweeney, Tom Godbey, Kine, C. E. Kopp, Donald Cameron and Neil Holmes. Graveside service at Boulder City Cemetery. Instead of flowers, the family requests that donations be made to the Boulder City Hospital, Inc. Luke was born August 2, 1894, in Stephen, Minn., the second of 8 children. After completing high school there, he attended St. Cloud Teachers' Institute. He then served in the infantry during World War I, earning six battle stars during 16 months overseas. Returning to the states, Luke farmed and worked in saw and paper mills. In 1923 he went to California, to work for Shell Oil. In 1926 he traveled to Venezuela to work in the oil fields, as division production engineer. On a vacation to Panama he met Lillian Hastings, a North Dakota school-teacher, and they were married Feb. 15, 1928. Their first son was born in Venezuela. The Whalens returned to the U.S. in 1930, and built a home in Long Beach, Calif. In 1932 he came to Boulder City to work for the Six Companies as pipe foreman. In 1936 he transferred to the U.S.B.R., where he soon became mixed gang foreman. When being given a Superior Performance Award in 1963, it was said that "he had the reputation of setting a good pace for his men and keeping it himself – with a goodly margin to spare." When he retired in 1964, he received a sledge hammer inscribed with the words "Hit It Again," often used by Luke in his eagerness to accomplish a difficult task. The Whalens were active in the American Legion and Auxiliary, serving in many offices. A past Commander of Post No. 31, Luke helped organize the Sons of American Legion Drum and Bugle Corps, the Sons of the Legion orchestra which played for teen dances for 7 years, and he coached the Legion baseball team for many years. He was Nevada Commander of the Sons of the Legion. He coached other local baseball teams for more than 20 years, and encouraged boys to build the field that used to be out by our one-time radio station. Luke was a charter member of the B. C. Recreation Association and the Recreation Board established to advise the

City Council. He helped Lee Tilman organize a community basketball program in 1951. Luke and Lillian both received PTA life memberships in 1952. By now, the Whalens had seven children, and Luke was named Clark County Father of the Year in 1954. (Lillian was named Boulder Woman of the Year in 1957.) In 1963, the Luke A. Whalen Field was dedicated in his honor, with appropriate ceremonies, and a plaque bears his name at the baseball field. Later, Luke also started playing golf. Along with his interest in all sports, he was also a trustee of the B.C. Cemetery Association, a Board member of the Knights of Columbus, belonged to the Plumbers and Pipefitters Union, and following his retirement joined the National Association of Retired Federal Employees and the American Association of Retired Persons. He is survived by his wife, Lillian, 652 California Ave.; five sons and two daughters. They are Dennis, attorney, Baton Rouge, Louisiana; Don, director at Fort Lewis College, Durango, Colo.; Brian, engineer, University of Nevada, Reno; Barry, business manager in Los Angeles, Calif,; Patricia "Pat" Nolan, R. N., Boston, Mass.; Karen "Kay" O'Brien, teacher, Tuba City, Ariz.; Luke Jr., dentist, Manteca, Calif. There were 22 grandchildren at the last family reunion. Sisters surviving are Lenore Kirkpatrick, Hemet, Calif.; Katherine Moldenaur, Seattle, Wash.; Margaret McGlynn, Grand Fork, N. Dak.; Frances McCallum, Pomona, Calif,; and Irene LeBlanc, Grafton, N. Dak.

Wheeler, Edith Beryl
Boulder City News, Thursday, 3 Mar 1983, 2:1-4.
Edith Beryl Wheeler, 73, of Boulder City, died Saturday. Mrs. Wheeler was born Nov. 16, 1909, in Joplin, Mo. She was a homemaker. She is survived by her husband, Clyde of Boulder City; daughter, Marian Crawford of Toluca Lake, Calif,; son, Steve of Grand Prairie, Texas; brothers, Grant of Spokane, Wash., and Kent and Jack Hamilton, both of Webb City, Mo.; sisters, Pane Paillipps of Eugene, Ore., and two grandchildren. The graveside service was at 10 a.m. Tuesday in Boulder City Cemetery in Boulder City. The family prefers donations to Alzheimer's Disease and Related Disorders Association Inc., 360 N. Michigan Ave., Suite 601, Chicago, Ill. 60601. Palm Mortuary handled all arrangements.

Wheeler, Houston
Boulder City News, Thursday, 29 Apr 1971.
Funeral service were held Monday at the masonic Temple for Houston Wheeler, 73, of La Guna Hills, Calif. Mr. Wheeler was a retired Bureau of Reclamation employee and longtime resident of Boulder City. He died last Friday in the Veterans Hospital in Long Beach, Calif. The deceased was born Nov. 7, 1897 in Oklahoma. He is survived by two daughters, Jeanne Traasdahl, Las Vegas; Joyce Braun, Monterey Park, Calif., and a son, Houston Jr. Pittsburg, Calif.

Whelden, Vernon
Boulder City News, Thursday, 22 Mar 1956, 9:5.
Vernon Whelden Dies Suddenly; Services Today
Masonic rites for Vernon Whelden, who died unexpectedly at the Boulder City Hospital Monday morning, will be held this afternoon at 4 o'clock at the Masonic Temple. The lodge will be opened on the Third Degree at 3 o'clock. Mr. Whelden underwent a routine operation at the Boulder hospital Sunday. No complications developed but he was suddenly stricken after the operation with a heart ailment and passed away. He had been a resident of Boulder City for about the last four years and was employed as an electrician at American Potash and Chemical Co. in Henderson. His widow, Flossie, who survives, is manager of the Black Canyon Motel in Boulder, where the couple lived. Mr. Whelden was born in Norton county, Kansas on May 31, 1884 and he and Mrs. Whelden were married in 1917. Before moving to Boulder City they had resided in West Plains, Mo. Other survivors include a daughter, Dorothy Vern Donaven of Hoodsport, Wash.; two brothers, Percy of Deertrail, Colo. and Ben of North Hollywood, Calif.; and two grandchildren, Patricia and Donna Donoven of Hoodsport. Mrs. Donaven and Mrs. Whelden's sister, Mrs. Lula Speicher of Whitney Point, N. Y., are in Boulder City this week to attend the services.

Whittington, Thelma Fern
Boulder City News, Thursday, 15 Nov 1990, 11:1-2.
Thelma Fern Whittington, 83, died Saturday Nov. 10. She was a 17-year resident of Boulder City. She was born Dec. 27, 1906 in Albia, Iowa. She is survived by two sons, Martin J. Long of Boulder City, and Larry E. Long of Chicago, Ill.; a sister, Darlene Johnson of Des Moines, Iowa; three grandchildren; and 2 great grandchildren. Graveside services were held at Boulder City Cemetery. Arrangements were handled by Palm Mortuary.

Whipple, John Lester
Boulder City News, Thursday, 18 May 1989, 29:3.
John Lester Whipple, 63, a Boulder City resident since 1964, died Monday, May 15 in Boulder City. Born in Mesa, Ariz., on July 22, 1925, he was a regional programmer for the government and a U.S. Marine Corps veteran of World War II. He is survived by his wife, Shirley L. Whipple of Boulder City; a son, Jeff Whipple of Green Oaks, Ill.; a daughter, Teresa Dodd of San Jose, Calif.; two sisters, Merrilee King of Westminster, Colo. and Nellie Ostler of Richland, Wash.; two brothers, Don Olsen of Layton, Utah and James Olsen of Santa Monica, Calif. and seven grandchildren. Funeral services are scheduled at 3 p.m., today, in the Boulder City LDS First Ward. Interment will be in the Boulder City Cemetery. Palm Mortuary handled arrangements.

White, Reverend Franklin M.
Boulder City News, Thursday, 15 Feb 1990, 20:3-4.
The Reverend Franklin M. White, 49, passed away Monday, Feb. 12, 1990 in Boulder City after a lengthy illness. He was born May 9, 1940 in Rahway, N.J. He had been Senior Pastor at Bethany Baptist Church for four years. He was a member of the Boulder City Ministerial Association and affiliated with Conservative Baptist Assn. of America. He had served in the United States Air Force. He leaves his wife Rita, sons Timothy and Daniel and daughters, Suzanne and Kristen, all of the home. His mother, Mary White of Oxford, N.J.; brother David White of Lake Tahoe, Calif. and sister, Sara White of Hackettstown, N.J. The viewing will be Thursday, Feb. 15 from 3 to 8 p.m., at Bethany Baptist. Services will be held Friday, Feb. 16 at 2 p.m., also at Bethany. Interment will be in the

Boulder City Cemetery. The family suggests Memorials be made in this name to Bethany Baptist Building Fund in lieu of flowers. Bethany Baptist is located at 210 Wyoming St., Boulder City, Nev. 89005.

White, James "Jack"
Boulder City News, Thursday, 2 Nov 1989, 30:3.
James "Jack" White, 72, a 25-year resident of Boulder City, died Wednesday. Born Sept. 29, 1917, in Bryan Co., Okla, he was a painting contractor. Survivors include three sons, Bob White of Honolulu, Hawaii, Jim White of Oildale, Calif. and Ron White of Bakersfield, Calif.; two daughters, Joanne Sparling of Oildale, Calif. and Judy Arlington of Las Vegas; and his sister, Brownie Dorman of Nuevo, Calif.; 22 grandchildren and 19 great grandchildren. Services were held, Palm Mortuary handled arrangements.

White, Thomas Sherman, M.D.
Boulder City News, Thursday, 30 Apr 1992, 10:1-2.
Thomas Sherman White, M.D. 87, a resident of Boulder City since 1955, died Sunday in a local hospital. Born in Portsmouth, R.I. on May 17, 1904. He was a retired medical physician and surgeon. He served in World War II, in the U.S. Army. He was a graduate of Defience College, Defience, Ohio, and a graduate of Albany Medical College. He was director of the Malaria & Tropical Disease Control in the South Pacific in the Army. He was a diplomat of the American College of Surgeons and a fellow of the American College of Surgeons. He was a member of the Boulder City group seeking the establishment of Boulder City as an independent entity when Boulder City was being separated from the government. He served as vice mayor of Boulder City for its first term. He was a member of the Boulder City Hospital staff from 1955-1973 and served as its chief of staff for 19 years. He was president of the Nevada State Medical Association at the time the association petitioned the board of regents to seek legislative funding for a feasibility study for the establishment for a state medical college. He was the past president of the Clark County Medical Society and a member of the Boulder City Rotary Club. The family suggests donations be made to the Dr. Thomas Sherman White medical scholarship at the University of Nevada Reno. Survivors include his wife, Juanita White of Boulder City and a daughter, Sally White Johnson of Fredericksburg, Texas, and five grandchildren. Services

were held. Palm Mortuary handled arrangements.

White, Velta S.
Boulder City News, Thursday, 5 Mar 1981, p.2
Velta S. White was a wonderful neighbor and a fine friend. That was the opinion of those at her funeral services, Saturday afternoon at the Church of Jesus Christ of Latter-day Saints in Boulder City. Bishop Karl Snow, who conducted the rites, remembered the years his family and the Whites were neighbors on Avenue G, and how his children called Velta "the candy door lady," and said she was a good influence on the children of the neighborhood. Jake Williams, in giving the eulogy, remarked on her hospitality at her home. Velta loved to crochet things for her family, and taught this and other skills at Relief Society. Patriarch R. Owen Gibson expressed his belief that Velta would always be helping others, in her continuing life. Speakers told of her early years in Utah, and how she married John "Barney" White when a young widow with two small sons, in 1936. They moved to Boulder City in the early 1940's, and Velta was employed at the U. S. Bureau of Mines. She belonged to the American Legion Auxiliary, and the B.P.O. Does. Teresa Denning played prelude music on the piano. A piano solo was presented by grandchild Donalane Cameron. Madeleine Tronier sang a solo, accompanied by Beverly Hirschi. Earl K. Leavitt gave the invocation, and Mads A. Gibson the benediction. The graveside dedication at Boulder City Cemetery was by Douglas Stoker, Pallbearers were sons Don and Wally Cameron; brothers-in-law Jim Whicker and Med Holley; grandson Karl Cameron, and family friend Walter Wright.

Whittaker, George Madison
Boulder City News, Thursday, 14 Aug 1975, 3:1.
Funeral services were held yesterday afternoon for George Madison Whittaker, 54, who died Sunday in the Southern Nevada Memorial Hospital. Rites were conducted at the Foursquare Gospel Church by the Reverend Marjorie Holman. Burial was in the Boulder City Cemetery. Mr. Whittaker had been ill only a few days. Pallbearers were Tony Restivo, Pete Cardoni, Don Tony, John Rohn, Ti Greene and David Whittaker. He was born September 5, 1920 in Mexico, Missouri. He served in the Navy Air Force during World War II. He was an expert tailor and did beautiful leather work. In 1967, the family moved to

Boulder City from Glendale, Arizona, and Mr. Whittaker has been employed by the Bureau of Fish and Wildlife Service of the U. S. Dept. of the Interior at the Fish Hatchery at Willow Beach. His survivors include his widow, Barbara Whittaker and daughter Teresa, at Space 103, Moore's Trailer Park; a son, David Wayne Whittaker, Cleveland, Mississippi; Two brothers, E. H. Whittaker, Los Angeles, Calif., and Glenwood Whittaker, Mexico, Mo.; and a sister, Wilma Armstrong, Niota, Illinois.

Wiebke, Fred
Boulder City News, Thursday, 16 July 1970, 2:5.
A 52-year service in the ministry closed last Saturday upon the death of Lutheran pastor, Fred Wiebke, 78, who passed away at his retirement home in Greeley, Colo. The funeral service will be conducted today at 2:30 p.m. in Bunker Brothers Chapel in Las Vegas. Reverend Wiebke is a former Boulderite and the father of Esther N. Gilleard. He made his home at 108 Wyoming St. from 1961 until last fall. He was born in Cook, Neb. and educated at Sterling Academy and Warburg Seminary in Iowa. On June 26, 1918 he married Freda Shubert and two days later was ordained. Reverend Wiebke served in five states in the midwest. His work was primarily with young people, and he was interested in 4-H Club work. He was given a 50-year pin by the American Lutheran Church in honor of his service. The renowed minister is survived by his sons, Almer B. of Colorado Springs, Colo., Clo.and Armin, China Lake, Calif.; a daughter, Mrs. Gilleard of Boulder City; seven grandchildren and nine brothers and sisters.

Wigley, Susan Lillian
Boulder City News, Thursday, 8 Jan 1953, p.1:4.
Wigley Infant Burial Today
Susan Lillian Wigley, who was born on Monday morning and died yesterday, will have private family burial rites in the Boulder City cemetery today, conducted by the Reverend Olaf Stoeve. Susan was born to Mr. And Mrs. Robert Wigley, 532 Avenue K, and is survived by her parents and two sisters.

Williams, Glen
Boulder City News, Thursday, 10 Mar 1988, 6:2.
Glen Williams, 39, of Boulder City passed away Monday, March 7, 1988. Glen was the manager of B & J Body Shop in Boulder City for many years. He leaves a wife Rana and two children. Local services at Boulder City LDS Chapel will be Friday. The hour is pending. Palm Mortuary in Henderson is handling the arrangements.

Williams, John
Boulder City News, Thursday, 3 Jul 1975, 9:8.
John Williams Services Held
Graveside services were held yesterday morning for John Williams, 78. The rites were conducted at the Boulder City Cemetery by the Reverend Louis Nimmo of Faith Baptist Church in Henderson. Mr. Williams died in a rest home in Huntington Park, California, after a long illness. He was born July 14, 1896, in Texas and was a retired printer. Mr. And Mrs. Williams had visited this area for many years, and came over in January to acquire property with the intention of moving to Boulder City. He is survived by his wife, Winnie, of Huntington Park. His sister-in-law is Ruth (Mrs. Don) Swartx, 171 Van Wagenen St., Henderson, who lived in Boulder City for more than 30 years. As Mrs. McCauley, she and her late husband operated a market in the Manix Building, and later also was employed by the U. S. Bureau of Mines.

Williams, Joseph F.
Boulder City News, Thursday, 13 July 1967, 1:5-6.
Joseph Williams Killed Near Ely
Requiem mass and burial services was conducted at 9 a.m. Wednesday at St. Christopher's Episcopal Church for Joseph F. Williams, 18, Boulder City, who was one of two youths killed early Sunday in a one-car rollover near Ely. The Reverend Robert Bateman and the Reverend Talley Jarrett will officiate. He is the son of Mr. and Mrs. William Williams, 725 New Mexico St. Mr. Williams is Public Information Officer for the Bureau of Reclamation, Region 3. Joe was employed by the Ely office of the State Highway Department and had completed his first year as a pre-medical student at College of the South, Sewanee, Tenn. on a four-year Fleischmann Scholarship. The youth was graduated from Boulder City

High School in 1966, second highest in his class and was named Most Inspiration Football Player in his senior year. Classmates plan to donate a trophy to be known as the Joe Williams Award which will be inscribed each year with the name of the outstanding football player. Joe was born Aug. 6, 1948 in Boulder City and received all of his schooling here. Besides his parents he is survived by two brothers, Kent, 23, and John, 14 as well as a paternal grandmother, Mrs. L. P. Williams, Stigler, Okla. and his maternal grandmother, Mrs. Fred A. Kent, Altus, Okla. Burial was in Boulder City Cemetery. In lieu of flowers, friends were asked to donate to the St. Christopher's Church Fund.

Williams, Leon A.
Boulder City News, Thursday, 8 Jan 1953, p.1:3.
L. R. Williams, Killed In Fall
Leon A. Williams, 632 Avenue M, prominent Boulder City Pioneer, died at the local hospital Tuesday at 9:09 a.m. of complications following a fall Saturday, from the roof of a home he was working on. Mr. Williams was born in Bethany, Missouri, January 4, 1898, and came to Boulder City in the early days to work on the Boulder Dam project. He was a member of the Chamber of Commerce and the Recreation association and owned and managed of the Hitching Post Motel and Boulder City Brick company. Surviving are his widow, Bessie, four sons, Frank Williams, Boulder City; Louis Williams, Reno, Nevada; Daniel A. Williams, Boise, Idaho, and Francis L. Williams, Sydney, Australia; and nine grandchildren; one brother, Harlen Williams, Boulder City; and three sisters, Mrs. Inez McAtee, Long Beach, California; Mrs. Grace McGillivary, Los Angeles, California, and Mrs. Luise McCall, Ulysses, Kansas. Funeral services will be conducted Saturday at 3 p.m. at the LDS church.

Williams, Lewis
Boulder City News, Thursday, 29 Jul 1954, 1:2.
Funeral Services Held Here for California Man
Lewis Williams 38, of Burbank, who died of a heart attack last week while in the area on business and visiting his brother Rick Williams, was buried Saturday in the Boulder City cemetery beside his father. He was honored with military rites, and graveside services were conducted by Herman Nelson of the Church of Jesus Christ of Latter Day Saints. He is

survived by his wife Kathryn, his mother Mrs. Charles Chester of Lovelock, Nevada; and three brothers, Francis of San Mateo, California; Daniel of Boise, Idaho; and Rick of 616 Avenue M.

Wilson, Doris I.
Boulder City News, Thursday, 30 Nov 1995, 12:3-4.
Doris I. Wilson, 81, died Tuesday, Nov. 21, 1995 in a local hospital. Born Oct. 9, 1914 in Prescott, Ariz., she had been a resident of Boulder City since 1972. She was a retired owner/operator of a drug store. She is survived by son Donald Toci of Mattawa, Wash.; and step-son Harlan Wilson of Elko; four grandchildren and eight great-grandchildren.

Wilson, George Lee, Sr.
Boulder City News, Thursday, 1 Nov 1956, 15:2.
Funeral Services For George Wilson Friday at 2 P.M.
Funeral services for George Lee Wilson, Sr., will be held tomorrow afternoon at the Grace Community church with the Reverend Earl S. Fox officiating. A resident of Boulder City since 1951, Mr. Wilson died of a heart ailment at his home Monday night at 620 Avenue M after a brief illness. Until Sept. 26, he had been employed at the Visitors Bureau in Boulder City for about five years. Mr. Wilson, 65, was born in Waterloo, Iowa and he and Mrs. Wilson came to reside in Boulder City from Brandt, South Dakota. He had lived most of his life in Iowa and South Dakota. In addition to his widow, Mrs. Cecile Fortier Wilson, survivors include two sons, Edward T. Wilson of Kahauli, Maui, T. H. And George L. Wilson, Jr. of Henderson; a daughter, Edith Christianson of North Las Vegas; a brother, Edd P. Wilson of Sioux Falls, South Dakota; two sisters, Mrs. C. Emil Carlson and Mrs. Mabel Olson, both of Sioux Falls; and 14 grandchildren.

Wilson, Jennifer J.
Boulder City News, Thursday, 12 Nov 1992, 9:1-2.
Jennifer Janene Wilson, 19, of Boulder City, passed away Sunday, Nov. 8, 1992, in a local hospital. Jennifer was born in Rock Springs, Wyoming, on Oct. 11, 1973. She and her family moved many times in her young life, small towns in Arizona, Colorado, to Death Valley and in 1985 to Boulder City. Jennifer had a great love for horses before moving to

Boulder City. She spent many summers with her family riding the ranches of Arizona. Because of her love for roping, she came to admire the team roping of Clay O'Brien Cooper and Jake Barnes. Her horse, a paint gelding which she raised and trained from a colt was lovingly named Clay. Jennifer attended BCHS where she lettered in track her junior year. Her senior year was devoted to her interest in horses and roping. She spent all her free time at the corrals with the B.C. Horsemen's Association. While not at the corrals "horsing around," Jennifer worked part-time at the Bureau of Reclamation in the IRM Department. The morning of June 1, 1991, two days before her graduation ceremonies, Jennifer was involved in a horseback riding accident. She was not riding her horse Clay at the time. Jennifer was airlifted by Flight for Life to UMC. Later, still in a coma, she was brought back to the Boulder City Hospital where she became a resident of the long term care. Jennifer's mother Margaret got a job working the night shift at the hospital to be near her daughter. Margaret and sister Tracy were often helped by others to decorate Jennifer's room to make things as homey and comfortable as possible. Posters of Garth Brooks, Clint Black and others adorned her room. Get well signs, signatures, happy thoughts were changed very few months. Many caring people helped through this ordeal, many gave their own time to help with therapy. During the National Finals Rodeo in December of last year, Jennifer's mother and sister had a chance to meet team roper Jake Barnes. When he learned of Jennifer's situation, he felt he had to meet her. He and his wife and family went to the hospital. There, he signed a T-shirt for her and at Christmas sent her a nightgown and roping tape of him and Clay. It's been a long year and a half for the family and friends of Jennifer Wilson whom so willing and unselfishly dedicated so much of their lives to the well-being of another. Her family and friends thank all those who showed love and support during this time. These words from author Thomas Wolfe, who died long before we feel his work was done, seem appropriate to Jennifer. "To lose the earth you know for greater knowing, to lose the life you have for greater life, to leave the friends you loved for greater loving, to find a land more kind than home, more large than earth." God speed, dear Jennifer. You were loved. Jennifer is survived by her mother, Margaret Wilson, a sister, Tracy, both of Boulder City; a brother Shawn Wilson of Arizona; father, William G. Wilson of Tennessee; grandparents Mr. and Mrs. Boyd Hicks, Vera Darton, great-grandmother Lucille McDaniel, all of Arizona. A memorial fund has been set up at the Boulder City Credit Union to help the family. Graveside services will be conducted at 10:30 a.m. today at the Boulder City Cemetery. *Editor's note: This information was supplied by a close friend of the family.*

Wilson, Robert E.
Boulder City News, Thursday, 12 Jan 1978, 13:4.
Graveside services will be held tomorrow at 2 p.m. at the Boulder City Cemetery for Robert E. Wilson, 79, who passed away January 10 at the Boulder City Hospital. Mr. Wilson was born December 19, 1899 in Prescott, Washington. He was a Marine Corps veteran of World War I and a member of the Bend, Oregon VFW. He was a retired railroad conductor. Survivors include his wife, Minnie of the home address at 1501 Nevada Highway, Boulder City; one daughter, Sherma Johnstone of McMinnville, Oregon; one son, Gary Wilson of Redmond, Oregon; seven grandchildren and one great grandchild. The Boulder City Veterans of Foreign Wars will officiate at the service. Palm Mortuary is in charge of arrangements.

Wilson, Victor "Paul"
Boulder City News, Thursday, 1 Oct 1968, 1:7.
Funeral service for Victor (Paul) Wilson, 705 Aztec Place, will be conducted by the Reverend Guy Holliday at 5:30 p.m. today at Grace Community Church. Mr. Wilson passed away Tuesday morning at B.C. Hospital. Burial will be in Boulder City Cemetery. The deceased was born April 13, 1901 on a ranch near Florence, Colo. At the time of his death he was a guide supervisor at Hoover Dam. He is survived by his widow Amalette (Ketch) Wilson of this city; his mother, Mrs. Alice (Granny) Wilson, ElJean Medical Hospital, Las Vegas; a son, Jack of Wells, Nev,; a grandson Danny of Boulder City; two granddaughters Rose Marie and Jeanie Wilson of Pueblo, Colo.; daughter Alice Rehamond, and granddaughter, Susan Houston, Tex,; a sister, Alice Neville, Boulder City, and two brothers, Joe of Green Valley, Wyo., and Frank of San Diego, Calif. Mr. Wilson was a member of Elks Lodge 1682 and an active member of the Fish and Game Commission board. The family requests in lieu of flowers that donations be made in Mr. Wilson's name to the B.C. hospital building fund or the American Cancer Society.

Wilson, William
Boulder City News, Thursday, 1 Sep 1988, 10:3.
William "Bill" Wilson, 20, died Friday in Terre Haute, Ind. He was an eight year resident of Boulder City. A missionary for the Church of Jesus Christ of Latter-day.

Winn, Mary
Boulder City News, Friday, 20 Apr 1951, 8:1.
Mary Winn Funeral Yesterday
Mary Winn, of 619 California Avenue, was buried yesterday morning in the Boulder City cemetery, with Bishop Herman Nelson conducting the services at the LDS Church. J. Donal Earl and Owen Gibson were the speakers. Mrs. Winn died Tuesday morning at the local hospital after a illness. She was born in July, 1886, in American Fork, Utah. She was very active in the LDS Church, and at the last Moapa Stake conference Mrs. Winn was set apart as a stake missionary. Last fall she received a pin for a year's perfect attendance at Relief Society. She had previously been a primary and Sunday school teacher. Survivors are her husband Jesse three daughters, Mrs. Magda Poter of Boulder City; Mrs. Jessie Lewis of Overton; Mrs. Udine Cooper of Napa, California; and two son, Verne Winn of Henderson; and Ray Winn, who recently returned from a mission and is now attending BYU in Utah.

Witherell, Robert "Bob"
Boulder City News, Thursday, 24 Dec 1992, 8:2.
Robert "Bob" Witherell, 81, died Dec. 20, 1992 in a local hospital. He was born July 9, 1911 in Olean, N.Y. and had been a resident of the Boulder City area for nine years. Witherell was a veteran of the United States Army serving during World War II. He was a member of Boulder City Masonic Lodge #37, F&AM and of Scottish Rite, Jamestown, N.Y. He is survived by his wife, Cleo J. Witherell of Boulder City; two nieces, Sally Earnest of Pittsboro, N.C. and Gail Walton of Meadville, Pa.; and a nephew, Richard Andrews of Clyner, N.Y. Arrangements were handled by Palm Mortuary in Henderson.

Withers, Iona F.
Boulder City News, Thursday, 24 Mar 1988, p.30.
Iona F. Withers, 80, died Monday, March 7, 1988 in a local hospital and was a resident of Las Vegas since October 1987. She was born in Huron, South Dakota on Dec. 29, 1907 and was a homemaker. She is survived by her mother Hannah Fortune of Las Vegas, sisters Louis Sanders of Las Vegas and Merna Bender of Boulder City and brother George Fortune of Indiana. No local services were held. Memorial services were held in Sunland, Calif. Palm Mortuary handled the arrangements and interment was in Boulder City Cemetery, Boulder City.

Wood, Carol Ann
Boulder City News, Thursday, 10 Jul 1986, 29:6.
Carol Ann Wood, 42, of Boulder City, died Saturday in Las Vegas. She was born Sept. 2, 1943, in San Diego. A three-year resident, she was an LPN. She is survived by her husband, Alan of Boulder City; son, Michael Malatino of New York; daughters, Karen Malatino of Henderson and Elizabeth Ann Hudson Wood of Boulder City; parents, Mr. and Mrs. Albert Goetz of Boulder City; sister, Norma Walter, of Hemet, Calif. The funeral was Wednesday at the Christian Center Church, Boulder City. Interment was in Boulder City Cemetery. Palm Mortuary, of Henderson handled the arrangements.

Wood, Estelle "Bill"
Boulder City News, Thursday, 11 Oct 1984, 8:1-2.
Graveside services were conducted Wednesday at 1 p.m. at Boulder City Cemetery for Estelle E. "Bill" Wood who died Saturday, September 29, at Valley Hospital, after a lengthy illness. Mr. Wood was born April 30, 1906 in Prarie, Oklahoma. He worked as an oil driller. In 1962 he moved to Las Vegas and resided there until becoming a resident of Boulder City in 1980. Mr. Wood is survived by his wife Nettie of Boulder; a brother, J.C. of Ponca City, Oklahoma; 3 stepdaughters, Barbara Titus of Boulder City; Beverly Smith of Pahrump; and Betty Larsen of Benson, Arizona; 3 stepsons, Bruce and Barry Faulkner of Boulder City; and Richard Kirby of San Francisco, California; 3 step grand children, Patricia Kirby of Las Vegas; and Eric and Brian Larsen of Benson, Arizona and 2 nieces and 2 nephews. Graveside services were conducted by Reverend Dan Murphy

of the Church of Christ on October 3, 1984. Funeral arrangements were handled by Palm Mortuary in Henderson.

Wood, Evelyn
Boulder City News, Thursday, 12 Dec 1968.
Graveside services will be conducted Saturday at 2 p.m. at Boulder City Cemetery for Mrs. Evelyn Wood who passed away sometime Monday night in her home at Cherry Lynn Apts. Palm Mortuary will handle the arrangements and burial will be in Boulder City Cemetery. She was born Nov. 9, 1902 in St. Joseph, Mo., and is survived by two brothers, Hank and Jack Williams and a sister, Ada Ausberry. Her husband, Lloyd, preceded her in death.

Wood, Lillie May
Boulder City News, Thursday, 15 Nov 1973.
Funeral services were held Monday, Nov. 5, for Lillie May Wood, 70, at the Bethany Baptist Church, with the Reverend Russell Fineber conducting. Interment was in the Boulder City Cemetery. Mrs. Wood died in Sunrise Hospital, Nov. 1., after an illness of several months. She was born September 6, 1900, in Staunton, Virginia. When Glen Canyon Dam was being erected, Mrs. Wood went to live at Page, Arizona, with her daughters. Her sons-in-law, W. E. "Butch" Webb and Charles M. Burns, worked with the late Earl Brothers. In 1964, the families moved to Boulder city, where the men helped Brothers develop William Beach. A few years ago, Mrs. Wood moved into the duplex at 901 Wyoming, sharing the house with the mother of Louise Brothers. A friendly person, Mrs. Wood enjoyed visiting with people around town, and loved to attend Bible classes. She is survived by two daughters, Kathleen Burns, 624 Sixth St., Boulder City; Audrey Webb, Willow Beach; two sons, Robert F. Wood of Oakhill, West Virginia, and Eugene II. Wood of Norfolk, Va.; several grandchildren, six sisters and two brothers.

Wood, Minnie Marie

Boulder City News, Thursday, 8 June 1978, 4:1-2.
Services today for Infant Wood
Graveside services will be held this morning at 11 a.m. at the Boulder City Cemetery for two day old Minnie Marie Wood who died June 4 in Salt Lake City. The infant was born June 2 in St. George, Utah. She is survived by her parents, Mr. and Mrs. Gilbert Wood of Boulder City; two brothers, Daren and Curtis Wood and a sister, Christine Wood all of Boulder City; grandparents, Mr. and Mrs. Jerry Morley of Boulder City, Eva Humes of Bountiful, Utah and Robert Humes of Overton, Nevada; and a great grandmother, Marie Morley of Boulder City. Palm Mortuary is handling the arrangements.

Wood, Nettie C.

Boulder City News, Thursday, 6 Aug 1987, 12:3.
Nettie C. Wood, 73, died Wednesday, July 29 in Las Vegas. She had been a resident of the area for 35 years. She was born I Yuma, Colo. on Aug. 22, 1913. She was a homemaker. Survivors include sons, Bruce Faulkner, Las Vegas; Barry Faulkner, Boulder City; Richard Kirby, California; daughters Barbara Titus, Boulder City; Beverly Smith, Las Vegas and Betty Larson, Sacramento, Calif.; three grandchildren. Funeral services were Saturday, Aug. 1 at 3 p.m. in the Palm Chapel in Henderson. Officiating was the Minister Hartley Simmons. Interment was in the Boulder City Cemetery.

Wood, Roy Melvin

Boulder City News, Thursday, 10 Mar 1983, 2:4-5.
Roy Melvin Wood, 87, died Tuesday at the Boulder City Care Center. He had been a resident of Boulder City for 41 years. He was born September 15, 1895 in Alvin, Texas and was retired from the Bureau of Reclamation as a Guard at the Dam. Roy is survived by his wife, Thelma, son Marvin Wood, and daughters Ardeen Sears and Norma Webb all of Boulder City and daughter Loretta Woodrum of Las Vegas; 1 sister and 6 brothers; also 17 grandchildren and 7 great grandchildren. Graveside services will be held Friday at 10:30 a.m. at the Boulder City cemetery. In lieu of flowers, the family requests donation to the intensive care unit of the Boulder City Hospital.

Wright, Ira Ross
Boulder City News, Thursday, 24 Oct 1991, 6:2.
Ira Ross Wright, 78, died Oct. 15. He was born March 6, 1913, in Wetzel County, W.Va., and had been a Boulder City resident for nine years. He is survived by his wife, Yvette Wright of Boulder City; two sons, Ross Wright of Boulder City and Brad Wright of Boulder City; two daughters, Lynette Wright of Seattle, Wash., and Gail Wright of Seattle, Wash.; also two sisters, Gertrude Halverson of Denver, Colo., three grandsons and one granddaughter. Arrangements were handled by Nevada Cremation or Burial Society.

Zamalloa, Arnold & Dorothy
Boulder City News, Thursday, 29 June 1972, p.1.
Residents here were shocked and saddened at the double tragedy Tuesday when Dorothy Zamalloa 46, fatally wounded her husband Arnold, 53, with shots from a .22 caliber pistol, then turned the pistol on herself and was killed instantly. According to Police Chief H. G. Smith, the couple had been separated and a divorce was to become final this week. Smith said Zamalloa arrived at the city garage on Nevada Highway where he was foreman, at 6:52 a.m., and as he was unlocking the gate, Mrs. Zamalloa pulled up in another car. She jumped out of the car with a gun in her hand, and according to witnesses, the only words spoken were when Zamalloa shouted "No, No, don't." She shot the gun four times and Zamalloa fell. She then fired one more shot at him, went behind the truck and shot herself through the temple. She died instantly. Zamalloa was taken to Boulder City hospital where he died about 7:58 a.m. Zamalloa began work with the Bureau of Reclamation in 1955 and transferred to the city garage in 1960. Mrs. Zamalloa had been living at the family home at 541 Sixth Street, with sons Donald 18, and John, 17.

Zamalloa, Paul
Boulder City News, Thursday, 20 Feb. 1954, 1:2.
Paul Zamalloa Graveside Rites Held Tuesday
Graveside services for Paul Zamalloa, six months old son of Mr. and Mrs. Arnold Zamalloa 541 Sixth Street, were held Tuesday afternoon at the Boulder City Cemetery, Bishop Leonard Stubbs officiated. The infant died at home Sat. He was born July 21, 1957. Surviving are two brothers, Donald and John, and a sister Darlene.

Boulder City News Articles Relating to the Boulder City Cemetery

Boulder City News, Saturday, 9 Mar 1943, p.1:4.
Any Organization, Person Interested Asked to Help Organize for Cemetery.
Any organization in Boulder City wishing to be represented at the meeting at which the Boulder City Cemetery association will be organized, tonight at 7:30 in the Municipal courtroom, should send a representative to the meeting, Chairman Tom Godbey of the committee announced last evening. Charter members of the association will have their names on the articles of incorporation, which have been drawn up tentatively for approval, with the organization represented named opposite the signature of the representative. This does not mean there is any bar to individuals not representing any organization attending and becoming charter members of the association, he said. Anyone interested in helping establish a suitable cemetery for Boulder City is welcome to attend. The meeting will determine the number of trustees and elect these from among the elect these from among the charter members of the association, and will set the meeting date for the annual election meetings in future years. Trustees will be divided by lot into one-year, two-year and three-year board members.

Boulder City News, Wednesday, 10 Mar 1943, p.1:3.
Boulder City Cemetery Association Elects Tom Godbey as Its Chairman
The Boulder City Cemetery Association was organized last evening with acceptance of articles of incorporation by representatives of many Boulder City organizations, and by interested individuals, and election of a board of trustees. The trustees elected named Tom Godbey as chairman of the board. Members to serve three years as trustees are Luke Whalen, Lee Hayward and Philip Brim. Two-year trustees are O. T. Painter, Mrs. John Abercrombie and W. T. Manning, and one-year trustees are Tom Godbey, Dave Laughery and Elton M. Garrett. The trustees, their first meeting, named officers, as provided by statute for cemetery associations. Lee Hayward was elected vice president, Elton M. Garrett secretary and Dave Laughery treasurer. The second Tuesday of March was set as the date for the annual election meeting. Mr. Hayward, Mr. Whalen and Mr. Manning were named a committee to prepare plans for landscaping and a

plan for financial provision for preliminary work of the association. Any Boulderite who wishes to be a charter member of the association may sign the articles of incorporation during the next two days by contacting the secretary.

Boulder City News, Saturday, 13 Mar 1943, p.1:1.
Incorporation of Boulder City Cemetery Association Complete; Articles Filed
Incorporation of the Boulder City Cemetery association under the laws of the State of Nevada was completed yesterday afternoon with the filing of the articles of incorporation with County Clerk Lloyd Payne in the county court house. In compliance with the law providing for such filing within three days after the organization meeting for any such association, the papers, including records of the proceedings of the incorporation meeting and provisions of the law relating to such associations, are of record and duly accepted as being complete. The articles of incorporation were signed by twenty-five Boulder City citizens, most of whom represented organizations, church groups and others.

Boulder City News, Saturday, 3 Apr 1943, p.1:1.
Operating Engineers Give $25 for Cemetery Work
A $25 donation toward work on the development of the Boulder City cemetery was voted by Operating Engineers' local 54 at a recent meeting, according to Tom Godbey, chairman of the Boulder City Cemetery association. The offer of help with donated labor also was made at the meeting. Plans are being formulated for landscaping and fencing of the cemetery tract, which is located southeast of the golf course.

Boulder City News, Tuesday, 23 May 1944.
Help Needed Getting Cemetery Fence Up for Memorial Day Ceremonies
Help is needed in getting the fence put up at the Boulder City cemetery, according to Tom Godbey, president of the Boulder City Cemetery association, who has expressed the hope of getting the job done in time for the Memorial day exercises. The fencing, 1100 feet of it, with stakes and braces and gates, was received recently and placing of posts has been under way for some days. Anyone who can help on this work from 4:30 p.m. on until dark is invited to participate in the "fence raising bee" every night until it is finished, according to Godbey. Setting of fence posts and

stretching wire are the main jobs now, and anyone who can bring along wire pliers is invited to do so, he stated. Memorial day ceremonies are being planned by the V.F.W. in conjunction with the Boulder City American Legion post, Godbey stated.

Boulder City News, **Saturday, 27 May 1944.**
Cemetery Fence Complete for Memorial Service
Erection of the fence for Boulder City cemetery was finished yesterday, with the help of the Auxiliary Firemen and others who faithfully aided President Tom Godbey of the cemetery association in the job. The Memorial Day services will be held at 2 p.m. Sunday at the cemetery.

Boulder City News, **Saturday, 2 Sep 1944.**
Cemetery Custodian Hut Remodeling "Bee" Today
Work of remodeling the custodian's house at the Boulder City cemetery will be commenced this evening by a group of volunteer workers, including members of the Cemetery association, according to Tom Godbey, president of the association. The work will begin at 5 p.m., and will include carpentering, some repair of plumbing work, some painting and some stuccoing, Godbey said, requesting that anyone who can help contact him or appear during the time appointed.

Boulder City News, **Thursday, 7 Sep 1944, 3:2-3.**
Cemetery, Recreation Funds to Be Sought
Plans for getting funds for the Boulder City cemetery maintenance, also additional funds for recreation in Boulder City, also plans for getting the football field resurfaced and for completing re-roofing of the U.S.O. building were discussed at last evening's meeting of the Boulder City Coordinating council. County officials will be asked to furnish funds for a caretaker for the cemetery, also to continue financial assistance for recreation on a basis similar to that of the summer, it was decided.

Boulder City News, **Tuesday, 19 Sep 1944.**
Boulder City Cemetery Association to Hold Annual Meeting, Elect
The Boulder City Cemetery association will hold its second annual meeting Wednesday evening of this week, for election of officers for the coming year, Tom Godbey, president of the association, announced last

evening. The meeting will be held in the Municipal building at 8 p.m., and each organization in Boulder City which wishes to send a representative to the meeting is invited to do so, Godbey stated. Any individual who is interested is invited to attend the meeting, said Godbey.

Boulder City News, Tuesday, 16 Apr 1946, 1:3.
Bunker Bill to Deed B.C. Cemetery Land Is Passed by House, Now to Senate
Congressman Berkeley L. Bunker's bill to deed the land on which the Boulder City cemetery is located to the Boulder City Cemetery association was approved yesterday by the house of representatives, according to word received from Nevada's congressman. The legislation, which has the approval of the Bureau of Reclamation, Department of the Interior, will go to the senate immediately, where it is expected early action will be taken. About thirty burials have taken place at the cemetery, most of these since the organization of the association, of which Tom Godbey is chairman.

Boulder City News, Wednesday, 22 May 1946, p.1:2.
B. C. Cemetery Bill Given Senate Committee Okay
Legislation for the deeding of land for the Boulder City cemetery took another hurdle yesterday when the state public lands committee of the United States senate acted favorably on HR-3966, the Boulder City cemetery measure, according to word received yesterday from Congressman Berkeley L. Bunker. It was expected the bill was to have been reported to the senate yesterday afternoon. The bill was passed some time ago by the house of representatives. The Boulder City Cemetery association, of which Tom Godbey is president, has worked with the Bureau of Reclamation in preparation of the setup for administration of the cemetery.

Boulder City News, Saturday, 15 Jun 1946, p.1:5.
You Can Buy Lots Soon in Boulder City, But They'll Be in Cemetery
It takes an act of congress to establish a cemetery in Boulder City. The act of congress has been passed, the senate having acted favorably on the measure yesterday, according to word received from Berkeley L. Bunker, Nevada congressman. When President Truman signs the bill, it will be possible for the Bureau of Reclamation to deed land for the cemetery to

the Boulder City Cemetery association, which was organized a few years ago under provisions of Nevada law. The land cannot be used for any other purposes. Many burials have taken place at the cemetery, and payments for maintenance have been made. Actual purchase of lots will become possible on a complete and final basis when President Truman and Bureau of Reclamation officials have made this possible.

Boulder City News, **Wednesday, 26 Mar 1947, 3:3.**
Cemetery Association To Elect Officers Tonight
Boulder City Cemetery Association will hold its annual election meeting this evening at 7 o'clock in the courtroom downstairs in the municipal building. Tom Godbey, president of the association, announced the election will involve filling of at least one trusteeship recently left open when Dr. D. S. Carder left for Washington, D.C. It is anticipated that land for the cemetery will be deeded to the association by the Bureau of Reclamation.

Boulder City News, **Thursday, 27 May 1947.**
Cemetery Lot Price Set At $25; Nicholson Is Named as New Trustee
R. H. Nicholson was elected trustee for the Boulder City Cemetery Association at last evening's annual business meeting, to take the place of Dr. D. S. Carder, trustee who has left for Washington, D.C. Luke Whalen and H. L. Hayward were reelected for three-year terms, the position of sextant was created, and Mrs. Ruth Getts was appointed to the job. Tom Godbey was reelected president, Dave Laughery treasurer and Elton Garrett secretary. Luke Whalen was designated grave digger. Inquiry regarding when the land is to be deeded to the association by the federal government, as authorized by Congress, was authorized, and plans made for such improvements as providing a tool chest, faucet repair, lighting for night digging and gate painting. Price of lots was raised to $25 each, and plans were made to contract with mortuaries for collecting for sale of lots, and first maintenance payment. A monument works will be contacted to arrange for handling of monuments by the Association. Financial report was made by Dave Laughery, treasurer.

Boulder City News, Thursday, 28 Nov 1947, 5:4-5.
Burial Lots in Boulder City Cemetery To Be Available for Purchase Shortly
by Elton M. Garrett

Lots will be available for purchase in Boulder City in the not too distant future – cemetery lots, that is. Such is word received by officers of the Boulder City Cemetery Association from the U. S. land office in Carson City. The 10-acre plot involved is now owned by Uncle Sam, as is all Boulder City Land. Final certificate to convey title for burial use was authorized in a recent decision, five years after Boulder City citizens organized in a committee and sent a request to Congress for this patent. The instrument to convey title to the land at sale price of $1 is to be issued from Washington, D. C. The cemetery association then will be able to sell lots, for burial purposes only. The federal government reserves the right to fissionable materials, rights for electric transmission and phone lines and for "water and sewage mains along thoroughfares such as driveways and walkways to provide the means of connecting the city facilities to such portions of Boulder City as may be constructed to surround the cemetery." Title to portions of said land may revert to the United States if used for any purpose other than a cemetery, or if the association violates "regulations hereafter promulgated by the Secretary of the Interior pursuant to the Act of June 25, 1946." Persons of all religious beliefs, as well as persons professing no religious beliefs, may be buried in the cemetery, it has been stipulated. It has taken as long to get action on this deed as it took to build Boulder Dam. During the construction days there was no burial place for Boulder City, and burials were in Las Vegas and elsewhere afar. The Bureau of Reclamation had no way of going into the "cemetery business." But bureau officials planned to set aside a certain plat of land for eventual use when legal means were found for administration of a cemetery. John Abercrombie, pioneer worker on the dam project, was the first person to be buried there and by October 17, 1942, there had been five burials, through there was nothing more but survey stakes. On that date a meeting of citizens was called and presided over by Tom Godbey, and I, as secretary, was asked to write a resolution requesting an act of Congress making possible a deed to the land for the cemetery. The resolution was sent to Congressman Jim Scrugham. I then perused Nevada statutes and wrote articles of incorporation for the Boulder City Cemetery Association, a non-profit organizations, and checked these for okeh of City Manager A. G. Boynton and the district attorney's office. On March 9, 1943, the association was organized under these articles: 25 citizens representing local organizations elected Godbey chairman, H. L. Hayward vice chairman, myself secretary and Dave Laughery treasurer. Other trustees were O. T. Painter, Mrs. Helen Abercrombie, W. T. Manning, Luke A. Whalen and Phil Brim. May 5, 1943 – Requests for donations sent to organizations. Nov 9, 1943 – Total of $135 received from unions and V.F.W. Auxiliary. Nov 9, 1943 – Trustees bid $76 for purchase of three-room cottage at 522 Seventh, to be used for caretaker, said bid accompanied by a $100 deposit check to the Bureau of Reclamation. Sep. 1944 – Officers asked County Commissioners for financial aid. Jack Higgins donated $10 to the association. Oct 6, 1944 – Report $300 spent for dwelling and its equipment, about $825 worth of work donated erecting fence, planting trees and lawn, etc. Sept 6, 1945 – Congressman Berkeley Bunker introduced H.R. 3966 in Congress; this bill was referred to the Public Lands Committee. June 25, 1946 (nearly 10 months later) – H.R. 3966 approved. May 12, 1947 – Application for title to land made by association to U.S. Land Office, Carson City. Nov 19, 1947 – Notice of favorable decision sent association officers from U.S. Land Office in Carson City.

Boulder City News, **Thursday, 12 Dec 1963, p.1.**
Civic Effort
Cemetery Project Gains Momentum
 A long-awaited civic improvement – that of beautifying the local cemetery – is speeding along with the help of community-minded clubs, and the sponsorship of the local Women's club. Club officials state that the following donations have already come in: Lions Club, $51; Rotary Club, $52; Women's Club, $25; Boulder Drove of Does and Elks Lodge, oleander bushes. Gene Dennison, director of the Department of Public Works is responsible for the design which will feature threes, plantings, bushes and flowers. The idea of enhancing the looks of the cemetery has lay dormant for over 20 years. It has been the desire of the board of directors – Tom Godbey, president; Elton Garrett, secretary and William Curry, treasurer – that the city take over the graveyard. But a unique section of the city charter precludes selling city land in quick fashion such as would be required for burial plots, so the city makes sure that the graves are tended through the offices of Sexton James Buchanan who

occupies a house adjacent to the cemetery, but leaves sales up to the board. The Women's Club is spearheading the improvements as the club's participation in the Sears Roebuck Foundation's community program for the year. "Individuals are asked to contribute to the effort as memorials as well as entire organizations," Mrs. Lillian Collins, chairman, added.

Boulder City News, Thursday, 20 Feb 1964, p.2:3-5.

PRESENTS ROSE – Members of the Purple Sage Desert Gardeners of Henderson presented an Hawaiian rosebush to Hoe & Grow Garden Club of Boulder City to be planted among other rose bushes at the entrance to the cemetery.

FORESTRY DIVISION – Department of Public Works Director Gene Denison, and Boulder Canyon Project Manager Dee Towne begin the happy task of planting 50 popular trees to be used as a windbreak at the local cemetery as part of the beautification plan. The trees were a donation from the State Forestry Department.

STATE AND JAYCEES
Still More Help On Cemetery Job
Under the direction of the Women's club and the able assistance of Gene Dennison of the city's maintenance division, the futures of the local cemetery is getting brighter each day. In a project first conceived by a NEWS editorial, the women's Club has been spear-heading a drive to beautify the unique little cemetery and civic, social and organizations through-out the city have rallied to the plea for money and plants as well as trees and shrubs to make the cemetery more attractive. One of the latest contributions has come from the Junior Chamber of Commerce, which has donated $50 to the cause. Another recent highlight of the drive came when the State Forestry Department sent 50 poplar trees to the women's Club with their best wishes. Donations of plants are steadily trickling in – two rose bushes at a time in most cases, not only from Boulder City residents, but also from donors in Las Vegas and San Diego. The Women's Club is also looking into the possibility of putting up a chain link fence around the cemetery.

Boulder City News, Thursday, 19 Mar 1964

DONATE TREES- (photo) The above members of Xi Zeta sorority, Joe Davis, Kathy Eby, Charlene Clark and Alberta Davis, are shown with the two live trees which have been donated as the group's share of the cemetery beautiful project.
Sorority Gives Olive Trees To Cemetery
Members of the Xi Zeta sorority, becoming interested in the cemetery beautification project, have presented two olive trees as their share in the civic program.

Boulder City News, Thursday, 12 Aug 1965, 1:1.

Cemetery Group Meets
Members of the B.C. Cemetery Association will hold an important meeting at 2 p.m. Saturday in the offices of Garrett Realty. The purpose of the meeting is to discuss a hike in cemetery lots to conform to a new state statute which makes it mandate to set aside a $1 per foot of each grave for perpetual care. The price of graves is now $50 per lot and the association is expected to raise that figure to $100. The city voted to assume the responsibility of the cemetery and when it takes over, there must be $25,000 in the perpetual care fund. The association has accumulated all but $500 of that amount which will be turned over to the city. Association members are Leo Dunbar, Sr., Luke Whalen, Elton Garrett, Lillian Collins, Bert Whitney, Morgan Sweeney, Tom Godbey, William Curry and Macie Felts. It has been in operation since 1942.

Boulder City News, Thursday, 14 Apr 1966, p.1:3-5.

Council Agrees To Take Over Cemetery Operation
Rising costs to the city for crews opening and closing graves and the problem of a land shift due to a primary street running through the cemetery, contrary to state law, overcame the reluctance of the City Council to assume the responsibility and allow the Boulder City Cemetery Association to go out of business as a private enterprise. It will be done by ordinance. Council was told Tuesday night that it is estimated it costs the city $81 per grave for opening and closing. The cemetery association charges $25 which it keeps. Utah street, as originally laid out, bisects the cemetery and rather than change the pattern or mix in a land-swapping deal, it seemed simpler to change the layout of the graveyard extension and allow Utah to pursue its original design. Assets of the

cemetery association include 10 acres, a caretaker's residence and more than $29,000 in cash and securities. The board of trustees was organized in 1943 and at the last meeting drafted another request that the city take over. A letter drafted by Elton Garrett, secretary of the association, reads in part: "With $20,000 investment in a savings & loan association of which $10,000 is insured, it is our belief that the city could accept the funds and securities which the Cemetery Association offers, establish a sound investment policy for that portion now required by law for perpetual care, establish procedures for plaing the required amount form the sale of each lot in this fund and utilize the remainder of the lot price for operation and maintenance. "We believe you will find you can adjust sales prices fo lots, now wols for $1000 for adults and $50 for babies; price of opening and closing graves now $25 each and sales price of concrete vaults $35 for adults and $20 for babies. "We believe that all records of lots, their sale and payments for them should be permanently in city hall rather than at the home of an officer of the Cemetery Association." Had the council not made the move Tuesday night, the association had requested it go to a ballot. The association was adamant against selling the facility to a private mortuary firm.

Boulder City News, **Thursday, 14 Dec 1967, p.1:8.**
Cemetery Charges Upped
The City Council Tuesday night passed a resolution raising cemetery fees. According to a department head in charge of operations at the city-owned facility burial costs lagged behind the rising cost of labor. New charges are: adult lot, $125; infant lot, $50; interment and adult vault, $35; infant interment and vault, $20; open and close a grave for an adult, $60 and for an infant $25. Charles for interment of cremains will be $25; monument setting, plain in the ground, $5, and in concrete, $15. The resolution also states that all lots, sold for immediate use will be on a cash basis. Those looking to the future may reserve a lot with a down payment of $25 per cent and a time payment plan of one year without interest.

Boulder City News, **Thursday, 15 Feb 1968.**
AT CEMETERY
Club Asks Help For Rose Garden
In the spring of 1964, the local B.C. Women's Club assumed the project of beautifying the local cemetery located on the desert south of the city. At this time all organizations in town were solicited for donations of money or certain shrubbery. The Hoe and Grow Garden Club had preciously been approached and urged to take over this project but since our organization is non-profit and not a money raising club, it was felt that with so few members it could not assume such a large responsibility. However, it was suggested that the Garden Club establish a Memorial Rose garden within the cemetery grounds and anyone having loved ones interred in the cemetery could donate a rose bush to this project and the club would have it planted and a marker placed beside the rose bush bearing the name in whose memory it had been planted and the name of the rose. After this was given publicity, a tremendous response followed and in a very short time the two 20-foot square beds were filled and further contributions had to be made in the form of climbing roses which were planted along the newly erected fence. At the beginning of this project, the cemetery was being handled not only by the Cemetery Association but also by the city. The Garden Club was advised to deliver the donated rose bushes to the Dept. of Public Works Superintendent Gene Denision and that he would see that they were planted and cared for. At the end of the summer when Mrs. John Reed who represented the club, inspected the gardens, the weeds were higher than the rose bushes and no cultivation had been done all summer. Upon investigation we were advised that the city did not have the extra help necessary to take care of the rose beds. Since the Garden Club had no funds available, Mrs. Reed assumed the expense of having a gardener dig out the weeds and put the two beds in proper condition. The Garden Club then purchased redwood chips and had them spread over the rose beds in order to keep down the growth of weeds. Each spring and fall the roses have been fed and fertilized. Thru the courtesy and generosity of Frank Turner the rose bushes have been pruned each year. In the meantime groups of women of the Garden Club have worked on the rose beds, digging out any shoots of grass or weeds shown coming thru the chips. The Garden Club also donated 32 of the floribunda roses as a border and also a cement bench which was mounted on a cement base by the city. A matching bench was donated by several contributions. There were put on either side of the

flagpole at the head of the gardens. The club, thru their efforts, was able to have donated to them thru the Palm Mortuary in Las Vegas, metal markers with the names on them which were placed in front of each rose bush. The Rose Garden has been outstanding in its appearance and our club has been complimented many times for contributing so nicely to the beautification of the cemetery. The rose bushes have now grown to the extent that our members do not feel it is physically possible for them to carry on this chore. The club recently hired help to put the rose beds in condition but voted that they could no longer afford to pay for this care and did not feel that they could do the work themselves. At this meeting it was voted to write a letter to the city manager asking that the city assume the care of the Rose Gardens especially since they had recently taken over the entire ownership and supervision of the cemetery. However, City Manager Dr. Guild Gray, replied that while he was sympatric with our dilemma, the city did not have nor could it employ the extra help needed to take care of this project. It is because of our present predicament that the Nevada State Federation of Garden Clubs have offered to prune our rose bushes next Saturday to save them from becoming bramble bushes. The Hoe and Grow Garden Club is bringing these facts to the attention of the residents of this community many of whom have contributed to the Rose Garden, in the hope that they might help as either to convince the City Council that this project should be cared for by the city or suggest any other means by which these beautiful roses may be property cared for. Originally the Garden Club never agreed to keep up the care of the rose beds, only, to plant the roses and place the markers beside them. It only assumed the care when the city did not follow thru as it was understood it would. Many of our women are employed and do not have the time to spend doing this gardening which has grown to be too much for a woman to assume over the past year. The club members are concerned for the contributors and don't want to sit by and see their investments not protected. Hoe and Grow Garden Club, Eldora N. Reed.

Boulder City News, Thursday, 15 Jan 1970.
Landmark Burned
Boulder firefighters in a practice session burned down the little, 26-year-old sexton's house at the B. C. Cemetery last week. The B. C. Cemetery Association was formed in 1943 with Tom Godbey as its president and Elton Garrett as secretary all through the years until the association dissolved recently when the city took over the responsibility. Capt. and Mrs. Bill Getts were the cottage's first tenants and the little house had been purchased from the Bureau of Reclamation on a $76 bid. It was formerly located at 552 Seventh St. The house was set on a foundation built with volunteer labor and donations of $166 were collected from several craft unions and organizations to put the home in shape.

Boulder City News, Thursday, 6 Sep 1973, 1:4-5.
Cemetery Extension Plans Readied
Mardi Corderman, city planner, said this week that the city's cemetery is being enlarged 1.75 acres to the south of the existing cemetery. The new area will consist of approximately 725 gravesites, and engineers are working on the plans at the present time. There are 1409 gravesites in the present cemetery. The present cemetery consists of 3.21 acres of land, and the city has reserved many acres in that area for cemetery use. According to the city, the front of the cemetery will be remodeled so that entrance can be made from Adams and Utah streets. There will be a paved parking area and a green belt for beautification. Miss Corderman said there will be a new marking system and map so that those coming to the cemetery may more easily identify their graves.

Boulder City News, Thursday, 14 Feb 1974, 1:1.
Cemetery Enlargement Underway
City crews removed a portion of the rear fence surrounding the Boulder City cemetery early this week in preparation for expanding the boundaries to include the approximately 1.12 acres, directly behind the current site. The new addition will be fenced to be included within the perimeter fencing . . . grass will be planted . . . and the present circular roadway changed to circle through the new portion. The new addition contains 596 plots, according to city officials.

Boulder City News, Thursday, 16 May 1974, 2:6.
Cemetery Fee Increase Discussed
A resolution increase cemetery fees was tabled by the City Council Tuesday after considerable discussion. The resolution was presented by City Manager Mayhlon Degernes who noted that the Cemetery Fund had been steadily declining in recent years. "The purpose for requesting a change in fees is because we're running out of money," he explained. "If we wish to make the cemetery reasonably self supporting, we must increase the rates." He added that cemetery fund began with $33,000 . . . and that is was now down to almost $24,000. It was noted that the latest drop is in large part because of recent expansion. As proposed by the City Manager, the cost of an adult lot would increase from $125 to $225; an infant lot would increase from $50 to $90; vaults would increase, as would grave services and monuments.

Boulder City News, Thursday, 30 May 1974, 6:5.
Cemetery Improvement Complimented
As a result of a program of expansion and improvement, the Boulder City Cemetery is now in the best shape it has been for many years according to many townspeople here. Comments in this regard were offered at the meeting of the City Council on Tuesday. Councilman Tom Cooper introduced the subject with words of commendation for the Public Works program which accomplished the feat. Several members of the audience spoke out in agreement. The project was under the direction of Public Works Director Robert Eads. Al Mayo, landscaping foreman, was in direct control of the program. He was assisted by Mike Quinn and M. C. Newbanks. Also taking part in the project were Bob Unverdorf, Howard Clarke and Richard Belding.

Legislative Reports Relating to the Boulder City Cemetery

Unpublished House Committee Hearings
Hpul-T.14

79th Congress, 1st Session
H. R. 3966

A BILL

Authorizing the Secretary of the Interior to convey certain lands situated in Clark County, Nevada, to the Boulder Cemetery Association for cemetery purposes.

By Mr. BUNKER

September 6, 1945
Referred to the Committee on the Public Lands

The Chairman. It has a favorable report and gives the history of the land. They suggested this:
"That title to all of said land shall rever to the United States in any of the following events," and provide for just corrective verbiage up in the provision of forfeiture, they want it worded a little differently.
You can explain that bill very quickly.
STATEMENT OF HON. BERKELEY L. BUNKER,
A Representative in Congress from the State of Nevada.
Mr. Bunker. This is the situation: Boulder City land is owned by the federal government. There is no cemetery and they have to carry people thirty miles to have them buried. And the Bureau of Reclamation will establish a cemetery there and are willing to, but in order to do so they have to turn this land over to the Boulder City Cemetery Association, and that is what this bill does.
Mr. White. It looks like in Boulder City that a man has to die before he can obtain title to a little piece of land.
Mr. Savage. This is an admission that people do not live forever down there.

Mr. Bunker. The fact that they only need this one cemetery is an admission that when they leave Nevada they pass away.

Mr. Holmes. I move it be reported favorably.

The Chairman. And the intent is you would forfeit under their amendment?

Mr. Bunker. Yes, we want the amendment.

The Chairman. But instead of saying, "title to all of said land shall revert to the United States in any of the following events," the Department suggests saying, "that title, to such of said lands as should, in the judgment of the Secretary, so revert, shall revert to the United States in any of the following events."

Mr. Savage. I move it be adopted.

Mr. LeCompte. That motion is seconded.

The Chairman. All in favor of the amendment to the bill say "aye", those opposed "no".

Mr. White. I now move that the bill be reported as amended.

Mr. LeCompte. The motion is seconded.

The Chairman. It has been moved and seconded that the bill be reported.

(The committee passed to the consideration of other bills.)

- - - - -

House of Representatives Report No. 1878
H. R. 3966
79th Congress, 2d Session
Union Calendar No. 548

IN THE HOUSE OF REPRESENTATIVES
September 6, 1945
Mr. BUNKER: introduced the following bill: which was referred to the Committee on the Public Lands

April 5, 1946
Reported with amendments, committed to the Committee of the Whole House on the State of the Union, and ordered to be printed
[omit the part struck through and insert the part printed in italic]

Boulder City Cemetery: Boulder City, Nevada 357

A BILL

Authorizing the Secretary of the Interior to convey certain lands situated in Clark County, Nevada, to the Boulder Cemetery Association for cemetery purposes.

1 *Be it enacted by the Senate and House of Representa-*
2 *tives of the United States of America in Congress assembled,*
3 That the Secretary of the Interior be, and he hereby is,
4 authorized to convey to the Boulder City Cemetery Asso-
5 ciation, a rural cemetery association incorporated pursuant

6 to the laws of the State of Nevada, for cemetery purposes,
7 upon such terms and conditions as he may prescribe and sub-
8 ject to such rules and regulations for the protection of
9 property and interests of the United States of America and

2.

1 for the preservation of the public health, safety, and wel-
2 ware in Boulder City, Nevada, and vicinity, as may there-
3 after be promulgated by him or pursuant to this authority
4 all right, title, and interest of the United State of America
5 in and to certain lands in Clark County, State of Nevada
6 heretofore withdrawn for reclamation purposes, described
7 as follows:
8 The east half of the southwest quarter of the northwest
9 quarter of the northwest quarter of the southwest quarter,
10 the southeast quarter of the northwest quarter of the north-
11 west quarter of the southwest quarter, the west half of the
12 southwest quarter of the southwest quarter, the west half of the
13 quarter of the southwest quarter, the east half of the north-
14 west quarter of the southwest quarter of the northwest quar-
15 ter of the southwest quarter, the northeast quarter of the
16 southwest quarter of the northwest quarter of the south-
17 west quarter, and the west half of the northwest quarter of
18 the southeast quarter of the northwest quarter of the south-
19 west quarter, section 10, township 23 south, range 64 east
20 Mount Diablo base and meridian. Nevada, consisting of ten
21 acres, more or less, by deed reserving a right-of-way thereon
22 for the construction, operation, and maintenance of electric

23	transmission lines and telephone lines constructed by the
24	authority of the United States or under permit from the
25	Secretary of the Interior: *Provided*, That title to all [crossout] such

3.

1	of said lands *as should in the judgment of the Secretary*
2	*so revert* shall revert to the United States in any of the
3	following events: (a) if any portion of said lands shall cease
4	to be used and maintained for cemetery purposes: (b) if any
5	portion of said lands shall be used for any purpose other
6	than cemetery purposes: or (c) if said association shall
7	violate any of the rules or regulations hereafter promulgated
8	by the Secretary of the Interior pursuant to this Act and
9	if the Secretary, whose decision shall be final, shall determine
10	in writing that as a result of such violation the interests of
11	the United States require a reverter of said lands: a reverter
12	resulting from any of the aforesaid events shall become
13	effective upon the filing for record by the Secretary with
14	the Recorder of Clark County, State of Nevada, of a decla-
15	ration that a reverter has occurred for reasons therein stated
16	and upon the service of a copy thereof upon the association
17	by regular mail addressed to it at its last known address.

- - - - -

House of Representatives Report No. 1878
79th Congress, 2d Session

AUTHORIZING THE SECRETARY OF THE INTERIOR TO CONVEY CERTAIN LANDS SITUATED IN CLARK COUNTY, NEV., TO THE BOULDER CITY CEMETERY ASSOCIATION FOR CEMETERY PURPOSES

April 5, 1946 – Committed to the Committee of the Whole House on the state of the Union and ordered to be printed

Mr. Bunker, from the Committee on the Public Lands, submitted the following
REPORT
[To accompany H. R. 3966]

The Committee on the Public Lands, to whom was referred the bill (H. R. 3966), authorizing the Secretary of the Interior to convey certain lands situated in Clark County, Nev., to the Boulder City Cemetery Association for cemetery purposes, having considered the same, report favorably thereon without amendment and with the recommendation that it do pass.

The amendment is as follows:

In line 24, page 2, delete the word "all" and substitute "such"; and in line 25, page 2, following the word "lands", insert "as should in the judgment of the Secretary so revert,".

EXPLANATION OF THE BILL

The purpose of this bill is to authorize the Secretary of the Interior to convey approximately 10 acres of land near Boulder City, Nev., heretofore withdrawn for reclamation purposes, to the Boulder City Cemetery Association for cemetery purposes.

Enactment of this legislation, as amended, was recommended by the Department of the Interior in a letter of March 11, 1946, as follows:

Hon. J. HARDIN PETERSON,
Chairman, Committee on the Public Lands,
House of Representatives.

MY DEAR MR. PETERSON: I am glad to comply with your request for a report on H. R. 3966, a bill authorizing the Secretary of the Interior to convey certain lands situated in Clark County, Nev., to the Boulder City Cemetery Association for cemetery purposes.

I recommend that the bill be enacted.

This bill, if enacted, would authorize the conveyance to the Boulder City Cemetery Association, for use as a cemetery, of approximately 10 acres of land, heretofore withdrawn for reclamation purposes, near Boulder City, Nev.

    For some time the residents of Boulder City have expressed the desire that a cemetery be established in or near the city. This Department has favored the establishment of such a cemetery. At one time consideration was given to the operation of a cemetery within Boulder City at Government expense. The site within the city which had been tentatively designated for that purpose became unavailable when it was included in Camp Williston, which was constructed by the War Department. The cemetery site described in the above-mentioned bill is located about 1 mile outside the limits of Boulder City, and the operation by the Government of the cemetery at this location would entail additional expense and the hiring of additional personnel, which, in my opinion, would not be justified. The Boulder City Cemetery Association, organized on March 9, 1943, pursuant to Nevada law, by residents of Boulder City, has requested the enactment of the above bill in order that it may operate the desired cemetery on the terms set out in the bill. In my opinion, these terms would adequately protect the interests of the Government.

    During the summer of 1941 the proposed cemetery site was tested and a suitable design prepared and staked. The first interment occurred on May 2, 1942. A total of 26 interments has been made to date.

    In anticipation of the enactment of legislation, such as this bill, which would enable ti to own and to operate the cemetery, the association has planted grass and shade trees. It has erected a cottage for the use of a caretaker, and it has made provision for water, electricity, and sanitary facilities. The association advises that it has also entered into agreements with the heirs of all but tow of the interred persons covering the care of the respective graves. These agreements provide for the purchase by the heirs of the respective cemetery lots from the association and that the association shall care for and maintain said lots in consideration of the payment of $5 a year or of $100 for perpetual care and maintenance. In some instances the heirs, in recognition of the association's need of funds, have paid the purchase price as well as the maintenance charges and have accepted receipts pending the associations delivery of deeds for the respective lots. The association has advised that it was unable to obtain agreements from the heirs of two fo the interred persons but has given its assurance that the graves of these persons will receive the same care as those covered by agreements.

The bill authorizes the conveyance in question to be made upon such terms and conditions as the Secretary of the Interior may prescribe. If this bill is enacted, I propose to require that the cemetery shall be available for the burial of persons of all religious persuasions as well as persons professing no religious beliefs. Operation of the cemetery by the association would satisfy an existing need. In my opinion, the association should be permitted to administer the cemetery which it has initiated and sponsored. The conveyance to the association of the cemetery site would enable the association to carry on its present plans for the development and maintenance of the cemetery.

Your committee may wish to consider the desirability of amending the first part of the proviso, beginning in line 24, on page 2 of the bill, to read as follows: "*Provided*, That title, to such of said lands as should in the judgment of the Secretary so revert, shall revert to the United States in any of the following events:". In my judgment, an amendment along these lines is advisable for administrative purposes and , particularly, to the end of avoiding, except in extraordinary cases, reversion to the United States of lands in which interments have been made.

The Director of the Bureau of Budget has informed me that there is no objection to the presentation of this report to your committee.

Sincerely yours,

Oscar L. Chapman,

Acting
Secretary of the Interior.

Senate Report No. 1365
Calendar No. 1392
79th Congress, 2d Session

AUTHORIZING THE SECRETARY OF THE INTERIOR TO CONVEY CERTAIN LANDS SITUATED IN CLARK COUNTY, NEV., TO THE BOULDER CITY CEMETERY ASSOCIATION FOR CEMETERY PURPOSES.

May 21 (legislative day, March 5), 1946 – Ordered to be printed.

Mr. Hatch, from the Committee on Public Lands and Surveys, submitted the following.

REPORT
[To accompany H. R. 3966]

The Senate Committee on Public Lands and Surveys, to whom was referred the bill (H. R. 3966), authorizing the Secretary of the Interior to convey certain lands situated in Clark County, Nev., to the Boulder City Cemetery Association for cemetery purposes, having considered the same, report favorably thereon without amendment and with the recommendation that it do pass.

The purpose of the bill is to authorize the Secretary of the Interior to convey approximately 10 acres of land near Boulder City, Nev., heretofore withdrawn for reclamation purposes.

The proposed legislation has the endorsement of the Department of the Interior and its aims and purposes are further detailed in the report of the Department to the chairman of the House Committee on the Public Lands, which report is hereinbelow set forth in full and made a part of this report:

Hon. J. HARDIN PETERSON,
    Chairman, Committee on the Public Lands,
        House of Representatives.

MY DEAR MR. PETERSON: I am glad to comply with your request for a report on H. R. 3966, a bill authorizing the Secretary of the Interior to convey certain lands situated in Clark County, Nev., to the Boulder City Cemetery Association for cemetery purposes.

I recommend that the bill be enacted.

Boulder City Cemetery: Boulder City, Nevada

This bill, if enacted, would authorize the conveyance to the Boulder City Cemetery Association, for use as a cemetery, of approximately 10 acres of land, heretofore withdrawn for reclamation purposes, near Boulder City, Nev.

For some time the residents of Boulder City have expressed the desire that a cemetery be established in or near the city. This Department has favored the establishment of such a cemetery. At one time consideration was given to the operation of a cemetery within Boulder City at Government expense. The site within the city which had been tentatively designated for that purpose became unavailable when it was included in Camp Williston, which was constructed by the War Department. The cemetery site described in the above-mentioned bill is located about 1 mile outside the limits of Boulder City, and the operation by the Government of the cemetery at this location would entail additional expense and the hiring of additional personnel, which, in my opinion, would not be justified. The Boulder City Cemetery Association, organized on March 9, 1943, pursuant to Nevada law, by residents of Boulder City, has requested the enactment of the above bill in order that it may operate the desired cemetery on the terms set out in the bill. In my opinion, these terms would adequately protect the interests of the Government.

During the summer of 1941 the proposed cemetery site was tested and a suitable design prepared and staked. The first interment occurred on May 2, 1942. A total of 26 interments has been made to date.

In anticipation of the enactment of legislation, such as this bill, which would enable ti to own and to operate the cemetery, the association has planted grass and shade trees. It has erected a cottage for the use of a caretaker, and it has made provision for water, electricity, and sanitary facilities. The association advises that it has also entered into agreements with the heirs of all but tow of the interred persons covering the care of the respective graves. These agreements provide for the purchase by the heirs of the respective cemetery lots from the association and that the association shall care for and maintain said lots in consideration of the payment of $5 a year or of $100 for perpetual care and maintenance. In some instances the heirs, in recognition of the association's need of funds, have paid the purchase price as well as the maintenance charges and have accepted receipts pending the associations delivery of deeds for the respective lots. The association has advised that it was unable to obtain agreements from the heirs of two fo the interred persons but has given its assurance that the graves of these persons will receive the same care as those covered by agreements.

The bill authorizes the conveyance in question to be made upon such terms and conditions as the Secretary of the Interior may prescribe. If this bill is enacted, I propose to require that the cemetery shall be available for the burial of persons of all religious persuasions as well as persons professing no religious beliefs. Operation of the cemetery by the

xiii.

association would satisfy an existing need. In my opinion, the association should be permitted to administer the cemetery which it has initiated and sponsored. The conveyance to the association of the cemetery site would enable the association to carry on its present plans for the development and maintenance of the cemetery.

Your committee may wish to consider the desirability of amending the first part of the proviso, beginning in line 24, on page 2 of the bill, to read as follows: "*Provided*, That title, to such of said lands as should in the judgment of the Secretary so revert, shall revert to the United States in any of the following events:". In my judgment, an amendment along these lines is advisable for administrative purposes and , particularly, to the end of avoiding, except in extraordinary cases, reversion to the United States of lands in which interments have been made.

The Director of the Bureau of Budget has informed me that there is no objection to the presentation of this report to your committee.

Sincerely yours,

Oscar L. Chapman,

Acting

Secretary of the Interior.

- - -

Boulder City, Nevada
City Code

This code was last updated by Ordinance 1191 passed February 25, 2003.

PREFACE

This city code of Boulder City, as supplemented, contains ordinances up to and including ordinance 1191, passed February 25, 2003. Ordinances of the city adopted after said ordinance supersede the provisions of this city code to the extent that they are in conflict or inconsistent therewith. Consult the city office in order to ascertain whether any particular provision of the code has been amended, superseded or repealed.

Sterling Codifiers, Inc., began supplementation of this code in January 2000. Prior to January 2000, supplementation of the code was done by the city.

Sterling Codifiers, Inc.
Coeur d'Alene, Idaho 83815

9-3-1: SHORT TITLE:

This Chapter shall be known and may be cited as *THE BOULDER CITY MUNICIPAL CEMETERY ORDINANCE* . (Ord. 744, 4-26-1983, eff. 5-18-1983)

9-3-2: CEMETERY TRANSFER:

The City Council, by the passage of this Chapter, does hereby accept the dedication of the cemetery property as contained in dedicatory deed from the Boulder City Cemetery Association; said cemetery property to be used for cemetery purposes only and in accordance with Public Law 39 - 79th Congress - 2 D Session, chapter 473 of the Public Laws of the United States of America. The City Council further, by passage of this Chapter, accepts the Cemetery Fund from the Boulder City Cemetery Association. (Ord. 744, 4-26-1983, eff. 5-18-1983)

9-3-3: DEFINITIONS:

For the purposes of this Chapter, the following terms, phrases, words and their derivations shall have the meaning given herein. When not inconsistent with the context, words, used in the present tense include the future, words in the plural number include the singular number, and words in the singular number include the plural number. The word "shall"

is always mandatory and not merely directory.
ADMINISTRATOR OF THE MUNICIPAL CEMETERY: The Director of Community Development.
MUNICIPAL CEMETERY OR CEMETERY: The Municipal Cemetery of the City of Boulder City.
SUPERINTENDENT OF THE MUNICIPAL CEMETERY: The Superintendent of Public Works. (Ord. 744, 4-26-1983, eff. 5-18-1983)

9-3-4: AUTHORITY OF CITY COUNCIL:
The City Council shall fix the following by resolution:
A. Value (sale price) of all unsold lots as presently exist or are provided in the future.
B. Interment fee.
C. Fee for opening and closing of grave.
D. Monument setting fee.
E. Disinterment fee.
F. Such other fees or charges as may be required. (Ord. 744, 4-26-1983, eff. 5-18-1983)

9-3-5: RULES AND REGULATIONS:
The Administrator, with the approval of the City Manager and the City Council, shall establish the rules and regulations for operation, administration and use of the cemetery. (Ord. 744, 4-26-1983, eff. 5-18-1983)

9-3-6: DUTIES OF THE ADMINISTRATOR OF THE MUNICIPAL CEMETERY:
A. Develop Plan: Develop the Municipal Cemetery Expansion Plan for inclusion in the Community Facilities and Services Plan of the Boulder City Comprehensive Plan.
B. Maintain Records: Maintain the administrative records of the Municipal cemetery to include:
1. Lot records of each deceased interred.
2. Lot records of each reserved lot.
3. Mailing of invoice for quarterly payments for reserved lots purchased on an installment basis.
4. Issue cemetery lot deeds on final payment of lots.
5. Update the Municipal cemetery map semi-annually. (Ord. 744, 4-26-

1983, eff. 5-18-1983)

9-3-7: DUTIES OF THE SUPERINTENDENT OF THE MUNICIPAL CEMETERY:

A. Operation And Maintenance: The Superintendent shall be responsible for the operation and maintenance of the Municipal cemetery, subject to any limitations and restrictions set forth herein, or contained in any applicable law or rules or regulations promulgated by the City Manager and City Council.

B. Supervise Interment: The Superintendent shall see that each lot is properly used or occupied, and shall cause graves to be dug to properly inter the deceased when called upon to do so.

C. Monument Setting: The Superintendent shall see that monuments are properly set on the lots in accordance with the current rules and regulations. (Ord. 744, 4-26-1983, eff. 5-18-1983)

9-3-8: RULES FOR INTERMENT:

No deceased person shall be interred in the cemetery until the Administrator has found:

A. Permit Obtained: That the burial permit has been obtained from the public health officer as required by law;

B. Payment Of Lot And Fees: That the lot in which burial is to be made has been fully paid for, or that satisfactory arrangement has been made to assure full payment for the lot and all other interment fees;

C. Right Of Use: That the person to be interred has the right to the use of such lot;

D. Capacity Of Lot: That the lot is not used beyond its capacity as set forth in the rules and regulations. (Ord. 744, 4-26-1983, eff. 5-18-1983)

9-3-9: RULES FOR DISINTERMENT:

No deceased persons shall be disinterred from a lot in the cemetery until the Administrator has found:

A. Request: That a request for disinterment has been processed through a local mortuary of the next of kin's choice;

B. Permit: That a disinterment permit has been obtained from the public health officer if the deceased is to be removed from the Municipal cemetery;

C. Reinterment: That if reinterment is to be in the Municipal cemetery, all provisions of Section 9-3-8 of this Chapter have been met. (Ord. 744, 4-26-1983, eff. 5-18-1983)

9-3-10: SALE OR RESALE OF LOTS:
A. Recording; Map: The Community Development Department shall record the sale of all lots on the Municipal cemetery map, to include reserved lots. The cemetery map shall be available for public inspection in the Community Development Department. There shall be no discrimination in the sale of lots, on any basis.
B. Resale: Cemetery lots may be sold from one individual to another. Resale of lots shall be administratively processed through the Community Development Department. (Ord. 744, 4-26-1983, eff. 5-18-1983)

9-3-11: CEMETERY FUND:
The established Cemetery Fund shall be a self-supporting special activity fund managed by the Finance Director. All fees and charges collected in connection with the cemetery, as well as the cemetery lot sale proceeds, shall be deposited to said Fund. All expenses and disbursements in connection with the cemetery shall be paid out of the Cemetery Fund. (Ord. 744, 4-26-1983, eff. 5-18-1983)

9-3-12: CEMETERY COLLECTIONS AND ACCOUNTS:
All fees and charges in connection with the cemetery shall be collected by the Finance Department. The Finance Department shall make all disbursements from the Cemetery Fund. The Finance Department shall keep full and detailed accounts of the receipts and expenditures of cemetery funds, and shall make appropriate financial reports as required by the City Council and budget procedures. (Ord. 744, 4-26-1983, eff. 5-18-1983)

9-3-13: OPERATIONS AND MAINTENANCE REPORT:
A. Required: The Superintendent shall make an annual report by November 1 to the Finance Director, which shall include:
1. Condition of cemetery.
2. Current fiscal year operation and maintenance expenditures.
3. Recommended changes to fees to ensure the Cemetery Fund remains a self-supporting activity fund to cover operation and maintenance costs. (Ord. 744, 4-26-1983, eff. 5-18-1983)

Obituary Index

Abercrombie, Fred, 138
    John, 138
Abernathy, Mabel, 269
Acosta, Imogene, 134
    Josie, 305
Acquist, Janet, 164
Adair, Connie, 1
    Dallas, 1
    Donald, 1
    Esther, 1
    Teresa, 1
Adams, Charles, 3
    Diane, 53, 54
    Doris, 2
    Fern A., 2
    Frank, 23, 202
    Frank M., 2
    Kathy, 3
    Marilyn, 3
    Mark Charles, 3
    Marlene, 3
    Matthew, 3
    Michelle, 3
    Ryan, 3
Adams, Ethel, 44
    Fern Ada, 1
    Frank, 1
    Frank G., 2
    Frank George, 1
    Leslie, 52
    Mark, 3
Adcock, Betty R., 3
    Earl, 3
    Mark, 3
Ahern, Don, 4
    Katherine, 4
    William, 4
Aikens, Daisy, 193
Aispuro, Buena Vertura, 238
Alldridge, Alvin, 219
    Jack, 219, 227

Allen, George, 87
    Laura May, 117
    Sheila, 68
Alvarez, Andrew T. "Andy", 4
    Carmen, 4
    Frank, 4
    Jennie, 4
Alvey, Mary, 47
Alwood, Patsy, 187
Alyce, Bette, 92
Anderson, Andrea, 85
    Andrea C., 86
    Bill, 5
    Bruce, 85
    Charlene, 80
    Dana, 6
    David, 5
    Elizabeth, 6
    Eric, 6
    Gwendolyn, 5
    Helen, 189
    Ira E, 5
    Irene, 5
    Irma, 169
    Juanita B., 5
    Kathleen Ryan, 258
    LuAnna Rae, 31
    Mark, 6
    Merril V., 5
    Orville G., 6
    Walter Eugene "Moose", 6
Andeway, Susan, 165
Andrew, Adam, 20
    Michael, 20
    Susan, 19
Andrews, Frank, 6
    John Stanley, 6
    Richard, 336

Anese, Father Joe, 125, 206, 228
    Reverend Joe, 160
    Reverend Joseph, 126, 163, 164
Angell, Clairmont, 10
    Victor, 10
Anglade, Diane Cowan, 11
Annese, Father Joe, 13, 36, 49, 108, 163, 225, 235, 284, 286
Apadaca, Maxine, 220
Apple, Donald Walter, 7
    Peter Gilbert, 7
    Timothy Scott, 7
Archer, Robert, 78
Archuletta, Joseph, 209
    Teresa, 178
Arden, Linda L., 84
Arelano, Doris, 257
Arlington, Judy, 328
Armstrong, Wilma, 330
Arnold, Edith, 7
    Gussie, 7
    Hazel, 7
    Jack, 7
    Mabel, 7
    N. W. Jack, 319
    Noah "Jack, 7
Arnts, Janet, 300
    Phil, 300
    Ralph, 300
    Sherrie, 300
Arp, Clarence, 23
Aschenbrenner, James, 257
    Leslie, 257
Ashbaugh, Don, 9, 53, 104, 294
    Patsy I., 150
Asher, Patsy, 203
Atkins, Don, 322
Atkison, Leonard, 72
Attig, Monnie, 79
Atwood, Chester J., 8
    Janet, 8
    Robert E., 8
    Terry, 8
Atz, William, 256
    Willma, 256
Ausberry, Ada, 338
Austin, Edith, 8
    Gene Douglas, 8
    Leona Mae, 8
    Rocklyn Gene, 8
    Robert, 185
    William, 8
Auten, Velma, 26
Averett, Virgil, 259
Aycock, Reverend Ralph, 87
A'Becket, Thomas, 208
Badger, Marjorie, 97
Bailey, Ginny, 24
    Hope, 32
    Joshua, 24
    LeGay, 24
    Mildred, 230
Baird, Walter, 164
    William, 164
Baker, Alice, 126
    Alyce, 140
    Clyde, 93
    Dorothy, 9, 150
    Emily Mae, 130
    Ernest, 232
    Frank, 227
    Harold, 232
    Kenneth, 232
    Lena, 9
    Pearl, 9
    Phillip, 232
    Ruth L., 43
    Sharon, 236
    William Emmett "Bake", 9
Baldus, Fr., 312
Baldwin, Leonard, 55
Ball, George, 27

Ballard, Bryce, 171
    Hirschi, 10
    Lynette Marie, 10
    Shelly Ann, 10
Balmer, Eugene, 11
    Kathryn E., 11
    Larry J., 11
    Michael H., 11
Banks, Bishop, 169
    Ireta, 169
    Nellie A., 11
    William "Bill" W., 11
Banner, Inez, 184
Barber, A. N., 55
Barbera, Jessica, 11
    Michael, 11
    Nicole, 11
    Tina Marie, 11
Barnes, Jake, 334
Barnson, Laurence, 92
    Lawrence, 227
Barrell, Gene L., 225
    Harold, 225
    Harold L., 226
Barrett, Kellie, 321
Barrick, Keith, 116
    Stephen, 116
Barrineau, Harry James, 12
    James R., 12
    Mary, 12
    Steve, 12
    Tanya K., 12
Barrow, Rita, 101
Barry, Ada, 108
    Lawton, 108
Barson, Miller Lawrence, 207
Barth, Norma, 189
Bartlett, Bud, 12
    Donald E., 12
    Elton, 12, 50
    Frank, 165
    Michael, 165
    Naturita, 12
    Walter, 165
    William, 50
    William E., 12
Bash, Jenni, 5
Basiliere, Adelina, 85, 86
Bass, Andrew, 25
    LaVerne, 25
    Melvin, 25
Bassett, Carlter, 198
    Porter, 138, 198
    Roe, 198
Bateman, Reverend Robert, 331
Batemann, Father Robert, 56
Bates, Billie, 4
    Elsie, 120
    Fredrick Elliot, 13
    Laura Ernestine, 13
    Russell Elliot, 13
Batson, Mildred, 203
Baxter, Stormie, 296
Bayo, Daniel, 13, 14
    Darin, 13, 14
    Dave, 14
    Dave J., 13
    Katherine, 13, 14
    Peter J., 14
Beach, Adam, 157
Beall, Marion, 202
Beanush, Ima, 259
Beard, Hobson, 259
    Ronnie, 18
    Vickie, 278
Beasley, Otis, 316
Beatty, Eulila, 238
Beck, Bays, 14
    Cora Cook, 14
    Margaret, 5
    Martha, 252
    Thomas, 14
    Thomas David 14
Beckwith, Ida May, 289
Beebe, Sharon 164

Bees, Bob, 15
    Lester, 15
    Lester Hoyt, 14
    Lucile E., 15
Beevers, Lela , 92
Beggs, Bernice, 15
    Charles, 16
    Chuck, 15
    Peggi, 15
    Terry N., 15
Behr, Mary L., 48, 49
Belding, Don, 49
    Ruthie, 270
Belknap, Bill, 169
    William, 58
Bell, Edith, 132
    Laura, 16, 51, 317
    Norman E., 16
    Vernon J. (Dutch) , 16
Belleville, Ella, 243
Bellis, G. Mike, 138
    Helen, 138
    Maude, 138
    Robert E., 138
    Tina, 138
Bellor, Betty, 17
    Elizabeth "Betty", 16, 17
    James, 17, 92
    James R., 16
    Jim, 295
Bender, Merna, 337
    Robert, 27
Beneda, Earl, 18
    James, 18
    Joseph, 18
    Lawrence R, 17
    Melba, 17
    Nellie, 18
    Robert , 18
    Stanley Robert, 18
Bennett, Andrea, 18
    Barbara, 18
    Betty Sue, 19

    Dave, 18
    David, 18
    Elizabeth, 18
    Haley Samantha, 18
    Jane, 18
    Mamie, 24
    Pete, 189
    Randy, 18
    Sarah Bessie, 18
    Waldo, 18
Benson, Billie, 20
    Craig, 19
    Don, 19, 20
    Earl, 19
    Lenoe, 19, 20
    Lucille "Billie", 19
    Steven, 19
    Taft, 19, 20
Bently, Mary A., 274
Berg, Florence, 289
Bernard, Carolyn Dawn, 285
    Coralyn, 284
    W. M., 285
    W. N., 284
Berry, Patricia, 289
    Suzanne, 208
Betlack, Charlotte, 157
Betts, Delbert, 113
    Devra, 113
Beuschlein, Louis, 125
Bezaire, Ruth, 150
Bicknell, Amy, 20
    Charles, 20
    Charles "Chuck", 202
    Deborah, 20
    Deborah S., 20
    Glen D., 202
Biddlestone, Delores, 218
Bidgenbach, Anna, 215
Bierce, Marguerite M., 21
    Walter, 21
    Walter B, 21
Bing, Alvin, 134

Bingham, Auretta, 301
Bird, Helen, 264
    Lavon, 12
    Thelma, 12, 50
Bisbee, Clair. A. "Biz", 21
    Gail, 21
    Roy, 21, 22
Bishop, William, 172
Bivins, Treca, 32
Black, Becky Lea, 312
    Betty JoAnn, 312
    Darrell W., 312
    Dave, 93
    Jeffrey L., 312
    Lucille, 193
    Minnie, 193
    Robert J., 312
    Terry Allen, 312
Blackwell, John, 23
    Nora E., 23
Blair, Edgar, 23
    Esper Mills, 23
    Hobart, 23, 275
    Hobert, 1
Blanset, Gene Quin, 204
Bloomer, Ruth, 283
Bloyer, Leona, 58
    Marie, 58
Boaz, D. J., 249
Bochmann, Bessie Dena, 23
    Karl H, 23, 24
Boehmer, Anna, 23
Boero, Sandra, 68
Bogart, Frederick L., 24
    LeFay, 24
Boggs, Martha, 114
Bohn, Kurt, 1
Bohte, Arleen, 125
    Jerry, 125
Bolser, P. J., 307
Boners, James, 143
Bonnell, Paul, 92

Boris, Beatrice, 24
    Marshall, 24
    Ron, 24
Bornhoft, Al, 134
    Jean, 80
Boston, Jemima, 241
Bouchard, Antoinette, 85, 86
Boucher, Laurie, 151
Bounty, Clay, 139
    Liann, 139
Bourget, Janelle, 25
    Jeffrey, 25
    June S., 25
Bourne, Al, 183
    Marilyn, 113
Bousman, Bill, 174
    Jerry, 174
    Larry, 174
Bow, Nora, 234
Bowers, Maurine, 31
Bowler, Jane, 208
Bowman, Mrs., 65
Bowser, Custis, 112
Boyce, Ann E., 2
    Ann Elizabeth, 1
    Harvey Walter, 1, 2
    Harvey Wood, 1
    R. Scott, 2
    Raymond, 1
    Rebecca, 1
Boyd, Joseph, 128
    Shirley, 181
Boyer, Carle, 25
    Gertrude Jetnnette, 204
    Sandra Jane, 25
    Winifred N., 25
Boynton, A. G., 22, 181, 227
Bozzano, Bernice, 26
    Bernice M., 26
    Carole, 26
    Gerald, 26
    Leonard, 26
    Silvio, 26

Brack, Reverend Lavern, 303
Bradley, Bob, 26
    Bruce, 26
    Darell, 26
    Deveda, 26
    Gary, 26
    Robert, 26
    Vernet, 26
Bradshaw, James, 138
Brady, George, 234
Brandt, Florence, 27
    Joseph Norma, 27
Brann, R. W., 22
Brannan, George, 127
    Jeff, 127
Brassel, Ruby, 123
Brasuell, Ruby, 122
Braun, Joyce, 326
Bray, Bette Jean, 283, 284
Brayton, Dennis, 27
    Kimberly, 27
    Sharon L., 27
Brenbarger, Evelyn, 28
    Todd, 28
    William P., 28
Brennan, Margaret, 28
    Richard P., 28
    Ruth, 72
Brewer, Wanda, 283, 284
Bridgman, Charles, 195
Brignall, Clifford, 130
Brincic, Joe, 127
Brinkerhoff, Cheryl, 212
    Chester William, 211
    Delora, 212
    Kay, 212
    Stephen, 212
    William, 212
Brisendine, Oneita , 23
Bristo, Glen, 264
Broadbent, Robert, 127
Brockett, Dale, 322
Bromley, Reverend William, 230

Brooks, Daniel L., 68
    Leonard J., 68
    Sharon Jean, 71
Brothers, Earl, 48, 300
    Louise, 338
Brotherton, James R., 249
Brown, Bob, 29
    David, 29
    Ernest, 29
    Kimberly Susan, 28
    Larry, 29
    Loeta, 28
    Marjorie, 247
    Mary, 29
    Myrtle, 97
    Quinten, 206
    Reverend David, 141
    Robert, 28, 29, 300
    Ted (Patricia), 71
    Udell, 206
    Verna , 212
Browne, Angela, 89
    Celeste, 201
Bruce, Clarence, 119
Brungardt, Guy, 156
Bryant, E. P., 22
    Ernest P., 181
Buckhart, Marilyn, 166
Budd, Elaine, 18
    John, 18
Buesgens, Marsha, 68
Bujarske, Bernard, 290
    Paul, 290
Bulloch, Bruce, 118
Bunch, Hazel, 161
Bunker, Archie Wendell, 30
    Gary, 30
    Marion Mott, 30
    Richard, 30
    Robert, 30

Bunting, Anthony Robert, 31
    Gordon P., 31
    L. Don, 31
    LaRue, 31
    Roger C., 31
    Sandra Lee, 31
    Warren Robert, 31
Burbridge, Rue Allena, 141
Burgan, Glynn Hyde, 31
    Paul, 31
Burger, Nora, 99
Burgess, Patricia J., 199
Burgett, Mary Jane, 270
Burk, Mertie T., 32
    Vern, 32
Burkhardt, Carmen, 135
Burkhart, Charles, 76
Burnett, Atrice O., 32
    Clayton Claude, 32
Burnett, Flora, 32
Burns, Brenda, 85
    Charles M., 338
    Denita Lynn, 156
    Derald, 85
    Harris Leroy, 264
    Kathleen, 338
    Lottie, 85
    Rex, 264
Burr, Gladys, 32
    John L., 32
    Lonnie, 32
Burrill, Marilou, 248
Burroughs, Ben, 291
Burson, Eunice, 63
Burt, Al, 168
    Alton, 119
    Elmo D., 33
    Julie, 224, 225
    LeRoy, 21, 169-171, 207
    Lester, 39
    Lucille, 170, 171
    Olive, 33
    Thomas, 33

Burton, Sarah, 46
Bush, David, 20
    Don, 20
    Mark, 20
    Samuel E., 33
    Stanley E., 33
Butterfield, Fran, 315
Butzerin, Hazel, 22
Buxton, Patricia, 96
Bybee, Anita, 142
Byrne, Adelaide, 293
    John, 293
Bywater, Joyce, 240
Cacace, Cyril, 34
    Fortunato "Forty", 34
    Gladys, 34
Cadaret, Margaret, 96
Cagle, Vivian T., 33
Cahill, Dorothy, 32
Caldwell, Jack, 134, 173, 301, 319
    Willa, 217
Caldwine, Willis, 290
Caless, Chelsea, 165
Callaco, Idie, 220
Callazo, Ida Mae, 220
Calvin, Maureen, 52
    Vanassa, 52
Cameron, Don, 329
    Donalane, 329
    Donald, 324
    Karl, 329
    Wally, 329
Camp, William, 184
Campbell, Delmar, 34
    Donald D., 158
    Ella, 298
    George, 229
    Heather, 34
    James R., 158
    Kathryn, 35
    Steel E., 34
    William, 153

Candelaria, Cesario, 35
    Gilbert, 35
    Julia, 35
    Pete, 35
    Rafael, 35
Caniglia, Andrew, 35
    Donald, 35
    Emido, 35
    Fannie, 35
Cannon, B. C., 255
    Claude, 255
    Bernard, 255
    L. E., 255
    Walter, 255
Cantrell, F. M., 37
Capito, Julia, 219
Caputo, Dorothy, 235
Card, Mildred, 117
Cardoni, Pete, 329
Carl, Dr. Ernest, 36
    Ermgard, 36
    Hugo, 36
Carlgren, Mitchell, 55
Carlman, Vicki, 239, 240
Carlson, C. Emil, 333
    Herbert J., 36
    Marie, 36
Carlton, Amy, 174
    Linda Diann, 174
Carlyle, Nancy, 213
Carmichael, Walter, 284
Carnes, Earl, 21
    Royanna, 21
Carney, Frances, 37
    Jerome D, 37
    Louie J., 37
Carpenter, Everett, 92
    Harold, 92
    Janet, 138
Carroll, Barry Wayne, 37
    Gary, 37
    Joann, 37

Carse, Cliff, 94
    Clifford C., 38
    Edward M., 38
    Joyce Carroll, 94
Carson, Charles T., 38
    Charles Victor, 39
    Jaylene, 273
Carter, Daisy, 247
    E. Paul, 295
Carter, Anneliese, 86
Carver, Benjamin S., 39
    Bud, 39
    "Dad", 39
    Georgia, 39
Casann, Josephine, 251
Casazza, Assunta, 251
    Michelina, 251
    Sabato, 251
Cascioppo, Cindy, 257
Case, Linda, 66
Castleberry, Sharon, 311
Cathey, Alva, 72
Cattoir, Debbie Davis, 70
Caven, Sally, 232
Caviglie, Father Caesar, 35
Cavis, Arthur B., 40
    Grant, 40
    Vergie, 40
Center, Cheri G., 84
Cerrington, V. W., 179
Chamberlain, Afton, 41
    Cal, 41
    Cecil, 41
    Gary C., 41
    Irma, 41
    Jaron, 41
    Judy, 41
    Kevin 41, 43
    Lamar E., 41
    Leone H., 41
    Roy, 41

Chambers, C. W., 192
    Clement, 42
    Clement W., 41
    Fred, 192
    Leila, 192
    Leila M., 42
    Leila McCollum, 42
Chandler, Janella, 44
    Richard, 208
    Robert, 208
Chapman, Clifford, 42
    Clyde, 42
    Elwood C., 42
    Gicela, 42
    Gloria, 42
    Lora, 200
    Valerie, 42
Chappell, M. L., 195
    Mrs., 195
Charest, Janice, 42
Charrette, Mary, 233
Chase, Dick, 221
Chastain, Terry, 319
Cheadle, Margaret Weller Titus, 43
Cheney, David, 43
    Louise O., 43
    Michael, 43
    Steven, 43
    Tomi, 43
Chesley, Dale A., 44
    Dave, 44
    John Albert "Bert", 44
    Opal, 44
Chester, Charles, 333
Childers, Thea, 148
Childress, Esther, 44
    L. Earl, 45
    Leslie Pryor, 44
    Stanley, 45
Chilson, Harry Orville, 45
    Rose, 45
Chipman, Kay M., 168

Chisum, Can, 278
    Carol, 278
    Christi, 279
Christanson, Gayle, 45
    Lyn, 45
Christensen, Frank, 236
    Phyllis, 2
    Sandy, 115
Christianson, Blanche, 270
    Gudrun 45
    Hans, 45
    Paul, 45
Christos, Cretia, 67
Chubbs, Gwenn, 147, 323
Churchill, R. L., 284, 285
Clair, Allen D., 46
    Charles R., 46
    Clifford R., 46
    Frances, 46
    Gilbert D., 46
    Joseph L., 199
    Marvin L., 46
    Orville D., 46
Clarahan, Shirley, 208
Clark, Charles (Chuck), 48
    Cleo F., 46
    Earl Jr., 48
    Erle, 47
    Erle Douglas "Pop", 46
    Fannie, 276
    G. Mabel, 47
    George, 92
    Guy W., 47
    Iva, 224
    Jack J., 47
    James, 47
    L. E., 294
    Lena, 48
    Lowell E. "Tex", 47
    Mabel, 47
    Marvel, 73
    Robert, 47, 48
    Robert C. "Sparky", 48

Wilba "Billie", 47
Winfield, 156
Winfield R., 47
Clarke, Howard, 210
    Robert, 210
Cleef, Rosella Jean, 189
Clegg, Arnold, 48, 49
    Blanche F., 48
    Jack, 48, 49
    John, 49
    William, 48, 49
Cleland, Julie, 229
Clements, Berni, 49
    Ila, 104
    Ila Godbey, 291
    James Alfred, 49
    Marie, 49
    Michael, 49
Cleveland, Burl, 79
    Dorothy, 77, 79
Clifford, Rose, 306
Clift, Barry, 84
    Barry L., 83
    Harvey, 84
    Harvey J., 83
    Ira Rolland B., 83
    Rolland, 84
Clough, Marquerite, 311
Cluver, Pastor Steve, 68
Cockrum, Jack, 245
Cody, Jack, 194
    James, 194
Coffin, Helen C., 49
Coggins, Clyde, 91
    Clyde A., 50
    Michael, 50
    Russell, 50, 173
Cohen, Marcella, 279
Cole, Dorene, 12
    Elsie Dorene, 50
    Etta S., 50
    J. E. "Bob", 202
    J. E. Jr., 50
    Jay, 189
    Jean S., 318
    Peter N., 50
    Roy, 167
    Steve, 189
    Steven, 50
Colhopp, Dorothy, 116
Collins, Diana, 52
    Elinor, 240
    Leona, 52, 53
    Lillian, 51, 52, 314
    Ray, 52, 53, 176
Colyar, Claudia, 157
    David, 157
    Jeni, 157
    Jesse, 157
Comeau, Diana, 305
Compton, Jane, 301
    Lloyd, 301
Condit, Mabel, 137
Conger, Charlotte M., 54
    Ethel F., 54
    Francis L., 54
    Frank, 54
    Isaac N., 54
    James, 54
    Joe, 54
    Mary E., 54
    William, 54
    William E., 54
    William P., 54
Conides, Eldra, 186, 200
Conine, Lee, 91, 92
Connelly, Fanny, 214
Conner, Cathy, 242
Conners, Myrtle F., 55
    Robert, 55
Connolly, Fanny, 62
    John, 289
Connor, Eva, 55
    Jeremiah, 55
    Jeremiah I., 55

Conrad, Louie, 43
    Warren, 43
Constantine, James, 245
Conti, Sadie, 304
Cook, Boyd, 289
    Charles, 289
    Constance, 56
    Ina, 56
    Jerry, 56
    Royce, 56
    Sue, 56
    Teresa Helene, 122
Cooke, Irma, 194
Coolbaugh, Yea, 204
Cooper, Clarence L., 241
    Clay O'Brien, 334
    Della H., 57
    Edgar E., 241
    Florence, 51
    Frank D., 56, 57
    Harold, 241
    Hazel, 57
    James, 57
    Linda, 202
    Melvin, 114
    Mildred, 254
    Robert M., 241
    Ronald, 114
    Theodore, 114
    Tom, 239
    Udine, 336
    Wilma, 239, 306
Corbin, Harold, 204
Corcoran, George, 39
Corderman, Edith, 58
    Edith E., 57
    Eugene, 57
    Gerald, 57, 58
    Marti, 57, 58
    Raini, 57
    Ralph, 58
    Richard, 57, 58
    Sissy, 57

Cordova, Dan L., 58
Corey, Maxie, 203
Corry, David, 144
    Steven, 144
Corwell, Barbara, 189
Cotterill, John R., 58
Coughlin, Flora, 225
    Frances, 225
Courthey, Ernest, 296
Courtney, Leo, 153, 289
Cowan, Anita, 59
    B. W., 138
    Ben, 59, 60
    Carl, 116
    Carolyn, 59
    Edna, 59, 60
    Eugene, 61
    Harry, 59
    Harry Welrose, 60
    Jacqueline, 61
    John, 59
    John R., 60
    LuElla, 61
    LuElla Meldrum, 60
    LuJean, 61
    Phyliss, 59
    Robert, 23
    Robert A., 11
Cowely, Bill, 62
    Margaret, 62
Craft, Elizabeth, 283
    Ila, 206
    William, 206
Crain, Al, 63
    Dell, 63
    Jacob A., 63
    Kristin, 63
    Timothy, 63
Crane, Virginia, 18
Crawford, Marian, 325
Crellin, Annie Henzie, 161
    Mr., 161

Crim, Helen, 225
    John, 225
Crincic, Catherine, 127
Criswell, Reverend Kenneth, 256
Criswold, Sharon, 132
Crossley, Ann, 63
    Harda, 63
    Joy D., 63
    Patrick, 63
Crowell, Benny, 195
    Maud Kathryn, 36
Cruz, Elsie, 35
Cudlip, Brad, 102
Culp, Julie, 64
    Sonia, 64
    Stuart W., 64
Cummings, Artie B., 64
    Edith, 208
Cunningham, Janice, 66
Cuppa, Elvira, 238
Curley, S. A., 195
Curry, C. E., 97
    Dennis, 65
    Gertrude, 65
    Gertrude Baker, 64
    Harry, 64
    Harry E, 65
    Herbert L., 65
    Nita , 65
Curtis, Christian, 66
    Henry, 66
    Henry Starr, 65
    Jesse, 65
    Julie, 66
    Maren, 66
    Nathaniel, 66
    Robert, 279
    Robyn, 279
    Shirley, 279
    Starr, 65, 66
    Vi, 66
Cysewski, Myrtle, 149

Dailey, James, 158
    Jane, 158
    Mary Jane, 158
Dake, Ed, 66
    Finis, 66
    Jack, 66
    Leo "Pete", 66
    Pat, 66
    Ron, 66
Daly, Georgia, 271
    Reverend Thomas, 122
Dana, David W, 67
    Florence W., 67
    Lee H., 67
Dane, Tim, 121
    Virginia, 121
Dangerfield, Genevieve, 119
Daniel, Frances, 274
    Mary, 190
    Richard, 188
Daniels, Beaulh, 189
Danneberger, Marion "Dan", 67
    Robert, 67
    Ruth, 67
Dart, Marilyn, 279
Darton, Vera, 334
Dastrup, Merrill, 288
David, Alice, 44
Davidson, Marshall W., 71
    Sandra K., 71
    Sheila F., 71
    Wanda M., 71
    Wanda Mae, 68
Davies, Morris E., 68
    Paul, 68
Davis, Amelia, 68, 109
    Andrea Leigh, 70
    Bill, 68
    Clint Michael, 70
    Donald, 71
    Donna Marie, 70
    Frank, 1
    Henry, 68

James, 71
Jeanette, 12
Jon F., 70
Joseph, 68
Kilene, 228
Kyle Clifton, 70
L. P., 295
Leonard, 68, 69
Mary Eleanor, 108
Nona, 71
Ralph, 70
Richard, 71
Robert, 71
Robert R., 71
Rosemary, 295
Velma, 70
William "Bill", 69
Dawson, Albert, 323
    Charles Earl, 71
    Ina Jean Smith, 71
    John C. "Jake", 71
    John S. "Jack", 71
    Patricia Ann Clawson, 71
Day, George, 21
Deaking, Rae Ola, 257
Dean, Donald W., 72
    Irene, 272
    Nancy, 272
    Rosabelle, 200
Deane, Amalee Estelle, 72
    Anne, 72
    Don, 72
    Donald W., 72
    Jerry, 72
    William, 72
Deatherage, W. E., 174
Debbold, Hazel L., 73
    Irving E., 72
    Lester I., 73
DeCamp, Joannie, 174
Decker, Rebecca, 179
Deem, Florence, 130
    George, 130

DeGrosa, Gary, 73
    Joseph John, 73
Dehm, Diane, 13, 14
Dejoria, Karen, 210
Delonney, Mazie, 90
DeMaggio, Mary, 26
Denison, Arlene M., 73
    Arthur, 73, 74, 202
    Elizabeth "Betty", 74
    Eugene Everett "Gene", 74
Denning, Robert, 21, 259
    Teresa, 264, 329
    Theresa, 323
Dennis, Don Michelle, 321
    Norma, 321
    Perry, 321
Denshire, Charles, 55
    Clifford, 55
Dent, John, 202
Denzer, Alvin, 74
    Dale, 74
    Gene V., 74
    George, 74
    Jeanette, 74
    Konye, 74
    Neil, 74
    Oak, 74
    Ray, 74
Derby, Kent, 184
    Marion, 184
    Mike, 184
Deres, Kathryn, 89
Derrick, Ardeen, 63
    JeDean 63
DeSalvio, Jean, 73
    Nellie, 73
Detmer, William, 303
Detrick, John S., 75
    Josephine, 75
    Orzal L., 75
    Virgil, 75
Diamond, Marvin, 153

Dickens, Richard, 92
Dickerson, George, 191
Dickhaus, Bette A., 140
Dickman, Beulah, 74
Diebold, Daniel, 75
    John, 75
    Linda F., 75
    Roger, 75
    Walter, 183
    Walter Harvey, 75
Dieleman, Jake, 267
Dinwiddie, Edler L. L., 272
Disney, Donna, 285
Dockter, Carol, 232
Dodd, Teresa, 327
Dodge, Delpha, 264
Doll, Vicki Lynn, 8
Donald, Ann, 295
Donat, Dolly, 26
Donaven, Dorothy Vern, 326
Donovan, Teresa A., 75
Donoven, Donna, 326
    Patricia, 326
Doolittle, Alice, 270
    Pops, 170
Door, Anna, 76
    Victor A., 76
Dorman, Brownie, 328
Dosch, Amanda, 76
    Autumn Regina, 76
    Brooke, 76
    John, 76
    Kathleen, 76
    Paul A., 76
    Paul Jr., 76
Dossett, Lucille, 87
    William, 167
Doty, Jack, 134
Doud, Marwood, 23, 156, 292
Douglass, Don, 314
    L. R., 14, 176, 307
    Louis R., 215

Downing, Bill, 221
    Leo, 221
Dowty, Helen, 46
Dresskell, Afton, 161
Drumm, Erma, 104
Du Charme, Bill, 183
    Gordon, 183
    Ronald, 183
Dubell, Frank, 235
    Walter, 235
Dubois, Eugenie, 77
Dudeck, Reverend John, 259
Dudley, Berta, 276
    Berta L., 276
Duggins, Jackie, 187
Dumais, Jean, 160
Dunagan, Charles, 78
    Charlie, 77
    James H., 77
    Lisa, 77
    Lucy, 77
    Lucy Jane, 78
    Ray, 77, 78
Dunbar, Harry Edgar, 78
    Jean, 181
    Leo, 1, 23, 60, 81, 185, 301
    Lorraine, 58
Duncan, Charles R, 79
Duncum, Iren, 72
Dunford, Charlene, 240
Dunham, Peter, 319
Dunlap, Burl T., 79
    Jack, 79
    Lola, 79
    Lola B., 77, 79
Dunn, Opal, 240
Dunphy, Connie, 80
    Helen, 80
    Helen G., 80
    James T., 80
    James T. Jr., 80
    Janice, 80

Mary, 80
Robert, 80
Thersa, 80
Duplaine, Peg, 157
Durante, Dorothy, 48, 49
Durden, Marie, 23
Dyer, Orville D., 167
Dyson, Albert W., 80
  Bernard, 80
  Virginia, 80, 219
Eads, Evelyn Francis, 80
Eagan, Loretta, 166
Earl, J. Donal, 336
  Jeanne, 264
Earnest, Sally, 336
Eaton, Bruce, 92
  Sid, 18
  Willis, 287
Echols, James, 81
  Orbin Ira 81
Eckhoff, Kenneth, 224
Eddings, Reverend John, 289
Eddy, Betty, 81
  Claud, 81
  Eugene, 81, 82
  Florence, 81
  Gene, 81
  Leo F., 121
  Marjorie, 81
Edelmann, Rebecca Daw, 2
Edwards, Bessie, 193
  Elbert, 176
  George, 296
  Zelda M., 248
Egertson, Reverend Paul W., 134
Elder, Charles, 48
  Ken, 309
  Kenneth, 311
Elgin, Katy, 219
Eliason, Carl, 39
Elich, Margaret, 189
Elinger, Helen, 178
Ellen, Bobbie, 18

Eller, Agnes, 82
  Agnes Emma, 82
  Dale, 82
  Leroy Charles, 82
Ellertson, Barbara, 68
Ellis, Alberta, 208
  James H. "Jim", 83
  John, 84
  John Brad, 83
  Opal, 83
  Opal N., 84
  Walter "Babe", 83
  William, 84
  William H., 83
Ells, Debi, 178
Elms, Mary, 95
Elsenson, Geneva, 23
Elsworth, Rawley, 307
Elwell, Madelaine, 40
Emerich, Bernice, 84
  William A., 84
  William W., 84
Emery, William Coleman, 141
Engle, Charles, 85
  Charlotte June, 84
  Jackie, 84
  James, 85
  John, 84, 85
  Johnny Lou, 84
  Kathie, 84
  LeRoy, 85
  Mary, 84
  Mirl, 84, 136
Englestead, Home, 12
Eno, Jerome, 85, 86
  John A., 85, 86
  Martha, 85, 86
Enright, Sheila Ann (Mrs. Robert), 74
Ericksten, Gladys, 51

Ernst, Carola, 86
    Georg, 86
    Hugo, 86
    Peter, 86
    Ursula, 86
Eskam, Eric, 279
    Ernest, 279
    Ernie, 116
    Phillis, 279
Estes, Donald G., 5
Estrada, Nancy, 234
Evans, Alma, 86, 87
    Annette, 88
    Arthur, 86, 87
    Edward, 88
    Ferrell, 86
    Florence, 88
    Joy, 88
    Lawrence E., 88
    Lois H., 88
    Norma Jane, 259
    Randell, 87
    Shirley, 58
    Terrell, 87
    William McKinley "Bill", 88
    Willie, 88
Ewing, Bill, 222
Ewy, Alberta, 321
Fabre, Debbie, 15
Fagan, Arleen, 89
    Arthur Samuel, 201
    Celeste Browne, 89
    Jack, 89
Fahner, Chaplain David W., 234
Fairchild, Patrici, 232
Falk, Virgini, 164
Fanning, Father Gerald, 198, 229
    Reverend Gerard, 263
Fare, Herman, 274
Farnsworth, Russell, 168, 258, 295
Farrell, George, 99
    Richard, 264
Farris, Angel, 266
    Jamie, 266
    Jennifer, 266
    Jessica, 266
Faulkner, Barry, 337, 339
    Bruce, 337, 339
Fehler, Wayne, 202
Fenlon, Robert L., 39
Fenton, Pat, 314
    Teddy, 25, 36, 51, 52, 53 57, 68, 89, 91, 104, 109, 130, 182, 195, 214, 264, 269, 290, 291, 301, 307, 313, 315, 322
    Steve, 53
Ferguson, Max, 214
Field, Lucille, 192
Fielding, John, 111, 295
    Mary Lou, 111
    Nancy, 145
Fields, J. N., 193
Figgins, Tom, 307
Figueroa, Irene, 6
Fincher, Reverend Russell, 32
Fineber, Reverend Russell, 338
Finigan, Evelyn, 89
    Lawrence, 89
Finmark, Betty, 38
Fiscus, Alice, 89
    Floyd, 90, 91, 92
    John, 90, 91, 92
    John Carpenter, 91
    John Jr., 91
    Lee, 90
    Mildred, 90, 91, 92
    Ruth, 91
Fisher, Al, 81
    Alfred, 229
    Faye E., 122
    Jean, 218
    Minnie Mae, 281
Fitzgerald, R. Gene, 47
Flahive, Reverend Florenc, 229

Boulder City Cemetery: Boulder City, Nevada 385

Flandrers, Ben, 1
Fleck, Eleanor, 283
Flemmer, Evelyn, 45
Fletcher, Dale E., 186
    John F., 186
Flint, Avera C., 215
Flury, Benjamin F., 92
    Florence, 92
Foley, Alin, 93
    Daniel, 93
    David, 93
    David, Jr., 93
    Joseph, 93
    Josie M., 269
    Naomi, 93
    Roger, 93
    Sara, 93
Fomsbee, Katherine, 37
Foos, Lyudia, 127
Foreman, Robert, 180
Forman, Jayne, 205
    Steve, 205
Forrest, Patricia, 206
    Robert, 323
Forrester, John, 212
Fortune, George, 337
    Hannah, 337
Foster, Baby, 93
    Bob, 93
    George, 94
Fourno, Frank, 94
    Joyce Carroll, 94
Fowler, Buck Wayne, 94
    Buck Wayne Jr., 94
    Catherine Violet, 94
    Julia, 35
    Kathryn, 273
    Richard Kenneth, 94
    Smitty G., 95
Fox, Christopher H., 140
    David E., 140
    Linda, 140

Reverend Earl, 23, 112, 120, 140, 322
Frampton, Earl, 20
    Paul, 19
Frances, Curly, 197
Francis, R. L., 92
    Richard L., 287
Frank, Wally, 240
Franklin, Albert, 227
Frazier, Shirley, 206
Freece, Dorothy, 254
Freeman, Evelyn, 203
Frejlach, Ken, 240
French, Helen, 22
    William, 21
Fresquez, Patti, 240
Friday, Hazel, 77, 78
Friedlan, Ed, 156
Fritz, Edna, 95
    Herbert L., 95
Fruenner, Frank, 110
Frye, Harry T., 242
Fulle, Mary, 139
Fuller, Grace E., 95
    Harry, 195
Furticella, Eva P., 96
    Nicholas A., 96
    Nicholas R., 96
Gabriault, Elzear, 96
    Jerome, 96
    Margaret, 96, 233
    Stephen, 96
Gabriel, Phyllis, 60
Gaffin, Stanley, 118
Gagliolo, Jack, 81, 275
Gaines, Casey, 11
    Mark, 11
    Michael, 11
    Walter, 11
Galbraith, Elaine, 198
Gale, Nellie, 161
    Ruby, 8
Gallaer, Mary E., 280

Gallio, Joe, 170
Gallo, Hannah, 303
    Mary, 73
Galloway, Gail, 204
Gant, Reverend Marvin, 319
Garbat, Agnes V., 96
    Dennis, 96
    Sue, 110
Gardner, Dorothy M., 97
    John B., 97
    Michael, 97
    Mikie, 97
    Misty Ann, 97
    Rosemary, 125
    Tony, 97
    Vicki, 97
Garehime, Betty, 173
    Jack, 81
    Jake, 173, 275
    Kurt, 82, 275
    Sannene, 82, 275
Garicia, Cail, 17
Garland, Walter, 189
Garnett, Betty, 21
    Clyde, 97
    Elton, 22, 60, 134, 153
    Frank, 97
    James, 22, 231
    Madelaine, 147, 258
    Perle, 97
    Ralph, 97
    Theodore R., 97
    Theodore Robert, 97
    William, 231
Garrett, Arlene, 158
    Elton, 205, 322
    Madelaine, 135, 322
    Perle, 128
    Thelma, 231
Garrison, L. L., 249
Garton, Donald, 243
    Forrest, 243
    Haldah, 243

    Harry, 243
Garvin, Barbara, 83, 84
    Desmond L., 83
Gaston, Veronica, 278
Gaterburg, Gail, 65
Gatlin, Dolores, 247
Gatterberg, Gail, 66
Gault, Doris, 160
Gayhart, Ray, 218
Gear, Roy, 112, 215
Gebauer, Reverend Ethan, 240
Gebbs, Louis, 1
Georgeson, Adelin, 98
    Jack W., 99
    R. L. "Pop", 98
    Robert W., 99
    Robina, 98
    William, 98
    William D., 99
Gerard, Father George, 72
Gerdes, Reverend Louis, 188
Gerth, Betty, 8
Gesaley, Mary, 244
Getts, Ruth, 135
    William, 22
Gibbons, Sharol L., 88
Giberson, Barbara, 298
Gibson, Bishop Owen, 93, 259
    Mads, 301
    Mads A., 329
    Owen, 322, 336
Gieck, Ann, 99, 321
    Debora, 99
    Fred, 99
    Fred Gary, 99
    Gary, 99
    John, 296
    John D., 99
    Kimberly, 99
    Oris, 99
Giesey, Darlene Alma, 100
    William, 100
    William Jay, 100

Gifford, Estella, 101
    W. T., 101
    William Thomas, 101
Gilbert, John, 101
    Reverend Ford, 147
    Reverend Ford L., 294
    Roy, 101
    Roy E., 101
Gilger, Archie E., 101
    Cindy, 102
    John Allen, 102
    Lyle, 101
    Roy D., 102
    Shellee, 102
Gill, Belle, 184
Gilleard, Esther N., 330
    Mrs., 330
Gillespie, Charles, 143
Gilligan, Joan, 206
Gillighan, Sonya, 36
Gilmore, Bruce, 102
    Connie, 102
    Earl, 102
    Irene, 102
    Kathleen Rae, 102
    Leah, 102
    Leonard, 102
    Lori, 102
    Patrick Edward, 102
    Patrick Kevin, 102
Gimbel, Reverend Dan, 213
Gino, Barney, 195, 229
Gise, Dorothy, 135
Giusto, Marge, 96
Glass, Clara, 103
    Donald, 103
    Lillian, 103
Glazier, Charles (Chick), 103
    Lois, 103
Gleason, Marie, 245
Glenn, Clayton, 202
Glover, Kay, 45
Godbey, Erma, 104, 292, 294, 322
    James, 104, 138
    Jim, 104
    Thomas, 40
    Thomas M., 103
    Thomas W., 104
    Tom, 104, 138, 156, 267, 292, 324
    Tom Jr., 104
    Tom Mayborn, 105
Godwin, Pastor Ted, 141
Goedert, Warren, 258
Goen, Lawence, 138
Goetz, Albert, 337
Goldsberry, Laura, 278
Goldsmith, Dorothy, 24
Gome, Tetra, 238
Goodard, Pamela Sue, 312
Goodbar, Lisa, 219
Goodrich, Alice, 260
Goodwin, Constance, 106
    James, 106
    Joseph P., 106
Goolsby, Christie, 70
Gordon, Berry, 106
    Bill, 106
    Fran, 242
    Gloria, 106
    Mabel, 106
    Pamela, 106
Gore, Cora, 136
    Laura, 123
Gotchall, Mary, 241
Gowan, Barbara, 29
    Ben, 29
Goyette, Cecile, 107
Graff, Beryl, 107
    Brad, 107
    Karl Hardy, 107
    Kenyon, 107
    Mark, 107
    Scott, 107
    Stanley, 107
    Todd, 107

Tona, 107
Grain, Leslie, 195
Grant, Claude, 19
Gray, Albert, 108
    George, 107
    Lawrence, 108
    Mary, 108
    Mary Jane, 233
    O. L., 227
    Rex, 108
Green, Earl L., 226
    Edward L., 226
    Ernest L., 226
Greene, Buford S., 108
    Malbone W., 108
    Mary Jane, 108
    Ti, 329
    William E., 108
Gregerson, Eugene, 197
    Larry, 19
    Nancy, 19
Gregg, Doug, 127
Gresh, Bertha, 109
Griesbaum, Dan, 110
    Richard, 110
    Robert, 110
    Teresa Matilda, 110
Griffen, Jesse, 85
Griffin, Carl, 303
    Gary, 110
    Lamar, 110
    Oluma, 303
Griffith, Fern, 46, 111
    Glen G., 111
Grimes, Annie Edna, 111
    Robert J., 111
    Stanley M., 111
    Walter L., 111
    William O., 111
    William Oliver, 111
Grinstrom, Carol, 112
    Gustas, 112
Grissom, Mollie, 87

Groberk, Donna, 36
Grunwald, Robert, 243
Guido, Mary R, 213
Guidry, Hermany, 170
Gurney, Robert J., 112
Gustad, Ingemar, 112
    Sophie, 112
Gustafson, Vivian, 157
Gutierrez, John, 113
    Linda, 113
    Nell, 209
    Rose, 113
    Sam, 113
    Samuel E., 113
Guyette, Grace L., 95
    Robert, 188
Hafen, Douglas, 286
    Sherman, 286
Hagan, Delbert, 113
    Mickie, 113
    Rosemarie, 113
Hagen, Ed, 202
Hahn, Alm, 32
Haiste, Anna, 260
Haley, Helen, 54
Hall, Carol, 175
    Douglas, 114
    Harry C., 114
    Harry E., 114
    Marion, 284
    Marion S., 285
Hallard, Edith, 247
Halleck, Eulah, 114, 115
    Harold G., 115
Halverson, Gertrude, 340
Hamdorf, Alan, 115
    David, 115
    Eugene H., 115
    Frank, 115
    Marlan, 115
    Mary Alice, 115

Hamilton, A. E., 92
  Bill, 205
  Dorothy Ellen May, 115
  Jack, 325
  Kent, 325
  Lloyd, 116
Hammer, Bill, 116
  Bill C., 117
  Donald, 117
  Glenn, 116
  Kenneth, 116
  Kenneth W., 117
  Marguerite Louise "Betty", 116
  William Glenn, 117
Hampststen, Michelle, 27
Haney, Dorothy, 10
Hanmore, Amelia, 207
Hanne, Reverend Walter, 178
Hannig, Julius L., 117
  Lavera, 117
  Lyle, 301
  Max, 117
  Ross, 117
  Smith, 117
Hansen, Wanda, 278
Hanson, Margaret E., 199
  Maxine, 264
  R. G., 40
Harbin, Ethelleen, 117
  Woody W., 117
Harbour, Bill, 53
Hardcastle, George, 118
  John Anthony, 118
  Lena, 118
  Louise, 118
  Maureen, 118
  Sheila, 118
Harding, Charles, 118
  Mary H., 118

Hardy, Bill, 119
  Derek, 119
  La Grande, 143
  Larry, 119
  LeGrande, 120, 156
  LeGrande Laird "Blackie", 119
  Legrande "Blackie", 119
  Mary, 119
  Ruth, 119
  Stanley, 119
  Thomas, 119
  William B., 119
Monreve, Ruth, 120
Hargrove, Jessie, 246
Harmer, Don, 1
Harmon, Myrtle, 32
Harnedy, Lulu May, 120
  Tim, 120
Harrigan, Phil, 229
  Phillip, 295
Harris, Ann, 118
  Betty, 55
  Bill, 121
  Bonnie, 232
  Clarence, 179
  Dalley, 67
  Deloris, 248
  Earl E., 310
  Gail, 121
  J. E. (Joanne), 226
  Jill, 67
  Julie, 157
  Murran W., 121
  Pat, 28
  Patricia, 28
  Sally, 67
  Shirley, 142
  Timothy, 67
Harrison, Dallas, 189
Hart, Louis Kemp, 152
Harter, Suzanne, 126

Hartley, Albert, 14, 21
    Orpha , 75
Hartling, Gervis, 232
Harvey, James, 121
    Jeanette, 64
    Lewis, 121
    Margaret B. Splawn, 121
Harwat, Irene, 126
Haser, Frances, 122
    Frank, 122
    Vincent, 122
Haskett, Dollie, 78
Hass, Merle, 26
    Vira, 27
Hastings, Lillian, 324
Hatcher, Ella Pear, 122
Hatfield, Alfred W., 122
    Alma, 220
    Richard, 123
    Richard J., 122
    Susie, 122
    Susie M., 123
Hauver, Luanne, 175
Havrilla, Nicholas, 60, 289
    Nick, 6, 23
Hawkins, Glen, 123
    Lois, 258
    Nellie Emma, 123
Haxton, Ida, 220
Hayes, Donald H., 123
    Esther, 104
    Frances, 123
    Howard, 303
    Lorna, 303
    Nancy, 123
    Phillip, 123
    William 123
Hayward, Dot, 270
    Lee, 22, 135
Heaton, Margie, 173
Heddens, Clifford, 188
Heersema, Nancy, 26

Hefty, Judith, 225
    Judy, 226
Hegberg, Gustaf, 194
Heil, Doris, 124
Hellenbrand, Alfred, 261
    Heather, 261
Heller, James I., 124
    Luella, 124
    Luella E., 124
Helms, Gaylord Sumner, 124
    John G., 124
    Murl D., 124
Henderson, Clyde, 125
    Emily, 125
    Madeline, 263
    Nancy, 125
    Nicholas, 125
    William A., 125
Hendrick, Charles, 161
Hendricks, Dona E., 125
    John W., 125
Hendrickson, Matilda Priscilla, 126
    Reverend Larry, 164
Hendrikx, Arlene, 175
Hengler, Anna, 126
    Charles, 126
    Edwin, 126
    Stella, 179
    William, 126
    William A., 126
Henry , Reverend Richard, 269
Herlihy, Loretta, 264
Hermanson, Folke, 257
Herndon, Kim, 178
Herron, Geraldine, 85
Hess, Robert, 169
    Sheila, 296
Hetrick, Rosemary, 230
Hewett, Christine, 189
Heyward, Jack, 81
    Gardiner, 127
    Jack, 195
    Neil, 127

Heywood, Ann, 128
    Anne Catherine, 127
    Gardiner, 128
    Grace, 128
    Grace Sharp, 128
    Jack, 127, 128
    John L., 128
    Neil, 128
    Reid, 128
Hibbard, Jeanne, 55
Hicks, Boyd, 334
Higginbotham, Melissa, 79
Higgins, Clark, 322
    Jack, 270
    Jeanne, 175
    Jeannie, 175
    Mary, 270
Hileman, June, 247
Hill, Alfred V., 129
    Dawn Rene, 218
    Dr. Fred, 129
    Fred, 129
    Frederick James, 130
    George, 130
    Gerri, 130
    Gerri M., 130
    Gerri. Marian, 130
    Kelly, 150, 151
    Mahlon, 130
    Mary M., 124
    Nancy, 130
    Nancy (Farris), 130
    Ruby, 129
Hiller, Charles O., 295
    Doc, 168
Hilliard, Agatha Edmonds, 150
    Carol, 50
Hilton, Claude, 130, 131
    Claude E., 132
    Ralph, 130
    Ralph D., 132
Hinderer, Harold, 133
    Ida Alice, 133

Hinds, Edward W., 132
    Julie, 132
Hines, Ruth, 175
Hinkens, Will, 188
Hinkle, Carolyn, 269
Hippensteel, Jackie, 149
Hirschi, Beverly, 329
Hixon, Emily, 46
Hoag, Vale, 203
Hodgkin, David, 133
    John F., 133
    Kathleen, 133
Hoffman, Ed, 134
    Edward John, 133
    Gladys, 133
    Gladys M., 134
    Tony, 134
Hogan, George, 34
Hogben, Father Joseph, 118
Holabaugh, Lottie, 133
Holberg, Charles Oscar, 135
    Clarence A., 135
    Lloyd D, 135
    Phyllis, 135
    W. C., 135
Holder, Eve Mae, 218
Holland, Florrie, 14
    Fred, 88
    Med, 329
Holliday, Reverend Guy, 18, 43, 46, 55, 60, 64, 81, 85, 86, 103, 111, 112, 115, 140, 143, 146, 148, 149, 161, 185, 203, 228, 242, 266, 273, 289, 296, 297, 306, 312, 335
Holloway, Robert, 319
Holman, Reverend Gene, 49, 123, 136, 199
    Reverend Margery, 70, 128
    Reverend Marjorie, 84, 329

Holmar, Reverend Gene, 122
Holmes, David, 136
    Grace L., 136
    Helen Hazel, 136
    Howard, 136
    Neil, 1, 324
    Richard, 136
    William, 136
    William H., 136
Holt, Bert, 136
    Charles, 136
    Hattie, 290
    Junior, 136
    Martha, 84, 136, 212
    William W., 136
    Woodrow, 136
Holton, Kerry, 13, 14
Holyoak, Cullen, 286
Homan, Margery, 62
Homes, Neil H., 202
Honer, Tommy, 190
Honeycutt, Bill, 137
    Lillian Votaw, 137
Hood, Justin, 138
    Lori Janine, 138
    Rich, 138
Hooper, Chester, 86
    Eugene, 167
    Jim, 167
    Mary Ann, 166
    Ralph, 167
    Rozanne, 167
    William, 167
Hoover, Paula, 187
Hora, Charlotte, 54
Horn, Alberta, 238
    Francis L., 54
Horne, Priscilla, 233
Horton, Belva, 223
    Elaine Abercrombie, 138
Hoskins, Howard, 139
    John K., 139
    Lena S., 139

Hostitler, Frances, 136
Houston, Susan, 335
Hovel, Lorraine, 274
Howard, Buckley, 60
    Cecilia, 139
    Kristen, 139
    Sarah, 139
    William Arlow, 139
    William R., 139
Huddleston, Daisy Moyer, 140
Hudlow, Florence, 126
    Florence E., 140
    Grant B., 140
    Joanne, 140
    Lloyd, 112, 126, 181, 300
    Lloyd J., 140
    Roberta, 314
Hudson, Jewel Norman, 141
    Ouida, 141
Hueftle, Bernice M., 141
    Leroy, 141
Huegele, Norine, 89
Huening, Alphonse H., 142
    Fred. H, 142
    Fritz, 142
    Theodore, 142
Huey, Marguerite, 153
Huff, Sheila, 169
Huffstedler, LaJoy, 18
Hughes, Beverly, 103
    Jack, 142
    Mildred B., 142
    Richard L., 142
    Ronald R., 142
    William E., 142
Hull, Hazel, 46
Humes, Eva, 339
    Robert, 339
Hunt, Hiram, 202
    Howard Clark, 142
Hunter, Charles, 322
    Charlie, 197
Huntley, Monte G., 143

Hurst, Gladys, 5
Hurt, Art, 6, 143
    Brian, 219
    Jack, 138, 143
    Lena, 48
    Lena (Mrs. Art), 10
    Ora, 143
    Robert H., 143
    William Art, 319
Husman, Cathy, 172
Hutchinson, George, 284
    Reverend Frank, 239
Hyde, Peggy, 176
    William, 169
Imlay, Dale, 1, 119, 286
    Dale F., 143
    Darin F., 143
    George, 143
    James Fenton, 143
    John, 143
    Kenneth, 143
    Luetta, 143
    Sidney Lynn, 143
    Wilma DeMille, 144
Insalata, Dorothy, 274
Irwin, Charles S., 261
Isenberg, Alice, 144
    Kurt, 144
    Richard Gene "Dick", 144
    Rick, 144
Isham, Jean, 210
Jackson, Gilbert, 266
    Leona, 266
Jacobs, Gayle Maureen, 144
    James, 144
Jacobson, Shirley, 41
Jacot, Daniel, 145
    Francis H., 145
    Mary Jean, 145
Jansen, Verlene, 26
Jarrett, Reverend Talley, 331
Jarvill, Luella, 110
Jeager, George, 208

Jefferson, Constance, 106
Jenne, Floyd, 145
    Floyd L., 145
    Lloyd, 191
    Rick, 145
    Wilma H., 145
Jennings, William, 298
Jensen, Cathy, 146
    Doc, 62
    Frank, 267, 296
    Helen, 115
    Jeffrey Allen, 146
    Lola, 62, 297
    Roy, 146
    Tina, 146
    Tony, 1
    Tracey, 146
Jenson, Floyd, 145
    Frank, 145
    Max, 145
    Vear, 145
Jesmer, Mary Elizabeth, 57
Jess, Fred, 168
    Nell, 48
Johnon, Hilma, 147
Johns, Harvey, 289
Johnson, Agnes, 140
    Allison, 24
    Allan, 146
    Billy, 140
    Carissa, 146
    Carrie, 78
    Cheyenne, 146
    Christopher Dean, 146
    Clarence, 140
    Clyde, 112
    Dale, 147
    Darlene, 268
    Dione, 3
    Elmo, 1
    Fay, 202
    Harry E., 146
    John Eric, 147

Kyle, 146
Lois, 260
Loren , 300
Lucille, 146
Lyle, 147
Mary, 209
Morris, 148
Nancy, 24
Rhett , 147
Richard, 148
Sally White, 328
Sandra, 147
Scott, 147
Susan , 30
Tami, 147
Thea, 148
Todd, 147
Traci C., 147
Veva, 148
Vernn, 147
Johnstone, Sherma, 335
Jolley, Donal J., 38
Jonasen, Bernice, 149
    Frederick A., 149
    Gordon P., 149
    Jonas (Joe) E., 148
    Karen Frederikke
      Andersen, 148
    Robert W., 149
    Walter (Wally) A., 148
Jones, Al, 149
    Albert R., 149
    Beatrice, 149
    Betty, 217
    Bob, 116
    Clifford R., 149
    Cora, 178
    D. A., 227
    Don, 168
    G. L., 217
    Gordon, 118
    Jim, 116
    Kathee, 312

Linda , 149
Mary, 300
Mary Kaye, 68
Robert, 188
W. D., 97
Jordahl, Marlene K, 88
Jordan, Gal C., 47
    Jim, 306
    June, 306
    Maxine V., 150
    Melba, 78
Kae, Joreena M., 66
Kaighn, Julia, 280
Kail, Debra Sue, 77
Kaiser, Frank, 150
    John, 150
    Otto, 150
    Otto H., 150
Kakaruk, Alice, 261
    George, 261
    Theresa, 261
Kaldenberg, Reverend, 291
Kamrowski, Bill, 143
    Dorothy, 143
Kangas, Micki, 313
Kania, Mary Ann, 263
Katchadoorian, Ann, 150
    Billie Sue, 150
    David, 150, 151
    Harry, 150, 151
    Joann, 151
Keehn, Judy, 85
Keele, Cal L., 249
Keillor, Kathi, 151
Keisling, infant, 151
    John, 151
Keith, Colleen, 68
    Richard, 159
    William, 159
Keller, Charles, 116
    Dallas, 116
Kelley, Cal, 259
    Marjorie, 255

Wayne, 119
Kelly, Barbara A., 152
    Earl J., 152
    Jennifer, 152
    Jim, 152
    Laura, 104
    Paul, 152
    Richard, 259
    Theresa, 152
    William R., 152
Kemp, Allan Richard, 152
    George Paul, 152
    Laura B., 152
    Norman Paul, 152
Kempf, Rose, 179
Kendall, Richard, 245
Kennedy, Addie, 153
    Bruce, 153
    Charles, 153
    Keith, 153
    Miriam, 203
    Robert E., 153
    R. Evans, 153
    Roger, 153
    Shirley, 149
    Winifred, 153
Kent, Fred A., 332
Keogh, James D., 154
    Lillian, 154
    Lillian Kay, 154
Keough, James, 154
    James J., 153
Kepler, Al E., 230
    Ed, 230
Keplinger, Lucy, 5
Kerr, Shauna, 107
Kervrat, Joe, 163
    Tony, 163
Kerzmann, Albert E., 154
    Jack A., 154
    Victoria E., 154

Kesterson, Pauline O., 155
    Robert, 155
    Sgt. J. N., 155
Ketchell, Pasto, 233
Ketterer, Irene, 232
Kickbush, Anselm Harold Charles, 156
    Autumn, 156
    Bill Edward, 156
    Brandon, 156
    Brian, 156
    Leota, 156
    Richard, 156
    Sharlene, 156
    Virginia Rose, 156
Kickhaus, Karl Eric, 140
Kilday, Duncan McKenzie "Irish", 156
    Stella, 157
Kilpatrick, Bud, 140
    Deanne, 140
    Michael, 140
Kimball, Charles, 227, 294
Kindy, Mary L, 189
Kine, Joe, 1, 170
    Joseph, 60, 81
    Joseph L., 202
King, Ethel C., 157
    Max, 260
    Merrilee, 327
Kingsley, Pat, 168
Kinnaman, Betty J., 142
Kinney, Clyde E., 157
    Herbert Clyde, 157
    Ina, 157
Kirby, Dorothy, 157
    Louise, 157
    Patricia, 337
    Richard, 337, 339
Kirchman, John, 158
    John Robert, 158
    Lila A., 158

Kirkpatrick, Josephine C., 158
    Lenore, 325
Kirtsman, Willcom, 66
Kish, Frank, 286
Kitchell, Reverend Jim, 179
    Reverend Marjorie, 277
Kitchens, Danny, 174
Kivett, Kittie, 102
    Warren, 296
Klann, Al, 12
    David, 159
    Elsie M., 159
    Gary, 159
    Paul, 156
Kleindeinst, Jack, 227
Klemmer, Brent, 159
    Pat, 159
    Raymond, 159
Klinger, A. G., 258
    Bessie, 160
    John A., 160
    Kristina, 160
    Michael, 160
    Patricia, 160
    Roy Arthur, 160
    Sarah, 160
Klunk, Sovieny, 280
Knause, Clark, 160
    Frances, 160
    Richard, 160
Knauss, Herb, 156
    Herbert, 161
    Herbert H., 161
    Herbert "Herb", 160
    Minnie E., 161
Knick, William "Bud", 186
Knight, Edna, 128
Knighton, Howard, 161
    Howard H., 161
    Kirk, 161
    Madeline, 161
Knox, Harold, 205
    Ruth, 239

Koenig, Arnold C. "Joe", 162
    David, 162
    Hester, 162
    John, 162
Koerner, Charles A., 163
Kohler, Peggy M., 89
Kooch, Patricia, 293, 294
Koontz, Alice, 104
    Patty, 151
Kopp, C. E., 324
Koppin, Darleen, 218
Korfman, Michelle, 163
Korn, Bill, 164
    Cynthia Lou, 164
    Vada Lou, 164
Kosappis, Christina, 239
Kothe, Catherine, 139
Kountz, Eleanor, 219
Kowalski, Edward Bernard, 164
    Rose Marie, 164
Krafft, Betty, 89
Kramer, Don, 47
    Fred, 47
    Susan, 47
Krause, Beverly, 164
Kuhl, G., 179
Kunde, Brian Phillip, 251
    Joan Miriam Richmond, 250
    Joan Miriam Sue Richmond 251
    Robert James, 251
Lacoe, Roseland, 115
LaCroix, Violet, 297
Lamb, Brandon, 165
    Clarence I., 165
    Dahlene C., 165
    Edith, 165
    Lucy, 165
    Lyle, 165
    Marvin D., 165
Lamour, Dorothy, 265
Lane, Olive, 219

Langley, Karen, 240
Lanska, Beverly, 165
    Charles, 165
    David, 165
    John, 165
    Noy, 165
LaPlante, Adrian, 166
    Emile, 166
    Joe, 166
    Olive, 166
Lappin, Joe, 227, 229
    L. S., 294
    L. W., 258
Larsen, Betty, 337
    Brian, 337
    Eric, 337
Larson, Betty, 339
Lasko, Bishop, 257
Laswell, Mary, 28
Laughery, Dave, 275
    Duane S., 69
    Maury, 308
    Nadean, 309
Laughran, Ann, 52
Laux, Michael, 21
    Mike, 92
Law, David, 210
Lawelin, William, 230
Lawellin, Marie, 229
Layman, Gusta Sparks, 278
    William, 278
Layne, Barbara, 141
    Jerrie, 257
Layton, John, 168, 183, 319
Lazaro, Bille A., 142
Le-Clair, Joy Lynn, 220
Lea, Melody, 189
Leaveitt, Earl K., 166
    Grant, 66
    Mary Ann, 166
Leavitt, Bonnie, 166
    Cherie, 166
    Danny, 166

    Earl, 166
    Earl K., 166, 329
    Eldon S, 255
    Grant, 166
    Grant J., 166
    Helen, 266
    Marge, 264
    Margie, 55
    Margie F., 166
    Mark Andrew, 167
    Mary Ann, 166
    Mathew David, 167
    Michael Earl, 167
    Valene, 236
LeBlanc, Irene, 325
Lechner, Sara L., 167
Lee, Jimmie, 170
LeFevre, George, 156
Legler, Rudolph, 112
    Sylvia, 23, 81, 138
Lehman, Florence, 99
Leicht, W. F. V., 38
    William, 296
Lektorich, Lynda Sue Richmond, 251
Leland, Maurine, 121
Lemke, Paula G., 176
Leonard, John, 167
    Laberta, 167
    Lionel, 138, 167
Leone, Oliver, 156
LeShander, Ruth S. MacPherson, 168
Leuke, Marg, 154
LeVan, Stell, 168
    William Mack, 168
Lewis, Anne, 168
    Beverly, 172
    Beverly E., 169
    Bob, 22, 169
    Chaire Raymond, 172
    Dean, 172
    Don, 172

398   Boulder City Cemetery: Boulder City, Nevada

Frank, 227
Helen, 169-171
J. Earl, 172
Jean E, 172
Jessie, 172, 336
Stella, 172
Sterling, 14, 172
Lieurance, Wes, 89
Ligion, Ralph, 21
Likens, Rodger Gene, 173
    Roger, 82, 275
Lilly, Virginia, 11
Limverakis, Elizabeth, 245
Linch, Mary, 56
Linck, Bonnie, 306
    Don, 134, 301
    Donald L., 39, 173
    John H., 173
    LaVona E., 173
Lindeberg, Floyd, 182, 183
Linick, Bonnie, 306
    Don, 306
Lins, Coleen, 150
Lisette, C., 86
Littler, Charles, 174
    Chuck, 174
    David F., 174
    Emily, 198
    Helen, 175
    Helen S., 174
    Lydia, 174
    Otto, 23, 174, 300
    Paul, 175
    Shirley, 174
    Ted, 175
    Theodore, 174
    William, 174
    William S., 175
Littleton, Robert, 27
Lively, Bob, 140
    Mill, 140
    Paul, 140

Lockhart, Malcom, 3
    Sidney, 3
Locks, Alan, 175
    Ed, 175
    Helen M., 175
    Leonard, 175
    Stephen J., 175
    Tom, 175
Lodge, Rebecca, 293
Loftis, William M., 249
Logue, Louise, 157
Loney, Emmett, 263
Long, Anna M., 75
    Charles Wm., 176
    Chuck, 176
    Frank, 176
    Frank L., 177
    Frank Leo, 176
    Jerry, 62
    Kevin, 176
    Larry E., 327
    Mahlon, 176
    Martin J., 327
    Olynnda, 176
    Paula, 176
    Pauline M., 176
    Wm., 176
Longpre, R. James, 233
    William, 233
Loose, Anne, 127
    Catherine, 127
    Dave, 127
    David, 127
    Gottfried, 127
    Lydia, 127
Lopez, Vicky, 70
Lorke, Yvone, 189
Lorts, Zenobia, 300
Lovell, Katherine, 8
Low, Kerry, 259
Lowe, George, 39

Lucero, Fidel, 178
    Lloyd, 177
    Reuben, 177, 178
    Ricky, 178
    Rosalie A., 178
Lueking, Carl Leslie, 178
    Fred, 179
    G. W., 179
    Hazel, 88, 178
Luizzi, Frank, 179
    Jack, 179
    Madeline, 179
    Nicola, 179
Lukowski, Diana, 107
    Michelle A., 107
    Walleen, 107
Lunda, Tillie, 178
Lundquist, Raynard, 185
Lusson, Collette, 187
Luther, Virginia, 80
Lynn, Mary, 261
Lyon, Eleanor, 58
    Merle, 16
Lyons, John E., 179
    Helen Zetta, 179
    Robert M., 179
Lytle, Edythe A., 179
    John Paul, 179
    Paul, 179
MacCormich, Dr. D. M., 176
MacCornack, E. A., 295
MacDonald, Irene, 180
    R. G., 181
    Richard G., 180, 181
Mace, George R., 183
    Terrill, 183
MacEachern, Kenneth 12
MacGregor, Bruce, 183
    Verna Mary, 183
Mackie, Beverly, 169
MacLeod, Ann, 182
    Margaret, 182
    Tom, 182

William "Bill", 182
Maddox, Doris, 184
    Doris C., 184
    Jackson P., 184
    Lee, 156, 184
    Terra, 184
Maddox, Jackson, 184
Madrigal, Steve, 254
Madsen, Cornelia Bates, 13
Magee, Martha, 133
Magis, Agnes, 55
Maglish, Ann, 96
Magruder, Pastor Ray, 212
    Reverend, 222
Mahanay, Patricia, 191
Maier, Lorraine, 311
Maiman, Henry, 24
    Ira, 24
    Milton , 24
Malatino, Karen, 337
    Michael, 337
Malinowski, Cynthia Lee, 228
Mallot, Billie, 242
    Jeanne P., 184
Malmsten, Georgia H., 185
    Roland, 185
Malone, George W., 316
Maloney, Ron, 163
Maloy, Darlene, 100
Maltby, Alta Grace Elridge, 185
    Clifford, 185
    Donald T., 185
    Richard A., 185
Manis, John, 238, 275
    Johnny, 171
    Mercedes, 238
Manix, J. C., 22
    Joe, 167
Mann, Emoline, 273
Manning, Basil, 186, 200
    Ivy, 186
    Larence, 186
    Lawrence, 200

Leslie Enid, 186, 200
R. W., 167
W. T., 229
Marble, Ethel, 245
March, Fred, 186
    Marijean, 186
    Patrick, 186
    Ron, 186
Marks, Arleen, 201
    Jack Fisher, 201
    Josephine Casann, 251
Markus, Alfonsas E. , 201
    James, 201
    John, 201
    Linda, 201
    Ruth, 201
Marshall, Ida, 291
    Shirley, 55
Martenson, Edna, 132
    Edna Hilton, 130
    Thern, 131, 132
Martin, Caroline, 187
    Claude H., 187
    Corrine, 187
    Essie L., 187
    Ethel, 297
    Lila, 291
    Lori Ann, 187
    Richard, 187
    Ruby, 228
Martz, Alvin, 187
    Claude, 187
    DeWayne, 187
    Dick, 187
    Esta, 187
    Harold, 187
    Irma, 187
    Linda, 187
    Lloyd P., 187
Marx, Mary Jane, 108
Masterson, John, 289
Mata, Stella, 4

Mather, Leslie, 188
    Linda, 188
    Mae, 188
    Robert L., 188
    Robert Lee "Bob", 188
Mathews, J. B., 51
Mathias, Albert Arthur, 188
    Alma, 188
Matthews, Mildred, 290
    Minnie Laura, 108
Matulic, Geraldin, 189
    Milan D., 189
    Sam, 189
Maugham, Chris, 189
    Della, 189
    Gregory Ray, 189
    Mardella "Delle" Coy, 189
Mauro, Karen, 282
May, Bernice, 139
Mayden, Jean, 210
Mayer, Pastor Ron, 24
    Pastor Ronald, 71
    Reverend Ron, 23, 271
Mayers, Reverend Ron, 131
Mayfield, Alice, 91
    Frances, 91, 92
McArthur, Estelle, 193
McAtee, Inez, 332
McBriade, Jerri, 240
McBride, Alvis E., 190
    Bobby, 190
    Clara, 190
    Delmos, 190
    Tommy, 190
    Willie, 190
McBroom, Muriel, 300
McCall, Luise, 332
    W. H., 195
McCallum, Frances, 325
McCandless, Jane, 218
McCardell, Ethel, 263

McCarthy, Agnes, 190
    Francis L., 190
    Kathleen, 191
    Kenneth, 190
    Mea, 190
    Pamela, 190
    Patrick, 190
McCauley, Mrs., 331
    Ruth, 299
McClure, Jack, 191
    Mike, 191
    Myron Cook, 191
    Ruby, 191
    Vincent, 191
McCollum, A. H., 192
    Alton, 42, 193
    Alton H. "Mac", 192, 193
    D. L., 193
    Daniel Luther, 192
    I. A., 192
    Irwin, 42, 192, 193
    Larry, 192, 193
    Lawrence, 193
    Mac, 193
    Martha, 193
    N. E., 192
    Norvell, 192, 193
    O. E., 192
    Orland, 193
    Orland E., 192
    Pauline, 193
    Pauline T. "Polly", 193
    Wardie Genevera, 193
McComb, Kent, 286
McConald, Pauline, 134
McCord, Mebra, 63
McCormick, Ella, 303
    Paul, 303
    William, 173
McCoy, Frances Jane, 31
    John, 194
    Mary Ellen, 194
    Raymond K., 194

McCready, Doug, 200
McCuin, Clarence, 194
    Luella G., 194
McCullough, Bill, 314
    Carmen, 200
    Karmen, 186
McDaniel, Lucille, 334
McDermott, Richard, 281
McDonald, Delores, 194
    Gerald, 194
    Lynn, 245
    Selma, 194
McDuff, J. W., 195
    Jimmy, 195
    Kate Files, 195
    Sally Ann, 195
McEwan, Gwen, 195
    John, 197
    John S., 197
    William C., 197
    William S., 197
McEwen, Miguel, 296
    Zita, 296
McFarland, Ernest, 216
McGary, Clara, 153
    Mrs., 153
McGee, James, 161
McGillivary, Grace, 332
McGlynn, Margaret, 325
McGonigle, William P., 92
McGrath, Virginia, 185
McHenry, Albert, 221
McHugh, Eileen, 198
    James P., 198
    Judith Ellen, 198
    Kenneth, 198
    Maureen, 198
    Richard T., 198
McIntyre, Bertha E., 198
    Douglas, 198
    Sherman, 198
McJilton, Mary Lou, 152
McKay, Douglas, 316

McKenzie, Ethel E., 198
    John D., 198
McKinnis, Clarence, 199
    Gary Phillip, 199
    George, 199
    Kelly, 199
    Phillip, 199
McLaughlin, Charles J., 199
    Charles M., 199
    Helena F., 199
    Margaret E., 199
McLean, Maxine, 217
McMurdy, Callie, 217
McNair, Ben, 200
    Jessie Lee, 200
McNeil, Robert John, 200
McSwain, Larry, 138
Mecham, Forest Ray, 202
    Leland, 203
    Marjorie, 209, 210, 247
    Ray, 209
    Robin, 203
    Russell, 203
Mechtley, Terry, 319
Medlin, Armine, 203, 204
    Eugene, 203
    Homer, 203
    Homer (Marilyn), 31
    James, 203
    John, 203
    Lucy Ellen, 203
    Thomas Hardy, 203
    Val, 203
    Val Martha, 203
    Victor, 31
Mehr, Precious, 82
Meisner, Ella, 291
    Florence, 81
    Lou, 81
Menser, Marjorie, 308
Mercadante, Michelina, 251

Mercer, Anita, 153
    Mrs., 153
    Ralph D., 153
Mercereau, Marji Ann, 62
Merchant, Leola, 92
Merrill, Betty, 204
    Carl, 6, 227, 319
    Glen, 204
    Mary, 139
    Mary Ann, 306
Merritt, Earl, 204
    James, 204
Messner, Bob, 46
    Vern, 46
Meyers, Grayson, 180
    Josephine, 180
    Leona, 218
Michael, Earl, 172
Michaels, Andy, 205
    Fred, 205
    Frederick Andrew, 205
    Mike, 205
    Randolph "Randy", 205
Milam, Charles A., Jr., 206
    Charles August "Gus", 206
    Ernst, 206
    Etta, 206
Milan, Carline R., 277
    Howard P., 277
    Robert D., 277
    William B., 277
Miles, Dorothy, 17
    Gordon, 17
Milka, Edward, 206
    Eleanor, 206
    John H., 206
    Robert, 206
Miller, Al, 208
    Anne C., 72
    Byron, 112
    Charles R., 207
    Doris Mather, 207

Edward N., 207
Frederick Nathan, 207
Jeanette, 207
Kathleen, 132
Larry, 136
Mack, 208
Warren, 208
Mills, Amos, 23
   Anna, 208
   Edith, 208
   Gordon, 173
   Home, 23
   Linda, 208
   Marguerite J., 208
   Otis, 23
   Ralph E., 208
   William, 23
Minish, Art, 135
Misun, Jack, 178
   Johnny, 178
   Rudy, 178
Mitchell, Al, 208
   Andrew, 191
   Benjamin F., 208
   Beulah M. (Billie), 13
   Merle, 202
Mlawsky, Carol, 73
Mobley, Lynn, 308
Moe, Jack, 294
   Samette, 294
Moen, Janet, 159
Moldenaur, Katherine, 325
Molin, Dorothy, 117
Moller, Elyse, 38
   N. R., 38
Monroe, Frances Estelle, 320
Montclair, C., 13
Mooney, Beulah, 123
   Beulah E., 209
   Cecil, 209
   Cecil Lloyd, 209
   Denzil, 209
   Dywen, 209

Hershel, 209
Hugh, 209
Trenie Leon, 209
Moore, Alexander Leslie, 209
   Claude, 92, 211, 212
   David G., 210
   David W., 210
   Elizabeth, 209
   Eugene T., 211
   Galen A., 210
   Harold G., 211
   Ivetta, 211
   James R., 209
   Karee, 210
   Kaycee, 210
   Machiel, 271
   Mel, 1
   Melvin R., 1
   Minnie L., 212
   W. A., 211, 212
Moore, Connie, 210
   David, 210
   Donna, 212
   Dorothy Ellen May, 115
   Douglas, 21
   Eldon, 212
   Jerry, 212
   Marian, 210
   Marvin, 212
   Norma, 277
   Patrick, 210
   Perry, 217
   Reverend Gary, 41
   Richard, 150
   Verna, 150
Mooring, Anita, 60
Morang, Mary Ann, 299
Moritz, C.J., 216
   Cora, 217, 302
   Cora T., 214
   E. A., 180, 215
   Ernest, 215
   Ernest A. "Ernie", 215

Holly, 217
Louis, 215
Robert, 217
Morlang, Henry "Red", 213
Morley, Claude, 217
    Jerry, 197, 207, 339
    Jerry H., 217
    Kay, 118, 217
    M. Marie, 217
    Marie, 339
    Robert E., 217
Morra, Patricia, 75
Morris, Ester, 17
    J. Dan, 213
    Jesse D., 213
    Monte, 1
    Perlie, 156, 296
    Ray V., 213
    Ray Vernon, 213
    Richard, 206
    Shirley, 213
    Thomas H., 213
Morrison, Lillian, 36
    Lloyd, 36, 191, 289
Mortiz, Cora Trimble, 214
    E. A., 181
Moseley, C. C., 9
Moser, Alpha L., 217
    John, 217
Moses, Clyde, 135
Moya, Jake, 218
    Jimmy Anthony, 218
    Moises, 217
    Moses, 218
    Ruby, 217
Moyer, Dorothy, 172
    Grace, 283, 284
Moyle, Janice, 172
Muchow, Glen, 229
Mueller, Joan, 117
Mull, Robert Lester, 218
    William Robert, 218
Mullens, Joanne, 311

Mulligan, Lela, 167
Munds, John, 167
Murchison, Jim, 4
Murphy, Nancy, 1, 323
    Pearl, 104
    Reverend Dan, 337
    Richard, 19
Murray, Wally, 19
Murry, Gladys, 134
    Pat, 134
Musgrove, Earl, 92
Musser, Howard, 147
Myers, Arthur L., 218
    John, 1, 228
    Naida Clarice, 1
    Reverend Neal, 111, 188
    Victoria, 218, 219
Naegle, Alan, 258
    Linda, 258
Natella, Emily, 172
Nay, Chris, 225
    Christine, 224
    Wanda, 99
Neely, Elenore E., 219
Neesley, Glenda, 116
    Reverend Stephen, 207
    Reverend Steve, 116
Neilson, Byron, 219
    Dustin, 219
    Fred, 197
    Kent, 219
    La Grande, 19, 20
    Lisa, 219
Nellis, Garold, 275
Nelson, Bishop Herman, 255, 264, 336
    Ed, 19
    Ervin, 172
    Ervin J., 169
    F. C., 227
    Grayce, 130
    Herman, 259, 332
    Kathleen, 49

Larry Leroy, 219
Marilyn, 202
Marsha M, 71
Michael, 219
Nellie, 281
Rachael Ann, 71
Randall, 219
Thora, 264
Tommy, 14, 19, 129, 202, 322
Ness, Letty Jo, 65
Neumann, Clarence, 267
Neville, Alice, 335
Newbanks, Alma, 220
Alma R., 220
Mack, 220
Mack, Jr., 220
Newby, Judy, 28
Newcomb, Mary, 260
Newman, Emma Nathalia, 220
Sandra, 117
Newquist, Mary, 123
Newson, Rose, 121
Nichell, Wilbur, 223
Nicholas, Father Robert, 210
Nichols, Claude, 227
Nicholson, Floyd, 223
Hallie, 222
Hallie O., 221
Joe, 223, 307
Leonard, 221
LeRoy, 112
T. L, 221
W. A., 227
Wesley, 212, 221, 289
Wesley Omer, 222
Nickell, Ann, 72
Betty, 102
Bill, 138
Charles L., 223
Gloria, 24
Mildred, 223
Tamara, 223

Nicks, James, 123
Jay, 29
Ruby, 29, 136
Walter, 123
Walter J., 212
Walter Jefferson, 209
Nicolls, Ann, 180
Nielsen, E. G., 92
Nielson, Hyrum, 259
Nienkamp, Roland, 24
Nilsen, Vivian, 186
Nisbet, Gladys, 304
Nixon, Bessie Jane, 223
Nobel, W. Phi, 258
Noble, Florence Virginia, 224
Phil, 227, 294
Nohner, Carolyn, 125
Nolan, Mary, 312
Patricia "Pat", 325
Noland, Lennie, 87
Noll, Lucy, 153
Norman, Bert, 224, 225
Charles R., 224
Floy B., 224
Helen, 224
Helen M., 225
John, 224
Northrop, Joan, 234
Novasconi, James, 225, 226
Lucille, 225, 226
Novello, Mark, 319
Novoselek, Dennise, 27
Nueezley, Reverend Steve, 46
Nunner, John, 21
Nutter, Darrell, 220
Shirley, 220
Steven, 220
Nybakken, Reverend Vernon, 268
Oakes, Lula, 21
Oberweiser, Pauline, 155
Ogden, Kay, 280
Ogsbury, Edra, 15

Oliver, Bob, 37
    Herbert, 37
    Kelly, 37
    Mary K., 80
    Robert, 37
    Vada, 37
    Vern, 37
Olmstead, Reverend Guy, 85
Olsen, Don, 327
    James, 327
    Louise, 106
Olson, Art, 119
    Bernice, 227
    Elmine, 113
    Judy, 36
    Mabel, 333
Orchard, Anthony K., 227
    Charles L., 227
    Yvonne, 227
    Yvonne C., 227
Orr, Judith, 176
Orton, G., 22
Osborn, Carolyn, 228
    Guy H., 228
    Hugh, 228
    Ida Mae, 228
    Ralph, 228
    Steven, 73
Osko, Reverend John, 12, 162, 247
Ostensen, Rulen G., 167
Ostergard, Della, 255
Ostler, Nellie, 327
Ott, Charles, 228
    Charles W., 228
    Christopher, 228
    Helen Elizabeth, 228
    Linnea, 228
    Roger, 228
Overbeck, Louise, 118
Overbey, Harry, 21, 319
Overfield, Jean, 70
Owens, Ruth, 97

O'Brien, Eva, 236
    Karen "Kay", 325
O'Connel, Margaret, 5
O'Connell, Margaret, 5
O'Hara, A. J., 226, 259
    Bill, 226
    Grady, 226
    Phil, 226
    William "Bill", 226
O'Neal, Charles C., 273
Pace, Marcel, 118
    Stella K., 228
Packard, Wayne, 150
Packenham, Sally, 247
Paddilla, Leonides, 4
Page, Deanna, 159
Pagora, Katherine, 164
Paillipps, Pane, 325
Palmer, A. R., 255
    Alice H., 229
    Nell, 133
    Norma J., 200
    Ted, 202
    Thomas, 229, 230
Palumbo, Angela M., 230
    David M., 230
    John A., 230
    Laura M., 230
    Marilyn E., 230
Panebianco, Jeanne, 107
Pankey, Peggy, 41
Paris, Kenneth, 260
    La Vada, 260
Park, Beverly, 84
    Billy, 230
    George, 230
    Preston Ray, 230
    William, 230
Parker, Billy, 280
    Bob, 17
    Charles, 280
    Elizabeth Anne, 231
    Irene, 17

Boulder City Cemetery: Boulder City, Nevada

Shirley, 173
Robert, 212
Parks, Brian, 233
    Kimberly, 233
    Larry, 233
Parl, Beverly, 83
    Billy, 83
Parmelee, Charles, 231
    Fred, 231
    Thelma G., 231
    Thomas L., 231
Parmenter, Bryan, 232
    Caralyn, 232
    Frank, 232
    Janalyn, 232
    Janice, 232
    Kayelyn, 232
    Mary, 232
    Marylyn, 232
    Richard, 232
    Scott, 232
    Sean, 232
Parrott, Wilburt, 236
Pasner, Francis, 82
Pate, Sarah C., 232
    William, 232
Patrick, Sadie, 16
Patten, Harold, 216
Patton, Arthur, 170
    Daisy, 306
    Doug, 320
    Ila, 32
    James, 114
    Marilyn, 114
    Myrtle, 290, 320
Pavlich, Lois, 55
Paxson, Loretta, 2
Payne, Terry, 41
Pearson, Sue, 231
Peart, Laurel Jeanne Bates, 13
Pease, Denny, 255, 306
    Denzel, 311
    Denzie, 156

Peasley, Ardeen, 40
    James, 40
Peckenpaugh, Carol, 136
Peevy, Mattie, 142
Pelham, Helen Jane, 232
    Henry, 6, 215
Pelham, George, 232
Pellow, Florence M., 233
Pendergrass, Phyllis, 224
Pendlebury, James, 233
    Martha, 233
    Thomas, 233
Penninger, Eulalia, 260
Pennock, Pat Bellow, 17
    Patricia J., 16
Penny, Johnny, 233
    Randy, 233
    Stanley, 233
Penrod, Grace, 99
Perkins, Vivian, 64
Perrault, Francis, 106
Perry, Mark, 55
Pesout, Donald, 234
    Ruth, 228
    Ruth Pace, 234
Peters, Dolores, 17
    Mary, 114
    Mary A., 234
    Wayne, 259
Petersen, Dee, 20
    Fred, 235
    Jim, 20
    Lucille A., 235
    Nancy, 235
Peterson, Charles, 171, 191
    Ellis Fritz, 234
    Ivan, 235
    Lucille, 234
    Mary E., 54
    Vere, 200

Peterson, C. F, 38, 295
　　Hjalmar, 228
　　Mary, 242
　　Richard, 309
　　Vere, 186
Petroff, George, 118
　　Mary J., 235
Pfankuch, Reverend Paul W., 226
Pherrin, J.B, 243
Phillips, Father Thomas, 201
　　Jayme, 210
　　John, 147
　　John Henry, 235
　　Marlene, 73
　　Martha, 242
　　Shirley, 43
　　William, 215
　　William L., 43
Piche, Joy, 247
Pickard, George W., 236
　　George William, 236
　　Leonard, 236
　　Minnie C., 236
　　Raymond, 236
Pickett, Lee H, 289
Pike, Douglas, 119
　　Edward "Ted", 119
　　Radny, 119
　　William, 119
Pilant, Cuba C., 237
　　Dan, 237
　　Daniel C., 236, 237
　　Jean H., 236
　　John, 21, 39, 183, 221
　　John R., 236
　　John Robert, 237
　　John W., 236, 237
　　Lula, 237
　　Richard, 39, 237
　　Richard N., 236, 237
　　Robert, 237
　　Robert L., 237
Pinkham, George, 310

Pitts, Darrell L., 294
Place, Adolf Edwin, 238
Playa, Sam, 189
Plott, William, 296
Pogue, Betty, 179
Polignone, Mike, 163
Polley, David, 231
　　Mary E., 231
Poncin, George Peter "Pete", 238
Pong, Nita Kay, 60
Pope, Lonnie, 70
Porter, Barbara, 138
　　Dick, 212
　　Tom, 118
Poter, Magda, 336
Potter, Irene, 239
　　Roy Willard, 239
Poulos, Basil, 239
　　Charles, 239
　　Flossie, 239
Powell, Minnie Lou, 258
Powers, Charlene, 167
Poyser, Ray, 38
Pratt, Mary, 50
Presquez, Patti, 239
Price, Bill, 240
　　Ethel R., 239
　　Gary, 239, 240
　　Ival, 240
　　Leo, 147, 239
　　Leo Edward, 240
　　Ronald, 239, 240
Pritchard, Alice, 153
　　J. Irl, 153
　　Cortez, 153
Pritt, Reverend Melvin, 301
Pritts, Melvin, 172
　　Reverend, 137
　　Reverend Mel, 3, 46, 57, 243, 277
　　Reverend Melvin, 182
Prittz, Reverend Mel, 26
Puckett, Audrey M., 240

Puckett, Charles, 240
    Gary, 240
Pulleyn, Arthur, 241
    David, 241
    Leon W., 241
    Olive, 241
    Ronald, 241
Pulleyne, Arthur, 241
    David, 241
    Leon, 241
    Olive D., 241
    Ronald, 241
Pulsipher, Alma, 20
    Dean, 19-21
    Elva, 19
    Louis, 92
Pulver, Joyce, 19
    Robert, 19
    William, 20
Pumphery, Beatrice E., 241
Purcell, Doris, 117
Puryear, Nelie, 242
    Tom, 242
Queenan, Martin, 140
    Sean, 140
Quinn, Herbert, 156, 242
    John "Jack", 242
    Michael, 242
Raddatz, Catherine, 55
    Cathy, 242
    Eva, 242
    John Walter, 242
Rader, Fred, 81, 135
    Ruth O., 229
Ragsdale, Dorothy, 268, 322
    Dorothy Weiler, 322
    Harold, 322
Rainey, Dean, 253
    Patty, 253
Ramsey, Donald, 243
    Douglas K., 243
    Haldah, 243
    Harry, 243
    Henry, 4
    Henry L., 243
    Jerry L, 243
    Mike, 163
    Nina, 243
    Ralph, 60, 185, 243
    Ursula, 243
    Wendel S., 243
Rasmussen, Fred, 129
    Ruby, 129
Ray, Helen Pherrin, 243
    Jeanne R., 213
    J. O., 190
Rayford, Brooks, 244
Raymond, Charles A., 244
    Doris, 244
    James N., 244
    James Nelson, 244
Rayner, Harry, 167
Raynor, Dale, 18
    Herman, 188
Ream, Donald, 232
    Orpha, 232
Reay, Roberta, 16
Reddington, Mary L., 244
    Walter, 244
Redford, J.A.C., 71
    Patrick A., 71
Reding, Nellie, 244
Reece, Erasmia Renee, 245
    Howard W., 245
Reed, Chloe, 126
    Joseph, 126
    Terri, 237
    Terri J., 237
    Theodora, 236
    William, 126
Reep, Donna, 293, 294
Reese, Bertrand "Bert" Samuel, 245
    Chester, 246
    Chester R., 246
    Douglas, 245
    Edward, 246

Edward L., 246
James, 246
John, 245
Leslie, 245
Margaret, 245, 246
Margaret Curdy, 246
Robert, 245, 246
Reeves, Socrates, 245
Rehamond, Alice, 335
Reid, Geraldine, 93
  Ruby, 218
Reinmiller, Lee, 246
  Mary R., 246
  Roger, 246
  Weldon R., 246
Remington, Edith H., 247
Renaud, Marge, 247
  Marguerite Louise Ashton, 247
  May, 39
Rennie, Don, 248
  Mary A., 248
Rennie, Minnie, 118
Reo, Darla (Mrs. John), 74
Restivo, Tony, 329
Reynolds, Andree, 248
  Elaine, 270
  Florence, 117
  Trevis Fenton, 248
  Wayne Alan, 248
Rhoades, Dusty, 171
Rhodes, Kathleen, 28
Rich, Mary, 264
Richards, Reverend Robert, 50, 273
  Reverend Robert W., 236
Richardson, Helen, 193
Richey, Charles, 250
  Charles A., 248, 249
  Mark, 250
  Mark A., 249
  Ruth, 250

Ruth A., 249
Richmond, Albert G., 250
  Caroline E. (Bradley), 250
  Ellen Claire, 251
  Maurice, 250
  Maurice Albert, 250, 251
  Maurice Albert, Jr., 251
  Susan Casazza, 250, 251
Riddle, Wardie Genevra, 192
Ridenour, Mary, 126
Riggs, Cora, 223
  Ivan W., 252
  Pat, 253
  Thomas, 253
  Thomas A., 253
  Tony, 253
Rignell, Carl, 254
  Eddie, 254
  May, 253
  Paul M., 253
Riley, Mary, 125
Ringell, Bob, 254
  May, 254
Rismiller, Donald, 254
  Ervin E., 254
  Gertrude, 254
  Robert, 254
  Walter, 254
Ritter, Carmen, 122, 123
  Nora, 122, 123
  Sandra, 273
Roark, C. E., 221
Robben, Janet, 47
Robeis, Lyda, 266
  Real, 266
Roberts, Belle, 123
  Frances, 122
  Gordon, 144
  J. C., 195
  John, 144
  Larry, 274
  Shelia, 145

Sophia, 119
Robertson, Ricky, 254
Robicheaux, I. J., 229
Robinson, Dick, 163
    Doug, 183
    Jeanie, 213
Robison, David, 255
    Michael, 255
    Rulon, 255
    Susan Kay, 255
    Wilfred, 255
Robles, Patricia, 266
Rocha, Betty, 213
Roche, Dorothy, 255
    Elizabeth, 256
    Glencora, 255
    Henry, 256
    Lyle, 256
    Walter L., 255
    Wilber, 256
    William Leonard, 256
Rockwell, E. W., 180
Roder, Fred, 259
Rodman, Sheila, 296
    Velma, 58
Rodriquez, Romy, 27
Rogers, Joan, 145
    Karen, 13, 14
Rohn, John, 329
Rohrbacker, Roy, 141
Rollins, Janet, 50
Romero, Linda, 13, 14
Romine, Ethel, 77
Romines, Mary Catherine Schutz, 262
Rosales, Conrad, 305
    Manuel, 305
    Margaret, 305
    Morris, 305
Rose, Karvel, 255
    Kenneth, 255
Roueche, Alton, 259
Rousey, Ruth, 87

Rousseau, Cecile, 77
    Dr. John, 235
    John, 268
    Reverend John, 292
Rovacchi, Betty, 81
Rowan, Sylvia, 26
Rowe, Jeanette, 117
    Unita M., 142
Rowland, Judy K., 243
    Rose, 236
Royer, Rae, 242, 256
    Rae M., 184
    William M., 256
    William Myrl, 256
Rua, Antone, 156
Ruby, R. N. (Dorothy), 16
Rudd, Amanda Chamblin, 257
    Betty, 257
    Betty Lou, 257
    Bryan, 257
    Daron, 257
    Daron J., 257
    Derrell S., 257
    Erin, 257
    Gordon J., 257
    Jeffery, 257
    Lauren, 257
    Mae, 270
Rudibaugh, Melinda, 35
Rundberg, Edna, 60
Rundell, Leola, 291
Rusch, Velda, 44
    Velda Ilene, 44
Russell, Charlotte, 31
    Donald, 47
    Genevieve, 31
    Glynna Sue, 31
    Jane, 31
    John (Carolyn), 31
    Lillian, 178
Rutan, Alice, 219
    Arelene, 219

Ruth, John H., 258
    Mary Ann, 258
    Matt, 134
    Matthew, 257
Ryan, Archie D., 258
    Bernice, 258
    George, 258
    Reverend John J., 167
Rybold, Rick, 319
Ryerson, Betty, 149
Safford, Blaine D., 258, 259
    Vee, 259
Sailor, Clifford, 212
Salisbury, Jay, 301
    Verna Lee, 268
Sallee, Harry James "Jim", 259
    M. L., 260
    Neal, 260
Salter, Lucille, 239
    Ros, 147
Sampson, John, 82
    Phillip, 82
    William, 81
Sanchez, Frank, 43
    Sophia, 35
Sandall, Maude, 128
Sanders, Beatrice, 101
    Louis, 337
Sansom, Barbara, 43
    Robert C., 43
Sargent, Cicele, 223
Sass, Ernest, 147
    Gladys L., 260
Saunders, Jaci, 23
    Jason, 23
Savage, C. A., 39, 229
    Doreen, 132
    Gloria, 132
Scarpelli, Irene, 274
Schaack, James, 185
Schaap, Cornelius J., 261
    Fremont O., 260
    Raae, 261

Schaller, Alan, 261
    Conrad, 261
    John, 261
    John L., 261
    Mary M., 261
Schareer, Antonio, 238
Schart, Hattie, 226
Scherer, Dallan J., 125
    Ronald J., 125
Scherrer, Kathleen, 159
Schiberg, Ruth, 309
Schideler, Joy, 8
Schilberg, Ruth, 308
Schlueter, Al, 261
    Alfred, 261
    Alfred H., 261
    Esther, 261
    Marion Ann, 261
Schmidt, Karen, 70
Schmitz, Gerald, 273
    Raymond, 273
Scholl, Kathy, 167
Schommer, Clara 134
Schoppe, Irwin, 270
Schultz, Helen, 27
    Patti, 27
Schutz, Clara, 262
    Harry Oliver, 262
    Ivan Harold, 262
Schwab, Jeannine, 149
Schwandenberg, Joyce, 254
Schwartz, Benita Louise, 262
    Leslie, 262
Schwecheimer, Sharalee, 207
Scott, Zevesta Z., 179
Scout, Cindy, 47
Scown, Shirley, 277
Scranton, C. A., 198
Searl, Ruth, 268
Searles, Richard, 216
Sears, Ardeen, 210, 247, 339
    Bill, 210
    Jeannie M., 262

Robert C., 262
William, 262
Searway, Brent, 284
Brenton , 285
I. J. , 284, 285
Sedillo, Adelina, 217
Sedwick, Katherine, 122
Segerblom, Cliff, 16, 314
Seiber, Jane, 241
Seible, Jerry, 119
Seigel, Paul (Judy), 16
Seiler, Mary L., 263
Selby, Kay, 273
Seley, Samuel, 263
Sepka, Chester J., 264
Donald, 264
Marcella, 264
Ted, 264
Seretko, Bonnie, 218
Serventi, Don, 92
Louis, 92
Setmer, Fred, 303
Herman, 303
Settle, Don, 264
Geraldine Engle, 264
Glen William, 264
William, 264
William Clyde, 264
Severson, Mary, 261
Seymore, Cobie, 116
Herb, 212
Shafer, Claude, 264
Cowboy" Claude, 264
Eddie, 265
Loeta, 212
Martha, 265
Randy , 265
Shamo, Luana L., 173
Shanahan, Alice, 255, 266
Leland R., 266
Patricia, 266
Stanley, 266

Shannon, James, 266
James A., 266
Jason, 266
Jeffrey, 266
Jeromy , 266
Joe, 266
John, 266
Shawn, 266
Sharp, Everett, 128
Everett E., 135
Melvin, 221, 222
Sharrow, A. L., 92
Shaw, Lucy, 243
Shay, Lynne Dee, 271
Sheek, Betty, 233
Kyle, 233
Shelton, Jessie F., 266
Marcus, 267
Sheppard, Finely, 124
Morris, 124
Sheridan, Maude, 267
Sherrod, Carl B., 268
Ruth, 268
Sherwood, Betty, 271
Dana, 268
Marguerite, 322
Marguerite L., 268
Shields, Mayetta, 268
W. I. "Bill", 268
Shilkaitis, Mary, 264
Shipp, Este, 171, 247, 317
Esther, 44, 51, 69, 72, 100, 115, 116, 133, 134, 148, 156, 202, 205, 266, 296, 320
John, 295, 296
John H., 202
Shoemaker, Billie Jean, 269
Dolores, 269
Gary, 269
Marjorie R., 269
Stanley L., 269
William, 269

Shope, Charles A., 269, 295
    Delores, 269, 292, 293, 320
    Herbert, 269
    Howard, 269
    Mary, 293
    Mary F., 269
    Nancy I, 269
Shoppe, Mabel, 269
Shortle, Emett, 271
    John F., 271
    Karen, 271
    Leo, 271
    Lori, 271
    Margaret, 271
    Michael, 271
    Robert, 271
    Sandra, 271
Shortt, Beverly, 271
    Delmont M., 271
    Margaret Helen, 271
Showacy, Louise, 236
Shreeve, Ormel Victor, 271
    Susanne, 271
Shubert, Freda, 330
Shuck, Clarence C., 272
    Clarence Jr., 272
    Douglas, 272
    Ina, 272
    Marie Lee, 272
Shultz, Hannah, 272
    Hannah E., 272
    John, 272
    John H., 272
    Richard, 272
    Stanley, 272
Shupp, Helen, 170
Sibon, John M., 244
Sigl, Georgia, 178
Simkins, Bishop Kenneth, 8, 83, 119, 166, 245
Simmons, Minister Hartley, 339
    Winnie, 186

Simone, Marianne, 280
Simpson, Anna M., 272
    Clarence, 94
    Jaylene, 94
    Sandra, 94
    Robert, 224
Sims, Elnora, 75
Singleton, Claude Lee, 273
    Cordie E., 273
    E. I., 273
    E. L., 273
    Edward G., 273
Sirkel, Edward Matthew, 274
    Helen Belle, 274
Skaggs, Palm, 70
Skee, Father Theodore Can, 231
Skerce, George, 122
    John Harry, 122
    Steven, 122
Skogen, Janet, 299
Slack, Amy, 274
    Bill, 286
    Lloyd, 274
    Rena, 274
    Richard, 274
    Robin Joann, 274
Slater, A. V., 211
    Mildred, 212
    Richard, 296
Slattery, Michael, 307
    Mike, 167
Slaveck, Raymond, 274
    Richard, 274
    Stephen, 274
    Virginia, 274
Sleeper, Claud, 275
    Florence, 275
Sliker, Emma, 133
    Ernest, 133
Smale, Rick, 319
Smee, Alvin B., 276
    Bert, 275, 276
    Dorothy, 276

Lucy Florence
  "Grandma", 276
Melvin R., 276
Melvin R. "Mike", 276
Melvin Robert, 276
Mike, 276
Pat, 276
Vida A., 276
Smiddy, Alice, 297
Smilanick, Pete, 147
Smiley, Mary Louise, 277
  William C., 277
Smith, Betty, 160, 311
  Beverly, 337, 339
  Butch, 278
  Claude, 116
  Cory, 278
  Curley, 90
  Elton R., 277
  Father Hugh, 4, 142, 158, 299
  Fr. Hugh, 146
  Gerry, 202
  H. G., 311, 340
  Harry, 227
  Hurlburt, 211
  James W., 1
  Juanita, 116
  Katherine, 95
  Laura Godbey, 322
  Lois, 277
  Mary A., 1
  Mary Addie Wilkins, 1
  Nell, 278
  Norman, 34
  Pearl, 212
  Reverend Hugh, 27, 112
  Reverend Hugh P., 281, 324
  Reverend Richard, 94
  Reverend Dr. Richard, 184
  Robert, 278
  Russel, 277
  Samuel Hood, 1
  Sharon, 311
  Terry, 278
  Thomas Clyde, 278
  Vida, 102
  William, 278
  William A., 278
Smithee, Marlene, 191
Smoot, Charlesetta Layman, 278
  Edna, 286
  Zeb, 278
Smythe, Arthur, 279
  Ida Mae, 279
Sneed, Andrew, 252
  Cheryl L, 252
  Emma Lee, 252
  John H, 252
Snethen, Jack, 48
Snow, Bishop Carl, 129
  Bishop Karl, 329
  Joyce, 107
Snyder, Edward, 168
  Helen, 6
  Roy, 168
Soder, Marion C., 279
Softchin, Frances, 280
  Frances E., 279
  John, 202
  John P., 280
  John Paul, 280
  Nellie, 280
  Sam, 280
Solomon, Bishop Bryant, 1, 282, 286
Sorensen, Dolores, 124
Souza, Manuel, 202
Sowers, Mary, 198
Spangenberg, Dorothy, 281
  Elizabeth, 219
  Glenn, 281
  Jane, 281
  Margie, 281

R. F., 280
Spann, J. H. (Joysa), 226
Sparks, Robert, 14
Sparling, Joanne, 328
Spearman, Gordon, 281
    Harvey, 281
    June, 281
    Millard, 221
    Millard Joseph, 281
    Millard "Pappy", 281
    Nina, 281
Speas, Reverend Clyde O., 281
Speicher, Lula, 326
Spellman, John Henry, 282
    John "Jack" F., 282
    Natalie, 282
    Wilbur, 282
Spelts, Ben, 282
    Grant Ardell, 282
    Ryan B., 282
    William, 282
Spencer, Elizabeth, 198
Spendlove, Clara, 212
Spickelmier, Bob, 282
    Robert, 282, 283
Spillan, Irene, 5
Spillian, Irene, 5
Spilsbury, G. C., 93, 259
Spitzig, Reverend Joseph A., 296
Sposato, Joseph A., 96
Sprague, Carlyle, 33
Sprouse, Gerald, 311
Stade, Howard, 146
    Paul, 146
Stagner, Helen, 103
    Ray, 235
Stahl, Roger, 160
Stakely, Carolyn, 60
Standfield, Georgia, 212
Stanley, John, 153
Stansmore, Olive, 137
Stanton, Martha, 85
Stauffer, Linda, 277

Stead, Florence D., 283
Stecker, Helen, 103
Stednick, John, 116
Steel, Carson, 35
Steele, Anne, 284
    Dedee, 284
    Esther, 283
    Etter, 50
    Kenneth, 283, 284
    Mike, 283, 284
    Pat, 283, 284
    Paul, 284
    Paul L., 283, 284
    Samantha, 284
Steeves, Barry, 284, 285
    Billy, 284, 285
    Grace, 284, 285
    Nancy, 284, 285
    Sandy, 284, 285
    William, 284
    William W., 284, 285
Stehwien, Boyd, 25
Stephens, Cecil W., 285
    Lee, 285
Stephens, Gary, 285
    O. N., 135
Stevens, Bob, 189
    Winona Esther, 189
Stevenson, William, 13
Stewart, Connie, 47
    Emma, 323
    Ernest, 323
    Gary, 3
    Gerald, 323
    Harold, 323
    John, 323
    Loletta, 323
    Mildred, 136
    William, 323
Stice, Sherl, 202
Stickles, Nancy, 15
Stien, Kathy, 62
Stienback, Kathy, 62

Stiver, Reverend Don, 128
Stivers, Father Don, 128, 315
Stock, June, 19
    Well, 19
Stockton, Rosemary, 89
Stoecker, Lillie, 161
Stoeve, Reverend Olaf, 81, 92, 192, 300, 330
    Reverend Olaf A., 155
Stoker, Beth, 168
    Edna Beth, 286
    LaMa, 286
    Stella, 286
    Sterling, 286, 296
    Stormie, 286
    Suzette, 286
Stokes, LaVon, 135
Stoller, Theresa, 26
Stoneham, Camille, 286
    Christine, 286
    Leo B., 286
Stoner, Charles A., 287
    Ezra, 287
Stoney, Stephen A., 287
    Stephen Richard, 287
Stoove, Reverend Olaf, 138
Story, Fannie, 72
    William, 72
    Wilson, 72
Stout, Archie, 288
    Cardon, 288
    Glen, 287, 288
    Marwood, 288
    Nathan, 288
    Shirley, 288
    Walter, 287, 288
Strafford, Dick, 289
Strange, Alice, 273
Stratton, Dorothy C. Jones, 289
    Harry, 289
    Robert L., 289
    Robert William, 289

Straus, Bob, 30
    Mary, 30
    Michael, 216
Strawn, Edna, 95
Strechlow, Susan, 278
Strehlow, Robert, 18
Strenge, Robert, 211
Strickland, Clifton, 289
    Kem, 189
Strickler, Minnie C., 290
Stripling, Bruce, 290
    Clarence, 290
    David, 290
    Edwin C., 290
Strong, G. R., 1
Struthers, Becky, 203
Stubbs, Al, 171
    Bishop Leonard, 65, 207, 340
    Glade, 207
    Leonard, 1, 33, 119, 169, 170, 225, 322
Stucki, McWane, 170
Stukas, Donald L., 291
    Leta A., 291
    Reverend R. H., 291
    Richard, 291
    Robert, 291
    Wilfred E., 291
Stultz, Robin, 8
Stypick, Helen, 118
Sucaansky, Betty, 274
Sudweeks, Suzette, 296
Sullivan, Alice, 294
    Alice Mae, 291
    Annie Fielding, 294
    Dolores, 261
    Doris, 136
    Eileen, 294
    Eileen C., 293
    Gerald, 294
    Helena F., 199
    James, 261, 294

James F., 294
Jane, 159
Joe, 291
Joseph Michael, 294
Joseph Monroe, 294
Leland, 18
Maurice, 261
Michael, 294
S. A, 135
Sammette, 292
Suzanne, 159
Verlene, 255
Winona, 278
Sulser, Joseph, 119
Super, Vinita, 125
Suriani, Carmine, 295
Surrie, Artie, 207
Sutherland, Roberta, 23
Ruth, 142
Swain, Mark, 119
Swallow, Kenneth, 289
Swan, Marian, 289
Swanson, Alice, 70
Bill, 70
Jim, 70
Joe, 70
Swarts, Jack, 289
Swartz, Don, 331
Donald, 258
Jack, 1
Ruth, 331
Swayze, Clara, 142
Sweeney, Bridget, 296
Eileen, 296
Morgan, 21, 92, 295, 300, 324
Sweet, Bessie, 60
Charles, 185
Swimley, Bonnie Marie, 204
Synder, L. J., 67
Szetela, Sharon, 96
Tabony, Larry, 310
Sgt, 311

Tabor, Alta Marie, 189
Florence, 189
Lloyd Ben, 189
Violet Esther, 189
Tadjiki, Karin, 271
Taft, Lucille, "Bille", 19
Tagert, Ernest, 108
Talbot, Addie, 296
Bessie, 286
Edna Beth, 286, 296
George, 286
George B., 296
Ned, 296
Robert, 296
Talley, Frances, 190
George, 267, 297
Nancy Ethel, 296
Tamasi, Ione, 231
Tannacakis, Despina, 245
Tanquary, Lois, 283, 284
Tarter, Richard, 18
Taylor, Edith, 95
Edith B., 297
Edward A., 297
Edward B., 297
Jo Ann, 178
K.V., 52
Kenneth, 52, 54
Richard, 95
Thomas T., 298
Tea, Father Clark, 159
Reverend Clark A., 215
Teal, Jean, 298
Teel, La Vern, 43
Templer, Darryl L., 148
Milo, 148
Veva, 148
Thames, Bert, 307
Theemiling, Louise, 28
Thiriot, Candace, 50
Thomas, Barbara, 70
Clara, 298
Evelyn, 299

George Franklin, 298
Gretchen, 160
Grover L., 223
James, 298
Laurona Ruth, 299
LaVerne, 263
LaVerne M., 299
Marty, 299, 300
Miranda, 299
Pam, 299, 300
Rose, 223
Thomas Michael, 299
Thomas W., 263, 299
Timothy, 299
Tom, 300
William F., 223
Thomlinson, Elizabeth, 300
   Morris Dailey, 300
   Philip, 300
   Rate, 300
Thompson, Carlis, 32
   Luella, 212
Thoni, Pastor Lee, 74
   Reverend Lee, 254
Thoreson, Anna, 235
Thormodsgaard, Kari, 233
   Neil, 233
   Rhonda, 233
   Tad, 233
Thormodsgaard
   Rhonda L., 233
Thurston, Dorothy, 86, 87
   Lois, 87
   Raymond, 86, 87, 300
   Virginia Lee, 300
Tibbits, Clara, 136
Tilman, Lee, 21, 325
Tilton, Thelma "Sammy", 319
Timme, Anne Marie, 46
   Glenn, 46
   Glenn, Jr., 46
   Mary, 45
Tindeland, Charlotte, 88

Tinger, Rose Marie, 113
Titus, Barbara, 337, 339
   Edgar Snow, 43
Toalson, Dorothy, 309
Tobler, Heber, 44, 173
   Heber J., 117
Toci, Donald, 333
Tofaya, Manny, 319
Tohlen, Eleanor, 232
Tomey, Marsha Rose, 236
Tompson, Geraldine, 298
Toms, Cecil, 233
Tony, Don, 329
Toomey, Mary, 296
Tornquist, C. H., 300
   Charles, 300
   Emmil, 300
Torongeau, Doris, 81
Torrence, Harry, 173
   Ray, 220
Torres, Carolyn, 323
Tougas, David, 6
   Norma, 6
Toulson, Dorothy, 308
Towne, Dee, 14
   Tracy, 29
Towner, Earl, 92
   Everett, 92
   Otis, 92
Toye-Bush, Helen, 33
Traasdahl, Jeanne, 326
   Osborne, 1, 92, 119
Tracht, DeWitt, 205, 301
Tract, Kenneth, 301
   Violet, 301
Trammel, John, 193
Trammell, Pauline, 193
Trasdahl, Osborn, 55
Trayler, Gertrude, 230
Trelease, Bill, 4
Trevathon, Dorothy, 260

Trever, Reverend Winston, 22, 39, 54, 135, 180, 181, 195, 211, 221, 267, 275
Troeger, Fred, 303
    Matilda Augusta, 303
Trollope, Aldon , 33
    Don, 33
    Leroy, 33
    Robert, 33
    Ted, 33
    Wildon, 33
    Zella, 33
Tronier, Madeleine, 329
Trost, Grace, 147
    Jack, 147
Troupe, Charles, 245
Trubachik, Inez, 178
    Mary, 178
Tucker, Amy, 87
    Bonnie, 240
Tudahl, Herbert, 303
Tudor, Ellen, 244
    Reverend Glen, 153, 154
Turcott, Cindy, 304
    Mary, 304
    Patrick G., 304
    Tomas L., 304
    Willard, 304
Turley, Dorothy, 141
    Merle, 141
Turner, Clara, 247
    Frank, 202
    Fred, 304
    J. E., 227
    Lucie, 304
    Lucie A., 304
    Mathew, 304
    Tammy, 56
    Thomas, 304
    Tom, 304
    Warren V., 304
Tyler, Clarissa, 301
Tyree, Chet, 116
Tyrell, Janiece, 220
Tyson, Duncann, 157
Ulivarri, Leah, 113
Underwood, Doris, 10
    Peggy, 290
    Ramona Wood, 305
Upchurch, Michael, 15
Ursin, Helen, 133
Valasity, Susan, 178
Valentine, Anthony, 305
    Anthony "T.J.", 305
    Barbara, 305
    Fred G., 305
    Frederic G. III, 305
    Mary Ann, 305
    Michael, 305
    Rodney, 305
Van, W. J., 274
Van Duren, Jean, 254
Van Hatten, DeeAnn, 116
Van Hoorebecke, Ricki, 246
Van Horn, George, 227
Van Kamp, Mary, 88
Vance, Anne, 26
VanDenBosch, Jason, 202
Vanderhoofven, Wenona, 26
Vanderpool, Margaret, 298
VanDover, Clifford E., 307
    Darrell, 307
    Darren, 307
    Miya, 307
    Sigrid, 307
VanZant, Ellen Mercy, 306
    Jack, 306
Vaughan, George, 306
    Gertrude, 306
    L. T., 306
    Larry, 306
    Richard, 306
Vaughn, Ben, 92
Verdugo, Viola, 305
Verser, Diane, 204
Vertin, Gladys, 233

Vetter, Carl, 153
Villareale, Christopher, 145
    Suzanne, 145
Vince, Ashley, 94
    Marian, 94
    Thomas, 94
Vinson, Shirley, 33
Voehlker, Louise, 221
Voelker, Edward, 222
    Louise, 223
Voorheis, James K., 307
Voss, Bill, 149
    Dick, 173
    Nadean, 307, 308
    Richard, 308
    Sharline, 117
    Wilfred, 92, 267
    Wilfred T., 6, 307, 308
    Wilfred "Bill", 319
Votow, Ida, 137
    William, 137
Vreeland, Walter, 295
Vrooman, Barrent, 309, 310
    Nicolas, 310
    Ronald, 310
    Thomas Edgar, 309
Wacaser, Everett, 27
Waddell, James, 200
    Wanda, 233
Wadsworth, Linda, 92
Wagner, Caren, 34
    Jessica, 34
    Mort, 39
    Phil, 48, 202
    Woodrow W., 264
Wait, Camilla Holtry, 281
Waite, Roy, 111
Waldie, Sandra, 187
Walkden, Jim, 147
Walker, Anna Mae, 188
    Bertha, 310
    Cal Victor, 310
    Darnell, 190
    Frank, 310
    John W., 183
    La Verne, 310
    Lois, 300
    Robert, 310
    Winfred, 296
Wallace, Ronald Floyd, 310
Walser, Nancy, 113
Walsh, Reverend Tim, 320
    Rita, 286
Walter, Norma, 337
Walters, Frank M., 311
    Gloria A., 311
    Kathleen, 311
    Mabel, 108
    Walt, 12
Walton, Gail, 336
Wammack, Eddie, 76
    Jim, 76
    Roger, 76
Wansley, Barbara J., 298
Ward, Agnes, 312
    Betty Jo, 312
    Billie, 225
    Cathleen, 125
    Cecil, 312
    Father, 52, 315
    Father Herbert A., 161, 282
    Floyd E., 313
    Harold V., 312
    Horace, 6, 319
    Jeffrey L., 312
    John A., 312
    John S., 39
    Ray, 312
    Theresa Othelia, 312
    William, 125, 312
    William J., 312
Warner, Robert, 275
Warren, Agnes, 245
    Richard, 227

Wartman, Al, 313
    Alvin, 308, 315
    Alvin N., 316
    Anna, 51, 313-315
    Doris, 313
    Frank, 315
    Frank Secord, 315
    Franklin S., 316
    Peter, 316
    Randall, 316
    Steven F., 316
Wascher, A. A, 1
Wastenberg, Louis, 18
Watkins, Dorothy Jean, 318
    James Eric, 318
    James L., 318
    Margo L., 318
    Paul L., 318
Watson, Arleigh, 37
    Clarence, 92, 227
Watts, Fields, 179
    H. O., 180
Weaver, Bill, 56
    Carol, 164
    Sue, 56
Webb, Audrey, 338
    Dick, 319
    Jim, 319
    Laura, 16
    Norma, 339
    Paul, 275
    Paul S. Jim, 319
    Richard "Dick" Sidney, 319
    Robert, 319
    Sammy, 319
    Sammy , 270
    W. E. "Butch", 338
Weese, Aubrey , 12
Wegren, A. R., 295
    Angus "Bud", 320
    Angus K., 320
    Car, 320, 321
    Frances, 320
    George, 320, 321
    George Francis, 321
    Gus, 321
    Kathie, 321
    Sallie, 320, 321
Wehr, Charlotte, 321
    Harold "Lefty", 321
Weiler, Lillian, 268, 322
    Marguerite, 322
Weir, Patricia, 198
Well, Teague, 170
Wellman, Erma Lorraine, 322
    Gene, 21, 323
    Henry Eugene "Gene", 323
    Richard, 323
    Thelma, 212
    Walter, 323
    William, 323
    William H., 211
Wells, Aileen, 239
    Michael, 323
    Steven, 323
Welsh, Robert, 112
Welsh, Peggy, 21
    R. B, 21
Wengert, Esther, 245
Wenta, Steve, 92
Wessel, Reverend E. A., 303
West, A. S, 191
    Arleigh B., 113, 215
    Eleanor, 113
    Joan, 207
    John, 113
    Richard, 113
Westen, John, 165
Westfield, Dolores, 42
Weston, Marguerite, 298
Wettengel, Eula, 123
    Lester, 123
    Louis, 123

Whalen, Barry, 325
    Brian, 325
    Dennis, 40, 325
    Don, 325
    Donald, 138
    Lillian, 325
    Luke, 167
    Luke Arthur, 324
    Luke Jr., 325
    Rosemary, 90
Wheeler, Edith Beryl, 325
    Grant, 325
    Houston, 326
    Jack, 138
    Steve, 325
Whelden, Ben, 326
    Percy, 326
    Vernon, 326
Whicker, Jim, 329
Whilhelm, Glenn, 258
Whipple, Jeff, 327
    John Lester, 327
    Shirley L., 327
White, Bob, 328
    Daniel, 327
    David, 327
    Franklin M., 327
    Helen, 246
    James "Jack", 328
    Jim, 328
    John, 135
    Juanita, 328
    Kay, 217
    Kristen, 327
    Mary, 327
    Mae, 78
    Pastor Franklin, 91
    Rita, 110, 327
    Ron, 328
    Sara, 327
    Suzanne, 327
    Thomas Sherman, 328
    Timothy, 327

    Velta S., 329
Whitener, Betty, 213
Whiting, Nancy, 138
Whittaker, Barbara, 330
    David, 329
    David Wayne, 330
    E. H., 330
    George Madison, 329
    Glenwood, 330
    Teresa, 330
Whittington, Thelma, 268
    Thelma Fern, 327
Widner, Chester, 229
Wiebke, Almer B., 330
    Fred, 330
Wiggins, Lloyd, 289
Wigley, Robert, 330
    Susan Lillian, 330
Wilcoxon, Helen, 85
Wilder, Reverend M. K., 272
Wilder, Christopher, 163
Wilhite, H. T., 258
Wilkerson, Debbie, 43
    Debra, 41
Willette, Nancy, 121
Williams, A. D., 7
    Bessie, 332
    Bishop Jacob, 10, 50, 55
    Bishop Jake, 9, 33, 119, 223, 274
    Clifford, 81
    Daniel, 333
    Daniel A., 332
    Danny, 82, 275
    Debbie, 82, 275
    Francis, 333
    Francis L., 332
    Frank, 332
    Glen, 331
    Jack, 195, 338
    Hank, 338
    Harlen, 332
    Helen, 116

    Jake, 196, 329
    James, 80
    John, 224, 331, 332
    Joseph F., 331
    Kathryn, 333
    Kent, 332
    L. P., 332
    Leon, 92
    Leon A., 332
    Lewis, 332
    Louis, 332
    Pearl, 224
    Ramon, 82, 173, 275
    Rick, 332, 333
    Roberta Sue, 218
    Robin, 82
    Sarah Brown, 80
    Shirley, 82
    William, 229, 331
    William J., 215
    Winnie, 331
Williamson, Ray, 87
Willis, Lucile, 15
Wilson, Alice (Granny), 335
    Amalette, 335
    Amalette (Ketch), 335
    Cecile Fortier, 333
    Dan, 249
    Danny, 335
    Darlene, 83, 84
    Doris I., 333
    Edd P., 333
    Edward T., 333
    Father David, 238
    Frank, 335
    George, 312
    George L., 333
    George Lee, 333
    Harlan, 333
    Helen, 172
    Jack, 335
    Jeanie, 335
    Jennifer, 334

    Jennifer Janene, 333
    Joe, 335
    Linda Sue, 218
    Margaret, 334
    Minnie, 335
    Paul, 98, 168
    Ray, 83
    Robert E., 335
    Rose Marie, 335
    Shawn, 334
    Sue, 112
    Tracy, 334
    Victor (Paul), 335
    Wilbur, 112
    William "Bill", 336
    William G., 334
Winder, Dorothy, 107
Wine, Joseph, 296
Winfrey, Rhonda, 57
Wingire, Esther, 303
    John, 303
Winkler, Ethel "Nanie", 296
    Guy, 297
    Ralph, 297
Winn, Jesse, 336
    Mary, 336
    Ray, 336
    Verne, 336
Winthrop, Walter L, 111
Wisham, JoElla, 305
    Ron, 305
Witherell, Cleo J., 336
    Robert "Bob", 336
Withers, Iona F., 337
Wolfenstein, Michael, 10
Wolsey, Ardell, 282
Wood, Alan, 337
    Barbara J., 100
    Billie, 66
    Carol Ann, 337
    Christine, 339
    Curtis, 339
    Daren, 339

Boulder City Cemetery: Boulder City, Nevada 425

Dell, 305
Elizabeth Ann Hudson, 337
Estelle E. "Bill", 337
Eugene II., 338
Evelyn, 338
Gilbert, 197, 339
J.C., 337
La Wauna, 305
Lillie May, 338
Lloyd, 338
Marvin, 6, 339
Minnie Marie, 339
Nathella, 305
Nettie, 337
Nettie C., 339
Robert F., 338
Roy Melvin, 339
Scott, 92
Thelma, 339
Van Dell, 305
Walt, 27
Wood-Layton, LaRene, 305
Woodard, Patty, 306
Woodrum, Loretta, 339
Woofe, Charmion, 227
Workman, Lucy E., 276
Wormser, Felix, 316
Wright, Arthur, 83
    Brad, 340
    Gail, 340
    Ira Ross, 340
    Katherine, 83, 84
    Konye (Mrs. Gary), 74
    Lynette, 340
    Ross, 340
    Walter, 329
    Yvette, 340
Wright, Carl, 275
    Donna, 145
    Walter, 179
Wylie, L.F., 217
    Maxine, 214, 217

Wythe, Debbi, 239, 240
Yeager, Pearl Jan, 88
Yeley, Ann-Marie, 89, 201
    Ryan Marks, 201
    Vicki Marks, 89
    Victoria Marks, 201
Yeoman, Sally, 113
Yerkes, Ruby, 290
York, Helen, 223
Young, Melva, 217
Youngblood, V. C., 164
Zamalloa, Arnold, 340
    Darlene, 340
    Donald, 340
    Dorothy, 340
    John, 340
    Paul, 340
Zander, Joel, 12
Zenoff, Morry, 253, 314
Zinggone, Helen, 152
Zoroya, Michael, 36
    Ted, 36
Zumwalt, Joan, 142
Zwiersybki, Mary, 110

www.ingramcontent.com/pod-product-compliance
Lightning Source LLC
Chambersburg PA
CBHW071015240426
43661CB00073B/2291